Chemical Dependency Counseling

4

EDITION

Dedicated to Angela Kaufman, Robert Reps Perkinson, Nyshie Perkinson, and Shane Perkinson, my anchors to love, hope, and joy.

Chemical Dependency Counseling

A PRACTICAL GUIDE

4 EDITION

ROBERT R. PERKINSON

Keystone Treatment Center,
Canton, South Dakota

Los Angeles | London | New Delhi
Singapore | Washington DC

Los Angeles | London | New Delhi
Singapore | Washington DC

FOR INFORMATION:

SAGE Publications, Inc.
2455 Teller Road
Thousand Oaks, California 91320
E-mail: order@sagepub.com

SAGE Publications Ltd.
1 Oliver's Yard
55 City Road
London EC1Y 1SP
United Kingdom

SAGE Publications India Pvt. Ltd.
B 1/I 1 Mohan Cooperative Industrial Area
Mathura Road, New Delhi 110 044
India

SAGE Publications Asia-Pacific Pte. Ltd.
33 Pekin Street #02-01
Far East Square
Singapore 048763

Acquisitions Editor: Kassie Graves
Editorial Assistant: Courtney Munz
Production Editor: Brittany Bauhaus
Copy Editor: Megan Markanich
Typesetter: C&M Digitals (P) Ltd.
Proofreader: Theresa Kay
Indexer: Kathy Paparchontis
Cover Designer: Bryan Fishman
Marketing Manager: Katie Winter
Permissions Editor: Adele Hutchinson

Copyright © 2012 by Robert R. Perkinson

Printed in the United States of America

Library of Congress Cataloging-in-Publication Data

A catalog record of this book is available from the Library of Congress.

9781412979214

This book is printed on acid-free paper.

14 15 10 9 8 7 6 5 4

Brief Contents

Detailed Contents

Preface

Things are changing in the addiction world, and the new health care parity and health care bills should make things better. As I travel around the country, giving workshops on addictive disorders, I often have the privilege of listening to the leaders in the field speak, and I find they are all saying the same thing. Addiction is a brain disease that needs long-term management. For decades, the field of addiction was living in the belief that treatment takes a few weeks. This is not true for any chronic disease, including hypertension, diabetes, asthma, or addiction.

Clients who get well need to come in to treatment for an individualized number of days, weeks, months, or even years and are then followed in continuing care for at least the next 5 years. That is when the relapse rate drops to around zero. Continuing care should include random drug screens, therapy, motivational enhancement contacts, treatment for co-occurring disorders, mandatory attendance at 12-step meetings, sponsorship, spiritual direction, lifestyle management, enhanced recreation, and support from the family and finding new friends in recovery. There is no easy fix or magic bullet; recovery is hard work. However, it is incredibly rewarding. We are fortunate to see our clients literally blossom into health before our eyes. Advancements in new treatments and medications will continue to change the field almost on a daily basis, so we must remain open to new treatments whenever possible. In any field, change occurs slowly in incremental steps.

Unfortunately, along with huge advancements in recovery, the field of addiction treatment is shrinking. This is a catastrophe because millions of our brothers and sisters will die, and millions will spend valuable time in prison. Most addiction programs today occur in outpatient settings with an average of 6 to 10 counselors working with 150 to 500 clients. This results in poor treatment outcomes. Research says that two thirds of clients relapse in the first year. Only 40% of these treatment programs offer individual sessions; they have no medical support and are overwhelmed with paperwork. The turnover of staff is dismal—about 50%—which is as high as the fast-food industry. Because of managed care, we have been trying to make treatment cheaper and more effective. This has led to cost cutting, usually staff cutting, and this leads to fewer professionals working with more clients. A few hospitals such as the Cleveland Clinic are doing things differently. They focus on the client first believing that better care leads to a more stable system, better outcomes, and greater financial rewards. They concentrate on prevention, treatment, and continuing care.

It is possible to treat addiction the right way the first time. Most addicts come through treatment three or four times. Most addicts eventually stop using on their own by making a motivated life changing decision usually made with the help of someone in recovery or a health care professional (McLellan, 2006). Still, many clients will not be able to recover without treatment. "I have spent my whole career looking at all of the kinds of things that have been tried—at least in the country—to reduce substance use problems, and treatment is by far the best" (McLellan, 2010, p. 26).

Because of third-party payers, thousands of treatment centers have closed. There are approximately 23 to 25 million diagnosed addicts in the United States on any given day, and only 2 to 2.5 million are in treatment. Worst of all, most professionals in the field are not using evidence-based treatments but treatments they learned in their own recovery or on the job training. These treatments do not work as well as evidence-based treatment programs. When we see a client, we want to know we are giving that person the best treatment in the world.

For the first time, science has shown us how to keep most addicts clean after only one treatment. If you read articles or hear speeches by the leaders in the field, you will read about this new revolution. Treatment that works developed in the programs where the cost of treatment was irrelevant because the cost of relapse was deadly to the public. This initially came from the work with physicians and then branched out to other professionals such as airline pilots. No one wants a pilot flying a plane or a physician doing surgery while intoxicated. No price was too high to pay these professionals to stay clean and sober. These people had to stay clean to protect all of our lives. These programs developed markedly higher recovery rates. If we develop similar programs for all substance abusers, most of our clients will stay clean and sober. It is obvious that this will be more effective and cheaper in the long run. Until now, third-party payers were reluctant to pay for treatment because it rarely worked. However, the treatment success rate in addiction is similar to the treatment of other chronic diseases. Third-party payers should be willing to pay for treatment that restores a client to health (Marlatt & Donovan, 2008; McKay, 2005; Skipper & Dupont, 2010; White, 2009).

There are many treatments for addiction, and most of them work, but it is important to note that when physicians treat their own, all of these physician health programs focus on 12-step facilitation as the core of treatment (Skipper, 1997; Skipper & Dupont, 2010). Studies show that if abstinence is the desired outcome, consistent involvement with 12-step meetings produces the best results. About 76% of treatment programs use the 12 steps as the basis for their program (Florentine & Hillhouse, 2000).

Robert L. DuPont, MD, the founding director of the National Institute on Drug Abuse (NIDA), said the following:

> Today, I see these fellowships as a modern miracle and the key to sustained recovery for most, but not all, addicts. . . . In fact, these programs created the entirely new concept of "recovery," which is much more than mere abstinence. The 12-step fellowships support a new and better way of life. (White, 2010, p. 43)

These programs for professionals also use evidence-based therapies such as motivational enhancement, cognitive behavioral therapy, and medication including disulfiram, naltrexone, acamprosate, and topiramate. Clients discharge into a prolonged tightly controlled continuing care program including workplace drug testing that lasts for 5 years or more. The change required is an emotional, interpersonal, and spiritual shift (Earley, 2009). This same treatment should be available for all clients.

This manual will concentrate on five evidence-based treatments:

1. Cognitive behavioral therapy

2. Motivational enhancement

3. Pharmacology

4. Skills training

5. 12-step facilitation

The Minnesota Model is the gold standard for alcohol and drug treatment. The research evidence for this treatment says that it is a good start, but continuing care in most programs is lacking. Two thirds of clients going through these programs relapse in the first year after treatment. This is exactly like the treatment of other chronic relapsing diseases such as hypertension, asthma, and diabetes. These chronic diseases have almost identical genetic concordance rates, about 50% to 60%; treatment compliance rates, about 50% to 60%; and relapse rates, about 50% to 60%. Health care has become an acute care business, but many chronic diseases need lifelong management. In acute medicine, clients learn what they need to do to stay healthy, but about half of them do not comply with treatment. Only half of substance abuse clients are encouraged to go to 12-step meetings, and we know that these meetings help addicts recover. Clients may be encouraged to get a sponsor, go to some kind of counseling, and take their medications, but most of them are not followed up, do not comply, drop out, and relapse.

This book outlines the best treatment in the world. The leading treatment centers and addiction professionals have contributed to and approved of this book. You might not work at a large treatment center that has all of these services available, but the more of these components you add, the better your treatment will become. The best treatment centers have a large, multidisciplined staff, but even these treatment centers fail miserably when it comes to continuing care. They fail because they are not paid for the continuing care that works. It must become a part of your mission to change this policy. Recovery does not take a set number of days, weeks, months, or years but usually takes a lifetime of vigilance and hard work.

You are reading this book because you are interested in working with addicts. Congratulations! You can be proud of yourself, because addiction treatment is effective and fun. You belong in one of the most rewarding professions in the world. In addition, with counseling you will watch your clients change from being at death's door to being happy, joyous, and free. You will be working with some of the most caring and dedicated professionals in the world. You will save lives and change the world. Because of whom you are and what you do, you will always be my hero.

—*Robert R. Perkinson*

Acknowledgments

Thousands of addiction professionals, mental health workers, and chemical dependency counselors shaped this book. Every comment, suggestion, or question I receive makes it better. I want to thank all of you for helping me over the years. As a field, we have been trying to develop and maintain a treatment book that all addiction professionals could be proud of and use every day. The work of training new staff is exhausting for everyone, and it became necessary for the major treatment centers to develop a standard treatment book that everyone coming on board could read, understand, and have available for review. It had to be practical, simple, and easy to use. It had to have feedback from the best treatment centers in the world. The following key professionals played a major role in developing the manuscript, sharing their training and expertise, and going over the manual in detail. These people never stop walking in the truth, and their light covers the earth.

Bob Bogue, *Clinical Supervisor, Keystone Treatment Center*

Julie Braaten, *Accreditation Coordinator, Keystone Treatment Center*

Bob Carr, *Director, Substance Abuse Program at the VA Regional Hospital in Sioux Falls*

Carol Davis, *Counselor, Betty Ford Center at Eisenhower*

Michael Ford, *Former President, National Association of Addiction Treatment Providers (NAATP)*

Luther Hegland, *Addictionologist, Keystone Treatment Center*

Charles and Jean LaCour, *Net Institute*

Cynthia Moreno-Tuohy, *Executive Director, National Association of Alcohol and Drug Abuse Counselors (NAADAC)*

Terry O'Brian, *Member of Board of Directors, Hazelden*

Donald P. Osborn, *President, National Association of Alcohol and Drug Abuse Counselors (NAADAC)*

Carol Regier, *Executive Director, Keystone Treatment Center*

Gene Regier, *Medical Director, Keystone Treatment Center*

Eleanor Sargent, *Project for Addiction Counselor Training, National Association of Alcohol and Drug Abuse Counselors (NAADAC)*

Nancy Waite-O'Brian, *Clinical Director, Betty Ford Center at Eisenhower*

Richard Weedman, *President Healthcare Network, Inc.*

All of the staff and clients of CRC Health and Keystone Treatment Center

1 The First Contact

Source: ©iStockphoto.com/lisafx.

Someone you know and love is dying of addiction. No one, even the addict, knows the extent of the disease that is poisoning his or her body. More than half of Americans drink, and many of them innocently fall victim to this silent killer. Addicts live their lives deeply alone, immersed in self-told lies. They could not tell you the truth if they wanted to, because they do not know what the truth is. They are living in a world of carefully constructed self-betrayal: "I am fine. I can stop anytime I want. I do not drink or use any more than my friends drink." "Everybody loves to gamble. It is so much fun, and I win." "I was born to use speed." At times, the addicts want to cut down or stop and they try, but they always fail—repeatedly they fail. Addicts live in world full of self-hatred and shame. They do not want anyone to know the terrible truth about their pain. They put on a false front of being fine. You might suspect something is wrong, and you would be right, but there seems to be little you can do to help an addict see the truth. Most addicts die of their addiction. Ninety-five percent of untreated alcoholics die of

"It's aged in oak."

M. Magus

1

alcoholism an average of 26 years early. The death certificate might read heart disease, cancer, or something else to protect the family, but the real reason is addiction.

Addiction is more than a behavior problem. Repeated drug use causes long-lasting changes in the brain, so the addict loses voluntary control. Addicts are obsessed with doing what they hate doing. The addiction is the only way they know how to feel normal. Not to use causes withdrawal, which is too painful to consider. In time, the addict's brain changes to the point that they cannot get high and they cannot get sober. This is when addicts feel hopeless, helpless, and powerless, and their lives are unmanageable. This is when many of them come in for treatment.

In America, 51.1% of the population drinks alcohol, and a little less than a third of them will have a substance use disorder sometime in their lifetime (Substance Abuse and Mental Health Services Administration [SAMHSA], 2007). In the United States, almost one million people die of substance abuse disorders annually. This does not count the people who die of diabetes, coronary artery disease, and cancer caused by drinking, smoking, poor eating, and lack of exercising. Heavy drinking or drug use contributes to illnesses in each of the top three causes of death: heart disease, cancer, and stroke. At least 13.8 million Americans develop problems associated with drinking. Over many years of following alcohol and drug problems, studies find that 78% of high school seniors have tried alcohol. Fifty-three percent have tried illegal drugs. Fifty-seven percent of high school seniors have tried cigarettes, and 27% are current smokers. Addiction is one of the most horrible plagues to attack the human race. According to the Centers for Disease Control and Prevention (CDC), 25% of Americans die as a direct result of substance abuse (Heron et al., 2009).

Millions of Americans are dying annually of preventable conditions.

- 443,000 die of tobacco products.
- 365,000 die of improper diet and exercise habits.
- 75,000 die of alcohol abuse.
- 75,000 die of microbial agents.
- 55,000 of toxic agents.
- 32,000 die of adverse reactions to prescription drugs.
- 26,000 die of automobile accidents.
- 29,000 die of firearms.
- 29,300 die of homicide.
- 20,000 die of sexual behavior.
- 17,000 die of illegal drugs ("Annual Causes of Death in the United States," 2011).

Treatment Works

Most addicts will quit on their own by making a highly motivated personal choice then working hard at recovery, usually with multiple attempts at quitting and periods of relapse and reevaluation. Most of the people who quit on their own have learned about treatment and recovery through someone who is in recovery, or from a health care professional. These people make the choice that the negative consequences of continued use outweigh the rewards of continued use. They go through the same motivational steps that a client needs to make in treatment (DiClemente, 2006b). Some clients cannot seem to quit on their own, and they need treatment. We know from many years of scientific experiments that addiction treatment works. For every dollar spent on treatment, the economy saves $7 in heath care and costs to society. Most clients who work a program of recovery stay clean and sober. To get clean, clients have to come out of hiding and use their journey to help others. By sharing our experience, strength, and hope, addicts in recovery give others reasons to get clean. Working the program means getting honest, going to recovery group meetings, and making conscious contact with a higher power of their own understanding (Johnston, O'Malley, Bachman, & Schulenberg, 2008; McLellan, 2006).

Your first meeting with an addict might be accidental or it might be by appointment. During the interview, you—if you look and listen closely—will sense something is wrong with this person, but you do not know what it is. You have a clinical thermometer inside of you that you will learn to trust. This is more than intuition; it is a gift. The skill is to watch the client so carefully and listen so intensely that you pick up cues that others miss. The person might look depressed and anxious. Her face may be red and swollen, his eyes watery and red, or the person may be markedly thin with scabs caused by "meth bugs." He might have a fine hand tremor or have difficulty sitting still. Sometimes the person's head hangs in depression that looks like shame. Something is wrong, and it will nag at you. That clinical thermometer feels uncomfortable, and you do not like it.

If you are reading this manual, you have probably been a natural born healer all of your life. When you were a little kid, you cared a little more about puppies and kittens than others did. People in school talked to you and told you secrets when they would not talk to anyone else. People recognize a healer when they see one.

There is another side of you that is very different. It has been in trouble with clients like this before. Sometimes being a healer is not good. Sometimes you have to tell people the truth when they do not want to hear it. They can rebel against you and fight. You have learned that sometimes it is best to let the truth go—or worse, lie to yourself and your clients and let them go. You hate that part of yourself, but you have learned how to live with it. After all, you live in a world full of litigation and managed care. Fear has overcome your best judgment many times.

And there is that client sitting in your office, crying out for the healer in you. Clients desperately need someone to tell them the truth. This time if you let the problem go, if you take the easy way out, the client may die. Addiction is like brain cancer. To let this client out of your office without confronting the truth is to be responsible for the client's death.

Yet you have confronted addicts before. Addicts seem to have two sides of them. One side knows they are in trouble while the other side knows they can continue the addiction safely. You and your client are in a life or death battle with the truth. The trick is to help the client win. You are up against a great enemy. Alcoholics Anonymous (AA) (2002a) says this illness is "cunning, baffling and powerful" (pp. 58–59).

The battle lines are drawn. The illness inside of the client is confident of victory. It thinks that you will take the easy way out. You will handle the acute problem and let the client go home. You will not ask the questions that could lead to the truth. That would be too much trouble; besides, you are too busy.

The enemy does not know that you are a healer. You will not lie, and you will not let the addict go home to die. You are going to fight. This is who you are, and it is who you will always be. To be anything else leaves you in shame.

The Motivational Interview

So you decide to take action. Either you do this yourself or you call in an addiction professional to do it for you. You suspect your client is addicted. Your client does not even want to know the reason because to know the truth confronts him or her with change. Your job is to go with the client toward the truth. It does no good to go against the client's idea of himself or herself. Arguing with the client will not work because the addict is an expert at giving every excuse in the world for abnormal behavior. If you argue, the client will win because he or she will leave your office convinced you are a bad person. Walk *with* the client toward the truth. Listen and seek out ambivalence about the negative consequences of continuing the addictive behavior. This is client-centered counseling, not self-centered counseling. You must listen so you can step into the client's world and connect with that gentle voice of reason inside of them. That healthy voice is there, and

Source: ©iStockphoto.com/AlexRaths.

your job is to connect with it, empathize with it, and pull for more. The other voice in clients' heads says something else is to blame. They might have a problem, but it has nothing to do with addiction.

As a professional, you are used to your clients being honest with you, but this one is going to lie. The client is not a bad person; he or she is a good person with a bad disease. The disease of addiction lives in and grows in the self-told lie. The client must lie to himself or herself and believe the lie or the illness cannot continue. The client will have a long list of excuses for his or her behavior:

My spouse has a problem.

The police have a problem.

The school has a problem.

My boyfriend has a problem.

I have a physical problem.

I am depressed.

I am anxious.

I have a stomachache.

I cannot sleep.

The excuses go on and on, and they might confuse you if you are caught up in them. They are all part of a tangled web of deceit. Remember, your job is to walk with the client toward the truth, not against the client toward the truth. You are going to spend most of your time agreeing with the client. When the client is honest, you are going to agree. When the client is dishonest, you are going to probe for the truth. Look at it this way: If the client is listening to you, you can work. If the client is not listening to you, anything you say is useless.

Watch the client's nonverbal behavior very carefully. You are a healer, and you have the gift of supersensitivity. Your intuition will tell you whether the client is going with you or resisting. When the client goes with you, you feel peace. When the client goes against you, you feel uncomfortable. When the client is ready, you will educate him or her about the disease. This is a gentle process, and it takes time. If you are in a hurry, this is not going to work.

The client has been using the addiction for a long time to relieve pain. All addictions tell the brain, Good choice! All organisms have a way of finding their way in a complicated lethal environment. They learn which foods are good and which are bad. They find the best way through the jungle. They learn what is safe and what is dangerous. We learn these things deep in the reptilian brain. What is good is remembered. If it is very good, it is remembered after one experience. The addiction has been good to this client for many years, but now it is destructive. The very thing that gave the client joy now gives pain. This process fools the client. Remember, the addiction has always said, Good choice! So how can it be a bad choice? You are fighting with the client's basic understanding of the world, and he or she will be convinced that you are wrong. You must help the client see that the addiction is no longer a good choice—it is a deadly choice. The addict cannot see this alone, but AA has an old saying: "What we cannot do alone, we can do together." The client cannot discover the truth without your help. You must guide the client toward a decision he or she finds impossible. You need to help clients see that they need to stop the addictive behavior.

What you are looking for is the truth. The client will rarely tell you accurate symptoms. You have to look for signs of the disease. You will continue to investigate—testing; smelling the air; ordering laboratory studies; and talking to family, friends, court workers, school personnel, and anyone else who can help you until you uncover the truth.

Your client cannot tell you the truth because the client does not know the truth. Addiction hijacks a client's thinking, a web of self-deception. Remember, you are the healer. You care for your clients even if they hate themselves. You are going to love them even though they are being deceptive. You are going to help them even though they do not understand what you are doing.

How to Develop the Therapeutic Alliance

From the first contact, your client is learning some important things about you. You are friendly. You are on his or her side. You are not going to beat up, shame, or blame your client. You answer any questions. You are honest, and you hold nothing back. You discuss every option in detail. You are committed to do what is best for the client. You provide the information, and the client makes the decisions. The client sees you as a concerned professional. In time, the client begins to hope that you can help. The therapeutic alliance is built from an initial foundation of love, trust, and commitment.

You show the client that he or she does not have to feel alone. Neither of you can recover alone. Both of you are needed in cooperation with each other to solve the problem. The client knows things that you do not know. The client knows himself or herself better than anyone else does, and he or she needs to learn how to share his or her life with you. Likewise, you have knowledge that the client does not have. You know the tools of recovery.

The client must trust you. To establish this trust, you must be honest and consistent. You must prove to the client, repeatedly, that you are going to be actively involved in his or her individual growth. You are not going to argue or shame the client; you are going to try to understand him or her. When you say you are going to do something, you do it. When you make a promise, you keep it. You never try to get something from a client without using the truth. You never manipulate, even to get something good. The first time a client might catch you in a lie, even a small one, your alliance is weakened.

If you work in a treatment facility or group practice, the client must learn that your staff works as a team. You can share with the whole team what the client tells you—even in confidence. The client will occasionally test this. The client will tell you that he or she has something to share, but that it can only be shared with you. The client wants you to keep it secret. Many early professionals fall into this trap. The truth is that all facts are friendly and all information is vital to recovery. You must explain to the client that if he or she feels too uncomfortable sharing certain information that the client should keep it secret for the time being. Maybe they can share this information later when they feel more comfortable.

The client must understand that you are committed to his or her recovery, but you cannot recover for the client. You cannot do the work by yourself. You must work together, cooperatively. You can only teach the tools of recovery. The client must use the tools to stay sober.

How to Do a Motivational Interview

In the first interview, you begin to motivate clients to see the truth about their problem. Questions about alcohol and other drug use are most appropriately asked as a part of the history of personal habits, such as use of tobacco products and caffeine. Questions should be asked candidly and in a nonjudgmental manner to avoid defensiveness. Remember that this is client-centered interviewing, not professional-centered, and the interview should incorporate the following elements (with the client being free of alcohol at the time of the screening) (DiClemente, 2006a; Prochaska, 2003):

- Offer empathic, objective feedback of data.
- Work with ambivalence.
- Meet the client's expectations.
- Assess the client's readiness for change.
- Assess barriers and strengths significant to recovery efforts.
- Reinterpret the client's experiences in light of the current problem.
- Negotiate a follow-up plan.
- Provide hope.

Example of a Motivational Interview

Professional: Hello, Frank, I am _____ (*your name*). Why did you come in to see me today?

Client: My wife wanted me to talk to you.

Professional: Why did she want that?

Client: I do not know.

Professional: I talked to your wife on the phone yesterday, and she said she was concerned about your drinking.

Client: She is always concerned about something. Her father was an alcoholic so she thinks everyone drinks too much. (*The client looks irritated.*)

Professional: Sounds like things are not going well at home? (*The professional mirrors the client's feelings and facial expression. When you mirror a person's expression, you validate his or her worldview.*)

Client: I do not know. It is just that she gets all worked up about everything.

Professional: Your wife said you have been drinking heavily every day. She is afraid for you.

Client: I work hard, and I like to come home and relax with a few beers. Is anything wrong with that? (*The client is obviously irritated with coming to the interview. So far, the client is saying,* My wife has a lot of problems.)

Professional: There's nothing wrong with relaxing. How do you relax? (*The professional goes with the client's point of view.*)

Client: I have a couple of beers. So what.

Professional: Your wife says you have been drinking a 12-pack a day.

Client: It is not that much.

Professional: Are you drinking more than a couple of beers a day? (*The professional is gently pulling for the truth.*)

Client:	Maybe a little more.
Professional:	Is it around 12?
Client:	I work hard, and I deserve to relax. *(The client is resisting, and the professional backs off a little. It is important to keep the client's ears open. Be empathic, tender, and understanding. Try to see the problem from the client's point of view. Once you enter the client's world and understand his or her point of view, you will get clues about what will motivate the client to change. This client is mad at his wife and he needs some help with that, but what is his real problem?)*
Professional:	I like to relax after a hard day, too. Your wife sounds afraid for you. What is frightening her?
Client:	My wife just sits around all day and watches television while I am working my tail off.
Professional:	So you really need to relax when you come home. Particularly if you feel like you are pulling the load all by yourself?
Client:	Yeah, she sits around and thinks about things to argue with me about.

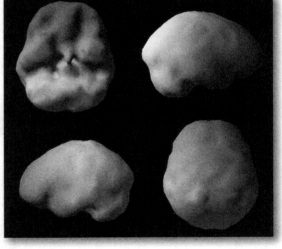

Professional:	Do you think your wife loves you? *(This is pulling the client toward the truth. Why is his wife worried about him?)*
Client:	Well, yeah, I think she does. *(The client visibly softens.)*
Professional:	It is great to have a wife who loves you. Sounds like you are a lucky man. *(The professional reinterprets the client's experience in light of the alcohol problem.)*
Client:	But I am not drinking too much. I am just drinking a few beers.
Professional:	You said it was 12. *(The professional reminds the client what he said earlier to cement the fact.)* What is the most beer you have ever drunk in a full day?

Client:	Oh, I do not know.
Professional:	Give me a guess.
Client:	Well, on the weekends I can drink up to a case if I am watching a ball game.
Professional:	That is a lot of beer. *(The professional determines the client is an alcoholic but does not jump the gun; the client is not ready yet.)*
Client:	Not if I am drinking all day.
Professional:	Did you know that if you drink more than three beers a day, more than three times a week, your organs are dying? Alcohol is a poison. It kills the brain, heart, kidneys, every cell in the body. If you are drinking more than three drinks per day, you are

More substance abuse pictures are available at www.brainplace.com.

literally killing yourself. That might be why your wife is worried about you? (*The professional believes the client's ears are open, so it is time to try a little education.*)

I want to show you a single photon emission computed tomography (SPECT) scan pictures of a healthy brain and a brain of someone who abuses alcohol.

The client quickly looks away. He does not want to see a picture of his brain dying. However, he did see it, and he could not make that fact go away. He has to rapidly deny the professional's statements and the pictures or admit that he has a problem. A part of him knows he has a drinking problem, and now it is confirmed. It is not only his wife's opinion but now a picture and a professional's opinion confirm the diagnosis. He has not admitted it yet, but he knows he has been drinking too much.

The professional begins negotiating and assessing the client's readiness for change.

Professional:	Bob, have you ever worried about your drinking?
Client:	No, honestly, I have not. (*This comes across as real. When the words and the client's affect match, they are probably telling the truth. Most addicts think their addictive behavior is normal.*)
Professional:	Maybe that is because you did not understand how much you could drink safely. If alcohol is killing you, do you not want to know?
Client:	Well, sure.
Professional:	Looking at these pictures, and thinking about how much you have been drinking, do you think you have been drinking too much? (*The professional is taking the biggest chance of all.*)
Client:	Maybe? (*Maybe is very close to a yes. The client has admitted that he drinks too much. That moves him from the precontemplation phase to the contemplation phase. For the first time, he is considering the negative consequences of his drinking. This is a huge step toward recovery.*)
Professional:	Did you know that 95% of untreated alcoholics die of their alcoholism? And they die 26 years earlier than they would otherwise.

The client says nothing.

Professional:	Knowing what you know now, would you like to learn how to drink less or even stop drinking entirely? (*The professional is negotiating how far the client is willing to go to get better.*)
Client:	I did not know it was that bad. (*Now the client is contemplating change. We are on the road to recovery. With a gentle approach, the professional can negotiate and listen to the client's life from his or her perspective, allowing the client to move toward the truth.*)
Professional:	Why don't we meet again with your wife and talk about what we can do to help you two feel better? Would that be all right with you?
Client:	If you think it will help.
Professional:	Most people who try to get better get better.
Client:	Okay, let's do it. (*A commitment to change has occurred. Now the client realizes he has a problem and is making plans to take action. These are the first giant steps toward recovery.*)

Questions to Ask the Adult Client

The National Institute on Alcohol Abuse and Alcoholism (NIAAA) has developed the following low-risk drinking guidelines:

Men should drink no more than two drinks a day and no more than four drinks on a single occasion.

Women and clients over 65 years of age should drink no more than one drink a day and no more than three drinks on a single occasion.

Pregnant clients and those with medical problems complicated by alcohol use should abstain completely ("U.S. Surgeon General Releases Advisory on Alcohol Use in Pregnancy," 2005).

We could also add that no person should ingest an illegal substance.

If a person cannot stop something they want to stop, it is an addiction.

At some time during the first interview, certain questions need to be asked to assess addiction problems. They have to be answered honestly to give you a clear picture of the extent of the problem. Most clients who have addiction problems will be evasive or deny their addiction, so the questions should be asked of the client, as well as a reliable family member.

The following questions and flags are taken from the American Society of Addiction Medicine (ASAM) (http://www.asam.org):

1. Have you ever tried to cut down on your drinking?

2. Have you ever felt annoyed when someone talked to you about your drinking?

3. Have you ever felt bad or guilty about your drinking?

4. Have you ever had a drink in the morning to settle yourself down?

5. Has alcohol or drugs ever caused your family problems?

6. Has a physician ever told you to cut down on or quit use of alcohol?

7. When drinking/using drugs, have you ever had a memory loss or a blackout?

Similar questions could be asked about gambling or any other addictive behavior. If clients answer yes to any one of these questions, it is a red flag for addiction. If they answer yes to two questions, it is probably addiction. Make sure you do not just ask the client. Ask family members, friends, and anyone else who can give you collateral information. (See Figures 1.1 through 1.5.)

Figure 1.1 Client History/Behavioral Observation Red Flags for Addiction

Tremor/perspiring/tachycardia

Evidence of current intoxication

Prescription drug-seeking behavior

Frequent falls; unexplained bruises

Diabetes-elevated blood pressure; ulcers nonresponsive to treatment

Frequent hospitalizations

Gunshot/knife wound

Suicide talk/attempt; depression

Pregnancy (screen all)

Figure 1.2   Laboratory Red Flags for Adult Alcohol/Drug Abuse

Mean corpuscular volume (MCV)—Over 95

Mean corpuscular hemoglobin (MCH)—High

Gamma-glutamyl transferase (GGT)—High

Serum glutamic-oxaloacetic transaminase (SGOT)—High

Bilirubin—High

Triglycerides—High

Anemia

Positive urinalysis for alcohol

Figure 1.3   Client History/Behavioral Observation Red Flags for Adolescent Alcohol Abuse

Physical injuries: motor vehicle accident (MVA), gunshot/knife wound, unexplained or repeated injuries

Evidence of current use (e.g., dilated/pinpoint pupils, tremors, perspiring, tachycardia, slurred/rapid speech)

Persistent cough (cigarette smoking is a risk factor)

Engages in risky behavior (e.g., unprotected sex)

Marked fall in academic/extracurricular performance

Suicide talk/attempt; depression

Sexually transmitted diseases

Staphylococcus infection on face, arms, legs

Unexplained weight loss

Pregnancy (screen all)

Figure 1.4   Laboratory Red Flags for Adolescent Alcohol/Drug Abuse

- Positive urinalysis for alcohol/illicit drugs
- Hepatitis A-B-C
- GGT—High
- SGOT—High
- Bilirubin—High

Figure 1.5   Interview Questions for Suspected Addiction Among Adolescents

Questions to Ask the Adolescent Client

1. When did you first use alcohol on your own, away from family/caregivers?

2. How often do you use alcohol or drugs? When was your last use?

3. How often have you been drunk or high?

4. Has your alcohol or drug use caused you problems with your friendships, family, school, community, etc.? Have your grades slipped?

5. Have you had problems with the law?

6. Have you ever tried to quit/cut down? What happened?

7. Are you concerned about your alcohol or drug use?

Questions to Ask the Parent/Caregiver

1. Do you know/suspect your child is using alcohol/other drugs?

2. Has your child's behavior changed significantly in the past 6 months (e.g., sneaky, secretive, isolated, assaultive, aggressive, hostile)?

3. Has the school, community, or legal system talked to you about your child?

4. Has there been a marked fall in academic/extracurricular performance?

5. Do you believe an alcohol/other drug assessment might be helpful?

What to Do If There Are One or More Red Flags

Once you have one or more red flags, you have several important actions to take:

1. Advise the client of the risk.

2. Advise abstinence or moderation. Men should be advised to drink no more than three drinks at a time and no more than three nights a week. Women should be advised to drink no more than two drinks at a time and no more than three nights per week. More drinking than this will result in disease. This is a harm reduction approach where you teach a client how to drink responsibly. This would not be appropriate for someone who has a serious drinking problem.

3. Advise against any illegal drug use.

4. Schedule a follow-up visit to monitor progress.

Natural History of Addiction

Addiction can begin at any age, and it often occurs in individuals with no history of psychological problems. When the addictive substance is readily available, inexpensive, and rapid acting, the incidence of use increases. Whenever the individual is ignorant of healthy alcohol or drug use, susceptible to heavily using peers, or has a high genetic predisposition to abuse or to antisocial personality disorder, abuse may increase. This is also true if the client is poorly socialized into the culture, in pain, or if the culture makes a substance the recreational drug of choice.

Risk Factors

Risk factor 1: Substance or behavior is readily available.

Risk factor 2: Substance use or addictive behavior is cheap.

Risk factor 3: The addictive chemicals reach the brain quickly.

Risk factor 4: Addiction is a pain reliever.

Risk factor 5: Addiction is more common in certain occupations (bartending).

Risk factor 6: Addiction is prevalent in the peer group.

Risk factor 7: Addiction is preferred in deviant subcultures.

Risk factor 8: Social instability is found.

Risk factor 9: There is a genetic predisposition.

Risk factor 10: The family is dysfunctional.

Risk factor 11: Comorbid psychiatric disorders are present (Vaillant, 2003).

How to Diagnose an Addiction Problem

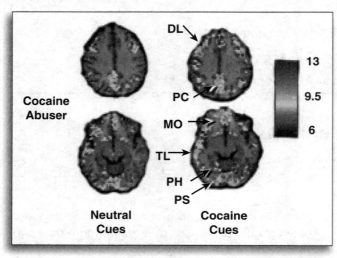

Source: From "Activation of Memory Circuits During Cue-Elicited Cocaine Craving", by S. Grant et al., 1996, *Proceedings of the National Academy of Sciences,* USA, 93, pp. 12040–12045.

In the assessment, you must determine if the clients fit into your range of experience and care. Do you have the ability to deal with his or her problem, or do you need to refer to someone else? Does the client have a problem with chemicals or an addictive behavior? Is he or she motivated to get better? Does the client have the resources necessary for treatment? Is the individual well enough to see you? For the most part, you will start by asking yourself certain basic questions: Does this person have signs and symptoms of addiction? Does he or she need treatment? Is he or she motivated for treatment? What kind of treatment does she or he need? For the benefit of third-party payers, it is important to use assessment instruments to document (1) diagnosis, (2) severity of addiction, and (3) motivation and rehabilitation potential. Third-party reviewers will often have more faith in a test battery than your clinical opinion.

There are a number of companies that sell inexpensive, disposable breathalyzers and drug screening instruments, including Prevent (1-800-624-1404); Bi-TechNostix (1-888-339-9964); Random Drug Screens, Inc. (1-803-772-0027); Drug Screens, Inc. (1-800-482-0693); hair screens; Pharmchec Drugs of Abuse Patch, which lasts 2 weeks; a new GGT alcohol screen that will test for alcohol injection for 80 hours after use; ankle bracelets that measure alcohol in the sweat of probationers 24 hours, 7 days a week. Order a number of these tests, and have them readily available for assessment, treatment, and continued care monitoring. Positive tests are only suggestive of drug and alcohol use, so before any legal or workplace action is taken, the test should be confirmed by both an approved immunoassay and gas chromatography/mass spectrometry, which can be administered and analyzed by a health care provider (SAMHSA, 2007). Two quick screening tests for alcoholism have been developed: the Short Michigan Alcoholism Screening Test (SMAST) (see Appendix 2), (Selzer, Winokur, & van Rooijen, 1975) and the CAGE questionnaire (Ewing, 1984; Selzer et al., 1975). The Michigan Alcoholism Screening Test (MAST) or SMAST has greater than 90% sensitivity to detect alcoholism. It can be administered to either the client or the spouse.

The Substance Abuse Subtle Screening Inventory (SASSI) (1-800-726-0526; www.sassi.com) was developed to screen clients when defensive and in denial. The SASSI measures defensiveness and the subtle attributes that are common in chemically dependent persons. It is a difficult test to fake, unlike the SMAST or the CAGE. Clients can complete the SASSI in 10 to 15 minutes, and it takes 1 or 2 minutes to score. It identifies accurately 98% of clients who need residential treatment, 90% of nonusers, and 87% of early stage abusers. This is a good test for those clients with whom you are still unsure about the diagnosis after your first few interviews—clients who continue to be evasive (Miller, 1985).

The Addiction Severity Index (ASI) and the Teen-Addiction Severity Index (T-ASI) (1-215-399-0980) are widely used, structured interviews for adults and teens and are designed to provide important information about the severity of the client's substance abuse problem. These instruments assess seven dimensions typically of concern in addiction, including medical status, employment/support status, drug/alcohol use, legal status, family history, family/social relationships, and psychiatric status. The tests are administered by a trained technician. The ASI is an excellent tool for delineating the client's case management needs (Kaminer, Bukstein, & Tarter, 1991; McLellan, Luborsky, & Woody, 1980).

The Adolescent Alcohol Involvement Scale (AAIS) is a 14-item, self-report questionnaire that takes about 15 minutes to administer. It evaluates the type and frequency of drinking, the last drinking episode, reasons for the onset of drinking behavior, drinking context, short- and long-term effects of drinking, perceptions about drinking and how others perceive his or her drinking (Mayer & Filstead, 1979; Mee-Lee, 1988; Mee-Lee, Hoffman, & Smith, 1992) (1-800-755-6299). The RAATE-CE is a 35-item scale that assesses treatment readiness and examines client awareness of problems; behavioral intent to change; capacity to anticipate future treatment needs; and medical, psychiatric, or environmental complications. The RAATE-CE determines the client's level of acceptance and readiness to engage in treatment and targets impediments to change.

How to Intervene

- Nonproblem Usage: If the client is low-risk for addiction, you should provide positive prevention messages that support the client has continued positive lifestyle. A client with a positive family history of addiction should be warned about their increased vulnerability to addiction and the need for vigilance.

- Problem With Addiction: The client who has had recurrent problems due to addiction should be encouraged to abstain from, or at least reduce, his or her addictive behavior. A client such as this should be strongly encouraged to abstain from all illegal drugs and addictive behaviors. You should discuss the biopsychosocial complications of addiction (see Appendix 8). A client who is encouraged to cut down on his or her addictive behavior should be provided with the brochure from NIAAA (see Appendix 9). It is essential that these clients be reassessed frequently to monitor their ability to comply with your recommended limits.

- Addiction: Addicts need to have their diagnoses carefully discussed with them and a treatment plan negotiated. You need to be empathic and address the problems that seem to be caused by or made worse by the client's continued addictive behavior. The client needs to hear that this illness is not his or her fault and that there is excellent treatment available that will help the individual to stay clean and sober. The client needs to hear that only 4% of addicts can quit on their own over the course of a year, but 50% can quit over the course of a year if they go through treatment. Seventy percent can quit over the course of a year if they also attend AA meetings regularly, and 90% can stay sober if they go through treatment, attend meetings, and go to continuing care once a week for a year (Hoffmann, 1991, 1994; Hoffman & Harrison, 1987). The client should also be told about the potential benefits of naltrexone, accamprosate, and disulfiram when used along with formal treatment programs. Carefully discuss the ASAM client placement criteria to help you and the client negotiate the best treatment plan possible to bring the addiction under control. (See Figure 1.6.) The following questions may be helpful in negotiating a treatment plan:

1. Is the client a danger to self or others (suicidal and homicidal ideation, impaired judgment while intoxicated, history of delirium tremens)?

2. Has the client ever been able to stay clean for 3 or more days?

3. What happened when the client stopped the addictive behavior in the past? How serious were the withdrawal symptoms?

4. Has the client ever been able to stay completely abstinent for long periods?

5. Why did previous attempts at staying clean fail?

6. How does the family understand alcoholism and its treatment?

Figure 1.6   Positive and Negative Prognostic Factors

Positive Prognostic Factors

- Lack of physical dependence
- Intact family
- Stable job
- Presence of prior treatment (prognosis improves for clients who have been through one to three treatments)
- Absence of psychiatric disease
- Presence of long-term monitoring arrangement, such as a Physician Effectiveness Program or Employee Assistance Program

Negative Prognostic Factors

- More severe, advanced dependency
- Presence of intoxication at office visits
- Loss of job
- Loss of home
- Loss of family
- Multiple, unsuccessful attempts at treatment
- Severe physiological dependence
- Coexisting psychiatric disorders
- Absence of long-term monitoring (Conigliaro, Reyes, Parran, & Schultz, 2003)

How to Assess Motivation

Constantly ask yourself about the client's stage of motivation and introduce appropriate motivating strategies to move the client up a motivational level. This book will give you many ways of doing this. No client is alike, so you must be creative in helping the client to see the inaccuracies in his or her thinking and move away from the lies toward the truth.

The Stages of Motivation

Precontemplation

The individual is not intending to take action in regards to his or her substance abuse problem in the near future.

Tasks: Try to increase awareness of the need to change; increase concern about the current pattern of behavior.

Goal: Make a serious consideration of change.

Contemplation

The individual examines the current behavior and the potential for change in a risk–reward analysis.

Tasks: Analyze the pros and cons of the current behavior and of the costs and benefits of change.

Goal: Write a list of the positive and negative consequences of continued use.

Preparation

The individual makes a commitment to take action to change and develops a plan for change.

Tasks: Increase commitment and create a change plan.

Goal: Create an action plan to be implemented in the near future.

Action

The individual implements the plan and takes steps to change and begins new behavior patterns.

Tasks: Implement change and revise the plan as needed while sustaining commitment in the face of difficulty.

Goal: Develop a successful action for changing behavior and establish a new pattern of behavior for a significant period of time (3–6 months).

Maintenance

The new behavior is sustained for an extended period of time and is consolidated into the lifestyle of the individual.

Tasks: Sustain change over time and integrate the behavior into everyday life.

Goal: Sustain long-term change of the old behavior and establish a new pattern of behavior (DiClemente, 2006a; Prochaska & DiClemente, 1983; Prochaska, DiClemente, & Norcross, 1992; Prochaska, Norcross, & DiClemente, 1994).

Motivating Strategies

Clients at different stages of motivation will need different motivating strategies to keep them moving toward recovery, and these stages are not static. Clients can shift back and forth through the stages for various reasons or spontaneously. Clients in the precontemplation stage underestimate the benefits of change and overestimate its cost. They are not aware that they are making mistakes in judgment, and they believe they are right. Environmental events can trigger a person to move up to the contemplation stage. An arrest, a spouse threatening to leave, or a formal intervention can all increase motivation to change. Persons in the precontemplation stage cannot be treated as if they are in the action stage. If they are pressured to take action, they will terminate treatment (Prochaska, 2003).

A client in the preparation stage has a plan of action to cut down or quit his or her addictive behavior in the near future. Such a client is ready for input from professionals, counselors, or self-help books. The client should be recruited and motivated for action. Action is the client changing his or her behavior to cut down or quit the addiction. This is the client who has entered early recovery and is involved in treatment (DiClemente, 2006a).

In the maintenance stage, the client is still changing his or her behavior to be better and is working to prevent relapse. A client who relapses is not well prepared for the prolonged effort it takes to stay clean and sober. All clients need to be followed in long-term containing care because addiction is fraught with relapse and clients need encouragement and support for years to stay in recovery. Addicts typically do not have the skills to work a program in early recovery. This takes time, commitment, and discipline, constantly trying to raise the client's consciousness about the causes, consequences, and possible treatments for a particular problem. Denial is unconscious, and one must help the client raise the material from unconscious to conscious. Clients can make a better decision consciously than they can without automatically thinking about the consequences of their addictive behavior. Interventions that increase awareness include observation, confrontation, interpretation, feedback, and education, pointing out the need to reevaluate the environment and change behavior. Encourage the client to reevaluate his or her self-image and explain how this is negatively affected by the addictive behavior. Encourage the client to learn the new skills of being honest, helping others, and seeking a relationship with a higher power (DiClemente, 2006a).

In order to help motivate clients to progress from one stage to the next, it is necessary to know the principles and processes of change (DiClemente, 2006a; Prochaska, 2003; Prochaska & DiClemente, 1983; Prochaska et al., 1992; Prochaska et al., 1994).

Figure 1.7 Processes of Change for the Client in Precontemplation Stage

1. Consciousness raising involves increasing the client's awareness of the causes, consequences, and responses to the alcohol problem.

2. Dramatic relief involves increasing the client's emotional arousal about one's current behavior and the relief that can come from changing.

3. Environmental reevaluation has the client assess the effects the alcohol problem has on one's social environment and how changing would affect that environment.

4. Self-reevaluation has the client assess his or her image of one's self free from alcohol problems.

5. Self-liberation involves the belief that one can change and the commitment and recommitment to act on that belief.

6. Counter-conditioning requires the learning of healthier behaviors that can substitute for drinking alcohol.

7. Contingency management involves the systematic use of reinforcers and punishments for taking steps in a particular direction.

8. Stimulus control involves modifying the environment to increase cues that promote healthy responses and decrease cues that lead to relapse.

The following process should be applied to clients in the precontemplation stage (see Figure 1.7) (DiClemente, 2006a; Prochaska, 2003; Prochaska & DiClemente, 1983; Prochaska et al., 1994).

Helping relationships combine caring, openness, trust, and acceptance, as well as family and community support for change.

2   The Drugs

Source: Comstock/Thinkstock.

Drugs of Abuse

It is not the purpose of this book to discuss all of the drugs of abuse. This is left to other texts such as *Uppers, Downers, All Arounders* by Inaba and Cohen (2007). All counselors should keep a copy of this excellent text close by their desk. Addicts are constantly inventing some new way to get high so the drug of abuse will always be changing. The major drugs of abuse seen in treatment are alcohol, cocaine, opioids, and methamphetamine (Centers for Disease Control and Prevention [CDC], 2009; www.cdc.gov).

All psychoactive drugs of abuse alter feelings, thoughts, and behavior. They directly affect the brain or the central nervous system (CNS). The specific actions of these drugs are highly complex. Feelings are altered when the drugs affect neurotransmitters and intercellular communications that seek a

"I'm going to quit tomorrow."

balance between excitatory and inhibitory functions. Every organism is driven toward establishing a balance between these two systems called homeostasis. Only humans seem to seek drug intoxication states. Other organisms avoid altered mind states because it makes vulnerable venerable to predation and death. The only way laboratory animals can be enticed to ingest drugs of abuse is to mix them with water or food. However, once addicted, animals use drugs compulsively to the point of choosing drugs over food, water, or sex. An addicted brain is a changed brain. Addiction is abnormal behavior that results from dysfunction in brain tissue. Addiction is just as physical a disease as heart disease or cancer (Leshner, 1997).

It is widely believed by many experts in the field that the level of drug use in the United States is the highest in the industrialized world. An estimated 21.1 million Americans used a drug illegally during the month prior to being surveyed in the 2008 National Household Survey on Drug Use and Health: National Findings (see Appendix 42). Nearly half of Americans (51.6%) 12 years old or over had used alcohol, 17.3% were binge drinkers, and 28.4% used tobacco products.

Specific drug action depends on the route of administration, the dose, the presence or absence of other drugs, and the clinical state of the individual. In general, psychoactive drugs can be classified by their primary action on the CNS.

Central Nervous System Depressants

The CNS depressants depress nervous tissue at all levels of the brain and nervous system. The CNS depressants include all sleeping medications, antianxiety drugs (also called minor tranquilizers), opium derivatives, cannabis, and inhalants (Hardman, Limbird, Molinoff, Ruddon, & Gilman, 1996; Inaba & Cohen, 2007; Schuckit, 1984).

Central Nervous System Stimulants

The CNS stimulants achieve their effect either by the stimulation of nervous tissue through blocking the actions of inhibitory cells or releasing transmitter substances from the cells or by the direct action of the drugs themselves. These drugs include all of the amphetamines and cocaine. Nicotine and caffeine also stimulate nervous tissue but to a much lesser degree (Hardman et al., 1996; Inaba & Cohen, 2007; Schuckit, 1984).

The Hallucinogens

The effect of these drugs is the production of an altered perception, thought, or feeling that cannot be experienced otherwise except in dreams. The hallucinations usually are of a visual nature. These drugs have no known medical usefulness. The most common hallucinogen currently found on the street is lysergic acid diethylamide (LSD) (Carroll & Comer, 1998; Inaba & Cohen, 2007; Jaffe, 1980).

The Reinforcing Properties of Drugs

Drugs of abuse are powerful reinforcers. Animals quickly learn to self-administer most of these drugs for their rewarding properties. Animals will press a lever more than 4,000 times to get a single injection of cocaine. They will continue to self-administer for weeks, alternating between self-imposed abstinence and drug administration. These animals generally die of drug toxicity and lack of food. They would rather use drugs than eat (Wise & Kelsey, 1998).

When given continuous access to drugs of abuse, animals show patterns of self-administration strikingly similar to those of human users of the same drug. These drugs are strongly reinforcing even in the absence of physical dependence. An addicted brain is a brain that has changed in chemistry, structure, and genetics to the point that the drug or addictive behavior undermines voluntary control. Chronic drug exposure alters neurons in dopamine-related circuits causing compulsive drug administration and poor inhibitory control. It is estimated that 40% to 60% of vulnerability to addiction is genetic (Thompson & Pickens, 1970; Uhl & Grow, 2004; Volkow & Li, 2009; Woods & Carney, 1977).

Tolerance and Dependence

Tolerance and physical dependence develop after chronic administration of any one of a wide variety of mood-altering substances. With increasing tolerance, the individual needs more of the drug to get the same effect. Tolerance and dependency develop as the nerve cells chemically and structurally counteract the drug's psychoactive effects. Tolerance is a complex generalized phenomenon that involves many independent physiological and behavioral mechanisms. It leaves the chemically dependent individual physiologically and psychologically craving the drug. The individual becomes obsessed with obtaining the drug for a sense of well-being. The chemically dependent person becomes inflexible in his or her behavior toward the drug despite adverse consequences. The intensity of this felt "need" or dependence may vary from a mild craving to an intense overwhelming obsession. At severe levels, the individual becomes very preoccupied with the drug (Inaba & Cohen, 2007; Kalant et al., 1978; Nestler, 1998; Wilcox, Gonzales, & Erickson, 1994).

Physical dependence is characterized by withdrawal symptoms. Withdrawal develops in an addicted individual when the drug is discontinued too quickly. Physical dependence occurs throughout the entire nervous system (Smith, 1977). The withdrawal symptoms are a rebound effect in the physiological systems modified by the drug. For example, alcohol depresses the CNS, whereas withdrawal stimulates the CNS. In studying the effects of withdrawal, look for the opposite effect that the drug was used for initially. Amphetamines are used to stimulate or to give energy, so amphetamine withdrawal causes depression and a lack of energy. The time required to produce physical dependence can vary. Withdrawal symptoms can develop in a day with large quantities of CNS depressants (Alexander, 1951; Inaba & Cohen, 2007). For most drug users, development of physical dependence is gradual, occurring over weeks, months, or years of chronic administration.

Cross-Tolerance

The ability of one drug to suppress withdrawal symptoms created by another drug is referred to as cross-dependence or cross-tolerance. Cross-tolerance drugs may partially or completely remove symptoms of withdrawal. All drugs of abuse cause intoxication and induce a psychological dependency. The individual is self-administering the drug to change his or her level of consciousness or to increase psychological comfort (Schuckit, 1984).

Alcohol

No one knows when alcohol was first produced, but it was most likely to be a natural occurrence. If any watery mixture of vegetable sugars or starches is allowed to stand for about 3 months in a warm place, alcohol will make itself. Yeast that exists in the air everywhere will land on the juice and begin to eat the sugar, making carbon dioxide and alcohol as waste. The alcohol content in the juice continues to rise until all of the yeast cells are killed. Therefore, alcohol is a poison to all living creatures even to the organisms that make it. Nature alone cannot produce anything stronger than 14% alcohol, but by distillation, the percentage can then be increased to 93% (Courtwright, 2001).

The early detection of alcohol abuse and dependency is complicated by denial that is found in the individual, in the family, and in society. Long-term alcohol dependence has profound effects on personality, mood, cognitive functioning, and a variety of physiological problems involving virtually all organ systems. The interaction of alcohol and other drugs may lead to fatal overdoses (Frances & Franklin, 1988).

Alcoholism is the result of a complex interaction of biological vulnerability and environmental factors. Environmental factors such as childhood experience, parental attitudes, social policies, and culture strongly affect the vulnerability to alcoholism. Genetic variables significantly influence the disease. There is no personality that causes alcoholism (Goodwin, 1985; Vaillant, 2003).

Alcohol-Induced Organic Mental Disorders

Alcohol Intoxication

Source: Jupiterimages/Thinkstock.

Alcohol intoxication is the most frequent organic-induced mental disorder. It is time limited, and it may occur with varying amounts of ingested alcohol. The intoxicated individual exhibits maladaptive behavioral changes due to recent ingestion. These changes may include aggressiveness, impaired judgment, impaired attention, irritability, euphoria, depression, emotional liability, and other manifestations of impaired social functioning. Although alcohol is a CNS depressant, its initial effects disinhibit the individual. Early in intoxication, the person may feel stimulated with an exaggerated sense of well-being. With further use, the person may slow down and become depressed, withdrawn, and dull. The person may even lose consciousness (Inaba & Cohen, 2007; Spitzer, 1987; Woodward, 1994).

Alcohol Amnesic Disorder (Blackout)

Alcohol amnesic disorder, or a blackout, is a period of amnesia during periods of intoxication. The person may seem fully conscious and normal when observed by others, but the person is unable to remember what happened or what he or she did while intoxicated. The disorder may last for a few seconds or for days. The severity and duration of alcoholism correlate with the frequency of occurrence of these blackouts (Goodwin, 1971; Goodwin, Crane, & Guze, 1969).

Wernicke-Korsakoff Syndrome

Wernicke-Korsakoff syndrome is a neurological emergency that should be treated by the immediate intramuscular administration of thiamine. The symptoms begin with a sudden change in organic functioning. The client becomes ataxic with a wide-based unsteady gait. The person may be unable to walk without support. The client is mentally confused and unable to transfer memory from short- to long-term memory. The client may be disoriented, listless, inattentive, and indifferent to the environment. Questions directed at the client may go unanswered, or he or she may fall asleep while being examined. The etiology of this syndrome involves a thiamine deficiency due to dietary, genetic, or medical factors. All clients with compromised mental functioning or a deficit in memory need to be examined by the medical staff as soon as possible to prevent further brain damage (Braunwald et al., 1987).

Alcohol Withdrawal

Alcohol withdrawal symptoms relate to a relative drop in alcohol blood levels. Withdrawal can occur when the individual is still drinking. The classic withdrawal symptom is a coarse fast frequency tremor observed when the client's hand or tongue is extended. The tremor is made worse by motor activity or stress. The client may experience nausea and vomiting, malaise, weakness, elevated pulse and blood pressure, anxiety, cravings, depressed mood, irritability, transient hallucinations, headache, and insomnia. These symptoms follow several hours after cessation or reduction in alcohol intake and peak within 72 hours. They usually disappear within 5 to 7 days of abstinence. The client in alcohol withdrawal is treated with a cross-tolerant drug similar in pharmacological effects to alcohol, usually one of the benzodiazepines. This stabilizes the client in a mild withdrawal syndrome (Mayo-Smith, 2009).

Alcohol Withdrawal Seizures

Withdrawal seizures may occur 7 to 38 hours after the last alcohol use in chronic drinkers. The tendency to seizure peaks within 24 hours (Adams & Victor, 1981; Mayo-Smith, 2009).

Alcohol Withdrawal Delirium (Delirium Tremens)

One third of clients with seizures go on to develop alcohol withdrawal delirium, or delirium tremens. This is characterized by confusion, disorientation, fluctuating or clouded sensorium, and perceptual disturbances (Adams & Victor, 1981; Mayo-Smith, 2009). Typical symptoms include delusions, vivid hallucinations, agitation, insomnia, mild fever, and marked autonomic arousal. The client frequently reports visual hallucinations of insects, small animals, and other perceptual disturbances. The client may be terrified. The delirium typically subsides after a few days, but it can continue for weeks (Gessner, 1979).

Sedatives, Hypnotics, and Anxiolytics

Benzodiazepines and barbiturates are useful medications with a potential for abuse and dependence. They are medically useful for a variety of symptoms such as insomnia and anxiety. Approximately 15% of the population uses a benzodiazepine each year (Gottschalk, McGuire, Heiser, Dinovo, & Birch, 1979; Inaba & Cohen, 2007). About 16% of clients abuse the sedatives that are prescribed by their physicians (Richels, Case, Downing, & Winokur, 1983). In 1977, 18% of young adults reported nonmedical use of sedatives (Abelson, Fishburne, & Cisin, 1977). There are no sharp lines that can be drawn among appropriate use, abuse, habituation, and addiction. Both the client and the physician might not recognize symptoms of dependence. Both might assume that the anxiety, tremulousness, and insomnia that develop when the drug is discontinued are a return of the original anxiety (Jaffe, 1980). Some of these clients have been on a succession of various benzodiazepines for years. When the medication is withdrawn, anxiety symptoms may increase for months. These clients must be followed by someone experienced in treating anxiety disorders. The therapist can work to reduce the anxiety symptoms while the client is experiencing withdrawal (Burant, 1990; Dickinson & Eickelberg, 2009; Geller, 1994; Juergens, 1994).

Diagnosis of sedative abuse may prove to be difficult. The abuse can start in the context of medical treatment for anxiety, medical disorders, or insomnia. Physical dependence can develop to low doses over several years or to high doses over a few weeks (Dietch, 1983). Intoxication, withdrawal, withdrawal delirium, and amnesic disorder are similar to those found with alcohol. Benzodiazepines have a much longer half-life, so withdrawal might not begin until 7 to 10 days after cessation of use. The client may have a protracted withdrawal that can last for months (Geller, 1994). Alcohol and opioid CNS depression may interact with sedative hypnotics and potentiate the depression. Adding small amounts of alcohol or opioids to the sedatives can quickly lead to overdose (Frances & Franklin, 1988). Treatment for sedative, hypnotic, or anxiolytic withdrawal is similar to that for alcohol withdrawal. A cross-tolerant sedative is administered to prevent severe withdrawal symptoms. This medication is gradually decreased until the client is clear of the drug.

Opioids

Opium has been around since humans first discovered that the opium poppy was not only good for food and oil but had medicinal and psychoactive properties. During the late 1960s, the use of heroin increased in the United States. Once centered in large urban areas, the use of heroin infiltrated smaller communities.

Members of lower socioeconomic groups continue to be overrepresented in this client population, but the use of heroin is now observed with greater frequency among affluent members of society. In 2005, there were 108,000 persons aged 12 or older who had used heroin for the first time within the past 12 months. A survey in 1977 indicated that 2% to 3% of young adults had tried heroin at some time in their lives. A large proportion of the individuals recently beginning heroin use are young. The existence of opioid addiction among physicians, nurses, and health care professionals is many times higher than that of any group with a comparable educational background (Courtwright, 2001; Gilman, Goodman, & Gilman, 1980; U.S. Department of Health and Human Services, 1999).

Rapid intravenous injection of an opioid produces a warm flushing of the skin and sensations in the lower abdomen described by addicts as similar to orgasm. This lasts for about 45 seconds and is known as the "kick" or "rush" (Inaba & Cohen, 2007; Jaffe, 1980). Tolerance to this high develops with repeated use. Physical signs of intoxication include constricted pupils, marked sedation, slurred speech, and impairment in attention and memory. Daily use over days or weeks will produce opioid withdrawal symptoms on cessation of use. The withdrawal symptoms are intense but generally not life threatening. Withdrawal starts approximately 10 hours after the last dose (Frances & Franklin, 1988; Inaba & Cohen, 2007). Mild opioid withdrawal presents itself as a flu-like syndrome with symptoms of anxiety, yawning, dysphoria, sweating, runny nose, tearing, pupillary dilation, goose bumps, and autonomic nervous system arousal. Severe symptoms include hot and cold flashes, deep muscle and joint pain, nausea, vomiting, diarrhea, abdominal pain, and fever. Protracted withdrawal may extend for months (Gold, 1994b; Kosten, Rounsaville, & Kleber, 1985; Tetrault & O'Connor, 2009).

The treatment of opioid addiction can be grouped into opioid maintenance with methadone or *buprenorphine* versus abstinence approaches. Choice of the proper treatment depends on the client's characteristics. The course of heroin addiction typically involves a 2- to 6-year interval between the start of regular heroin use and the seeking of treatment. The need to participate in criminal activity to procure the drug predisposes the addict to further social problems. Treatment takes total psychosocial rehabilitation.

Many heroin addicts cannot or will not give up using opioids. Methadone or buprenorphine maintenance programs can return these clients to a productive lifestyle. Methadone substitutes long-acting methadone for short-acting heroin. Methadone has a half-life of 24 hours whereas heroin has a half-life of 4 to 6 hours. Buprenorphine clings tightly to the mu-opioid receptor. Research over the past 15 years has shown that buprenorphine and buprenorphine combined with the opioid blocker nalaxone is a safe and effective alternative to methadone for opioid maintenance therapy. Buprenorphine with or without naloxone is also used to ease withdrawal symptoms. Levomethadyl acetate hydrochloride (LAAM) is no longer used because of its history of causing fatal cardiac arrhythmias. Buprenorphine has a ceiling dose, and low toxicity reduces the danger of overdose. Buprenorphine along with the opioid antagonist naloxone also helps to prevent the client from getting high on other opioids such as heroin during maintenance therapy (Tetrault & O'Connor, 2009).

Worldwide opioid maintenance remains the major modality for the treatment of opioid dependency. The research supporting methadone or buprenorphine maintenance benefits to the heroin user are well documented (Institute of Medicine, 1995; Lowinson, Marion, Herman, & Dole, 1992; Tetrault & O'Connor, 2009). Methadone has been found to be medically safe even when used continuously for 10 years or more (Leshner, 1998). Methadone is administered to the client orally at established methadone clinics. Although a mainstay of treatment, these programs reach only 20% to 25% of addicts, with program retention rates from 59% to 85% (Stimmel, Goldberg, Rotkopf, & Cohen, 1977). Opioid detoxification should be slow to avoid relapse. The drug should be removed in weeks rather than days. Total abstinence might be the only alternative for many clients (Tetrault & O'Connor, 2009).

Buprenorphine is related to morphine but is a partial opioid agonist that possesses both agonist and antagonist properties. Partial agonists exhibit ceiling effects; increasing the dose has effects only to a certain level. Therefore, partial agonists usually have greater safety profiles than do full agonists such as heroin, morphine, and certain analgesic products chemically related to morphine. This means that buprenorphine is less likely to cause respiratory depression, the major toxic effect of opiate drugs, in comparison to full agonists such as morphine and heroin. Another benefit of buprenorphine is that the withdrawal syndrome seen on discontinuation with buprenorphine is mild to moderate and often can be managed without administration of narcotics (Tetrault & O'Connor, 2009).

Cocaine and Amphetamines

Moderate doses of psychoactive stimulants produce an elevation in mood, a sense of increased energy and alertness, and decreased appetite. Task performance that has been impaired by boredom or fatigue improves. Some individuals may become anxious or irritable. Cocaine addicts describe the euphoric effects of cocaine in a way that is indistinguishable from that of amphetamine addicts. In the laboratory, research participants familiar with cocaine cannot distinguish between the two drugs when both are given intravenously (Fischman et al., 1976). Animals use the drugs in a similar fashion, and the toxic and withdrawal symptoms of the drugs are indistinguishable. There is a difference in the half-lives of the drugs' effects. Cocaine's effects tend to be brief, lasting a matter of minutes, whereas amphetamine effects last for hours (Griffith, Cavanaugh, Held, & Oates, 1972; Inaba & Cohen, 2007; Wesson & Smith, 1977).

The user of a psychoactive stimulant such as cocaine or methamphetamine at first feels increased physical strength, mental capacity, and euphoria. The person feels a decreased need for sleep or food. A sensation of "flash" or "rush" immediately follows intravenous administration. It is described as an intensely pleasurable experience. With time, tolerance develops, and more of the drug is necessary to produce the same effects. With continued use, toxic symptoms appear. These include gritting the teeth, undue suspiciousness, and a feeling of being watched. The

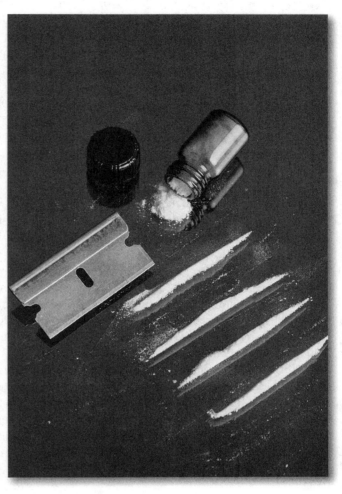

Source: Comstock/Thinkstock.

user becomes fascinated with his or her thinking and the deeper meaning of things. Stereotypical repetitious behavior is common. The individual may become preoccupied with taking things apart and then putting them back together. The mixture of another CNS depressant drug, such as an opioid (speedball) or alcohol, can be used to decrease irritable side effects. The client often becomes addicted to both drugs (Wesson & Smith, 1977).

Pattern of Use

Stimulants may be injected or taken intranasally every few minutes to every few hours around the clock for several days. Such a "speed run" usually lasts until the individual has exhausted the drug supply or is too paranoid or disorganized to continue. Stopping administration is followed within a few hours by deep sleep. On arising, the individual feels hungry and lethargic. Sometimes the individual is depressed. Cocaine is inhaled, smoked, or injected intravenously. Cocaine users who try to maintain the euphoric state will ingest the drug every 30 to 40 minutes (Inaba & Cohen, 2007; Wesson & Smith, 1977). Animals given free access to stimulants develop weight loss, self-mutilation, and death within 2 weeks (Jaffe, 1980). Given a choice between food and cocaine, monkeys consistently choose cocaine (Aigner & Balster, 1978).

A toxic psychosis may develop after weeks or months of continued stimulant use. A fully developed toxic syndrome is characterized by vivid visual, auditory, and tactile hallucinations and paranoid delusions indistinguishable from paranoid schizophrenia (Griffith et al., 1972; Inaba & Cohen, 2007). Unless the individual continues to use the drug, these psychotic symptoms usually clear within a week. The hallucinations are the first symptom to disappear (Jaffe, 1980). Craving for the drug, prolonged sleep, general fatigue, lassitude, and depression commonly follow abrupt cessation of chronic use (Inaba & Cohen, 2007; Post, Kotin, & Goodwin, 1974).

Adolescent cocaine or methamphetamine abuse leads to more rapid and severe consequences than adult stimulant abuse. Cocaine's price has decreased to the point where it costs as little as $5 to get high. During the mid-1980s, the distribution of the ready-to-smoke freebase cocaine known as "crack" spread nationwide (Courtwright, 2001; Featherly & Hill, 1989). With the potent freebase form, there is an almost instantaneous euphoric high that is extremely desirable (Frances & Franklin, 1988). Cocaine's half-life is less than 90 minutes, but the euphoric effect lasts for only 15 to 30 minutes (Jaffe, 1980).

The Stimulant Abstinent Syndrome

The stimulant abstinent syndrome has three phases. The first phase is the crash, where the individual reports depression, anhedonia, insomnia, anxiety, irritability, and intense craving. These symptoms can last for 7 to 14 days. In the second phase, low-level stimulant craving continues along with irritability, anxiety, and decreased capacity to experience pleasure. Over several days, the negative consequences of stimulant use fade, the person feels more normal, and the craving for stimulants increases, especially in the context of environmental cues. The third phase consists of several weeks of milder episodic craving triggered by environmental stimuli. Many clients will appear to have a major depression shortly after cessation of stimulant use. These clients may become suicidal. Most of these symptoms will clear, but some symptoms, such as sadness and lethargy, can last for months (Gawin & Kleber, 1986a; Inaba & Cohen, 2007; Schuckit, 1984).

The treatments for stimulant rehabilitation are similar to the treatment for alcoholism. The euphoria that stimulants offer needs to be replaced by more adaptive coping skills. Stimulant intoxication can be managed with the benzodiazepines or propranolol. Stimulant psychosis might have to be treated with antipsychotic medication. Clients who are psychotic need to be kept in a quiet place, supported, and reassured. Antidepressants such as desipramine may ease the withdrawal syndrome (Gawin & Kleber, 1986b).

Phencyclidine

Phencyclidine (PCP) is an anesthetic initially manufactured for animal surgery. For a short time, it was used as a general anesthetic for humans. Street use of PCP became widespread during the 1970s, when it was introduced as a drug to be smoked or snorted (Jaffe, 1980). It is still epidemic in certain eastern U.S. cities (Caracci, Megone, & Dornbush, 1983; Inaba & Cohen, 2007).

In humans, small doses of PCP produce a subjective sense of intoxication with staggering gait, slurred speech, and numbness of the extremities. The user may experience changes in body image and disorganized thought, drowsiness, and apathy. There may be hostile or bizarre behavior. Amnesia for the episode may occur. With increasing doses, stupor or coma may occur, although the eyes may remain open (Domino, 1978). Animals will self-administer PCP for its reinforcing properties (Balster & Chait, 1978). Psychoactive effects of PCP generally begin within 5 minutes and plateau in 30 minutes. In contrast to the use of hallucinogens, the use of PCP may lead to long-term neurological damage (Davis, 1982; Inaba & Cohen, 2007).

Few drugs are able to produce a more wide range of subjective effects than can PCP. Among the effects that users like are increased sensitivity to external stimuli, stimulation, mood elevation, and a sense of intoxication (Carroll & Comer, 1994). Other effects, seen as unwanted, are perceptual disturbances, restlessness, disorientation, and anxiety. Smoking marijuana cigarettes laced with PCP is the most common form of administration (Frances & Franklin, 1988). PCP produces several organic mental disorders including intoxication, delirium, delusional mood, and flashback disorders (Spitzer, 1987). Acute adverse reactions to this drug generally require medication to control symptoms. Benzodiazepines usually are the drug of choice, but antipsychotics might become necessary.

Dissociative Anesthetics (Phencyclidine, Ketamine, and Dextromethorphan)

PCP and ketamine are dissociative anesthetics, and ketamine is still legally marketed. In recent years, ketamine has developed greater popularity as a club drug. Dextromethorphan (DXM) is widely available as an over-the-counter cough and cold medication. Dissociative anesthetics produce a range of intoxicated states that are grouped into three stages. Clients, particularly adolescents, use large doses of DXM to get a "high" that they describe as feeling numb.

Stage I: Conscious with mild psychological effects

Stage II: Stuporous or light coma, yet responsive to pain

Stage III: Coma, unresponsive to pain

Clients may emerge from one state to the other, and many of them become agitated and delirious. Treatment is largely supportive by getting the client in a quiet room and reassuring them that the intoxicated state will improve over time. Sedatives and antipsychotic medications may be necessary to calm psychotic and agitated states (Wilkins, Danovitch, & Gorelick, 2009).

Hallucinogens

There is no clear line that divides the psychedelics from other psychoactive drugs that cause hallucinations. Anticholinergics, bromides, antimalarials, opioid antagonists, cocaine, amphetamines, and corticosteroids can produce illusions and hallucinations, delusions, paranoid ideation, and other alterations in mood and thought similar to psychosis. What seems to distinguish the psychedelic drugs from the others is the unique characteristic to produce states of altered perception that cannot be experienced except in dreams (Carroll & Comer, 1994; Inaba & Cohen, 2007; Jaffe, 1980).

The psychedelic most available in the United States is LSD. The psychedelic psilocybin has long been used in religious ceremonies by Southwest American Indians. Fortunately, the use of this drug is on the decline.

Hallucinogens are not reinforcing to animals, only to humans. Using more than 20 times is considered chronic abuse. Hallucinogens produce a variety of organic brain syndromes including hallucinogen hallucinosis, delusional disorder, mood disorder, and flashback disorder (Spitzer, 1987). Flashbacks may occur in as many as 25% of users (Naditch & Fenwick, 1977). Chronic delusional and psychotic reactions, and rarely schizophrenoform states, have been reported in some psychedelic users (Vardy & Kay, 1983).

The Psychedelic State

During the psychedelic state, there is an increased awareness of sensory input often accompanied by a sense of clarity. There is a diminished ability to control what is experienced. The user experiences unusual and vivid sensory sensations. Hallucinations are primarily visual. Colors may be heard, or sounds may be seen. Frank auditory hallucinations are rare. Time seems to be altered. The user frequently feels like a casual observer of the self. The environment may be experienced as novel, often beautiful, and harmonious. The attention of the user is turned inward. The slightest sensation may take on profound meaning. There commonly is a diminished ability to differentiate the boundaries of objects and the self. There may be a sense of union with the universe. The state begins to clear after about 12 hours (Freedman, 1968; Inaba & Cohen, 2007). The intoxicated client generally can be talked down without sedation. This client needs to be placed in a quiet environment free of excess stimulation. A sedative occasionally may be necessary to calm the client.

Cannabis

Cannabis is an India hemp plant that has been used for medicinal purposes for centuries. Marijuana is a varying mixture of the plant's leaves, seeds, stems, and flowering tops. The psychoactive ingredient in cannabis is delta-9-tetrahydrocannabinol (THC). Hashish consists of the plant's dried resin, and it contains a higher percentage of THC (Turner, 1980).

Source: Comstock/Thinkstock.

Marijuana remains the most commonly used illegal drug in the United States. Surveys reveal that 31% of teenagers, 40% of young adults, and 10% of older adults have tried marijuana. It is generally acknowledged that marijuana use among adolescents peaked during the 1970s. Daily users of marijuana dropped from 10.2% in 1978 to 5.0% in 1984 (Frances & Franklin, 1988).

Cannabis produces effects on mood, memory, motor coordination, cognitive ability, sensorium, time sense, and self-perception. Peak intoxication with smoking generally occurs within 10 to 30 minutes. Most commonly, there is an increased sense of well-being or euphoria, accompanied by feelings of relaxation and sleepiness. Where individuals can interact, there is less sleepiness and there often is spontaneous laughter (Hollister, 1974; Inaba & Cohen, 2007; Jones, 1971). Physical signs of use include red eyes, strong odor, dilated pupils, and increased pulse rate. With higher doses, short-term memory is impaired, and there develops a difficulty in carrying out actions that require multiple mental tasks. This leads to a tendency to confuse past, present, and future. Depersonalization develops with a strange sense of unreality about the self (Melges, Tinklenberg, Hollister, & Gillespie, 1970). Balance and stability of stance are affected even at low doses (Evans et al., 1973). Performance of simple motor skills and reaction times are relatively unimpaired until high doses are reached (Hollister, 1974; Jones, 1971).

Marijuana smokers frequently report an increase in hunger, dry mouth and throat, an increase in vivid visual imagery, and a keener sense of hearing. Subtle visual and auditory stimuli may take on new meanings (Cloptin, Janowsky, Cloptin, Judd, & Huey, 1979; Inaba & Cohen, 2007). Higher doses can produce frank hallucinations, delusions, and paranoid feelings. Thinking becomes confused and disorganized, and depersonalization and altered time sense increase. Anxiety to the point of panic may replace euphoria. With high enough doses, the client has a toxic psychosis with hallucinations, depersonalization, and loss of insight. This syndrome can occur acutely or after months of use (Chopra & Smith, 1974; Nahas, 1973; Thacore & Shukla, 1976).

Chronic smoking of marijuana and hashish has long been associated with bronchitis and asthma. Smoking affects pulmonary functioning—even in young people. The tar produced by marijuana is more carcinogenic than that produced by tobacco (Secretary of Health, Education, and Welfare, 1977). Individuals using marijuana chronically exhibit apathy, dullness, impairment of judgment, concentration, and memory problems. They lose interest in personal appearance, hygiene, and diet. These effects have been observed in young users who regularly smoke a few marijuana cigarettes a day. These chronic effects take months to clear after cessation of use (Jaffe, 1980; Tennant & Grossbeck, 1972).

The pharmacological effects of marijuana begin within minutes after smoking. Effects may persist for 3 to 5 hours. THC and its metabolites can be found in the urine for several days or weeks after a single administration. THC is a highly lipid soluble, and its metabolites tend to accumulate in the fat cells. They have a half-life of approximately 50 hours (Hollister, 1974; Secretary of Health, Education, and Welfare, 1977). Tolerance to and dependence on marijuana develop, and abrupt cessation after chronic use is followed by headaches, mild irritability, restlessness, nervousness, decreased appetite, weight loss, and insomnia. Tremor and increased body temperature may occur (Gold, 1994a; Jones, Bennowitz, & Bachman, 1976; Wikler, 1976). Because the withdrawal symptoms tend to be mild, detoxification usually is not necessary (Frances & Franklin, 1988).

Inhalants

Inhalants include substances with diverse chemical structures used to produce a state of intoxication—gasoline, airplane glue, aerosol (spray paints), lighter fluid, fingernail polish, typewriter correction fluid, a variety of cleaning solvents, amyl and butyl nitrate, and nitrous oxide. Hydrocarbons are the most active ingredients in these substances (Frances & Franklin, 1988; Inaba & Cohen, 2007).

Several methods are used to inhale the intoxicating vapors. Most commonly, a rag soaked with the substance is applied to the mouth and nose, and the vapors are breathed. The individual may place the substance in a paper or plastic bag and inhale the gases. The substance also may be inhaled directly from containers or sprayed into the mouth or nose (Spitzer, 1987).

Dependent individuals may use inhalants several times per week, often on weekends and after school. Inhalants sometimes are used by children as young as 9 to 13 years of age. These children usually use with a group of friends who are likely to use alcohol and marijuana as well as the inhalant. Older adolescents and young adults who have inhalant dependence are likely to have used a wide variety of substances (Spitzer, 1987).

Whereas high doses of these agents produce CNS depression, low doses produce an increase in CNS activity and a brief period of intoxication. Intoxication can last from a few minutes to 2 hours. Impaired judgment, poor insight, violence, and psychosis may occur during the intoxicated period. Inhalants are easily acquired and they are cheap. This makes them attractive to children who cannot drink legally. Animals will self-administer inhalants for reinforcement. There is a strong cross-tolerance with inhalants and the CNS depressants. Studies of inhalers have found indications of long-lasting brain damage (Cohen, 1979; Sharp & Brehm, 1977; Sharp & Carroll, 1978). Long-term damage to the bone marrow, kidneys, liver, and brain also has been reported (Frances & Franklin, 1988). There have been a number of deaths among inhalant abusers attributable to respiratory depression or cardiac arrhythmia. These deaths often appear to be accidental (King, Smialick, & Troutman, 1985).

Nicotine

Crew members who accompanied Columbus to the New World were the first Europeans to observe the smoking of tobacco. They brought the leaves and the practice of smoking back to Europe. Tobacco addiction is the number one preventable health problem in the United States (Courtwright, 2001). Cigarettes are responsible for more than 443,000 premature deaths each year in the United States (CDC, 2010). About 4,000 different compounds are generated by the burning of tobacco, but tobacco's main psychoactive ingredient is nicotine. Nicotine produces a euphoric effect and has reinforcing properties similar to cocaine and the opioids (Henningfield, 1984). Tolerance to some of the effects of nicotine quickly develops, but even the chronic smoker continues to exhibit an increase in pulse and blood pressure after smoking as little as two cigarettes. Nicotine has a distinct withdrawal syndrome characterized by craving for tobacco, irritability, anxiety, difficulty in concentrating, restlessness, increased appetite, and increased sleep disturbance (Hughes & Hatsukami, 1986; Inaba & Cohen, 2007; U.S. Surgeon General, 1979).

Tobacco addiction has many properties similar to opioid addiction. The use of tobacco usually is an addictive form of behavior (Frances & Franklin, 1988). Tobacco produces a calming, euphoric effect, particularly on chronic users. Nicotine in cigarette smoke is suspended on minute particles of tar, and it is quickly absorbed from the lungs with the efficiency of intravenous administration. The compound reaches the brain within 8 seconds after inhalation. The half-life for elimination of nicotine is 30 to 60 minutes (U.S. Surgeon General, 1979).

Chronic use of tobacco is causally linked to a variety of serious diseases ranging from coronary artery disease to lung cancer. The likelihood of developing one of these diseases increases with the degree of exposure that is measured by the number of cigarettes per day. Cigarette smoking men have a 70% higher death rate than do nonsmoking men. Smoking in women is increasing along with smoking-related diseases (Braunwald et al., 1987).

About 50 million Americans are still smoking, and most of them want to quit. More than 90% of successful quitters do so on their own without participating in an organized cessation program. Smokers who quit "cold turkey" are more likely to remain abstinent than are those who decrease their daily consumption of cigarettes gradually, switch to cigarettes with lower tar or nicotine, or use special filters or holders. Quit attempts are nearly twice as likely to occur among smokers who receive nonsmoking advice from a physician. Heavily addicted smokers who smoke more than 25 cigarettes per day are more likely to participate in an organized cessation program (Pierce, Fiore, Novotny, Hatziandreu, & Davis, 1989).

Counselors need to advise their clients against smoking and help them quit (see the American Cancer Society Guide to Quitting Smoking, Appendix 60). Smokers can and do quit. All smokers should consult with the staff physician for advice on not smoking. Self-help material can be presented to the clients who request more information. A pharmacological alternative, such as gum containing nicotine or a nicotine patch, can be substituted to ease withdrawal. Formal smoking cessation programs, such as the American Lung Association's "Freedom from Smoking" clinic, may be beneficial for heavier smokers (Glynn, 1990). The 12 steps can be useful in giving smokers support in their attempts to quit. Some clients will want to quit smoking while in treatment. This should be highly encouraged and supported.

Club Drugs

Club drugs are typically used by teenagers and young adults at bars, clubs, concerts, and parties. The most common club drugs include Ecstasy (3–4 methylenedioxymethamphetamine or MDMA), gamma hydroxybutyrate (GHB), Rohypnol, ketamine, methamphetamine, and acid (LSD).

MDMA

MDMA is a synthetic drug with effects similar to methamphetamine and the hallucinogen mescaline. MDMA can decrease the body's ability to regulate temperature resulting in dehydration, hyperthermia, and death. MDMA damages serotonin neurons in as little as 4 days. Twenty minutes to 1 hour after ingestion, MDMA causes stimulation and mild distortions of perception. The user also feels a calming effect that heightens empathy for others and the desire to dance. Physical dependence is generally not a problem, but tolerance can quickly develop with any amphetamine-like substance. Starting in 1990 in Europe and then spreading to the United States, there has been an increase in "rave" clubs. Flyers are handed out during the week and a few hundred to 1,000 teenagers get together at an empty warehouse to dance (Inaba & Cohen, 2007).

GHB

Since about 1990, GHB has been abused in the United States. The drug causes the user to feel euphoric and sedated. It also has anabolic (bodybuilding) effects and is used to increase growth hormone production, build muscle mass, and decrease water retention. It has been called liquid Ecstasy. GHB is usually dissolved in water or alcohol by the capful or teaspoonful. The effects last 3 to 6 hours and can cause amnesic effects; it can be used by sexual predators to lower the inhibitions and defenses of women (Inaba & Cohen, 2007).

Ketamine

Ketamine is an anesthetic that was initially used to put animals to sleep for surgery. About 90% of the ketamine used on the street is stolen from veterinary supplies. Ketamine is also known on the street as "special K" or "vitamin K." Doses of ketamine can cause dreamlike states and hallucinations. In high doses, it can cause delirium, amnesia, impaired motor function, high blood pressure, depression, respiratory problems, and death.

Rohypnol

Rohypnol is a powerful benzodiazepine that is often mixed with alcohol to cause decreased inhibitions and sedation. Rohypnol can incapacitate victims and prevent them from resisting sexual assault. It can produce "anterograde amnesia," which means the user cannot remember the events they experienced while under the effects of the drug (Inaba & Cohen, 2007).

Polysubstances

Few drug abusers abuse only one drug. There is a strong correlation between misuse of heroin and alcohol problems, abusers of stimulants frequently use depressants to cut irritable side effects, and alcoholics are at a higher risk for abusing other depressants and stimulants (Schuckit, 1984).

In Western society, youths begin drug use with caffeine, nicotine, and alcohol. If they go on to use other drugs, then the next drug of choice most likely will be marijuana or prescription opioids followed by one of the hallucinogens, depressants, or stimulants. These drugs first are taken on an experimental basis. They are reinforcing and lead to few serious consequences. Marijuana is seen as a step on the road to the use of other substances. Once the illegal barrier is crossed, it becomes easier to take a second and a third drug (Gould & Keeber, 1974; Kandel, 1978).

The effects of a drug may be either increased or decreased by adding an additional drug. Depressants taken together may potentiate the effect of either drug taken alone. Depressants and stimulants taken together may decrease the level of side effects encountered when one of the drugs is used alone. Marijuana has been shown to potentiate the effects of alcohol; it may increase the likelihood of a flashback from hallucinogen use (Schuckit, 1984). More than half of the clients who go to a polydrug clinic report the use of three or more substances (Cook, Hostetter, & Ramsay, 1975).

The most common multiple drug withdrawal syndromes are those seen following concomitant use of multiple depressants or depressants and stimulants. Depressants produce the most severe and life-threatening withdrawal symptoms. When depressants and stimulants are used together, the withdrawal syndrome more closely follows the clinical picture of depressant withdrawal, but it probably includes greater levels of sadness, paranoia, and lethargy (Schuckit, 1984).

Treatment Outcome

The Treatment Outcome Prospective Study (TOPS) is the largest and most comprehensive study of drug abuse treatment ever completed. It collected data on more than 10,000 clients admitted for chemical dependency treatment nationwide. The clients were in 37 different programs that varied from methadone maintenance, to residential, to outpatient treatment. The major finding was that treatment works. Drug abuse is significantly reduced after treatment, and the amount of decrease is greater in clients who remain in treatment longer. Clients needed to remain in treatment at least 6 months before a significant impact on drug abuse was achieved. Associated problem behaviors decreased (e.g., criminal behavior, family problems, suicidal thoughts).

This study found that drug addiction is a chronically relapsing condition usually requiring prolonged or repeated treatment (Hubbard et al., 1989).

The overwhelming weight of evidence from a large number of outcome studies and epidemiological studies indicates that treatment contributes significantly to positive behavior change in chemically dependent clients (Anglin & Hser, 1990; Gerstein & Harwood, 1990; Hoffmann, 1994; Hubbard, 1992).

The Institute of Medicine's Committee for the Study and Treatment and Rehabilitation Services for Alcoholism and Alcohol Abuse (1990) and many individual reviewers (e.g., Anglin & Hser, 1990; Hubbard & DesJarlais, 1991) have concluded that chemical dependency treatment changes clients for the better. Other studies confirm that the benefits of these changes considerably outweigh the costs of treatment (e.g., Hubbard, 1992).

Follow-up studies of proprietary programs reviewed by the Institute of Medicine (1989) found abstinence rates between 40% and 60% during the first year after treatment. Similar results were found in studies of state and private programs (Hoffman & Harrison, 1987; Hubbard & Anderson, 1988; Institute of Medicine, 1989).

Comprehensive Assessment and Treatment Outcome Research (CATOR) is the largest independent evaluation service for the chemically dependent field in the United States. Since 1980, CATOR has collected data on more than 50,000 adults and 10,000 adolescents who have entered treatment programs. CATOR finds that there are large differences in the clinical characteristics of clients admitted to inpatient programs versus outpatient programs. Cocaine dependence is much higher in the inpatient group; marijuana and stimulant dependence also is higher. Half of the inpatients are dependent on illicit drugs, whereas only one third of the outpatients are so addicted. Nearly 20% of inpatients admit to using at least two drugs other than alcohol on a weekly basis, whereas only 8% of outpatients admit to such heavy use. Recent ingestion is more common in the inpatient population, with 44% using alcohol or drugs within the past 24 hours of admission, compared to 23% of outpatients.

Detailed analysis of the CATOR research has encouraging words for chemical dependency counselors. A client who completes treatment—either outpatient or inpatient—has a 50% chance of staying clean and sober for the year following treatment. If the client completes treatment and attends Alcoholics Anonymous (AA)/Narcotics Anonymous (NA) once a week for the next year, then he or she has a 70% chance of staying sober. If the client completes treatment and attends one AA/NA meeting and one continuing care session per week, then he or she has a 90% chance of remaining sober for the next year. These are fantastic results: Fully 90% of clients can stay sober if they complete treatment and attend AA/NA and continuing care on a regular basis (Hoffmann, 1991, 1994).

3

The First Hours of Treatment

Source: ©iStockphoto.com/tack5.

The First Hours

The first thing that clients need when they come into treatment is a warm welcome. Most clients coming into treatment feel demoralized and ashamed. They feel like the scum of the earth. These people need you to show them encouragement, support, and praise. You show them that they are persons of worth, that they are important, and that they matter to others. Nothing gives this feeling better than a warm welcome. A warm welcome helps them to understand that they are entering a caring environment. They do not need to be afraid.

"That machine has to pay out soon. She's been sitting there for 48 hours."

How to Greet Clients

You need to convey to clients that you understand how they feel and that you will do everything in your power to help them. When greeting a new client, it is as if you are welcoming a long-lost brother or sister back into your family. This person is not different from you; this person is you. Treat the person the same way in which you would want to be treated yourself. The more the client senses your goodwill and unconditional positive regard, the less alienated and frightened the client will feel.

If you feel as though you can shake a client's hand, then do this. Make it a warm handshake. As you do these things, you are developing your therapeutic alliance, and you are giving the client the most important thing that he or she needs—acceptance.

The initial words you choose are important. Clients remember your words. Clients come back after years and describe their first few hours in treatment. They remember the exact things that people said. Because coming into treatment is a highly emotional experience, they seal them inside their hearts. You want them to remember the good things. Think of it like this: These people have been living a life full of no love, no light, no beauty, and no truth. You are walking them toward a new life full of love, light, beauty, and truth. Life in the darkness is lonely and painful. As you welcome them home, the client should clearly see that he or she is entering a new world full of hope.

Examples

Introduce yourself and say something like the following:

"Welcome. You have made a very good choice. I am proud of you. This is a victory not only for you but for all of the people in the world that you will help recover."

"This is a new start. Good going." (Give the thumbs-up sign.)

"Please ask us if there is anything you need. We are going to serve you and take good care of you."

"I know this was a difficult decision for you, but you will not be sorry. This is the beginning of a new life you have not even dreamed about."

"Try everything in your power to stay in treatment. If you feel uncomfortable, tell one of the staff. We are here to give you the best treatment possible. You will feel better every day."

Notice how each of these statements welcomes the client and enhances his or her self-esteem. Welcome. You are a good person. You made a good choice. We are going to take good care of you.

Ask whether the client wants anything. How can you help? Nothing shows that you care better than to offer to get the client something small—juice, food, milk, or coffee. This shows that you care and, more importantly, that the client is worth caring for. You are giving the client new ideas. Treatment is not going to hurt. The staff is willing to respond to the client's needs. "This treatment thing might be okay," the client begins to think. "I just might be able to do this."

How to Handle Family Members

If the client came into treatment with family members, then make sure to tour the facility with the family as a whole. This helps the client to make the transition between the family at home and the new family in treatment. When you have all the information that you need from the family members, they should be encouraged to leave. To have them linger unnecessarily can be detrimental to the client's transition. The client needs to focus on himself or herself and to orient to treatment. Family members who cling are rare, but they do exist. These people need to be separated from the client and given reassurance that the client is in a safe place. Someone in the family program might be willing to talk to the family members for a while to encourage them and answer any questions they might have. Remember that you are bonding with the client and his or her family members. You want them all to see you as someone they trust.

Beginning the Therapeutic Alliance

From the first contact, your clients are learning some important things about you. You are friendly. You are on their side. You are not going to hurt, shame, or blame them. This is disease like cancer, hypertension, asthma, and diabetes. People should not be ashamed for being sick. No one wants to become an addict, just like no one wants to have cancer.

Freely answer any questions about treatment and the treatment center. Take the client on a tour, and introduce him or her to other clients. Be honest, and hold nothing back. You provide the information, and the client makes the decisions. The client sees you as a concerned professional. The client begins to hope that you can help him or her. The therapeutic alliance is built from an initial foundation of love, trust, and commitment.

Give the client the idea that you are going through treatment with him or her. The client does not have to feel alone. Neither of you can do this alone. Both of you are needed in cooperation with each other. Clients know things that you do not know. They have knowledge that you do not have. They know themselves better than they know anybody, and they need to learn how to share themselves with you. Likewise, you know things that they do not know. You know the tools of recovery. You have to share these tools and help the clients to use them. This is a cooperative effort. It is as if you are on a wonderful journey together.

The Importance of Trust

Your clients must develop trust in you. To establish this trust, you must be consistent. You must prove to the clients, repeatedly, that you are going to be actively involved in their individual growth. When you say that you are going to do something, you do it. When you make a promise, you keep it. You never try to get something from the clients without using the truth. You never manipulate, even to get something good. The first time your clients catch you in a lie—even a small one—your alliance will be weakened.

Clients must understand that you are committed to their recovery but that you cannot recover for them. You cannot do the work by yourself. You must work together cooperatively. You can only teach the tools of recovery. The clients have to use the tools to establish abstinence.

Dealing With Early Denial

The first few hours of treatment are not a time for harsh confrontation. It is a time for listening, supporting, and encouraging the client to share what they can share. The great healer in any treatment is love (treating the other person like you would want them to treat you), and love necessitates action in truth. All clients come into treatment in denial. They have been dishonest with themselves and others. They are lying, and they will lie to you. Your job is to search for ambivalence and inconsistencies in their story that reveals the lies as gently as possible. Reflect the truth. You do not want to hurt the clients or incur their wrath, but you must be dedicated to the truth. This program demands rigorous honesty.

Clients lie to themselves in many ways. They do not want to see the whole truth because the truth makes them feel guilty and anxious. They keep the uncomfortable feelings under control by deceiving themselves. They distort reality just enough to feel reasonably comfortable. They defend themselves against the truth with unconscious lies called defense mechanisms. "As long as we could stop using for a while, we thought we were all right. We looked at the stopping, not the using" (Narcotics Anonymous [NA], 1988, p. 3).

Clients minimize reality by thinking that the problems are not so bad. Then they rationalize by thinking that they have a good reason to use drugs. Then they deny by stubbornly refusing seeing the problems at all. Treatment is an endless search for truth.

Those who do not recover are people who cannot or will not completely give themselves to this simple program, usually men and women who are constitutionally incapable of being honest with them. There are such unfortunates. They are not at fault. They seem to have been born that way. They are naturally incapable of grasping and developing a manner of living which demands rigorous honesty. (Alcoholics Anonymous [AA], 2001, p. 58)

Your job as an addiction counselor is to help the clients learn the truth knowing that the truth will set them free from the slavery to the lies.

Example of an Initial Contact

Approach the client. Reach out and take the client's hand. "Hi, Ralph." Use the client's first name. "I am _____ [your name]. I am going to be your counselor. How are you doing?"

The client looks at the floor and then at the wall. (*You know the importance of silence and wait.*)

The client finally looks up. "I am okay, I guess."

"The first few days are going to be the hardest. After that, it is going to be a lot better. This is the beginning of recovery. Is there anything I can do for you right now to make you feel more comfortable?"

"I do not think so," Ralph says, looking relieved.

"If you feel uncomfortable, I want you to tell the nurse or one of the staff, okay? If you cannot find anyone else, come and see me. My door is always open to you. We want you to feel calm and tranquil through withdrawal, not anxious or tense. Do not try to get through this by yourself. Let us help you. How you feel is important to us." (*The therapeutic alliance is being established.*)

The client might never have experienced unconditional positive regard before. It might seem strange to the client. To many clients, it is unbelievable. They come into treatment with preconceived ideas about how treatment is going to go. Many think that they are going to be punished. When they are greeted with love and affection, it comes as a great surprise. Your words of support and concern are as soothing as a warm bath.

All chemically dependent clients, at some level, want to punish themselves. They feel guilty about what they have done, and they are waiting for the executioner. They expect to be treated poorly. When you treat them with respect, they ask themselves why people are treating them so nice. *Could it be that I am worth it?*

Tell your clients that they are important. The staff cares about how they feel and what they want. You are here to help. You want to help. You are going to respond to the clients' needs. It might be tough for a while, but things are going to get better.

How to Check for Organic Brain Dysfunction

Clients need to be checked for medical problems, particularly organic brain syndrome, as quickly as possible. Some clients coming into treatment are organically compromised and need immediate medical treatment to prevent further damage. Clients may be intoxicated, may be in withdrawal, or may have a serious vitamin deficiency called Wernicke's encephalopathy.

You should be familiar with how to check a client for these cognitive problems. The Cognitive Capacity Screening (see Appendix 1) is an excellent way of screening for organic brain problems (Jacobs, Bernhard, Delgado, & Strain, 1977). The Mini-Mental State Examination is a similar assessment test (Folstein, Folstein, & McHugh, 1975). Either of these tests is a brief 10-minute assessment of how the brain is functioning. The test is simple and comes up with a score. If the client falls below the cutoff score, then inform medical professionals of the possible organic problems. If you notice anything unusual about how the client moves, acts, or speaks, then tell a physician or nurse. Always count on your medical staff or the client's family physician. They are more skilled at these examinations than you are.

The Initial Assessment

During the first few hours, you must determine whether clients fit into your program. Do they have a problem with chemicals? What is their level of motivation? Do they have the resources necessary for treatment? Are they well enough to move through your program? The criteria for admission are different for different facilities. For the most part, you will start by asking yourself certain basic questions about a client. Does this person have a problem with addiction? Does he or she need treatment? Is this person motivated? What kind of treatment does he or she need?

Referral

The counselor will need to establish and maintain relationships with civic groups, agencies, other professionals, governmental entities, the general recovery community to ensure appropriate referrals; identifies service gaps; and helps address unmet needs. You will need to network and communicate with a large community resource base. You need to have knowledge and understand the functioning of these agencies:

Source: Andrea Morini/Thinkstock.

- Civic groups and neighborhood organizations
- Health care systems
- Employment and vocational opportunities
- Rehabilitation services
- Faith-based organizations
- Governmental entities

- Criminal justice systems
- Child welfare agencies
- Housing administrations
- Child care facilities
- Crisis intervention programs
- Mutual and self-help groups
- Advocacy groups

The counselor needs to have knowledge about community demographics, political and cultural systems, criteria for receiving community services, access to funding opportunities, state and federal legislative mandates and regulation, confidentiality rules and regulations, effective communication styles, and community resources for both affected children and other household members. If you decide to refer, you must advocate for the client working with others in the community as a team. You need to respect interdisciplinary service delivery, respect the clients and the agency's services, collaborate and cooperate with respect, and appreciate strength-based principles that emphasize client autonomy and skills development (Substance Abuse and Mental Health Services Administration [SAMHSA], 2006).

Two quick screening tests for alcoholism have been developed: the Short Michigan Alcoholism Screening Test (SMAST) (see Appendix 2) (Selzer, Winokur, & van Rooijen, 1975) and the CAGE questionnaire (Ewing, 1984).

The Substance Abuse Subtle Screening Inventory (SASSI) was developed to screen clients when they were defensive and in denial. The SASSI measures defensiveness and the subtle attributes that are common in chemically dependent persons. It is a difficult test to fake, unlike the SMAST or the CAGE questionnaire. The SASSI gives the clients the opportunity to answer honestly about their problems with chemicals, but it also measures the clients' possible abuse using questions that do not pertain to chemicals (Creager, 1989; Miller, 1985). Clients can complete the SASSI in 10 to 15 minutes, and it takes only 1 or 2 minutes to score. It accurately identifies 98% of clients who need residential treatment, 90% of nonusers, and 87% of early-stage abusers (Miller, 1985).

The Addiction Severity Index (ASI) is a widely used structured interview that is designed to provide important information about what might contribute to a client's alcohol or drug problem. The instrument assesses seven dimensions that typically are of concern in addiction: (1) medical status, (2) employment/support status, (3) drug/alcohol use, (4) legal status, (5) family history, (6) family/social relationships, and (7) psychiatric status. The ASI is administered by a trained technician and takes about 1 hour (McLellan, Luborsky, & Woody, 1980).

The Recovery Attitude and Treatment Evaluator-Clinical Evaluation (RAATE-CE) is a measure of client readiness. It assesses client resistance and impediments to treatment. The instrument is a structured interview that measures five scales: (1) degree of resistance to treatment, (2) degree of resistance to continuing care, (3) acuity of biomedical problems, (4) acuity of psychiatric problems, and (5) extent of social/family/environmental systems that do not support recovery (Mee-Lee, 1985, 1988).

As the counselor, you need to constantly ask yourself about clients' stage of motivation and introduce appropriate motivating strategies to move the clients up to the next level. The manual will give you thousands of ways of doing this. No two clients are alike, so you must be creative in helping the clients to see the inaccuracies in their thinking and move them toward the truth. The *precontemplation* stage is where the individuals are not intending to take *action* with regard to their substance abuse problem in the near future. *Contemplation* is where the individuals intend to take action within the next 6 months. *Preparation* is where the persons intend to take action within the next month. Action is where the persons have made overt attempts to modify their lifestyles. *Maintenance* is where the individuals are working a recovery plan and attempting to prevent relapse. If you can move the clients up to the next stage, then you can be sure that treatment is working (Prochaska & DiClemente, 1983; Prochaska, DiClemente, & Norcross, 1992; Prochaska, Norcross, & DiClemente, 1994).

Clients at different stages of motivation will need different motivating strategies. In the precontemplation stage, clients underestimate the benefits of change and overestimate its cost. They remember the good things about addiction and forget the bad. They are not aware that they are making these mistakes in judgment and believe that they are right. Environmental events can trigger persons to move up to the contemplation stage. An arrest, a spouse threatening to leave, or an intervention each can increase motivation to change.

Clients in the preparation stage have a plan of action to cut down or quit their addictive behavior. These clients are ready for input from their doctors, counselors, or self-help books and should be recruited and motivated for action. Action is where the clients are changing their behavior to cut down or quit the addiction. These clients have entered early recovery and are actively involved in treatment.

In the maintenance stage, clients are still changing their behavior to be better and are working to prevent relapse. People who relapse are not well prepared for the prolonged effort needed to stay clean and sober. All clients need to be followed in continuing care because they need encouragement and support to stay in recovery. Addicts typically do not have the skills needed to work a program in early recovery. This takes a time commitment and discipline.

As the counselor, you constantly try to raise your clients' awareness about the causes, consequences, and possible treatments for a particular problem. Interventions that can increase awareness include observation, confrontation, interpretation, feedback, and education. You point out the need to reevaluate the environment and how to change behavior. Encourage the clients to reevaluate their self-images and how they are negatively affected by the addictive behavior. Encourage the clients to learn the new skills of honesty, helping others, and seeking relationships with a Higher Power (Prochaska & DiClemente, 1983; Prochaska et al., 1992, 1994).

Laboratory tests can be used to corroborate suspicions about excessive alcohol use that have been generated by the history and physical. None of the tests alone or in combination can diagnose alcoholism, but they add to the certainty of the diagnosis and warn clients of physical complications. High serum levels of liver enzymes can represent alcohol-induced hepatic injury. Ethyl glucuronide (EtG) testing is the newest way to test for alcohol consumption and can detect alcohol use up to 80 hours after drinking (1-800-724-1970; www.red woodtoxicology.com). The problem is the test is too sensitive. It will pick up any alcohol use, including using common products such as hand sanitizers or aftershave. Therefore, this is not a good stand-alone biomarker to test for relapse. Gamma-glutamyl transferase (GGT) is elevated in two thirds of alcoholics. There are many sources for an elevated GGT, and GGT only elevates with heavy drinking. Aspartate aminotransferase (AST) and alanine aminotransferase (ALT) are elevated in about one half of alcoholics. Alteration of fat metabolism causes elevated serum triglycerides in about one fourth of alcoholics. Alkaline phosphatase is elevated in about one sixth of alcoholics. Total bilirubin is elevated in about one seventh of alcoholics. Mean corpuscular volume (MCV) is elevated in about one fourth of alcoholics. Uric acid is elevated in about one tenth of alcoholics. A newer biomarker is carbohydrate deficient transferin (CDT) and is now widely available. It has moderate sensitivity and picks up drinking at least five drinks a day for 2 weeks. This biomarker has been shown to be a good measure to identify relapse. The advantage of CDT over GGT is that fewer things can cause elevation. However, CDT is not as sensitive to heavy alcohol use, resulting in false positives. The best biomarkers for monitoring abstinence are using a combination of urine alcohol and EtG. A follow-up test of CDT could be used to confirm heavy alcohol use (Brostoff, 1994; DuPont, 1994; SAMHSA, 2009b; Wallach, 1992).

How to Conduct a Crisis Intervention

Clients who are severely dependent and unwilling or unable to see the severity of their addiction need a crisis intervention. Crisis intervention is a confrontation by a group of concerned family and friends. This confrontation must be gentle and supportive, and it is best to use a trained interventionist to help you develop the intervention strategy. If you want to do the intervention yourself, first read the books *Love First: A New Approach to Intervention for Alcoholism and Drug Addiction* by Jeff and Debra Jay (2001) and *No More Letting Go: The Spirituality of Taking Action Against Alcoholism and Drug Addiction* by Debra Jay (2006). These excellent texts carefully discuss the intervention techniques. Basically, an intervention has to be carefully organized, rehearsed, and choreographed. Each member of the group should be a caring significant other and not an addict. Each person writes a letter stating exactly how the client's addiction has negatively affected his or her life. In this letter, group members share their love and concern for the client and ask that the client enter treatment. The client is told it is not he or she that is the problem but the illness. It is a lethal problem, and it needs treatment. Each person reads his or her letter of concern and love for the

Source: ©iStockphoto.com/clearstockconcepts.

client and asks him or her to go into treatment that day. The treatment setting has been arranged and the client's bags are packed. The intervention needs to be held at a neutral location when the client is clean and sober, not in the client's home or office where the client may feel more comfortable. It is difficult for the wall of denial to hold up under all of this love, and most of the time, the client agrees to go into treatment. If the client refuses, the truth has still come out, and this often leads to treatment later. Each participant is encouraged to exhibit the following behaviors:

- Show positive regard for the client and negative regard for the addiction.
- Give specific situations where the addiction negatively affected them.
- Validate that addiction is a disease, and it is not the client's fault.

Figure 3.1   Example of an Intervention Letter

Barbara, you are my closest friend, and I cannot tell you how much your friendship has meant to me. We have grown up together. Our kids love to play ball together, and you and I enjoy being close friends. There is no one in my life who has had a more positive effect on my life than you. Thank you for all of the years you have stood by me. When I made mistakes, you were always there to comfort me and give me good advice like a sister. Now comes the hard part of this letter, and I might not handle this very well so bear with me.

Lately, I have been concerned with your drinking. I see you driving the car with the children after you have had too much to drink. In fact, after the Halloween party on Saturday, you were so drunk you could hardly walk, yet you insisted on driving your children home. We all tried to stop you, but you would not listen to anyone. Barbara, addiction is a disease, just like the alcoholism that killed your father. It is genetic and life threatening. I am here to ask you to get the treatment that you need to get well. It hurts me too much to see you suffer. You and I know you cannot drink in a healthy way anymore. These problems have happened too much. My own kids do not want to come over here anymore, and I avoid you myself. This hurts me too much for it to go on. Please help yourself and your family, and get the help you need. The counselor has set up treatment for you today at a great treatment center, and we would all be incredibly proud of you if you would go for help. I love you very much. Please do this for all of the people who love you.

Love,

Nancy

Save the best letter for last. This is someone very tender and special to the client. It might be the client's child, a friend, or family member. It is someone whose letter breaks your heart. It is very difficult for denial to work in this atmosphere of love and truth. Most clients agree and go to treatment. Remember that no intervention is a failure. Even if the client refuses to get treatment, the truth came out and that is always a victory.

Interventions and treatment are going to take time. If you are a primary care physician, emergency room doctor, cardiologist, or surgeon, you might not have the time to struggle with this problem. All addiction treatment is a long journey toward the truth, and this journey is slow and painful. Clients have to face the demons they have hidden from for years. They need to walk into the dark forest of fear and need a trustworthy guide. They need someone with time, energy, patience, and love, a person who has been on this journey many times and come out alive. At some point, you need to decide if you are going to take on this problem yourself or refer to an addiction professional. Remember that addiction is a chronic relapsing brain disease. It is only at the 5-year sobriety point that the relapse rate drops to around zero (Vaillant, 2003).

Therefore, if you take this battle on, it is going to be a long one. If you look at addiction programs around the country, you will see that about half of the clients who leave treatment stay sober for the next year. Ninety percent of clients who work the program stay clean and sober. Therefore, if you want to take on this job, remember that you are in a 5-year fight for the client's life. You must do everything in your power to make sure that the client works the program. Because of protracted withdrawal, dual diagnoses, organic brain syndrome, and many other factors, about half of all addicts are not able to work their program on their own. They do not have the spiritual, mental, or physical skills necessary to work a self-directed program of recovery. These clients may need years in a structured facility or a highly structured continuing care program.

Sometimes you will want to refer an addict to an addiction professional. There are excellent alcohol and drug counselors and physicians that specialize in addiction. They are used to the battle, and they have specialized training to deal with the special problems of addiction. A treatment facility locator can be found at http://findtreatment.samhsa.gov. Other times, you will want to try to help the client yourself but remember you are in for a 5-year battle. Never forget that you are the healer, and you will do everything in your power to keep your client sober.

Once the diagnosis of addiction has been made, you will need to decide what level of care the client needs to get the best help possible in the least restrictive environment. This is why the American Society of Addiction Medicine (ASAM) developed the client placement criteria.

American Society of Addiction Medicine Patient Placement Criteria

All clients need to be assessed constantly in the following six dimensions:

1. Acute intoxication and/or withdrawal complications

2. Biomedical conditions and complications

3. Emotional, behavioral, or cognitive conditions and complications

4. Readiness to change

5. Relapse, continued use, or continued problem potential

6. Recovery/living environment

These are the areas of assessment that have been developed by the ASAM in the second edition of its handbook, *ASAM PPC-2R, ASAM Patient Placement Criteria for the Treatment of Substance-Related Disorders, Second Edition-Revised* (Mee-Lee, 2001). All counselors need to have a copy of this document and use these criteria in deciding which level of care clients need. (A copy of the criteria can be obtained from the ASAM,

4601 North Park Avenue, Upper Arcade, Suite 101, Chevy Chase, MD 20815.) The manual details specific criteria for admission, continued stay, and discharge for all levels of treatment, adult and adolescent.

For brevity, the present book concentrates on the criteria for admission and discharge of adult and adolescent outpatient and inpatient treatment. These are the criteria that you, as the counselor, will use most often. The criteria are as objective and measurable as possible, but some clinical interpretation is involved. Psychoactive disorders are no different from any other medical evaluation. Assessment and treatment are a mix of objectively measured criteria and professional judgment. The six dimensions that need to be assessed are as follows:

1. Acute intoxication and/or withdrawal complications
   a. What risk is associated with the client's current level of intoxication?
   b. Is there significant risk of severe withdrawal symptoms based on the client's previous withdrawal history and amount, frequency, and recency of discontinuation of chemical use?
   c. Is the client currently in withdrawal? To measure withdrawal, use the Clinical Institute Withdrawal Assessment of Alcohol (see Alcohol Withdrawal Scale, or Appendix 4), the Benzodiazepine Scale (Busto, Sykora, & Sellers, 1989), the Narcotic Withdrawal Scale (see Appendix 5) (Fultz & Senay, 1975), or the Clinical Opiate Withdrawal Scale (COWS).
   d. Does the client have the supports necessary to assist in ambulatory detoxification (or "detox") if medically safe?

2. Biomedical conditions and complications
   a. Are there current physical illnesses, other than withdrawal, that may need to be addressed or that may complicate treatment?
   b. Are there chronic conditions that may affect treatment?

3. Emotional, behavioral, or cognitive conditions and complications
   a. Are there current psychiatric illnesses or psychological, emotional, cognitive, or behavioral problems that need treatment or may complicate treatment?
   b. Are there chronic psychiatric problems that affect treatment?

4. Readiness to change
   a. Is the client objecting to treatment?
   b. Does the client feel coerced into coming to treatment?
   c. Does the client appear to be complying with treatment only to avoid a negative consequence, or does he or she appear to be self-motivated?

5. Relapse, continued use, or continued problem potential
   a. Is the client in immediate danger of continued use?
   b. Does the client have any recognition of, understanding of, or skills with which he or she can cope with his or her addiction problems to prevent continued use?
   c. What problems will potentially continue to distress the client if he or she is not successfully engaged in treatment at this time?
   d. How aware is the client of relapse triggers, ways of coping with cravings, and skills at controlling impulses to continue use?

6. Recovery/living environment
   a. Are there any dangerous family members, significant others, living situations, or school/working situations that pose a threat to treatment success?
   b. Does the client have supportive friendships, financial resources, or educational vocational resources that can increase the likelihood of treatment success?
   c. Are there legal, vocational, social service agency, or criminal justice mandates that may enhance the client's motivation for treatment?

Clients must be able to understand treatment. They must be intellectually capable of absorbing the material. They must be physically and emotionally stable enough to go through the treatment process. They cannot be actively harmful to themselves or to others. They cannot be overtly psychotic. They cannot have such a serious medical or psychiatric problem that they cannot learn.

Diagnostic and Statistical Manual

Criteria for Diagnosis

To make a diagnosis, use the criteria listed in the current edition of the *Diagnostic and Statistical Manual of Mental Disorders (DSM)* published by the American Psychiatric Association. (A copy of the *DSM* can be obtained from the American Psychiatric Association, 1400 K Street, N.W., Washington, DC 20005.) A new edition comes out every few years, so there will be changes in the criteria from time to time. The 2000 criteria (American Psychiatric Association, 2000) are listed in Appendix 3.

Diagnosis: Drug Abuse

A. A maladaptive pattern of psychoactive substance use leads to clinically significant impairment or distress indicated by one or more of the following occurring within a 12-month period:

1. Recurrent substance use resulting in a failure to fulfill major role obligations at work, school, or home (e.g., repeated absences or poor work performance related to substance use; substance-related absences, suspensions, or expulsions from school; neglect of children or household)

2. Recurrent use in situations where use is physically hazardous (e.g., driving an automobile or operating a machine when impaired by substance use)

3. Recurrent substance-related legal problems

4. Continued substance use despite having persistent or recurrent social or interpersonal problems caused or made by the effects of the substance (e.g., arguments with spouse about consequences of intoxication, physical fights)

B. The symptoms never met the criteria for psychoactive substance dependence for this class of substance.

Questions for You to Ask the Client

1. What are your drinking and drug habits?

2. Was there ever a period in your life when you drank or used drugs too much?

3. Have drugs or alcohol ever caused problems for you?

4. Has anyone ever objected to your drinking or drug use?

If you are unable to diagnose abuse, then check with the family. The client may be in denial, and you might get more of the truth from someone else. A family member, particularly a spouse or a parent, might give you a more accurate clinical picture of the problems.

If you diagnose abuse, then move on to the dependency questions.

Diagnosis: Chemical Dependency

A maladaptive pattern of substance use leads to clinically significant impairment or distress, as manifested by three or more of the following, occurring at any time during the same 12-month period:

1. Tolerance, as defined by either of the following:
   a. A need for markedly increased amounts of the substance to achieve intoxication or desired effect
   b. Markedly diminished effect with continued use of the same amount of the substance

2. Withdrawal, as manifested by either of the following:
   a. The characteristic withdrawal syndrome for the substance
   b. The same (or a closely related) substance taken to relieve or avoid withdrawal symptoms

3. The substance is often taken in larger amounts or over a longer period of time than was intended.

4. There is a persistent desire or one or more unsuccessful efforts to cut down on or control substance use.

5. A great deal of time is spent in activities necessary to obtain the substance (e.g., visiting multiple doctors, driving long distances), to use the substance (e.g., chain smoking), or to recover from its effects.

6. Important social, occupational, and/or recreational activities are given up or reduced because of substance use.

7. The substance use is continued despite knowledge of having a persistent or recurrent psychological or physical problem that is likely to have caused or been made worse by the use of the substance (e.g., current cocaine use despite recognition of cocaine-induced depression, continued drinking despite recognition that an ulcer was made worse by alcohol consumption).

Specify if:

With physiological dependence: Evidence of tolerance or withdrawal

Without physiological dependence: No evidence of tolerance or withdrawal

Explain to the client that the diagnosis is your best professional judgment. It is important that the client makes up his or her own mind. The client needs to collect the evidence for himself or herself and to get accurate in his or her thinking. Does the client have a problem or not? This is a good time to explain about denial and how it keeps clients from seeing the truth.

Pathological Gambling

Diagnostic criteria for 312.31 Pathological Gambling

Persistent and recurrent maladaptive gambling behavior is indicated by five (or more) of the following:

1. is preoccupied with gambling (e.g., preoccupied with reliving past gambling experiences, handicapping or planning the next venture, or thinking of ways to get money with which to gamble)

2. needs to gamble with increasing amounts of money in order to achieve the desired excitement

3. has repeated unsuccessful efforts to control, cut back, or stop gambling

4. is restless or irritable when attempting to cut down or stop gambling

5. gambles as a way of escaping from problems or of relieving a dysphoric mood ͵ helplessness, guilt, anxiety, depression)

6. after losing money gambling, often returns another day to get even ("chasing" one's losses)

7. lies to family members, therapist, or others to conceal the extent of involvement with gambling

8. has committed illegal acts such as forgery, fraud, theft, or embezzlement to finance gambling

9. has jeopardized or lost a significant relationship, job, or educational or career opportunity because of gambling

10. relies on others to provide money to relieve a desperate financial situation caused by gambling

The gambling behavior is not better accounted for by a manic episode.

How to Determine the Level of Care Needed

Once you know that the client has a significant addiction, you must decide the level of care the client needs. There are five levels of care generally offered across the United States:

Level 0.5: *Early intervention.* Early intervention is an organized service delivered in a wide variety of settings. Early intervention explores and addresses problems or risk factors related to substance use and assists clients in recognizing the harmful consequences of inappropriate substance use. Clients who need early intervention do not meet the diagnostic criteria of either chemical abuse or chemical dependency, but they have significant problems with substances. The rest of the treatment levels include clients who meet the criteria for psychoactive substance abuse or dependency.

Level I: *Outpatient treatment.* Outpatient treatment takes place in a nonresidential facility or in an office run by addiction professionals. Clients come in for individual or group therapy sessions, usually fewer than 9 hours per week.

Level II: *Intensive outpatient/partial hospitalization.*

Level II.1: *Intensive outpatient treatment.* This is a structured day or evening program of 9 or more hours of programming per week. The program has the capacity to refer clients for their medical, psychological, or pharmacological needs.

Level II.5: *Partial hospitalization.* Partial hospitalization generally includes 20 or more hours of intense programming per week. This program has ready access to psychiatric, medical, and laboratory services.

Level III: *Residential/inpatient services.*

Level III.1: *Clinically managed, low-intensity residential services.* This is a halfway house.

Level III.3: *Clinically managed, medium-intensity residential services.* This is an extended care program oriented around long-term management.

Level III.5: *Clinically managed, high-intensity residential services.* This is a therapeutic community designed to maintain recovery.

Level III.7: *Medically monitored intensive inpatient treatment.* This residential facility provides a 24-hour structured treatment. This program is monitored by a physician and is able to manage the psychiatric, physical, and pharmacological needs of its clients.

Level IV: *Medically managed intensive inpatient treatment.* This 24-hour program has the resources of a hospital. Physicians provide daily medical management.

Criteria for Outpatient Treatment (Adults)

An adult client qualifies for outpatient treatment if he or she meets the diagnostic criteria for psychoactive substance use disorder as defined by the current *DSM* and if the client meets all six of the following criteria:

1. The client is not acutely intoxicated and is at minimal risk for suffering severe withdrawal symptoms.

2. All medical conditions are stable and do not require inpatient management.

3. All of the following conditions exist:
   a. The individual's anxiety, guilt, and/or depression, if present, appear to be related to substance-related problems rather than to a coexisting emotional/cognitive/behavioral condition. If the client has emotional/cognitive/behavioral problems other than those caused by substance use, then the problems are being treated by an appropriate mental health professional.
   b. Mental status does not preclude the client from comprehending and understanding the program or from participating in the treatment process.
   c. The client is not at risk for harming himself or herself or others.

4. Both of the following conditions exist:
   a. The client expresses a willingness to cooperate with the program and to attend all scheduled activities.
   b. The client may admit that he or she has a problem with alcohol or drugs, but the client requires monitoring and motivating strategies. The client does not need a more structured program.

5. The client can remain abstinent only with support and can do so between appointments.

6. One of the following conditions exists:
   a. The environment is sufficiently supportive to make outpatient treatment feasible. Family or significant others are supportive of recovery.
   b. The client does not have the ideal support system in his or her current environment, but the client is willing to obtain such support.
   c. Family or significant others are supportive, but they need professional interventions to improve chances of success.

Criteria for Inpatient Treatment (Adults)

An adult client needs inpatient treatment if he or she meets the *DSM* diagnostic criteria for substance use disorder and meets at least two of the following criteria:

1. The client presents a risk of severe withdrawal or has had past failures at entering treatment after detox.

2. The client has medical conditions that present imminent danger of damaging health if use resumes or concurrent medical illness needs medical monitoring.

3. One of the following conditions exists:
   a. Emotional/cognitive/behavioral problems interfere with abstinence and stability to the degree that there is a need for a structured 24-hour environment.
   b. There is a moderate risk of behaviors endangering self or others. There are current suicidal/homicidal thoughts with no action plan and a history of suicidal gestures or homicidal threats.

    c. The client is manifesting stress behaviors related to losses or anticipated losses that significantly impair daily living. A 24-hour facility is necessary to address the addiction.

    d. There is a history or presence of violent or disruptive behavior during intoxication with imminent danger to self or others.

    e. Concomitant personality disorders are of such severity that the accompanying dysfunctional behaviors require continuous boundary-setting interventions.

4. Despite consequences, the client does not accept the severity of the problem and needs intensive motivating strategies available in a 24-hour structured setting.

5. One of the following conditions exists:

    a. Despite active participation at a less intensive level of care or in a self-help fellowship, the client is experiencing an acute crisis with an intensification of addiction symptoms. Without 24-hour supervision, the client will continue to use.

    b. The client cannot control his or her use so long as alcohol or drugs are present in the environment.

    c. The treatments necessary for the client require this level of care.

6. One of the following conditions exists:

    a. The client lives in an environment where treatment is unlikely to succeed (e.g., chaotic, rife with interpersonal conflict that undermines the client's efforts to change, nonexistent family, other environmental conditions, significant others living with the client who manifest current substance use and are likely to undermine the client's recovery).

    b. Treatment accessibility prevents participation in a less intensive level of care.

    c. There is a danger of physical, sexual, or emotional abuse in the current environment.

    d. The client is engaged in an occupation where continued use constitutes a substantial imminent risk to personal or public safety.

Criteria for Outpatient Treatment (Adolescents)

An adolescent client qualifies for outpatient treatment if he or she meets *DSM* criteria for substance use disorder and the following dimensions:

1. The client is not intoxicated and presents no risk of withdrawal.

2. The client has no biomedical conditions that would interfere with outpatient treatment.

3. The client's problem behaviors, moods, feelings, and attitudes are related to addiction rather than to a mental disorder, or the client is being treated by an appropriate mental health professional. The client's mental status is stable. The client is not at risk for harming himself or herself or others.

4. The client is willing to cooperate and attend all scheduled outpatient activities. The client is responsive to parents, school authorities, and staff.

5. The client is willing to consider maintaining abstinence and recovery goals.

6. A sufficiently supportive recovery environment exists to make outpatient treatment feasible:

    a. Parents or significant others are supportive of treatment, and the program is accessible.

    b. The client currently does not have a supportive recovery environment but is willing to obtain such support.

    c. The family or significant others are supportive but require professional intervention to improve chances of success.

Criteria for Inpatient Treatment (Adolescents)

To qualify for inpatient treatment, the adolescent must meet the *DSM* criteria for substance use disorder, all of the dimensions for outpatient treatment, plus at least two of the following dimensions:

1. The risk of withdrawal is present.

2. Continued use places the client at imminent risk of serious damage to health, or a biomedical condition requires medical management.

3. History reflects cognitive development of at least 11 years of age and significant impairment in social, interpersonal, occupational, or educational functioning, as evidenced by one of the following:

    a. There is a current inability to maintain behavioral stability for more than a 48-hour period.

    b. There is a mild to moderate risk to self or others. There are current suicidal/homicidal thoughts with no active plan and a history of suicidal/homicidal gestures.

    c. Behaviors are sufficiently chronic and/or disruptive to require separation from the current environment.

4. The client is having difficulty in acknowledging an alcohol or drug problem and is not able to follow through with treatment in a less intense environment.

5. The client is experiencing an intensification of addiction symptoms despite interventions in a less intense level of care; the client has been unable to control use so long as alcohol or drugs are present in his or her environment; or the client, if abstinent, is in crisis and appears to be in imminent danger of using alcohol or drugs.

6. One of the following conditions exists:

    a. The environment is not conducive to successful treatment at a less intense level of care.

    b. The parents or legal guardians are unable to provide consistent participation necessary to support treatment in a less intense level of care.

    c. Accessibility to treatment precludes participation in a less intense level of care.

    d. There is a danger of physical, sexual, or emotional abuse in the client's current environment.

Source: ©iStockphoto.com/ keeweeboy.

The Client's Reaction to Intoxication

Clients in these acute organic brain syndrome states can seem to be relatively normal or extremely bizarre. They can be actively psychotic, relaxed and comfortable, or in a panic. They can experience intense flashbacks. High doses of amphetamines, cocaine, or phencyclidine (PCP) may produce organic delirium. Disorganized thinking and a reduction characterize delirium in the ability to maintain attention. The client will not be able to follow a conversation. The disorganized thinking is manifested by rambling, irrelevant, or incoherent speech. This delirium usually is brief (less than 6 hours) after amphetamine or cocaine use, but it can last for up to a week after PCP use (Schuckit, 1984; Spitzer, 1987).

Acute use of amphetamines, cocaine, or PCP may result in a delusional state. Delusions are false beliefs that are intractable to logic. The client may feel that someone or some group is out to get him or her. The client may think that he or she has strange or unusual powers.

These delusions usually are brief, lasting from several hours to several days, but in some clients, they can last for up to a year, even in the absence of further drug use. Hallucinogen use can result in the development of delusions (Vardy & Kay, 1983). Brief psychotic states also have been reported following cannabis use (Hollister, 1986).

During acute intoxication and withdrawal, it is not unusual to see clients complaining of hallucinations. These hallucinations usually are visual or tactile and rarely are auditory. Lights may seem too bright, or sounds may seem too loud and startling. This is a transient psychotic state. The clients may see trailing of objects (e.g., when the clients move a hand, they see a brief image extend behind the solid object like a jet contrail). The walls or floor might seem to move, or the clients might see bugs or other things that are not there. The clients may feel something unusual on or under their skin. These hallucinations usually are brief, but the clients will need to be reassured and supported. The clients' brains are chemically correcting. These negative experiences are used to give the clients evidence that they need to stop abusing chemicals.

What to Do With an Intoxicated Client

Never argue with intoxicated clients. This will get you nowhere. They probably are not going to remember the conversation anyway. Briefly introduce yourself, let the medical staff examine and treat these clients, and let the clients sleep. Intoxicated clients and clients in withdrawal will mainly be the responsibility of the medical staff. These staff members will be watching the clients carefully and monitoring their vital signs.

There is an old idea that has been floating around the field for years that clients should hurt in withdrawal. The theory goes that this will help clients to learn that they have a problem. To do this would be a medically unsound practice. It is inappropriate to subject clients to severe withdrawal symptoms just to teach them a lesson. Some of them would die. Clients should be medicated to a point where they stay in mild withdrawal. This hurts enough.

Intoxicated clients who want to talk will have to be reassured and educated. They are not bad people. They are sick. If they want to talk a lot, then let some of the other clients do the talking. Join in if you must. The clients will definitely need to trade off. This is very tiring work, but it is beneficial for them to see the intoxicated clients so messed up. It reinforces for the other clients that they never want to go through this again.

Clients need to be educated about withdrawal. What can they expect? The main thing that clients need to hear is that things are going to get better. With every hour that passes, things are going to improve. The staff is not going to let the clients feel too uncomfortable. Things are going to feel uncomfortable sometimes, but the staff is not going to allow the pain to reach intolerable levels.

Many of the clients' thoughts and feelings now are chemically induced. The clients need to understand that they are going to have some wide mood swings in acute withdrawal. Most clients will be feeling depressed, agitated, irritable, and crabby at various times. They need to have their fears and concerns put to rest. Let them talk. Answer their questions. Listen. These clients need a lot of attention.

Detoxification

Except for the hallucinogens, PCP, and the inhalants, prolonged drug or alcohol use is accompanied by the development of drug tolerance and

Source: ©iStockphoto.com/Scrofula.

physical dependence. In the case of withdrawal from the central nervous depressants (alcohol, barbiturates, and benzodiazepines), tremulousness, sweating, anxiety, and irritability may give way to life-threatening seizures and delirium. Opioid withdrawal is not life threatening, although the client feels uncomfortable (Group for the Advancement of Psychiatry Committee on Alcoholism and the Addictions, 1991). Withdrawal from central nervous system (CNS) stimulants may be accompanied by a "crash" characterized by depression, fatigue, increased need for sleep, and increased appetite (Gawin & Ellinwood, 1988; Kasser, Geller, Howell, & Wartenberg, 1998).

Detoxification is the gradual safe elimination of the drug from the body. Some drugs, such as alcohol, are detoxified quickly, usually within a few days, but the benzodiazepines may take weeks or months (Burant, 1990; Schuckit, 1984). Many clients are suffering from polysubstance withdrawal, and this can complicate the clinical picture. The drugs most likely to cause serious physical problems are the depressants. These clients can deteriorate rapidly.

How Clients React in Detoxification

Most any physical or mental symptom can present itself in withdrawal. No heavy confrontation is necessary. These clients are sick and irritable. They are sleeping poorly. They have powerful cravings. This is where many clients walk out of treatment. They feel as though they cannot stand the symptoms anymore. These clients need medication, reassurance, and support. You must be gentle. Keep telling them repeatedly that it will get better. If they stay clean and sober, then they never will have to go through this misery again.

In withdrawal, clients are restless and have strong cravings. This physiological and psychological need for the substance is the primary motivating force behind drug addiction. The clients' bodies are driving them to return to their drugs of choice. The cells are screaming for relief. The clients have been in withdrawal hundreds of times before, but they always have treated it by getting intoxicated again. Now they are going to stick it out, striving for recovery. All of these clients think about leaving treatment, but when they get to feeling a little better, they reach the greatest chance of actually going out the door. You must be on top of this by constantly assessing where the clients are both physically and psychologically.

   • The clients need to keep a journal of each day they are in treatment. What happened? What did they learn? What do they need to work on? As they journal, they need to think about their recovery skills and how they need to use them.

   • The clients need to rate their cravings and try to uncover the situations, feelings, or thoughts that trigger the craving. Clients need to keep up with their Daily Craving Record (see Appendix 66) for at least the first 90 days of recovery. Check this record often throughout treatment to see how the client is doing in recovery. Identify situations, thoughts, and feelings that trigger craving, and make a plan to cope with each trigger. Watch for triggers that happen repeatedly because they are driven by inaccurate thoughts. For example, the client may have a trigger that he or she calls feeling angry. "When I get angry, I want to drink." You know that all anger comes from hurt so you try to answer the questions, how come people hurt the client so often or how come other people are seen as being too aggressive. Once you pull for the thinking that comes before the feeling, you will get more and more data about how to help the client see these situations and to cope with each situation appropriately.

   Detoxification should be managed in a room that is reduced of excessive stimulation. The area needs to be quiet and without bright lights. Familiar people, pictures, a clock, and clothes are helpful. Soft conversation that reassures clients and keeps them oriented is best. The staff should display a positive attitude of mutual respect. Reassuring touches, such as taking a pulse and putting a hand on a shoulder, are helpful (Baum & Iber, 1980).

Once the acute withdrawal syndrome has passed, clients remain in a protracted abstinence syndrome for weeks or even years. Relapse is higher during this period of physiological adjustment. The protracted abstinence syndrome varies depending on the drug of dependency. Typically, it is a symptom constellation opposite of that which the client was using the drug to produce (e.g., the client using stimulants to increase energy will experience lethargy) (Geller, 1990).

The AMA Threat

Clients in an inpatient or outpatient setting can present an AMA threat (leave treatment *against medical advice*). They usually isolate themselves first from the treatment peers and staff. Addictive thinkers must lie to themselves and believe that the lies are the truth for the illness to work. The addiction cannot exist in the light of the truth. The disease has a much better chance of working in isolation. That is why clients must not be left alone in early treatment until they have stabilized.

The illness cooks a stew of inaccurate information—minimization ("My use is not that bad"), rationalization ("I have a good reason to use"), projection ("It is not my problem, it is their problem"), and denial (a stubborn refusal to see the truth). All of these defenses are used to distort reality.

You may first get wind of an AMA threat as you assess a client, or you may learn of it from another client or from a staff member. The client shares that he or she is thinking about leaving treatment. You must intervene when you see this problem developing. As the client tells more and more lies to himself or herself, the client becomes convinced that the lies are the truth. The client keeps collecting information that proves that the illness is right.

For the most part, clients' reasons will be inaccurate. They are distortions of reality. Clients might not be aware that the real reason why they are leaving treatment is to use their drugs of choice. Clients delude themselves. They are craving, but many of them do not know it. They believe the inaccurate thinking.

Example of an AMA Intervention

The intervention desperately needed here is the truth. Every time the client brings up a reason for leaving treatment, you challenge him or her with the truth. Be gentle. The truth is on your side, and a big part of the client wants to know the facts. Do not talk to the illness side of the client. Talk to the side that wants to get well.

Client: I have to get out of here. I can quit on my own.

Counselor: You have tried that before, and you have always failed.

Client: This time I can do it.

Counselor: Your meth addiction is worse now than it has ever been. It is not better. It's worse.

Client: I will go to meetings. That is all I need. I know how to stay off drugs.

Counselor: You may do that for a while, but it is very likely that you will begin using again.

Client: I think I can do it this time.

Counselor: You have had that thought a hundred times before. Give the disease some credit. It is stronger than you are. The 12-step program says that no human power can remove our addiction. It is unlikely that you will lick this problem on your own.

Client: I will go to church.

Counselor: I believe you need treatment.

Client: I have some marital problems that I need to work out. I cannot do that in here.

Counselor: The best thing you can do for your marriage is to stay in treatment and get into a stable recovery. Why don't we call your wife and see if she wants you to leave?

Client: I have to get out of here. I do not fit in.

Counselor: Why don't you try to help someone else?

Client: I am not like these people. Their problems are much worse than mine are. Some of them are criminals.

Counselor: Weren't you arrested twice?

Client: Yes.

Counselor: But you are not like these people?

Client: No.

This conversation can go on for quite some time. The longer you expose the lies that the client is telling himself or herself, the better the chance of keeping the client in treatment. If you have to, see whether the client will agree to stay in treatment for one more day or even one more hour. The longer the client stays, the more opportunity you have to help him or her see the truth.

How to Develop and Use the AMA Team

The AMA team is a group of three or more of the treatment peers selected by the staff to help other clients who are at risk of leaving treatment early. Have them share their experiences, strengths, and hopes with the client. Often, this group will be more effective than you are. It is easier for a client to trust people who are in treatment. In an outpatient setting, if you do not have an AMA group, then maybe one of the clients further along in the program will agree to encourage the client to stay.

If there are any consequences that a client will face if he or she leaves treatment, this is the time to bring these things out. The client may have been court ordered into treatment. The client's employment may be in jeopardy. A spouse or parent may have given the client an ultimatum—get treatment or else. Use every angle you can so long as it is based in the truth. The family may even have to involuntarily court commit the client into treatment.

The client must be gently told the truth until he or she hears it. There is a healthy side of the client—the side that is sick of this problem and wants to recover. The truth is a very powerful tool. It is even more powerful when delivered in an atmosphere of encouragement and support.

Some counselors believe that they have to hammer away at a client's denial aggressively until they literally "break through it," but it cannot be like a war. The therapeutic alliance builds on mutual acceptance, trust, and unconditional positive regard. It is impossible to trust someone who is verbally beating on you. This behavior harms your relationship and makes your job even harder than it already is. You will get angry with clients. That is normal; everyone does. Try to treat clients the same way in which you would want to be treated.

How to Use the In-House Intervention

If all else fails, then you might have to arrange an in-house intervention. Here you gather the client's family and concerned others together and have them tell the client why they want him or her to stay in treatment.

Have each of the participants write a letter stating how the client's addiction has adversely affected the participant. The participants need to give specific examples of how they were hurt. They share how they are feeling now and ask for what they want. They write down exactly what they are going to do if the client does not agree to stay in treatment. A spouse could state that she has been humiliated in front of friends. If the client does not stay in treatment, then she will divorce him. An employer could say that he is weary of the client calling in sick. If the client does not stay in treatment, then he will be fired. The kids could say that they are embarrassed by the client and want out of the home. Parents could talk about the lies and mistrust in the home and say that they are going to withdraw their financial support.

In an intervention, the family members are going to need a lot of encouragement. You need to help them with their letters and practice the intervention without the client present. Once the group is gathered, bring the client in and have each member share his or her letter. If the client is still unwilling to stay in treatment, then you can open the group up for discussion. Again, every time the client gives the family a good reason for leaving, you and the family will tell the client the truth.

How to Respond to Clients Who Leave AMA

Do everything in your power to keep your clients in treatment, but if they decide to leave early, then wish them well and invite them to come back if they have further problems. Many clients will leave for a time and then return. Whatever happens, remember that when the clients were in treatment you told them the truth. Clients leaving treatment are no reflection on you or your skills. You did not lose. You planted the seed of the truth that will grow later.

Programs that are more genuinely caring will keep more clients than will programs that are harsh and confrontational. The key balance is to confront the clients in an atmosphere of support. An encouraging and supportive environment is attractive, and everyone wants more. You will know that you have struck the right balance when many of your clients are reluctant to leave treatment at the end of their stays. They have felt so accepted, loved, and supported that they do not want to leave an environment in which they have made major growth.

4 The Biopsychosocial Interview

Source: Jupiterimages/Thinkstock.

The Biopsychosocial Interview

Now kick back and relax. Get yourself a cup of coffee. When the client has settled into treatment, it is time to hear his or her whole story. This is an exciting time because everyone's story is fascinating, like a detective story. You are searching for the leads necessary to develop a treatment plan. The biopsychosocial assessment will be one of the most valuable times you spend with your client. Every client is interesting and has a never-ending puzzle of human and environmental interactions. Do not worry about being bored. This is a great mystery, and you are the detective. You need to search out and find the problems.

The purpose of the biopsychosocial is to find out exactly what the problems are and where they came from. Then you need to decide what you are going to do about them. All diseases have biological, psychological, and social factors that contribute to dysfunction. These ingredients mingle together, leaving the client in a state of "dis-ease." The client does not feel easy; he or she feels "dis-easy." There are no major psychiatric diseases that do not have biopsychosocial components. All addiction affects the cells (*bio* from biology); the emotions, attitudes, and behavior (*psycho* from psychology); and the social relationships (*socio* from sociology).

To do your biopsychosocial, you will need the Biopsychosocial Assessment form (see Appendix 31) and a quiet place where you will not be disturbed. The interview will take at least 1 hour or maybe more. Many beginning counselors are bogged down in this interview because they become overwhelmed with information or they try to begin treating the problems too early. This interview is not for treatment; it is for assessment. The best way of keeping out of these traps is to let the client do most of the talking. You ask the questions and let the client tell his or her story while you write it down. Ask for more information only if you are confused or uncertain about what the client is describing. You must understand the facts and how the client feels about the situation.

It will take you a while to become a skilled interviewer. It takes keen insight to see the problems clearly, as they develop. You will get better at this as you become more experienced.

How to Conduct the Interview

Begin the biopsychosocial interview by telling the client what you are going to do: "The purpose of this interview is to see exactly what the problems are, where they come from, and what we are going to do in treatment. From this information, we will develop the treatment plan. You need to keep things very accurate here. Just tell me exactly what happened."

Now relax and begin your interview. Do not be in a hurry. This is fascinating and fun. Ask the following questions, and write the answers down in the blanks provided on the biopsychosocial form.

Date:

Client name:

Age:

Sex:

Marital status:

Children:

Residence:

Others in residence:

Length of residence:

Education: Mark the highest grade completed.

Occupation:

Characteristics of the informant: Mark down whether or not you trust the information that the client is giving you. Is the client reliable? If so, then write "reliable informant." If for some reason you do not trust the information the client is giving you, then write why you mistrust it. You might want to write "questionable informant."

Chief complaint: This is the chief problem that brought the client to treatment. Use the client's own words. If someone else gives you the chief complaint, then list that person as the informant. "What was the chief problem that brought you to treatment?"

History of the present problem: This is everything that pertains to the chief complaint. One good approach with histories is to say something like this: "As they are growing up, kids have a real accurate idea when things are right with them and when things are wrong. Go back into your childhood and tell me where you think things began to go wrong for you. From that point, tell me the whole story including what is bringing you into treatment now."

Let the client tell his or her story, and for the most part, you just copy it down. Use as many direct quotes as you can. Guide the client only when you need to do so. You want the story to flow in a rough chronological order. Most clients will do this naturally, but everyone jumps around a little. Stop the client if he or she is going too fast or if you do not understand something. Do not let the client ramble and be caught up in irrelevant details. Look for the problem areas.

The history of the present problem must contain the following information:

- *Age of onset:*
- *Duration of use:*
- *Patterns of use:* How does the client drink? Is this client a binge drinker or a daily drinker? Does the client drink all day or only after work? How often does the client drink?
- *Consequences of use:* These are physical, psychological, and/or social problems caused or made worse by drinking.
- *Previous treatment:* Who did the client see? What was the treatment? What were the results?
- *Blackouts:*
- *Tolerance:*
- *Withdrawal symptoms:*

Past history: A history of the client's life, from infancy to the present, is the next phase of the interview. The categories include the following:

- *Place of birth:*
- *Date of birth:*
- *Developmental milestones:* "Did you have any problems when you were born? Problems walking, talking, toilet training, reading, or writing? Did anyone ever say that you were a slow learner?" Cover developmental problems and intellectual problems here. Determine as best you can whether the client can understand the material presented in your program. Most recovery material is written at a sixth-grade level. Clients who read two grade levels below this are going to need special assistance.
- *Raised with:* This includes primary caregivers, brothers, and/or sisters and what it is like to live with them.
- *Ethnic/cultural influences:* "What is your ethnic heritage?" This includes race, sexual orientation, marital status, religious preference, culture, disability/ability, ethnicity, geographic location, age, socioeconomic status, and gender. An inner-city black teenager is going to be a lot different from a Midwestern farmer. You need to know about the person's culture and be able to step into the person's worldview from his or her perspective. How does the culture relate to things such as time orientation, family, sharing, cooperation, and taught customs that guide relationships? (For further information on cultural differences, read the book *Counseling the Culturally Different: Theory and Practice* [Sue & Sue, 1999]. This book will help you to become culturally competent, which is essential to understanding the client and offering good treatment.)
- *Home of origin:* "When you were growing up, how did it feel in the house where you were raised?"
- *Grade school:* "What kind of a kid were you in grade school? How did you get along with the other kids and the teachers?"
- *High school:* "What kind of a student were you in high school? Did you get in any trouble?"
- *College:* "What were you like in college?"
- *Military history:* "Were you ever in the armed services? For how long? What was your highest rank? Did you get an honorable discharge?"
- *Occupational history:* "Briefly tell me about your work history. What kind of work have you done?" Include the longest job held and any consequences of drug or alcohol use.
- *Employment satisfaction:* "How long have you been at your current job? Are you happily employed?"
- *Financial history:* "How is your current financial situation?"
- *Gambling:* "Do you gamble? Have you ever tried to cut back on your gambling?"
- *Sexual orientation:* "How old were you when you first had sex? Have you ever had a homosexual contact?"
- *Sexual abuse:* "Have you ever been sexually abused?"
- *Physical abuse:* "Have you ever been physically abused?"

- *Current sexual history:* "Are you having any sexual problems? Are you HIV infected? Do you have AIDS or any sexually transmitted disease?"
- *Relationship history:* Briefly describe this client's relationship and friendship patterns. Does the client have any close friends? Is the client in a romantic relationship now? How is that going? Include consequences of chemical use. Some helpful questions include the following: "Do you have close friends? Have you ever been in love? How many times? Tell me a little bit about each relationship."
- *Social support for treatment:* "Does your family support you coming into treatment? What about your friends?" Thoroughly assess the client's recovery environment. How supportive are family and friends going to be about recovery?
- *Spiritual orientation:* "Do you believe in God or a Higher Power or anything like that? Do you engage in any kind of religious activity?"
- *Legal:* "Are you having any current problems with the law? Have you ever been arrested?" List the year and cause of each arrest.
- *Strengths:* "What are some of your strengths?"
- *Needs:* "What are some of the things you need to do to get into recovery?"
- *Abilities:* "What are some of your abilities that might help you stay in recovery?"
- *Personal preferences:* "How do you prefer to learn a recovery program, person to person contact, group therapy, audio visual material, reading, any cultural preferences . . . ?"
- *Weaknesses:* "What are some of your weaknesses or some of your qualities that are not so good?"
- *Leisure:* "What do you do for play, entertainment, or fun? What has been the effect of your chemical use?"
- *Depression:* "Have you ever felt depressed or down most of the day, almost every day, for more than 2 weeks?" If the client has signs of depression, this needs to be flagged for the medical staff.
- *Mania:* "Have you ever felt so high or full of energy that you got into trouble or people thought that you were acting strangely?" Mania is a distinct period of abnormally elevated, expansive, or irritable mood. This mood must be sustained for at least 2 full days.
- *Anxiety disorders:* "Have you ever been anxious for a long time? Have you ever had a panic attack?"
- *Eating disorders:* "Have you ever had any problems with appetite or eating, gorging, purging, starving yourself, or anything like that?"
- *Medical history:*
- *Illnesses:* "Have you ever had any physical illnesses? Even the small ones, such as measles, mumps, or chicken pox?"
- *Hospitalizations:* "Have you ever been in a hospital overnight?" Write down the reason for each hospitalization.
- *Allergies:* "Do you have any allergies?"
- *Medications at present:* "Are you taking any medication?" List each medication and dose schedule.
- *Family history:*
- *Father:* "How old is your father? Is he in good, fair, or poor health? Any health problems? What is he like? How did he act when you were growing up?"
- *Mother:* "How old is your mother? Is she in good, fair, or poor health? What was she like when you were growing up?"
- *Other relatives with significant psychopathology:* "Did anyone else in your family have any problems with drugs or alcohol or any other kind of mental disorder?"
- *Mental status:* This is where you formally test the client's mental condition.
- *Description of the client:* Describe the client's general appearance. How would you be able to pick the client out of a crowd? Note the client's age, skin color, sex, weight, hair color, eye color, scars, glasses, mustache, and so on.
- *Dress:* How is the client dressed? Describe what the client is wearing and how he or she is dressed. Is the client overly neat, sloppy, casual, seductive, or formal?
- *Sensorium:* Is the client fully conscious and able to use his or her senses normally, or does something seem to be clouding the client's sensorium? Is the client alert, lethargic, or drowsy? Intoxicated clients will not have a clear sensorium.

- *Orientation:* The client is oriented to person, place, and time if the client knows his or her name and location and today's date.
- *Attitude toward the examiner:* What is the client's attitude toward you—cooperative, friendly, pleasant, hostile, suspicious, or defensive?
- *Motor behavior:* Describe how the client is moving. Anything unusual? Does the client move normally, restlessly, continuously, or slowly? Does the client have a tremor or tic?
- *Speech:* How does the client talk? Any speech or language problems? Does the client talk normally, or is he or she overly talkative or minimally responsive? Do you detect a speech disorder?
- *Affect:* How is the client feeling during the interview—appropriate, blunted, restricted, labile, or dramatic over production?
- *Range of affect:* What is the client's capacity to feel the whole range of feelings? Affect ranges from elation to depression. During the interview, you should see the client cover a wide range of affect. Does the client's range of feelings seem normal, constricted, blunted, or flat?
- *Mood:* What is the feeling that clouds the client's whole life? The client might be calm, cheerful, anxious, depressed, elated, irritable, pessimistic, angry, neutral, or any other sustained feeling.
- *Thought processes:* Does the client have a normal stream of thought? Is the client able to come up with clear ideas, form these ideas into speech, and move the speech into normal conversation? If the client is hard to follow, then write down why. Describe what the client is doing that makes the conversation difficult. Are the client's thought processes logical and coherent, blocked, circumstantial, tangential, incoherent, distracted, evasive, or persevered?
- *Abstract thinking:* "What does this saying mean to you? People who live in glass houses shouldn't throw stones." An abstract answer might be, "Do not talk about people because you might have problems yourself." A concrete answer might be, "They might break the glass." Ask the client, "How are an egg and a seed alike?" An abstract answer might be, "Things grow from both." A concrete answer might be, "They are both round." Using such questions, determine the client's ability to abstract. Is it normal, or is it impaired?
- *Suicidal ideation:* "Have you ever thought about hurting yourself or anything like that?" Describe all suicidal thoughts, acts, plans, and attempts.
- *Homicidal ideation:* "Have you ever thought about hurting someone else?" Describe all thoughts, acts, plans, and attempts.
- *Disorders of perception:* Disorders in how the client perceives can be assessed by asking questions such as the following. "Have you ever seemed to hear things that other people could not seem to hear, like whispering voices or anything like that? Have you ever seemed to see things that other people could not seem to see, like a vision? Have you ever smelled a strange smell that seemed out of place? Have you ever tasted a strange taste that seemed out of place? Have you ever felt anything unusual on or under your skin?"
- *Delusions:* "Have you ever felt that anyone was paying special attention to you or anything like that? Have you ever felt that someone was out to hurt you or give you a hard time? Have you ever felt like you had any strange or unusual powers? Have you ever felt like one of the organs in your body was not operating properly?" A delusion is a false belief that is fixed.
- *Obsessions:* "Have you ever been bothered by thoughts that did not make any sense, and they kept coming back even when you tried not to think about them? Have you ever had awful thoughts like hurting someone or being contaminated by germs or anything like that?" Obsessions are persistent ideas, thoughts, impulses, or images that are experienced, at least at first, as intrusive and senseless.
- *Compulsions:* "Was there anything that you had to do repeatedly and you could not stop doing it, like washing your hands repeatedly or checking something several times to make sure you had done it right?" Compulsions are repetitive, purposeful, and intentional behaviors that are performed in response to an obsession, according to certain rules, or in a stereotyped fashion.
- *Intelligence:* Estimate the client's level of intellectual functioning—above average, average, low average, borderline, or retarded.

- *Concentration:* Describe the client's ability to concentrate during the interview—normal, mild, moderate, or severe impairment.
- *Memory:*
  a. *Immediate memory:* Tell the client, "Listen carefully. I am going to say some numbers. You say them right after me: 5–8–9–3–1." After the client has completed this task, tell him or her, "Now I am going to say some more numbers. This time I want you to say them backward: 4–3–9." Clients should be able to repeat five digits forward and three digits backward.
  b. *Recent memory:* Tell the client, "I am going to give you three objects that I want you to remember: a red ball, an open window, and a police car. Now you remember those, and I will ask you what they are in a few minutes." Clients should be able to remember all three objects after 5 minutes.
  c. *Remote memory:* The client should be able to tell you what he or she had for dinner last night or for breakfast this morning. The client should know the names of the last five presidents of the United States. The client should know his or her own history.
- *Impulse control:* Estimate the ability of the client to control his or her impulses.
- *Judgment:* Estimate the client's ability to make good judgments. If you cannot estimate from the interview, then ask the client a question. "If you were at the movies and were the first person to see smoke and fire, what would you do?" The client should give a good answer that protects both himself or herself and the other people present.
- *Insight:* Does the client know that he or she has a problem with chemicals? Does the person understand something about the nature of the illness?
- *Motivation for treatment:* Is the client committed to treatment? Estimate the level of treatment acceptance or resistance.

Summary and Impression

Begin with the client's childhood and summarize all that you have heard and observed. Include all of the problems you have seen and give your impression of where the client stands on each of the following dimensions:

1. Acute intoxication or withdrawal complications

2. Biomedical conditions and complications

3. Emotional/cognitive/behavioral conditions and complications

4. Readiness to change

5. Relapse, continued use, or continued problem potential

6. Recovery environment

Diagnosis

Diagnose the problem using the *Diagnostic and Statistical Manual of Mental Disorders* (DSM–IV–TR) (2000).

Disposition and Treatment Plan

List and describe all of the problems that need treatment and how you plan to treat each problem.

A Sample Biopsychosocial Interview

Now let us go through an actual interview so that you can see how it works. We describe how you should be thinking as we go through the interview.

The client comes into the office. She is tall and thin and is dressed in white jeans and a white sweatshirt. She smiles as she sits down. She makes good eye contact and relaxes. Her face is pretty. She does not appear to be in any acute distress.

Counselor: Give me your full name—all three names please—and spell them all.

Client: Jane J-A-N-E Roberts R-O-B-E-R-T-S.

Counselor: How old are you?

Client: Twenty-eight. *(The client seems to relax even more. She sits farther back in the chair and crosses her legs.)*

Counselor: Are you married?

Client: No.

Counselor: Have you ever been?

Client: No.

Counselor: Do you have any kids?

Client: No.

Counselor: What is your current hometown?

Client: Sioux Falls, South Dakota.

Counselor: Who lives with you?

Client: No one.

Counselor: How long have you lived there?

Client: About 5 years.

Counselor: How much education do you have?

Client: High school.

Counselor: Are you currently employed?

Client: Yes.

Counselor: What do you do?

Client: I am a self-employed beautician.

Counselor: What was the chief problem that brought you to treatment?

Client: I knew I could not go on drinking the way I was.

Counselor: When kids are growing up, they have a real accurate idea of when things are right with them and wrong with them. Go back into your childhood as early as you feel is important and tell me where you think things began to go wrong with you in your life, and from that point, tell me the whole story including what brings you to treatment now.

Client: I think that as a child I do not remember an awful lot about my childhood. I do not remember many good things. I did not have a bad childhood. I have never been abused physically or sexually or anything like that. But I always felt left out, abandoned, lost, alone a lot. (*This is where the problems start. The client grew up feeling left out, abandoned, lost, and alone.*)

I think I knew that I was loved, but I was not shown it very much. Going to a Lutheran school was hard on me. I never felt like I was like the other kids. (*The client continues to feel isolated in school.*)

One year I was a class officer, and that made me feel very good. I was not sports-minded. I did not feel that anyone was working with me with what I could do. My father died when I was a baby. My mother did not listen to me. I would ask her a question, and she would just look at me. I could never get any answers. (*This seems to be where the client began to feel unheard, abandoned, and lost.*) I remember asking her about how boys and girls were different. She just said, "Don't you know?" I never got any information about my period. I did not get it until I was old anyway, about 17, and by then I had to find out some things from my friends. I read a book about how to take care of myself. (*The client is angry with her mother. This may or may not have influenced her drinking. It certainly increased her feelings of isolation and loneliness, and it influenced her ability to establish and maintain close interpersonal relationships.*)

I hear from other members of my family that my father was strict. I did not hear good things about him, but I did not hear bad things either. He did not like drinking, and my mom would hide her alcohol from him. (*The client seems to long for her father. It is in the sadness of her voice. Her mother might have had a drinking problem. It sounds as though it caused some family conflict.*)

I think my mom talked to me about this. She may have had a problem. She hid her wine bottle down in the basement. Going through school was hard because I did not fit in with the group. I remember making up stories and trying to buy the clothes they wore to fit in, but I never did. They all caught on about what I was trying to do. It did not work. I could not afford many things. When I was older, I was very glad to get out of the house. I did not date much, but when I did, I immediately fell in love. I felt like, great, somebody likes me. When they would go out with others, I was devastated. I kept grasping at them to come back. (*These relationships sound addictive. This is a problem. Listen to the powerful feeling statements she makes: "When they would go out with others, I was devastated. I kept grasping at them to come back." The client begins to use relationships to fill the empty void. She is trying to replace her dead father and her distant mother with a relationship with a man.*)

One day my girlfriend and I were eating lunch, and these guys came up to us. They asked if we wanted to go out for a ride and have a few drinks with them. They were cute, you know, so we decided to go. There was this one, he said his name was Mark, he was older, and we got along really well. He impressed me. I could tell he really liked me a lot, more so than anyone else I had ever dated. I ended up going with him for quite a while. About a year later, I found out he was married. His name was not Mark. It was Andy. He had a wife and a kid. I finally called him up and told him that I knew the truth but that I loved him anyway. This was a very passionate man. He loved me. He showed me he loved me. I do not care what you say—he was able to love two people at the same time. (*The client becomes involved in another addictive relationship. This time it is with a man who is addictive himself. The intense sexual excitement that this man offers fools her into thinking that he really loves her.*)

We continued that relationship for a long time. There was a lot of pain in that relationship. I just broke up with him about 2 years ago.

Counselor: When did you start dating him?

Client: When I was about 21, I went with him for 4 years, and two of those years he was married, 2 he was not. (*This is passive and dependent? She does not look passive. She makes good eye contact and seems to feel comfortable. We must let the story unfold to get the answer.*)

Counselor: How old were you when you first had a drink?

Client: It was in my early teens, at a party.

Counselor: Did you drink much in high school?

Client: No, only very occasionally.

Counselor: Okay, go on with your story. You are going out with Andy, and Andy's married.

Client: We kept seeing each other. He kept promising that he was going to get a divorce. He did not want to lose me. It kept going on for years and years. I would get angry with him when I found out that he was seeing somebody else other than his wife and me. I would blow up, then I would finally settle down, and we would continue to see each other. Every time I would get frustrated with him, I would seek someone else out.

                 I would find someone else who was interested in me. I had several affairs. Andy would get very angry if he found out that I was dating someone, but I felt he did not have the right to get angry. He was married. (*There is an honesty problem here. The client was lying to both men.*)

                 I went out with this guy once. He was everything I had ever dreamed of. He was tall and dark with a hairy chest. He was beautiful. I went out with him for quite a while. He really liked me, but I kept seeing Andy. The relationship with this guy, the new guy, Rob, began to get abusive. The relationship with Andy was abusive, too. They would both hit me, slap me, sometimes. They both tried to choke me. A couple of times, they raped me out of anger. Andrew was not ever a violent person, but then all of a sudden he got violent. He put me down a lot. He put me down all the time.

Counselor: Did he make important choices for you? (*The counselor probes the dependency problem.*)

Client: No, I never did that.

Counselor: Is it hard for you to make decisions without some sort of reassurance from someone else?

Client: No, I do not have any problem there, but I am attracted to men with power. They can tell me anything, and I would believe it. I do not know what it is about powerful men, but I am real attracted to that. Andy finally got a divorce, and I lived with him. He is a banker and very wealthy. I thought things were going to be a lot better. He was still controlling and manipulative, but I thought everything was going to improve. I always knew that eventually I was going to be abandoned. (*Here we see the fuel for the addictive relationship. The client chronically fears abandonment, like the abandonment that she felt as a child. This leaves her feeling anxious and vulnerable. She will do anything to keep her man, but at the same time, she fears that she will lose him.*)

                 He was very demanding, but I could get what I wanted by being very diplomatic. It took me a long time to learn how to do that. He always wanted me to do all kinds of things. I kept the house and the grounds immaculate. I worked and kept house and did the yardwork and worked at my job. (*The client is not assertive. She has learned how to lie and manipulate to get what she wants.*)

                 All this time, I was drinking a lot. I was hiding my drinking. I would hide my beer cans. Sometimes he would come home, and I would be drunk.

Counselor: How much were you drinking then?

Client: At least a six-pack.

Counselor: Did you ever have a blackout?

Client: Oh, yeah, I had plenty.

Counselor: Did you ever have a real bad hangover?

Client: Yes.

Counselor: Hands ever get shaky?

Client: No, but I would be sick. I would feel terrible—headache, upset stomach.

Counselor: What happened then?

Client: I came home one night and caught him with another woman. He denied what was going on, but I knew. I could tell from her reaction that she did not know about me. I talked to her, and in time we both got together with him again. I swear to God, he has the ability to love two women at the same time. I can tell he loves me.

Counselor: Healthy relationships are based on trust.

Client: I know that. This woman and I were never mad at each other. We both knew that he was so intense that he could love us both.

Counselor: It is not right to lie to you.

Client: I like that. That makes sense. I finally broke up with him. I did not know anyone. It was very hard, but I did it. He was furious. That was the last time he raped me. He was out of his mind.

Counselor: You do not rape somebody that you love either.

Client: It was finally over. I fell in love with a new guy, Dave. I fell in love so fast. He was a dream come true. We had long talks about things. This guy did not work out because I realized that I was doing all of the giving again. I am starting to realize my pattern. I do all the giving, and I love men with power. It took me a long time to realize that. He would go to my house, watch TV, and eat all my food. He never took me anywhere. I said, "Are you getting tired of me or what?" I realized that there was something I was not getting here. I had such feelings for David. I cannot remember ever feeling like that. He was such a heartthrob.

Counselor: It is easy to get love and lust confused. (*The counselor continues to teach the client and to show her how she has been confused about relationships. Notice that these interventions are very brief. This is not the time for therapy. It is the time for assessment.*)

Client: That relationship ended, and I started going out with another guy. He was an alcoholic in recovery, so I cut down on my drinking some. I only saw him once a week. It was nice. One night Andy just walked in on us. It was crazy. He just came right in as if he owned the place. I had my own place then. I was finally making the break with him, and he could not believe it. Bryan handled it very well. Andy finally left. You know, I like a man with power. I have this thing about a man with power. I do not know what it is.

Counselor: Well, you have felt powerless in your life. Someone with power would make you feel safe.

Client: Yeah, a strong man makes me feel safe. Anyway, my drinking kept on increasing, my relationships kept going to hell, and here I am.

Counselor: Anything in particular bring you into treatment now?

Client: I went out and got drunk again, and I woke up with such a hangover. I said to myself, I have to do something about this, now. I made the call right then.

This concluded the history of the present problem. Then the counselor moved right into the history.

Counselor: Where were you born?

Client: Livingston, South Dakota.

Counselor: When is your birthday?

Client: June 28, 1983.

Counselor: Did you have any trouble when you were born?

Client: No.

Counselor: Any trouble walking, talking, toilet training, reading, or writing?

Client: No.

Counselor: You were raised with whom?

Client: My mother and two younger sisters.

Counselor: What is your ethnic heritage? Irish? German? Do you know?

Client: I am Irish.

Counselor: Your home of origin, growing up with your mother and sisters. How did it feel in that house?

Client: I felt alone. I did not like it.

Counselor: What kind of a kid were you in grade school?

Client: I was timid, not very outgoing.

Counselor: What kind of a kid were you in high school?

Client: I was scared, scared to relate.

Counselor: You seem to have made real progress with that timid thing. You do not seem timid anymore.

Client: Yeah, I really have. I do not think I am timid anymore.

Counselor: Great. Were you ever in the armed services?

Client: No.

Counselor: Ever go to college.

Client: No.

Counselor: Give me a brief occupational history. What kind of work have you done?

Client: I worked as a secretary for 5 years. I have been at my current job for about 5 years.

Counselor: Are you happily employed?

Client: Yeah, I like my job.

Counselor: How is your current financial situation?

Client: Good. I am not rich, but I get along okay.

Counselor: Do you have any sexual problems?

Client: No.

Counselor: Have you ever had a homosexual contact?

Client: No.

Counselor: Are you currently involved with a guy?

Client: Yes.

Counselor: How long has that been going on?

Client: About 3 months.

Counselor: And how is that going?

Client: Great.

Counselor: Do your friends and family support your coming into treatment?

Client: Yes.

Counselor: Do you feel like there is any kind of a Higher Power or God or anything?

Client: I believe in God.

Counselor: Do you attend church?

Client: I go to the Lutheran church.

Counselor: Are you having any problems with the law?

Client: No.

Counselor: Have you ever had any problems with the law in the past.

Client: No.

Counselor: What are some of your strengths or some of your good qualities?

Client: I am caring. I get along with people real well. I think I am intelligent.

Counselor: What are some of your weaknesses?

Client: A drinking problem.

Counselor: What do you enjoy doing for fun?

Client: I enjoy biking. I hike and jog.

Counselor: Have you ever had a period of time where you felt down or depressed most of the day most every day?

Client: No.

Counselor: Have you ever felt real anxious?

Client: No.

Counselor: Ever felt so high or filled with energy that you got into trouble or people thought you were acting strangely?

Client: No.

Counselor: Ever had any eating problems—gorging, purging, starving yourself, anything like that?

Client: No.

Counselor: Are you intensely afraid of anything?

Client: No.

Counselor: Ever had any illnesses, even the small ones—measles, mumps, or chicken pox?

Client: Measles, mumps, and chicken pox.

Counselor: Ever been in a hospital overnight?

Client: No.

Counselor: Do you have any allergies?

Client: No.

Counselor: Are you taking any kind of medication here?

Client: They have me on a Valium come-down schedule.

Counselor: For what?

Client: I have been taking Valium for about 5 years. I am withdrawing from that. (*Current problems are covered in the history of the present problem. The counselor did not know about the Valium until now. This happens often. The counselor now has to flip back to the history of the present problem and add this part.*)

Counselor: How much of the Valium were you using?

Client: I was using it every day for sleep.

Counselor: Did you find yourself using more?

Client: Yes, I had to increase what I took so it would work.

Counselor: Twice as much?

Client: More.

Counselor: Did you ever stop using?

Client: No.

Counselor: How much would you take every night?

Client: I got up to about 30 mg. (*Once this information was gathered, the counselor resumed the client's past history.*)

Counselor: Okay, how old was your father when he died.

Client: In his 20s.

Counselor: How old is your mother?

Client: Fifty-three.

Counselor: Is she in good, fair, or poor health?

Client: She is in good health.

Counselor: What kind of a person is your mom?

Client: She is quiet and demanding.

Counselor: Has anyone else in your family had any problems with alcohol, drugs, or any other kind of mental disorder?

Client: I think my mother had a drinking problem.

This concludes the past history. Now you would complete the mental status, which we will not bore you with here, and you are ready to dictate the biopsychosocial interview. The client has said a lot, and it was important for her to share these things, but you need to tell the story in an abbreviated form. Keep in the main parts of her story, but exclude all of the details. At the end of the biopsychosocial interview, come up with a problem list and a preliminary treatment plan.

To view Jane's biopsychosocial interview as it was completed, see Appendix 6.

5   The Treatment Plan

Source: ©iStockphoto.com/digitalskillet.

The treatment plan is the road map that a client will follow in his or her journey through treatment. The best plans will follow the client for the next 5 years where the relapse rates drop to around zero (Vaillant, 2003). No two road maps will be the same; everyone's journey is different. Treatment planning begins as soon as the initial assessments are completed. The client might have immediate needs that will need to be addressed. Treatment planning is a never-ending stream of therapeutic plans and interventions. It always is moving and changing. I have written an excellent treatment-planning book and computer program that makes treatment planning easy: *The Addiction Treatment Planner* (Perkinson & Jongsma, 2009). The book and computer program write your treatment plan with point-and-click easiness and have been approved by all accrediting bodies.

How to Build a Treatment Plan

The treatment plan builds around the problems that the client brings into treatment. The problem list details each problem. It must take into account all of the physical, emotional, and behavioral problems relevant to the client's care. It must take into account the client's strengths, weaknesses, needs, abilities, and personal preferences. It must address each of the six dimensions that you are following.

The treatment plan details the therapeutic interventions, what is going to be done, when it is going to be done, and by whom. It must consider each of the clients's needs and come up with clear ways of dealing with each problem. The treatment plan flows into discharge planning, which begins from the initial assessments.

The Diagnostic Summary

After the interdisciplinary team members assess the client, they meet and develop a summary of their findings. This is the diagnostic summary. This is where members of the clinical team—the physicians, nurses, counselors, psychologists, psychiatrists, recreational therapists, occupational therapists, physical therapists, dietitians, family therapists, teachers, pastors, pharmacists, and anyone else who is going to be actively involved with the client's care—meet and develop a summary of the client's current state and needs. The team members discuss each of the client's problems and how to treat the problem. From this meeting, the diagnostic summary is developed. This details what the problems are, where they came from, and what is going to be done about them. It is much better to do this as a team. As you see your team function, you will see how valuable it is to have many disciplines involved.

The Problem List

The treatment team will continue to develop the problem list as the client moves through treatment. Add new problems as the client continues in treatment. Nothing will stay the same. A problem list and treatment plan must be fluid. It is modified as conditions change.

How to Develop a Problem List

A treatment plan must be measurable. It must have a set of problems and solutions that can be measured. The problems cannot be vague. They must be specific. A problem is a brief clinical statement of a condition of the client that needs treatment. The problem statement should be no longer than one sentence and should describe only one problem.

All problem statements are abstract concepts. You cannot actually see, hear, touch, taste, or smell the problem. For example, low self-esteem is a clinical statement that describes a variety of behaviors exhibited by the client. You can see the behaviors and conclude from them that the client has low self-esteem, but you cannot actually see low self-esteem.

Problems are evidenced by signs (what you see) and symptoms (what the client reports). A problem on the treatment plan is followed by specific physical, emotional, or behavioral evidence that the problem actually exists. List the problem, add "as evidenced by" or "as indicated by," and then describe the concrete evidence you see that tells you that the problem exists.

Examples of a Problem List

Problem 1: Inability to maintain sobriety outside of a structured facility

As evidenced by: Blood alcohol level of .23

As evidenced by: The client's family report of daily drinking

As evidenced by: Alcohol withdrawal symptoms

As evidenced by: Third DWI

As evidenced by: History of third treatment for addiction

Problem 2: Depression

As evidenced by: Hamilton Depression Rating Scale score of 29

As evidenced by: Psychological evaluation

As evidenced by: Client's two suicide attempts in the past 3 months

As evidenced by: Depressed affect

Problem 3: Acute alcohol withdrawal

As evidenced by: Blood alcohol level on admission .23

As evidenced by: Coarse hand tremors

As evidenced by: Blood pressure 160/100, pulse 104

As evidenced by: Restless pacing; self-report of strong craving

As evidenced by: Profuse sweating; mild visual disturbances

Goals and Objectives

Once you have a problem list, you need to ask yourself what the client needs to do to restore himself or herself to normal functioning. A person who has a drinking problem needs to stop drinking and must learn the skills necessary to maintain a sober lifestyle. A person who is depressed needs to reestablish normal mood. A person who is dishonest needs to get honest with himself or herself and others. Writing goals, objectives, and interventions in a treatment plan is made much easier for counselors by using *The Addiction Treatment Planner* or *The Addiction Treatment Planner With Disk* (Perkinson & Jongsma, 2006, 2009) plus the *TheraScribe 5.0* computer program. These plans conform to the highest standards set by accrediting bodies such as the Joint Commission on Accreditation of Healthcare Organizations (JCAHO, 1988).

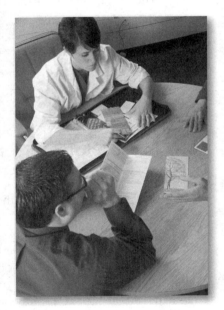

Source: Jupiterimages/ Thinkstock.

How to Develop Goals

A goal is a brief clinical statement of the condition you expect to change in the client or in the client's family. You state what you intend to accomplish in general terms. Specify the condition of the client that will result from treatment. All goals label a set of behaviors that you want to create.

Goals should be more than the elimination of pathology. They are directed toward the client learning new and more functional methods of coping. Focus on more than just stopping the old dysfunctional behavior. Concentrate on replacing it with something more effective.

Examples of Developing Goals

Instead of: The client will stop drinking.

Use: The client will develop a program of recovery congruent with a sober lifestyle. (The client is learning something different.) It often helps to put the goals in the clients own words. Client statement: "I need learn how to stay sober."

Use: The client will learn to cope with stress in an adaptive manner. Client statement: "I need to learn how to cope with my stress."

Instead of: The client will stop negative self-talk. (The client does not learn or use something differently; the client just avoids something that he or she already knows.)

Use: The client will develop and use positive self-talk. Client statement: "I need to start telling myself the truth." (Now the client learns something different that is incompatible with the old behavior.)

Use: The client will develop a positive self-image. (The client learns something new and more adaptive.)

The client or the client's family must be the subject of each goal. No staff member or staff intervention are mentioned. Identify one goal and condition at a time. Make each goal one sentence.

Examples of Goals

1. The client will learn the skills necessary to maintain a sober lifestyle.

2. The client will learn to express negative feelings to his or her spouse.

3. The client will develop a positive commitment to sobriety.

4. The client will develop a healthy diet and begin to gain weight.

5. The client will learn how to tolerate uncomfortable feelings without using chemicals.

6. The client will learn to share positive feelings with others.

7. The client will develop the ability to ask for what he or she wants.

8. The client will develop the ability to use anger appropriately.

9. The client will sleep comfortably on a regular basis.

10. The client will learn healthy communication skills.

How to Develop Objectives

An objective is a specific skill that the client must acquire to achieve a goal. The objective is what you really set out to accomplish in treatment. An objective is a concrete behavior that you can see, hear, smell, taste, or feel. An objective is stated so clearly that almost anyone would know when he or she saw it. Goals usually are abstract statements that you cannot actually see happen. You cannot see someone learn or see his or her self-esteem. You can see an individual express 10 positive things about himself or herself. One way of seeing whether you have a goal or an objective is to use the "see Johnny" test developed by Arnold Goldman: "If you can see Johnny do it, then it is an objective; if you cannot, then it is a goal." (Goldman [1989] gives lessons on treatment planning in *Accreditation and Certification: For Providers of Psychiatric, Alcoholism, and Drug Abuse Services* [PO Box 742, Bala Cynwyd, PA 19004]. Richard Weedman also has done a lot of work in this area. He wrote *Client Records in Addiction Treatment: Documenting the Quality of Care* [JCAHO, 1992]. A copy can be obtained from JCAHO, One Renaissance Boulevard, Oakbrook Terrace, IL 60181. These materials should be read if you have problems with treatment planning.)

Remember, if you can see it, then it usually is an objective. If you cannot see it, then it usually is a goal.

Can you see the client read about Step One in the "Big Book" (Alcoholics Anonymous [AA], 2002a)? Yes. (Objective)

Can you see the client understand the illness of addiction? No. (Goal)

Can you see the client gain insight? No. (Goal)

Can you see the client improve his or her self-esteem? No. (Goal)

Can you see the client complete the Step One exercise? Yes. (Objective)

Can you see the client keep a daily record of his or her dysfunctional thinking? Yes. (Objective)

Can you see the client share his or her feelings in group? Yes. (Objective)

All goals and objectives help the client change. Individuals must change how they feel, what they think, and/or what they do. Each goal should have one or more objectives. The best way of developing goals is to ask these questions. How can you know for sure that the client has achieved the goal? What must the client say or do to convince you that the treatment goal is completed?

State the goal aloud, add on the words "as evidenced by" or "as indicated by," and then complete the sentence describing the specific objectives that will tell you that the goal has been reached. Each goal will need at least one objective. Each goal and objective will need a number or a letter that identifies it. Each objective will need a completion date. This is the date by which you expect the objective will be completed. If the client passes this date without completing the objective, then the treatment plan might have to be modified.

Examples

Goal A: The client will develop a program of recovery congruent with a sober lifestyle, as evidenced by the following:

1. The client will share in recovery skills group three times when he or she tried to stop drinking but was unable to stay sober.

2. The client will make a list of the essential skills necessary for recovery.

Goal B: The client will learn to use assertiveness skills, as indicated by the following:

1. The client will discuss the assertive formula and will role-play three situations where he or she acts assertively.

2. The client will keep an assertiveness log and will share the log with the counselor daily.

3. The client will practice assertiveness skills in interpersonal group.

Objectives must be measurable. You must be able to count them. You or the client can count all thoughts, feelings, and actions. The client can count his or her thoughts by keeping a daily record of his or her thinking. The client can count feelings by keeping a feelings log. You can keep a record of every time a client acts angry around the unit.

To achieve the goal of maintaining a sober lifestyle, an alcoholic might need to develop one or more of the following skills:

1. Verbalize that he or she has a problem, or verbalize an understanding of the problem.

2. Develop and practice new behaviors that are incompatible with the problem. Read the Big Book.

3. Practice the 12 steps of AA.

4. Go to meetings.

5. Learn how to cope with uncomfortable feelings.

6. Develop a relapse prevention plan.

All depressed clients will need to develop one or more of the following skills:

1. Learn how to say positive things to themselves.

2. Develop recreational programs to add fun to their lives.

3. Grieve and learn how to accept the deaths of loved ones.

4. Get accurate in their thinking.

5. Improve the dysfunctional interpersonal relationships with their spouses.

6. Take antidepressant medication.

How to Develop Interventions

Interventions are what you do to help the client complete the objective. Interventions also are measurable and objective. There should be at least one intervention for every objective. If the client does not complete the objective, then new interventions are added to the plan.

Interventions should be selected by looking at what the client needs. They may include every treatment available from any member of the multidisciplinary team. They may include any therapy from any staff member such as group therapy, individual therapy, behavior therapy, cognitive therapy, occupational therapy, recreation therapy, or family therapy. The person responsible for the intervention needs to be listed below the intervention so that the staff knows who is responsible.

Examples

Intervention: Assign the client to write a list of five negative consequences of his or her drug use.

*Responsible professional _____

Intervention: In a conjoint session, have the client share the connection between drinking and marijuana use.

*Responsible professional _____

Intervention: In group, encourage the client to share his or her anxious feelings.

Intervention: Have the client develop a personal recovery plan that includes all of the activities that he or she plans to attend.

*Responsible professional _____

How to Evaluate the Effectiveness of Treatment

In treatment, it is vital to keep score of how you are doing. It is the only way in which you will know whether treatment is working. Feelings, thoughts, and behaviors are counted. The staff can count them, or the client can count them. The client must record thoughts and feelings, being internal states. Behaviors are recorded by the client or by the staff. Clients and the staff will record feelings, thoughts, and behaviors and keep a log of these data. The log of the staff is called the clinical record or the chart.

How to Select Goals, Objectives, and Interventions

Goals, objectives, and interventions are infinite. It takes clinical skill to decide exactly what the client needs to do to establish a stable recovery. Every treatment plan is individualized. Everyone is different, and every treatment plan is different. For the same goal, you may have widely different objectives. You need to ask yourself three questions:

1. What is this client doing that is maladaptive?

2. What does the client need to do differently?

3. How can I help the client behave in a new way?

These questions, if asked carefully, will uncover your goals. Once you have your goals, ask yourself this question: What does the client need to do to achieve these goals? These are your objectives. Then ask yourself what you can do to help the client. Each client will need to do the following three things:

1. Identify that he or she has a problem.

2. Understand exactly what that problem is and how it affects the client.

3. Apply healthy skills that will reduce or eliminate the problem.

Examples of Goals, Objectives, and Interventions

Problem 1: Pathological relationship with alcohol, as indicated by a blood alcohol level on admission of .32, three DWIs, and family report of daily drinking

Goal A: Develop a program of recovery congruent with a sober lifestyle, as evidenced by the following:

Objective 1: Norman will identify with his counselor 10 times when alcohol use negatively affected his life by 6-1-2010.

> *Intervention:* Assign the client the homework of making a list of 10 times when alcohol use negatively affected his life.

> *Responsible professional _____

Objective 2: Norman will complete his chemical use history and share in group his understanding of his alcohol problem by 6-1-2010.

> *Intervention:* Assign the client to complete a chemical use history exercise and then have him share his answers in group.

> *Responsible professional _____

Objective 3: Norman will share his powerlessness and unmanageability with his group by 6-10-2010.

> *Intervention:* In a one-to-one counseling session, teach the client about powerlessness and unmanageability and then have him share what he learned in group.

> *Responsible professional _____

Objective 4: Norman will share in group his understanding of how he can use his Higher Power in sobriety by 6-15-2010.

Intervention: Clergy will meet with the client and explain how he can use a Higher Power in recovery.

*Responsible professional _____

Objective 5: Norman will take all medications as prescribed and report side effects to the medical staff.

Intervention: Physician will examine the client and order medications as indicated while the medical staff monitors for side effects.

*Responsible professional _____

Objective 6: Norman will develop a written relapse prevention plan by 6-25-2010.

Intervention: In a counseling session, teach the client about relapse prevention and help him to develop a written relapse prevention program.

*Responsible professional _____

Objective 7: Norman will discuss his codependency with his wife by 6-30-2010.

Intervention: In a conjoint session, help the client to discuss his codependency with his wife and how this problem relates to substance abuse.

*Responsible professional _____

In developing goals and objectives, the client must move through the following events:

1. Identify that he or she has a problem.

2. Understand how the problem negatively affects the client.

3. Learn what he or she is going to change.

4. Practice the change.

Let us take another problem.

Problem 2: Poor impulse control, as indicated by numerous fights, abusiveness to spouse, and self-report that he loses control when angry

Goal A: Learn to use angry feelings appropriately, as evidenced by the following:

Objective 1: Thomas will discuss with his counselor five times when he used anger inappropriately by 7-2-2010.

Intervention: Assign the client the homework task of listing five times when he used anger inappropriately.

*Responsible professional _____

Objective 2: Thomas will share in group his understanding of what he needs to do differently to cope with his anger by 7-10-2010.

Intervention: Have the client share in group five tools he can use to cope with anger effectively.

*Responsible professional _____

Objective 3: Thomas will visit the staff psychologist to learn and practice stress management techniques by 7-2-2010.

Intervention: The staff psychologist will teach the client stress management techniques such as progressive relaxation, biofeedback, and systematic desensitization.

*Responsible professional _____

Objective 4: Thomas will keep a daily log of his angry feelings and discuss the log with his counselor once a week.

Intervention: Assign the client to keep a daily log of angry feelings and to use subjective units of distress to rate each situation on a scale from one to 100.

*Responsible professional _____

Objective 5: Thomas will share his hurt and his angry feelings in group by 7-21-2010.

Intervention: Encourage the client to share his feelings log in group.

*Responsible professional _____

Objective 6: Thomas will practice sharing his hurt and his anger with his spouse in a conjoint session by 7-30-2010.

Intervention: In a conjoint session, have the client share his hurt and angry feelings with his wife, and make a written contract to separate and contact the sponsor or counselor when angry.

*Responsible professional _____

Objective 7: Thomas will attend a violence group once a week.

Intervention: Refer the client to an anger management group and make the first appointment with the client present.

*Responsible professional _____

Samples of a complete biopsychosocial, diagnostic summary, and treatment plan are given in Appendix 6.

Treatment Plan Review

The interdisciplinary team reviews the treatment plan at regular intervals throughout treatment. At a minimum, the treatment plan is reviewed at all decision points. These points include the following:

1. Admission

2. Transfer

3. Discharge

4. Major change in the client's condition

5. The point of estimated length of treatment

Most facilities have a daily staffing where the client's progress is briefly discussed and a weekly review where the treatment plan is discussed. It is at these meetings that the treatment plan will be modified. Problems, goals, and objectives will change as the client's condition changes. Treatment team review is where the staff finds out how the client is doing in treatment and what changes need to be made.

Documentation

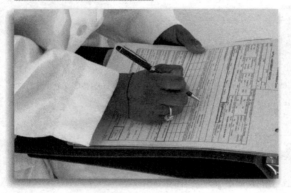

Source: ©iStockphoto.com/nano.

The staff keeps a written record of the client's progress through treatment. This document is called the client record, commonly called the chart. The staff keeps progress notes that document what happens to the client during treatment. Progress notes have to be typed or written in black ink.

Each progress note needs to be identified with one or more treatment objectives. For example, a progress note on Goal A, Objective 7, would begin with the notation *a (7)*. This helps the staff to keep track of how the client is doing with each objective.

Progress notes include the following data:

1. The treatment plan

2. All treatment

3. The client's clinical course

4. Each change in the client's condition

5. Descriptions of the client's response to treatment

6. The outcome of all treatment

7. The response of significant others to important events during treatment

How to Write Progress Notes

Keep your progress notes short, and write with a black pen only. Progress notes must include just enough detail to describe what is going on with the client. For the most part, describe things in behavioral terms. Any entry that includes your opinion or interpretation of events is supplemented by a description of the actual behavior you observed. What did you see or hear that led you to that conclusion? Describe exactly what the client did or said. Direct quotations from the client make an excellent progress note.

The client's progress in meeting the goals and objectives is recorded on a regular basis. The efforts of the staff in helping the client to meet treatment goals and objectives are recorded. The progress notes will be used by the staff to see how the client is doing in treatment. A person who has never met the client should be able to know the client's story by reading the client record. Before you chart, ask yourself this question: If you were a counselor just coming in to take over this case, what would you need to know? It is a good idea to write a short progress note on each client each day. This is not essential, but it will keep you thinking about the treatment plan and the client's progress through the treatment plan on a daily basis.

Examples of Progress Notes

6-12-2010 (10:30 am)

Jane discussed her denial exercise in group. She verbalized an understanding of how denial had adversely affected her, stating, "I cannot believe how dishonest I was to myself. I really did not think I had a problem even after all that trouble. I lied to Andy too, about everything." The client was able to see how denial was a lie to herself and to others. After the session, the client was able to verbalize her need to get honest with herself and others. "I have been lying about everything. It is about time I got honest with myself."

6-14-2010 (3:15 pm)

Jane was tearful in an individual session. She mourned the loss of her love relationship with her past partner. The group helped her to see how destructive the relationship had been for her. The treatment peers reinforced that Jane was worth being treated better than her partner was treating her. Jane expressed that she is extremely angry with her mother. "I hate her. She never spent any time with me. She only wanted me as a slave. She wanted a housekeeper, not me." It seemed to give Jane some relief to hear other clients express that they had similar feelings about their mothers. "I thought I was the only one who felt like that," Jane stated.

6-15-2010 (11:00 am)

Jane's facial expression is sad. She has been isolating herself. She did not eat breakfast. She was seen crying alone in her room. I went in, and she was able to express her feelings. "I am so ashamed of myself. I would never be able to live this down." Jane expressed that she was feeling guilty about sharing with group her anger at her mother. I reassured Jane and told her to bring up her feelings in group this afternoon.

Formal Treatment Plan Review

Once a week, the staff will do a formal treatment team review. This requires a more detailed look at how the client is doing in each problem area. The staff members present must be identified along with their credentials.

6-16-2010 (11:45 am)

Treatment plan review: Present, Dr. Roberts, MD; M. Smith, CCDC Level II; T. Anderson, RN; F. Mark, CCDC Level I; Dr. Thomas; M. Tobas, PhD; E. Talbot, RN; A. Stein, LPN. The staff feels that Jane is adjusting well to treatment. She is more talkative and seems to feel more comfortable. She has made some friends with several treatment peers including her roommate. Her mother came to see her on Sunday, and Jane reported that this visit went well.

Problem 1: Jane continues on her Valium comedown schedule. She has reported only mild withdrawal symptoms. She is sleeping well. She continues to be mildly restless. She was encouraged to increase her level of exercise to 20 minutes daily.

Problem 2: Jane has completed her chemical use history and Step One exercise. She shared in interpersonal group her powerlessness and unmanageability. She was open in group, and she verbalized that she has accepted her disease of addiction. She was somewhat more reluctant to accept her problem with Valium, but the group did a good job of explaining cross-tolerance. The client should complete the cross-tolerance exercise and report her findings to the group.

Problem 3: The client continues to take her iron supplement. Her hemoglobin is within normal limits.

Problem 4: The client is over her cold. Problem 4 is completed.

Problem 5: The client has written a letter to her mother and father (even though he passed away years ago), describing how she felt about her childhood. The client shared her letter in group, and she was surprised to find out that many of the other clients had similar experiences. The client stated that she is feeling more comfortable sharing in group, and she appears to be gaining confidence in herself.

Jane met with her counselor, and the counselor encouraged Jane to accept her new AA/Narcotics Anonymous (NA) group as the healthy family that she never had. Jane expressed hope in becoming involved with this healthy family.

Problem 6: Jane is working on the relationship skills exercise. She has been practicing asking for what she wants. It is still very difficult for her to share some of her feelings, particularly her anger, in group. When she shares her anger, she tends to feel guilty.

Problem 7: Jane completed the honesty exercise and the chemical use history that opened her eyes to how dishonest she has been. Jane made a contract with her group to be honest and asked the clients to confront her if they felt that she was being dishonest. Jane is keeping a daily log of her lies and when she is tempted to lie. She has been able to identify many lies she was telling in her life and is able to verbalize her understanding of how her lies keep her isolated from others.

Problem 8: Jane is working on the assertiveness skills exercise. She is practicing the assertive formula. She tends to feel guilty when she says no, but she is getting better at it. She will say no to someone five times a day for 3 days and keep a log of how she feels about each situation.

Discussion of Continuing Care

During the discussion of the treatment plan, it is always a good idea to begin continuing care planning. This will include a 5-year follow-up plan run by the continuing care case manager. This is a formal contract negotiated with the client and significant others. The plan includes an agreement that the client work all aspects of the continuing care plan with detailed consequences if the client fails to meet his or her obligations. The plan should include the following:

- Client sends in a log of 12-step meetings by the 10th of every month. The case manager sets the number of meetings each week.
- The client will meet regularly with his or her 12-step sponsor.
- Client will agree to attend all therapy recommended by the primary counselor with a report from the primary care giver as often as deemed necessary.
- Client will agree to up to one random drug screen a week for the first 6 months and up to one random drug screen a week for the next year and a half. The client can use the PharmChek Drugs of Abuse Patch that lasts for 7 days or longer (www.pharmchem.com) or use an alcohol ankle bracelet, the Secure Continuous Remote Alcohol Monitor (SCRAM), that measures alcohol from the sweat 24 hours a day, 7 days a week.
- The client will take all medications as ordered.
- If the client fails to meet any of his or her obligations, he or she is sent a letter explaining the deficiency and asking that it be corrected.
- If the client fails to answer the letter an appointment will be set up with the continuing care case manager.
- If the client still fails to comply with the contract, the consequences agreed upon are implemented. This might include contacting the clients, professional board, employer, probation officer, drug court judge, family members, etc. The client has initially signed a release of information to all such individuals and has written each of them cosigned by the continuing care case manager. These letters are signed, sealed, stamped, and mailed if necessary. The continuing care manager must be very careful to design consequence that leads the client back into treatment.

6

Individual Treatment

Source: ©iStockphoto.com/killerb10.

All of the treatments that counselors work with on a daily basis revolve around changing clients' thoughts, feelings, and behaviors. People think in two ways: in words and in images. If you close your eyes and think of the word *tractor*, that is thinking in words. If you close your eyes and see some sort of a tractor in your mind, that is thinking in images. Thoughts happen extremely quickly, so quickly that we do not pick all of them up. Some are conscious, and some are unconscious. There is a constant stream of thought. It never stops.

Feelings give us the energy and direction for problem solving. All feelings have a specific movement attached to them. The feeling of fear gives us the energy and direction to run away from an offending stimulus. The feeling of sadness gives us the energy and direction to recover a lost object. Good problem solving necessitates using feelings appropriately.

"We don't have oral sex for a relationship. We have it for recreation."

Behavior is movement. Anytime a person moves, he or she is exhibiting behavior. Speech is movement. Drinking is movement. Going to Alcoholics Anonymous (AA) meetings is movement. These all are behaviors. Behaviors are the easiest things to see, count, and record. Whenever possible, conduct your treatment using the client's behavior as your guide. Behavior will tell you whether your treatment is working.

The Therapeutic Alliance

Source: Hemera Technologies/Thinkstock.

All individual treatment will revolve around the relationship that you have with your clients. This is the therapeutic alliance. If the clients like and trust you, then they will listen to you and will want to change to please you.

How to Develop a Therapeutic Alliance

The therapeutic alliance should be growing and improving from the first moment you meet your clients. You need to be constantly encouraging and supportive. You should give the clients the feeling that you are going to walk with them as a trusted guide. This relationship is based on love, trust, and commitment. The clients are afraid to tell anyone the truth. The clients probably never have told anyone the whole truth. You are going to be different. You are going to be confidential and consistently act in the clients' interest. You are going to show the clients unconditional positive regard. No matter what the clients do, you are going to be there for them. You are not always going to tell the clients what they want to hear, but you are going to tell them the truth, and you are going to encourage the clients to see the truth in themselves. You are going to expect the clients to improve and work with you. You cannot do all of the work yourself. The client has to struggle to get clean. You are going to encourage the clients to see the fact that they can recover if they work a program of recovery. You believe that the clients have the resources necessary, or else you would not have accepted them as your clients. You believe that the clients can do it.

Clients will have great doubts about themselves. They have tried to lick their addictions many times before and always have failed. Many clients have lost hope that they can recover. Self-efficacy is clients believing they can succeed. This confidence builds over the weeks of treatment by constantly reinforcing the clients when they complete some small task in the program. This may be as little as coming to group on time or as big as confronting their parents with their real feelings.

The solid basis of a good therapeutic alliance is to constantly encourage, support, and educate. Encourage means to reward the client when she or he tries something new. You give the client confidence by assigning tasks that the client can successfully complete. Support means to help clients to do something that they cannot do by themselves. The client might not be able to talk to a spouse, probation officer, or employer at first. You might have to help him or her to do that. As the counselor, you look for good behavior from the clients. When you see the clients doing something right, you point it out and praise them for it. Try not to miss an opportunity to reinforce the client for good behavior. That gives the client confidence.

How to Be Reinforcing

"Good job. I knew you could do it."

"You are doing great. I am proud of you."

"I am so impressed."

"That took great courage."

"This is going to pay off for you."

"Keep coming. You can do it."

These statements reinforce clients. You are going to support the clients warmly as often as you can. Be sensitive to the clients' needs. Constantly ask yourself this question: If you were in this client's situation, how would you want to be treated? Then treat the client that way.

Make good eye contact when you give praise or make a point. Clients have learned that they cannot trust anyone. The clients do not even trust themselves. You are going to prove to the clients, with your actions, that they can trust you.

Be gentle. Do not hammer your ideas home aggressively. That wounds the therapeutic alliance. Let the power of the truth work for you. A whisper of truth is much more powerful than an angry confrontation. Your clients are injured already. They do not need to be broken. They need to heal in an atmosphere of love and trust.

Help the clients to move toward greater self-understanding. Help the clients to identify exactly how they have kept themselves isolated, and teach them new ways of reaching out to others. The clients have been hiding from themselves for a long time. They have been feeling lost and alone. They need to come out from the darkness created by the disease and into the light of the truth.

How to Use Empathy

Empathy is stepping into the client's world and understanding it from his or her perspective. Whenever you put yourself in someone else's position, you are practicing empathy. It often is helpful to recognize the feelings or thoughts of the clients that stimulate something from your own experience. You do not have to experience the same intensity of feelings that grips the clients, but you need to relate to the feelings and understand them. Feel yourself walking in the clients' shoes. What if this was happening to you? How would you feel? What would you be thinking? What would you need? What would you want? Your empathic responses will not always be correct—you can misperceive the clients—but they will improve over time. A good test of empathy is that your comments should deepen the clients' narrative flow (Havens, 1978). Empathic accuracy can be further determined by reflecting the clients' feelings. Repeat to the clients your understanding of what they have just said. The clients will clarify any misunderstanding. Their words and behavior should continually deepen your understanding of their life (Bettet & Maloney, 1991).

Be sensitive to your own feelings. How are the clients affecting you? Are some of your own issues being triggered? How can this give you insight into yourself and the clients?

Transference and Countertransference

Transference is clients responding to you with the same feelings, thoughts, and behaviors that they developed for other people in their lives. Countertransference is you responding to clients in the same way that you responded to other people. We all have internal maps about how the world and people function. We trust these maps to help us navigate in the world. We learned maps from our primary caregivers and from significant others in our lives. If you had a father who was demanding, then you learned that people, particularly men, are demanding. If you had a mother who you could not trust, then you learned that people, particularly women, are not trustworthy. These maps profoundly influence the client's whole life and therapy. Sometimes they are accurate, and sometimes they are inaccurate. Constantly check your maps, as well as the clients' maps, for accuracy.

There are counselors who are insensitive to themselves and others. These counselors can do great damage to their clients. They demand immediate disclosure before their clients are ready. They are not sensitive enough to know that the clients are not ready to share. They need to trust you first. Clients are making some very quick decisions about you:

- Can I trust this person to try to understand me?
- Can I trust this person not to hurt me?
- Can I trust this person to act in my interest?
- Does this person know what he or she is talking about?

Clients are given the opportunity to share. They should never be forced or manipulated into sharing. The best intervention for someone who is keeping a secret is to tell that person that he or she can keep the secret; that is a person's right. An individual does not have to share everything with everyone, but there is a consequence for keeping secrets. If you cut someone off from the truth, then you cut yourself off from feeling close to that person. The formula is this: The more you can share, the closer you can get, and the closer you can get, the more you can share. Intimacy (into-me-see) can occur only in an atmosphere of truth.

Some of the keys to developing a positive therapeutic alliance are a forward-leaning posture, good eye contact, a reinforcing facial expression, good listening skills, unconditional positive regard, and the skill of engaging the clients on a feeling level. It helps if you can engage the clients using your own feelings. This increases the feeling of intimacy.

Examples of Empathic Statements

"Bob, you scare me sometimes. I have to wonder how your wife and kids must feel when you raise your voice like that."

"I feel very close to you right now."

"You seem confused. What do you want from me right now?"

"That makes me feel really sad. I am sorry that happened to you."

"I can feel that you are angry. What happened?"

"Ralph, I am scared for you."

How to Be Confrontive

A good confrontation is one individual stating how another person is making him or her feel. The formula is as follows:

1. I think _____. (Describe the client's behavior: "That is the third time that you have said nothing is wrong.")

2. I feel _____. (Tell the client how the behavior makes you feel: "I feel a bit frustrated.")

3. I want _____. (Describe exactly what you want the client to do: "I want you to describe how you are feeling.")

These actions need to be described in behavioral terms. Exactly what did the person do to make you have a certain feeling?

"When I hear you deny you have been drinking, I feel frustrated. I want you to look at what has really been happening in your life. Didn't you just get your third arrest for drunk driving?"

"I feel scared when I hear you say that you want to hurt yourself. What are some of the other alternatives?"

"When I see you sit there with that blank look on your face, I feel really sad. You seem to want to cry. Can you tell me what you are thinking?"

A positive therapeutic alliance fosters mutual independence. It is an intense investment in energy. There is a lack of defensiveness and a sense of mutual positive regard. You develop similar modes of communication. You are in accord. You constantly affirm the client's worth as an individual.

A Guide to Treatments That Work is a wonderful book developed by Peter Nathan and Jack Gorman (2007). Every mental health professional should make sure that she or he has easy access to this text. Better yet, Oxford University Press, the publisher, has published a number of client workbooks and therapist guides that show the client and the therapist exactly how to treat a number of psychiatric problems. This is how you can make sure you are using evidence-based treatments that are demanded by third-party payers. The authors found that certain psychopharmacological and psychosocial therapies have consistently been shown to have better outcomes.

Behavior Therapy

In treatment, counselors concentrate on change. Clients have maladaptive feelings, thoughts, and behaviors that keep them from functioning normally. The clients are unable to reach their full potential in life because of something they are doing wrong. When there is something wrong with their actions, behavior therapy is needed. All behavior is movement. Changing how clients move will help them to function better. Clients who always lash out in physical violence when they are mad are in for a world of hurt. They must understand how to do something different when they are mad. They must learn how to practice new behaviors until this becomes automatic.

Source: Jupiterimages/Thinkstock.

How Clients Learn

To understand all types of therapy, you need to know how the brain works. The brain is like a jungle. Imagine, for a moment, that you have crash-landed an airplane in the jungle. There are thick branches and vines everywhere. All you see is thick vegetation. As you recover from the crash, you get thirsty. You hear a creek running to the right of the nose of the plane. You look for the easiest way of getting to the creek, but you only see jungle. The jungle is the same thickness in all directions. Finally, your thirst overcomes your fear, and you strike out for the creek. When you do, you make a pathway. It is not much, and it will not last long, but it is there. By passing through the jungle once, you have made a pathway of least resistance. Naturally, on the way back, you take that pathway again. It is the easiest way. As you go through repeatedly, you make more of a pathway until in time you have a nice smooth trail. Every time you go to the creek, you take the easiest way. That is exactly how the brain works, and that is how learning takes place.

Habits

Humans are creatures of habit. Habits are learned behaviors. They are easy pathways in the brain. Habits must be practiced to remain an active part of the person's behavior. Suppose that someone has a drinking problem. This is a habit. The person has this wide pathway in the brain. We could call this the drinking pathway. When this person feels uncomfortable, he or she takes a drink. The person has been doing this for years. We need to teach this person another way of relaxing. The first time the person takes the new way in the brain, it is going to be difficult. Just like the jungle, there are thick vines and branches in the way, it hurts, and all the time the person has this other way tempting him or her back to drinking. The old pathway is better established. As the counselor, you encourage the client to try something new. You support the client, you reward the client, and finally he or she tries the new way. It is not easy, but the client does it. Now you encourage the client to try it repeatedly. The client begins to build a new pathway in the brain, and as he or she does, the old pathway gradually begins to grow over. It never will grow over completely. The client may think about drinking. This will be tempting sometimes, but the more the client takes the new pathway, the more it becomes the pathway of least resistance. Soon it will be the easiest way, and the client will take the new way automatically.

You can see from this analogy that every time you go one way in the brain, it is important. Each time you go through the brain the same way, you are making a better and more long-lasting pathway.

Changing a Habit

People drink for a reason. Let us say that they drink when they feel tense. Every time people feel tense, they reach for a drink. Once people come into treatment, they decide that they cannot drink anymore, but they still have times when they feel tense. They need to learn a new way of dealing with that tension. They need to learn a new skill. They may learn that every time they feel tense, they talk about it, they exercise, or they go to an AA meeting. The more clients practice the new behavior, the more comfortable and habitual it becomes. Soon the new behavior will become second nature. Every time the clients feel tense, they use the new skill.

What Is Reinforcement?

New behavior is learned by encouraging clients to try something new and then reinforcing them for the new behavior. Reinforcement increases the frequency of a behavior. It increases the chances that the new behavior will happen again. A reinforcer does one of two things for the clients:

1. It gives the clients something positive.

2. It allows the clients to escape from something negative.

Behavior does not exist, nor does it continue to exist, without reinforcement. If you take the reward away, the behavior will vanish. It will extinguish.

What Is Punishment?

Punishment decreases the frequency of a behavior. It works in two ways:

1. It introduces something negative.

2. It removes something positive.

The best punishment for someone is to allow that person to suffer the natural consequence of his or her behavior. For example, someone who does a poor job of completing a step exercise has to do it over again. This usually is punishment enough. There are some bad things about punishment, so you need to use it sparingly. Punishment cannot teach someone a new behavior. It can only teach them to avoid an old behavior. Punishment takes the client's mind off what he or she did and puts it on to what you are doing. The client can miss the point. Treatment centers need to be set up with a clear consequence for maladaptive behavior. The rules and the consequence for breaking the rules must be clear.

The Behavior Chain

To understand people and behavior therapy, you need to understand the behavior chain. At every point along the chain, clients can change or can do something differently. Treatment is learning what to do and when to do it. These are the tools of recovery.

The first event in the chain is the *trigger*. This is the stimulus or event that triggers a response. After the trigger comes *thinking*. Here the person evaluates what the stimulus means. Much of this thinking is so fast that it is not consciously experienced. The thoughts generate *feelings*. The feelings give energy and direction for action or *behavior*. All behavior has a positive or negative *consequence*. The behavior chain looks like this:

Trigger → Thinking → Feelings → Behavior → Consequence.

Let us look at an example. Larry is addicted to cocaine. He is riding down the street and hears a particular song on the radio (trigger). He begins thinking about the "good old days" when he enjoyed using cocaine (thinking). This thinking leads him to crave cocaine (feelings). He decides to ride over to a drug dealer's house just to see how his "old friend" is doing (behavior). Larry uses cocaine (consequence).

Now let us plug in some tools of recovery. Larry is riding down the street and hears a particular song on the radio. He recognizes this song as one of his triggers. He tells himself that he no longer has the option of using cocaine (new thinking). He thinks about the misery that cocaine caused him (new thinking). He experiences some craving, so he decides to give his sponsor a call (new behavior). He goes to a meeting with his sponsor (new behavior). He does not use cocaine (new consequence).

The Importance of Reinforcement

Every time you encourage people or pay attention to them, you reinforce them. You must try to reward clients only when they act in the way that you want them to act. If possible, you must ignore, or give a negative consequence for, all maladaptive behavior. Behavior therapy is going on constantly in treatment. You need to look for positive things to reinforce. Reward your clients as often as you can. See yourself as someone who is constantly looking for behavior to reinforce.

Examples of Reinforcing Statements

"I liked what you did in group today."

"Thank you for joining in this afternoon."

"You look better after you exercise."

"You told the truth. That is great!"

"I saw you working on your assignments this afternoon. Good going."

How to Use Punishment

When maladaptive behavior is displayed, the first thing you need to do is share your feelings. Remember the formula. I feel _____ when you _____.
I would prefer it if _____. This tells the client how you are feeling, what the client is doing that is causing you to have that feeling, and what you want the client to do differently.

"Tom, I feel frightened when you raise your voice. I would prefer it if you speak more quietly."

If the maladaptive behavior continues, then warn the client of an impending consequence.

"Tom, if you do not lower your voice, I am going to leave the room."

If the behavior continues, then administer the consequence: Leave the room.

Let us go through another example. Tim, an adolescent client, begins to throw food.

"Tim, it makes me angry when you throw food. I would prefer it if you would eat normally."

Tim keeps throwing the food. He laughs with the other adolescents.

"Tim, if you do not stop throwing food, you will be restricted to your room for 1 hour."

Tim defiantly throws food again.

"Go to your room. You are restricted to your room for 1 hour."

When a Client Breaks a Rule

If a rule is broken, then a consequence is given. To let the behavior slide tells the client that rules do not count. It is a common early mistake for counselors to want to avoid giving consequences. They do not want to hurt clients' feelings, and they want to be friends. If you will examine this desire carefully, you will see how wrong it is. A good counselor does not want to teach people to do bad things. You do not want to let clients continue their maladaptive behavior. That would be helping them to stay sick.

Let us go through a few behavioral objectives. Remember that in behavior therapy you want to teach the client to do something differently.

Objective 1: The client will go to five treatment peers and share the feelings exercise with them. (This exercise comes with a built-in reward because sharing feelings brings people closer together. As the client shares his or her feelings, the client draws closer to others. This is a powerful reinforcement.)

Objective 2: The client will list 10 times when he lost his temper with his children. He will discuss each situation with his counselor. He will verbalize other means of dealing with his anger (by 9-20-2010). (In this objective, the client also feels closer as he or she shares the truth. You also would want to reinforce the client for being honest and ask the client how he or she feels after the disclosure.)

Objective 3: The client will keep a feelings log for the next 5 days (completed by 9-15-2010). (In a feelings log, the client charts his or her feelings. This allows the client to keep up on his or her improvement. This is a powerful reinforcement.)

Objective 4: The client will give a 20-minute speech to the group on his or her powerlessness and unmanageability (by 9-25-2010). (Giving the group a talk is a positive new behavior. If the client is going to teach something to others, then the client must first learn it himself or herself.)

Objective 5: The client will meet with his or her counselor and spouse in five conjoint sessions before the end of treatment. (During each session, you would want to reinforce each person for building better communication skills. When someone compromises, reinforce him or her.)

Objective 6: The client will ask two treatment peers a day for help with his or her program. The client will record each situation and share weekly with his or her counselor. (A client who is reluctant to ask for help needs practice in doing so. The illness tells the client that he or she is not worth helping and that other people do not want to help the client. Nothing works better to dispel these inaccurate beliefs than to actually have people help the client.)

Objective 7: The client will give three treatment peers a compliment each day. The client will keep a log of each situation and discuss with his or her counselor (by 9-25-2010). (By having a client say reinforcing things to others, you set up a natural reinforcing situation. You need to talk with the client about how the other people responded.)

Objective 8: The client will keep an anger log and share weekly with his or her counselor (by 9-30-2010). (Keeping an anger log will make the client more aware of his or her anger. If the client is more aware, then he or she can catch the anger earlier and use a specific skill to deal with the feeling. For example, every time the client gets angry, he or she could back away from the situation until the client can get accurate in his or her thinking. Then the client can do something different such as talking about his or her anger.)

Why We Concentrate on Behavior Therapy

The reason why behavior therapy is so good is that you can see it happen. The new behavior either occurs or does not occur. The more you reinforce a new behavior, the quicker it develops into a habit. It is important to reinforce the behavior as quickly as you can after it occurs. Practice is important. The more a client practices a behavior, the more of a habit it will become. You can role-play certain situations to solidify and practice the new skills. We ask for progress, not perfection. Most old behaviors fall away slowly. It will be months before the triggers stop creating old responses.

Do not drink or use drugs, read the "Big Book" (AA, 1976), go to meetings, seek a Higher Power, call your sponsor, share how you feel, ask for what you want, and tell the truth—all of these are essential parts of the program. They all are placed in behavioral terms. They can be changed and counted as they change. If you monitor behavior, then you will know exactly how your clients are doing in treatment.

Cognitive Therapy

Source: ©iStockphoto.com/track5.

Another essential element in addiction treatment is how people think. Thoughts precede feelings, and feelings initiate action. Clients have to think about drinking before they drink. People think in words or in images. If I were to ask you to close your eyes and think about the word *wagon*, you could do that. If I were to ask you to close your eyes and see a wagon, you could close your eyes and see some sort of an image of a wagon. That is thinking in imagery.

How Chemically Dependent People Think

Because of the disease, clients do not think accurately. They have separated themselves from reality. They are distorting the truth to protect themselves. Most clients come into treatment in some form of denial:

"I do not think I have a drinking problem."

"I never had any problems with marijuana."

"Everybody I know drinks as much as I do."

"My husband is overly sensitive. His dad was a heavy drinker."

"Anybody can get arrested for drunk driving."

"I may have an alcohol problem, but I am not an alcoholic."

The client who said these things had a severe drug problem. All of these thoughts were inaccurate. She was addicted to alcohol and cannabis. She was drinking and using cannabis all day, every day.

The psychology of addiction demands repressing the truth from consciousness. Repression is a mental process where we keep the facts hidden from ourselves. This information is kept secret to protect us from the painful reality of our situation. If drug addicts will see the whole truth, then they will see their addictions. The addicts will see that they are dying from addiction. This truth creates tremendous fear. The addicted individuals protect themselves from experiencing this fear by not seeing reality. An addict might have gotten an eighth DWI but still does not think that he or she has a problem. The addict might see only half-truths. The addict might see that the police are out to get him or her or that the addict's spouse is overreacting. The addict does not see the whole truth or the seriousness of the addiction.

Defense Mechanisms

The illness of addiction cannot operate without lies. Addicts must lie to themselves until they believe the lies or else the illness cannot continue. All of the lies are inaccurate ways of thinking. Cognitive therapy corrects the thoughts and gets the clients accurate. Cognitive therapy is a fearless search for truth.

Minimization distorts reality and makes it smaller than it actually is. When minimizing, the addict says, "It is not so bad." When an alcoholic pours whiskey, he or she does not use a shot glass; the alcoholic pours. If we take that poured drink and measure how many shots are in it, we might find four or five shots in the glass. To the alcoholic, this is *one* drink. However, it is not one drink; it is five drinks. "I am only having three," the alcoholic says innocently to himself or herself. "What is the problem?"

Rationalization is a good excuse for drinking or using drugs. Probably the most common excuse is as follows: "I had a hard day." Therefore, for the addict, "Anyone who has had a hard day needs to relax. Therefore, I need a few."

Clients can rationalize almost anything. Rationalization is blaming.

"The police were out to get me."

"My wife does not understand me. That is why I drink."

"I have been having financial problems."

"I cannot sleep if I do not drink."

"My boss really gets on my nerves. I need a drink."

The essential element here is that these clients are fooling themselves. They really believe that their behavior is not their fault. Something else is to blame. In treatment, these clients need to accept the responsibility for their own behavior. Being an adult means making all of your own decisions and living with the consequences.

Denial is the most common defense in addiction. It is primitive and distorts reality more than does any other defense mechanism. In denial, clients refuse to experience the full impact of reality. Suppose that you are walking downtown on a hot summer day. Along the sidewalk, people are standing holding buckets of ice water. As you walk past, they throw the ice water in your face. You see the water and you see the people, but you do not experience the full shock of the water. Denial is a dissociated, unreal world. A drug addict might be losing his or her spouse, children, job, friends, money, and freedom, but the addict does not experience the full impact of this reality. The addict does not see why everyone is worried.

All clients who come into treatment are in some form of denial. They are not seeing what is right in front of their faces. It is incredible how strong denial can be. Clients can be at death's door and still believe that they are fine.

Applying Cognitive Therapy

Cognitive therapy is correcting the lies that clients have been telling themselves. It is the process of getting the thinking accurate. As the counselor, you help the clients to see the truth. First, the clients need to see the lies in operation. Have a client do the following exercise in your office or in group.

Place a chair in the center of the room, and explain to the client that he or she has an internal dialogue going on all of the time. The dialogue is between the illness and the healthy side of the client. The illness wants to use alcohol or drugs. The healthy side wants to be healthy and happy. Have the client sit in one chair and role play the illness. Have the illness side talk the healthy side into drinking or using drugs. It will be helpful if you model the exercise first. The dialogue will go something like this:

"John, you have had a pretty hard day. Nobody is going to know if you have just a couple of beers. Your wife is not going to find out. Why don't you stop by the bar for just a couple? It would taste good. You can handle a couple of beers. You can stop whenever you want to. Remember all the good times we had drinking. Remember the women. You can talk to them better if you have had a couple of beers. You do not have to call your wife. She will not know. You can hide it. It will not matter."

As the client talks, you can see all of the lies he is telling himself:

1. "I have had a hard day."

2. "Nobody is going to know."

3. "Just a couple."

4. "You can handle it."

5. "You can stop."

6. "Remember all the good times."

7. "Remember the women. They liked you better when you were drunk."

8. "You can talk to women better when you have had a couple of beers."

9. "You do not have to call your wife."

10. "She will not know."

11. "You can hide it."

12. "It will not matter."

Now you challenge each of the client's inaccurate statements.

"Do you think that having a hard day is worth risking your life?"

"When is the last time you went in a bar and just had a couple of beers?"

"Haven't you proven to yourself that you cannot stop? If you could stop, what are you doing in here?"

"How are you going to feel if you start hiding from your wife again?"

Repeatedly, challenge your clients' inaccurate thoughts. In treatment and in recovery, the clients must be committed to reality. They have to live in reality and solve problems using the whole truth.

Clients are inaccurate not only about their drugs but also about their self-images. They might call themselves stupid, inadequate, or ugly. They might have an exaggerated sense of their own importance. The best way of correcting these inaccurate thoughts is in group, but individual therapy also is valuable. Someone who thinks that he or she is worthless, helpless, or hopeless needs to see what is real. Many clients will argue with you about these things. The inaccurate thoughts seem to have a life of their own.

Client: I cannot live without Bob. I cannot.

Counselor: You cannot? What would happen to you if you were shipwrecked on an island in the South Pacific? There was no one on this island but you. You have plenty of food and water, but you are all alone.

Client:	Oh, I would be okay.
Counselor:	But Bob would not be there. Wouldn't you die?
Client:	That is different. That is a different situation.
Counselor:	No, it is not. You just said you *could not* live without Bob. Now you tell me you could live without anyone.
Client:	Well, I do not *want* to live without him.
Counselor:	That is better, but that is not quite accurate either. Would you kill yourself if you did not have Bob in your life? Is it impossible to live without Bob?
Client:	No, it is possible to live without Bob, but I love Bob. I want Bob in my life.
Counselor:	Good, that is accurate. You want Bob in your life. You do not need him in your life for survival. Seeing the relationship more accurately will give you feelings that are more accurate. If you need Bob for your survival and Bob leaves you, then you will die. That is scary. It is too scary, and it is not accurate.

Automatic Thoughts

Thinking occurs extremely quickly. There is a never-ending stream of conscious and unconscious thought flowing though a person's mind. Most of this thought is not registered on the screen of consciousness. The more a behavior or thought process is practiced, the more unconscious and automatic it becomes. You do not have to think consciously of each of the hundreds of little decisions you make while driving a car. You make most of these decisions unconsciously out of habit—how to turn the wheel, when to put on the brake, when to speed up a little bit. These decisions are made without conscious thought.

Beck, Rush, Shaw, and Emery (1979) found out that many people who were depressed were having certain thoughts that were leading them to feel depressed. It was the private ways in which these individuals were interpreting events that were critical to their uncomfortable feelings. They were thinking inaccurate things that were involuntary, persistent, and plausible and that often contained a theme of loss. This thinking was keeping them down. Most of these thoughts occurred automatically, totally out of the clients' awareness. The important thing to note here is that these thoughts profoundly affect feelings and behavior.

Beck (1967, 1972, 1976) reported that three elements were essential to the psychopathology of depression: (1) the *cognitive triad*, (2) *silent assumptions*, and (3) *logical errors*.

The cognitive triad consists of the negative views of clients about themselves, their world, and their future. In general, depressives view themselves, their world, and their future as lacking something that is a prerequisite for happiness. For example, they may view themselves as inadequate, incompetent, and unworthy. They may view their environment as demanding and unsupportive. They may view the future as hopeless, frightening, and full of inevitable pain.

Silent assumptions are unarticulated rules that influence depressives' feelings, thinking, and behavior. For example, a client may believe one or more of the following:

"I will only be happy if I am good looking, intelligent, or wealthy."

"When I make a mistake, people think less of me."

"It is weak to ask for help."

"I have to please everyone all of the time."

These stable beliefs develop from early experience and influence the individual's responses to events. They give rise to automatic thoughts.

Logical errors are the inaccurate conclusions that clients draw from negative thinking. They can over generalize, drawing conclusions about their ability, performance, and worth from one incident:

"He does not love me, so I am unlovable."

Logical errors can magnify or minimize by exaggerating or diminishing the importance of an event:

"The class laughed. Everyone thinks I am a fool."

"I got all As this quarter, but 2 years ago I got a C."

"I cannot do college work like other people."

How to Correct Inaccurate Thoughts

Let us go through an example of how to correct automatic thoughts. The first time that clients hear about interpersonal group, they usually feel frightened. The clients might not stop and think, Why are we afraid? They just feel scared. Feeling like this, the clients might try to do something to prevent themselves from going to group. They might fake that they are sick or tired.

Uncover the Thoughts and Feelings

Using cognitive therapy, you first would ask clients how they were feeling. Write each feeling down. Then ask the following: "What were you thinking between the time that you heard about interpersonal group and the feeling you felt? What thoughts came to mind?" The clients might be able to respond here, or you might have to suggest some thoughts. In cognitive therapy, you will have to suggest to the clients thoughts that they might have been having. Do not stop until you have brought out a short list of thoughts such as the following:

"The people in group will not understand me."

"I would make a fool of myself."

"This is going to be humiliating."

"They are going to put me on the hot seat."

"They are going to make me talk."

Pull on clients' automatic thoughts. Ask and then make suggestions. Remember, these are thoughts that the clients do not try to have. They are unconscious and happen automatically. Once you see the powerful negative message that these thoughts give the clients, you will understand why they feel afraid.

Score the Inaccurate Feelings

It will help to have clients score each feeling on a scale of 1 (*as little as possible*) to 100 (*as much as possible*). Let us say that a client felt fear at 90. Ask whether the client was feeling any other feelings as well, and ask the client to score each of these. Our client also was feeling angry with a score of 50. The client was angry because the group was going to try to "make me talk." The client also was feeling sad at a score of 70 because "this is going to be humiliating. I am going to make a fool out of myself. These people will not understand me." If we add up all of the negative feelings, the client was feeling 210 units of distress.

Getting the Thoughts Accurate

Now we help the client to challenge his or her automatic thinking. We know that many of these thoughts are inaccurate.

Counselor:	Your thought was that these people will not understand me. What do you think is accurate?
Client:	Well, they have the same problem as I do. They should be able to understand me. At least they will try to.
Counselor:	How about, I am going to make a fool out of myself.
Client:	I do not really think I am going to make a fool out of myself. It could be a little embarrassing.
Counselor:	Yeah, you could do something a little embarrassing. What do you think would happen if you did?
Client:	I do not know.
Counselor:	Do you think the other clients might understand and be sympathetic?
Client:	I think they would try to understand.
Counselor:	So, even if you did do something a little embarrassing, it would not be the end of the world.
Client:	No.
Counselor:	Now what about, "This is going to be humiliating." Do you think the group is going to humiliate you?
Client:	No, I do not. I have met a few of the clients already, and they seem very nice. I do feel humiliated, though, just being here . . . you know, in treatment.
Counselor:	Do you think the other group members could relate to that?
Client:	Sure.
Counselor:	How about, they're going to put me on the hot seat.
Client:	Well, they might. I have heard about the groups where they hound you and attack you until you spill your guts.
Counselor:	Let me assure you that the staff here does not work like that. We do not have a hot seat. We give people the opportunity to talk. If they do not want to talk, that is fine. What if it was one of those heavy confrontational groups? Could they make you talk if you did not want to?
Client:	Probably not.
Counselor:	So what is accurate here?
Client:	I can talk if I want to. I really want to talk. I want to get better.
Counselor:	Good. Let us go back and score your feelings again using accurate thoughts. You hear that there is an interpersonal group at 10 o'clock. You think, These people are nice. They have the same illness as I do. They should be able to understand me. I want to talk and get better.

Scoring the Accurate Feelings

Counselor:	Now, thinking accurately, how much fear do you feel?
Client:	About 35, I guess.
Counselor:	How much anger?
Client:	None.
Counselor:	How much sadness?
Client:	40.

Compare Inaccurate and Accurate Thoughts and Feelings

Counselor: When you were thinking automatically, you were feeling 210 units of distress, but when you get accurate, your pain dropped to 75. That is a drop of 135 points.

Client: Amazing.

Counselor: Yes, and these thoughts go on all the time. You automatically think the worst, so you feel bad. There is some real reason to feel uncomfortable—bad things could really happen—but if you get accurate, you can live in reality. You can feel the real world. You have been living and feeling in a world created by your distorted thoughts.

Uncovering the Generalizations

As clients keep track of their negative thoughts, you will see that their thinking ends up with certain generalizations or themes. These stable attitudes or beliefs develop over time. They usually can be traced to early childhood experiences. These beliefs are very tenacious. A client who believes that "I do not get along with people" might base that belief on something that happened to him or her as a small child. The inaccurate thinking keeps the person from seeing reality. Themes are based on evidence that clients have collected over a number of years. The clients act on these beliefs as if they were absolute facts. The clients no longer challenge them. The automatic thoughts are used as evidence from which these inaccurate conclusions are drawn. You must help the clients to uncover these distorted attitudes and beliefs. They are not accurate, and they need to be corrected.

Clients might believe that they are unlovable. The clients are convinced inside of their own thinking that this is a fact—"I am unlovable." These clients will begin to build evidence from their experience that will support this belief. The clients will begin to tell themselves things such as they are unlovable for various reasons—"I am ugly," "I am stupid," or "I am bad." None of these things is true, but the clients believe that all are true. Naturally, this leads to uncomfortable feelings. Clients who think that they are unlovable feel depressed and lonely.

In cognitive therapy, your job is to get clients thinking accurate. Most of the clients' thinking is automatic, and you will have to train the clients to keep track of their thoughts. David Burns's (1999) *The Feeling Good Handbook the New Mood Therapy* is an excellent overview of the various forms of cognitive therapy (Burns, 1999). Reading this is a good way of beginning to think in cognitive terms. In time, you will pick up clients' inaccurate thinking quickly. You rarely will want inaccurate thinking to pass by unnoticed. Stop clients at every opportunity and correct them.

Client: I have messed up my whole life.

Counselor: Your whole life?

Client: Yeah.

Counselor: Is any part of your life still intact?

Client: No. I have screwed up everything.

Counselor: You still have your job.

Client: Well, yeah.

Counselor: You still have your wife and kids.

Client: Yeah, they're still with me.

Counselor: And your boss is supporting your treatment.

Client: Yeah.

Counselor:	So, let us get accurate. You have not messed up everything. You just feel like you have.
Client:	(*Laughs.*) Now that I think about it, I have a few things left. I still have my job, my wife, my kids, and my house.
Counselor:	You have many things. You have not messed everything up. Why don't we make a list of the things you still have? Carry this list around with you, and when you think you made a mistake, take out the list and read it to yourself.

This is cognitive therapy at its best. The client corrects inaccurate thinking, develops accurate thoughts, and then practices accurate thinking.

Solidifying Accurate Thinking

It is helpful to have clients carry around note cards with accurate thoughts written on them. When they feel bad, they take out the cards and read them to themselves. Sometimes they need to look at themselves in the mirror and read the cards to themselves. Clients will not catch the inaccurate thinking at the thinking stage. Thinking happens too quickly. They will have to catch the inaccurate thoughts at the uncomfortable feeling stage and then backtrack to find out what the thoughts were. Have clients keep a feelings log in which they jot down every time they have an uncomfortable feeling and the situation that caused the feeling. Then have them score each feeling on the scale of 1 to 100. Once they have a few days of a log, call them in and begin to filter out what thoughts were occurring during the situation.

John came in with his feelings log. On Thursday at lunch, he felt hurt and angry when a treatment peer made the following comment about his sweater: "Where did you steal that old sweater?" John felt angry with 70 and hurt at 80. He felt 150 units of emotional distress.

Example of a Cognitive Therapy Session

Counselor:	What were you thinking when he said that?
Client:	He does not like me.
Counselor:	What else?
Client:	That is about it.
Counselor:	Were you thinking that people do not like you very much?
Client:	Yeah, I was.
Counselor:	Were you thinking that nobody likes you?
Client:	Exactly.
Counselor:	Nobody has ever liked you?
Client:	(*Nods his head.*)
Counselor:	How about nobody will ever like you?
Client:	Well, I know that.
Counselor:	Bob says to you, "Where did you steal that old sweater?" You think that he does not like you, nobody likes you, and nobody will ever like you.
Client:	Yes.
Counselor:	Now, what is accurate? Bob says, "Where did you steal that old sweater?" What do you think is an accurate way of thinking about that situation?

Client: Bob was just having fun and making a joke.

Counselor: So, to get you to like him, Bob tells a joke.

Client: I think so.

Counselor: Why does Bob tell you a joke?

Client: Because he wants me to like him.

Counselor: Right, Bob likes you and wants you to like him, so he tells you a joke. He ribs you about your sweater. Your automatic thinking takes over and says that he hates you, everyone hates you, and everyone will always hate you. Thinking these thoughts, you feel hurt and angry. Now thinking accurately, how do you feel?

Client: I feel good. Bob likes me.

Counselor: Right.

Interpersonal Therapy

Addiction wounds relationships. Interpersonal therapy heals relationships and restores an atmosphere of love and trust. In recovery, clients are encouraged to love God, to love others, and to love themselves. If one of these relationships is not healed, then the clients will continue to feel uncomfortable and will be vulnerable to relapse.

How to Develop Healthy Relationships

In the AA/Narcotics Anonymous (NA) program, when we are talking about relationships, we are first talking about spirituality. Spirituality is defined as the innermost relationship we have with ourselves and all else. The first thing that clients must do in developing a healthy relationship is to surrender. Step One demands an admission of powerlessness and unmanageability. Without surrender, the clients will continue to try to control themselves and other people. This leads to disaster as the "self will run riot" (AA, 2001, p. 62).

The next step is to believe that a power greater than ourselves can restore us to sanity. This relationship with a Higher Power is an essential part of the AA/NA program. Clients must seek the God of their own understanding and establish a relationship with that Higher Power.

Relationships with a Higher Power, self, and others are based on love, trust, and commitment. Love is not a feeling. It is an action. Trust necessitates truth, and commitment takes consistency of action. Action without truth is not enough. Truth without action is not enough.

Building a Relationship With a Higher Power

In building a relationship with a Higher Power, clients must be willing to accept that some sort of a Higher Power is possible. The best way of showing this is to ask the clients this question: "Do you think that there is a power greater than yourself?" For most clients, this is enough. However, for some, you have to demonstrate by asking the following: "If you wanted to leave this room and the group was determined to keep you in, could you leave?" The answer here is obvious to even the most stubborn. The group has greater power.

Now, can clients *begin* to turn their wills and lives over to this new power? This will start with the group. Can the group be trusted? Does the group make good decisions? If the clients can begin to deal with doubt and faith in a group, then they have come a long way toward developing trust in a Higher Power. The clients must see the group members love each other. The clients must see the group be committed to the truth even when it hurts.

Much later in the program, clients are encouraged to begin thinking about a Higher Power. Willingness again is the key. If the clients will seek a Higher Power through prayer and meditation, then they will begin to make progress in this area. Some clients will want to do some reading about spirituality, and all of them need to talk with a clergy person who is familiar with the 12 steps.

Developing a Relationship With Self

The relationship with self begins to heal when clients begin to treat themselves well. They stop hurting themselves with drugs and alcohol. They stop saying bad things to themselves. They begin eating three meals a day. They sleep properly. They begin to get regular exercise. All of these simple skills have a profound effect on the clients' feeling of self-worth. People of great worth are worth treating well.

Building Relationships With Others

Interpersonal relationships heal when a client uses good interpersonal relationship skills.

1. The client must share how he or she feels.

2. The client must ask for what he or she wants.

3. The client must be honest.

4. The client must be actively involved in the other person's individual growth.

If one of these skills is missing, then the relationship will be unstable. It will feel unstable, and the individuals involved will feel frightened. Each of these skills is developed and practiced.

Clients must practice identifying and sharing their feelings. This takes education, individual therapy, and group work. There are only a few primary emotions. Plutchik (1980) theorized that there are eight:

1. Joy

2. Acceptance

3. Anticipation

4. Anger

5. Fear

6. Surprise

7. Disgust

8. Sadness

Other emotions are various combinations of the basic eight. For example, jealousy is feeling sad, angry, and fearful all at the same time. All feelings give energy and direction for movement. Feelings motivate behavior directly related to survival. For example, fear activates escape behavior. Escape protects the organism from a dangerous situation. Surprise activates orienting behavior. Sadness gives the organism the energy and direction to recover the lost object.

In therapy, you must educate clients about their feelings. For example, in many homes, anger is an unacceptable emotion. A child learns that anger is dangerous, so the child learns to repress anger. The child does not feel it. The child may feel fear every time that he or she feels angry. A client needs to use all of his or her feelings to function normally. A person who cannot feel anger cannot express anger. A person who cannot express anger is handicapped. This person cannot adequately protect himself or herself. Anger is necessary to establish and maintain boundaries around ourselves. If a person cannot do this, then people will violate the person's boundaries and he or she will be victimized.

Have your clients list situations in which they felt each feeling and then discuss how the clients could have responded properly. You will find that cultural differences abound. For example, in the United States, women are not supposed to act angry, so when they feel angry, they cry. Men are not supposed to cry, so when they feel sad, they act angry.

As a counselor, you are teaching clients to use feelings in problem solving. When a client has a feeling, he or she should listen to this feeling. What is the feeling telling the person to do? The client should then consider options of action.

Client: I got so mad.

Counselor: What did you do?

Client: I just stood there. I did not know what to do.

Counselor: What were your options?

Client: I could have hit him.

Counselor: What else could you have done?

Client: I could have walked away.

Counselor: What else?

Client: I was so mad that I did not know what to do.

Counselor: Could you have told him you were mad?

Client: Oh, yeah, but he would not have cared.

Counselor: You could have told him you were mad and what he did that made you mad.

Client: What good would that have done?

Counselor: We have to hold people accountable for what they do. Anger gives us the energy and direction to fight for our rights. One of the best ways to use your anger is to tell people you are angry. That holds them accountable.

How Clients Use Feelings Inappropriately

Many clients use their feelings inappropriately. They make the wrong movements when they have feelings. People who are fearful tend to avoid fear-producing situations. They shy away from everything. People who are angry can constantly be fighting. They fight everybody about everything. These clients need to learn how to use their feelings appropriately. Their feelings can get to be the problem. Some of these clients need behavior therapy. They need to learn how to act appropriately when they feel certain feelings. A client who was abused and terrified by his father might respond to all people with fear. This client needs to identify and understand how the relationship with his father influenced how he responds to everyone. He needs to understand that most people are going to treat him well.

How Clients Learn Relationship Skills

People learn what to expect from the world by the experiences they have had. It is from these experiences that we draw maps about what the world is like. We learn what to do in certain situations. Childhood experiences are very powerful. They condition us and give us attitudes about what the world is like. The most important relationship for us was with our primary caregiver. This person usually was the mother, but it could have been someone else. If this person was healthy and loved us, then we felt safe and important. We grew up feeling that the world was a safe place. If our primary caregiver was not healthy, then we learned other things. We might have learned that the world was an abusive place or a sad place. The first relationship was very important. As the counselor, you must help clients to develop accurate maps of the world.

How to Change Relationships

In therapy, you will see clients' relationship maps in how they relate to you. The clients will react to you as if they reacted to significant others in the past. This is transference. When you react to the clients using your old maps, it is countertransference. As the clients respond to you, watch for the inaccurate ways in which they interpret what you do. If the clients act frightened of you when there is nothing to be frightened about, then you can be sure that you are dealing with a transference issue. As you treat the clients with encouragement and love, they will have the opportunity to redraw their maps. Maybe the world is a safe place after all. In the relationship with you, the clients will see how healthy persons relate to each other. They will observe and be able to model after you. You will teach the clients how to communicate and how to relate to other people with love and trust.

Clients may have a relationship problem that they will need to address with some other person. In the family program, you will have the opportunity to work with the family. Here you can teach all of the family members healthy communication skills. You can teach them how to listen to each other and how to develop empathy for each other. Have them repeat each other's thoughts and feelings. This makes sure that each person understands what the others are saying. Teach them how to use "I feel" statements. Teach them how to reinforce each other. Teach them how to inquire for more information until they understand. Burns's (1999) *The Feeling Good Handbook* has some communication exercises that can be helpful if you are interested in pursuing this therapy further.

How to Handle Grief

Grief issues can need attention in interpersonal therapy. When clients have lost significant others, they will have to work through the grief. The clients will have to experience pain and say good-bye to the lost loved ones. Having the clients talk about the good and bad times that they had with the lost loved ones is important. Have the clients write good-bye letters to the loved ones. Have them read the letters to you or to their interpersonal group. The clients need to gain the support of other people. The Higher Power concept can be greatly beneficial here. God knows everything, and everything fits into God's plan. "Nothing, absolutely nothing happens in God's world by mistake" (AA, 1976, p. 449). The clients can be encouraged to trust in a Higher Power's judgment. Work and grief work go together. We turn our will and our lives over to the care of God as we understand God. Grief work is a good time to build a closer relationship with the Higher Power.

How to Choose the Therapeutic Modality

Individual therapy helps to prepare clients for group work. The clients will transfer what they learn from you in individual therapy to the group as a whole. From the group, the clients will transfer what they have learned to people in society. Individual therapy gives you an opportunity to discuss some things with your clients that are not appropriate for the group. There is no need for a client to share every intimate detail in group. Some things are best left for individual therapy. Sexual abuse and other sensitive issues can generate a great deal of shame, and the group might not understand. If a client decides to share something with you but does not want to share this issue with the group, then the client is given this opportunity, but remember that everything of importance must be discussed with the clinical staff. The client does not have to talk to the staff, but you do. You need the help of your colleagues, particularly in sensitive situations.

Individual therapy gives clients the opportunity to have a healthy interpersonal relationship with another person. This is very healing. The clients finally will tell someone the whole truth and see that person's reaction. As you continue to care for the clients, even when they tell you the worst, it teaches the clients something that they never have known: They are persons of worth. Nothing battles the disease better than this fact.

7 Group Therapy

Source: ©iStockphoto.com/clearstockconcepts.

The most powerful motivation for change in most addiction programs is the group. The group is a microcosm of the world in which the client lives. In group, there are people who clients identify with their mothers, fathers, brothers, sisters, friends, and enemies. Therefore, they can work through many issues by interacting with group members. The whole group is seen as the client's dysfunctional family, and the client can learn how to resolve family conflicts by working with the group. Clients can grow from a group in ways that they cannot grow in individual therapy. The group serves as a healthy family from which clients can develop normal social interaction. From the treatment center group, clients transfer relationships to their 12-step group that is by no accident called a home group. Addiction requires long-term treatment, and this is how it occurs. Other groups such as rational recovery or other treatment groups work just as well as 12-step groups, but some of them are expensive. Long-term treatment is necessary for the underlying character defects that fuel addiction. In 12-step groups, the treatment is good, it is supportive, and it is free. The group has special characteristics that make it uniquely effective in helping clients to overcome their problems.

Benefits of the Group Process

1. *Healthier members instill hope.* There are clients in the group who are further along in treatment. These clients look better and act better. They use effective communication skills. They do not deny their

disease. They confront other clients gently and with the truth. They encourage each other. They are not afraid to share. This has great impact on clients coming into treatment. They see that people get better as they stay in treatment longer.

2. *Clients can model healthy communication skills.* They see members sharing their feelings and asking for what they want. Group members are not shamed for having feelings or thoughts. The world does not end if someone gets angry or cries. Clients watch as problems and feelings are worked through until they are resolved.

3. *Clients become aware that they are not alone in their pain.* They hear the stories of the other clients, and the stories are very similar. The group members can laugh together about the mutual pain. No one else but fellow alcoholics would understand riding around the block waiting for the liquor store to open or hiding the bottle so well that even the alcoholic could not find it. It is comforting for clients to hear someone else discuss problems that they have experienced themselves. Clients often feel like they did the worse thing possible, and they find to their amazement that everyone in the group did the same thing. The clients begin to feel as though they are not bad, but the disease is bad.

4. *Information is exchanged.* Clients share their experiences, strengths, and hopes. In these stories are examples of how to handle difficult situations. Group members learn from each other's experiences. If members never have relapsed, then it is informative to hear about someone who has had that experience.

5. *A feeling of family develops.* The group members feel close. They accept each other and try to love each other. Interpersonal trust and intimacy develops. Clients carefully keep each other's confidentiality and learn how to watch out for each other.

6. *Clients learn that they can be accepted for who and what they are.* Even when clients are at their worst, the other group members still accept them. They are supportive and encouraging. This comes into direct conflict with what clients always have believed—that if they told the truth, they would be rejected.

7. *Clients learn the power of the truth.* Using real feelings, in real situations, and with real people, clients learn to solve real problems. People do not go away from the group sulking or worse off than when they came in. They go away feeling loved and supported. It is your responsibility to make sure that every group ends in a positive light.

8. *Clients can express their feelings freely.* They can express their pain in a supportive atmosphere. They can ventilate feelings and still feel accepted. They can practice sharing feelings to see whether they are appropriate to the situation. People who never have acted angry can act angry and see the positive effect of their anger.

9. *By listening to each other and sharing together, clients feel a new sense of self-worth.* They begin to feel worthy of the group's time and energy. The group members show each other that they all are worthwhile individuals.

10. *Clients learn what works and what does not work in interpersonal relationships.* They see what brings people together. They come to understand that the more they share, the closer they can get, and that the closer they can get, the more they can share.

Preparation for the Group

Before each group, have someone read the Preparation Statement about the group process. This sets the stage for group and prepares the members for the work ahead. It sets a few simple rules about how the group functions.

The Preparation Statement

Interpersonal group is an experience designed to help us learn more about how we feel, think, and act. Addiction blinds us to the truth about ourselves. It keeps us from experiencing reality. We develop defenses that keep us from seeing ourselves as we really are. We present to the world a false front that we ourselves believe to be true. If we are ever going to accept ourselves and begin the process of recovery, then we must know whom we are. We can do this only by learning how other people see us. The group members will act as mirrors, showing to us those parts of ourselves that we do not see. They will reflect our feelings, thoughts, and behaviors.

The spirit of this group is love. We share, care, and help each other to grow as individuals. With all of our heart, we encourage you to share your experience, strength, and hope. Be open to listen and talk. Our experience has shown that only those who participate fully recover.

A main focus of the group is feelings. Many of us never have dealt honestly with our feelings before. We know that doing this is frightening and painful, but it is necessary. You must be willing to be yourself. It is a tremendously rewarding experience to be accepted for who you really are.

The group has only two rules. First, there will be no physical violence. We need to feel free to express ourselves without the fear of physical harm. The second rule is confidentiality. What you see here, what you hear here—let it stay here. We will now begin the session by introducing ourselves and stating why we are in treatment.

The reader of the preparation statement gives his or her first name and the reason why he or she is in treatment. For example, "I am Shirley, and I am an alcoholic." If someone in the group does not want to call himself or herself an addict, that is fine, but that person does have to give a reason why he or she is in treatment. For example, "I am Frank, and I got a DWI."

The Agenda Group

As the counselor, you then have each group member choose an agenda and someone in the group to share it with. The agenda is a current matter of concern for the client. It has to be a real problem that generates real emotion. Some clients will try to choose something easy, but do not let them. If they will not, or cannot, choose something important, then choose something for them. You write down all of the agenda items on the blackboard or a large pad for everyone to see.

Client	Agenda	Share With
1. Bob	Feeling confused	Frank
2. Frank	Scared about family program	Shirley
3. Shirley	Mad at a treatment peer	Tom
4. Tom	Disgusted with self	Jose
5. Jose	Fear about going to jail	Nancy
6. Nancy	Sad about loss of marriage	Francis
7. Francis	Angry at staff	Bob

How to Choose the Order of the Agenda

Once the agendas are up on the board, you choose an agenda that seems to be the most therapeutic. Choose something that will generate emotion and will teach the clients about addiction. The best agendas usually are those that deal with problems the group members are currently having with each other. It is always best to deal with the here and now rather than with the there and then.

The group members will start with the agenda item that you choose and will move as far through the list as they can. As the counselor, you choose the next agenda each time. You will have a good idea—which agendas need to be dealt with during a particular day. A client starts by telling a problem to the person with whom he or she has chosen to share the problem. For example, Shirley talks to Tom about being mad at her treatment peer. Tom answers first, and then anyone in the group can add what he or she feels is important. You watch for and reinforce appropriate feedback. Most new counselors talk too much. Let the group do most of the talking and only speak if someone is not being understood or is being hurt. Then you clarify the issue and redirect the group toward understanding, encouraging, and supporting each other.

How to Give Good Feedback

A person giving good feedback will do the following:

1. Talk about the specific behavior.

2. Give feedback in a caring manner.

3. Give the other person a chance to explain.

4. Avoid being judgmental.

5. Use "I feel" statements.

6. Share the positive as well.

7. Avoid giving advice.

How to Receive Feedback

To receive feedback appropriately, a client must do the following:

1. Ask for it.

2. Receive it openly.

3. Acknowledge its value.

4. Be willing to discuss it.

5. Make no excuses.

6. Indicate what he or she intends to do with it.

7. Listen to everyone.

How to Run a Group

As the counselor, you should not talk much in group. Intervene only when necessary to keep the group moving along therapeutically. So long as the truth is coming out and people are being accepted, the group is doing well. It is a common early mistake for counselors to talk too much. This discourages the other members from sharing. It is also common for the clients to get into the habit of talking only to the counselor.

When this happens, draw other people into the discussion. "John, how do you feel about that?" is enough to take the focus off of you and onto other group members. Let the silent periods raise the group's anxiety. Someone will talk if you wait. If you always talk, then no one else will.

For the most part, the clients who are doing the most sharing are getting the most out of group. You must encourage quieter members to share. A simple question, such as "Tom, how do you feel about that?" often is enough to get someone started.

If someone is becoming a problem in the group, then let the group handle it. Do not try to handle everything yourself. Asking a question such as "How do the rest of you feel about Bob right now?" is enough to let the group work for you. Sometimes people try to monopolize the group, and they need to spend more time listening. Look at Jane, who is talking too much and playing counselor for everyone, and gently say, "Listen."

You need to make sure that no one is harmed in the group process. If things are getting too hot and angry, then focus on the client's pain. Hurt comes before anger, and it defuses anger to talk about the pain. If someone is getting hurt, then you must step in and give the group direction. Statements such as "How would you want to be treated right now?" go a long way toward giving the group solid direction.

How to Know Which Therapy to Use

Behavior, cognitive, interpersonal therapy, and skills training can all be effective in a group setting. Your skill is to use the best therapy for the particular problem. If a client is behaving in a way that is maladaptive, then behavior therapy comes into play. If the client is thinking inaccurately, then cognitive therapy is necessary. If the problem is in a relationship, then interpersonal therapy is most appropriate. If the problem is the client needs to learn a certain skill, the skills group will be most effective.

The Honesty Group

There are special groups that are particularly effective in dealing with specific problems. You can plug in one of these exercises anytime you feel that it is appropriate. The honesty group helps clients to see how they lie to themselves. For many of these groups, as the counselor, you will model the exercise for the group first. By being creative, you can come up with many effective groups like this.

In the honesty group, you might say, "Today we're going to see how the illness operates inside of your thinking. We all have a constant dialogue going on inside of our heads. This conversation is between the illness, who just wants to drink or use drugs, and the healthy side, who wants to get clean and sober." Place an empty chair in the center of the group. "We are going to put a chair in the center of the group. In this chair, we are going to put our illness. This side of us wants to get high. In the chair that we are currently sitting in, we are going to put the healthy side of us, the side that wants to stay clean and sober. Now each of us is going to spend some time in each chair. We are going to start in the illness chair and try to convince the healthy side of us to drink or use drugs. I am going to go first."

Example of the Honesty Group

The counselor, Judy, sits in the center chair and leans toward the empty chair in which she was just sitting. From the illness side of herself, she tries to talk herself into drinking or getting high. She might say something like this:

"Judy, you are doing great. I am very proud of you. You have been sober for a long time. You have been going to meetings. That is great. You have your life back together.

"You know, when you feel like it, I would like to do something. I want to go for a ride in the car, maybe on a nice spring day. I am not in any hurry. I can wait. I want to for a ride, relax, and drink three beers. No one is going to know. Nothing bad is going to happen. You need to relax, Judy. You have been working too hard. You deserve a break. Come on, it is just three beers. Remember all the good times we had drinking. Remember how good it felt."

Judy looks at the group. "That is how my illness still tries to get me drunk. Now, I am going to trade chairs and answer the illness from the healthy side of me." She moves to her original chair and leans back. "Well, illness, you seem to forget a few things. You always forget. You remember selectively. See, I remember the misery. I remember trying to drink three beers and throw up three beers at the same time. I remember losing my husband and my kids. I remember the shame of losing my job." She sits forward in her chair. "I also remember that we have tried this before, about a hundred times. We have tried drinking only three beers, or two, or one, and it goes okay for a while, but eventually I get drunk and bad things happen. Illness, I know how good I feel in recovery. I have regained my self-respect. I have my children back. I have a good job. I have found God for the first time in my life. In addition, you want me to give all of this up for three beers. You keep your three beers. I do not want to have anything to do with you."

Now the clients should have the idea. The counselor picks someone whom he or she thinks can do a good job, and the exercise is repeated. Most of the clients will not have as long a dialogue as the counselor, but it is important to see each person's illness at work. This exercise is excellent at uncovering who has a good recovery program and who is still struggling.

Clients usually will feel more comfortable in playing the illness role. This may show how little it is going to take the client to go back to using. The counselor will see all manner of seductions perpetrated by the illness. It is good for the clients to see how they have been deceiving themselves.

Uncovering the Lies

About halfway through the group, hand each of the clients a blank piece of paper. Then tell them this: "It is important that you see how the illness works. The illness must lie to operate. It cannot exist in the truth. You must lie to yourself and believe the lie before you can ever go back to drinking or drugging. What we are going to do now is uncover the lies. Every time you hear the illness lie, I want you to wave your paper. This is your white flag of surrender. Wave it loud so it rattles." The counselor asks the next client to start with his dialogue.

Bob smiles at the group and sits in the illness chair. "Well," says Bob, "you have had a hard day." (The group members rattle their papers.) "Why don't you stop by the bar and have a couple of beers? That is not going to hurt you." (The group members rattle their papers again.) "Your wife will not know." (The group members rattle their papers and laugh. Bob laughs with them.) "You can drink just a few." (Rattle.) "Just a couple." (Rattle.) "Remember all the good times we had." (Rattle.) "You need to relax and enjoy yourself." (Rattle.)

This is educational and fun. The clients never will forget those white flags going up after they speak to themselves. When the clients speak from their healthy side, the flags stay quiet. It is sobering to experience the lies try to work in front of treatment peers.

Have the group members discuss the exercise. In which role did they feel the most comfortable? Why? What are they going to do to keep from lying to themselves? How can they begin to keep the illness in check? How do they feel about the illness part of themselves and the healthy part of themselves? What is the goal of the illness? What is the goal of the healthy side? What is it like to have what seem to be two people in the same body?

How to End Each Group

End each group with a chance for the members to share the positive things that they learned about themselves. Keep this sharing time positive. At Keystone Carroll Treatment Center, we begin each group with the serenity prayer and end with the Lord's Prayer. The group members put their arms around each other or hold hands as they pray.

The Euphoric Recall Group

This group examines euphoric recall and how this differs from reality. As the counselor, you stand at the blackboard and ask each client to give an example of what drinking or using drugs did for him or her when that person first started using. You pull out all the positive things that the clients were getting from early use.

How to Uncover Euphoric Recall

Counselor: Tony, what did drinking do good for you? What was it giving you that was good?

Tony: It made me relax.

Counselor: Good. (The counselor writes "It made me relax" on the blackboard. Then the counselor moves to the next person in the group.)

How about you, Sally? What did drugs do good for you?

Sally: It was easier for me to talk to people.

Counselor: Okay, good. (The counselor writes, "It was easier to talk to people" on the blackboard.)

As the counselor, you go around the group at least twice. You need a long list of the positive things that chemicals did for the group members. Do not put down the same thing twice. You should come up with a list that looks something like this:

1. It made me relax.

2. It was easier to talk to people.

3. I felt more intelligent.

4. I felt stronger.

5. It made me brave.

6. It made me feel wanted.

7. I felt more attractive.

8. I could sleep.

9. I felt happy.

10. I could be creative.

11. My problems did not bother me anymore.

12. I could get along.

13. I was funny.

14. I felt comfortable.

15. People liked me.

16. I could talk to women.

You make as long a list as the blackboard will allow and then state, "Now, here are some of the good things that drinking and drugs did for you. I assure you that we could make a longer list of the good things that chemicals gave us early in use. This is why we were drinking and using drugs."

How to Help the Clients See the Truth

You then draw a line down the middle of the blackboard.

Counselor: Now let's see what happened to each of these things when addiction set in. Tony, after you became an alcoholic, did alcohol still make you relax?

Tony: I was tenser. I could not relax.

Counselor: How about it, Sally? After drug addiction took over, was it still easier for you to talk to people or did you feel more isolated?

Sally: Lonely. I felt totally alone.

   You write down what each person says. Be sure to read off what the client got good out of early use before asking him or her what happened when drug addiction took over. What the group members are going to find out is that once addiction set in, they ended up with the opposite of what they were using for. People who were drinking to sleep cannot sleep. People who were using to be social ended up alone. Your second list will look something like this:

1. I was tenser.

2. I could not talk to anyone. I was lonely.

3. I felt stupid.

4. I felt weak.

5. I felt inadequate.

6. I felt like no one wanted me.

7. I felt ugly.

8. I could not sleep.

9. I was very sad.

10. I could not think.

11. I had more problems.

12. I could not get along with anybody.

13. I was not funny anymore. I was sad.

14. I could not get comfortable.

15. I felt as though no one liked me.

16. I could not talk to anybody.

   The group members need to take a long look at both sides of the blackboard. You emphasize that the illness side of them will use euphoric recall to seduce them into using drugs and alcohol again. The clients have to get in the habit of seeing through the first use. They need to remember the painful consequences that come with continued use. The group members discuss what they learned for a brief period, and then you need to speak again.

Counselor: You see how the illness uses the good stuff to get you to use again. Now, what are you going to do when the illness side of you begins to gain strength? What are the tools of recovery that will put hurdles in the way of the first drink?

Tony:　　　　Call your sponsor.

Bob:　　　　Go to a meeting.

Sally:　　　Turn it over.

The counselor writes each of the new coping skills on the blackboard.

1. Call your sponsor.

2. Go to a meeting.

3. Turn it over to your Higher Power.

4. Get some exercise.

5. Talk to someone.

6. Read some Alcoholics Anonymous (AA)/Narcotics Anonymous (NA) material.

7. Remember the bad stuff.

8. Remember how good you have felt when clean and sober.

9. Ask for God's help.

10. Do something else that you enjoy.

Help the clients to make a long list and then discuss it with the group.

The Reading Group

In reading group, clients read a portion of the "Big Book" (AA, 2002a) or the "Twelve and Twelve" (AA, 1981) and discuss it with each other. It is necessary to have a counselor present to facilitate this discussion. Gently encourage all members of the group to share. People do not have to share, but if they do, they get more out of treatment. The first 164 pages of the Big Book, and all of the steps in the Twelve and Twelve, are read during treatment. There will be clients who do not feel comfortable reading for one reason or another. Encourage all of them who can comfortably read to do so. If a client feels too uncomfortable reading, then he or she can pass. This

Source: ©iStockphoto.com/digitalskillet.

material is read out loud chapter by chapter, paragraph by paragraph, or line by line. The clients discuss the subject matter to help them understand and internalize the material.

The Relapse Prevention Group

A relapse prevention group is run once a week. This group concentrates on high-risk situations and develops coping skills for dealing with each situation. The first group introduces relapse and concentrates on the triggers that might trigger using. These are the environmental situations that make clients vulnerable to using drugs and alcohol. Clients learn that there is such a thing as lapse (the use of a mood-altering chemical) as well as relapse (continuing to use the chemical until the full-blown illness becomes evident again). For most clients, the time period between lapse and relapse is less than 30 days. If a lapse occurs, then immediate action needs to be taken to prevent relapse. All clients must develop coping skills for dealing with a lapse.

The Trigger Group

Clients tend to relapse in certain situations, which include environmental stressors and personality characteristics. To prevent relapse, addicts need to develop individual coping skills, self-efficacy, and lifestyle balance, which might increase the probability of finding themselves in a high-risk situation. Relapse prevention includes teaching effective coping strategies and enhancing self-efficacy, along with cognitive interventions designed to prevent the occurrence of relapse episodes. It is essential that the clients not see a lapse as a failure or a lack of willpower but as an opportunity to learn more about the disease (Marlatt & Donovan, 2008).

How to Uncover the Triggers

Discuss each trigger with the group. Ask the clients to list the feelings that make them vulnerable to using. In what situations do they continue to use? How do they feel before they use? Are they more vulnerable when they are angry, frustrated, bored, lonely, anxious, happy, or joyful? Ask the group what they think are high-risk situations including social pressure, interpersonal conflict, inaccurate painful thoughts, uncomfortable feelings, low motivation for change, environmental stress, and lack of lifestyle balance. Generally, the counselor is trying to reduce stressors and increase pleasurable activities. Relaxation training and stress management exercises are used to help the clients reduce their response to relapse triggers. An environmental or interpersonal trigger throws the client into withdrawal that often leads to craving and relapse. The trigger can set of a cascade of symptoms including craving, inaccurate thinking, and addictive behavior or with training it can result in behaviors that are incompatible with relapse. A person who craves and then goes to a meeting or calls his or her sponsor is going to have a different outcome than someone who craves and drives to the bar.

Social pressure can occur in one of two ways: (1) direct social pressure or (2) indirect social pressure. Direct social pressure is someone directly encourages the client to drink or use drugs. Indirect pressure is when the client is in a social situation where people are drinking or using drugs (Marlatt & Gordon, 1985).

The Drug Refusal Skills

After discussing a wide variety of triggers, the group goes through drug refusal exercises. The counselor is the role model in the situation and talks to the group about the skills needed to say no to drug or alcohol use:

1. Refuse in a firm and unhesitating voice: "No thank you."

2. After refusing, change the subject. "I do not drink. How did you get here tonight?"

3. Suggest an alternative such as having something to eat or going for a walk. "Want to get some pizza?"

4. Avoid giving excuses. "I have got to work tomorrow." Just tell it like it is. "I do not drink."

5. If the person is persistent, walk away. "See you later."

At first, let the refusal exercises be easy, and then have more than one person encourage the person to use. The first time that a client goes through this, anxiety and craving usually are generated. The first attempt at refusal tends to be rather pathetic, but with practice, the client gets better. Each client needs to practice until he or she can say no and feel reasonably comfortable.

The group has a lot of fun with these exercises, but this role-playing delivers a powerful message: It is hard to say no and feel good about yourself. It is a new skill, and it has to be practiced repeatedly until it feels comfortable. The exercise provides excellent protection against relapse if the client can continue the exercises until he or she feels comfortable saying no. For each client, try to reenact the exact situation that makes him or her most vulnerable to relapse. For example, if the client is vulnerable to a sexual situation, then set up this situation as exactly as you can. A situation in which a significant other encourages the client to use is not difficult to set up. What is the client going to say? What is the client going to do? What if the other person gets mad? Have the client go through each situation until the group members believe that he or she has developed the skills necessary to say no, and then have the group make a long list of the hurdles that the client can put in the way of the first drink or use. What can the client do that will prevent use even when in a high-risk situation?

The Inaccurate Thinking Group

The second group focuses on thinking. What thinking occurs between the trigger and the feeling of craving? This is where the client's inaccurate thinking takes over.

"It will not hurt to have a couple of beers."

"No one will know."

"I can handle it."

"I never had any problem with pot."

"I can use a little pot."

"I never really had a problem anyway."

"I deserve a drink."

"I had a hard day."

"I would show them."

All of these, and more, are given as examples of inaccurate thinking at work.

Have group members discuss what they think about before they use chemicals. How is the sick part of them trying to trick them into thinking that they can still drink or use drugs normally? Use the chair technique again. Have the clients talk to the empty chair and talk the healthy side of them into using drugs or alcohol. Each of these thoughts must be placed on the blackboard and exposed as a lie. Discuss the inaccurate thoughts carefully until the clients understand that they all are lies. Then replace the inaccurate thoughts with accurate thoughts and have the clients practice the accurate thinking. Go over exactly what new thoughts the clients are going to use. They are taught a sentence to plug into their thinking whenever they feel the desire to use alcohol or drugs:

"Drinking (using drugs, gambling, etc.) is no longer an option for me."

Have clients practice thinking this sentence several times. Have them write it down and carry it with them. Every time they feel craving in treatment, they are to first think this new thought and log the situation that triggered the craving. These triggers are discussed in further groups. Every time clients are in a high-risk situation, they will think the new thoughts and then consider the other options for dealing with the situation. Drinking and using drugs no longer are an option, so what are they going to do? If they are in a high-risk situation, then they need to use their new coping skills. Have the group put on the blackboard a variety of options available other than drinking or using. It will end up looking something like this:

1. Call someone.

2. Turn it over to your Higher Power.

3. Think "That is no longer an option for me."

4. Call your sponsor.

5. Go to a meeting.

6. Think through the first use.

7. Think about how good you feel in recovery.

8. Remember how miserable you were before treatment.

9. Exercise.

10. Call the treatment center.

The Feelings and Action Group

The third group focuses on feelings and behaviors. The group members need to know that most chemically dependent persons are particularly vulnerable to anger and frustration. How are they going to handle these feelings in sobriety?

Feelings are used to give the clients energy and direction for problem solving. Have the group members discuss the feelings that make them vulnerable to relapse, and come up with coping skills to deal with each feeling. Any number of positive or negative feeling states can lead to relapse. The clients need to learn how to cope with good and bad feelings without chemicals.

When clients are having intense feelings, they need to share these feelings with others. This allows the clients to feel accepted and supported. They need to develop better problem solving skills and to practice problem solving in treatment. The following steps need to be followed when solving a problem:

1. Stop and think. Exactly what is the problem?

2. Consider the options. What is the best thing you can do for yourself and/or the other person right now?

3. Develop an action plan.

4. Carry out the plan.

5. Evaluate the effect of your action.

The Lapse Group

The fourth group is a lapse group. What are clients going to do to prevent a lapse, and what are they going to do if they have a lapse? How are they going to feel? What are they going to do specifically? What hurdles are they going to put in the way after the first use to prevent continued use? Remember that for most clients the elapsed time between lapse and relapse is less than 30 days.

Group members put on the blackboard the actions they are going to take to prevent a lapse. Make a long list, and have all clients copy the list to take home with them.

1. Work a daily program of recovery.

2. Attend regular meetings.

3. Read AA/NA material.

4. Do daily meditation.

5. Have daily contact with sponsor or other AA/NA member.

6. Get daily exercise.

7. Develop enjoyable hobbies.

8. Attend church, or work on spiritual program.

9. Say daily prayer.

10. When wrong, promptly admit it.

11. Be honest. Do not lie.

12. Eat right.

13. Get enough sleep.

14. Take a daily personal inventory.

Have each client make an emergency card of phone numbers to call if he or she is feeling vulnerable. Have the client carry this card in a wallet or purse at all times. The phone numbers should include those of the following: sponsor, several 12-step group members, the treatment center, the local 12-step hotline, a religious contact, and any other person who may be able to respond to the person positively.

In group, clients should role-play calling these numbers and practice asking for help. This is a very difficult skill for some people, and they need to be desensitized to the situation. Have someone else in the group play the other party. A client needs to get in the habit of calling someone when he or she feels uncomfortable. Just out of treatment, the client should call someone every day until he or she feels comfortable. The client should make every attempt to go to a 12-step meeting every day for 90 days. The first 3 months out of treatment are when the client is the most vulnerable to relapse. Every effort is made to stay sober during these first 90 days. After the 3 months, the client can discuss with his or her sponsor and continuing care group how and when to cut back on meetings.

Signs and symptoms of impending relapse developed by Gorski (Gorski, 1989; Gorski & Miller, 1986) are given to a client and his or her significant others. Each symptom is discussed so that the client understands and can identify the symptom. These warning signs include the following:

1. Apprehension about well-being

2. Denial

3. Adamant commitment to sobriety

4. Compulsive attempts to impose sobriety on others

5. Defensiveness

6. Compulsive behavior

7. Impulsive behavior

8. Tendencies toward loneliness

9. Tunnel vision

10. Minor depression

11. Loss of constructive planning

12. Plans beginning to fail

13. Idle daydreaming and wishful thinking

14. Feeling that nothing can be solved

15. Immature wish to be happy

16. Periods of confusion

17. Irritation with friends

18. Easily angered

19. Irregular eating habits

20. Listlessness

21. Irregular sleeping habits

22. Progressive loss of daily structure

23. Periods of deep depression

24. Irregular attendance at meetings

25. Development of an "I do not care" attitude

26. Open rejection of help

27. Dissatisfaction with life

28. Feelings of powerlessness and helplessness

29. Self-pity

30. Thoughts of social use

31. Conscious lying

32. Complete loss of self-confidence

33. Unresolved resentments

34. Discontinuing all treatment

35. Overwhelming loneliness, frustration, anger, and tension

36. Start of controlled using

37. Loss of control

Clients and their significant others should be given a copy of the warning signs. It is possible to prevent relapse. In taking a daily inventory, the clients should list any relapse symptoms that they saw in themselves and come up with a plan for dealing with the symptoms as soon as possible. Any symptoms resistive to change are discussed with a client's sponsor or 12-step group.

Clients might not recognize the early warning signs, so someone else needs to check them. That is why a sponsor, the continuing care group, and regular attendance at meetings are so essential. The clients need to listen to everyone. A closed mind is a sure way of ending up in trouble.

Clients must understand that relapse is a process. It does not begin with using alcohol or drugs. Some of the symptoms will occur long before actual drug use begins. The one symptom that everyone should notice is a decrease in attendance at meetings. Any decrease in attendance at meetings should be carefully discussed with a client's family, sponsor, and group.

The Spirituality Group

Spirituality group should be conducted once a week. This group is run by a clergy person trained in the group process or by a member of the counseling staff who has a solid spiritual program. At the beginning of each group, the group leader (or someone the leader has chosen) reads the following to prepare the group for the spiritual process: "Spirituality is the innermost relationship we have with ourselves and all else. Religion and spirituality are different. Religion is an organized system of faith and worship. Spirituality deals with three intimate relationships: We will explore how to improve our relationship (1) with ourselves, (2) with others, and (3) with a Higher Power. We are going to call this Higher Power 'God.' You may call your Higher Power something

Source: ©iStockphoto.com/CEFutcher.

else if you like. We only ask that you be willing to consider the possibility that there is a power greater than you are. We will begin the group by giving our names and the reason why we are here."

How to Develop Healthy Relationships

The first group discusses the concept of a healthy relationship. What are the essential components of a good relationship? What are the clients' experiences with relationships with self, others, a Higher Power, and religion? What hurdles seem to stand in the way of these relationships? What makes them worse? What makes them better? Many clients see a Higher Power as punitive. They see a Higher Power as they saw their fathers or mothers. These transferences, attitudes, and beliefs need to be discussed with the group. The pastor or counselor should be free to discuss his or her own relationships with self, others, and the Higher Power of his or her own understanding.

As the counselor, you must be willing to accept how other people experience a Higher Power. You will see a wide variety of individual beliefs. This is good. Each person has his or her own understanding of what the Higher Power is like and what the Higher Power can do. In the atmosphere of unconditional acceptance, the group members can freely explore their own concepts of a Higher Power. They must see that a Higher Power and religion are not going to be shoved down their throats in this program.

It is a mistake to allow formal religious doctrine to enter into this group. Do not allow one group member to try to convince others about some religious principle or belief. Neither AA, NA, nor Gamblers Anonymous (GA) has any religious affiliation. People can talk about their religious preferences, but for the most part, they should discuss spirituality rather than religion. They need to talk about their own spiritual journeys.

How to Develop a Healthy Relationship With a Higher Power

The second group specifically delves into the relationship with a Higher Power. The group members write letters to a Higher Power in which they ask for what they want and share how they feel. Then the clients write down what they think the Higher Power answers back. They may come up with questions that they would ask a Higher Power if the power was sitting next to them and then write down the answers. This makes the conversation with the Higher Power a dialogue rather than a monologue. In Step 11, it says, "Sought through prayer and meditation to improve our conscious contact with God as we understood him, praying only for knowledge of His will for us and the power to carry that out" (AA, 2001). The group members share this material with each other. The group is encouraged to view the relationship with the Higher Power as essential to the program. Clients are encouraged to share their knowledge of a Higher Power with each other. What do they want a Higher Power to be like? What does a Higher Power want from them? How can people have a relationship with a Higher Power?

The group needs to process through how God communicates with them. The relationship with God needs to be presented as a simple dialogue between two people. Clients are taught to contact God in a variety of ways. Nature, scripture, prayer, meditation, church, and other people all are ways in which God can speak to them. Each of these ways needs to be discussed, and clients in the group should give examples of when they felt close to or far away from a Higher Power.

The Eleventh Step Group

The third group seeks ways of improving conscious contact with God. Prayer and meditation are defined and discussed. Prayer is described as talking to God, whereas meditation is described as listening for knowledge of God's will. Clients are encouraged to begin to talk to God. They need to discuss various methods of prayer and meditation. They are encouraged to look for God in themselves and in each other. What do they see in themselves that is good? Clients explore the moral law. We all know what is right and wrong. Why do we all have the same laws? Is it possible that some life force gives us these laws? If that is possible, then who might that force be? Clients are asked to explore several philosophical questions. If there is a God, then why did not God make himself more knowable? If there is a God, and if God is all good, then why do bad things happen?

The Meditation Group

The fourth group does an exercise in an attempt to contact God directly. The clients are told that God may communicate with them in many different ways, thoughts, feelings, images, other people, scripture, music, nature, and so on. God often communicates with them inside of their own minds. God may contact them in words or in images inside of their own thinking. The clients are told that the group members will try to establish a conscious contact with God, as they understand God, and that they will try to receive a direct communication from God. It is explained that God may communicate with them in one of three ways:

1. In words inside of their thinking

2. In images inside of their thinking

3. In no words or images, but the communication will be known

Give the group members a piece of paper and tell them to write down any communications they receive. Then play some soft music and take the group members through an imagery exercise. You can take them through the exercise yourself, or you can order a book, *God Talks to You* (Perkinson, 2000), and a meditation tape, *A Communication From God*, on the Web (www.godtalkstoyou.com). If you want to do it yourself, then speak these words slowly and rhythmically:

"Close your eyes and concentrate on your breathing. Just feel the cool air coming in and the warm air going out. As you concentrate on your breathing, you will begin to relax. Your arms and legs will begin to feel heavy and warm. There is no right way or wrong way to pray. Prayer is just a dialogue with God. He knows exactly what you need to experience. Say these words to God. God, I am sorry I have not treated myself the way that I should have, I am sorry I have not treated others the way that I should have, and I am sorry I have not treated you the way I should have. Please come into my life and make me the person you want me to be. Then ask God a question, 'God what is the next step in my relationship with you.'" Wait for 2 to 5 minutes for the answer to come inside of the clients' mind, body or spirit. Then have the clients open their eyes, and have them write down what they experienced. Go around the group and have each person share what he or she received. If a client received no communication, then have that person discuss what happened when things were silent. How did the client feel? What did the client think? What did the client see in his or her mind?

When everyone has shared his or her communication, have the group members decide whether they believe that this communication came from God. Have them describe the characteristics of the person who delivered the message. What was that person like?

Most 12-step groups begin with the serenity prayer and end with the Lord's Prayer or the Gallic Prayer. Those clients who do not feel comfortable praying can remain silent. At all points in spirituality group, you need to concentrate on spirituality and not on religion. You must be willing for each client to find his or her own unique relationship with the Higher Power of his or her own understanding.

If this is done properly, then it will be the most important turning point for most of your clients in treatment. AA (2002a) says at the end of the chapter on how it works that

> Our description of the alcoholic, the chapter to the agnostic and our personal adventures before and after make clear three pertinent ideas: (a) we were alcoholics and could not manage our own lives, (b) probably no human power could have relieved our alcoholism, and (c) God could and would if God was sought. (p. 60)

Addicts who follow a genuine spiritual journey will find the peace that AA calls serenity. They need to feel the incredible joy of a Higher Power's love, which is so much better than any drug. For more information about this procedure, I recommend you get the book *God Talks to You* (Perkinson, 2000). The text will tell you how to help clients make conscious contact with God and then to help clients make progress along the spiritual journey.

The Childhood Group

In the childhood group, clients come to understand how they developed the tendency to lie about themselves. They come to understand the great lie. The great lie is that if you tell people the whole truth about yourself, then they will not like you. The truth is the opposite of this: If you do not tell people the truth about yourself, then they cannot like you. Most of the clients have been living their lives as though the great lie were the truth. They need to hear that they are created in perfection in the image of God. There is no reason for them to lie. The group members need to see that they could not be themselves and that they pretended to be someone else. They wore a variety of social masks and played a variety of roles. They thought that it was the only way in which they could ever be loved.

How to Explore Early Parental Relationships

The group explores early parental relationships. The clients had to pretend to be someone else to their parents. They knew that their parents would not love them for who they were. This belief system resulted in the clients feeling empty and unloved. They did not get what they wanted from their homes of origin. Addiction is an attempt to avoid this empty feeling. Most addicted persons come out of their childhoods feeling inadequate and unloved by parents and others.

Have the group members write a letter to their parents. This work is based on some of the work of Bradshaw (1990). As the counselor, you introduce the exercise like this. "Write a letter to your parents using your nondominant hand. This makes the letter look like a small child wrote it. Write them about how you felt as a child growing up. Tell them how you were feeling and what you wanted that you did not get."

After the group members write their letters, have each client read his or her letter to the group. Then have the other members of the group respond, each in turn, as if they were the *healthy* parent hearing the letter. If the client feels comfortable, then have the group members reach out and touch the client as they respond. The group should sound something like this.

John reads his letter. "Dear Mom and Dad. Mom, I wanted you and Dad to stop fighting. I wanted you to pay more attention to me. Dad, I wanted you to take me fishing and tell me you loved me. I wanted you to stop drinking. I wanted you to tell me everything was going to be all right. I was afraid."

Joyce, a group member, reaches out and touches John's arm. She speaks as if she is John's healthy mother. "John, I am sorry your dad and I were fighting. We were having problems. It was not your fault. I love you."

Meg, another group member, leans over to John. She, too, plays the role of a healthy mother. "I am sorry your dad and I were fighting. We did not mean to frighten you. We both love you very much."

Frank speaks as the healthy father. "John, I am sorry I was drinking. I am sick. I am going to try to get some help. I would love to go fishing with you."

How to Begin to Heal Early Childhood Pain

After all of the group members have read their letters, you take the group through this imagery exercise. This exercise must be positive. It must emphasize that the clients are now going to be their own champions in recovery. They are going to take over the parental role. They are going to try to forgive their parents and reach for their Higher Power. You should speak very slowly, pausing briefly after each sentence.

"Close your eyes and relax. Feel yourself becoming more comfortable. See yourself drifting back through time. See your high school. What was that building like—was it brick or wood? See yourself walking the halls of that school. How did you feel at that time in your life? Did you feel happy? Did you feel frightened? Feel the feelings that you were feeling then. See your grade school. See the playground. See a special friend. What is your friend wearing? See yourself playing a favorite game with your friend. How did you feel in that school? Reexperience the feelings that you were having at that time.

"See yourself walk up the street where you lived as a small child. See your house up ahead. You walk up the front walkway and peek in your window. Which room was yours? Go inside your house and see yourself as a small child. How did you feel in that house? Did you feel safe? Did you feel loved? Feel the feelings you were feeling then. See your mother. How did you feel when she was there? See your father. How did you feel about him?

"Walk over to yourself as a child, and smile. Imagine that the child looks up at you. Tell the child, 'I am from your future. I am going to be your champion from now on. You can trust me. I am going to keep you safe. I am going to see to it that good things happen to you. You are important. You matter to me. I want to listen to how you feel. I care for what you want.' Tell the child that it is time for you to leave. You are growing up. You are not going to blame your parents anymore. That would not do any good. They were trying as hard as they could to love you. You pick the child up, and the child wraps his or her arms around you. You carry the child out of the house. Your parents come out on the porch and wave good-bye. Your Higher Power appears beside you. Your new AA/NA group members are ahead. 'Come on,' they say. 'You can do it. We'll help you.' You walk up the street feeling confident, trusting yourself, trusting your Higher Power, and trusting your new support group. You feel happy and at peace. Everyone is smiling. You and the child are laughing together. You take the child and place him or her into your heart, where the child will stay. You feel yourself coming back to this time, back to the treatment center, back to your chair. Take a deep breath. Feel your toes wiggle and your eyelids flicker. When you feel comfortable, open your eyes."

The group then discusses the exercise. It is important that the group not delve deeply into old childhood pain. If you keep pulling on these memories, they can overwhelm clients. Most of these wounds are left to the second year in recovery. Clients in early recovery need to concentrate on working a self-directed program of recovery. Once their program is stable, usually in the second year, they can begin to work through some of the origin issues. In early recovery, you want to connect the clients to their feelings and not work through every issue. You want them to feel supported by their new group and their Higher Power. This will give them new hope that even the old pain can be resolved.

Men's Group/Women's Group

Men's group and women's group are run once a week. In these groups, men and women can gather and discuss things that would be more difficult in mixed company. Sexual issues and sexual abuse issues can be more easily shared in this atmosphere. The special relationship of a mother to a daughter or of a father to a son is explored in greater depth in these groups. How can you be a good mother or father? What did you want from your parents? What did you want to say to your mother or father that you never said? What did you want the relationship with your father or mother to be like? What is it like to be a man? What is it like to be a woman? What are the special problems that men and women face?

The group needs to discuss how to have healthy relationships with the opposite sex. They need to consider addictive, dependent, and normal relationships as well as how they differ. Women can discuss the premenstrual syndrome that may make some of them more vulnerable to relapse. Men need to discuss anger and how to use it appropriately. Men and women can role-play various situations. Both groups need to discuss boundaries and how to establish and maintain appropriate boundaries around themselves.

The Community Group

Community group is where the client population meets to discuss problems that they are having with each other or the staff. This group usually runs first thing in the morning and lasts for only a few minutes. Some programs run this group daily and some weekly. A daily group is best if the clients feel supported.

A daily meditation is read during this group. Any rules of the treatment center that have been broken need to be discussed. Have the group members join hands or put their arms around each other and commit themselves to helping each other through treatment.

The Personal Inventory Group

At the end of every treatment day, the clients have personal inventory group. In this group, they evaluate their day. They need to consider how they grew in the program and how they slipped backward. At a minimum, they need to consider each of the following points:

1. What did I do to love myself today?

2. What did I do to love others today?

3. What did I do to love my Higher Power today?

4. Was I honest?

5. What uncomfortable feelings did I have?

6. What did I do with my feelings?

7. What character defects caused me problems?

8. How have I been doing in my program?

9. What am I grateful for?

10. What do I need to do differently tomorrow?

Once clients have considered their personal inventories, they need to share positive experiences from the day. Then they need to go through a relaxation exercise to wind down. This exercise can be taped or given by the counselor. Have the clients sit in a comfortable place and pay attention to their breathing. Then have them imagine a relaxing scene. They can imagine that they are at the beach, in the mountains, down by a river, or in the desert. Take them through the scene for about 20 minutes, and then call it a night.

Skills Training Group

The skills training group is where you teach the clients how to use skills to reduce the chances of relapse. An excellent coping skills training manual has been developed by Monti, Kadden, Rohsenow, Cooney, and Abrams (2002). All counselors should read this book and bring it with them to the skills training group. Then you can read the rationale for learning a skill, teach the skill, be a role model for the skill, and role-play each skill with the clients. If the clients role-play situations, it is much more likely that they will use this skill in recovery. If the clients just hear about the skill, or watch someone else use the skill, it is less likely that the skill will be effective. When you practice a behavior, you use sight, hearing, touch, smell, and a variety of muscle movements. This uses most of the brain, so when challenged, the person has a much higher chance of remembering the skill and using it. Practice solidifies the skill until it becomes automatic. Use the skills listed in the aforementioned book to fit your client population. Some clients have these skills but some need practice. We will discuss two skills groups, but you will want to use more.

Assertiveness Skills Group

Open the assertiveness group by discussing communication skills, including verbal and nonverbal communication. "It is important that we learn good communication skills in treatment. This begins with nonverbal communication. You can say the same thing a number of ways that will make the communication different. Your facial expression, body posture, what you do with your hands and feet, and your tone of voice are just as important as what you say. Let us say it is 10 pm and you have something real important to do tomorrow at school or work, like take a test, and you need to get a good night's sleep. In the apartment upstairs, someone sounds like she or he is bouncing a basketball, and you cannot sleep. You have waited for the person to stop playing, but the bouncing goes on and on. Let me show you three ways to talk to the neighbor upstairs, and you tell me which way is most likely to be effective."

Have someone else in the group play the part of the neighbor. Then role-play someone who is too passive. You knock gently at the door. The neighbor opens the door. You keep your eyes on the floor, shuffle your feet, stumble over your words, and make nervous gestures with your hands. You speak in a voice that is so quiet you can hardly hear it, asking the neighbor if he or she could stop the bouncing noise. "Excuse me . . . well . . . maybe. I have got a test . . . you know an exam thing . . . tomorrow, and I was wondering . . . if you could, maybe . . . , if you really want to . . . stop bouncing that ball or whatever it is. I cannot sleep . . . really much . . . or at all with that . . . noise. Please, do you think you could stop? I do not want to be a bother to you or anything. Please . . . okay . . . thanks." Then wait for the person playing the neighbor to respond.

Then role-play someone who is too aggressive. This time you bang on the door. Get too close to the neighbor's face, raise your voice, clench your fists, and act in a threatening manner, using the word *you*.

"Are you crazy? How do you expect anyone to sleep with you bouncing that ball all night? This is not a basketball court. It is an apartment building. If do not stop this racket, I am going to make sure you get kicked out of here."

Then role-play the same scene by being assertive. Here you stand straight, over an arm's length from the person, use good eye contact, keep your voice and face relaxed. "I live downstairs, and I cannot sleep with the bouncing ball. I have an important day tomorrow and need to get to sleep. I would appreciate it if you would stop bouncing the ball. Thank you. Have a nice night."

Then ask the group which way is most effective and why. Then have each member of the group role-play the person who needs to sleep. Then ask the group to come up with other situations that they have encountered or might encounter in recovery. Role-play the passive-aggressive and assertive roles until all members seem to understand the difference.

Skills

1. Personal space: Stand at over an arm's length from the other person.

2. Facial expression: Keep everything relaxed.

3. Posture: Stay relaxed with arms to the side, hands open.

4. Tone of voice: Remain calm.

5. Hands and feet: Do not engage in nervous gestures.

6. Words: Be specific about the facts, using "I statements." Remember the assertive formula: I feel _____ when you _____. I would prefer it if _____.

Problem Solving Skills Group

Life is full of problems, and many of them will show themselves in recovery. Clients need to know the steps involved so they can solve problems effectively. If clients do not have effective problem solving coping skills, they are likely to return to their old skills, such as rage, withdrawal, or drug and alcohol abuse. If clients have problem solving skills, they are not left helpless to a problem; they have precise steps that they always use when confronted with a difficult situation. Fear, depression, or anger might start to trouble these clients, but if they become aware of these uncomfortable feelings and shift toward problem solving skills, they will be on the road to problem resolution.

It is essential that the clients learn how to handle a situation where they are encouraged to drink or use drugs. Social pressure includes being in a situation where other people are using or being directly encouraged to use. Going into a casino or bar is indirect social pressure, and being encouraged by a friend to use is direct social pressure. Each of these situations can easily cause craving and relapse unless the client knows how to deal with the situation. The clients will go through this group again in relapse prevention groups, but they need all the practice they can get with this one.

Begin the group by introducing the refusal situation: "Many times during recovery you will be asked or encouraged to become involved in your addictive behavior again. If you are not careful, this could lead to craving, inaccurate thinking, and relapsing. We will try to avoid using people, places, and things, but it is inevitable that at some point you are going to be encouraged to drink, use drugs or gamble, etc. There are three ways to act when you are encouraged to drink or use drugs.

1. You can answer too passively, making the other person think you are not sure or you are conflicted or confused. This results in confusion because the other person is not sure about your answer.

2. You can be too aggressive and make the other person afraid or angry, hurting your relationship.

3. You can be assertive, clear, and firm about your decision not to drink or use drugs.

Then the counselor sets up a role-play situation where he or she is encouraged to use. "Let us pretend that we are at a family reunion. Your cousin walks over to you holding a tray of large plastic cups. You and your cousin get drunk together every year. He asks you if you want a drink. You could answer him too passively; look down; make nervous gestures with your hands; speak in a soft, hesitant voice, or make a lame excuse: 'No . . . thanks anyway . . . not today. I am taking some medication, and I do not want to mix things up.' You could answer too aggressive: 'If you ask me anything like that again, I am going to kill you.' Better yet, you could be assertive: 'No, thank you.' If your cousin asks you again, you say no again and then suggest that you do something else together or say, 'No thanks, I quit drinking,' and then walk away.

Skill Set 1

1. Say, "No thank you," in a firm, controlled voice.

2. Make good eye contact.

3. Do not make nervous gestures with your hands or feet.

4. Give suggestions about something else you could do.

5. If the person keeps asking, say, "No thanks," and then calmly walk away.

Give each member of the group an opportunity to walk through the drug refusal exercise. Then ask the group to come up with other situations they have experienced or might experience and practice a few more times to solidify the behavior.

Skill Set 2

1. Write the problem down. Be specific about exactly what happened.

2. Get accurate about the other person's intent.

3. List each possible alternative action.

4. Consider the positive and negative consequences of each action.

5. Choose the best alternative, and carry the action out.

6. See if the problem moved toward resolution.

Then come up with a role-play situation. It could be something like this. Imagine that you have come home from a hard day. You are exhausted, but you are an hour late getting home. The minute you enter the door, your spouse looks at you with a cold glare and says, "You are probably drunk. I knew you could never stay sober." You might want each member of the group to work through the same role play or you might want to make up a specific role play for each client. After each member has tried the steps, see if the group can come up with other situations and work on them using the problem solving skills.

8 Recovery Skills

Source: Hemera Technologies/Thinkstock.

Recovery skills are client homework. They educate a client about the tools of recovery. The client completes each exercise and shares what he or she has learned in recovery skills group. The group decides to accept or reject the contract based on how well the client completes the exercise. If the contract is rejected, then the client has to do it over again. The contract group meets daily. As the counselor, you decide which recovery skills to give based on the problem list and the treatment plan.

Recovery skills are used as specific objectives. They help a client to identify a problem, understand the problem, and learn new skills to overcome the problem. These tools of recovery are individualized for each client. The types of recovery skills are infinite. You will want to develop some of them on your own. You will use a few recovery skills more often. There are some, such as the Chemical Use History (see Appendix 7), that you will use on every client. This chapter discusses the recovery skills that you will use most often. You can order a wide variety of other recovery skills from treatment facilities (e.g., Hazelden, Educational Materials, PO Box 176, Center City, MN 55012).

The Chemical Use History

The Chemical Use History (see Appendix 7) is designed to give clients and their counselors a detailed account of the clients' use of drugs and alcohol. This is an excellent way of breaking through the clients' denial. It is very beneficial for the clients to see the whole thing written down at one time. There is nothing like writing down the history of the clients' chemical abuse and presenting it in front of their treatment peers for breaking through the denial system.

Clients need to address each drug that they took and process through any problems that the drug caused them in their lives. They need to identify specifically when they started using and detail their patterns of use. Where do they use and with whom? What happens when they use? What are the consequences? Each problem caused or made worse by use is identified and discussed with the group.

Most clients will hedge, at least to some degree, in presenting their chemical use history. Remember that these clients come into treatment in denial. They do not know what the truth is. You and the group need to be ready to press a client when group members feel that the client is not being completely honest. The group members can give examples of how they answered certain questions when they came into treatment. This solidifies that the client is not trying to lie. The client is fooled by the denial process.

As you work through the chemical use history, you will be able to firm up clients' diagnoses. Periods of intense intoxication; blackouts; withdrawal symptoms; using to avoid symptoms of withdrawal; and all consequences in the home, work, and school are covered. The feeling of shame and humiliation is identified, and the group needs to support the clients when they have these feelings. The clients need to feel like they are not alone. Now the clients are with their brothers and sisters in this program.

Honesty

Source: ©iStockphoto.com/clearstockconcepts.

The Honesty exercise (see Appendix 8) helps clients to see how they have been distorting reality. All clients use denial, in its many forms, to keep themselves from experiencing the pain that the truth would bring. If they were to see the whole picture about themselves, then they would realize that they were deathly ill and needed treatment. This fact would create tremendous fear in the clients, and they would have to do something about their problems.

Clients keep from feeling this fear by minimizing, rationalizing, denying, blaming, distorting, projecting, intellectualizing, diverting, and engaging in countless other ways of not seeing the truth. The other clients in recovery skills group will need help with this exercise. Clients will be unable to uncover most denial self-statements without help from the counselor or group. The Honesty exercise just gets them started in this process. Treatment should be an endless search for the truth.

It is an eye-opening experience for clients to realize just how much they have been lying to themselves and to others. Clients usually feel guilty about lying to others, but they do not realize that the persons to whom they have lied the most were themselves.

Clients need to process how they feel about themselves when they lie and learn the consequences of dishonesty. If clients lie, then they will be lonely and will not be able to solve problems in the real world. They need to understand why dishonesty leads to empty relationships. If you tell people lies about yourself, then people cannot know the real you, and you will feel unloved, empty, and alone. If clients lie to themselves about the real world, then they cannot use the facts to solve problems. If problems are not solved, then they escalate until the clients go crazy, get sick, and/or use drugs.

Love, Trust, and Commitment

The Love, Trust, and Commitment exercise (see Appendix 9) builds self-esteem. Clients come into treatment not understanding what love is. They might have love confused with sex. Clients need to develop a new, positive relationship with themselves. They have been saying bad things to themselves for a long time: "I am no good. I am bad. I am stupid. I am ugly. I am unlovable." These thoughts dominate the clients' thinking and keep them feeling discouraged, depressed, and anxious.

Using the Love, Trust, and Commitment exercise, clients build a positive relationship with themselves and others. For this, they will need to understand the essential ingredients in a healthy relationship. They need to understand where their original feelings of inadequacy and rejection come from. They need to explore their first relationships with their primary caregivers and how these relate to their current relationships with themselves and others.

Clients need to learn what it means to trust themselves and to commit themselves to their own individual growth. What do they need to see from themselves that will show them that they are trustworthy? What do they need to see from themselves that will show them that they are committed to their own recovery?

Clients need to learn how to be supportive and encouraging to themselves and to others. They need to say positive things to themselves. They need to give themselves a lot of praise whenever they try to do something well. These skills will need to be practiced on a daily basis.

Many clients will have considerable difficulty in working through this exercise. Some might even fight and say that there is nothing positive to say. They have a hard time thinking up anything good to say. These clients need the help of the group. Each group member might have to come up with something positive to say about such a client. It might be a long time before the client believes these things, but if he or she keeps trying, then the new ideas will begin to take hold.

Clients need to develop a personal plan that will help them to treat themselves well. They need to act as if they are persons worthy of good things. They need to learn how to praise themselves and others, and they need to practice this skill. A compliments group often is helpful to get this process started. In this group, each member comes up with positive things to say about each other member.

Feelings

The Feelings exercise (see Appendix 10) is designed to help clients identify their feelings and use them appropriately to solve problems. The clients are told that all feelings are motivators. Feelings give energy and direction for movement. Each feeling is connected to a specific motor activity. Fear gives the energy and direction to run away from danger. If clients cannot use their fear, then they cannot run and they are handicapped. Similarly, if they cannot act appropriately on their anger, then they are more vulnerable to the world. If clients cannot feel, then they cannot adapt to their environment.

Chemically dependent people treat their feelings with drugs or alcohol. They do not use their feelings to solve problems. The Feelings exercise takes the clients through each feeling, connects them with the physical cues that accompany each feeling, and teaches them how to problem solve.

The main point that clients need to get is this: Each feeling needs to be carefully processed. Clients need to stop, think, and plan before they act. Each feeling is directing the clients to take some sort of action. The clients must have the skill of identifying each feeling and understand what each feeling is directing them to do. Then the clients need to process through their options of action, decide which is the best, and act.

Clients in treatment need a lot of practice in properly identifying their feelings. They have old skills that will constantly get in the way. For example, when men feel hurt or frightened, they often act angry. That is confusing. Once the clients are able to identify the real feeling—the pain—they can address the problems more accurately.

Women often cry when they are angry. This is confusing to them and to others, and it muddies the waters of problem solving. Their husbands might react to the tears when in fact the real problem is that the women are angry. You and the group help the clients to get at the core feeling and then process through the feeling to resolve the problem.

Bob might come to group acting angry and sullen. When it comes time for him to talk, he might not talk about the anger at all. He might talk about his fear. Bob might not even be aware that he is angry. Perhaps in his home of origin, he could not get angry or else he would incur the wrath of his father. As a child, it was dangerous for Bob to feel angry, so he did not feel it. He repressed it and felt scared instead. The group might need to teach Bob how he is really feeling by processing the situation with him. What happened to Bob that caused the feeling? How would the rest of the group have felt in a similar situation? One group member reflects Bob's anger to him: "Bob, you say you feel scared, but you look angry."

Clients who have felt feelings for the first time in their lives can express their feelings in group in a non-threatening environment. They are not rejected for their feelings. They are accepted and loved no matter how they feel.

Clients need to know that all of their feelings are friendly and are great and wise counselors that need to be listened to and acted on. Acting too quickly on feelings is a mistake. This causes impulse control problems, which make the clients vulnerable to relapse. Feelings are processed carefully and acted on rationally. That takes a lot of practice.

Relationship Skills

Source: ©iStockphoto.com/1911.

Most clients have poor interpersonal relationship skills. They manipulate, distort, accuse, blame, shame, project, sulk, rage, and harbor deep-seated resentments. They are trying to control the world and everyone in it, and they are furious when not everything is going their way. The Relationship Skills exercise (see Appendix 11) is designed to teach and practice healthy interpersonal relationship skills.

Clients learn that love is not a feeling. It is an action in truth. You cannot love and lie. Love is the interest in and active involvement in people's individual growth. Self-love is the interest in and active involvement in your own individual growth. To love, you have to be there for yourself or for the other people when they need you. Chemically dependent people cannot do this. Sometimes they are too intoxicated or hungover. No drug addict is completely trustworthy.

Clients are taught that commitment means stability over time. Commitment is developed by working a daily program of recovery. Clients must take the time necessary to nourish themselves and others.

Clients need to be encouraging and reinforcing to themselves and others. They practice the skill of giving praise. Some clients will need specific social skills training. They need to learn how to do simple things such as making good eye contact and standing at an acceptable interpersonal distance. As the clients practice good interpersonal skills, it is important that they recognize how they feel when they are using healthy skills compared to the old skills they have been using.

It is inevitable that clients will use their old methods of coping with conflict while in treatment. When this happens, you and the group can help these clients to stop and use their new skills. Nothing solidifies learning better than watching the consequence of the old behavior compared to the new behavior. The clients will see that the new skills work better and result in better problem solving. The old skills tend to make the problem worse.

Clients will need a lot of practice in sharing how they feel and in asking for what they want. Most of them are trying to tell people what they want to hear rather than the truth. This results in the clients feeling unknown. They need to share their feelings and watch the other members of the group respond appropriately.

Many clients are reluctant to share their feelings. They never have asked for what they wanted. They have been taught that this is selfish or that other people simply do not care. It is a new experience for these clients to see the power of the truth.

Compromise is necessary for healthy relationships. Clients have to practice working through issues until every party is satisfied with the result. This is called the "win-win scenario." Each party in a conflict shares how he or she feels and what he or she wants, until the problem is resolved. New options have to be constantly thrown out by the group for consideration. The primary principle is this: Treat other people the same way in which you want to be treated.

Clients are taught that all people need to be respected equally regardless of race, color, creed, education, or belief system. Healthy relationships demand caring for how other people feel and caring for what they want.

Addictive Relationships

Many clients coming through treatment for chemical addiction are just as addicted to some other person as they are to their drugs of choice. Addictive relationships can be as destructive as alcohol or drugs. They leave the clients feeling empty, abandoned, and unlovable. People can be so hooked on other people that they cannot see the truth.

The Addictive Relationships exercise (see Appendix 12) is designed to teach clients the difference between healthy and addictive relationships. It teaches them what they need to do if they are in relationships that are addictive. These unhealthy relationships are fueled by powerful sexual feelings that the clients mistake for love. The clients become caught up in the excitement of emotionally chaotic relationships.

Addictive relationships are characterized by the same loss of reality as is involved in addiction. The clients are unaware that these relationships are bad for them and are convinced that they are the best things that have ever happened in their lives. Lies permeate these relationships, which are filled with feelings of intense fear, anger, and pain.

An addictive relationship must use lies to keep going. The partners must feel that they have to stay in the relationship to feel normal. They fear that without the relationship, they will be lonely forever. "I will never have anything as good as this. I cannot live without her."

Addictive relationships are filled with verbal and physical abuse. They are demoralizing and end in feelings of anger and abandonment. Clients who have addictive relationships typically will have a pattern of these relationships rather than just one.

Clients use these relationships in a similar way as they use drugs. The relationships distract them from their real pain and fill their lives with something to obsess about. The clients will need to make the decision either to get out of these addictive relationships or to take the relationships into long-term treatment.

Communication Skills

The Communication Skills exercise (see Appendix 13) teaches healthy communication skills. It is essential that these skills be practiced in group as well as in individual sessions. The clients need to be constantly reminded to use these skills.

Good communication necessitates being able to listen well and speak clearly. Active listening pulls out more of a person's communication until the entire message is perceived.

Words are symbols for thoughts and feelings. They are accompanied by nonverbal cues that often are more accurate than the words themselves. Clients who tell you that they are doing well with flat, unemotional voices and downcast eyes are telling you with their words that they are fine, but with their actions, they are telling you another thing entirely.

To develop good listening skills, clients need to practice repeating what the other person said. People often have different communication patterns, or family rules, that other people do not understand. In certain cultures, for example, friends argue vehemently about things. That is just how they communicate. In other cultures, this behavior might be considered insulting. Clients who are used to using an angry tone of voice to get their point across need to hear how it adversely affects other people. They might not know how scary it is.

Many clients need to develop empathy skills. They have to practice understanding and personally relating to how other people are feeling. This will take a lot of trial-and-error practice. Clients must try to relate personally to what other people are saying by directly relating it to their own personal experience.

As clients watch you validate the other members of the group, they will begin to be more reinforcing to each other. Clients need to be encouraged to use "I feel" statements when they speak. Many chemically dependent persons constantly blame others for their problems. "You" is perceived as the problem rather than "I." Statements that begin with "You" usually are headed for trouble. In the great scheme of things, we know much more about "I" than we do about "you."

Clients need to be reminded to be positive in their interactions with each other. A positive attitude needs to be soundly reinforced by all staff members. Clients who are not positive need to see how their attitude clouds their whole day. They need to practice saying positive things to themselves and others, even if they do not feel positive.

Clients with poor communication skills need to go through the Communication Skills exercise with at least five of their treatment peers. These skills have to be practiced repeatedly until they are used automatically. The more the clients practice, the better communicators they will become.

Self-Discipline

The Self-Discipline exercise (see Appendix 14) is for those individuals who have a difficult time in delaying gratification and accepting responsibility for their own actions. They constantly blame other people for their problems. They think that they would be fine if other people would leave them alone. Clients with these problems often have antisocial traits. They have had no experience with success. They never have worked at a goal long enough to reach the goal.

These individuals need to see themselves achieve objectives in gradually escalating steps. They can accomplish things if they settle down and try. Most of these individuals have a low frustration tolerance, and they have serious problems with impulse control. They act out too quickly on their feelings, particularly anger and frustration.

Begin with a simple task, such as one of the recovery skills, and walk the clients through it. Do not get frustrated with them when they procrastinate. That is all they know how to do. Have them sit down for a few minutes at a time and work through a page of the exercise. When they have accomplished something, reinforce them. Tell them that they can do it if they try and that you have confidence in them. These clients need to see themselves be successful. They need to feel like they can do things that are difficult. Self-discipline is not an easy skill, and many times, it will be frustrating. However, remember that if the clients are reinforced for doing something, then the behavior will increase.

Clients need to see how poor self-discipline leads to failure. To accomplish this objective, the clients need to process through several of their problems with you. Take a problem that caused them quite a bit of pain, such as getting arrested or failing at something they really wanted, and walk them through the problem. Where did they go wrong? What else could they have done? Who was responsible?

Let us take someone who was arrested for drunk driving. This person might be blaming the police. "They have always been out to get me." However, who was drunk? Did the police make this person drive drunk? In what way is the client responsible?

Clients must understand that if other people are responsible for everything bad that happens to them, then other people are in control of their lives. They need to re-achieve control by taking back the responsibility for their own behavior.

Clients with poor self-discipline do not understand the rules. They break the rules of society to get their own way. They do not understand that the rules are there to keep them safe. The spiritual part of the program can be a benefit here. The clients need to understand that God did not make the rules to keep us from having a good time. God made the rules so that we could be safe and happy. The same thing goes for the laws of the state. The legislature makes the rules to protect its citizens.

These clients usually will break some rules in treatment and will blame others for their rule breaking. You must walk them through these violations and help them to see that it was their choice to break the rules. Breaking the rules resulted in their getting caught and experiencing pain. If they could learn how to obey the rules, then they would feel better all of the time.

Clients with self-discipline problems have poor problem solving skills. They go for the pleasure first, being unable to delay gratification long enough to achieve long-term goals. They need to process several problems with you while in treatment. If they want job training, how are they going to get that? What are they going to have to do specifically? If they want to stay sober, how are they going to get that? They must learn and practice working on a problem on a daily basis until the problem is solved. These individuals usually have such low frustration tolerance that they are unable to feel much pain without acting impulsively. People who can tolerate little pain cannot work at anything for very long. They must see themselves take off a small piece of a problem and work on it until the whole problem is resolved.

Impulse Control

Clients who have impulse control problems act too quickly on their feelings. They need only a little of a feeling to move into action. If they feel angry, then they act angry immediately. This leaves them vulnerable to relapse. Craving is a feeling. If they move too quickly when they crave, then they will relapse into using substances. The Impulse Control exercise (see Appendix 15) helps the clients to develop control over their feelings.

These clients need to stop, think, and plan before they act. This takes a great deal of practice, particularly when the clients are feeling strong emotions.

Clients must be able to identify each feeling, understand why they are having the feeling, consider the options of action, plan their response, and then act. When they are having strong feelings, the clients need to stop and analyze their feelings carefully. They cannot continue to act too quickly on their feelings. That leads to disaster.

Clients need to understand the behavior chain and practice analyzing their behavior carefully. They need to understand how their poor impulse control led to excessive drinking or drug use. They have developed a habit of moving immediately from craving to drug use. They will need to develop another plan and practice that plan many times in treatment.

These individuals are particularly vulnerable when they are feeling angry and frustrated. They have a low frustration tolerance, and they desire immediate gratification. They need to understand how this has led them into trouble. Most of them will have to work through the Self-Discipline exercise.

These individuals will need to learn assertiveness skills and will need to role-play interpersonal conflict. When they act impulsively in treatment, they need to process through the situation until they understand how they could have handled it better.

As clients become more skilled at identifying their feelings, they can begin to address the real feelings. What underlies most anger is pain. As the clients begin to solve real problems in real time and with real people, they feel less frustrated and more in control.

When angry, these clients must take a "time-out" and walk away from such situations. They cannot stay in situations where they have lost control before. Teach them and their significant others to use the time-out sign of a referee when they are feeling too angry. They also can say "Time-out" as they make the sign. Their partners then agree to say nothing except, "Okay, time-out." The clients then leave these situations to get their thinking accurate. They might have to call other people to process the problem with a third party before they come back into the original situations. The clients must promise to come back within a previously specified length of time to continue to work on the problems. Both members of a couple need to write this plan down and follow it every time they have a significant conflict. Everyone who gets angry knows when he or she is beginning to "lose it." At the earliest possible opportunity, someone needs to make the time-out sign and then follow the prearranged contract.

All anger, fueled by pain, is there to make the pain stop. To be angry, clients must establish other people to blame. They must think that the other people purposely did things wrong that hurt them. This rarely is accurate. Other people are just trying to meet their needs. They rarely are trying to hurt others.

Clients with impulse control problems will need to come up with a written plan that they carry with them at all times. When they are feeling strong emotions, they need to carry out the plan. They can call their sponsors, go to meetings, read some Alcoholics Anonymous (AA)/Narcotics Anonymous (NA) material, turn the situations over, talk with friends, and so on.

Relapse Prevention

Relapse prevention is one of the most important aspects of addiction treatment. Approximately two thirds of clients will use their drugs of choice within a year of leaving treatment (Hunt, Barnett, & Branch, 1971; Marlatt & Donovan, 2008).

Most clients (60%) lapse within 3 months of leaving treatment. This is the period of highest risk, and it needs the greatest attention. The clients must be willing to do almost anything to prevent relapse during this period. They need to see themselves as clinging to an ice-covered cliff with their recovery skills the only rope. The most important thing that they can do is go to meetings. Clients who are working a daily program of recovery will not relapse. They cannot work the program and use at the same time. The two are incompatible.

Relapse is a process that begins before the first use. A client begins to feel under stress. The client's new tools of recovery are not used, so the problems continue to escalate. The client reaches a point where he or she thinks that the only option is to drink or use drugs.

The Relapse Prevention exercise (see Appendix 16) is designed to help the client develop the skills necessary to prevent relapse. Relapse prevention takes working a daily program of recovery. The client must take his or her personal inventory at the end of every day. If any of the relapse symptoms become evident, then immediate action must be taken.

The client checks every day for symptoms that he or she is having problems that need intervention. The client will develop a written plan detailing the exact skills that he or she will use when craving or considering relapse. The client carries an emergency card full of telephone numbers of people he or she can call if problems arise.

Other people need to be encouraged to check the client daily for relapse warning signs. This is a good reason to go to daily meetings and to hang around other recovering persons. Other people often can see what the client is unable to see for himself or herself.

Clients need to identify high-risk situations that may trigger relapse and develop coping skills to deal with each situation. The more clients can practice these skills, the better off they will be. In groups, clients need to role-play high-risk situations and help each other deal with relapse situations. High-risk situations might include negative emotions, social pressure, outcome expectations, access to substances, self-efficacy, lifestyle imbalance, and coping skills (Marlatt & Donovan, 2008). Individuals who choose to indulge are vulnerable to the abstinence volition effect, which are the guilt, hopelessness, and loss of self-efficacy that occurs when someone violates his or her own rules. Self-efficacy can be measured using the Alcohol Abstinence Self-Efficacy Scale (see Appendix 63) (Marlatt & Donovan, 2008; Marlatt & Gordon, 1985).

Using the Relapse Prevention exercise, clients develop the skills necessary to deal with each of the high-risk situations and practice these skills in group. All clients must role-play drug refusal situations until they can say no and feel reasonably comfortable. They must examine and experience all of their triggers, see through the first use, and learn about euphoric recall.

All clients must develop a written plan for a lapse. What are they going to do if they use again? Whom are they going to contact? What are they going to say? This must be role-played in group so that the clients can see that the people on the other end of the phone are not going to be angry with them.

Clients must understand the behavior chain and develop skills for changing their thoughts, feelings, and actions when they have craving. Using imagery and drug paraphernalia, the clients need to experience craving and learn experientially that craving will pass if they move away from their drugs of choice.

When you are discussing relapse with clients, you need to discuss the benefits of medications that cut relapse rates. Naltrexone and acamprosate both reduce the craving for alcohol and other drugs and decrease some of the reinforcing properties of addiction. These medications consistently cut the relapse rates in half. Naltrexone is an opioid antagonist that is helpful in many clients, particularly those with chronic histories of relapse. Naltrexone blocks some of the reinforcing properties of alcohol by blocking the action of endorphins (opium-like chemicals that exist naturally in the brain to kill pain). Endorphins give addicts the euphoric effects that trigger craving. Several studies have shown that alcoholics who take naltrexone daily can decrease relapse rates by as much as 50%. The alcoholic still may drink, but the intense craving is not triggered, so he or she can bring the drinking under control more quickly (O'Malley et al., 1992; Volpicelli, Alterman, Hayashida, & O'Brian, 1992). Naltrexone now comes in a depot injection (Vivitrol) that lasts for one month. These medications can be life-saving, so all clients need to be educated and given a prescription.

Acamprosate works by affecting gamma-aminobutyric acid (GABA) and excitatory amino acid (glutamate) neurotransmission rather than affecting the endogenous opioid system. The medication cuts craving and increases the number of days abstinent (Kranzler, Ciraulo, & Jaffe, 2009; Littleton, 1995, 1996). One of these two medications should be encouraged to be used in everyone who can afford it. Drug companies will often give price breaks to clients who are indigent. These drugs must be used in addition to working a program of recovery.

Stress Management

The Stress Management exercise (see Appendix 29) helps clients to cope with stress. The inability to deal with stress effectively fuels addiction. The clients have been using chemicals to deal with the uncomfortable feelings caused by stress.

Stress is the physiological response of the organism to a stressor. A stressor is any demand made on the body. This can include psychological or physiological loss, absence of stimulation, excessive stimulation, frustration of an anticipated reward, conflict, or the presence or anticipation of painful events (Zegans, 1982).

Source: ©iStockphoto.com/hidesy.

Selye (1956) found that if rats were presented with a problem to which there was no solution, they got sick. There was a generalized stress response that affected most organ systems. Initially, the body's response to stress is adaptive, but chronic stress is damaging. Severe stress has been linked with many diseases including kidney impairment, malignant high blood pressure, atherosclerosis, ulcers, anxiety, depression, increased infections, and cancer (Selye, 1956; Zegans, 1982).

To learn how to deal with stress more effectively, chemically dependent clients need to do three things: (1) relax twice a day, (2) maintain regular exercise, and (3) learn coping skills for dealing with stressors (Benson, 1975).

Many clients resist developing these programs, and some will be unable to do so, but as many as possible need to be encouraged to practice these techniques. The clients who have the most trouble will have problems with self-discipline. They have not learned how to work toward a long-term goal. They will moan and complain whenever you mention the exercise or relaxation program. What they are really complaining about is they do not want to be told what to do. What is behind that is the inability to stick to things that they want to do. They have just failed too much and are unwilling to go to any length to stay clean and sober. Many of these clients will have antisocial traits. You have to show them, repeatedly again, why it is important to develop these programs.

If people relax twice a day for 10 to 20 minutes, they reap many benefits. They learn how to control their feelings, decrease tension, and decrease psychosomatic problems. In general, these people are happier and healthier. They learn that there is something that they can do to make themselves feel normal (Benson, 1975).

Clients can go through one of the formal relaxation techniques listed in the Stress Management exercise, or they can pray and meditate quietly twice a day. The important thing is that they practice relaxing. The more they do this, the better they will feel.

Once clients know what it feels like to relax, they can develop techniques to stay more relaxed during the day. If something stresses them, then they can use one of the techniques to recapture their serenity. The Higher Power can be used as an adjunct to this process. The clients can turn things over and relax.

It is very difficult to get some chemically dependent individuals to maintain an exercise program. This is like pulling teeth for some people, but you should encourage them. Research has shown that exercise is important, not only for cardiovascular fitness but also for a sense of psychosocial well-being (Folkins & Sime, 1981; Greist et al., 1979; Ledwidge, 1980; Stern & Cleary, 1981).

It has been demonstrated that hospitalized alcoholics can increase fitness levels in as little as 20 days. This increase enhances not only their physical fitness but also their self-concepts (Gary & Guthrie, 1972). A strong exercise program is important for developing a new sense of self-efficacy. Many chemically dependent people come into treatment thinking that they cannot do anything. When they see their strengths develop, they feel a new sense of power and control. They feel like they can do it. This is a key, particularly to adolescent clients who are concerned about their body images.

Rigorous exercise produces natural opioids in the body that will give clients a natural high (Appenzeller, Standefer, Appenzeller, & Atkinson, 1980). They feel better all day after working out. The clients must be encouraged to develop a stretching, strength, and cardiovascular fitness program. The exercise or recreational therapist will help them to individualize the program.

In learning new coping skills, clients need to learn assertiveness skills, social skills, and how to increase their involvement in pleasurable activities. The clients need to be shown what they are doing that makes their lives difficult. If they are frowning at everybody all of the time, they are not getting positive responses from the world. They need to learn how to be pleasant and how to ask for what they want. They need to practice sharing how they feel.

The Stress Management exercise helps clients to develop pleasurable activities. They need to learn how to have fun clean and sober. They must be encouraged to reach out and try different things. If they sit at home and wait for the wonders of sobriety to overtake them, then they are going to be disappointed. They must reach out to others and become actively involved in their AA/NA groups and communities.

Many of these clients do not know how to have fun without chemicals. Chemicals have been their whole lives, and they are all that they know. The clients need to be shown that sobriety can be fun. This will be very difficult for many clients when they are grieving the loss of their drugs of choice. The pleasure of the drugs must be replaced by pleasure from the environment. This requires doing something new.

The best way to get clients motivated is to show them that drugs and alcohol are no fun for them anymore. Once addiction clicks in, the drugs lose their ability to make the clients feel better. The clients feel miserable when intoxicated and when clean. A new lifestyle must be developed to help the clients to enjoy their sobriety. New hobbies and interests have to be tried until the clients develop a leisure program that fits.

9 The Steps

Source: ©iStockphoto.com/sagaYago.

The 12 steps are the core of treatment for most addiction treatment programs. More individuals have recovered using the principles of the 12 steps than using any other treatment. Alcoholics Anonymous (AA) currently has some 1.5 million active members worldwide, including more than 700,000 members in the United States. AA works, and it is free. The only requirement for membership is the desire to stop drinking. Narcotics Anonymous (NA) and all of the other 12-step groups developed their programs directly from the 12 steps of AA. The programs are almost identical. "The program," as it is called by 12-step groups, has been broadened to cover many types of problems including not only NA but also Gamblers Anonymous (GA), Overeaters Anonymous, Drugs Anonymous, Cocaine Anonymous, and Pills Anonymous (Emrick, 1987).

"My husband's divorcing me, my kids don't want to see me anymore, I was arrested by a stupid policeman who wouldn't listen, and I'm being held in some clinic. I need money for a cab fast."

133

Treatment programs differ as to which steps they address in treatment. Some programs address only Step One, some address Steps One to Three, and others address Steps One to Five. This must be individualized. Some clients will be able to embrace only the First Step, and that is fine if they do a good Step One. For most clients, it is beneficial to complete at least Steps One to Three while in treatment. The more steps the clients can complete, the better off they are in recovery and the further along they are in the program. Working through the Fifth Step takes a great burden of guilt and shame off clients. If they complete the Fifth Step, then they will not have to carry the heavy burden of guilt into early sobriety.

If your center works only on the First Step, then that will give you more time to work on powerlessness and unmanageability. This chapter teaches you how to take the client through Steps One to Five, assuming that some inpatient programs will go this far. Rare is the program that goes further than Step Five, but some long-term programs work all 12.

As you take clients through the steps, you must make sure that they are internalizing the material. The clients must be able to identify each problem, understand the problem, and learn coping skills for dealing with the problem. They must be able to verbalize to you a solid understanding of each step and how they are going to apply the step in their lives.

You will be able to tell when clients are complying and when they are understanding and internalizing the material. The level of commitment to sobriety will be evident in their behavior, in what they do, and in what they say. If you watch how they act with you and with their treatment peers, then you will have a good idea as to whether they are internalizing the information or not. If you are hearing one thing in individual sessions and a client's peers are hearing another thing, then one of you is not getting the truth. The client has to be confronted in group with the inconsistency of his or her behavior.

The Committee

Clients are constantly torn between the side of themselves that wants to use alcohol and drugs and the side that wants to get clean and sober. There often is a constant, and often turbulent, internal war going on inside of a client's head. Each side tries to take control over the client's behavior. Each side has its good and bad arguments. Sometimes it is hard for the client to know who he or she is or what he or she wants. It feels as though there is more than one person talking to the client inside of his or her head.

It is useful to label the three voices. Freud called them the id, the ego, and the superego. In treatment, we call these voices the disease, the Higher Power, and the client. One train of thinking is the disease process. This side only wants clients to use drugs or alcohol, and it does not care how it gets the clients to do it. If the clients feel miserable, this is all the better. Another voice is the voice of the Higher Power. The Higher Power only wants the clients to love themselves and others and to reach for their full potential in life. This voice is incredibly supportive. The third voice is the clients' own thinking. Here the clients are trying to figure out things for themselves.

As you move clients through the steps, you must be careful not to continue to the next step until they have a solid foundation in the steps below. If the clients have not embraced a good Step One, then there is no use in moving on to Step Two. If you have to work on Step One the whole time the clients are in treatment, that is fine, but do not try to move up in the steps until the clients have a firm foundation of the steps below. The steps must be built one on top of the other. The first building block is Step One.

Step One

"We admitted we were powerless over alcohol—that our lives had become unmanageable" (AA, 2001, p. 59). Assign the client to complete the Step One exercise in *The Alcoholism and Drug Abuse Client Workbook* (Perkinson, 2011). Copy Appendix 17, which is the same thing. The workbooks were made to be cheaper than copying the exercises at the end of the book. The book is attractive so the clients like it and often take it home and read it again, reinforcing learning. If you give the client xeroxed copies, most of them will throw them away. Order the books from Sage Publications (800-818-7243; www.sagepub.com), and give them the following priority code: A030504. This will give you 40% off and save you hours at the copy machine.

It is vital that all clients complete a solid Step One in treatment. Step One is the most important step. Without it, recovery is impossible. Step One necessitates a total surrender. Clients must accept as true that they are addicted and that their lives are unmanageable so long as they use mood-altering chemicals. Until this conscious and unconscious surrender occurs, the clients cannot grow. So long as they believe that they can somehow bring their lives under control and learn to use addictive behavior normally, they have not accepted their disease, they are stuck in the illness, and they cannot break free.

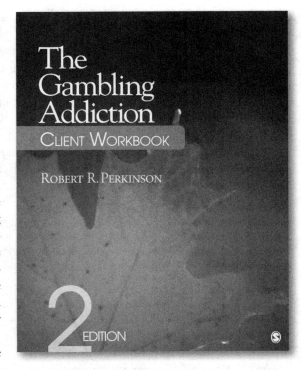

Step work is mainly group work. Clients complete the Step One exercise and present the exercise in group. The group members help the clients with the step, ask questions, and help you decide whether the step is completed successfully. You usually should not make this decision without the support of the group. Particularly in an inpatient setting, things go on in treatment that you, as the counselor, do not know about. The clients may be complying with treatment and may be pretending that they are working when, in fact, they really are not internalizing anything. The treatment peers are more likely to see these lies. They see the clients in casual interaction and notice the inconsistencies.

In Step One, clients must learn to accept as fact that they are addicted, that they are powerless, and that their lives are unmanageable. They must understand that they cannot live normally so long as they use mood-altering substances.

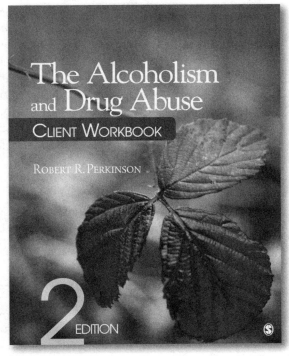

The best way of convincing clients to surrender are to show them repeatedly that they get into trouble when they drink, use drugs, or engage in addictive behaviors. They do not get into trouble every time—just sometimes—but they never can predict when the trouble is going to occur. They might drink a couple of beers and go home, or they might drink more and get arrested for drunk driving. The clients must process through many of their problems in detail until they realize that they never have been able to predict when they were going to have addiction problems. This is one of the primary reasons for processing through Step One.

How do clients feel about having blackouts? It is very scary for clients to know that they were awake doing things and that they cannot remember what they did. Did the clients do embarrassing things while intoxicated or gambling? What were they, and how do the clients feel about what they did? How do they feel about not doing things with their families, at school, or at work because they were too intoxicated or hung over? You must get at the real stories—exactly what happened—and examine how the clients feel. Talk about the shame, humiliation, depression, and anxiety caused by the addiction. How depressing is it to know that the clients' families are falling apart? How did it feel to be unable to keep promises?

Sometimes clients used chemicals more, or for a longer period, than they originally had intended. Once they began using, the addiction took control. Even when they promised themselves that they were going to stop or cut down, they kept on using. The clients must understand that once they start using they never know what they are going to do.

Most addicts want to hold on to the delusion that they still are in control. Clients do not want to admit that they are powerless and that their lives are unmanageable. They were having problems sometimes, they think, but only occasionally. The fact is that when the clients had problems, the problems usually were directly related to the addiction. The clients got into trouble obtaining the substances, using the substances, gambling, or recovering from substance use. Addicts do things when they are intoxicated that they never would do when sober. They need to look at each of these things and see the painful consequences of their addictions. They need to take a careful look at their addiction histories—at the lies, the crimes, the inconsistencies, and the people they have hurt. They need to understand that so long as they use drugs or alcohol, they will hurt.

Step Two

"[We] came to believe that a power greater than ourselves could restore us to sanity" (AA, 2001, p. 59). Read the Step Two exercise (see Appendix 18) before continuing with this chapter.

The beginning of clients' spiritual program is Step One. This is the surrender step, and it is essential to accept powerlessness and unmanageability before the clients reach toward a Higher Power. The essential ingredient of Step Two is willingness. Without willingness to seek a power greater than themselves, the clients will fail. "There is one thing more than anything else that will defeat us in our recovery; this is an attitude of indifference or intolerance toward spiritual principles" (NA, 1988, p. 18). The clients have admitted that they are powerless and that their lives are unmanageable. They must now see the insanity of their disease and search for an answer to their problem.

The word *sanity* in AA means soundness of mind. To have a sound mind, a person must be able to see and adapt to reality. The person must be able to see what is real. No person who is an addict sees reality accurately. The person is living in a deluded world of his or her own creation. The mind of an addict is irrational. The person cannot see what is real, so he or she cannot adapt to reality.

In Step Two, clients look at their insane behavior. They see how crazy they were acting and reach for an answer. They must conclude that they cannot hold onto their old ways of thinking. If they do, then they will relapse into old behavior.

How to Help Clients Accept a Higher Power

Many clients rebel at the very idea of a Higher Power. They must be gently encouraged to open the door just a little and to seek. They must be encouraged to be honest, open-minded, and willing. They need power. They are powerless. They need someone else to manage. Their lives are unmanageable.

At first, you encourage clients to see that some sort of a Higher Power can exist. The clients must look at their interpersonal group and see that the group has more power than they do. You can say something like this to a client: "If you wanted to leave this room, and the group wanted to keep you in, do you think you could leave?" The matter becomes obvious. The group could force the client to stay inside of the room. It might take some wrestling, but the group has more physical power than the client does. The client could then be asked if he or she is willing to place his or her trust in the Higher Power of the group.

Trust is a difficult issue for most addicts, and they will need to process their lack of trust with the group. This is a good issue for group work. If clients cannot trust the group as a whole, can they trust anyone in the group? If they cannot trust anyone, can they trust themselves? Are they willing to try to trust—to be open to the possibility? If they are unable to trust themselves and are unable to trust anyone else, then they are lost. They will have to start somewhere. This reality will have to be driven home. The clients cannot really trust themselves. That should be obvious. There were times when they were out of control, they were powerless, and their lives were unmanageable.

The best way of having clients learn to trust the group is to develop a caring group. The members are actively interested and involved in each other's growth in this group. They gently help each other to search for the truth. The group members are kind, encouraging, and supportive. The group members never are hostile and aggressive. They do not put each other down; that is counterproductive. If you have an aggressive and highly confrontive group, then you destroy trust. People must learn to confront each other in an atmosphere of love and unconditional positive regard. It is your job to teach the group this process.

Once clients trust the group, they can begin to transfer this trust to the 12-step group. The clients should attend as many meetings as possible while in treatment. Gradually, the clients will feel safe and will begin to share. This builds trust. As the group, members are interested in a client, and as they show love to the client, the client's confidence in the group grows. This probably is the first time in the client's life when he or she has told someone the absolute truth. When the group does not abandon the client, it is a tremendous relief. This will show on the client's face and will be etched into his or her heart.

Clients see people further along in the program doing better. These people look better and sound better. The clients cannot miss the power of the group process. It changes people right in front of their eyes. They will see new members come in frightened or hostile, and they will watch them turn around. They will watch the power of group support. Soon they will be offering new clients encouragement. They will learn how helpful it is to share their experiences, strengths, and hope.

Once clients see how insane they were acting and accept that the group has the power to restore them to sanity, they have come a long way toward embracing Step Two. By trusting the group, the clients open the door to a Higher Power. This basic building block of trust is vital to good treatment. Clients can miss seeing a Higher Power in others. These clients, on discharge, might feel that a Higher Power is the only answer they need. They might think that they do not have to go to meetings so long as they have a good spiritual program. These clients will not work a program of recovery, and they ultimately will relapse. All clients must be encouraged to trust the group process. They need other people to flag for them what they do not see in themselves.

Step Three

"[We] made a decision to turn our will and our lives over to the care of God *as we understood Him*" (AA, 2001, p. 59). Read the Step Three exercise (see Appendix 19) before continuing with this chapter.

Most clients will have some difficulty with Step Three. They need to be reminded to turn problems over to their Higher Power. Addicts are self-centered, and they need to learn how to be God-centered. Clients can be so self-centered that they constantly set themselves up for unnecessary pain. They think that the whole world, and everyone in it, should revolve around them. When people do not cooperate with their self-aggrandizing plans, they are furious. They think that their spouses, children, and friends always should obey their every whim. Previous relationships in which their partners have been involved are seen as humiliating and self-degrading. They believe that everything should go exactly the way in which they want it to go. They believe that they are deserving of special honor and privileges. They care very deeply about what they want and how they feel, but their ability to empathize with others is seriously impaired (B. Carr, personal communication, 1992).

A client might get furious when someone does something simple such as turn up the heat or fail to fix the car. When the world does not cooperate by doing exactly what the client wants, he or she goes into a rage. A more serious form of this character defect is called narcissistic personality disorder.

Clients correct this defect by learning empathy for others and turning their will and their lives over to the care of a Higher Power. Our program is a set of spiritual principles through which we are recovering from a seemingly hopeless state of mind and body (NA, 1988, p. xvi).

The worst thing that you can do is push clients faster than they are ready to go. The decision to turn things over is the clients' decision. All you can do is encourage them.

You have one big thing going for you in Step Three. When the clients finally do turn things over, they feel immediate relief. They feel this relief emotionally, and this is the most powerful way of learning. They will feel that the stress of trying to figure out the problem is reduced. The pressure will be off, and they will feel better. Nothing works better than to show the clients how this tool of recovery works. If you give a chemically dependent person a good feeling, then he or she will want to re-create the feeling. That is what the person was doing with chemicals—seeking immediate relief from pain. The Third Step is the new answer that clients have been waiting for. They must experience it to believe it.

Many clients will stubbornly resist Step Three. Even people who have been in the program for years have difficulty with Step Three. Meetings are full of people talking about turning over the controls and then taking them back. Step Three is a decision that must be made every day.

There is a great hope here for clients in Step Three, and they will feel it. If there is a God, and if God loves them and will help them, that is great.

This newfound hope must not be shattered by religion. Religion can make people feel excluded. Religious doctrine must be kept out of the program as much as possible. If clients want to use a religious structure, that is encouraged so long as it does not immerse them in guilt and remorse. The Higher Power is presented to the clients in an atmosphere of forgiveness.

How to Help Clients Embrace Step Three

The key to Step Three is willingness. Once clients are willing to seek a Higher Power of their understanding, they have come a long way toward completing Step Three. The clients will find relief in talking about a God that loves them and forgives them.

When you hear clients say that they are willing to turn it over, you can tell them that they are well on their way to recovery. The problems might not be solved immediately, but the clients are moving in the right direction.

Clients need to trust and turn things over to the group. The group has more collective wisdom than the client, and the group members can be helpful in solving problems. As the clients use the power and support of their group, they are learning about how to turn things over to their Higher Power.

Some clients have serious problems with the word *God*, and that is fine. They do not have to use the word if they do not want to. Many clients have had the word *God* crammed down their throats for so long— since they were children—that they are sick of it. If you try to do the same thing, then they will revolt. Remember that even God gives total freedom of thought and action.

Step Four

"[We] made a searching and fearless moral inventory of ourselves" (AA, 2001, p. 59). Read the Step Four exercise (see Appendix 20) before continuing with this chapter. Much of this exercise was developed by Lynn Carroll during his years at Hazelden and at Keystone Treatment Center.

Step Four is where clients make a thorough housecleaning. They rid themselves of the guilt of the past and look forward to a new future. Detail is important here. You must encourage the clients to be specific. They must put down exactly what they did. The clients will share their Step Four with someone of their choice in Step Five. They will go over the assets part of the Fourth Step in group. The assets part of the Fourth Step allows the clients to share the good things about themselves with their treatment peers. This keeps them from decompensating into a negative attitude. Step Four can be very painful for many clients, and they must be encouraged to look at the good parts of themselves.

Step Four was developed directly from spiritual principles. To get rid of guilt, if someone admits his or her wrongs and asks God for forgiveness, then God wipes the slate clean. You should discuss the grace of the God with your clients. They need to know that there is no way of earning God's forgiveness. God offers it free. God wants to set us free and give us an opportunity to start over again.

To do this, clients must be honest. They must share their wrongs with God, with themselves, and with one other person. The other person is necessary because clients need to see a nonshaming face respond to their wrongs. Remember that the illness has been telling them that if they tell anyone the whole truth about themselves, then they will be rejected. The only way of proving this to be wrong is to do it. The clients no longer will be excessively burdened with guilt if they do their Steps Four and Five properly. They might have a difficult time forgiving themselves, but God will forgive them. Faith can do for them what they cannot do for themselves.

There will be a tendency for clients to leave things they consider bad out of the Fifth Step. The "Big Book" (AA, 2002a) says that this is not a good idea. "Time after time, newcomers have tried to keep to themselves certain facts about their lives. Trying to avoid the humbling experience, they have turned to easier methods. Almost invariably, they got drunk" (AA, 2002a, pp. 72–73).

Clients are encouraged to share everything that they think is important no matter how trivial it might seem to be. If it causes them any degree of guilt or shame, then it needs to be examined. The clients need to come face-to-face with themselves. All of the garbage of the past must be cleaned out. Nothing can be left to fester and rot. The clients who leave things out will feel unforgiven.

The Fourth Step is where clients identify their character defects. Once identified, the clients can work toward resolution. Clients often will come upon material suppressed for years. As memory tracks are stimulated, deeper unconscious material will surface.

Clients need to concentrate on the exact nature of their wrongs rather than accuse or blame other people. This is a time to take full responsibility. They do not make excuses. They ask for forgiveness. Yes, there likely were mitigating circumstances, but this is not a time to find out who was right and who was wrong. It is the time to dump the guilt and the shame.

The illness of addiction projects on the screen of a client's consciousness his or her wrongs. This makes the client feel bad. By drowning in his or her guilt and shame, the client cannot pull free. The client wallows in self-pity.

Clients who get too depressed doing their Fourth Step need to stop and concentrate on their good qualities. They are not all bad. They need to be shown that they are valuable persons who deserve to be accepted and loved. They have done many good things in their life and they need to focus on these attributes. Some clients might have to wait quite a while before doing their Fifth Step. Absolute honesty is a requirement of their readiness.

Some clients are so used to being negative about themselves that they cannot come up with their assets. These clients need to have the group help them to see the positive things about themselves.

Step Four must be detailed and specific. The clients must cover the exact nature of their behavior. This is the only way for them to see the full impact of their disease. They should not color their stories to make themselves seem less guilty or responsible.

Most of all, Step Four, like all of the steps, is a time of great joy. The clients finally face the whole truth about themselves. The truth is that they are wonderful creations of God. As they rid themselves of the pain of the past, they are ready to move forward to new lives filled with hope and recovery.

Step Five

"We admitted to God, to ourselves, and to another human being the exact nature of our wrongs" (AA, 1976, p. 57). Read the Step Five exercise (see Appendix 21) before continuing with this chapter.

Your job in Step Five is to help a client match up with the right person with whom to share the Step Four inventory. Who this person is and what he or she is like is vitally important. This person stands as a symbol of God and all of the people on Earth. This step directly attacks the core of the disease of addiction. If it is done properly, then the client will feel free of the past. The person chosen should be in the clergy, if possible, because a minister better symbolizes a Higher Power. Someone else in the program will do if he or she is chosen carefully and has a good spiritual program. The person chosen needs some experience in hearing Fifth Steps, and this person must have an attitude of acceptance and unconditional positive regard. The person must be nonjudgmental and strictly confidential. It is helpful if this person is working a 12-step program. The person should not look uncomfortable when the client is sharing sensitive material. If this person looks uncomfortable, then the client may take this negatively. The client needs to see a nonshaming face.

The purpose of the Fifth Step is to make things right with the self, with others, and with God. Clients should see themselves accurately—all of their positive and negative points—all at the same time. At the core of the illness of addiction is this firmly held belief: "If I tell anyone the truth about me, they will not like me." This is not accurate, but the clients have been living as if it were true. They have not been honest with themselves and others for a long time—perhaps since childhood. They have pretended to be someone else to get the good stuff in life. The only way of proving to people that this held belief is wrong is to show them. This is the purpose of having another person hear the Fifth Step. If this person does not reject the client, then the belief is proved wrong. A new accurate thought replaces the old one: "I have told someone the truth, and that person still likes me." This is a tremendous relief to the client, who has been living his or her life convinced that he or she was very unacceptable to others. This is a deeply held conviction, and it causes great pain. The client must come to realize that unless he or she tells the truth, the client never will feel loved.

In the Fifth Step, clients must come to realize that they are good people. They have made mistakes and have done bad things. However, they are not bad; they are good. God will forgive them, and they can forgive themselves. They can start over, clean and new. Clients have varying degrees of spirituality and religious beliefs. You and the clergy must help the clients see that forgiveness has taken place. All religious systems provide for the forgiveness of sin.

Many clients will be tempted to hold something back in their Fifth Step. They do not want to share some part of their past. They do not think anyone can understand. The clients must be warned against this tendency. If they hold anything back, then the illness is still winning. All the illness needs to stay in operation is something important kept secret. All major wrongs must be disclosed. The whole truth must come out. The clients must stop living double lives.

After the Fifth Step, most clients experience a feeling of relief. The truth sets them free. In time, the clients will need to process the feelings with you. Some clients feel no immediate relief, but if they are honest, then they feel the relief later. Sometimes this takes a little while to sink in. The Fourth and Fifth Steps are a profoundly humbling experience, but once they are over, there is a feeling of relief. The person giving the Fifth Step should be encouraged to end the step with a prayer asking for forgiveness. The person listening to the step also should end the session in prayer. The person who has heard the step should tell the client that he or she understands what the client has said, that God forgives the client, and that he or she believes in the client's basic goodness.

10 The Lectures

Source: ©iStockphoto.com/track5.

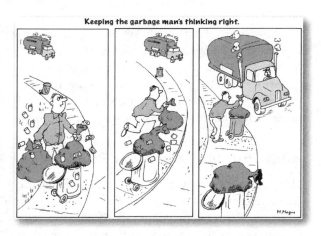

Once or twice a day, clients go to lecture. The lectures last 30 minutes to 1 hour. All professional staff members will take their turn in educating the clients about the various aspects of the program. The physician will lecture on medical aspects, the psychologist on psychological aspects, the dietitian on diet aspects, and so on. As the counselor, you will be responsible for lecture topics relevant to addiction. You can use any of the exercises in this book to come up with your speech. If the clients hear the material more than once, that is better at first they have a difficult time remembering material and it should be repeated. Each of the 12 steps should be presented in lecture. Other topics might include the disease concept, spirituality, relapse prevention, feelings, relationship skills, communication skills, impulse control, anger management, stress management, and defense mechanisms, to name a few.

Many of these topics have been discussed already, and it would be redundant to present them again. You can use any of this information in developing your lecture program.

The lecture schedule should be flexible enough to allow for something that the current client population needs. You should read the "Big Book" and *Twelve Steps and Twelve Traditions* (Alcoholics Anonymous [AA], 1976, 1981, 2002a) to round out your lectures. It is not difficult to talk to the client population, and you soon will learn to breeze through the lectures. Those of you who are frightened of public speaking will need to make an outline of each talk and follow it carefully. The structure will give you the confidence you need and soon you will be speaking like a trained presenter. PowerPoint presentations or using a blackboard is also very helpful. People learn best when using all parts of the brain, visual, auditory, tactile, movement, verbal, interpersonal, intrapersonal, musical, nature, feeling, reading, and writing. The more parts of the brain you can use, the more people will acquire the information. Some people learn best through movement, some visual and some auditory. Make your presentations full of different kinds of stimulations and clients will learn better. If you can make people laugh, cry, and learn they will remember.

Examples of several lectures are presented in what follows, but it is important to develop your own personal style. You must use your creativity. Only the important points of each lecture are given. Your job is to fill in the lecture with examples and stories of your own. You can use some of your own stories or stories that you have learned from clients. The clients do not need to hear a lot of confusing research or references in these lectures. They will be less confused if you put forth the facts in a simple and straightforward manner.

The Disease Concept

This morning we are going to talk about the disease concept of addiction. It is important for you to know that you have an illness. *Dorland's Illustrated Medical Dictionary* (1965) defines disease as "a definite morbid process having a characteristic train of symptoms; it may affect the whole body or any of its parts, and its etiology, pathology, and prognosis may be known or unknown" (p. 428). During the late 1940s, E. M. Jellinek began to study alcoholism in more than 2,000 members of AA. He found that alcoholism had a characteristic set of signs and symptoms and that it had a definite progressive course. In 1956, the American Medical Association formally recognized alcoholism as a disease. Up until that time, medical science, and society in general, thought that someone who was chemically dependent was a person with a moral problem or someone with a weak will. The American Psychiatric Association has also classified substance abuse and dependence as a disease.

This illness has a certain set of signs and symptoms. It has a particular treatment and course. Not one of you asked to be chemically dependent. It is not your fault. You should not feel guilty. That would be unduly hard on you. You would not blame someone for having cancer or heart disease, even though some of their behaviors may have contributed to their disease. If you eat a certain way or smoke cigarettes, then you increase your chances of coronary artery disease. If you drink or use drugs, then you increase your chances of becoming chemically dependent.

Addiction Is Not a Moral Problem

Many years ago Americans thought of drinking, drug abuse, and gambling problems as a weakness of moral character or a weakness of will. The addict was considered too weak or inadequate to say no to the addictive behavior. Today, animal experiments and experiments with humans have shown that an addict's brain is a changed brain. Scientists found out that animals will press a lever and ignore all other survival behaviors to stimulate with an electric current or a drug that stimulates the ventral tegmental area (VTA) area and the nucleus accumbens in the midbrain, which exists to help the organism survive. This area takes precedence over all other higher levels of the brain, such as thought or choice. This center produces dopamine, which tells the organism that engaging in a survival behavior, eating, sex, drinking, avoiding predation, and even killing is pleasurable. This area is so powerful that an animal will press a lever to get an electrical stimulation or drug stimulation, avoiding all other survival behaviors, to the point of death. In other words, the animal chooses a drug over food to the point of starvation. Over time, the drug takes the highest level of survival behaviors. The organism choses the drug first and sees the drug as the most important for survival. For an addict the drug equals survival. Drug dopamine spikes in the midbrain are far higher than normal pleasure spikes such as eating or sex so in time the addict only feels pleasure when using drugs. All other survival behaviors feel pleasure less. Chronic addiction leads to long-lasting changes brain tissue to the point that voluntary control is undermined. Recent imaging studies have revealed changes in brain activity that are important for normal motivation, reward, and inhibitory control are changed in addicted individuals. This provides the basis for the idea that addiction is a disease of the brain and addicted behavior is the result of dysfunction of brain tissue. Dopamine extends to the frontal cortex telling the brain that the drug is the most important behavior—so important that the prefrontal cortex uses glutamate to make a hypermemory of drug use. The drug and everything surrounding the drug and drug use is laid down as a superhighway in the brain. In time, the conscious part of the prefrontal cortex that inhibits drug use goes offline (hypofrontality), and all inhibitory control is lost. The addict cannot say no to drugs because to do so signals death (McCauley, 2009; Volkow & Li, 2009). The addict can still choose not to use for short periods of time under intense threat or incarceration, but they can't choose not to crave, and craving is miserable, suffering, and automatic. It always leads the addict back to the only thing that will help him or her survive. Every counselor and patient needs to watch the video *Pleasure Unwoven* by Kevin McCauley (2009). This is a wonderful DVD that beautifully shows why addiction is not a choice but a disease.

Addiction Is Not Due to a Weak Will

Please do not think that a weak will had anything to do with your addiction. We find that addicts are incredibly strong and resourceful people. More than 90% of chemically dependent persons are able to keep functioning even when they are deathly ill. You know how it goes. You come to work and you have this incredible hangover, your head is throbbing, and you feel like you are going to throw up. Your coworker comes in and asks how you are doing. "Fine," you say cheerfully. You are there, you feel terrible, but you made it to work. That takes a strong will.

Addiction Has Genetic Components

There are no medical diseases other than microbes that do not have powerful genetic links. We all are genetically predisposed to certain physical and mental illnesses. We are more likely to acquire the same diseases that the members of our families have had. Cancer, hypertension, asthma, diabetes, and coronary artery disease run in families; depression and anxiety run in families; and addiction runs in families. For example, cells are programmed at birth to do certain things when alcohol is in the body. Many sons of alcoholics need to drink more before they feel intoxicated. They have a programmed need to drink more before they get the same effect. You may have noticed in your drinking or drug use that you could use more than other people could. This is because some people who are predisposed to chemical dependency metabolize drugs differently. It seems that many people who are chemically dependent were predisposed to the illness before they were born (Anthenelli & Schuckit, 1994; Volkow & Li, 2009; Woodward, 1994).

Addiction Is a Social Problem

To be chemically dependent, you need to use chemicals. This is a psychosocial issue. In some societies, drinking and drug use are not tolerated. For example, Muslims and Mormons have a strong religious belief against the use of drugs. They consider use to be a sin. There is less chemical dependency in these groups. In France, drinking is a regular part of life. It is not uncommon for a French person to have wine with breakfast, lunch, and dinner. Understandably, France has a higher incidence of alcoholism.

Addiction Is a Psychological Problem

Certain psychological factors also have to come into play. There is no specific addictive personality, but people do have to drink to become alcoholic. Drinking, using drugs, and gambling are highly reinforcing to some people, and to other people they are not. Not everyone who drinks or even uses drink a lot becomes an alcoholic. You have to like drinking to drink. All behavior, including addictive behavior, increases if it is reinforced. If the reinforcement is taken away, the addiction slows down and eventually stops. Addictive behavior makes a person feel good so finding out other ways to feel good decreases addiction.

Addiction is a biopsychosocial disease. It has biological components, psychological components, and social components. Two or more of these elements appear to be necessary for addiction to exist.

Someone has a drug problem if he or she continues to use a drug despite persistent physical, psychological, or social problems associated with that drug. Anyone who continues to use despite persistent negative consequences is an abuser. Obviously, if you get into trouble when you use chemicals, then you should not use chemicals.

Addiction Is a Physiological Problem

Addiction is characterized by tolerance and withdrawal symptoms. As you use cocaine, the cocaine tells your brain to wake up. The cells of your body gradually catch on to this abnormal wake-up signal, and they produce chemicals that tell the brain to go to sleep. The cells counteract the drug. Ultimately, it will take more of the drug to produce the same effect. As you take in more of the drug, the cells counteract even further. This is a vicious cycle called tolerance. You will find that you are using more of the drug now than when you started.

People who are addicted know it—at least on some level—and they try to cut down. They might change from beer to wine or from hard liquor to beer. They might decide to use only after 5 o'clock or only on weekends. They might even move or change jobs.

The Obsession

People who are having problems with addiction will find that more and more of their time is taken up using the substance. People first use cocaine once in a while. They occasionally use at parties. As their illness progresses, however, they find themselves using more often, during the week, even when they are alone. More and more of their time is spent in getting cocaine, using cocaine, and withdrawing from cocaine. The more they use, the more they need. The more they need, the more they use.

People who are chemically dependent find themselves intoxicated or hungover when they need to do something else. The homemaker might be high when she is supposed to be taking care of the children. She might be drunk at work. She might have to call in sick because she is too hungover to work. More and more, the disease takes over, usually over a long period. The drug becomes the center of the universe. Dinnertime revolves around those first drinks. There begins a morning hungover ritual and an evening get-high ritual. Eventually, the person gives up normal activities. The person does not go fishing or camping. The person quits school or is fired. Sexual activity decreases. Recreational activity decreases. With more time needed for the addiction, time with family and friends decrease. Any activity can go, but the addiction stays and grows more and more important.

The Problems

Eventually, problems begin to develop. There are social consequences caused by the addiction: problems with the spouse, problems with the law, problems at school, problems with friends, and problems with parents. The problems begin to mount, but the addict keeps dealing with the problems in the same way. The person gets relief the only way he or she knows how: with the addiction of choice. The addiction becomes the addict's best friend. It is the only thing the person relies on for help. It always helps to ease the pain. It works, and it works every time.

By this time, people around the addict are complaining. They are warning that something is wrong. Someone might even have the unmitigated gall to talk to the person about the problem. When someone does this, the chemically dependent person hammers that person to the floor. "It is not my problem," the addict shouts. "It is your problem." The lies escalate, and the addict begins to be caught in a web of lies. People challenge the addict with the truth. All of this leads to more addictive behavior, and the cycle goes on.

Finally, some crisis breaks through the lies the addict has been telling himself or herself. Some glimmer of the truth seeps in, and the person comes into treatment. The person is still in denial. This person is still lying to himself or herself. The person still cannot see the full impact of the disease. But here this person is in treatment.

Most people who are addicts die because they never see treatment. Very few make it into treatment. Of those who do make it into their first treatment, most will achieve a stable program of recovery. They might have to come through treatment several times but you will abstain from the addiction, or you will die.

You will find treatment centers dedicated to the truth. We must tell the truth to get clean and sober. We must give up all that control we have been working on and turn our will and our lives over to the care of others. If you work this program, then you will find relief. If you hang on to your old ways, then you will live in pain. The choice is yours.

Defense Mechanisms

Today we are going to talk about where all the lies come from. How did we end up being such liars? In addition, we tell incredible lies. We lie when we think we have to, and we lie when we do not have to. We lie to get out of trouble, and our lies get us into more trouble. We lie to increase our pleasure, and we lie to wallow in our self-pity.

This illness must lie, and it must continue to lie, or it cannot exist. The illness cannot live in the light of the truth. You cannot tell the truth to yourself and continue to be an addict. With the truth, you would realize your problem and get some help for it.

All of the lies exist to protect us from a painful truth. The truth is that we are out of control, and if we keep up the addictive behavior, then we are doomed. The truth causes us great anxiety, so we defend ourselves from the truth. We distort the truth just enough to feel like nothing is wrong.

Source: ©iStockphoto.com/ YazolinoGirl.

Minimization

The first lie we tell ourselves is called minimization. This is where we take reality and make it smaller. We think the problem is not that bad. If an alcoholic takes an 8-ounce glass, fills it up with ice, takes a shot glass full of whiskey and pours it over the ice, and holds the glass up to the light, the alcoholic will be disappointed. A shot glass full to the brim with whiskey makes a disgustingly small splash in an 8-ounce glass.

If you are an alcoholic, you are not going to use a shot glass. If you have a shot glass at home, it is gathering dust. You are going to pour your whiskey until you see some color in that glass. Now, if we were to take this drink and measure how many shots are in it, we are going to find about four shots in the glass. Here is how we minimize. We think, and believe, that we are having one drink. However, it is not one drink; it is four drinks.

We can do the same thing with beer cans. If you are a beer drinker, you probably have a considerable collection of empty beer cans at the end of the week. When you take out the garbage, you have maybe two big plastic trash bags full of cans. As you are taking out the garbage, you may think, "Boy, I hope the garbage person does not think I am drinking all this beer." At that time, you may put one of the bags on your garbage pile, and the other one on your neighbor's pile.

Those who are into cocaine, remember when you have just picked up your stash. You have this nice big pile of cocaine on your kitchen table. You feel self-satisfied. You have more than enough. Your treasure chest is full. You are content. You feel a great peace. This is going to last a long time. However, the next morning, you are wondering who got into your stash. Where did it all go? You used it all; that is where it went.

We can minimize about our mounting problems. Everyone gets a couple of DWIs, right? Almost everybody gets a divorce. It is not so bad to spend a couple of nights in jail. We are good persons. We are not bad. We were just unlucky; the cops were after us. We take what is real and make it look smaller. We lie to ourselves, and we believe the lie.

Rationalization

The next lie we tell is called rationalization. This is where we have a good excuse. Probably the most commonly used excuse for drinking is "I had a hard day." It follows, then, that if I had such a hard day, I deserve to get blasted. Anyone who had the hard day that I had would need to relax. Let us have a few beers or a couple of joints. In rationalizing, we might blame our problems on someone else. "If you would just lighten up," we might say, "I could straighten things out." We might think remorsefully of all that we could have been if we had been born wealthy or been given the right breaks. We look at all of those successful people, and we hate them. We never had such a chance, we tell ourselves. There is no God. If there was a God, then where was God when we needed him?

Denial

The last type of lie that we tell ourselves—and this one is the most characteristic of addiction—is denial. Denial is a stubborn and angry refusal to see the truth. Here we refuse to see what is right before our eyes. We block out what is real until we really do not see it at all. The best way of showing you how this works is to give you an example. You are walking down the street on a very hot day. It is 95 degrees in the shade. Sweat is pouring down your face. As you walk up the road, watching the heat waves rise up off the asphalt, people are standing along the side of the road with pails full of ice water. As you pass each of them, they throw their buckets full of ice water in your face. In addition, when they dunk you they yell the following words: "Your wife's divorcing you! That is your third DWI! The boss will not put up with you anymore! You are in trouble with your parents again!" You see the pails of water, you see the people throw them in your face, and you hear the words that are shouted at you, but you do not experience the full reality of what is happening. You do not get the full emotional impact of the problems. With your whole life falling apart, you are walking up the street as if nothing was happening at all. The people around you are amazed. Why don't you see? Why don't you understand? Why can't you see what is happening to you? It is because you are denying reality. The mind has a way of cutting off the painful truth and living in a numb zone.

How to Begin to Live in the Truth

You cannot see what is happening to you because you are lying to yourself. You cannot see the truth because you believe the lies. You are completely fooled. In treatment, the full reality of what has been happening to you will be before you. It will be painful, but the truth will set you free. Treatment is an endless search for the truth, and you must be willing to listen to what others say. You must try to be open to what people tell you about yourself. We will reflect to each other what we see. We will try to find the truth together. What we cannot do alone, we can do together.

The Great Lie

It is important for you to know how the psychology of addiction gets going. During childhood, we come to believe in the great lie. This lie is at the core of addiction. We do not hear this lie from our parents or from our friends. We do not hear it from our teachers or from television. It is more powerful than that. We hear this lie inside of our own thinking, inside of that most personal part of ourselves. The lie is this: "If I tell people the whole truth about me, they will not like me."

Once we hear this lie and believe this lie, we know that we never will be loved for who we are. Therefore, to get any of the good stuff out of life at all, we have to pretend to be someone we are not. We try to be someone else. We watch those people who are popular, and we copy them. We are very careful about what kind of clothes we wear. We copy people's mannerisms and their fine little gestures. We find ourselves cocking our heads in a certain way when we laugh or smile. We are hoping to fool the people. We hope that they cannot see our real selves. We want them to see our pretend selves.

How the Great Lie Works

As this coping behavior occurs, it works. Some people do like us for the new selves we are trying to be. We become pleased to know that we are not going to be alone. The people we are fooling will love us. We begin to wear specific costumes and to play certain roles. We might wear the nice girl costume or the cowhand costume. We might wear the hippie costume or the yuppie costume. We know that it is a costume—we know it is not us—but the people are fooled and the lie goes on.

We Never Feel Accepted

You must look carefully at what is happening. We have fooled people into liking us, but they do not really like us. They do not know us. We are keeping who we are secret. As we keep doing this—making this effort to be loved—our emptiness grows and our pain increases. We try hard. We copy everyone who looks cool. We put on the best false front that we can, but in time we realize that it isn't going to work. We feel more and more lonely and isolated. We have known all along that we were not going to be loved, not for the real us. No one was going to love us.

The Promise of the Disease

When we are lonely enough in this process, when we are isolated enough, and when we are hurting enough, the illness comes along and offers us a smorgasbord of answers to our pain. Sex, money, power, influence, drugs, gambling, and alcohol all are there—and more—and we begin to feed from this cafeteria of behavior. For a while, things get better. All of these things relieve the pain for a little while. We find ourselves irresistibly drawn to this table of wrongs. We spend more time doing it. We eat, drink, stuff, cram, push, and shove. We find that more and more of our lives center on the use of these things. We get up on the table and stuff ourselves. We begin to lose our morals and values. We eat, consume, vomit, and stuff ourselves even more. In time, there never is enough. There is not enough sex. There is not enough money. There is not enough power. There is not enough booze. AA says that one drink is too much and that a thousand never is enough.

Truth

Finally, you begin to get sick from this cafeteria of wrongs. You realize an awful fact: The answer is not in these things. It is a terrible point of grief when you finally realize that the answer is not in your drug of choice. This is not a happy time, but by now, you are addicted. You cannot stop. You might be addicted to sex, and you want to stop what you are doing, but you cannot stop. You might be addicted to money, and you want to stop chasing money, but you cannot stop. You want to stop drinking. You promise yourself that you will stop, but you cannot stop. You are addicted.

Somehow, by the grace of God, you finally come to treatment. Maybe you are ready to surrender. I hope so, because if you are not, then you are in for a lot more misery. If you are ready to surrender, and if you are ready to try something new, then this program is for you.

A Program of Rigorous Honesty

One of the things that you must be willing to do is tell the truth all of the time. Nothing else will stop the great lie. The truth will set you free. You are enslaved to your addiction, but the truth will set you free of your chains.

In treatment, probably for the first time in your life, you will have the opportunity to get honest. If you do not, and if you hold anything back, then you will return to chemicals. You do not have to tell everyone the truth, but there is a psychological law at work. The law is this: The more you can share, the closer you can get; the closer you can get, the more you can share. As intimacy grows, you tell more of the truth. In your Fifth Step, you will tell someone the whole truth at one time. You will tell that person exactly what happened. Time after time, we have had newcomers decide to hold something back in their Fifth Step. They did not want to tell that one thing. Invariably, these people get drunk because they do not prove to themselves that people will like them if they tell the whole truth. They keep the emptiness, loneliness, and isolation. The pain grows, and eventually they relapse.

It is vitally important that you find out the truth about yourself. God created you in perfection. You are God's masterpiece. You were created in the image of God. God loves you and wants you to be happy. For some of you, this will be difficult to hear and difficult to believe. How could God love you? Where was God when you needed God? If there is a God, then where is God? These are the questions that you will seek the answers to in this program.

Normal Development

Today we are going to talk about normal development and how things go wrong for addicts. As infants, we cannot see very well. Our eyes are developing, and everything looks hazy. An infant knows only when it feels comfortable and uncomfortable. When it feels uncomfortable enough, it cries. It cries out in the only way it knows how. This cry is at such a pitch and timbre that parents cannot ignore it. Those of you who have heard the cry of an infant have experienced the pain. The infant cries out into the haze, "Help me! Help me!" It is the only thing the infant can do to show he or she needs help. Without someone coming to help, the infant will die.

The Primary Caregiver

But out of the haze, someone comes, and that someone meets our needs, and we feel comfortable again. In healthy homes, this someone always comes, at all hours of the day and night, and as we grow older, this someone has a particular sight, sound, taste, and smell. Later still, it has a name—mother.

A great trust develops between mother and child. We learn that whenever we cry out, mother will come. It happens repeatedly. It happens every time, and we learn to trust in mother. She is always there.

The Struggle for Independence

As we grow older, we begin to struggle for independence. We begin to do things for ourselves. We reach out and grasp things. We learn language, and we ask for things. During the second year, we learn the power of the word *no*. Mother can be all ready to go home, she can have her hands full of packages, she can be walking out the door, and we can say no. Oh, the power of that word. The whole world seems to stop and revolve around us. "No!" People get very upset with that word. It is very powerful.

The Fear of Abandonment

Somewhere between 3 and 5 years of age—and this depends on the maturity of the child—we learn a terrifying fact: Other people can say no, too. This fact strikes terror in a child's heart. We know that we need other people for survival. What will happen if we cry out in the night and someone does not come? We develop a new fear—the fear of abandonment. We never get over this fear. We carry it with us for the rest of our lives. It is the fear of life and death itself. When something goes wrong in our lives, this fear can come back very intensely. Lovers and spouses panic when one partner attempts to leave the other. They fear that if that person leaves, then they will die. You hear them say things such as "I cannot live without her" and "I cannot live without him."

Learning the Rules

As a frightened child, we go to our parents and search out an answer. "Mom, Dad, how can I be sure that when I cry out you will always come?"

"These are the rules," the parents say. "These are the rules about how to be a good boy and a good girl. If you obey the rules and you cry out, we will come. But if you are a bad boy or girl, and if you break the rules, we might not come." As a child, we nod our head reverently. We want to live!

The Development of Insecurity

Now the parents hit us with a crippling blow, and from this blow, we will get another new feeling—insecurity. They do not tell us all the rules. The rules are too complicated, and the rules keep changing. Sometimes things are against the rules, and sometimes they are not. Sometimes we are punished for things, and sometimes we are not punished for the same things. We spend the rest of our lives trying to learn the rules. In every situation, the rules are a little different. It is very complicated, and it causes a great deal of anxiety.

The Peer Group

As we move out of the home and into the peer group, things are very different. The peer group does not love us just because we are a part of the family. The peer group loves us because we have a function. We are a good leader or a good follower, we are funny, we laugh, we are strong, or we are loyal. If we do not have a function in the group, then we are rejected.

Little boys and little girls are very different by this age. Boys struggle for power, and girls struggle for connection. Boys work to control, and girls work to cooperate. Boys work at being the ones who can solve the problem, and girls work toward who is the closest to whom. It is not that either of these personality styles is better or worse. They are just different. Both are necessary for healthy family roles.

If we have been told how wonderful we are every day of our lives, then we might be ready for school by 6 years of age. In the best of circumstances, school is a struggle. It is a very new situation with a new set of rules. We are not rewarded for our individuality or our creativity. We are rewarded for our ability to cooperate. We are supposed to be quiet and stay still. It goes against everything that a child is, but we try to cooperate, we try to be quiet, we try to stay still. We remember that we do not want to be abandoned.

Adolescence

Adolescence is a time of great change. There is a huge hormone dam. It leaks, cracks, and finally breaks, releasing a flood of chemicals into our bodies. These hormones say one thing—mate. They say this loud and clear. We begin to mate in our dreams, in class, and in every waking moment. The opposite sex becomes exciting, irresistible, and new. We try even harder than ever to fit in, because with all these changes going on it is even more critical to be accepted. We struggle to fit in much more than we struggle for our individuality.

Society tells us to prepare to leave our parents, who have been at the very core of our survival. We begin to question the morals and values of our parents. We begin to make decisions on our own. We prepare ourselves for the commitment of adulthood. We must know who and what we are. We try out many different things in an attempt to find ourselves.

For most chemically dependent persons, it is here, during early adolescence, that chemical use gets going. Here we first try chemicals, and they make us feel good. Soon we begin to use chemicals to deal with our problems. Here is where our emotional development stops. If we treat our feelings with chemicals, then we do not learn to use our feelings to solve problems. If we continue to use mind-altering chemicals, then we do not have our real feelings anymore. Most chemically dependent persons are emotionally stuck in adolescence. They still do not know how to use their feelings appropriately to solve problems.

Adulthood

The dividing line between adulthood and adolescence is the ability to make long-term commitments. Adults are emotionally stable and mature. They can commit to career, family, and home. They can build a nest and rear healthy young. Adulthood should really be a long, smooth ride. It is a gradual building of knowledge and skill. Financial problems fall to the wayside as we reach our full economic potential.

Somewhere during our 60s, the decision comes: Should we retire? If we like our work and if it gives us joy, then of course we should keep working. If we do not like our work, then we should retire and do something that we do enjoy. We deserve it.

During later life, there inevitably will come a time of terminal illness. We will acquire a disease from which we will not recover. This usually is coronary artery disease or cancer, but it can be many others. If we are close to God, then this is not such a scary time. We will have the hope of eternal life. If we do not know God, then this time may be more difficult. However, in normal life, everyone dies.

We have discussed the normal life cycle, and we have seen where it usually goes wrong in addiction. The illness can occur at any stage in life, but it usually gets started in adolescence. The moment we begin to use chemicals to excess, we cannot live a normal life. It is impossible. We cannot use our feelings in real time, and with real people, to solve life's real problems. In treatment, you will learn the skills necessary for living a normal life. These are the tools of recovery. If you learn these skills, then your life will stabilize and you ultimately will live a normal life again.

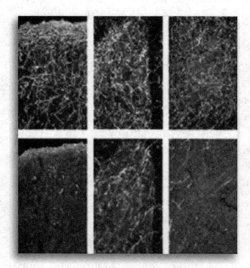

Source: From "Long-Lasting Effects of Recreational Drugs of Abuse on the Central Nervous System", by U.D. McCann, K.A. Lowe, & G.A. Ricaurte, 1997, *The Neuroscientist, 3,* 399–411.

Physical Addiction and Recovery

This morning we are going to talk about the physical changes that occur in addiction. The cell is the basic building block of the body. It has a cell wall that protects the cell from harm, a nucleus that is the brain of the cell, and a variety of other specialized parts with specialized functions called organelles. The nucleus is made up of deoxyribonucleic acid, or DNA, and it decides how the cell is made and how the cell works. It is the manager of the cell in the same way as the brain manages your body. The cell wall is an actively selective membrane that chooses what comes into and out of the cell.

How Drugs Affect the Cell

Drugs pass through the cell wall in a variety of ways and influence how the cell operates. This is a very involved process, and we do not know exactly what each drug does. What we do know, however, is important, and you must understand some of this in your recovery program. Alcohol is a drug. One of its effects is that it dehydrates protoplasm. It sucks water out of the cell. This prevents the cell wall from operating properly. This happens in every cell in the body, but it has its most noticeable effect on the central nervous system (CNS). It suppresses higher cortical centers in the brain. This reduces people's normal ability to perceive the environment. It tells the brain to go to sleep. This inability to perceive accurately makes us feel less inhibited. We lose the normal constraints that the world puts on us. We miss the subtle cues. It makes us feel free.

The brain of the cell picks this up as a problem and changes things in the cell to correct the problem. Alcohol tells the brain to go to sleep. The cell tells the brain to wake up. At first, these changes are transient chemical changes or subtle changes in metabolism that will quickly return to normal after alcohol leaves the body. However, if the alcohol keeps coming, then the cell produces permanent changes in the cell wall. One way in which it does this is by making tunnels, or chloride channels, through the cell wall. This provides for easier transport of atoms across the cell wall. The more that alcohol stays around, the more of these chloride tunnels are needed.

How Drugs Affect Behavior

Now let us see what is happening to you behaviorally. You start drinking, and one beer gets you that feeling you are after. One beer is all that you need, but eventually, the cell produces those changes and you need two beers to get that same feeling. In a few weeks, or months, or years, you are going to need three beers, and then four, and five, and six, and so on. The more beer you drink, the more the cell corrects with those chloride channels. This is called tolerance. You need more and more of the drug to get the same effect. All chemically addicting drugs create this physiological pattern.

Tolerance

It is important for you to know that these changes in the cell may take years to develop, but once tolerance is there, it is there permanently. The cell never changes back completely the way it was before. It never forgets. That is why you never can use drugs normally again. You have developed permanent changes in the cells in your body. If you were drinking a fifth a day, staying sober for 20 years, and then start drinking again, you will be drinking a fifth a day within 30 days. It took you years to develop tolerance, but this time it is there already. This never will change. You can recover completely from some of the psychological and social effects of this disease, but you never can recover from the physical changes that have taken place in your cells. Your cells never forget.

Cross-Tolerance

This is why cross-tolerance is such a problem. Alcohol, pot, sedatives, and sleeping pills all tell the brain to go to sleep, and the cells counteract that drug in some of the same ways. If you develop tolerance for one of these drugs, then you will develop tolerance for all of them. You cannot leave treatment and say to yourself, "Well, I am sure glad I got that alcohol problem licked, but I never had any problem with pot. I can have a little pot now and then." This would spell disaster for you. Taking a little pot is like taking a little alcohol because of the cross-tolerance.

What we find in addiction treatment is that once you are addicted to one mood-altering chemical, you are addicted to all of them. You have learned things physically, psychologically, and socially that will cross over to any other mood-altering chemical. If your drug of choice is whiskey, and if you go out of here and smoke a little dope, then you will be back to the whiskey very soon.

Withdrawal

The cells produce all of these short- and long-term changes to counteract what the drug is doing, so you can guess what happens when the drug is removed. All of these cellular changes are still there and the drug is gone. The cells are producing wake-up signals to the brain to counteract the go-to-sleep signals that the alcohol is producing, and all of a sudden, there is no alcohol. What happens is called acute alcohol withdrawal. The cells are screaming for you to wake up, and no alcohol is telling you to go to sleep. Acute withdrawal has been driving alcoholics to the liquor store every day. They go to sleep under the effects of alcohol and in a few hours, they wake up feeling nervous and restless. They cannot sleep. Their stomachs feel upset. They have headaches. Their hands shake. All of these are withdrawal symptoms.

Some of you learned that what you needed was a drink or a Valium to get you back to sleep, but if you have that drink or that pill, then the cycle starts all over again. Acute withdrawal is not fun. It produces the opposite effect of the drug that you are using. If you were using a sedative drug, then withdrawal will tell you to wake up. If you were using a stimulant drug, then the withdrawal symptoms will tell you to go to sleep.

The length of acute withdrawal differs depending on the drug you were taking. With alcohol, withdrawal usually is over within a few days. With cannabis or certain other benzodiazepines, it can be weeks or even months. Once acute withdrawal is over, protracted withdrawal extends the problems for about 2 years. Protracted withdrawal is characterized by random mood swings, sleep problems, and generalized feelings of stress. These symptoms will wax and wane over the next few months. Do not think that you are crazy or think that anything is wrong. Just recognize the symptoms for what they are (Geller, 1994).

The first 3 months out of treatment will be the hardest for you because of the extended withdrawal syndrome. This is where people tend to relapse, so do everything in your power to work a daily program of recovery in early sobriety. The daily program will put hurdles in the way of the first use.

How We Learn

Drug use is a habit. We get into the habit of drinking or using in certain situations or when having certain feelings. A habit is some movement or thought that is so practiced that it has developed a nice smooth pathway in the brain. Whenever we even randomly approach that area in the brain, we are very likely to take that pathway because it is so well traveled and easy to follow.

You have developed certain habits in your drinking or drug use. You might use when you celebrate, or when you feel angry, or when you are frightened or sad. You might always drink after work or always drink a certain kind of beer. These pathways in your brain are well developed. What treatment is all about is teaching you to get what you want by doing something else other than using your old behavior. It is a process of learning new behaviors. For example, if you want to feel less angry, then you will need to talk to someone about how you feel and try to work through the problem. The second you realize that you are on one of your old pathways, you need to stop and change direction. Drinking or drug use no longer is an option for you. You need to find other methods for dealing with your problems.

Alcoholics Anonymous

The idea behind AA got started in 1935. Bill Wilson, one of its founders, had gotten drunk again. He was at the end of his rope. He was afraid to go home. He was afraid he was going to kill himself. He hated himself. His spouse was still sticking by him, but he could not trust himself anymore. He had tried to quit drinking countless times, in countless ways, and he had always ended up drunk. Here he was in the hospital again. He did not know whether he wanted to live or die, but he knew that he did not want to live this way anymore. Medical science had given up on him as hopeless. He had nowhere to go. He was trapped.

A Spiritual Awakening

In his room alone, feeling very powerless, Bill looked up toward heaven, and he cried out, "If there is a God, show me. Give me some sign." At that moment, Bill's room filled with a great white light. He felt incredibly filled with new hope and joy. "It was like standing on a mountaintop with a strong clear wind blowing through me. However, it was not a wind of the air. It was a wind of the spirit." Bill felt like he had stepped into another world full of goodness and grace. There was a wonderful feeling of presence that he had been seeking all of his life. He never felt so complete, so satisfied, and so loved. Bill had finally surrendered, and when he surrendered, God came into his life. Notice that God came into his life with such power and force that Bill never denied God again.

Bill never took another drink, but his spiritual awakening did not fully resolve his problem. He still had a craving for alcohol. One day, he passed a bar and felt himself being pulled into it. He thought that if he could just talk to another drunk, he might be able to pull himself back together. He got on the phone and after making a few calls, he finally found one: Dr. Bob Smith. Dr. Bob was a hopeless alcoholic. He had destroyed his medical practice, and he was waiting to die. He reluctantly agreed to see Bill, but he had no hope that Bill could help him. Dr. Bob would have no nonsense. He had talked about his alcohol problem with the best, and now here was some other guy—a drunk—who was coming over to try to help him. He was in no mood for help.

Two Alcoholics Talking to Each Other

When Bill got there, Dr. Bob was surprised to learn that Bill was not there to keep him sober. "No," Bill said, "I am not here to keep *you* sober. I am here to keep *me* sober." Well, this was the new concept—one alcoholic talking to another to keep himself (or herself) sober. Dr. Bob was going to give Bill only a few minutes, but they talked easily, and Bill stayed for hours. Dr. Bob began to open up and speak as frankly as Bill was doing. Having common experiences, they could speak to each other without shame. They talked about the helplessness and hopelessness that they had been feeling—the feeling of total powerlessness. They talked about all of the problems that alcohol had caused them. Bill told Dr. Bob about the spiritual experience that he felt had saved him.

These two persons became great friends, and AA was born. They began to meet with other alcoholics. They began to carry the program to others. Dr. Bob got drunk one more time—when he was away at a convention—but when he returned he was more determined than ever to stay sober.

A bunch of alcoholics began getting together to help each other stay sober. To everyone's amazement, it worked. Hopeless cases began to recover. Of course, the group members had their setbacks, but the way to recovery had been found. The group would not have the name AA for 4 more years.

The Big Book

Bill dictated most of the first chapters to his secretary. He had considerable resistance when he came up with the 12 steps. Some of the group members were adamantly opposed to including so much God talk in the program. They did not want to scare drunks away with all of the spiritual talk. Bill listened quietly, but he knew that he was right. The only concession he made was to add the phrase "God, *as we understood Him.*" That made some members of the group feel more comfortable.

As the program developed and people began to stay sober, Bill was offered a job as the first alcohol counselor. A hospital wanted to incorporate the program and use it to help alcoholics. The group was opposed. Group members were afraid that it would make the program commercial and that this would destroy an essential element of the group. This time Bill agreed, and AA remained a free self-supporting program.

Another problem was money. The group needed money to pay for expenses and to reach out to alcoholics who were still suffering. They went to John D. Rockefeller, and he gave the group $5,000. They had asked for $50,000, but Rockefeller felt that financial backing would weaken the program.

With the individual stories written by the new groups, Bill completed the Big Book in 1939. The groups ordered 5,000 copies to be printed. They did not sell many until an article written by Jack Anderson appeared in the *Saturday Evening Post* (Anderson, 1941). This gave AA national exposure, and the mail began to pour in. AA now has more than 1 million members and has meetings all over the world.

The Twelve Steps

The program is made up of 12 steps. You will hear these steps read at every meeting:

1. We admitted we were powerless over alcohol—that our lives had become unmanageable.

2. [We] came to believe that a power greater than ourselves could restore us to sanity.

3. [We] made a decision to turn our will and our lives over to the care of God *as we understood Him.*

4. [We] made a searching and fearless moral inventory of ourselves.

5. [We] admitted to God, to ourselves, and [to] another human being the exact nature of our wrongs.

6. [We] were entirely ready to have God remove all these defects of character.

7. [We] humbly asked Him [God] to remove our shortcomings.

8. [We] made a list of all persons we had harmed and became willing to make amends to them all.

9. [We] made direct amends to such people whenever possible except when to do so would injure them or others.

10. [We] continued to take personal inventory, and when we were wrong promptly, [we] admitted it.

11. [We] sought through prayer and meditation to improve our conscious contact with God *as we understood Him*, praying only for His will for us and the power to carry that out.

12. Having had a spiritual awakening as a result of these steps, we tried to carry this message to alcoholics and to practice these principles in all our affairs. (AA, 2001, pp. 59–60)

There are many slogans in AA that will help you to reorganize your life and your thinking—slogans such as "one day at a time," "easy does it," "keep it simple," "live and let live," and "let go and let God." These slogans have great meaning, and they will help to keep your program on track.

Meetings

It is hoped that, after treatment, you will attend many AA or Narcotics Anonymous (NA) meetings. The more meetings you attend, the greater your chances of achieving a stable recovery. You need to ask someone further along in the program to be your sponsor. That person will guide you through the steps and will be there for you in times of need.

You will find this program to be a healthy family. The regular meeting that you attend will be called your home group. There is a stable set of rules. People will care about you. They will respond to how you feel. They will care for what you want. They will be there for you when you need them.

The choice is yours. We strongly recommend that you throw yourself into this program with all the enthusiasm and courage you can muster. Tell your group the truth. Do not hold back. AA says, "Rarely have we seen a person fail who has thoroughly followed our path."

Feelings

Most chemically dependent people have difficulty with their feelings. They do not know how to identify their feelings and do not know to use their feelings effectively. All feelings give us motivation. They give us specific energy and direction for movement. If you cannot use your feelings effectively, then you cannot adapt to the changes in your environment.

The reason why we, as chemically dependent persons, do not use feelings appropriately is we learned not to trust our feelings. We learned that there was something wrong with our feelings. We learned this from watching people respond to us when we were having feelings. When we were children and we were feeling afraid, we heard, "There's nothing to be afraid of." When we were angry, we learned that we were bad. "There's nothing to be angry about," our parents said.

Look at what this does to us as children. We begin to think, "I am having feelings that I shouldn't be having. I am afraid when there is nothing to cause me to feel afraid. I am angry when there is nothing to be angry about." We believe our parents. We can reach only one conclusion: Something is wrong with us. We are not feeling right, or we are having the wrong feelings at the wrong time.

We might be further confused when we get to school and are teased when we have feelings. The other kids tease us when we cry. They do not take us seriously when we are in love. We all know that feelings are one of the most basic things about us. It is one of the things that make us who we are as people. If there is something wrong with our feelings, then there is something wrong with us. "Something is wrong with me," we think. "I cannot trust myself."

Once we cannot trust who we are, we have to become someone else. We begin to search for that person who we want to be. We copy other people who we respect. We imitate various roles to see whether the roles fit us. Whatever we do, we do not share our feelings. We have been taught not to do that. We keep our feelings more and more to ourselves until sometimes we do not know how we feel anymore. Boys are not supposed to cry, so they get angry instead. Girls are not supposed to get angry, so they cry when they are angry. More and more, we separate from ourselves. We become more isolated.

All Feelings Are Adaptive

Each feeling has a specific action attached to it. Fear gives us the energy to run away. Anger gives us the energy to fight. Acceptance gives us the energy to move closer. You may have more than one feeling at the same time, and this can be confusing. However, if you break the feelings down into their basic units, then you always can figure out what the feelings are telling you.

There are eight primary feelings: (1) anger, (2) acceptance, (3) anticipation, (4) joy, (5) disgust, (6) sadness, (7) surprise, and (8) fear. More complicated emotions are combinations of the basic eight. For example, jealousy is when you feel sad, angry, and fearful all at the same time. When you feel jealous, you have to break the feelings down into their smaller units. Each feeling has to be identified and dealt with. What exactly are you frightened of, and what can you do to relieve your fear? What exactly are you angry at, and what can you do with your anger to make the situation tolerable? What makes you so sad, and what action can you take to help you feel more comfortable? As each of the feelings is addressed, you will have a more complete picture of the problem.

Remember that all feelings have movement attached. Fear moves you away from an offending stimulus; so does disgust. Sadness gives you the direction to recover the lost object. Anger gives you the direction to fight. Anticipation and surprise are orienting responses that prepare your body for action. Joy and acceptance give you the direction to move closer and stay with the object that gives you those feelings.

You must learn how to identify your feelings and use them to help you take action. It is a mistake to keep your feelings quiet. Sharing your feelings is an essential skill in interpersonal relationships. You cannot be close to someone if you do not know how that person feels and vice versa. You do not have to act on all of your feelings—that would not be wise—but you do have to process or deal with each feeling that is important to you.

Assertive Skills

In treatment, we are going to learn the assertive formula. This is an excellent way of dealing with your feelings appropriately. This is what we are going to say when we have an uncomfortable feeling:

I feel _____.

When you _____.

I would prefer it if _____.

Start by describing your feelings. That will be one or more of the eight feelings that we discussed. Then describe the behavior of the other person that triggered that feeling. Exactly what did they do or say that made you feel uncomfortable? Then tell that person what you would prefer him or her to do.

Let us say that your husband is an alcoholic and that he is 2 hours late from work. You are scared and angry. He could be drunk again. He could have been involved in an accident. He could be having an affair. Just as your worry reaches its peak and you begin to call the police, he comes home. Using the assertive formula, you would say, "I feel scared and angry when you come home late. I would prefer it if you would call me and let me know where you are." Now this statement gives him knowledge about how you are feeling, what he did to give you that feeling, and what he can do to improve things. This is good communication.

What if you feel as though someone in your group is in denial and lying to himself or herself? You might say something like this: "I feel sad when I hear you say you do not have a drinking problem. I would prefer it if you would try to see the truth about what you are doing to yourself."

In group, you will have people reflect your feelings to you. They are not trying to hurt you. They are trying to get you to see the truth. They might tell you that they experience you as mad or sad when you do not really know how you feel. It is important to listen to your group members and to try to see what they see. Maybe they can see a side of you that you cannot see.

It is vitally important for you not to feel ashamed of your feelings. You can have your feelings whether or not you have a good reason for having them. They do not have to be logical and make sense to be important. You will learn how to trust your feelings in treatment. You will learn that all of your feelings are great and wise counselors.

11 Special Issues

Source: ©iStockphoto.com/imbarney22.

There is a high comorbidity rate among psychiatric diagnoses and addition. These addiction have another set of specific problems that complicate treatment (Frances & Franklin, 1988; Mueser, Drake, Turner, & McGovern, 2006). If these clients are treated for their dual diagnoses, then their chances of recovery improve. If they are not treated for their secondary problems, then their chances of recovery are significantly reduced (Mueser et al., 2006; Ries & Miller, 2009; Woody et al., 1984). These clients need different treatment. For example, most clients are depressed when they enter treatment. For some of these clients, the depression is serious. Without treating the depression, these clients will be at greater risk for relapse.

One way of evaluating these clinical phenomena is to make a distinction between the primary and secondary diagnoses.

The disorder that occurred first is called primary, and the problem that appeared second is called secondary. When the disorder appearing first is abuse of substances, it is highly likely (but not always true) that the secondary problems will improve rapidly (within days or weeks) once abstinence is achieved (Schuckit, 1994).

The Psychiatric/Psychological Assessment

All clients need to be carefully screened for comorbidal problems during the initial assessment process. This screening must be done by a mental health profession with the special skills necessary for this examination. The assessment must include the following:

1. A systematic mental status examination with special emphasis on immediate recall and recent and remote memory

2. A determination of current and past psychiatric/psychological abnormality

3. A determination of the dangerousness to self or others

4. A neurological assessment (if indicated by the psychiatric/psychological assessment)

5. An evaluation of cognitive functioning including any learning impairment that might influence treatment

This assessment will signal to the staff problems that need further treatment. The mental health professional will flag for you serious psychopathology, but you still need to keep him or her informed if you believe that something else is going on other than addiction. You see the client on a daily basis, and you are the most likely to know when things are not going well. Sometimes more of the client's abnormal behavior will become evident as he or she moves through the treatment program.

How to Develop the Treatment Plan

Once the client is diagnosed with a secondary problem, the treatment team will develop a treatment plan. Sometimes you will not be formally involved in the treatment (the mental health professional may do it), but you will deal with the problem on some level, so you need special skills. If you ever feel that you are in over your head with a client, then you must inform the staff. You might need to refer the client for further consultation or treatment. Do not strike out on your own with these clients. Use the treatment team to guide you.

It would be beyond the scope of this book to cover all of the psychopathology that you will experience as a counselor, but we discuss what you will see most often. You should familiarize yourself with the latest edition of the *Diagnostic and Statistical Manual of Mental Disorders* (*DSM–IV–TR*) (American Psychiatric Association, 2000). Keep this manual close to you for reference. It is not your job to diagnose these clients, but you should be alert for the major problems you will see and become familiar with methodologies to treat the problems.

All of the major psychiatric diseases, like addiction, have a biological component, a psychological component, and a social component. You must consider all three parts of the problem in developing a treatment plan.

Some psychiatric diseases require Psychotherapeutic Medications (see Appendix 55). There is an old idea in 12-step programs that all medications are bad. This no longer is appropriate. Many clients need their medication to survive. For example, a certain type of depression is treated very well with antidepressant medication. If you deprive these clients of the treatment they need, then some of them will die. Fully 15%

of people who have serious depression eventually kill themselves (Hirschfeld & Goodwin, 1988). Many psychiatric clients need their medication for normal functioning. Let the physician make this decision. Once the decision is made to treat the client with medication, it is vital that you support this decision.

The Depressed Client

By far, the most common secondary diagnosis related to addiction is depression. Depression is a whole body illness that involves a client's body, mood, and thinking. It affects the ways in which clients eat and sleep, feel about themselves, and think about things. There is a consistently high rate of depression in substance abusers (Dorus, Kennedy, Gibbons, & Raci, 1987; Hesselbrock, Meyer, & Kenner, 1985; Nunes & Weiss, 2009). Most chemically dependent individuals will come into treatment with some degree of measurable depression.

Source: Andrea Morini/Thinkstock.

Excessive use of alcohol and other chemicals results in depressed mood. This depression can be organic, psychological, or interpersonal. You will first pick up depression in the mental status examination or in the psychological testing. Client depressed mood can range from mild to severe. The best way of measuring the severity is to use a psychological instrument such as the Hamilton Depression Rating Scale (HAM-D) (Hamilton, 1960) (see Appendix 30). The primary symptom of depression is the inability to experience pleasure. This is called anhedonia. Depression clouds the clients' whole lives. The anhedonia is persistent and pervasive. The clients feel numb as though life is dead. The joy is gone. They feel sad or down most of the day almost every day. They sleep poorly: They either undersleep or oversleep. Their appetites are off. They have a diminished ability to concentrate. They might feel helpless, hopeless, worthless, or excessively guilty. When people feel this bad, they might think that they would be better off dead. They may be suicidal.

How to Assess Depression

To assess depression, you will have the Hamilton score, the mental status examination, the history of the present problem, and the past history. The client is asked, "Have you ever felt sad or down most of the day, almost every day, for more than 2 weeks?" If the answer to this question is yes, then the client needs to see someone on the staff experienced in depression. As the counselor, do not try to evaluate the extent of the depression yourself. It gets complicated and takes quite a bit of diagnostic skill. You should be familiar with the types of depression listed in the *DSM–IV–TR*. Some depressions are chronic and mild, and some can be acute and life threatening.

How to Treat Depression

Depression can be treated by you if you work with the clinical team. Depression is treated in three ways: (1) with antidepressant medication, (2) with psychotherapy cognitive therapy behavioral therapy, and (3) with interpersonal therapy. If the clients are placed on medication, then you need to be supportive of these decisions and encourage the clients to comply. In behavior therapy, you will encourage the clients to change their actions. For example, you will help the clients to develop leisure time activities that will increase their opportunity to experience joy. What the clients do will change how they feel. In cognitive therapy, you will help the clients to correct their inaccurate thinking. In interpersonal therapy, you will help the clients to resolve interpersonal conflicts.

Psychopharmacology

The biology of depression is centered on a chemical problem in the brain. Certain neurotransmitter systems (e.g., norepinephrine, dopamine, and serotonin) become deregulated or out of balance. This chemical problem can be corrected chemically with medication. (For a complete list of all psychotherapeutic medication protocols, see Appendix 55.) There are four groups of antidepressant medications commonly used in treating depression: selective serotonin reuptake inhibitors (SSRIs), tricyclics, monoamine oxidase inhibitors (MAOIs), and lithium. Lithium, carbamazepine, and valproic acid are the current treatments for bipolar affective disorder. The doctor might have to try a variety of antidepressant medications or a combination of medications before finding the right one. Depression has strong genetic links, and certain genes predispose some people to manic or depressive episodes. Affective disorders can be caused by physical, psychological, or interpersonal problems, or they can occur without environmental precipitant. There is not always a psychological or social cause of the disease, but it always has psychological and social effects that need treatment.

If the physician decides to put the client on antidepressant medication, there usually will be a 3- to 6-week delay before the client begins to feel better. You must encourage the client during this period. Keep telling the client that the depression is going to get better. This encouragement will instill hope in the treatment and will increase client compliance. There are side effects of antidepressants that the client needs to discuss with the physician. Mostly, this will be mild sedation and an overall drying effect experienced as dry mouth, urinary retention, and constipation. Some of the newer antidepressants can cause an increase in anxiety, weight gain, loss of appetite, and sexual dysfunction. Be sure to chart any symptoms that the client reports and to discuss them with the clinical team.

Because it takes these drugs 3 to 6 weeks to work, you might not see the antidepressants take effect in every client. The client might respond only after he or she has left treatment. Once you see this change take place, however, you will be totally convinced. The dramatic effect that these drugs produce will win you over. They contribute in a major way to the treatment of depression.

Medication never should be the only treatment for depression. Studies have consistently shown that clients who undergo medication plus psychotherapy have a better prognosis (Beitman, Carlin, & Chiles, 1984; Conte, Plutchik, Wild, & Karasu, 1986; Ries & Miller, 2009).

The two major psychological treatments for depression are behavior therapy and cognitive therapy. In the biopsychosocial, you will try to uncover any psychosocial stressors that may have precipitated the depression. Certain depressions are caused by specific environmental events such as a death in the family or a divorce. If you can determine what caused or made the depression worse, then you will have come a long way toward knowing where to concentrate treatment.

Behavior Therapy

Behavior therapy of depression centers around teaching the client new skills and increasing positive reinforcers in the client's environment. This increase in pleasure-oriented activity elevates mood. Studies have shown that depressed people do not do fun things. They tend to sit and feel helpless, hopeless, and depressed. Your behavioral intervention will increase the clients' activities. You will have them begin an exercise program; increase social interaction with treatment peers; and become more involved in games, sports, and hobbies. You must be specific in what you are recommending, and you must make sure that the clients are following through with your recommendations.

Monitor depression with a weekly HAM-D. You can give this test daily if it is necessary. As the client gets better, the HAM-D score will drop.

A word about psychological testing is appropriate here. Testing will give you a general indication of what is going on. A test is not able to be certain about anything. The scores need to be considered in light of the total clinical picture. You need to trust your clinical judgment more than you trust a psychological test. If the tests show that the client is not depressed and you believe that he or she is depressed, you could be right. This issue needs to be discussed with the clinical team. You will make more accurate judgments together.

An increase in goal-oriented behavior is essential to behavioral treatment of depression. Depressed persons have a difficult time in doing anything, and they will need encouragement to set goals. If they need to increase their level of social interaction, then you can get them to go through a communication exercise with one or two peers each day. You can get them to play pool or cards with someone once a day. The recovery skills are very helpful here, and most of these clients will need to work through the recovery skills with you or with a treatment peer. Relaxation skills and stress reduction skills will be important to some of these clients. Depressed clients might need to learn assertiveness, communication, and social skills. You can work through these issues with your clients and come up with specific behaviors for the clients to learn.

In groups, depressed clients will need to be encouraged to talk in both individual and group sessions. They need to talk about how they feel, and they need to detail what they are going to do to feel better. You cannot let these clients ruminate about how bad they feel. They need to be encouraged to do something different. Have them go for a bike ride, take a walk, play basketball, play pool, swim, talk to someone, call a friend, become involved in a hobby, listen to music, read pleasant material, breathe the clean air, pray, meditate, eat something good, listen to the sounds of nature, give a gift, help someone in the program, do a job until it is well done, take a hot bath, or kick the leaves. You can have fun coming up with new ideas for them to try.

As the clients try these new fun behaviors, they will naturally begin to feel better. When they do, you need to reinforce them and show them that it is what they are doing that is influencing how they feel. You must chart the new behaviors and the responses of the clients. Place some quotations in their charts regarding what the clients say about their new behaviors.

Cognitive Therapy

Cognitive therapy concentrates on how a client thinks. This therapy was developed by Albert Ellis during the early 1960s (Ellis, 1962). It was further refined for depressed clients by Aaron Beck and colleagues (Beck, Rush, Shaw, & Emery, 1979). These researchers found that many depressed feelings come from negative self-talk. This tends to be inaccurate thinking, and it needs to be corrected. All clients who are depressed should read *Coping With Depression* (Beck & Greenberg, 1974). This monograph will explain cognitive therapy and will get the clients started.

Using the technique developed by Beck et al. (1979), the clients keep a daily record of their dysfunctional thinking. This is accomplished by having the clients write down each situation that makes them feel uncomfortable during the day. The clients need to be specific about this situation, stating exactly what happened that triggered the uncomfortable feelings. Then the clients make a list of each uncomfortable feeling that they had following the situation. Did the clients feel fear, sadness, disgust, or anger? Then the clients rate the intensity of each feeling on a scale from 1 (*as little of that feeling as possible*) to 100 (*as much of that feeling as possible*). These numbers are called subjective units of distress. Only the negative feelings are of interest to you. The clients add up the scores—the total of the subjective units of distress that they felt during the situation.

Now you help the clients to determine what they were thinking between the situation and the negative feelings. Ask the clients what they were thinking, and then be willing to make suggestions. The clients will not be able to come up with all of these thoughts by themselves because the thinking is out of their awareness. The thoughts that you are after are negative, and they lead directly to uncomfortable feelings. Pull for as many of these negative thoughts as you can, and write all of them down. This is uncovering the automatic thinking that occurred between the situation and the uncomfortable feelings. It must be emphasized that the clients do not try to think these thoughts. They are automatic and come without conscious effort.

Once you have a list of the negative thoughts and feelings, have the clients go back and develop accurate thoughts. Go over what happened again, and help the clients to decide what they should have been thinking. What would have been an accurate judgment of that situation? Once you have a list of the accurate thoughts, re-rate each of the feelings based on an accurate evaluation of the situation. You will come up with new subjective units of distress based on accurate thoughts rather than inaccurate thoughts.

The clients will be amazed at how their inaccurate thinking directly causes their uncomfortable feelings. The clients need to keep actively involved in cognitive therapy the whole time that they are in treatment. Each time the clients go through an uncomfortable situation, they need to keep a record of the thinking. In time, the clients will be able to catch themselves in inaccurate thinking, stop this thinking, and get their thinking accurate. Once the clients are accurate, they will feel much better.

An Example of Cognitive Therapy

Let us go through an actual cognitive therapy session. In this session, the counselor uses the first time that the client hears about interpersonal group as the situation that caused uncomfortable feelings. The first time that any client hears about this group creates quite a bit of anxiety. The client is Kim, a 17-year-old female who is rather shy and avoidant. Her Beck depression score is 24, which puts her in the severely depressed range.

The counselor introduces the cognitive therapy session.

Counselor: Kim, I want you to begin to get accurate in your thinking. When you do this, you will feel more comfortable. What we are going to do now is go through an actual situation and see if we can uncover some of your inaccurate thoughts. The first time you heard about interpersonal group, how did you feel?

Kim: Scared.

Counselor: How scared did you feel on a scale of 1 (*as little scared as possible*) to 100 (*as scared as possible*)?

Kim: I do not know.

Counselor: We're just going to guess. How scared do you think you were feeling on a scale of 1 to 100?

Kim: (*Pauses.*) About 85, I guess.

Counselor: Great, 85. How else were you feeling?

Kim: Oh, I do not know.

Counselor: Were you feeling angry?

Kim: No, I was not feeling angry.

Counselor: Were you feeling sad?

Kim: Yeah, I guess I was.

Counselor: How sad were you feeling on a scale of 1 (*as little sad as possible*) to 100 (*as sad as possible*)?

Kim: About 60.

Counselor: Good. How else were you feeling?

Kim: (*No response.*)

Counselor: Were you feeling surprised?

Kim: No.

Counselor:	Were you feeling any anticipation?
Kim:	No . . . I was feeling discouraged.
Counselor:	How discouraged?
Kim:	About 75.
Counselor:	Good. Now if we add up all those negative feelings, we get 230 subjective units of distress. When you hear about interpersonal group, you feel 230 units of uncomfortable feelings. Now, what were you thinking between hearing about interpersonal group and the feelings you felt? What thoughts ran through your mind?
Kim:	I will not fit in.
Counselor:	Great. What else were you thinking?
Kim:	I would be treated like an outcast.
Counselor:	What else?
Kim:	They will think I am a psycho.
Counselor:	Okay, what else?
Kim:	They will get the idea that I am not serious about treatment.
Counselor:	What else were you thinking?
Kim:	That is about it.
Counselor:	Were you thinking, "They're not going to like me"?
Kim:	Yeah, I was.
Counselor:	Okay, let us put that down. Were you thinking, "I would have to talk"?
Kim:	Yes.
Counselor:	Were you thinking, "They will make me talk about things I do not want to talk about"?
Kim:	Definitely.
Counselor:	Any other thoughts?
Kim:	They will not understand me.
Counselor:	Good. Now I have written down all of your automatic thoughts. It is important to recognize that these thoughts came to you automatically. You did not try to think these thoughts. They came on their own. You will find that before you have negative feelings, you will always have rapid thoughts before the feelings. This is where you make assumptions or judgments about the situation. It is where you internally evaluate the situation and how it directly applies to you. Do you understand?
Kim:	Yeah.
Counselor:	Good. Now we need to get accurate. Go back to the situation and think about it. You hear about interpersonal group. What is accurate thinking about that situation?
Kim:	They might be able to help me in group.
Counselor:	That is right. That is what they are there for. What else is accurate?
Kim:	I will not have to talk if I do not want to.

Counselor: Good. What else is accurate?

Kim: I would try to fit in. We all have problems in common.

Counselor: That is right. What else?

Kim: They will try to make me feel like a part of the group.

Counselor: Yes. What else?

Kim: They have some of the same problems as I do.

Counselor: That is very true. What else?

Kim: That is all I can think of.

Counselor: How about, "They will try to be supportive of me"?

Kim: Yeah, that is true.

Counselor: How about, "If I want to get help, I should try and share as much as I can"?

Kim: That is right.

Counselor: Okay, now let us go back and rate each of the negative feelings we rated before. You hear about interpersonal group, but this time you think accurately. You think, "They will try to make me feel like a part of the group. They might be able to help me. They will try to support me. They will try and understand me. I will not have to talk, but if I want help here, I should try and share as much of myself as I feel comfortable sharing." How much fear do you feel when you are thinking accurately?

Kim: About 20.

Counselor: How sad do you feel?

Kim: I do not feel any sadness.

Counselor: How discouraged?

Kim: About 5.

Counselor: Great. Now let's see. When you are thinking automatically and inaccurately, you score 230 units of distress. But when you stop and get accurate, you feel only 25 units of uncomfortable feelings. How do you feel about that?

Kim: That is amazing.

Counselor: Yes, it is. Many of these inaccurate thoughts come out of childhood. We judge situations automatically as if our inaccurate thoughts are accurate. No wonder you were feeling bad about interpersonal group. You were thinking, "I will not fit in. I would be treated like an outcast. They will think I am a psycho." What we are going to do over the next few weeks, Kim, is to keep account of each situation that makes you feel uncomfortable. Then we are going to uncover the inaccurate thinking that leads to your uncomfortable feelings. Then we are going to challenge these thoughts and get accurate. You need to live in the real world. You can no longer live in the painful world of your inaccurate thinking. You need to commit yourself to reality.

In cognitive therapy, you can decrease your clients' negative feelings substantially if you get the clients accurate. You must make this therapy formal. The clients will be unable to do this therapy on their own. They will not be able to uncover their inaccurate thoughts or to get accurate without your help. You will need to make suggestions. As the clients understand that they have been getting their depressed feelings from inaccurate thoughts, they will feel better and their depression will begin to lift.

As the clients bring in their dysfunctional thoughts, you will begin to see patterns in their thinking. Some of the same thoughts will come up repeatedly. These thoughts give the clients false information from which they make false assumptions. They collect the inaccurate thoughts and reach conclusions based on false information. These conclusions must be challenged with accurate information. It is not uncommon for clients to reach conclusions such as "I am stupid," "I am ugly," "I am unworthy," "No one will ever love me," "I am inadequate," and "Everyone is better than I am." They live their lives as if these false conclusions were true.

You will have some interesting therapy sessions with these clients. Many of their false assumptions are held onto quite rigidly. You might have to get the support of the group to help convince the clients that they are wrong. It is not uncommon for a strikingly beautiful person to think that he or she is ugly. Many clients will fight to hold on to their inaccurate opinions of themselves.

Trust in you and in the group is important here. The clients will need to trust others to make accurate judgments. This is difficult. The old ideas die hard; they seem to have lives of their own. With work, the clients will get more accurate. You should see the clients in cognitive therapy at least once a week. The more the clients keep up on their thinking, the more rapidly they will improve.

Interpersonal Therapy

Interpersonal therapy of depression has been outlined by Klerman, Weissman, Rounsaville, and Chevron (1984). This therapy seeks to heal interpersonal problems that leave the clients feeling depressed. For example, many clients will come into treatment with abnormal grief reactions. They have had a loss of a love object or self-esteem that they have not dealt with. Some clients are involved in interpersonal disputes. These unresolved conflicts leave the clients feeling lost and depressed. Some clients are in a role transition that they cannot deal with. Some clients are impoverished. They have no socially reinforcing situation from which they can gain pleasure.

Clients in interpersonal disputes will have to work toward resolving the interpersonal problems. In addiction treatment, you often will see spouses who are being rejected by their significant others. The drinking and drugging have taken their toll, and the spouses have left their relationships. The clients may come into treatment in a frantic attempt to save their relationships. These clients may feel hopeless and solely responsible for the problems.

Treatment begins with helping the clients to identify the problems. The clients need to plan what they are going to do. What are all of the possible actions that the clients can take regarding the problems? The clients will need to improve communication skills. They should work through the Relationship Skills exercise (see Appendix 11) and the Communication Skills exercise (see Appendix 13). They will need to practice these skills with their peers before they bring these skills into play in their current conflicts. If possible, you need to meet with the clients and the significant others to work toward resolution.

At times, the client will need only to renegotiate a dispute with a significant other. This is the easiest type of conflict to resolve. First, you need a commitment from each party to work on the problem. At times, there is an impasse, where one member of the couple is not willing to cooperate. You cannot do much here except to encourage the client to hope that in recovery this other person will change. Often a spouse needs to see recovery to know that it is real. Many marriages reconnect after a few months or years of sobriety. The client must understand that the other person has been devastated by the disease. It is the disease that is the problem. The best thing that the client can do now is to get into a stable program of recovery and turn the situation over to the Higher Power: "God, grant me the serenity to accept the things I cannot change, the courage to change the things I can, and the wisdom to know the difference."

Grief

Clients in an abnormal grief reaction need to work through the grief process. Normal grief is much like depression, but it lifts without treatment within 2 to 4 months. The persons gradually deal with the loss and move on with their lives. Sometimes the persons suffering a loss do not grieve until much later. This is a delayed grief reaction. They postpone the grief because they cannot deal with it at the time of its occurrence. Persons with a delayed grief reaction will feel numb at the actual loss. It is only later that they begin to experience the pain.

Some clients will drink or use drugs that prevent them from feeling the pain. Grief can be unresolved for years. When clients come into treatment with a significant loss of a close family member or friend, you must consider how they handled the grief process. Did they work the death through, or do they still need grief work? Is the issue resolved, or are the clients still stuck in the grief process? Many persons who have had abortions have unresolved grief.

Normal grief runs through a range of highly charged feeling states. The loss of a loved one leads to at least 1 year of disturbance, and 3 years of disturbance is not uncommon. Normal bereavement reactions include states of shame, guilt, personal fear of dying, and sadness. In normal grief, anger at the person who died, at the self, and at persons who are exempted from the tragedy are common. In pathological grief, the client becomes frozen in one or more of these stages for weeks, months, or years (Karasu, 1989).

People in the unresolved grief process need to talk about their grief. To accept the reality of their loss, they need to experience their pain. They need to talk about it in individual sessions and in group. They need to share the good and bad memories. They need to discuss the events prior to, during, and after the loss. They need to adjust to a new environment. This may include coming to terms with living alone, managing finances, learning to do the chores, facing an empty house, and changing social relationships. They need to begin to withdraw emotionally from the lost person, reinvest in new relationships, and acquire new interests to substitute for the loss. They need to be reassured that they have a program full of people, which makes it impossible that they ever will be lonely again. They need to see what they lost accurately, with all of the good and bad qualities. People who see only the good things will not work through the grief.

These clients need to develop new relationships in the program. They need to be encouraged to increase their social interaction with treatment peers. Do not let them huddle up in your office bemoaning their fate. Get people further along in the program to stick with them and keep them out with the client population.

Suicide

Most clients who are depressed consider suicide to relieve their pain. There is a 15% mean suicide rate in alcoholics (Talbott, Hales, & Yudofsky, 1988). Suicidal ideation begins with clients thinking that everyone would be better off if they were dead. Remember that the primary symptom of depression is the absence of pleasure. When all of life's pain remains and all of the pleasure leaves, it is logical for the clients to consider death. The incidence of suicide is about 20 times higher in drug abusers (Blumenthal, 1990). Clients who are a suicide threat will move through three phases of increasing lethality.

1. They will have increasing suicidal thoughts.

2. They will plan their suicide.

3. They will carry out their plan.

Your job is to recognize the process and reestablish hope. No clients commit suicide if they can see that they can live lives that have meaning and worth. All clients who are depressed need to hear that depression is an illness from which people recover. Depression is treatable and curable. The depression is not their fault. A sickness happened to them. It is not a punishment.

On the HAM-D, Question 2 assesses hopelessness and Question 8 assesses suicidal ideation. Both of these questions, when answered positively, should be taken seriously. The higher the score, the greater the risk.

In the mental status examination, all clients are formally assessed for suicidal risk, but you also can ask the suicidal questions anytime during treatment when you believe that they may be important. The questions are as follows:

1. Have you ever wanted to go to sleep and not wake up? (If the answer is yes, then ask the client about that. What was going on?)

2. Have you ever thought about hurting yourself? (If the answer is yes, then ask the client what was happening.)

3. If you were to hurt yourself, how would you do it? (If the client has a suicidal plan, then write it down.)

4. If the above answer is yes, have you carried any of that plan out? (Carefully assess any actions the client has taken to arrange for or to commit suicide.)

These four questions accurately assess suicidal risk in escalating order of severity. Clients who have suicidal ideation, have an active plan, and have carried out any part of the plan should be transported to a psychiatric unit. These clients are in danger of hurting themselves and need more structure. A psychiatric facility has rooms and wards that are specifically designed to reduce the possibility of suicide. Clients who are suicidal usually are afraid of themselves or are resigned to their death. Each of these signs is an ominous indicator of serious intent.

Most clients who come in for addiction treatment have thought about suicide but do not have an active plan. If they do have a plan, then they developed one outside of the treatment center. Clients who have been actively considering suicide and who have been considering a plan in treatment need to be transported. Do not leave these clients alone, not even for a second. Wait until you turn them over to the care of professionals.

Do not make decisions about suicidal clients by yourself. This is outside of your level of expertise. All of these clients need to be examined as soon as possible by a mental health professional. This covers you and your staff, and it will give you confidence in the decisions reached.

Clients who are experiencing suicidal ideation with no plan can stay in treatment. They will need extra support, and they will need to be watched more carefully than will other clients. You do not want these clients isolating themselves. You want them to be with people who are supporting and encouraging them. These clients need to feel that they are in a safe environment, and they need to be certain that the staff is going to respond to their needs. Once these clients begin to feel hope, their suicidal ideation will subside.

The Angry Client

Source: ©iStockphoto.com/JodiJacobson.

Anger and resentments are poison for chemically dependent persons. "Resentments is the 'number one' offender. It destroys more alcoholics than anything else" (Alcoholics Anonymous [AA], 2001, p. 64). It is not very far from that burning angry feeling to the chemicals. Anger has a lot of energy behind it. This angry energy is going to have to go somewhere, and it is important that it be directed positively into the recovery program. Anger at the illness can be constructive.

Anger necessitates blame. Clients must believe that someone purposely did something wrong that ended up hurting them or else the anger cannot continue. Each of these beliefs must be checked out for accuracy. The clients must stop and think before they act.

How to Handle a Violent Client

Clients who are acting violent do not belong in a treatment center. Like the actively suicidal client, these clients belong in a more secure psychiatric facility. Psychiatric hospitals have the equipment and the staff to deal with violent clients. Most addiction centers do not have this expertise. If your client makes overt attempts, acts, or threats of substantial bodily harm to himself or herself or other persons, then the client should be transferred. Keep as many staff members with this client as necessary to transport him or her safely. Do not hesitate to call the police. Apprise the officers carefully of your situation, and tell them to bring enough backup to manage the situation. Get an immediate consultation from your psychiatrist or psychologist, and follow his or her orders carefully. The doctor can order a chemical or mechanical restraint if this is necessary.

How to Handle an Angry Client

Clients who are feeling angry, or are verbally acting angry, usually can be managed in your facility. It is rare for a client to go through treatment without expressing anger. Most of your clients have unresolved anger issues. Chemically dependent persons tend to harbor deep anger and resentments. They boil and fume for years over some real or imagined slights. This all comes from the desire to be in control. "Each person is like an actor who wants to run the whole show; [the actor] is forever trying to arrange the lights, the ballet, the scenery, and the rest of the players in his [or her] own way" (AA, 2001, pp. 60–61). When people do not do what chemically dependent people want them to do, the latter become furious.

The treatment for angry clients revolves around having them complete the Anger Management exercise (see Appendix 32), where the clients learn about their anger problem and learn specific skills to deal with angry feelings. Most people feel sad and fearful along with the anger. All of the feelings need to be expressed. The clients need to verbalize how they see the whole situation while you support them. Do not argue with angry clients. Stay out of their reach and use a calm voice. Do not stand in the way of an exit. Let them rant and rave if they want to do so. The clients need to feel that they are important. If you listen to them, even when they are angry, it validates them as people.

Angry clients are feeling afraid and will need a lot of reassurance. The clients often feel that their anger is so repulsive that they will be rejected for expressing it. You need to show them that their anger is friendly so long as it is used appropriately. Anger exists to help us establish and maintain boundaries around ourselves. It keeps us from being violated. Anger is adaptive. People who cannot get angry will have their boundaries violated.

Help your clients to see that all anger comes from hurt. Anger is there to make the pain stop. First, something violates the clients physically or emotionally, and then they get angry. If the clients learn to hold people accountable by expressing all of their feelings, then they might not even get angry.

Assertiveness Skills

Clients do not have to act aggressively to show that they are angry. They need to be taught assertiveness skills. They need to see that assertiveness skills work and bring people closer together. Aggressive skills, on the other hand, drive people away. The book *Your Perfect Right: A Guide to Assertive Living* (Alberti &

Emmons, 1995) is an excellent resource for you and your clients. If your clients need assertiveness training, then they can read assigned parts of this book as homework. Assertiveness skills need to be practiced repeatedly in individual sessions, in role-playing, and in group.

The Importance of Forgiveness

Clients with an anger problem must learn how to forgive. They can use the Higher Power for this if they cannot forgive themselves. They want to be forgiven, and God will forgive them as they learn to forgive others.

Forgiveness is difficult. Clients never will forget what happened, but they can understand the persons who hurt them by understanding their own disease.

> We realized that the people who wronged us were perhaps spiritually sick. Though we did not like their symptoms and the way they disturbed us, they, like ourselves, were sick too. We asked God to help us show them the same tolerance, pity, and patience that we would cheerfully grant a sick friend. (AA, 2001, p. 67)

All clients who are angry and resentful need to read the following passage from the "Big Book":

> And acceptance is the answer to *all* my problems today. When I am disturbed, it is because I find some person, place, thing, or situation—some fact of my life—unacceptable to me, and I can find no serenity until I accept that person, place, thing, or situation as being exactly the way it is supposed to be at this moment. Nothing, absolutely nothing happens in God's world by mistake. Until I could accept my alcoholism, I could not stay sober; unless I accept life completely on life's terms, I cannot be happy. I need to concentrate not so much on what needs to be changed in the world as on what needs to be changed in me and in my attitudes. (AA, 1976, p. 449)

Have clients who are angry keep an anger diary. Take them through some cognitive therapy. Every time they feel angry, they should write down the situation and uncover their automatic thoughts. As these inaccurate thoughts are uncovered, the clients will see why they have been so angry. They take the slightest look or word as an attack. They need to work through the impulse control exercise and begin to practice the assertive formula repeatedly.

I feel _____.

When you _____.

I would prefer it if _____.

How to Teach the Client to Recognize Anger

These clients need to learn the specific changes in their bodies when they are getting angry. They need to learn how this feels. Do they feel tightness in their chests? Do their faces feel flushed? As early in the anger process as possible, the clients need to back out of the situation and use their new assertiveness skills. The initial response needs to be delayed until they can stop, think, and plan. This requires a lot of practice. Have the clients write down every time they use assertiveness skills and every time they lapse back into aggressive behavior. You will be able to show them the damage that they are doing to relationships with their old behavior. You also will show them how assertiveness skills bring people closer together.

Disengagement

It often will help angry clients to disengage from the current situation and detach as if the situation is happening to someone else. It is here that the clients can step back from themselves and see themselves as if they were their own counselors.

"I am feeling some anger."

"This is interesting."

"I need to check this out."

"What is going on with me right now?"

By stepping out of themselves and checking out the anger, clients will be more likely to get accurate and make better judgments. They can even laugh at themselves. They can recognize their anger, smile at themselves, and realize that getting angry is a silly thing to do to themselves. The clients can then take two deep breaths, breathing in slowly through the nose and out slowly through the mouth. As they exhale, they feel a warm wave of relaxation move down their bodies. The clients should practice this technique in your individual and group therapy sessions.

Time-Out

Clients who have a tendency to become verbally or physically violent must move away from an escalating situation as soon as possible. They must move away from the situation as far as necessary to recover their normal feelings. One useful technique to use if the anger happens in a family is to develop a "time-out" contract. This is a written contract between two or more people in which they agree that either party can say time-out at any time. Once one person has said "time-out," the other party can only say okay, time-out. At this point, the couple separates and agrees to return in an hour to further process through the problem. When they are separated, it is important that they do not rehash the argument over again in their minds. Otherwise, they might come back even more furious than when they left. When separated, it is important that they both tell themselves certain things to get their thinking more accurate (McKay, Rogers, & McKay, 1989).

1. No one is completely right or wrong.

2. It is okay to disagree.

3. The other person is not trying to hurt me. The other person is trying to meet his or her needs.

4. Do I need to call someone and talk about this? If I do, then I need to do that right now.

5. I will turn this situation over to my Higher Power.

The clients need to keep with them a list of these statements along with several numbers of people to call at all times.

How to Keep Your Cool as a Counselor

It is not easy dealing with people who are angry. They may verbally abuse you, and you need to keep calm. The worst thing that you can do is to lose your temper. Anger from the counselor can do a lot of damage. Concentrate on feeling yourself relax. Feel your arms and legs become heavy and warm. Focus on your breathing, and breathe slowly. If you are getting angry, then excuse yourself and take a few minutes outside of the room. Let someone else take over for a while. The best thing that you can do for angry clients is to remain calm and take good care of yourself.

The Homicidal Client

Clients who are experiencing homicidal ideation need to ventilate their feelings and then process through their options. They are not thinking clearly. They need help in processing through their options to a logical conclusion. It is not unusual for some clients to feel like killing someone, even someone they love. You will find homicidal thoughts to be a common element in dealing with angry clients. Most clients are just blowing off steam, thinking about homicide, wanting the ultimate revenge.

The Duty to Warn

If staff members determine that a client presents a serious danger of violence to another person, then they have the obligation to protect the intended victim (*Tarasoff v. Regents of the University of California*, 1976). This is an unusual event, but it does happen, and it should be carefully discussed with the clinical staff. There is a delicate balance between duty to warn and confidentiality. Whenever you have a client seriously threatening another person, it is necessary to staff the problem and document the staff decision in the client record. This client might have to be transferred to a more secure facility, or the threatened person might have to be warned.

Persons who have homicidal ideation usually can be reasoned with if they can be guided to see the truth. What is going to really happen if they kill someone? They need to process through the whole idea from beginning to end. Is killing someone taking good care of themselves, or will it put themselves in harm's way? What good is going to come of homicide? Is murder going to do the world any good? Is it going to do the clients any good? What does God want from them? These persons will need to be encouraged to turn the situation over to the perfect judge—God.

Homicidal intent is assessed in escalating order of severity:

1. Have you ever thought about hurting anyone or anything like that? (If yes, ask the client who. Ask what happened.)

2. If you were to hurt that person, how would you do it? (If the client has a plan, then write it down.)

3. Have you carried out any of that plan? (Get the details of the client's behavior.)

Clients with homicidal ideation who have a plan and have carried out any part of that plan are considered seriously homicidal. They must be watched. They must not be discharged or allowed to leave without being processed by the clinical staff. If the clients are imminently harmful to others by overt attempts, acts, or threats within the past few hours, then they might have to be detained against their will and transported to another facility. A psychiatrist, psychologist, physician, and/or police officer are necessary for these decisions. Your job is to keep the appropriate personnel informed of the clients' conditions. Let them take over the responsibility for these clients when they can.

Personality

Personality is composed of two basic parts: (1) temperament and (2) character. Temperament is the general psychological tone of the client. Some people are more sensitive to incoming stimulation. Some people seem dull and unresponsive. Character is what we learn about what to do and how to behave. It is shaped by the family and the social environment. Temperament and character are the primary elements in all personality disorders (Millon, 1981).

What Is Personality?

Personality is the enduring way in which a person thinks, feels, and acts. Personality is stable, well learned, and resistive to change. Personality makes up the total person. It is the pattern of behavior that a person evolves as the style of his or her life or how the person adapts to the environment.

A state is a person's current condition. This is transient, flexible, and easily manipulated by environmental stimulation. A person may feel sad, or even depressed, by the loss of his or her car keys. Once the keys are found, the person immediately returns to his or her normal state of thinking, feeling, and acting.

A trait is a long-standing tendency to react in a particular way to a set of circumstances. A trait is fixed and resistant to change. This is how a person has acted for years. A person might feel frightened of social interaction. This person fears doing something to embarrass or humiliate himself or herself in a group. This tendency may be persistent.

Personality disorders are patterns of inflexible and maladaptive traits that cause significant impairment. These patterns are not time limited. They are chronic. Personality disorders become evident by late adolescence and often last a lifetime. The symptoms of personality disorder can be relieved. The client can learn how to function better and more comfortably.

The Antisocial Personality

Source: BananaStock/Thinkstock.

You will see many antisocial personality disorders in your career. There is a higher incidence of this disorder in substance abusers (Khantzian & Treece, 1985; Weiss, Mirin, Griffin, & Michaels, 1988). This personality disorder has at its biological base the tendency to act aggressively and impulsively. These clients have a diminished capacity to delay or inhibit action, particularly aggressive action (Siever & Davis, 1991; Siever, Llar, & Coccaro, 1985). These clients act too quickly on their feelings. They have a tendency to act before they think. They do not feel the same arousal levels that normal people feel, so they can push the limits further (Eysenck & Eysenck, 1976). These biological tendencies leave these individuals vulnerable to a variety of problems. When most people break the rules, they are afraid of being caught. Antisocial persons do not feel this fear as much. They have difficulty in anticipating the effects of their behavior and learning from the consequences of their past.

A Disorder of Empathy

Antisocial clients do not feel normal empathy. They can break the rules of society to get their own way. They can openly defy authority and break the law without suffering much guilt or remorse. They do not feel at fault, and they have a tendency to blame others for their faults. They lack insight and fail to learn from experience. This is easy to understand. If they do not feel responsible for their actions, why should they change?

Antisocial clients begin to get into trouble with society by their early teens. They are in trouble at home, at school, and often with the police. As they grow older, they are unable to sustain work, and they fail to conform to the social norms with respect to lawful behavior. This is one of the most difficult disorders to treat. These clients can spend more time trying to outwit the staff than trying to work the program.

How to Treat the Antisocial Personality

Treatment for these clients revolves around teaching them the consequences of their behavior and learning how to think in a new way. They need to stop blaming others and accept responsibility for their own actions. They must see how their choices lead directly to painful consequences. At every opportunity, you need to show them how their decisions and actions got them into trouble. (An excellent resource for corrective thinking is the Truthought Corrective Thinking Process listed in Appendix 54 [Barriers in Thinking].

An excellent manual can be obtained from Truthought, PO Box 222, Roscoe, IL 61073; 815-389-0127.) They will love to argue the point so that they can place the blame on someone else, but you are not going to allow them to do this. You are going to constantly direct them to see the truth.

You may hear these kinds of statements from a client with an antisocial personality:

"I did not know that was a rule."

"She did not explain it properly to me."

"He did it. I did not do it."

"I was just standing there. What are you looking at me for?"

These clients are used to lying their way out of everything. They need to keep a daily log of their honesty and work hard at learning from their behavior. Each time they do something wrong, take them aside and take them through the behavior chain. Cover the trigger, thoughts, feelings, actions, and consequences carefully. They need to see their patterns repeatedly.

Working with the antisocial personality can be a frustrating experience, but these clients can do well in recovery. They will need a lot of structure in early sobriety. A halfway house or some other facility can be helpful during those first few months out of treatment.

These clients have little self-discipline and have poor impulse control (see Appendixes 14 and 15). They will need to work through each of these problems in treatment. They need to stop, think, and plan before they act. This will be learned only with practice. The clients need to learn to stick to a task until it is completed. The recovery skills in treatment give them an opportunity to learn this new skill. They are notorious for procrastinating at their work or for doing barely enough to get by. The group will have to reject these poorly done recovery skills and put up with these clients' anger to show the clients what is required. Sobriety necessitates a long-standing commitment.

How to Deal With a Rule Violation

You need to be familiar with the rules of your facility. These clients will push the limits and will argue that they are right. If they can find a way around a rule, then they will break the rule. Rather than being very negative, this provides the staff with an opportunity to intervene and teach these clients. The clients need to see what is causing their pain. The rules do not exist to keep them from having a good time. The rules exist to keep them safe. They need to practice turning things over rather than trying to manipulate everything.

If an antisocial client is caught breaking a rule, have him or her write a report on the incident and present it to the group. This is not intended to shame the client. It is intended to help the client see the consequences of this behavior. The group encourages the client and supports him or her in trying to bring the antisocial behavior under control. The group and the counselor should constantly reinforce prosocial behavior.

Learning empathy and appropriate guilt is a difficult skill. An antisocial client will do most of this work in group. When someone in the group is having a strong feeling, the antisocial client can be asked to relate to the feeling. Have the clients ever felt in a similar way? The client tries to match his or her experience with the feeling of the other person. If the feelings can be matched, then empathy will begin to develop.

When an antisocial client takes advantage of someone in treatment (this is inevitable), he or she needs to see the other person's pain. Take the client through the behavior chain that revolved around the incident.

Moral Development

Moral development occurs in stages.

1. It is right so long as I can get away with it. (no rules)

2. It is right if it is within the law. (rules outside of self)

3. It is right because I believe it is right. (rules internalized)

Antisocial clients are stuck in the first stage of moral development. A spiritual program can do wonders for these clients. If they can see that a Higher Power is there and watching, then they can begin to develop some external control.

Cognitive therapy is helpful with these clients, but they must learn to be honest. Sometimes they will deny or hide what they are thinking to prevent reprisals. It is very important for these clients to know that you understand them and do not blame them for their antisocial thinking. The clients need to feel like they can share their antisocial thoughts and acts with you. Clients must never be shamed for their thinking. They are held accountable only for their actions.

It is very easy to get into a "bad guy" role with antisocial clients. They might feel like you are pushing them around or being unnecessarily controlling. They want you to be the problem. That is why the rules, and the consequences of breaking the rules, need to be very clear from the outset. Then when the client breaks a rule, all you have to say is, "It is not me doing this to you. It is you doing this to yourself. You knew the rule and you broke it. There is a consequence for that. I hope that next time you will think before you act."

How to Deal With the Family of an Antisocial Client

The family of an antisocial client usually is in chronic distress. The family members need to be educated in how the client manipulates them. Communication patterns need to be improved. The family must hold the client accountable for his or her actions. This means allowing the client to suffer the consequences. This means no more enabling.

Antisocial clients are not used to being loved, and they often are suspicious of anyone who tries to get close to them. They wonder what you really are after. They look for the hidden motive. Once they see you consistently act on their behalf—even when they are being difficult—they will begin to come around. The worst thing that you can do with these clients is get angry with them. This is playing their game, and they know it better than you do. They are used to dealing with people's anger. They know just how to manipulate this situation. They will just blame you.

If you establish a good therapeutic alliance, there will come a time when antisocial clients will want to please you. This gives you great power as a reinforcer. By carefully selecting when to give positive reinforcement, you can effectively shape the clients' behavior. A day without a violation of the rules should be soundly reinforced, perhaps by congratulating the clients in front of the staff or the client population. A day without a lie is cause for celebration. The more positive attention you can give these clients for prosocial behavior, the further along they will be in their treatment program.

The Borderline Client

The biological component of borderline personality disorder is a tendency to act impulsively plus emotional instability. The affective instability is characterized by rapidly changing moods that are overly reactive to environmental emotional stimulation (Linehan, 1993; Siever & Davis, 1991; Siever et al., 1985). These clients overreact when they encounter emotional events such as relationship problems, separation, criticism, and frustration. They need long-term psychotherapy and many times psychopharmacology to stabilize their psychiatric symptoms. Dialectical therapy is very helpful for borderlines (Linehan, 1993). They feel too much too long and this raises havoc with self and interpersonal relationships. Borderlines do not have a sense of self and they tend to feel alienated and abandoned easily. When having extreme feelings, it is very difficult to think normally. The emotional shift can be quick and extreme, rarely lasting more than a few hours. It is common for borderline clients to attempt to control these affective shifts with self-damaging behavior such as suicide attempts, sexual acting out, and overusing mood-altering chemicals (Widiger & Frances, 1989). These clients grow up immature and unstable. They experience their feelings as being outside of their own control, controlled by environmental events. The environment becomes a major regulator of self-esteem and well-being. The boundaries between the clients and their environment become blurred (Siever et al., 1985). These clients do not feel safe and do not trust others because whenever they have trusted in the past, bad things inevitably occurred. Many of these clients have a history of childhood physical or sexual abuse. Dialectical behavior therapy has been designed to help borderline clients develop the skills necessary to cope with borderline feelings and situations. Clients are taught how to tolerate stress, regulate emotions, develop stable interpersonal relationships and use a state of mindfulness to stay in the moment and non-judgmental.

Interpersonal Relationships

When borderline clients sense supportive relationships with other persons, counselors, staff members, or loved ones, they feel uncomfortable. At first, they adopt an engaging, clinging, overly dependent style of relating. You are the greatest counselor in the world, and you can do no wrong. You are the only person who can help them. When the relationship is threatened through normal treatment, whether real or imagined, the clients shift to angry manipulation. Then you become the worst person in the world, and you cannot help anyone. The clients may become self-destructive to regain control. The clinging dependency is rapidly replaced by devaluation of the goodness and worth of the other person (Gunderson & Zanarine, 1987).

Borderline clients tend to throw temper tantrums and will often use one staff member against another. They seem to flourish in an atmosphere of conflict, splitting people into having all good or all bad characteristics. This split often occurs with the same person hour by hour. At times, the other person is the best, and at times, the other person is the worst. This can be very difficult for you to deal with, but remember that these clients need to feel safe. Staff members need to work together to prevent the clients from manipulating. Constantly ask the clients, "What do you need to feel safe right now?" Then try to support the clients. After they calm down, try to help them to see the emotionally charged situation more accurately.

Emotional Regulation

Borderline clients have extreme feeling shifts and act impulsively on their feelings. They repeatedly become involved in self-destructive behavior. They often cut themselves to feel some relief. This can also work by holding an ice cube, which causes pain but not self damage. Borderlines have chronic abandonment fears. They have a difficult time distinguishing who they are at any point in time. They often have attempted to hurt themselves, and they tend to become involved in dangerous activities such as shoplifting, sex, substance abuse, and reckless driving. They lack a life plan. They chronically feel empty and bored.

How to Treat the Borderline Client

Borderline clients bring all of this psychopathology into the treatment program. They can act out of control, and they can be very disruptive. You must provide a stable framework from which they can grow. They are emotionally immature and unstable. They will try your patience and push the limits of their relationship with you. Use the *Skills Training Manual for Treating Borderline Personality Disorder* (Linehan, 1993). You will find this very helpful in teaching borderlines skills to use when they feel uncomfortable.

You must remain alert and active in their treatment. They need a lot of direction and input. They need to be confronted on their maladaptive behavior. Use the group if the clients are not under control. Meet with the clients and the whole staff if necessary. The clients need to identify the feelings and motivations behind their acting out. Often this comes as a shock to them. Self-destructive behavior will become unwanted if you draw the clients' attention to the consequences. They need to get real about what they are doing and what happens when they do it. They are often in a mess, and they rarely believe that the problem is their fault. They need to see how their behavior affects what happens.

Setting Limits

Treatment centers on setting limits, learning impulse control, and developing skills for dealing with feelings. The staff will have to keep up on these clients to make sure that they do not pit one staff member against another. Often a borderline client will believe that one staff member is the enemy and someone else is a trusted friend. Without staffing this client, two staff members might end up in confrontation with each other. In such a situation, the staff needs to bring the client in during staffing. Here everyone can get the same story at the same time.

Dealing With Transference

Transference and countertransference can be a real problem with these clients. They seem to have a way of creating strong feelings and relationships among staff members. You might end up feeling angry, guilty, or frustrated. You might feel helpless. At first, the clients might see you as their savior, and then they might see you as their persecutor. It feels like an emotional roller-coaster ride. It is common for some to see these clients as "poor little things" who just need nurturing and for other staff members to see these clients as angry manipulators who need limits. Consultation with other staff members is essential. This will keep you in balance. This is the clients' problem, not yours. Borderline clients can form overly intense relationships with their counselors. You need to maintain your boundaries. Do not become overly involved. Do not do anything for borderline clients that you would not normally do for someone else.

Stress Tolerance

When borderline clients are feeling uncomfortable, they need to do something. They need a specific plan of action when they have strong feelings. They can exercise, talk to someone, turn it over to a Higher Power, become involved in something else, go to a meeting, read recovery material, and so on. They should not always talk to you when they are upset; this fosters dependency. It is notorious for borderline clients to say that they have to talk to you right now. You need to teach them that they cannot always come to you. You cannot always be there for them. They need to develop other coping skills.

Cognitive therapy is important. Clients need to be able to see a person's good and bad qualities at the same time. When the clients are extremely angry with someone, help them to see the person's positive characteristics. Borderline clients would rather be joined in attacking someone, but you should encourage them to look for the good. The clients need to see themselves and others more realistically. Cognitive therapy will help them to uncover their unconscious thoughts and motivations. They need to see why they feel and act the way they do. What are they after? How can they get what they want more appropriately?

Dealing With the Family

Two family issues may be important with the borderline client. The family may be overinvolved and need to let go, or the family may have a history of abuse or neglect. Both of these issues need further counseling than you can provide in an inpatient program. They will need long-term psychotherapy. You can just help the family to get started. The family members must be referred to make sure that they address the problems in continuing care. The borderline client often has clinging dependency needs or extreme anger at his or her family members.

Everyone in a borderline client's family needs to be educated about the client's diagnosis and become actively involved in treatment. They will be relieved to know that there is an illness called borderline personality disorder, and they need to understand the signs and symptoms. Most family members will be amazed that other people have this disease and that treatment is very effective.

Behaviorally, clients need to work through the Impulse Control exercise (see Appendix 15), the Relationship Skills exercise (see Appendix 11), and the Communication Skills exercise (see Appendix 13). They need to practice these skills with their treatment peers. They need to rehearse and role-play problem situations in interpersonal group.

Borderline clients are a challenge for you and the staff. They take a lot of energy. It is important to remember that these clients have an illness. They did not ask for their disease, nor did they create it themselves. They are frantic for love and affection with no idea about how to get it. They should work through the Love, Trust, and Commitment exercise (see Appendix 9) to help them understand exactly what love is. They need to practice establishing relationships without unrealistic expectations.

These clients will need to be referred to outpatient psychotherapy in continuing care. They might need the structure of a halfway house or some other long-term facility. Long-term involvement with a 12-step group is very beneficial to these clients. They can learn to function well over the years.

The Narcissistic Client

Narcissistic clients can be difficult to deal with emotionally. They have a grandiose sense of their own self-importance and capabilities. They feel as if they are so special that everyone should treat them as if they were unique and amazingly talented. They think that they have special skills, beauty, power, or abilities. If you do not treat them in a special way, they get mad and reject you, destroying the therapeutic alliance. It is very difficult for them to hear the truth about themselves because they cannot tolerate criticism. They are excessively sensitive to having any flaws. When they are confronted with a problem that they have, they tend to dissolve into shame and worthlessness. When they become extremely angry and resentful, it is called narcissistic rage. Narcissistic clients do not think they need to learn anything from you. They know everything already. They tell everyone else what to do.

These clients spend a lot of time with big plans and schemes for unlimited success or power. They want to rule over others rather than be one of the common people. They believe that they deserve to be treated special due to their outstanding achievements, brilliance, beauty, or ability. They believe that only the special people of the world, those of a similar high caliber, can understand them. They think that they should interact only with the beautiful people.

It is very easy to counter transfer with these clients and get angry, but if you do, then you will destroy your therapeutic alliance and they will think of you as inadequate. The best way of treating these clients is as if they really were the ruler. If you treat them as if they are the ruler and you are the servant, then you will go a long way toward getting them to listen. They often need to see that you are special too, with special powers and abilities. After all, only the greatest professional could help them. Once they see that you are wonderful, you can then show them that you have faults and that you have made some mistakes. If you and these clients can agree that both of you are wonderful but that both of you have made some mistakes, the clients are beginning to get accurate in their thinking.

Give these clients the Narcissism exercise (see Appendix 33), which allows them to learn about their narcissistic traits. The most important thing for narcissistic clients to do is get honest with themselves and others. After they do that, they need to turn their wills and their lives over to the Higher Power. This is very difficult for them to do because they have been playing God for a long time.

Narcissistic clients grew up as the kings or queens of their households, and they need long-term psychotherapy to improve. At home, they were in total control of the household. Their every whim was met. One of their primary caregivers often doted on their every word and told them that they were wonderful. The adults in their homes used these children to build their own inadequate self-esteem. If their children were wonderful, then they were wonderful.

Narcissistic clients are interpersonally exploitative because they are only interested in their own needs. They are not capable of understanding that other people have feelings, wants, and needs. Their relationships start in a blaze of glory but end in despair. A high relapse trigger for them is sex, and they often fall in love in treatment. They can become convinced that any new relationship, no matter how bad it might seem to others, is going to be ideal and wonderful. It is as if they are blind to the truth, making the same mistakes repeatedly. They need love and attention so much that when they get it, they tend to idealize the other persons, and this sets these relationships up to fail.

Narcissistic clients need to spend time developing empathy for others. In group, when someone is having a feeling, have the narcissistic client try to connect with the other client's feeling.

Most of the time, you inevitably will end up disappointing narcissistic clients. You will not be empathic in the right way, in the right amount, or at the right time, and they ultimately will decide that you are not enough for them. Every relationship ends up this way. That is why the Higher Power concept works. God is the one that can be enough. God always is available. God has all the power. God is smart enough. When you feel these clients' disappointment, carefully explain the ABCs of AA: (a) that we were alcoholic and could not manage our own lives, (b) that probably no human power could have relieved our alcoholism, and (c) that God could and would if God were sought. When narcissistic clients see that no one can meet their needs except God, things can change. It is to be hoped that the clients will begin a genuine search for their Higher Power. God is the only one that seems good enough for them anyway.

The Anxious Client

Source: © Can Stock Photo Inc. / gina sanders.

Anxiety is a vague generalized fear. Some children are born with a nervous system that is more sensitive (Kagan, 1989; Kagan, Reznick, & Gibbons, 1989; Kagan, Reznick, & Snidman, 1987). This increased physiological responsivity can heighten the sensation of unpleasant experience. These children have a low threshold for subjective fear and a high arousal in anticipation of adverse consequences (Siever & Davis, 1991). Children with such a heightened response to the environment can become shy and inhibited. It takes less of an adverse experience to upset them (Rosenbaum, Biederman, Hirshfeld, Bolduc, & Chaloff, 1991).

Anxious clients are afraid, but they are not sure why. These individuals are hypervigilant and tense. They look for the impending disaster. They believe that the ax is falling. They feel a sense of dread and impending doom. Most of these clients are avoidant. They avoid social situations. They feel uncomfortable in groups and fear doing something that will humiliate them.

There are a high percentage of anxiety disorders in clients who end up abusing depressants (Dorus et al., 1987; Hesselbrock et al., 1985). Clients attempt to reduce their anxious feelings with drugs that suppress central activity.

How to Measure Anxiety

Anxiety can be tested with a variety of psychological tests including the Hamilton Anxiety Rating Scale (HAM-A) (see Appendix 64). The test scores will help you to determine the effectiveness of your treatment. The Self-Rating Anxiety Scale (Zung, 1971) and the State-Trait Anxiety Inventory (Spelberger, 1983) can be used to measure anxiety. The tests are simple and can be given as often as necessary.

Multiple somatic complaints accompany anxiety. Clients may feel sweaty palms, a pounding heart, trembling, light-headed, dizzy, or numb. They may feel as though their lives are threatened. They may think that they are having a heart attack. The anxiety may go on for a few minutes, or it may last most of the day.

There are nonaddictive medications that can suppress or block certain forms of anxiety. Panic disorder is improved or eliminated with certain antidepressant medications such as the selective serotonin reuptake inhibitors.

Mood stabilizers or other psychiatric medications can also be helpful. Feel relieved when doctors order medication for your clients. Physicians can be trusted to treat these clients with medication appropriately.

Outside of the chemical dependency field, anxiety often is treated with benzodiazepines. These central nervous system (CNS) depressants are contraindicated in chemically dependent persons because they can be highly addictive. Clients who come into chemical dependency treatment taking these drugs will have to be withdrawn.

The Psychological Component of Anxiety

The psychological part of anxiety disorders centers around an inaccurate perception of threat. This threat can be real or imagined, but it is exaggerated to the point where it interferes with normal functioning. To these clients, all of the fears are real. The intensity of the fear is preparing them to escape a dangerous situation. Clients can be immobilized by fear. They can freeze and be unable to move. This is no joke, and you will get nowhere pretending that these clients have no worries. You must try to relate to, and understand, the intense fear that these clients are feeling. Clients can be intensely afraid of spiders even if there are no spiders. They can be terrified of a group even if there is no logical reason to be afraid. These clients need gentle support and encouragement. They need to feel as though someone understands them.

There are many forms of anxiety disorders, and the feared objects are incredibly variable, but you can approach all anxiety in the same general way. You need to know the following things about an anxious client:

1. What is the client afraid of?
2. Where did the fear seem to come from?
3. Is the fear accurate or inaccurate?
4. What can the client do to reduce the fear?

Anxiety disorders are not character disorders. In character disorders, the clients blame everyone else for everything. In anxiety disorders, the clients blame themselves for everything.

How to Use Relaxation Techniques

Anxious clients need to learn how to relax. They cannot be anxious and relaxed at the same time. The two physiological states are incompatible. The clients will have to be taught how to relax using relaxation techniques. There are many relaxation tapes on the market. You can use relaxing music, sounds of nature, or imagery. Get a few, and have the clients listen to a relaxation exercise twice a day. You can take clients through a relaxation exercise yourself by doing the following exercise.

Make sure that you will not be interrupted. Have the clients sit or lie down in a quiet comfortable place. Read these words in a slow, quiet voice:

"Close your eyes and pay attention to your breathing. Feel the cool air coming in and the warm air going out. As you focus your attention on your breathing, feel yourself beginning to relax. There is no right way or wrong way to do this exercise. There is just your way. Feel yourself becoming calm. Your arms and legs are feeling heavy and warm. Inside of your mind, as completely as you can, in your own way, see ocean waves. Do not worry about how you are seeing these waves. Just see them as completely as you can. Match the waves with your breathing. As the wave builds, you inhale, and as the wave washes on a shore, you exhale. See yourself standing on an island, on a white sandy beach, looking at the waves. You are feeling at peace. With each breath and each wave, you feel more relaxed. It is warm, and you can feel the sunshine on your cheeks and on your arms. You are on an island. This is your island inside of your own mind. You are safe here. There is no one else on the island except you. There are palm trees and lush green vegetation on the island. There is a trail on the island, and you turn and see yourself take that trail. You are not in a hurry. You have plenty of time. You are walking slowly. There are flowers along the trail of every imaginable color and hue. You begin to walk up a hill, and as you walk up the hill, you become tired. Your arms and legs feel heavy. You come to a ridge that overlooks a lush green valley filled with waterfalls. You wander for as long as you like in this valley feeling at peace."

You can add any other relaxing scene to modify this exercise. When the clients have been relaxing for 10 to 20 minutes, you need to bring them out of the state of relaxation. Say something like this:

"You walk out of the valley and down the trail. You walk back on the beach and watch the waves. They build and wash on the shore. You feel yourself becoming more awake and aware of yourself. You wiggle your toes and fingers. You feel yourself in this room and in your chair. Your eyelids begin to flicker. When you feel comfortable, open your eyes and become fully awake."

While the clients are relaxed, you can give them some positive affirmations. The clients are good persons. They have talents. They have a Higher Power. They have people who support them. How the clients feel is important. They are going to take care of themselves. The clients are going to commit themselves to being honest. They should help you to develop these positive self-statements. Use this exercise to build a more positive self-image.

The Daily Log

These clients will need to score the level of relaxation after each exercise from 1 (*as little as possible*) to 100 (*as much as possible*). They also need to keep a log of their daily anxiety using the same scale. The clients score their general anxiety level at the end of each day. The clients should log any situation that caused or made their anxiety worse. This plus the psychological testing will give you a good idea of where the clients are in working their program.

Cognitive Therapy

Anxious clients need to see you in individual sessions at least twice a week. You will take the anxious situations and go through the same cognitive therapy suggested for depression. The clients can complete *Mastering Your Fears and Phobias: Workbook* (Craske, Antony, & Barlow, 2006), *Coping With Anxiety and Panic: SCT Method* (Beck & Emery, 1979), or *Panic Attacks: How to Cope, How to Recover* (Greenberg & Beck, 1987) to introduce them to the cognitive techniques. (Some of these pamphlets can be ordered from the Foundation for Cognitive Therapy, 133 South 36th Street, Room 602, Philadelphia, PA 19104.)

Anxious clients often exaggerate the level of threat by inaccurately perceiving and judging the situation. They can do this in many ways. They may make any of the following cognitive distortions:

1. Catastrophizing

   "I am going to pass out."

   "I am going crazy."

   "I am losing control."

2. Exaggerating

   "This is the worst thing that could happen."

   "I fail at everything."

   "I would make a fool of myself."

3. Ignoring the positive

   "They hate me."

   "Nobody likes me."

Each of these clients' inaccurate thoughts needs to be challenged for accuracy. The clients will need to keep track of their automatic thinking while in treatment. You cannot just do this for a few days. Cognitive therapy takes weeks of concentrated effort.

If it is medically possible, these clients need to exercise for 20 minutes a day at a training heart rate (220 minus age times 0.75). The clients might have to build up to this level of fitness. The exercise will burn off excess stress hormones that the clients are producing. They will be more relaxed for 24 hours following the exercise.

Anxious clients need to understand what triggers their anxiety and prepare for anxious moments with accurate thinking and relaxation techniques. These clients must learn that they can cope with anxiety using the tools of recovery. They are not going to die or go crazy from anxiety. They need to slow the anxiety cycle by stopping and thinking when they feel anxious. What are they thinking? Is it accurate? Then they replace negative thinking with positive thinking. At any time, they can use a relaxation technique to block the anxious symptoms.

Post-Traumatic Stress Disorder

The essential feature of post-traumatic stress disorder (PTSD) is the development of troubling symptoms following exposure to an extreme direct personal experience that involves actual or threatened death or serious injury, or a threat to one's personal well-being or witnessing another person going through a similar trauma. The person's response must involve intense fear, helplessness, or horror. The person persistently avoids any stimuli that are associated with the trauma and has a general feeling of numbness. These symptoms have to cause significant distress and impairment in psychological, social, or emotional functioning. To test for PTSD, use the PTSD Checklist Civilian Version (PCL) (see Appendix 61) or the PTSD Checklist Military Version (PCL) (see Appendix 62).

These clients will need to reassure the client and educate them about PTSD. They need to understand how the past trauma clouds their whole life and undermines a feeling of well-being. The client can then be referred to a professional that specializes in PTSD treatment. Cognitive behavioral therapy seems to work best with these clients helping them to identify and overcome the impact of the traumatic event, the meaning of the event, and how to identify stuck points that interfere with the acceptance of the trauma. This is done by helping the client to remember the details of the trauma and it is meaning. The client writes and reads an account of the trauma both with the counselor, therapy group, or a concerned other. The client is asked to rewrite and reread the account throughout treatment. This is done when the client has practiced relaxation exercises and can reexperience the trauma with his or her emotions under control. These clients tend to overgeneralize and establish inaccurate beliefs about the world. For example, they might think everyone is going to hurt them. These inaccurate beliefs have to be challenged and replaced with accurate information. It is essential that these clients feel safe during treatment—by the counselor remaining relaxed and supportive during the therapy sessions. Most of the time the trauma has lead these clients not to trust themselves or they feel like they have to control everything so they will feel safe. The counselor needs to discuss how these fears and controlling mechanisms interfere with normal relationships and a feeling of intimacy. It often helps to have the client write down the event or events that caused the trauma in detail. Then the client reads this over to himself or herself and listens to the reading to begin to deal with the trauma. You will find that the client has generalized the traumatic feelings to people, places, and things that should not be traumatic. The client needs to think of events outside of the traumatic event to see things accurately. Have the client write down these events repeatedly until the client uncovers more and more of the memory. If it is safe, the client can share the traumatic events with his or her counselor or group. Once the client has put the trauma into perspective and learned how to cope with stress, they are ready to terminate PTSD treatment. They will still need to work a daily program of recovery to stay clean and sober.

Panic Attacks

If these clients come to you when they are having a panic attack, you need to be calm and reassuring. Have them look at you and slow their breathing—slow, deep breaths. Then begin one of your relaxation techniques to distract the clients from their feelings. Tell them the anxiety will pass. You might want to take them on a walk and have them look at the scenery—at the blue sky and the clouds. You might have them contact their Higher Power and have the Higher Power begin to fill them with peace. Have the clients float in their anxiety and go with it. Reassure them that nothing bad is going to happen and that you are going to stay with them until they feel comfortable.

These clients will need to practice distracting themselves when feeling anxious. They can notice some fine details in the room or in the environment. They can look for styles of clothing or shoes. They can read something or estimate the cost of things. They need to develop a simple coping imagery, such as a trip to the beach, to replace the fearful thoughts. The coping fantasy can be any relaxing situation in which the clients feel comfortable and in control.

Anxious clients usually are easy to work with. They are frightened, but they are responsible individuals. They are willing to do almost anything to get better. These clients need a lot of love. It will be hard for them to accept your rewards. They often do not feel worth it, but you should give reinforcers lavishly. When they feel praised by their treatment peers for their work in group, it is a triumph. Clients with a history of panic disorder should complete the *Mastery of Your Anxiety and Panic: Workbook* (Barlow & Craske, 2006).

The Psychotic Client

Psychotic clients persistently mistakenly evaluate reality. They have disturbances in cognitive/perceptual organization. They are unable to perceive important incoming stimuli, process this information in relation to experience, and select appropriate responses (Siever & Davis, 1991). This mistaken evaluation of experience results in tenacious false beliefs (Klein, Gittelman, Quitkin, & Rifkin, 1980). If you walked into a restaurant and a person turned around and looked at you, you would not think much about it. However, a psychotic client might mistakenly evaluate this situation and think, "That person is after me." This mistaken evaluation has the force of reality, and it results in distorted conclusions. "The mob sent that person to kill me."

Hallucinations and Delusions

The hallmark of psychosis is hallucinations and delusions. Hallucinations are false perceptions. They can seem to come from any sense organ. Clients may hear voices, see visions, have a strange taste or smell, or feel something unusual on or under their skin. To psychotic clients, these false perceptions are as real as reality itself.

Delusions are false beliefs that are intractable to logic. The clients may believe that they are being watched by someone, that they have strange or unusual powers, or that one of their body organs is not operating properly. No rational argument will deter them from this irrational belief. Some clients have social or cultural beliefs that might seem odd, but if they occur in a normal social context, they are not considered psychotic. For example, someone could believe that he or she has the power to read minds, but that person has been trained culturally in this belief. Psychosis is a persistent mistaken perception of reality that is not accounted for by social indoctrination or normal life experiences.

All psychotic states are due to an abnormal condition of the brain. Chronic disorders, such as schizophrenia and schizoid personality disorder, seem to result from a core vulnerability expressed in a relative detachment from the environment, often with defects in reality testing. This seems to be due to inherited neurointegrative dysfunction. These individuals do not develop normal interpersonal relationships. They lack empathy and a sense of connectedness. Their relationships are shallow and not satisfying (Siever et al., 1985).

Acute organic brain syndromes, including intoxication and withdrawal, can produce psychotic symptoms. Many other psychiatric conditions, such as schizophrenia and major depression, can create psychosis. Acute organic brain syndrome must be ruled out first because it can be life threatening. Psychosis can be transient, as in some forms of acute alcohol withdrawal, or it can be chronic in some forms of schizophrenia.

How to Treat the Psychotic Client

In psychotic clients, there is a mix of psychotic and real perception being evaluated. Your job is to respond to, and reinforce, the healthy side of these clients. Rarely will you respond to a psychotic statement other than to reassure the clients and point out reality to them. Even in the most florid psychotic states, clients have some hold on reality and do remember what happened. The environment of a client having active hallucinations needs to be reduced to its lowest level of stimulation. A quiet room, without a radio or television, is best. Keep calm yourself. There is no reason for you to be afraid. A conversation with a psychotic client might go something like this:

The client, Mary, is lying in her bed, covers drawn up to her chest. She is looking at the walls with a frightened look on her face. The counselor walks over and sits in a chair beside the bed.

Counselor: How are you doing, Mary?

Mary: Okay, I guess. . . . I keep seeing colors. The walls seem to be moving, as if they are breathing.

Counselor: That is withdrawal, Mary. We are treating you for that. It will pass. Just hang in there.

Mary: And I see spiders on the wall.

Counselor: I know that seems real to you, but the bugs are not real. They are coming from the withdrawal. There are no spiders on the wall.

Mary: But I see them.

Counselor: It seems real, doesn't it? Shows you how tricky the mind can be. You are going to be feeling a lot better soon. I am proud of you coming into treatment. That took a lot of courage.

Mary: Thanks.

Counselor: Can you tell me a little bit about your drinking?

The counselor did not try to prove to the client that there were no spiders. The counselor just told the client the truth and reassured her. Then the counselor began to get some history of the client's problems.

There may be clients who will have psychotic symptoms throughout treatment. These clients might need to be treated with antipsychotic medications that are the mainstay of the treatment for psychosis. The psychotic symptoms probably will gradually decrease in intensity over time. The hallucinations will go first, with the delusions gradually decreasing over the next several months. Some of the delusional material may be persistent, lasting for years or even the client's entire life. Once these beliefs are set, they are very tenacious to change.

Do not allow psychotic symptoms to trouble the other clients. Psychotic clients rarely are dangerous. For the most part, you can ignore the symptoms in group. If they do come up, a frank explanation might be necessary. The other clients will understand so long as they know they do not have to feel frightened. The group can be helpful in assisting the client to test reality and to gain social skills.

Diseases such as schizophrenia and mania can be difficult to manage and they need psycholopharmacological intervention (see Psychotherapeutic Medications, or Appendix 55). Clients who are not in good control will need to be transferred to a more structured psychiatric facility. The psychotic clients that you work with will be having perceptual and thought disturbances. It is useless to argue with clients about their delusional material. These beliefs are well defended and intractable. For the most part, you will reassure, support, and try to take them through your program.

Many psychotic clients will have an unusual affect. The range of feelings may be flat, they say few words, are not goal directed, have attention problems. The clients usually have a strange feel to them. Their behavior might not fit the circumstances. They may have little or no motivation. With the flat affect, you can help the clients to identify and use their feelings. Motivation can be improved by having the clients do many small tasks that can be separately reinforced. Do not set the clients up to fail by asking them to do things that are too difficult for them.

These clients usually need social skills training. They might have to be taught how to sit, walk, talk, smile, and use interpersonal space and eye contact appropriately. They might have to learn what appropriate conversation is and what it is not. They might need to practice communication skills and interpersonal relationship skills.

Clients who are chronically mentally ill will need help in becoming acquainted with community resources. They need to be referred to the appropriate agencies for follow-up. Social, vocational, and housing needs all will have to be appropriately addressed.

Insight-oriented therapy, or therapy that is highly confrontive, is contraindicated with these clients. If painful material is uncovered, then the psychotic symptoms may worsen. With these clients, it is best to stay with the here and now.

The clients will need to learn problem solving skills in treatment and will need to practice these skills. They need to identify the problem, consider the options, plan their actions, and carry out the plan. The clients should check the problem later to see whether their plan has been successful.

The Family of the Psychotic Client

The client's family will have to meet with the staff to be educated about the disease. The psychologist or psychiatrist should do this because he or she knows more about the psychopathology. If you do not have anyone on staff that has this expertise, then you might need to refer the client to an outside agency. The family is important in preventing a relapse with the client. An emotionally unstable family will increase the client's chance of relapse (Brown, Monck, Carstairs, & Wing, 1962). A family needs to be educated to keep criticism and over involvement to a minimum.

The great healer in any good treatment program is love. You can actively care for and respond to these clients even though they make you feel a little uncomfortable. They are just people who have a difficult disorder. They need all of the love and encouragement that you can give them. It is incredibly rewarding to see these people improve.

Acquired Immune Deficiency Syndrome

Some clients in need of treatment for addiction will have acquired immune deficiency syndrome (AIDS), will have AIDS-related complex (ARC), or will test positive for HTLV-III antibodies. Needle sharing among intravenous drug users places them at high risk for contracting this disease. AIDS can affect the CNS, and it can affect thinking, feeling, and behavior, even in the absence of other symptoms (Gabel, Barnard, Norko, & O'Connell, 1986; Perry & Jacobsen, 1986; Stulis, 2009). Clients with AIDS can develop a psychosis characterized by delusions, hallucinations, bizarre behavior, affective disturbances, and mild memory or cognitive impairment. The cause of this psychosis is yet to be established (Harris, Jeste, Gleghorn, & Sewell, 1991).

Approximately 30% of all AIDS cases are intravenous drug users. They are the second leading risk group for infection for transmission of the disease to the adult heterosexual population (Centers for Disease Control [CDC], 1990).

More than one third of AIDS clients develop symptoms of AIDS dementia complex. This organic brain disease may complicate the diagnosis and treatment of chemically dependent individuals because of the complicated cognitive, emotional, and behavioral changes that can occur. The course of AIDS-related dementia is variable. Early signs and symptoms may be subtle. AIDS dementia complex generally progresses to severe global impairment within months. Depression and psychosis are frequent complications (Perry & Jacobsen, 1986).

The High-Risk Client

All high-risk clients, homosexuals, intravenous drug users, and sexual partners of high-risk individuals should be routinely screened and educated about HIV infection and risk, particularly if they present with signs of organic or psychotic impairment, fever, or weight loss. Informed consent should be obtained before testing. Clients who are seropositive without active symptoms of AIDS can be safely taken through the program.

AIDS clients will have special issues revolving around their disease. Uncertainty of diagnosis, guilt about the previous lifestyle, fear of death, exposure of lifestyle, changes in self-esteem, and alienation from family and friends all can be important elements in treatment. The catastrophic nature of this illness will have to be dealt with on an individual basis. If possible, the clients need to be referred to a facility that specifically deals with AIDS for continuing care.

The AIDS and Chemical Dependency Committee (1988) of the American Medical Society on Alcoholism and Other Drug Dependencies recommend that treatment be provided for these clients. The clients need to be assessed on a case-by-case basis and referred for follow-up by a physician familiar with AIDS. Clients with AIDS do *not* require isolation techniques any different from clients with active hepatitis B. Hepatitis B precautions should be followed carefully. Caps, gloves, masks, and other kinds of protective wear are *not* necessary in routine contact. Nevertheless, use gloves when dealing with bodily fluids. The principle of confidentiality is particularly important in protecting these clients (AIDS and Chemical Dependency Committee, 1988).

The Client With Low Intellectual Functioning

Clients with low intellectual functioning have defects in learning and in adaptive skills. Most of these clients will have low average to borderline intelligence many times due to fetal alcohol spectrum disorders. You occasionally will see someone in the mildly mentally retarded range. Intelligence below this is not amenable to the normal treatment program.

How to Treat the Client With Low Intelligence

Some of these clients will need a specialized treatment plan. These clients have difficulty with abstract reasoning. Their program will have to be tangible and concrete. Many of them will have deficiencies in social skills that will need remediation. Social skills training can be very helpful here as the group teaches them how to communicate and solve problems effectively. Most of these clients will need an advocate or a group home in their community to assist them in developing and maintaining life skills.

Abstract thought is more complicated than concrete thought. To have normal abstract thought, clients must easily shift from one aspect of a situation to another, keeping in mind simultaneous aspects of the situation. They must be able to grasp how the parts fit into a whole. They must be able to separate the parts and put them back together again mentally. Clients with good abstract thought can plan, organize, and think in complex symbols.

Concrete thought is immediate and tangible. It is set in the current situation without the ability to generalize to other situations. Use of complex symbols or the ability to see all of the parts is not present. The ability to effectively plan and understand complicated issues is impaired if the client can think only concretely. Most of these clients only think concretely so they have difficulty planning, organizing, resisting primitive impulses, and learning from experiences. Many of them have to be reminded of the rules repeatedly because they forget or cannot generalize rules from one situation to another.

The Client Who Cannot Read

Some of these clients cannot read nor do the written exercises. Most of the reading material in the 12-step program is written at a sixth-grade level. Clients with reading levels two or more grades below this are going to have difficulty. The psychologist can help you to determine the extent of these problems and can give you advice on how to present the program. If the clients can read a little, then they should be encouraged to do so. The encouragement and praise that they receive will more than offset minor problems.

If the clients cannot read, then the program will have to be presented to them in oral form. They can watch videos and hear 12-step material on tape. Every treatment center has audiovisual material around for just such a purpose. The clients will need more individual attention and additional support in group. Some of the group sessions will be over their heads, and that is okay so long as they are getting the basic program. The program can be made simple enough for most anyone to follow.

You will have to do a lot of repeating with these clients, and you need to keep asking them to repeat what you said. This is the only way of being sure that they understand. Many of these clients learn to be great head-nodders when they do not understand. If they can repeat the program to you, then they are learning it. Give them a few key phrases to learn by heart. Check on them from time to time to see whether they are learning the phrases and understanding what they mean. "Do not drink. Go to meetings. Turn it over to your Higher Power."

These clients may need occupational rehabilitation in continuing care. They may qualify for locally supported programs such as Social Security. They may need a halfway house or other structured facility in continuing care. The Division of Vocational Rehabilitation is an excellent program for many of these clients.

The Family of the Client With Low Intelligence

The family of a person with low intelligence might not know of their loved one's disability. The family will need to be informed about the client's liabilities. These clients can be some of the best AA/Narcotics Anonymous (NA) members. They can be fiercely loyal and consistent. They often are willing to do jobs that other members find distasteful. It is very reinforcing to watch them bond with the group and find a place for themselves.

The Elderly Client

Source: ©iStockphoto.com/azndc.

Most counselors do not realize how prevalent addiction is among the elderly. A recent study revealed that substance abuse was the third-ranked mental disorder in a large geriatric mental health population (Reifler, Raskind, & Kethley, 1982). The elderly are vulnerable to becoming addicted to a variety of over-the-counter or prescription medications, and they tend to take a variety of medications without proper medical supervision. Any medication or illicit drug tends to have more effect on the elderly than on younger persons. Drugs usually have one third more power in older individuals for a variety of physiological factors. There appears to be no age-related change in liver detoxification, but there is a decline in brain cells that results in higher concentration of alcohol and other substances. With normal aging, there is a decline in extracellular and intracellular fluid and an increase in body fat that result in a greater effect of many drugs on the CNS (Gambert, 1992).

Elderly clients often have outlived their psychosocial support system. Their spouses may have died or been incapacitated, and their children may be unable to care for them. Loss of family and friends, coupled with retirement and loss of job and self-esteem, may lead elderly clients into a depressive state where substances are used to ease the pain. A study at the Mayo Clinic's inpatient alcohol unit found that 44% of elderly clients were compromised organically from chronic alcohol or drug use but that they went through treatment with no appreciable difference in treatment outcome (Morse, 1994). Only 10% of elderly clients have a dementia that is serious enough to hamper them in retaining a recovery program. Many clients suffer from mild cognitive defects including impairment of orientation, concentration, short-term memory recall, and abstract thinking.

Atkinson and Kofed (1984) found a number of risk factors that contributed to the vulnerability of the elderly to substance abuse. Biological sensitivity to chemicals, loneliness, pain, insomnia, depression, and grief all were predisposing factors.

Symptoms of substance abuse often are overlooked in the elderly in medical settings because they suffer from multiple pathological conditions. Changes in cognition or behavior may be blamed on an illness or old age rather than on substance abuse.

For a variety of reasons, the elderly may start drinking heavily after they retire. They have more time on their hands, and drinking or drug use can easily become a habit using relatively small amounts of substances. It is most common for these clients to drink or use alone. Like any addict, there is a strong desire for the clients to hide their use. This may be easy to do when they live alone and have no one to check on them periodically.

The good thing about recovery is that it gives clients a new family. They do not have to live alone anymore. The clients can use their support group to reestablish social connections and develop new leisure activities. They develop a sense of belonging by helping other addicts, and this improves their self-worth. This gives elderly clients, who often are ready to die, a reason to live. The clients have to know that their recovery group needs them. God trained them in addiction, they have grown wise over the years, and now they need to heal. They can do this by going to meetings and sharing their experience, strength, and hope. It might take a while before elderly persons realize this truth. The best way of having them learn it is to have them help someone in treatment. They can help someone go through detox or can help someone earlier in recovery. Once they see that their lives have meaning and worth for others, they are on the road to recovery.

The Client With Early Childhood Trauma

Many chemically dependent clients were raised in severely dysfunctional families, and some of them were abused as children. Some of these clients will meet the criteria for PTSD from the abuse, but all of them will be adversely affected. For the most part, you need to leave severe early childhood trauma for treatment later in the recovery. Before addressing early childhood trauma, it is best if the client has been working a self-directed program of recovery for about a year. The clients will need to maintain a stable recovery before they tackle the intense pain of these issues. To immerse them too deeply in the old trauma now may not be appropriate. Some clients are so preoccupied with the abuse that it has to be addressed earlier in treatment. The best way to determine this is the extent of the client's preoccupation with the traumatic material. If they are obsessed with thoughts, intrusive memories, and dreams, it seems best to let the clients vent some of their story to provide them some relief. Eye movement desensitization and reprocessing (EMDR) can be helpful with some of these clients.

If clients disclose abuse in individual sessions or in group, they need to be supported. They need to hear that it was not their fault. Little children are not responsible for what adults do. If a client who discloses abuse is an adolescent, then the situation will have to be reported to the proper authorities. This is to protect the child from further harm. Do not do this without consulting with the clinical staff and carefully documenting it in the client record.

How to Deal With Sexual Abuse

If a client is stuck in treatment because of this pain, then it will have to be addressed to relieve the pressure. This is a clinical decision. If the client is too vulnerable for this issue, then he or she will feel anxious and you will feel uneasy yourself. If you can, transfer this issue to the psychiatrist or psychologist. You might have to refer the client to an outside mental health professional. Clients with PTSD from childhood trauma will need to reexperience the trauma in a safe environment. They will need to tell their stories many times. Details are important. The stories need to include the events before, during, and after the trauma. Therapy begins with a safe relationship with the therapist.

Clients may decompensate when this material comes out. If staff-members are supportive, this should not last long. The clients may experience feelings of derealization or depersonalization. This can be frightening to an unskilled counselor. If at any time you feel that you are in over your head, stop and get the help of someone more experienced.

Sexual abuse is not a topic for most groups. The material is too disturbing and explosive. These matters need to be addressed in individual sessions. Events such as rape and insults to self-esteem and security are particularly likely to cause long-term problems. The more extreme and long-lasting the trauma, the more likely the events are to cause psychological damage.

These clients ultimately need to see the past events in a new context and attempt to forgive themselves and the offenders. The clients no longer are children, and these things are unlikely to happen again. The clients now have power and control that they did not have before. They will need to see themselves as competent and capable of handling stressful situations now. You can role-play situations for them and help them to develop skills for getting themselves out of trouble. "If that happened to you now, at your present age, what would you do?" The clients can learn that they can take care of themselves.

People who were involved in traumatic events often become anxious when they have to deal with similar situations in their current life situations. A spouse who was sexually abused as a child may feel frightened or numb when called on to perform sexually in his or her marriage. This client may need some of the techniques you used with the anxious client.

Cognitive Therapy

Cognitive techniques are necessary to correct the negative self-talk of these clients. They often call themselves bad or evil in their own thinking. They think that no one will like them because they have been bad. This negative self-talk will have to be exchanged for positive affirmation.

These clients will need to develop trust. The Love, Trust, and Commitment exercise (see Appendix 9) is a good one for them to start with. First, they need to reestablish a trusting relationship with themselves and then hopefully with you. This trust ultimately can be transferred to the group. The clients need to be encouraged to see their new support group as the healthy home that they never had. The home group will be there for them when they need it. The group has a stable set of rules that do not change.

These clients need to learn interpersonal relationship skills and to practice these skills with their treatment peers. They need to work on honesty. The cocoon of individual therapy is important here, and the clients must know that they can trust you. You need to be consistent and nonjudgmental. You need to be honest about how you feel about the abusive issues.

How to Learn Forgiveness

As these clients develop a good spiritual program, they need to try to forgive the perpetrators. By seeing the abusers as spiritually sick, the clients are relieved of some of the anger and the feeling of responsibility. When the clients are ready, they can be encouraged to pray for the perpetrators. They can turn the judgment over to the perfect judge. God will judge all humankind. The judgment will be perfect because God sees into everyone's heart.

Small steps in trust will be beneficial with these clients. You may find the clients sharing their abuse with other clients who have had similar experiences. The Fifth Step is tremendously beneficial for these clients. If the step is done properly, they will feel relieved of the guilt and rage.

Love in the Treatment Center

"I found out from another client that he liked me. After that, it preoccupied my mind. I jumped ahead and thought of marriage with this guy, and I did not even know him. It was hard to concentrate on the lectures or the steps because I could not wait for us to have a break so I could be with him. He told me how violent he was, but that did not faze me. I thought he was changing. The staff talked to me about it, and I started to think and realize it was wrong, but I needed to have a man in my life."

These thoughts and feelings are all too familiar. Two clients, during those fragile first few weeks of sobriety, have become romantically involved. These clients can lose the focus of treatment. They do not respond well to the interventions of the staff who are trying to get them to see the mistake they are making. They are in love, and to them it is real. It is difficult for these clients to realize that what they are feeling is not love at all and that the intense feelings they are experiencing are sexual. In their passion for each other, they are confused. It feels like love, it feels like the real thing, it is heaven, and it is the answer to what they have been looking for. They came into treatment feeling worthless and unimportant, and this other person has restored their sense of value. They have been made whole again. These clients do not realize that they are particularly vulnerable to such feelings in early sobriety. Feelings, which were deadened by chemicals before treatment, are just beginning to blossom new and untested. Their whole treatment program is at stake.

One client described the consequences of love in the treatment center like this: "After treatment, we had sex right away, and it all went downhill from there fast. He got too jealous. I was totally bending over backward for him, buying him cigarettes and pop. Even when I told him I only wanted to be friends, he wanted me back. He got drunk and threatened to kill me, so I went back with him for a while. I finally got the courage to tell him the truth. When he finally left, I felt so guilty."

The Importance of the Unit Rules

It is prudent for treatment programs to develop a set of unit rules that discourage these relationships from developing. The rule that only three or more clients may pair off together at any one time is a valuable one. Then if staff members see two clients pairing off, they can intervene.

How to Deal With Clients in Love

The first intervention attempted should be individual counseling with each client. These sessions should focus on educating the clients about what love is and what it is not. The clients can explore the Addictive Relationships exercise (see Appendix 12) with you and use this opportunity to learn and grow in treatment. They must be helped to see the reality of the situation. With assistance, they can begin to see the situation accurately. Is this really the best time for romance? Is this the person they want to spend their life with? What is their history? The clients and counselor must carefully collect all the evidence possible. They must get accurate and explore all of the options available. What is going on? Why? What do the clients hope to gain? What does it mean to the clients? Can they get their needs met in another way? Do they see the danger? What is love? What are romance and sexual attraction? How do they differ? How are they alike? The complexities of the feelings and motivations must be thoroughly explored. The dangers of this relationship at this time must be emphasized and addressed.

Disciplinary action might become necessary to prevent further problems. Considerable clinical skill is necessary here. Transference and counter transference issues may arise. The clients may resist your attempt to end the relationship that they see as beneficial. The staff must be sensitive to how in love these clients feel. Disapproving looks and derogatory comments will tend to intensify the feelings and draw the clients closer together.

The next intervention that you might need is conjoint counseling. Here the relationship can be addressed with both parties at the same time. If the clients have separate counselors, then both counselors should be involved in this session. The clients should be warned that they are placing each other's treatment at risk. It is not right to risk someone else's sobriety. If the problem persists, then it becomes an issue for the group. Now everyone's treatment is threatened, and the client population needs to respond. If the group cannot stop it, then the transfer of one client to another facility, or dismissal from treatment, becomes a viable option.

Love in the treatment center is a crisis from which all clients can grow. They can learn more about themselves. They can learn more about how to develop healthy relationships and the challenges that will confront them in sobriety. They must be encouraged to focus on their own recovery. The clients need to concentrate on supporting and encouraging themselves.

The Pathological Gambler

"Gamblers Anonymous (GA) has been, and is, the single most effective treatment modality for the pathological gambler" (Custer, 1984a). This point continues to be true today. The American Psychiatric Association's *Treatments of Psychiatric Disorders* states, "In general, an approach which utilizes several treatment modalities, including participation in Gamblers Anonymous, appears warranted at this time" (Karasu, 1989, p. 2466).

GA is a 12-step program modeled after the 12 steps of AA. The program provides hope to recovering individuals. Many clients recover by going to GA alone, but some clients, particularly those with concomitant psychiatric disorders, need the structure of inpatient or outpatient treatment (Custer, 1984b; Karasu, 1989).

All clients with gambling issues need to be thoroughly assessed for their gambling problem and take the South Oaks Gambling Screen (see Appendix 53). Gamblers tend to leave things out of their gambling history (see Appendix 68), so you must be careful to collect all of the problems caused by gambling. It helps to use the financial forms (see Appendix 51) to assess the amount of debt and develop a pay budget to pay back debtors.

Clients who have entered gambling treatment need to do a minimum of three things to begin recovery: (1) get honest with themselves, (2) embrace the first few steps of GA, and (3) develop a good relapse prevention program. These steps provide the foundation for recovery. The recovery skills presented in this book are client work. They educate about the disease of pathological gambling, teach the tools of recovery, and have clients apply the tools in their daily lives. Each client completes each exercise and shares his or her answers with the recovery skills group. The group decides by majority vote to accept or reject the contract based on how well the client completes the exercise. If the contract is rejected, then the client has to do it over again.

Recovery skills help a client to identify the problem, understand the problem, and learn coping skills for dealing with the problem. The types of recovery skills are infinite. You will want to develop some on your own, but there are a few exercises that you will use with nearly every client. The following recovery skills are the ones that you will use most often. If there is no pressure relief group in your local GA chapter, then you will have to help the client make a payback plan using the pressure relief group and financial forms in Appendix 51.

Honesty

The Honesty for Gamblers exercise (see Appendix 34) helps clients to see how they have been distorting reality. All clients use denial, in its many forms, to keep from experiencing the pain of the truth. If they see the whole picture about themselves, they hurt. They realize that they are sick and need help. This creates tremendous fear. Clients keep from feeling this fear by minimizing, rationalizing, denying, blaming, distorting, projecting, intellectualizing, diverting, and utilizing dozens of other ways of not experiencing the truth.

Clients cannot uncover denial without getting help from others because denial tends to be unconscious. The Honesty for Gamblers exercise gets them started in this search for the truth. It is the job of the counselor and treatment center to set up an atmosphere of love and trust and then to give clients the opportunity to search for and share the truth with each other. The truth sets people free. Treatment is an endless search for truth.

Working through the Honesty for Gamblers exercise is an eye-opening experience for clients. They come to realize how much they have been lying to themselves and to others. They feel guilty about lying to others. However, clients usually do not realize that they have lied to themselves more than to anyone else. This comes as a startling revelation.

Clients need to process how they feel about themselves when they lie, and they need to learn the negative consequences of dishonesty. First, if they lie, then they will hurt. If they do not tell people the truth, then they will not be known or feel loved. Second, without truth, clients cannot solve problems accurately. To solve problems, you need the facts.

The 12 steps should be the core of treatment for pathological gambling. More individuals have recovered using the principles of GA than using any other treatment. GA works, and it is free. The only requirement for GA membership is the desire to stop gambling.

Treatment programs differ in terms of the steps that they address. Some programs address Step One, some address Steps One to Three, and others address Steps One to Five. This must be individualized. Some clients will be able to work only through Step One, and that is fine if they do a good Step One. For most clients, it is a benefit to complete at least Steps One to Three while in treatment. The more clients can do, the better off they will be in recovery. Working through the Fifth Step takes a great burden off the clients. If they complete the Fifth Step, then they will not have to carry as much guilt and shame into abstinence from gambling.

If your program works only on the First Step, that will give you more time to work on powerlessness and unmanageability.

As you take clients through the step exercises, make sure that they are internalizing the material. They must be able to identify the problem, understand the problem, and learn coping skills for dealing with the problem. They must be able to verbalize a solid understanding of each step and how they are going to apply the step in their lives.

You will be able to tell when clients are just complying and when they are actually understanding and internalizing the material by their level of commitment to remain free of gambling. This will be evident in their behavior. If you watch how clients act with you and with their treatment peers, you will have a good idea of whether they are internalizing the information or not. If you are hearing one thing in individual sessions and a client's peers are hearing another thing around the treatment center, then someone is not getting the truth. This client needs to be confronted with the inconsistency of his or her behavior.

Clients often feel torn between various parts of themselves. There seems to be a side that wants to gamble and a side that wants to stop. There seems to be a side that wants to love and a side that wants to hate. There is a constant, and often turbulent, internal war going on inside the clients' thinking. Each side tries to take control of the clients' behavior. Sometimes it is hard for a client to know who he or she really is. It feels as though there is more than one person talking inside the client's own head.

Freud (2000) called these internal voices the id, ego, and superego. Berne (1964) called them the child, adult, and parent. In recovery, we call the voices the illness, self, and Higher Power. One train of thinking is the thought process of the disease. This side only wants the clients to gamble, and it does not care how it gets them to do it. If the clients feel miserable, that is all the better. Another voice is that of the Higher Power. The Higher Power wants the clients to love themselves, others, and the Higher Power. This voice is supportive. The third voice is the clients' own thinking.

As you move these clients through the steps, do not move a client to the next step until he or she has a solid foundation of successfully completing the step below. If the client has not embraced a good Step One, then there is no use in moving to Step Two. If you have to work on Step One the whole time that the client is in treatment, that is fine. Some clients do that. However, do not try to move up in the steps too quickly. The steps must build on top of each other. The first building block is Step One.

Gambling Step One

"We admitted we were powerless over gambling—that our lives had become unmanageable" (GA, 1989b, p. 38).

It is vital that all clients complete a solid Step One for Gamblers (see Appendix 35) in treatment. Step One is the most important step because without it recovery is impossible. Step One necessitates a total surrender. The clients must accept as true that they are pathological gamblers and that their lives are unmanageable. Until this conscious and unconscious surrender occurs, these clients cannot grow. So long as clients think that they can bring the gambling under control, they will not accept their disease. "The idea that somehow, some day, we will control our gambling is the great obsession of every compulsive gambler. The persistence of this illusion is astonishing. Many pursue it into the gates of prison, insanity, or death" (GA, 1989a, p. 2).

Step work is mainly group work. The clients complete the step exercise and present the exercise in group. The group helps the clients with the step by asking questions, giving constructive comments, and deciding whether the step is successfully completed. As the counselor, you usually should not make the decision to clear the step without the support of the group. The clients may be only complying with treatment, pretending that they are working, when in reality they are not internalizing the information. The treatment peers sometimes are more likely to see this manipulation. The peers see the clients in casual interaction, and they may notice the inconsistencies.

In Step One, the clients must learn to accept that they are pathological gamblers and that they are powerless over gambling. Their lives are unmanageable. They also must understand that they cannot live normally so long as they gamble.

The best way of convincing clients to surrender is to show them that they get into trouble when they gamble. They do not get into trouble *every* time, but they cannot predict when the trouble is going to occur. They may place a few bets and go home, or they may gamble away the farm. The key point is inconsistency once they place the first bet.

Clients need to process through many of their problems until they realize that they cannot predict their behavior. Have clients share exactly what happened when their gambling got out of control. Talk about the fear, shame, humiliation, and depression caused by gambling. How depressing was it to know that their families were falling apart? How did it feel to be unable to keep promises?

Sometimes the clients gambled more, or for a longer period, than they originally had intended. Once they began gambling, the addiction took control. Even when they promised themselves that they were going to stop or cut down, they kept on gambling. Clients must understand that once they place the first bet, they do not know what they are going to do.

Most gamblers want to hold on to the delusion that they are still in control. They do not want to admit that they are powerless and that their lives are unmanageable. Sure, they were having problems sometimes, but they think that they were having problems only occasionally. The fact is that when clients had serious problems, they usually were related to gambling. Gamblers do things when they are gambling that they never would do otherwise. They need to look at each of these behaviors and see the painful consequences of their addiction. They need to take a careful look at their gambling histories—at the lies, the crimes, the inconsistencies, and the people they have hurt. They need to understand that so long as they gamble, they will be in pain.

Gambling Step Two

"[We] came to believe that a power greater than ourselves could restore us to a normal way of thinking and living" (GA, 1989b, p. 39).

The beginning of the clients' spiritual program is Step One, or the surrender step. It is essential to accept powerlessness and unmanageability before the clients reach toward a Higher Power. The essential ingredient of Step Two for Gamblers (see Appendix 36) is willingness. Without being willing to seek a power greater than themselves, the clients will fail. They have admitted that they are powerless over gambling and that their lives are unmanageable. Now the clients need to see the insanity of their disease and search for an answer.

In Step Two, the clients look at their insane behavior. They see how crazy they were acting and reach for an answer. They must conclude that they cannot hold onto their old ways of thinking and behaving. If they do, then they will relapse.

Many clients rebel at the very idea of a Higher Power. They are encouraged to open the door, just a little, and seek a Higher Power of their own understanding. They are encouraged to be honest, open-minded, and willing. They need power; they are powerless. They need someone else to manage; their lives are unmanageable.

At first, you encourage the clients to see that a Higher Power can exist. The clients are encouraged to look at their interpersonal group and see that the group has more power than they do. You can say something like this to a client: "If you wanted to leave this room but the group wanted to keep you in, do you think you could leave?" It soon becomes obvious to this client that the group members could force the client to stay inside the room if they so desired. The client is then asked to try to place his or her trust in the Higher Power of the group.

Trust is a difficult issue for most gamblers, and they need to process their lack of trust with the group. This is good group work. If clients cannot trust the group as a whole, can they trust anyone in the group? If they cannot trust anyone, can they trust themselves? Are they willing to try? If they are unable to trust others, then they are lost. Clients who obviously cannot trust themselves are out of control.

The best way of helping clients learn to trust the group is to create a supportive group. The members are actively interested in each other in this group. They are involved in each other's recovery. They gently help each other to search for the truth. The group members are kind, encouraging, and supportive. They are confidential. The group members never are hostile or aggressive. They do not put each other down. This is counterproductive. If you have an aggressive, highly confrontational group, you will destroy trust. People must learn to confront each other in an atmosphere of unconditional positive regard. It is the counselor's job to teach the group this process.

Once the clients trust the group, they can be encouraged to transfer this trust to the GA group. The clients in treatment should attend as many regular meetings as possible. Gradually, they will feel safe enough to share. This builds trust.

As the group becomes involved in the clients' growth, confidence in the group process grows. This probably is the first time in these clients' lives when they have told someone the whole truth. When the group does not reject these clients, the clients feel a tremendous relief. This will show on their faces.

The clients also see people further along in the program doing better. These people look better and sound better. The clients cannot miss the power of the group process. It changes people. Clients see new members come in frightened or hostile and watch them turn around. Clients watch the power of group support. Soon the group will be offering the new clients encouragement. Clients learn how helpful it is to share their experiences, strengths, and hopes. Once these clients see how insane they are acting and accept that the group has the power to restore them to a healthy way of thinking and living, they have embraced Step Two. By trusting the group, the clients open the door to a Higher Power. This basic building block of trust is vital to good treatment. Clients who move too quickly to the concept of God miss the power of the group. They miss seeing the Higher Power in others. These clients sometimes believe that God is the only answer they need. They might think that they do not have to go to meetings so long as they have a good spiritual program. These clients might not work a program of recovery, and they probably will relapse. All clients are encouraged to trust the group process.

Gambling Step Three

"[We] made a decision to turn our will and our lives over to the care of this power of our own understanding" (GA, 1989b, p. 40).

Most clients have difficulty with Step Three for Gamblers (see Appendix 37). They need to be reminded to turn problems over to their Higher Power. Clients can be so self-centered that they set themselves up for pain. They think that the whole world should revolve around them. When people do not cooperate with their plans, they are furious. They think that their spouses, children, and friends should obey them. They believe that everything should go exactly the way in which they want events to go. They believe that they are deserving of special honor and privileges. They care very deeply about what they want and how they feel, but their ability to empathize with others is seriously impaired. Clients correct this defect in treatment by learning empathy for others and turning their will and their lives over to the care of a power greater than themselves.

The worst thing that a counselor can do in the Third Step is to push clients faster than they are ready to go. The decision to turn things over is the clients' decision. As the counselor, all you can do is encourage, educate, and support. However, you have one big thing going for you in Step Three. When clients turn something over, they feel immediate relief. They feel this relief emotionally, and this is a powerful way of learning. Nothing works better than showing clients how this tool of recovery works. If you give gamblers a good feeling, they will want to re-create that feeling. That is why they were gambling. The Third Step is the answer that these clients have been waiting for. They must experience it to believe it.

Many clients resist Step Three. Even people who have been in GA for years have difficulty with it. Meetings are full of people talking about turning things over and then taking them back. Step Three is a decision that is made every day.

There is great hope for clients in Step Three, and they usually feel it. This newfound hope must not be confused with religion. Religion is an organized system of faith and worship. Spirituality is the innermost relationship that you have with yourself and all else. If the clients want to use a religious structure, that is encouraged so long as it sets the clients free and does not immerse them in guilt or remorse.

The key to Step Three is willingness. Once clients are willing to seek a Higher Power of their own understanding, they have come a long way toward completing Step Three. As soon as you hear clients say that they are willing to turn it over, they are well on their way to recovery. Clients need to trust and turn things over to the group. The group has more collective wisdom than does the individual client, and the group can be helpful in solving problems. As clients use the power and support of their group, they learn how to turn things over.

Some clients have serious problems with the word *God*. They feel better if they use the words *good orderly direction* (for each letter in *God*). Clients do not have to use the word *God* if they do not want to. Many clients have had God and religion crammed down their throats for so long that they are sick of it.

Gambling Step Four

"[We] made a searching and fearless moral and financial inventory of ourselves" (GA, 1989b, p. 42). Much of this exercise was developed by Lynn Carroll during his years at Hazelden and at Keystone Treatment Center. The material has been expanded and adapted for use with gamblers.

Step Four for Gamblers (see Appendix 38) is where clients make a thorough housecleaning. They rid themselves of the guilt of the past and look forward to a new future. Detail is important here. You must encourage clients to be specific. They must put down exactly what they did. The clients will share their Fourth Step inventory with someone in the Fifth Step. Another part of Fourth Step group work involves each client's assets. This work allows clients to share good things about themselves with their peers.

To do a good Step Four, clients must be honest. They will relieve themselves of the guilt if they do their Steps Four and Five properly. They might have a difficult time in forgiving themselves, but they can feel that their Higher Power has forgiven them. Faith can do for them what they cannot do for themselves.

There is a tendency for some clients to leave something bad out of the Fifth Step. This is not a good idea. Clients are encouraged to share everything that they think is important, no matter how bad it might seem. If it causes them guilt or shame, then it needs to be shared. Clients need to come face-to-face with their problems. All the garbage of the past must be cleaned out. Nothing can be left to fester and rot.

The Fourth Step is where clients identify their character defects. Once these defects are identified, the clients can work toward resolution. Often clients will come upon material suppressed for years. As memory tracks are stimulated, deeper unconscious material may surface.

Clients need to concentrate on the exact nature of their wrongs. Do not let them accuse or blame someone else. This is a time to take responsibility. They should not make excuses. They should just ask for forgiveness. Yes, there were mitigating circumstances. This is not a time to find out who was right and who was wrong. It is time to dump the shame.

Clients who get depressed doing their Fourth Step need to concentrate on their good qualities. These clients are not all bad. They need to be shown that they are valuable persons who deserve to be loved. Some clients might have to wait quite a while before doing their Fourth Step. Absolute honesty is a requirement.

Some clients are so used to being negative about themselves that they cannot come up with their assets. These clients need to have the group help them to see the positive things about themselves.

Step Four must be detailed and specific. Clients must cover the exact nature of their behavior. This is the only way for them to see the full impact of their disease. They should not color their stories to make them seem less guilty or responsible.

Most of all, Step Four (like all of the steps) is a time of great joy. Clients finally face the whole truth about themselves. The truth is that they are wonderful. As they rid themselves of the pain of the past, they are ready to move forward to new lives filled with hope and recovery.

Gambling Step Five

"[We] admitted to ourselves and to another human being the exact nature of our wrongs" (GA, 1989b, p. 44).

As the counselor, your job in Step Five for Gamblers (see Appendix 39) is to help the client to match up with the right person to share with. Who this person is and what each is like is vitally important. This person stands as a symbol of the Higher Power and all people on Earth. This step directly attacks the core of the disease. If it is done properly, the client will be free from the past. The person chosen should be someone who understands the program and who has experience in hearing Fifth Steps. This person needs an attitude of acceptance and unconditional positive regard. The individual must be nonjudgmental and strictly confidential. It is helpful if this person is working a 12-step program himself or herself. The person should not look uncomfortable when a client is sharing painful material. The client needs to see a nonshaming face.

The purpose of the Fifth Step is to make things right with self, others, and the Higher Power. The clients should see themselves accurately—the positive *and* negative points, all at the same time. At the core of the illness is this firmly held belief that if the clients tell anyone the truth about themselves, then that person will not like them. This is not accurate, but the clients have been living as if this were the truth. The clients have not been honest with themselves and others for a long time, perhaps since childhood. The clients have pretended to be somebody else to get the good stuff in life. The only way of proving to these clients that their held belief is wrong is to show them. This is the purpose of having another human being hear the Fifth Step. If this person does not reject the clients, then the inaccurate thinking is proved wrong. A new accurate thought replaces the old one: The clients can tell the truth, and people will still like them. This is a tremendous relief to clients. They have been living their lives convinced that they were unacceptable to others. This is a deeply held conviction, and it causes great pain. Clients must come to realize that unless they tell the truth, they never will feel loved.

In the Fifth Step, clients need to come to realize that they are good persons. They have made mistakes. They have done bad things. They are not bad; they are good. They need to forgive themselves and start over, clean and new. Clients have varying degrees of spirituality and religious beliefs. You must help each client see that forgiveness has taken place.

Many clients will be tempted to hold something back in the Fifth Step. They do not want to share some part of their past. They do not think that anyone can understand. Clients must be warned against this tendency. If they hold anything back, then the illness will win. All major wrongs must be disclosed.

After the Fifth Step, most clients experience a feeling of relief. The truth sets them free. In time, clients will need to process these feelings with you. Some clients feel no immediate relief. If they were honest in the step, they will feel the relief later. Sometimes it takes a while to sink in. Steps Four and Five are profoundly humbling experiences. Once these steps are over, there is a profound feeling of relief.

Gambling Relapse Prevention

Relapse prevention is one of the most important aspects of treatment. In studies of many different addictions, approximately two thirds of clients seem to relapse within the first year of leaving treatment (Hunt, Barnett, & Branch, 1971; Marlatt & Gordon, 1985; Shaffer & LaPlante, 2008).

Most clients relapse within 3 months of leaving treatment. This is the period of highest risk. Clients must be willing to do almost anything to prevent relapse. They need to see themselves as clinging to an ice-covered cliff with their recovery support group holding the only rope. The most important thing that they can do is go to meetings. Clients who are working a daily program of recovery will not relapse. You cannot work the program and gamble at the same time. These behaviors are incompatible.

Relapse is a process that begins long before making the first bet. If the new tools of recovery are not used and problems begin to escalate, then clients reach a point where they think that their only option is to gamble.

The Relapse Prevention for Gamblers exercise (see Appendix 40) assists gamblers in developing a relapse prevention plan. Some of this work was done with alcohol or other addictions, but it is applicable for gambling problems (Shaffer & LaPlante, 2008).

Relapse prevention requires that clients work a daily program of recovery. The clients must take their personal inventory at the end of every day. If any of the relapse symptoms become evident, then immediate action must be taken.

Other concerned individuals need to check clients daily for relapse warning signs. This can be done by family members, sponsors, or coworkers. This is a good reason for clients to go to daily meetings and hang around other recovering persons. Often other people can see what clients are unable to see for themselves.

The clients need to identify high-risk situations that might trigger relapse and to develop coping skills to deal with each situation. The more clients can practice these skills, the better off they will be in recovery. In group, clients need to role-play high-risk situations and help each other to develop relapse prevention plans.

Each client will be different. Marlatt and Gordon (1985) found that most relapses occur when clients are experiencing the following high-risk situations:

1. *Negative emotions:* These include particularly anger and frustration. They also can be negative emotions such as boredom, jealousy, depression, and anxiety.

2. *Social pressure:* This is being in a social situation where people are gambling or being directly encouraged to gamble by someone.

3. *Interpersonal conflict:* This can be a conflict with a parent, spouse, child, boss, friend, and so on.

4. *Positive emotions:* Something positive happens and the client wants to celebrate. This can be a promotion, wedding, birth of a child, graduation, and so on.

5. *Testing personal control:* The client gambles to find out whether he or she can control the gambling.

Using the Relapse Prevention for Gamblers exercise, clients develop the skills necessary to deal with each of the high-risk situations and then practice the new skills until they become good at them. All clients must role-play gambling refusal situations until they can say no and feel relatively comfortable. They must examine and experience all of their triggers, see through the first use, and learn how to deal with euphoric recall.

Clients must develop a plan for a lapse. What are they going to do if they gamble again? Whom are they going to contact? What are they going to say? This must be role-played in group to give the clients practice.

The clients must understand the behavior chain. They also must develop skills for changing their thoughts, feelings, and actions when they have problems. Using imagery, the clients need to experience craving and learn experientially that craving will pass if they move away from the situation and use their new tools of recovery. No gambler should carry money in early recovery. It is a relapse trigger. Someone else, such as a spouse, has to manage the client's money and give him or her only enough to buy the essentials, such as lunch, that he or she needs each day. This is a humbling experience for most gamblers but is necessary to prevent relapse.

12 Adolescent Treatment

Source: Digital Vision/Thinkstock.

Adolescent treatment must be different. You cannot use the same program for adolescents that you use for adults. Teenagers have not developed the skills that adults have. The client's biopsychosocial level of development must be assessed and used to develop an appropriate age-level treatment plan. Adolescents are not socially and emotionally mature. Adults have a stable identity. Adolescents are developing an identity. Only at the age of 15 does an adolescent have an idea of who he or she is. Adolescence is the age at which tremendous physiological changes occur in the body, mind, and spirit. The clients' emotional and physical structure is in transition from childhood to adulthood.

The Normal Adolescent

Studies have shown that most adolescents are well adjusted. They get along well with their peers, teachers, and families. Despite greater demands, most youth are rising to the challenge and developing higher levels of skill and maturity than were common in prior generations (Block, 1971; Csikszentmihalyi & Larson, 1984;

Source: Jupiterimages/Thinkstock.

Douvan & Adelson, 1966; Larson, Brown, & Mortimer, 2003; Offer & Offer, 1975; Offer, Ostrov, & Howard, 1981; Santrock, 2010; Vaillant, 1977; Westley & Epstein, 1969). Adolescence should be understood as a transitional stage that allows individuals to adjust to growth, development, and change. Each cycle of life brings new challenges and opportunities, but all of the changes will be incorporated into the basic personality structure. At the end of high school, the majority of American adolescents enter a new phase of life called young adulthood.

Normal adolescents do not feel inferior to others. They do not believe that other people treat them badly. They feel relaxed. They believe that they can control themselves, and they have confidence that they can handle novel situations. They feel proud of their body image and physical development. They feel strong and healthy. They have embraced the work ethic. They feel good when they do a good job. They are not afraid of their sexuality, and they like the recent changes in their bodies. They do not perceive any major problems between themselves and their parents. They are hopeful about the future, and they believe that they will be successful. They do not believe that they have major problems (Larson et al., 2003; Santrock, 2010).

Most adolescents have strong egos and are able to cope well with internal and external stimuli. They have mastered previous developmental stages without serious problems. They accept social norms and feel comfortable in society. These adolescents are free of adolescent turmoil, and they comprise 80% of the adolescent population (Offer, 1986; Santrock, 2010).

Puberty

Puberty is a period of rapid physiological development involving massive hormonal and bodily changes that take place primarily in early adolescence. Puberty is accompanied by changes in the endocrine system, body fat, muscle size, new brain connections, height, weight, bone density, and secondary sexual characteristics. Heredity is an important factor, but it does not totally determine these events. Puberty takes place between the ages of 9 and 16 for most individuals. Environmental factors can influence its onset and duration (Blakemore, Berenbaum, & Liben, 2009; van den Berg & Boomsma, 2007).

From the first whiskers of boys and the budding of the breasts of girls is a giant hormone flood. Hormones are like a light switch; they might look small, but once switched on the whole room lights up. Androgens are the main male sex hormones, and estrogens are the main class of female hormones. Both sexes secrete each of these hormones but in different quantities. Testosterone is an androgen that plays an important role in male development including development of external genitals, increase in height, voice changes, and increased sexual desire. Estrogens play an important role in female pubertal development including breast development, uterine development, and skeletal changes (Cameron, 2004).

The hypothalamus, pituitary gland, thyroid gland, and the gonads all play a role in growth and skeletal maturation. The hallmark of puberty is the reactivation of the hypothalamic-pituitary-gonadal axis. In the United States, puberty begins at approximately 9 to 10 years of age in girls and 10 to 11 years of age in boys. For girls, the mean beginning of the growth spurt is 9 years of age and for boys 11 years of age. During their growth spurt, girls increase in height about 3.5 inches per year and for boys about 4 inches per year. Because of these dramatic changes, during puberty adolescents understandably become preoccupied with their bodies. Throughout puberty, girls are less happy with their bodies, probably because their body fat increases, and boys become more satisfied—probably because of an increase in muscle mass (Santrock, 2010).

Some adolescents mature early and some mature late. This is often called early and late bloomers. Recent research shows that it is an advantage to be an early-maturing boy and a disadvantage to be an early-maturing girl. Early-maturing boys felt good about their early increase in height, muscle mass, and secondary sexual characteristics. Early-maturing girls have more problems in school, were more independent, and more popular with boys than late bloomers. In the sixth grade, early-maturing girls were more satisfied with their body image, but by the tenth grade, late maturing girls were more satisfied with their body image. By late adolescence, early-maturing girls are shorter and stockier, while late maturing girls are taller and thinner. The late maturing girls have body images that more closely match the American ideal of beauty—tall and thin (Simmons & Blyth, 1987).

Early maturing increases vulnerability to a number of problems. Early-maturing girls are more likely to smoke, drink, be depressed, have an eating disorder, request independence from their parents, and have older friends. Their bodies are more likely to elicit responses from males that lead to earlier dating and earlier sexual experiences. Because of their cognitive and social immaturity, combined with early physical development, early-maturing girls are easily lured into problem behaviors. They look older and appear to be more capable of taking on more mature responsibilities when they are not ready. Early-maturing adolescents of both sexes take more risks, especially sexual risks (Santrock, 2010). It is important for parents, mentors, and other responsible adults to monitor adolescent behavior. When adolescents are in tempting and dangerous risk-taking situations with minimal adult supervision, they become more vulnerable to negative outcomes. Parents play the most important role and are the best at protecting their children from the negative consequences of risky behavior (Arria et al., 2008).

Adolescents reach a level of health, strength, and energy that they will never again have in their lives. They develop a sense of uniqueness and invulnerability that convinces them that they will never suffer from poor health. Risk taking increases from ages 10 through 15 and then declines and remains stable through the remainder of adolescence and early adulthood. Even 18-year-olds are more impulsive, less future-oriented, and more susceptible to peer pressure than adults in their mid- to late 20s. This leads adolescents to seek experiences that create intense feelings, such as loud music, horror movies, amusement rides, sex, and use of alcohol and drugs (Dahl, 2004).

Ages 13 to 16

The period of ages 13 to 16 brings an enormous change in physical and psychological development. Throughout adolescence, girls remain about 2 years ahead of boys in their level of maturity. Some adolescents bloom early, and some bloom late, each having a different psychological challenge. Early bloomers may be expected to perform with individuals of their size, whereas late bloomers suffer from the problems of self-esteem that result from looking more immature than their peers look.

Adolescents of this age group experience a great deal of ambivalence and conflict, and they often blame the outside world for their discomfort. As they struggle to develop their own identity, dependence on parents gives way to a new dependence on peers. These adolescents struggle to avoid dependence and may disparage parents, devaluing past attachments. These early teens often find a new ego ideal that leads to idealization of sports figures or entertainers. Adolescents at this stage are particularly vulnerable to people who they would love to emulate. It is sometimes useless to try to get these adolescents to connect past, present, and future behavior. Because they think concretely, they have difficulty connecting current behavior with future negative consequences or connecting current negative consequences with their past choices. These adolescents spend most of their time in the present but they can learn in treatment to do positive things to get positive results. Nothing works better with adolescents than being reinforcing. When they succeed, tell them that you are proud of them. Punishment and control does not work as well as being reinforcing. You should be reinforcing the clients about 90% of the time and giving negative consequences about 10% of the time. Many counselors think this loses them control but in reality, this gains control. If your clients care about you and respect you, they will do anything for you. Nothing is more powerful than love, and these adolescents are starved for it.

The development of a self-concept is crucial at this stage. These adolescents must explore their own morals and values, questioning the accepted way of society and family to gain a sense of self. In treatment, they need to spend a lot of time processing the positive and negative consequences of their behavior. Because these clients have difficulty with connecting past, present, and future behavior, it helps to show them how this works on paper or a blackboard.

Counselor:	It says here that you got arrested for breaking into a gas station.
Client:	I did not do anything.
Counselor:	Then how did you get arrested?
Client:	One of my friends told the cops I broke into the store.
Counselor:	I am getting confused. Let's write down on the blackboard exactly what happened.
Client:	Sure.
Counselor:	Okay, you were riding around with your friends, right?
Client:	Right.
Counselor:	Had you been drinking?
Client:	Yeah, we were drinking beer.
Counselor:	So you decided to get in a car with people who were drinking beer?
Client:	Yeah.
Counselor:	But you could have said no, and you knew you were on probation, and you knew that one of the requirements of your probation was not to drink alcohol. Let us write that on the blackboard.
Client:	Yeah, but I was not going to drink.
Counselor:	Did you drink?
Client:	I had a few beers.
Counselor:	So you made a decision to drink beer when you knew it was against the law and you knew it was against a court order. Let's write that on the blackboard.
	Now, what happened with the gas station?
Client:	We ran out of beer.
Counselor:	So what happened then?

Client: Well, I knew of this gas station that was down a gravel road that had beer.

Counselor: Was the gas station open?

Client: No, it was three o'clock in the morning.

Counselor: But you decided to drive down to the gas station anyway? Were you hoping it would be open?

Client: No, I knew it was closed.

Counselor: How did you know that?

Client: We steal beer from there all the time. The owner leaves the back door open.

Counselor: Let us put all these decisions on the blackboard. (*The counselor writes them all down.*) Then what happened?

Client: The cops stopped us and found beer in the car.

Counselor: How much beer did they find?

Client: Five cases.

Counselor: What happened then?

Client: I got arrested for being in possession of alcohol.

Counselor: But you said you were not guilty of anything? Let us look at all the choices you made that resulted in your arrest. (*The counselor points the decisions out one by one.*) At any time, you could have made a decision that would have had a different result. That is what we are trying to learn in treatment—to make better decisions. To tell yourself that you didn't make any bad decisions is lying to yourself. We have a list of many decisions you made that resulted in a negative consequence. In treatment, we are going to practice thinking through your decisions so you can end up with different results. Now, looking at all the decisions you made, do you think you did anything that resulted in you getting arrested?

Client: Yeah, I shouldn't have gotten in the car.

Counselor: And?

Client: I drank when I knew it was wrong.

Counselor: And?

Client: I shouldn't have told my friends about the gas station.

Counselor: And?

Client: And, I shouldn't have had my friends steal the beer.

Counselor: That is right. Now copy all these decisions down, and carry them in your pocket. Take them out each day for a week and read them through. Your decisions are important. They make you the person you want to be.

As the counselor, you cannot create the client you want. You can only show the clients how to develop positive social, emotional, nutritional, and recreational skills. Adolescents make up their own minds who they are and what they believe in. They must reassess the facts that were accepted during childhood and must accept, reject, or modify these societal norms as their own. The here and now thinking of earlier childhood gives way to a new capacity for more abstract thought. These adolescents may spend long periods contemplating the "meaning of life."

Ages 16 to 19

In our culture, we expect a gradual development of independence and self-identity by 19 years of age. The physical manifestations of approaching adulthood require numerous psychological adjustments—in particular the development of how one views the self in relation to others. The vast majority of adolescents attain their adult size and physical characteristics by 18 years of age, and the earlier differences between early and late bloomers no longer are evident. The process of abstract thinking changes along with physical development, becoming more complex and refined. Late adolescents are less bound by concrete thinking. A sense of time emerges where these individuals can recognize the differences between the past, present, and future. They can adopt a future orientation that leads to the capacity to delay gratification. These individuals develop a sense of equality with adults.

In the brain, adolescents are developing the prefrontal cortex, which controls executive functioning such as focusing attention, prioritizing, planning, organizing, and resisting primitive impulses. In childhood and early adolescence, the amygdala, the site of many primitive emotions, takes priority; later in adolescence the prefrontal cortex thinks through behavioral options and can inhibit maladaptive risky behavior. It is here where a person learns how to resist primitive impulses. This is the first area of the brain to go off-line in addiction. Drug addicts cannot plan, organize, or resist primitive impulses because the prefrontal cortex is not working. The prefrontal cortex comes completely online at about age 20 (Lerner & Steinberg, 2009).

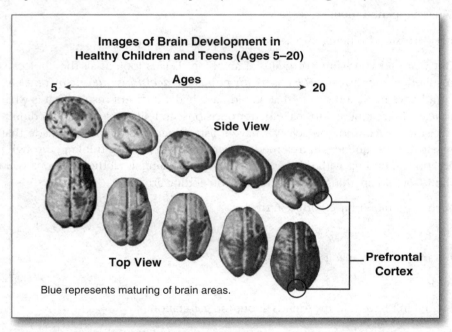

Images of Brain Development in Healthy Children and Teens (Ages 5–20)

Ages — 5 ⟵——————⟶ 20

Side View

Top View

Prefrontal Cortex

Blue represents maturing of brain areas.

Source: From PNAS USA, 2004, May 25; 101(21):8174–9. Epub 2004 May 17.
Copyright © 2004 National Academy of Sciences, U.S.A.

Self-certainty and an internal structure develop while teens experiment with different roles. By 19 years of age, most adolescents are considering occupational choices and have begun to develop intimate relationships (Weedman, 1992).

Interesting Adolescent Facts

- In general, throughout puberty girls are less happy and have more negative body images than boys (Bearman, Presnall, Martinex, & Stice, 2006).
- Adolescents have a sense of uniqueness and invulnerability that convinces them that they will never suffer from poor health (Santrock, 2010).

- The three leading causes of death in adolescents are (1) accidents, (2) homicide, and (3) suicide (National Vital Statistics Reports, 2008).
- When given the opportunity, adolescents will sleep an average of 9 hours and 25 minutes a night (Tarokh & Carskadon, 2008).
- Forty-five percent of adolescents get less than 8 hours of sleep on school nights (National Sleep Foundation, 2006).
- Adolescent girls engage in more self-disclosure in close relationships and are better at active listening than boys (Leaper & Friedman, 2007).
- In a recent national survey, 63% of high school seniors (64% of boys and 62% of girls) report they have experienced sexual intercourse (MMWR, 2006).
- The overwhelming majority of adolescents growing up in a gay family have a heterosexual orientation (Tasker & Golombok, 1997).

Children and adolescents who experience a heavy media diet of violence are more likely to perceive the world as a dangerous place and to view aggression as more acceptable (Wilson, 2008).

The Chemically Dependent Adolescent

Troubled adolescents comprise about 20% of the adolescent population. These adolescents come from family backgrounds that are not stable. There often are histories of mental illness in these families, the parents often have marital conflicts, and the families often have economic difficulties. The moods of these adolescents are not stable, and they are more prone to depression. They have significantly more psychiatric disturbances, and they do well only with the aid of intense psychotherapy. They do not grow out of it (Larson et al., 2003; Masterson & Costello, 1980; Offer, 1986; Santrock, 2010). It is in this troubled group that addiction often develops.

In this country, the average first use of mood-altering chemicals for boys is 11.9 years and for girls is 12.7 years (U.S. Department of Justice, 1983). Adolescents usually use alcohol or drugs for the first time under peer pressure. They want to be accepted and to be a part of the group. Children are likely to model after the chemical use of their parents. Children with alcoholic parents are at greater risk for becoming chemically dependent. More and more adolescents are using prescription drugs found in the medicine cabinets of their parents. Individuals who begin drinking before the age of 14 are more likely to become alcohol dependent (Hingson, Heeren, & Winter, 2006; Spalt, 1979; U.S. Department of Health and Human Services, 2009).

Adolescents who continue to use will increase drinking to a regular pattern (usually weekends). They may experiment with other drugs, particularly prescription medication taken from their parents or friends. The use of opioids is becoming more often the second drug of abuse. Hydrocodone is now one of the most prescribed medications in the country, so opioids are widely available. Adolescents begin to use drugs to communicate, to relate, and to belong. With regular drinking, tolerance develops. The adolescents need more of the drug to get intoxicated. Emotional changes may first be noticed here by their families. The adolescents may become irritable and more noncommunicative. They may begin to spend more time alone in their rooms. They may begin not caring for themselves or for others. Polarization of parents and children begins to occur (Morrison & Smith, 1990; U.S. Department of Health and Human Services, 2009).

As addiction further develops, adolescents no longer can trust themselves when using chemicals. The choice to use these drugs no longer is available to them; they have to use to feel normal. The continued use of chemicals eliminates the ability to think logically and rationally. Rationalization, minimization, and denial cut the adolescents off from reality (Soujanen, 1983).

Chemically dependent adolescents gradually change their peer group to include drinking and drug-using friends. They begin to use chemicals to block out the pain. They no longer use for the euphoric effect. They drink to escape pain. Anger, blackouts, and drinking alone are strong indicators of addiction in the adolescent population. With the progression of the disease, family conflicts increase. The adolescents may run away, withdraw, or act out at home and at school. They withdraw from family and community activities.

Problems with the police and school officials increase and become serious. The adolescents may become verbally abusive to parents and more rebellious to authority figures. Life begins to center around the drug or addicted behavior of choice. Daily use begins, and these addicted individuals begin to use to maintain rather than to escape. The adolescents attempt to cut back or quit, but they are unable to stay clean and sober. Physical deterioration begins. Hiding and lying about drugs becomes more common. The adolescents feel more intensely isolated and alone. Concern is now openly expressed by parents, teachers, and even peers. Gradually, the adolescents lose all self-esteem and depression begins. Persistent chemical use leads to incarceration, institutionalization, or death (Chatlos & Jaffe, 1994; Morrison & Smith, 1990).

Addiction stops emotional development and the addicted adolescent stays immature. Their prefrontal cortex goes off-line so they become unable to focus attention, plan, organize, inhibit primitive impulses, and learn. To develop normally, adolescents must learn to use their feelings to give them energy and direction for problem solving. When feelings are consistently altered by alcohol or drugs, this no longer is possible. The major coping skill of addicts is their addiction.

Adolescent addiction can occur extremely quickly—within weeks—because adolescent emotional development is immature. Adolescents do not have the internal structure to bring themselves and their lives under control. They cannot delay the onset of addiction for years, as can adults.

The Adolescent Chemical Dependency Counselor

Source: ©iStockphoto.com/monkeybusinessimages.

Working with adolescents can be among the most rewarding work in the field. By making an early intervention in an adolescent's life, you can save him or her years of misery and certain death. Adolescents can be frustrating, but to see them blossom from hurting children into children who can laugh, play, and learn is a wonderful thing to watch. Just being a part of their recovery will make you feel good about yourself.

Becoming an adolescent counselor is not for everybody. These clients have a lot of energy, and the counselor has to have a high frustration level to deal with a certain amount of disorder without feeling too uncomfortable. As the counselor, you must be able to withstand people challenging you face-to-face and toe-to-toe. You must have good impulse control. If you have a weak spot, these clients will find out what it is and use it against you. They are expert manipulators. It is normal for them to want to manipulate you and the system.

Adolescents almost never decide to come into treatment on their own. They are forced into treatment by other people, their parents, or the courts. Most of their homes are dysfunctional, and many have chemically dependent parents. These clients come into treatment angry and resistive. Where most adults are ready to surrender, most adolescents are ready to fight. The staff must be willing to endure this initial resistance. These clients gradually will change their attitudes about chemicals as they settle down and process more of the facts.

Unlike adults, adolescents are not frightened by the physical consequences of addiction. It does little good to threaten them with talk about addiction being a deadly disease. The adolescents need more time before they will pay attention to this information. They think that they are invincible when it comes to physical problems. Adolescents are resistive to the initial part of the program, and they need more structure in treatment. This allows them to learn self-discipline and social responsibility. A good way of adding structure is to develop a level system (see Appendix 22) in which the clients move up in rank as they progress through the program. At each level change, the clients earn increased freedom and responsibility. A point system (see Appendix 22) is used in conjunction with the level system to increase the structure. In the point system, the clients earn points for working the program and lose points for resisting. Points can be given for a clean room, a neat appearance, level of commitment, participation in group, completion of exercises, positive interaction with treatment peers, and so on. More resistive adolescents will need more structure (Davidson & Seidman, 1974; Kazdin & Weisz, 2003; Phillips, 1968).

The Point System

Most adolescent programs these days will need a point system (see Appendix 41). Points give you more advantage, and rewards are instantaneous, providing for faster behavior modification. With a point system, clients earn privileges as they accumulate points. They can earn telephone calls, soft drinks, free time, visits from guests, television or radio time, snacks, and so on. They lose points for breaking the rules. Each treatment center needs to develop its own point or level system geared to its specific client population. Each center will be different, and the systems will have to be constantly revised or updated. Various point systems, sometimes called token economies, have been developed for these purposes (Cohen & Filipczak, 1971; Phillips, 1968).

In the point system, the clients earn points for each goal that they complete during the day. Points can be given or taken away as the staff desires. For example, clients will be required to keep their rooms clean. They will be given points for completing this goal or will lose points for failing to complete the goal. They can earn or lose a certain number of points per day for keeping their rooms clean. They can be scored on participation in group or on commitment to treatment.

The staff must make sure that reinforcers are positive. The clients turn in points for positive reinforcers, candy, television time, or trips to the recreation room. The clients can earn greater privileges by saving points. For example, a "fun" video might cost 100 points. A telephone call to a family member might cost 200 points. This teaches the clients self-discipline and how to delay gratification. Clients with serious conduct disorders need this kind of structure (Graziano & Mooney, 1984; Herbert, 1982; Kazdin & Weisz, 2003; Ollendick & Cerny, 1981).

A point system adds structure because it gives the staff more control. This tends to shape behavior more quickly. Token reinforcement programs for adolescent clients have existed for a long time and have a proven record of accomplishment (Kazdin & Weisz, 2003).

The Primary Elements in Adolescent Treatment

The most important thing that occurs in adolescent treatment is the change in perceptions, attitudes, and behaviors that revolve around addictive chemicals. The clients must come to realize that they have a problem, come to understand the problem, and develop recovery skills. Adolescents must be habilitated rather than rehabilitated. They have never developed the skills necessary to lead a normal sober lifestyle. They need to learn these skills for the first time. They must stop using chemicals so that they can grow and mature normally. Healthy role models are essential to this process. The staff on any adolescent unit must show the clients how to deal with problems. Clients further along in the program also will model coping skills. Clients must be shown how to treat each other with respect at all times. New adolescents room with someone further along in treatment to show him or her the ropes and be a good role model.

The Rules

Adolescents will constantly test the rules and each staff member. The staff must rigidly adhere to the rules of the treatment center. It is a manipulation for an adolescent to try to get special privileges from you. If they can get you to bend a rule even a little, then they have you right where they want you. Your rules do not mean anything because they can be manipulated.

Communication Skills

Adolescents need to focus on developing communication skills (see Appendix 13). They need to practice identifying their feelings and sharing their feelings with their treatment peers. They must practice telling each other the truth. In the skills groups learned from *Treating Alcohol Dependence: A Coping Skills Training Guide* (Monti, Kadden, Rohsenow, Cooney, & Abrams, 2002), the clients role-play nonverbal communication, assertiveness, drink and drug refusal skills, and how to develop a supportive support network at home. As the clients develop new skills, they can transfer this behavior to their families during family visits (Monti et al., 2002).

As open communication begins, the clients build trust. They usually transfer trust from the treatment peers, to you (the counselor), and to the parents, in that order. Mutual respect is necessary, and the clients must hear you be positive about treatment. A positive attitude will take you a long way with these clients.

It is important for you to know that adolescents are not trying to hurt you. They are not mad at you. They are just mad at their lives. Most of their anger is transferred from the family and environment from which they came. If they act out, then you must provide the structure of consequences. Do not hesitate to give these consequences. They are learning tools. Explain to the adolescents that it is not you who is doing this to them. They knew the rule, and they broke it. They knew the consequence, and now they must accept it.

It is normal for adolescents to push the limits and break the rules. They will try to manipulate their environment just as they did at home and at school. This is all that they know how to do. You cannot blame them for using the old skills that have worked for them. Treatment will teach them what is wrong with the old skills, and it will teach them new skills to get what they want more appropriately.

Honesty

Lying is a good example of an old behavior. Adolescents have learned how to lie to get their way. They lie to get out of trouble. They lie to get what they want. This works for them, at least to some degree, and the lying increases. As the lying grows, they feel more lonely and isolated. What they do not understand is that lying and loneliness are directly connected. If they lie, they will be lonely. Most adolescents do not understand this, but they will learn it with education. Once they learn why they are telling the truth, they will be motivated to be honest. All adolescents complete the Honesty exercise (see Appendix 8).

Adolescents need to practice honesty. Just because they understand the principle does not mean that the behavior changes. They must practice it repeatedly. They need to experience the natural rewards that come when they use a new skill. As the clients set up natural reinforcers, the behavior ultimately will become automatic.

Exercise

Adolescents need a challenging exercise program. They need to exercise at a training heart rate at least once a day. This needs to be about 1 hour of fun activity that can turn a bad day into a better one. Sometimes adolescents do not like each other, but if they play games with each other, the interpersonal dynamics change. They need to be actively involved in sports and other athletic events. Weight training, playing sports, and jogging are excellent accompaniments to any program. These are exercises where the adolescents can see their gains and feel good about themselves. Adolescents care about how they look, and exercise can show them they are gaining in strength, flexibility, and endurance. Boys get to feel like a pro athlete if they play a game well. This helps them to identify with positive role models who are clean and sober. The girls get to learn activities that can control their weight and shape their body to be more attractive. It is particularly important that the adolescents do activities that they know they cannot do. This improves self-efficacy and proves they can stay clean and sober. Hiking, walking, rock climbing, backpacking, and camping makes kids work together to accomplish goals. They have to help each other or the activity will fail. In rock climbing, for example, you have to trust your belayer to save your life if you fall. This brings trust and pride in the accomplishment. Not every program has a ropes course, but these are excellent activities to show adolescents that they can do what they know they cannot do. This means they can stay sober even if they have always thought they could never live without drugs or alcohol. Many of these kids have never done any healthy activity, such as a hike or picnic, so it is a new world for them where they can succeed and work together to accomplish goals. When adolescents are acting out by destroying property or not complying with treatment, there is nothing like fun exercise to turn the group around.

Fun in Sobriety

Adolescents need to learn how to have fun in sobriety. One of the things that they are worried about is that they will not be fun if they stop using drugs and alcohol. They do not want to be boring to their friends. They need to see that they can feel good without chemicals. The only way of doing this is to take the clients out on recreational activities and have them experience firsthand that they can still enjoy themselves. Trips to the zoo, an amusement park, a pizza parlor, an ice cream stand, or a video arcade all can be used to show the adolescents that they can still have fun in sobriety.

The Reinforcers

Adolescents are very concerned about how they look and how they get along with their friends. If you are searching for a reinforcer, you always can hook into one of these. Adolescents desperately want to be loved, no matter what they say. These children are starving for genuine love, compassion, help, attention, encouragement, and praise. They need people to listen to them, and they need a chance to prove what they can do. Most of these clients feel like failures in the real world. They are mad at themselves, and they are mad at everyone else. They have felt overwhelmed by their dysfunctional home situations. Many of these children come from homes of severe abuse and neglect. They have been beaten down by society, and many of them have given up. You will see these clients flourish in an environment of love. You will see the real child be reborn. It is a beautiful thing to watch.

Spirituality

Adolescents have more difficulty with spirituality than do adults. Most adolescents still have their health, and they are not as ready to surrender. They need to be shown a Higher Power is there for them. This takes a spiritual program of action rather than of words. You need to seek a clergy person with particular skills in working with adolescents. The clients should trust this person and not feel intimidated by him or her. The clients need to explore spirituality in spirituality group. The best way of hooking adolescents into a Higher Power is to have them directly experience a Higher Power's presence. This is done using the meditation exercise discussed in Chapter 5.

Some of the adolescents will resist a Higher Power, but they cannot deny their own experiences. Some of these clients have been involved in Satanism, and it takes a great deal of skill to get them to a place where they can be open to a Higher Power. The best therapist here often is another peer. Peers have a way of trusting each other about this sensitive issue. Adolescents will explore spirituality if they do not feel as though they will be shamed by their peers. A peer further along in the program is an excellent model.

Group Therapy

Source: ©iStockphoto.com/clearstockconcepts.

Group therapy with adolescents is different. The level of sharing is shallower at first. Adolescents are inexperienced with their deeper feelings. They do not have the skills necessary to share openly. They feel just as deeply as adults do, but most of them never have practiced communicating their feelings. Early attempts to share feel clumsy and awkward, and the adolescents fear being humiliated in group. Once older members of the group begin sharing, the way is paved for new members. Role-playing works well for adolescents. They do not feel as vulnerable when playing a role. They can role-play drug refusal situations or parent–child conflicts.

Adolescents need to role-play the skill exercises in group. For example, you can hold denial court for those clients who remain in denial. This is an active group. The adolescents enjoy and benefit from the experience. In denial court, the clients divide and play the roles of defense attorney, prosecuting attorney, judge, and jury. The client who is in denial is called to the stand and is examined and cross-examined by the attorneys. The client tries to prove to the court that he or she is not an addict. The group holds the trial and reaches a verdict.

The clients can act out the thoughts that exist inside of someone's head at certain decision points. One client can pretend to be the illness while another pretends to be the healthy side. The two sides try to get the adolescent in question to behave in certain ways. These three—(1) the illness, (2) the healthy side, and (3) the person—can be placed in a variety of situations to see how all sides respond. Use your creativity and come up with group exercises. What you are after is active participation by all of the group members. Once the group members start talking, let them go, with only occasional guidance from time to time. The best treatment will be between the clients further along in the program and those just coming into the program. Once they get the hang of it, the adolescents will enjoy group. It draws them closer together. They feel supported, listened to, and understood. They lose that sense of separateness that has haunted them all of their lives.

Give each client a paper bag and many old magazines. On the outside of the bag, have them glue on pictures that shows how they want the world to view them. Then on the inside of the bag glue on how they really feel inside. Then have the group discuss the differences from the outside person they are pretending to be and the real person inside.

If possible, have a ropes course where the clients can learn self-efficacy. Ropes courses challenge the clients to work together to accomplish a goal. All of these exercises can teach adolescents that they can do something they know they cannot do. If they can do this, maybe they can stay clean and sober.

Peer Pressure

Peer pressure is vitally important to adolescents, and they can easily be swayed to use drugs by their peer group. Peer pressure comes in two forms: (1) being in a social situation where chemicals are available and (2) being actively encouraged to use chemicals by friends. The adolescents need to spend a lot of time role-playing drug refusal exercises. They need to practice exactly how they are going to say no. Most of the adolescents will need to work through the Peer Pressure exercise (see Appendix 23). Sometimes the adolescents will attempt to gang up on the staff because of something that happens between a staff member and a client. This is a good sign because the group members function to help each other. This process should be encouraged, and the staff should carefully listen to the complaint. Try to compromise and reach a decision that is agreed on by all. The center rules must not be broken or manipulated in the process, but the situation can be explored to determine exactly what happened and who is responsible. This can be a difficult process, but once the whole truth comes out, it will be clear where the client or staff member went wrong. Everyone makes mistakes, and Step Ten says, "When we were wrong, we promptly admitted it" (Alcoholics Anonymous [AA], 2001, p. 59). This goes for the staff as well as for the clients. It is a great learning experience for the clients to see the staff struggle to be fair and impartial. It is not easy.

Continuing Education

Continuing education is necessary for adolescents—even those who have dropped out of school. They should have a thorough educational assessment, including an examination of school records and psychological testing. From these data, the schoolteacher develops individual educational treatment plans. Some clients will need intensive remedial work, and some can continue regular assigned schoolwork. School is an excellent opportunity to develop self-discipline. The clients need to determine what they want from further education, and they need to help develop a plan for reaching their goals. Do not allow clients to slough off school because they are dropouts. Quitting is old behavior. All adolescents need continuing education.

Continuing Care

During the discussion of the treatment plan, it is a good idea to begin continuing care planning. This will include a 5-year follow-up plan run by the continuing care case manager. This is a formal contract negotiated with the client and significant others. The plan includes an agreement that the client work all aspects of the continuing care plan with detailed consequences if the client fails to meet his or her obligations. The plan should include the following:

• Client sends in a log of 12-step meetings by the 10th of every month. The number of meetings each week is set by the case manager based upon client needs.

- Client will meet regularly with his or her 12-step sponsor/mentor/coach.

- Client will agree to attend all therapy recommended by the primary counselor with a report from the primary care giver as deemed necessary.

- Client will agree to up to one random drug screen a week for the first 6 months and up to one random drug screen a week for the next year and a half. The client can easily use the PharmChek Drugs of Abuse Patch that lasts for 7 days or longer (www.pharmchem.com) or use an alcohol ankle bracelet, the Secure Continuous Remote Alcohol Monitor (SCRAM), that measures alcohol from the sweat 24 hours a day, 7 days a week. Readwood Toxicology Laboratory (www.redwoodtoxicology.com) has also developed an ethyl glucuronide (EtG) alcohol screen that will show any alcohol use for the last 80 hours. This test is often too sensitive as it picks up any alcohol use including shaving lotion and hand sanitizers.

- Client will take all medications as ordered.

- Client needs a school and community advocate so she or he has many healthy adults to contact if she or he needs encouragement or support. A school teacher, counselor, coach, or youth pastor can often be elicited to pay special attention to a new student and keep encouraging him or her to work toward positive life skills.

- If the client fails to meet any of his or her obligations, the client is first sent a letter explaining the deficiency and asking that it be corrected.

- If the client fails to answer the letter, an appointment will be set up with the continuing care case manager.

- If the client still fails to comply with the contract, the consequences agreed upon will be implemented. This might include contacting the clients, professional board, employer, probation officer, drug court judge, family members, etc. The client has initially signed a release of information to all such individuals and has written each of them cosigned by the continuing care case manager. These letters are signed, sealed, stamped, and mailed if necessary. The continuing care manager must be very careful to design a consequence that leads the client back into treatment.

Continuing care is essential for adolescent clients, and many of them will need long stays in a halfway house or group home. If you send them back to a sick home and community, they will be using. Adolescents do not have the internal structure necessary to stick to a recovery program on their own. Just going to meetings is not enough. The continuing care program should continue to teach the tools of recovery and show the clients that they can have fun in sobriety. The group members need to go on outings and do fun things together. They can attend concerts or go to the zoo, parks, games, dances, and so on. This establishes a new peer group and solidifies recovery.

The Parents Support Group

As the adolescents are going through treatment, the parents attend at least two groups per week. Again, this is individualized and based on the needs of their families. All parents attend a parents support group and a weekly conjoint session with the clients. The parents support group encourages the parents, supports them emotionally, and teaches them the tools of recovery. This is a 12-step group. The clients' families concentrate on working the steps, developing healthy communication skills, and learning a behavior program to follow in continuing care. All parents need to read *Parenting Your Out-of-Control Teenager: 7 Steps to Reestablish Authority and Reclaim Love* by Scott Sells (2001) and discuss each chapter in this book with other parents. A parent support group that teaches parenting skills is an essential component in any adolescent program.

The Behavioral Contract

The Behavioral Contract (see Appendix 24) is the primary method by which clients and their families hold each other accountable for their actions. The contract is necessary to show the clients and families that they can function together in an atmosphere of mutual support. A point system will be necessary for more seriously disturbed adolescents. All parents need to be taught behavioral contracting and the point system.

Using the approach of Alexander and Parsons (1973), the parents negotiate a behavior contract with the adolescent. The contract is jointly developed by the client, the family, and the counselor. The family is taught how to negotiate future recovery skills on its own. The benefit of behavioral contracting has been widely confirmed by a variety of studies (Alexander, 1974; Sanders & Glynn, 1981; Wells & Forehand, 1981, 1984).

If the adolescent has a more serious behavior problem, then the parents will need to develop a point system. The parents will need intensive training and practice in this procedure before the child comes home. The training is divided into three phases. In the first phase, the parents are taught basic social learning concepts (Patterson, 1977; Patterson & Gullion, 1976). In the second phase, they are taught how to define, track, and record deviant and prosocial behaviors. In the third phase, the parents learn how to develop a point system where the adolescent earns or loses points contingent on positive and negative behaviors. Points are exchanged *daily* for rewards previously selected by the child. The parents are taught to use positive social reinforcers (e.g., smiles, pats on the back) for appropriate behaviors and "time-out" procedures for inappropriate behaviors. As the counselor, you must work closely with the parents, particularly shortly after discharge. Daily phone calls from the case manager might be necessary to make sure that the parents and other mentors are following the program. The parents and the client need to attend continuing care for at least 1 year following treatment. Some will attend for years depending on their specific needs.

Phases of Adolescent Treatment

Adolescent treatment seems to go in phases. When the adolescents come into treatment, most of them are angry. This may be expressed overtly or covertly. They may be overly aggressive toward the staff, or they may be quiet and sulk. This defiant period is a good indication that the clients have been out of control. They are attempting to use old skills to bring order to a new situation.

In 1 or 2 weeks, the adolescents will begin to comply with the staff, but they still have not begun to internalize the program. They have learned how to get along in treatment, but they do not think that they have a problem, and they are planning to go back to their old behavior when they leave treatment.

As the adolescents begin to feel the genuine love of the staff and the group, they begin to take a real look at themselves. They see the negative consequences of their addiction. They realize that they do not want to go on living like that. This is positive movement, and it depends primarily on trusting other people. Many of these clients never have trusted anyone, but as they open up to the group and continue to be accepted, they soften. When they behave at their worst and the staff still sticks with them, a light comes on in their heads. The adolescents, who came into treatment defiant and trusting no one, begin to reach out to others. They feel loved and understood for the first time in their lives.

As trust develops, denial becomes more evident. The clients begin to see the truth. The clients are encouraged to transfer this trust of the group to trust of their new AA/Narcotics Anonymous (NA) group. Many adolescent clients hate group when they come into treatment, but in time, they learn to like it. It is the only time in their lives when people have dealt with real feelings. The clients are encouraged to see their new AA/NA group as a healthy family. In this family, the clients can grow and develop normally. The goal is to stay involved with a 12-step group and a Higher Power for life.

13   The Family Program

Source: David Sacks/Thinkstock.

The purpose of the family program is to begin to heal the many wounds caused by addiction and to improve the client's recovery environment. A family system that has been altered by the disease may reinforce addiction. Frequently, a family crisis brings the client into treatment. Including the family in the treatment program increases the chances that the client will engage and stay in treatment.

You should carefully evaluate the client's social system and move it toward being supportive of recovery. If anyone in the family needs intervention for a mental disorder of substance abuse, it is your job to refer that person to the appropriate professionals.

If the family is not supportive, then you should intervene with education and counseling to change the attitudes and behaviors that will make the client's recovery possible. It should be obvious that the client will do better in recovery when supported by his or her family. This is motivational enhancement like you used on the client to bring them out

"Your father needs a little nap."

of denial and into the truth. At first, you need to listen to each family perspective so carefully. From there, you can understand their needs from their prospective. Once each family finally feels heard, you can move into family meetings without the client and finely into meetings with the family including the client. You will find that everyone has unmet needs and they have maladaptive ways of getting their needs met. You need to help each family member learn and practice new coping skills to get their needs met appropriately.

Each primary relationship needs to be examined carefully. You should send each significant person the Family Questionnaire (see Appendix 25). This will give you a good idea of how the family members are functioning and explore what they think about the client and his or her addiction.

By the end of the family program, you should know how each person is functioning and how the family is functioning as a unit. The family is like a mobile, or a group of objects suspended by strings. They are all connected, so if you touch one part of the mobile the whole system moves. This is how a family works. If one person changes, the whole family system changes. You need to gather enough data to show you how the family members are coping with their environment. Many families will need financial aid or therapy of some sort in continuing care.

The First Family Contact

The client's family should be contacted within the first few hours of the client's admission. Once you have met the client, you need to speak with the family members either in person or over the phone. You need to speak to them and light a spark of hope about recovery. Explain that their loved one has a chronic relapsing brain disease that will need to be managed for life. In time, the family will commit to an active recovery program for at least the next 5 years. The family members will be relieved to have the client in treatment, but they will feel frightened that treatment might not work. Do not give them unrealistic expectations, but reassure them that the client is safe and has a new opportunity to recover. The family members should be immediately encouraged to begin attending 12-step meetings such as Al-Anon, Alateen, or Alatot. Give them a list of meetings in their area, and stress that they need to get some support right now from people who understand the disease. The best place to feel understood is with people who are in recovery.

How to Handle the Early Against Medical Advice Risk

The family must be warned that the client may attempt to leave treatment early against medical advice (AMA). It is not uncommon for clients to want to go home after the first few hours in treatment. You want to reduce the possibility that the client will call the family and have someone come and pick the client up. You need to make it clear that this is very common and is to be expected in early recovery. It is not a matter of concern so long as it is handled properly. Tell the family to say a firm no along with some gentle encouragement. That usually is enough to keep the client in treatment. If the client is a serious AMA risk, you might have to plan an in-house intervention with the family. Some clients come into treatment not yet ready to surrender to the disease. The family may need to tell the client that if he or she leaves treatment early they will file an involuntary commitment. Most states allow this for substance abuse. Here the client is brought into custody by the police and sent to a qualified mental health professional for a formal evaluation. If the professional believes the client is chemically dependent and because of this dependency is harmful to himself or herself or others, the court can order a client into treatment. Your most important job early on with the family is to instill hope. If the client works the program of recovery, there is over a 90% chance that the client will stay clean and sober.

The family members may have a lot to tell you over the phone, but you want them to save this information for the forms that you will be sending them. The first contact with them is to reduce fear and to support their decision for treatment. The forms take a history of the problem and give the family members an opportunity to provide input into the treatment process.

Common Family Problems

Source: ©iStockphoto.com/Alina555.

No one can grow up in an addicted family, or live in one, without it changing him or her. Clients who live in addicted homes live in a chaotic whirlwind. These clients grasp at anything that will help them to regain control. Their environment has been totally out of control for a long time. They do not know what is going to happen next. They cannot predict or trust anyone. They live in fear, anger, confusion, and mistrust. They desire, more than anything else does, to achieve stability in their families.

Codependency

A codependent person is obsessed with controlling the person who is out of control (Beattie, 1987; Weinhold & Weinhold, 1989). Addiction adversely affects everyone in the home. Codependents, adult children of alcoholics, and children of alcoholics are some of the names given to these suffering persons.

These people have been seriously damaged by addiction. They have learned to live in an addicted world, and this takes using maladaptive skills. They learn to stuff their feelings and to keep secrets. Their motto is do not trust, do not talk, and do not feel. They focus their lives totally on the addicted person. They do not have time for themselves and their own needs.

Codependents are as blinded and reality distorted as are addicted persons. They do not think about their own problems because their own problems are too painful. They would rather think about other people. Their whole lives revolve around the sick persons. Codependents become so obsessed with helping and controlling the other persons that they lose the ability to think. They cannot see reality. Over the years, in an unbearable situation for most, they have developed an incredible tolerance for neglect and abuse. They keep thinking that if they just do enough—if they figure it out—then everything will work out.

Guilt

Family members often feel incredible guilt. They think that they are at fault. The addicted person keeps denying responsibility, and someone must be held accountable, so the family members often take the blame. The spouse might feel that everything would be okay if he or she could just be the right kind of husband or wife or could just do the right thing.

These people attempt to control their out-of-control environment in any way they can. They whine, wheedle, threaten, cry, bemoan, seek counseling (for themselves), manipulate, and lie. Each attempt at control works to some degree, and it is kept tucked away in their behavioral repertoire to be used later.

The wife might start calling her husband to make sure that he got to work. She feels responsible for her husband getting to work on time, and her anxiety builds as the time approaches for him to be there. The little boy of the family might try to do especially well in school in hopes that the drinking or drug use will stop. The child is anxious because he feels a direct relationship between his grades and the family problems. Family members will go to incredible lengths to control the addiction. They pour out bottles. They threaten using friends. They scold, argue, hide money, cry, get depressed, get anxious, go to church, talk to the boss, and make excuses. They chase addicted friends away from the house. They talk to the family physician or their clergyperson in trying to get support.

Loss of Control

As more and more energy is expended in trying to control someone else, the family members lose contact with themselves. They become so involved in the addicted person that they lose who they are. They do not know what they want. They do not know how they feel. They cannot ask for what they want. They cannot share how they feel. This leaves their interpersonal relationships empty, isolated, and alone. They cannot use their real feelings to solve problems. Therefore, their problems escalate out of control. They are on a treadmill, frantically trying to keep the family together.

Shame

Codependency is deeply rooted in the feeling of shame. The family members feel as though something is wrong with them. They believe that the reason why the family is in such a mess is that they are not good enough. They are not working hard enough or long enough. If they could just figure this whole thing out, then things would be better. They are battered and beaten. They keep trying, but they keep failing. They never can keep up with the increasing nightmare.

Caretaking

Family members of an addicted person learn to be caretakers. They are obsessed with taking care of the addicted person. In their frantic attempt to take care of someone else, they lose contact with their own needs. In group, they will be able to tell you how the addicted person is feeling, but they will be unable to tell you how they themselves are feeling. Their whole lives are caught up in taking care of the other person. This happens to divert the family members from feeling the pain in their lives. In group, you must redirect the family members to stop concentrating on the other person and to explore their own pain. This will not come easily for them because many of them have been feeling numb. You must listen with your whole body to step into this other person's life. You must remove yourself and how you feel and tune into the family members' perception and level of coping skills.

Enabling

The family members will have a long history of making excuses for the addicted person. They have been protecting the addicted individual from facing the severity of the problem. They help the addicted individual get out of trouble. They will lie because they are ashamed of the reality of their family life. Children will lie to friends, the spouse will call the boss, the father or mother will make excuses, and the siblings will pretend that nothing is wrong. Enabling is the major way in which the family members protect themselves from the reality of the situation. They fear that if they do not enable, then their world will collapse. The truth is that they are living with an addictive individual and their lives are out of control, but they keep the family from falling into disaster by shoring up the situation.

The family members must realize that they have kept the illness alive by protecting the chemically dependent individual from the reality of his or her behavior. By their constantly getting the addicted individual out of trouble, the addicted individual could not learn the truth. To protect themselves, the family members allowed the illness to go unchecked. They fed into the denial of the disease.

Inability to Know Feelings

People in addicted homes are so separated from reality that they do not know how they feel. Their feelings have been suppressed for so long that all they feel is numb. They have let go of the pain and live in lives full of false beliefs. They have learned to keep their feelings hidden because they fear that if they expressed themselves, the drug addict will get worse. Some family members who have been subjected to incredible abuse think they feel fine.

Inability to Know Wants

The family members do not know what they want. Their lives are centered on the addicted individual. They only know what the addict wants. That is the primary focus of attention. Most family members are trying to hold on to their sanity and to keep themselves, and the family, from going under. They have no time for the superficial wishes and wants of normal people. They only have vague hopes that everything can be better. They are so used to the broken promises that they do not listen anymore.

Lack of Trust

The family members have learned to trust no one. The people who they trusted ultimately abandoned them repeatedly. Therefore, they lie to everyone—parents, friends, brothers, sisters, neighbors, and fellow employees. They tell no one their secrets. They never trust that they will be safe and comfortable again. They have had their dreams shattered so often that they are afraid to dream anymore.

People Pleasing

The family members of the addicted person learn to be people pleasers. They will do anything to prevent someone from feeling bad. This comes from the attempt to be responsible for other people's pain. If someone is hurting, the family feels anxious and numb. The pain is their fault, and they have to do something about it. They feel that their wants and wishes always are secondary to the needs of someone else. They get to the point where they feel guilty when they get anything; someone else might be deprived.

Feelings of Worthlessness

The family members feel worthless. They feel as though no one cares for how they feel or for what they want. They feel profoundly inadequate and unlovable. They feel rejected by others. They do not feel as though they have a fair chance in life, and somehow they feel as though this is fair—that it is their entire fault anyway. This would not be happening to them if they were better persons. This is all they deserve. This is the best they can get.

Dependency

Codependent persons do not trust their own decisions. They feel incapable of dealing with life. Something always goes wrong with their plans. The very thought of leaving the addicted individual terrifies them. They cling to that person. The more they try to control things, the more things lapse out of control. They develop a profound sense of inadequacy and indecisiveness that keeps them locked in to an intolerable situation.

Poor Communication Skills

The family members have poor communication skills. They learned a long time ago the credo of the addicted family: "Do not talk, do not trust, and do not feel." These individuals do not talk to their friends or other family members. They are cut off from everyone. They feel afraid of open communication. If they talked openly, then the truth might come out and the family would be destroyed. They constantly tell other people what they think these people want to hear rather than how or what they really think or feel. Each of them may need to work through the Communication Skills exercise (see Appendix 13).

How to Treat Family Members

Before reading this section, read the Codependency exercise (see Appendix 26). The exercise will show you what the family members need to work on in treatment. It must be emphasized that each family—and each family member—must be treated individually. No one intervention works for everyone. All families will need individually developed treatment plans. No two families are the same.

The first thing that the family members need is support. They need to feel listened to and like you understood them. They need to be encouraged to share the reality of their lives. They need to feel as though they are in a safe place where others care for how they feel and will respond to what they want. These people are not used to being cared for; they are used to caring for someone else. Some of them will resist any attempt by you to help them. They will tell you that they are fine. They want you to help their loved one, not them. They have identified that person as the "sick" one. Addiction makes the whole family sick.

In treatment, the family members will need to realize that they have a problem. Each member of the family will work through the Codependency exercise (see Appendix 26). This should open their eyes to what they have been doing, which is maladaptive. This exercise gives basic information about codependency and helps each family member to identify the problems that he or she is having.

These individuals have been living in an addicted world, and they are suffering whether they realize it or not. They have learned survival skills that are inappropriate for normal living. They will need to examine exactly what they are doing wrong and learn how to do it in another way. They need to practice the tools of recovery in the family groups and with the client. You must try to see the family as often as they need to be seen both during treatment and in continuing care. You might have to refer the family to a marriage and family therapist to continue their growth. Many families, or family members, will have to be referred to outside agencies. They have severe mental, emotional, spiritual, marital, and family problems that need further treatment. It is your job to refer them to appropriate therapists. Make sure you have a list of therapists in the family's hometown that can work with the family and family members for years.

The family members need to understand that they are powerless over the disease and that their lives have been unmanageable. If they think that they can still control things, then they might try to work the client's program for him or her, and that is a setup for relapse. The family members need to admit to the client that they have problems, too. The family members need to identify exactly what the problems are, understand the problems, and learn what they are going to do differently in recovery.

Some family members come into the program ready to unload and blame the client for everything. This is not going to do anybody any good. Addiction is a family disease. Everyone is affected, and everyone needs to bear some responsibility. Everyone needs to keep the focus on what he or she can do to make things better. All of the eight core feelings need to be explored. Do not let the family get by with sharing only the feelings with which they feel comfortable.

Do not think that you can handle all of the family problems in treatment. All that you can do is start the family members off in the right direction and give them some practice in the tools of recovery. You will see the family members in conjoint sessions. In these sessions, try to get the family members to share the whole truth with each other. If a family member withholds the truth or lies, then the illness will have a foothold and, just like a cancer, will grow until it ends in relapse.

Each family member needs to write a letter to the client stating how the person feels and asking for what he or she wants. The client does the same thing for each family member. The family will read each other these letters in the conjoint sessions. It is from these letters, and from the questionnaires, that you will get a good idea of what needs to be worked on in the conjoint sessions. Only with the whole truth can you help the family to move closer to a healthy lifestyle.

The only truth that can be withheld is something that will injure someone. Use your best judgment here. Alcoholics Anonymous (AA) (2001) says, "[We] made direct amends to such people wherever possible, except when to do so would injure them or others" (p. 59). Sometimes a truth is too painful or harmful to the client or to others to disclose.

After the family members have been involved in the family program long enough to break through initial resistance, they should be given the Codependency exercise (see Appendix 26) to complete at home. Each family member will then read his or her answers to the group. As the family members do this, they will begin to bond together and understand how addiction has affected them.

The Family Program Schedule

The family program begins at admission and in most facilities lasts for 1 week, but you should have weekly family sessions if possible. This gives the family members enough time to get started in their own recovery. The family group meets separately from the clients for the first few sessions. The family members are oriented to the program and hear several lectures. They learn about the disease concept of addiction and how it affects the family. The family members need to see people talk about their problems rather than keep them secret.

The family program members need to share their experiences, strengths, and hopes with each other. A family group, without the clients, should meet at least once a day. Here each family member needs to tell his or her story in brief autobiographical form. This helps to remove the intense shame and guilt that the family members have been feeling. For the first time, family members do not feel alone anymore when hearing each other's stories. The counselor should continue to educate them about addiction and codependency in the groups. The family members need to see how the tools of recovery offer better solutions to their problems.

Many times, family members are so beaten up by the disease that it is difficult for them to share. If you wait and extend the silence, then they will begin talking. They really want to talk. They have been closed up for a long time, and they long for closeness, openness, and love. These people are people pleasers, and they will want to please you. They feel uncomfortable and anxious in extended silence. Try to create an atmosphere that is so tender and kind that people who are very afraid can search for and share the truth. If you ask a question and remain quiet, then someone will get the idea and start sharing. Once the ice is broken, it will become easier for others.

The group needs to be introduced to the Al-Anon, Gam-Anon, or Narconon program and should attend a 12-step group once a day throughout the family week. It is essential that the family members bond with their 12-step group as quickly as possible. This will happen only with regular attendance at meetings. They should be encouraged to begin daily prayer and meditation.

As the family group members share, they will feel understood and supported by the group. Most groups begin to bond after 1 or 2 days. Many tears will be shed as they hear each other's stories. Once the group of family members has bonded, the clients can be brought into the group. This must not be done until the family members are supporting each other. The clients have bonded in treatment, and they are supporting each other. This prevents the addict from eventually coming into the groups and attempting to take control. The family members need a solid support system to prevent the illness from shaming and blaming others. The groups with the family members and addicted clients in them will be able to address the problems more fully.

How to Work With the Family in Group

Source: ©iStockphoto.com/Alina555.

You cannot solve each family problem in these groups. You need to concentrate on the process. Help the family members to gain support from each other and eliminate dysfunctional communication skills. You should have each person share and work toward group acceptance. This is the first time in years that these people have had anyone listen to them.

You should not let one family member interrupt, manipulate, or speak for another. You must explain how these techniques are used for control. With group support and encouragement, the clients and their family members will have the opportunity to express themselves fully. Quiet family members, who have been intimidated at home, will find new strength from the group. This group work prepares the family members for flowing smoothly into continuing care.

Family members are encouraged to keep a daily journal during the family program. At the end of the day, they write down the important things that they learned. They write down how they did that day, and they make plans for what changes they need to make the next day. This is their daily inventory. What do they need to do next? How can they be more actively involved in uncovering the truth? This log can be shared periodically in group.

The family members will need to learn and practice healthy communication skills (see Appendix 13) and healthy interpersonal relationship skills (see Appendix 11). They can work through each of the exercises, just as the client in treatment did. You will develop a treatment plan for each family. What does this family member need specifically? The family members need to identify that they have a problem, understand the problem, and learn skills to deal with the problem. They must see that they have a problem or else they will not continue to go to continuing care and support groups.

The Conjoint Session

Once the family has practiced the tools of recovery for a few days, you will begin to see the family in conjoint sessions. This is where you meet with the family members and the client and work out a family recovery plan. You may want to meet with the spouse more regularly, but you need at least several sessions with the whole family. All family members need to hear the plan of recovery and understand their responsibility. They need to know exactly what they are expected to do. This is a family disease, and everyone will have to do things differently to make recovery work.

In the conjoint sessions, the family members will read the letters that they have written to the client. Each family member will share how that person feels and will ask for what he or she wants from other family members. All of them need to understand that they are developing a program of recovery. Every family member is responsible to act in a manner that is conducive to recovery. Not all of the problems are going to be solved now. First, the family members must enter into a personal recovery program. They need to take one day at a time. They are not going to address all of the problems now.

You occasionally will get resistance from the family. Some family members are not willing to cooperate. Some are chemically dependent or are not interested in recovery. Some individuals have an investment in keeping the client sick. They might fear that if the sick person gets well, their role in the family will be threatened. Out of fear, they want things to stay the same. If you are sensitive and listen hard enough, you will understand these needs and be able to respond to them. The family needs to see the truth about this dynamic, and the problem needs to be worked through. The family members who want the client to remain sick cannot see that everyone will be better off in recovery. They are trying to meet their own needs. Once they see the truth, you will see these family members turn around.

At the end of the family program, there will be a short process whereby the family members say goodbye to each other. For the first time in their lives, they have felt unconditionally accepted, known, and loved. They do not want to leave this warm supportive atmosphere. If you have encouraged them to seek this support in their outside 12-step meetings, this will not be overly difficult, but some pain will be involved. They need to transfer a good feeling to their new support group. All of the family members will need continuing care, and some will need further counseling or treatment. This must be arranged before the family goes home. At the last session, make sure you have a big group hug. The family now should be bonded and ready for the rigors of continuing care.

To see the family members come into the family program frightened and sad, and then to see them go out with new hope, is a very rewarding experience. The family members never will forget the major role that you played in restoring their lives. You lead them from the darkness into the light. They will be eternally grateful.

14   The Clinical Staff

Source: ©iStockphoto.com/Alina555.

The staff of any treatment center is the lifeblood of treatment. A good staff can do effective treatment anywhere. The clinical staff had a great deal of respect for each individual member of the staff and listen carefully to each other. No one staff member is more important than another is. All are equal and essential for recovery. They work together like a symphony all playing the same masterpiece.

A good staff is fun. The staff members enjoy working together and supporting each other in the war against addiction. A good staff laughs a lot. Sometimes you have to laugh to keep the disease from getting you down.

Everyone has input into the clients' treatment plans, but everyone has his or her own area of specialization. Professional boundaries are important and should be respected and guarded. To question another person's skills or decisions when you do not know their profession is silly. Let them do what they are trained to do and trust that they have you and the client's best interest at heart. If you stay within your own boundaries—the boundaries of the chemical dependency counselor—then you will be a lot better off, you will feel better, and you will give better quality treatment. All staff members are experts in their chosen fields. They are licensed or certified by their respective boards, and you have to believe that they know what they are doing.

The Physician/Addictionologist

Source: Comstock Images/Thinkstock.

The medical doctor is in charge of all medical treatment. This physician has the most training in the total disease process. A physician completes a premedical bachelor's degree, 3 or 4 years of advanced medical training, and at least 1 year of interning. Many physicians go on to specialize in one or more areas of medicine. Physicians can have a specialty in addiction called addictionology.

All clients must have a complete history and physical examination given by a physician. If you have any questions about any type of physical disease or medical treatment, then the physician is the person to rely on. It is important to establish a professional working relationship with the physician. He or she is a wealth of information. Do not be intimidated by professionals with advanced degrees. They are just people like you—fallible and human. Discuss your client's case with them, and respect their judgment. Good physicians are easy to talk to and readily admit that they do not know everything. They often need you to tell them how the client is responding to treatment.

The physician will be in close contact with you, particularly if your client has a medical condition that requires treatment. Close consultation with the physician will prevent you from assuming that behavior caused by an organic disease is a psychological problem.

The physician is in charge of any medication order. If you believe that your client needs pharmacological treatment, then you need to tell the physician or nurse. Once you have discussed this issue carefully with the medical staff, your job is over. The physician will examine the client and make the determination based on his or her own clinical judgment. Do not argue with the physician or the nurse about what they are doing. They know more about it than you do. Trust them to do their job. You must keep the medical staff advised about your client's condition if they are not doing well or might be having side effects to the medication. Let them know your concerns and leave it to them to treat the medical condition.

The Psychologist/Psychiatrist

All treatment centers should have a consulting psychologist or psychiatrist. The psychologist/psychiatrist has advanced training in the diagnosis and treatment of mental disorders. A psychiatrist is a medical doctor with 3 years of residency in psychiatry. A psychologist has a 2-year master's degree and a 4-year doctorate degree with 1 year of internship during the doctoral training and 1 year postdoctorate. These two professionals are the best-trained mental health professionals. Only psychiatrists can order medications, and usually only psychologists are heavily trained in psychotherapy, particularly evidence-based cognitive behavioral therapy and psychological testing.

Two thirds of chemically dependent clients have a concomitant psychiatric diagnosis. They have problems such as depression, anxiety, and/or personality disorders in conjunction with their addiction. Clients will not do well in recovery unless these disorders are treated effectively (Frances & Franklin, 1988; Ries & Miller, 2009; Talbott, Hales, & Yudofsky, 1988; Woody et al., 1984). It is important to have a professional in your center who can deal with these coexisting problems.

The Joint Commission on Accreditation of Healthcare Organizations (JCAHO) and the Commission on Accreditation of Rehabilitation Facilities (CARF) requires that all clients in inpatient substance abuse treatment receive a psychiatric/psychological evaluation. This examination includes a mental status examination, a determination of current and past psychiatric/psychological abnormality, a determination of the degree of danger to self or others, and a brief neuropsychological assessment. It is from this examination that you will learn about any secondary diagnosis and will develop a treatment plan. The psychiatrist or psychologist will tell you what to do. Follow his or her directions as precisely as you can. Use this professional as a valuable information source. This professional understands the development of personality and the forces that motivate behavior. If you are confused by a client, talk the situation over carefully with the psychiatrist or psychologist.

The Social Worker/Mental Health Counselor

Social workers and mental health counselors are wonderful mental health professionals. They usually have been through a 2- to 3-year graduate program and are licensed by the state. These mental health professionals have many fine qualities. They are excellent therapists and group leaders. They understand the community of mental health professionals and are often charged with testing and treating co-occurring disorders and arranging for continuing care placements in continuing care, including referrals to other professionals, halfway houses, and group homes. These professionals are good at about anything and can handle almost any mental health task except ordering medication. They are a lot like mental health professionals or professional counselors who have a master's degree in counseling and have many things to offer you and your clients.

The Nurse

There are two types of nurses: (1) registered nurses and (2) licensed practical nurses. Registered nurses complete a registered nurse's degree from an accredited institution. Most go on for a bachelor's degree. Licensed practical nurses complete a 1-year vocational–technical program in nursing.

Nurses are frontline medical personnel. They take responsibility for the client in the absence of the physician. In an inpatient setting, they usually are guiding the ship and are available 24 hours a day. There is a tendency in some centers for there to be some conflict between the nursing staff and the counseling staff. This is a big mistake for all concerned. A good clinical staff has little of these turf battles. Each staff member should feel comfortable with his or her unique function in the treatment setting.

Nurses are second in command in medical treatment. Only the doctor has more medical authority. The physician writes the orders, and the nurses carry them out. In many facilities, there are standing orders that allow nurses to make medical decisions. This is necessary to reduce response time and to prevent the physician from being called every time a decision is made. If a nurse tells you to do something, then you should carry out this order as if it came from the physician.

Nurses will listen to you and help you. You will find them to be supportive. They tend to be caring people who are willing to go the extra mile to provide good quality care. They are used to charting and usually are wonderfully self-disciplined.

The Clinical Director

The clinical director has the primary responsibility for making sure that the clinical team provides the best possible treatment. This individual develops and implements the whole treatment program. He or she has advanced training and experience in treating addiction and co-occurring disorders. The clinical director makes sure that the team is working well together and is accomplishing its goals. The clinical director decides who does what, when, how, and with whom. This person leads the clinical team and the client population. The clinical director has administrative experience. This individual usually sees the clients and the staff who are having more severe problems. All program and policy changes go through the clinical director.

The Clinical Supervisor

The clinical supervisor is an addiction counselor with several years of experience in counseling and supervision. This individual's primary responsibility is to supervise the counseling staff. The clinical supervisor will be doing some hands-on work with the clients and will be sitting in on some of your individual sessions and groups. He or she makes up the work schedule. You should use this person often. The clinical director and clinical supervisor are your mentors. This person will set a good example for how to take a client through treatment effectively. If you have any questions about treatment planning, charting, or therapy, then these are the first people to ask. You should receive continuing education from the supervisory personnel. If you feel as though you have any weak points in your training, then ask them for in-service training sessions to build your expertise.

The clinical supervisor will be going over your charts to be sure that you are treating the clients according to JCAHO or CARF. JCAHO and CARF require specific standards of care to be met before it will allow a facility to receive accreditation. (You can order a copy of the standards by contacting JCAHO, 875 North Michigan Avenue, Chicago, IL 60611 or CARF International, 4891 E. Grant Road, Tucson, AZ 85712 USA, 520-325-1044 or 888-28106531 voice/TTY, 520-318-1129 fax.)

The Chemical Dependency Counselor

Chemical dependency counselors must meet state standards set by a certification board. They take specialized college courses and work for at least 1 year in a treatment setting under a qualified supervisor. In most states, they have to pass a national examination and are state certified. Counselors must show competency in 12 core function areas: (1) screening, (2) intake, (3) orientation, (4) assessment, (5) treatment planning, (6) counseling, (7) case management, (8) crisis intervention, (9) client education, (10) referral, (11) reports and record keeping, and (12) consultation. Many counselors are involved in their own recovery programs, but many are not. It does not seem to matter. It is the on-the-job training in addictions and personal experience that gives addictions counselors their unique professional character. They are excellent highly qualified health care professionals.

The Rehabilitation Technician or Aide

Rehabilitation technicians, sometimes called aides, usually are individuals with no formal training in addiction. Sometimes they are people who are getting their degrees in addiction and need experience. These people do a variety of work assigned by supervisory personnel. They work with the clients, sometimes individually and sometimes in groups. They work under the direct supervision of the counseling staff. It is your responsibility to help them to function effectively around the client population. Many times, the tech or aid says just the right thing at just the right time to turn a client toward recovery. Never forget that they are smart, willing, and able to go the extra mile for you and your clients.

There often is some conflict about how far these people should go in treating clients. For the most part, the care they offer should be highly structured and supervised by someone on the clinical staff. You will find that much of the real work in treatment is offered by these individuals. You must see to it that they offer quality care. The only way of doing this is to listen to them, talk to them, and educate them. They might be in recovery and know the 12-step program well, but you can still improve their skills by extending yourself to support, educate, and encourage them. They are working harder than you often think and are having more effect than you can possibly imagine.

The Recreational Therapist

Source: Paul Sutherland/Thinkstock.

The recreational therapist is a certified coordinator in charge of getting the clients involved in fun, constructive exercise and leisure time activities. This individual will be doing an activities assessment to see what the clients are doing for entertainment, play, or fun. The activities coordinator will develop an exercise program for each client. Most addiction clients have lost the capacity to have fun in sobriety. They need to be encouraged to develop healthy recreational activities and hobbies. They need to learn how to have fun clean and sober. It is important that you encourage your clients to become active in pleasure-oriented activities in recovery. The clients who enjoy sobriety will be more likely to stay sober. One of the most important things that clients can do in their recovery program is to establish regular exercise habits. All clients should be encouraged to exercise on a daily basis. The recreational therapist needs to be a lot of fun to be with and very encouraging. Most addicts have not exercised or enjoyed recreational activities in a long time, so they need someone fun to encourage them to try new activities.

Clinical Staffing

The clinical staff makes up the treatment team. The staff usually meets once a day, usually at each shift change, to discuss the clients' status. Once a week, the staff meets for a more formal clinical staffing. Here the clients will be discussed in more detail, and each problem on the problem list will be evaluated.

The staff must be constantly kept informed about how the clients are doing in treatment. In these meetings, treatment plans will be updated. A multidisciplinary staff can take clients through treatment much more effectively. More expertise comes into play, and many heads are much better than one.

Clinical staffing is your opportunity to discuss a client with the whole team. You can get advice and help from everyone at the same time. The client is reassessed throughout treatment to determine current clinical problems, needs, and responses to treatment. The assessment includes major changes in the client, family, or life events that could complicate or alter treatment. A client could have just learned that his wife is divorcing him or that he is being prosecuted for a crime. Someone in the client's immediate family could die or become ill. All changes in treatment need to be documented in the client record.

The atmosphere of clinical staffing is a professional one. The principal matter of concern is the clients. You must assume that all members of the professional staff are willing and able to help. The staff members should be supportive of each other. Treating addiction is emotionally draining, and everyone occasionally will make mistakes. The atmosphere in clinical staffing should be one of mutual respect. You should enjoy clinical staff meetings. They should be educational, and they should help you to develop your professional skills.

How to Present a Client

You will present each of your clients to the clinical staff and will discuss how treatment generally is going. If you have any questions, now is the time to ask them. The first time that you present a client, you need to be thorough. As the client remains in treatment, you need to cover just the pertinent issues. An outline for case presentation is handy to use your first few times. The outline might look something like this:

1. Identifying data

2. Present illness

3. Past history

4. Family history

5. Social history

6. Medical history

7. Mental status examination

8. Most likely diagnosis

9. Formulation
    a. Predisposing factors
    b. Psychosocial stressors
    c. Stress that precipitated treatment

10. Further assessment you propose

11. Treatment plan

12. Prognosis

Your presentation should sound something like this:

Jason Roberts is a 43-year-old black male who just got his third DWI. He has been drinking heavily for the past 20 years. He is divorced with two children. He lives alone. He came to treatment after spending the night in jail. He is working on his chemical use history and problem assessment form. He is doing well around the unit so far. He is in good physical health except for some mild withdrawal symptoms. His CWIA scores have averaged around 8 to 14. He seems to be getting along well with his treatment peers. In group, he did admit to a drinking problem. He seems committed to treatment. He says he does not want to go on living this way anymore. I talked to his oldest son this morning, and the family is supportive of treatment. He is in some withdrawal, but he seems to be handling that okay. He needs to visit with the psychologist to rule out other psychiatric disorders. He is depressed and reports he is not sleeping well. His diagnosis is alcohol dependence—severe—with a possible substance induced depression or a major depression. He will be working through the steps, and we will probably address his depression depending on the psychologist's report.

The case presentation globally advises the treatment team of the client's condition and describes how the client is doing in treatment. After you present the client, each member of the treatment team can comment. The physician or the nursing staff may have something to share about withdrawal or the medical condition for which the client is being treated. The dietitian may make a report on the client's diet. The recreational therapist may have a comment on how the client has been using his or her leisure time. The other counselors may have something to say about what they see. As the primary counselor, you collate this material and enter the staff's input into the client record. These progress notes do not have to be very long, but they do have to show that the treatment team is reassessing the client and changing the treatment plan where necessary.

Team Building

A good staff is constantly building the team. These staff members are actively encouraging each other and reinforcing each other's work. When you see someone do a good job, you say so: "You did a good job with Mark this morning. I was impressed with how you handled yourself." These comments are very reinforcing to fellow staff members. The staff members often put so much energy into the clients that they forget that they have needs, too. This is emotionally difficult work, and everyone needs support. A good team knows this. Each member goes out of his or her way to treat each other well.

New team members are welcomed and are assisted in adjusting to the flow of treatment. Every treatment center is different, and new staff members need orientation on both an intellectual and an emotional level. A good team's members constantly talk each other up to insiders as well as outsiders. They never talk someone on the staff down. You can share the truth about someone without damaging his or her reputation. The members of a good staff communicate well together. They share openly how they feel and what they think. They work together as a group. If a personal problem develops between staff members, then the problem is handled by a supervisor.

A good staff's members never gossip about each other. Gossip is one of the most harmful things that can occur in any staff organization. Gossip will cause a team to fail. Everyone's life outside of the center should be private. Unless someone decides to confide in you, keep out of the issue. Do not spread damaging rumors about anyone. A good way of checking yourself is to refuse to repeat anything unless you have the permission of the person in question.

Good staff members get support, not treatment, from their fellow staff members. It is a mistake for someone in recovery to think they no longer need their 12-step meetings because they have the support of the clinical team. The clinical staff does not exist to treat you; it exists to treat the clients. If you want to see someone on the staff for a brief consultation about a problem, that is fine, but keep it short. Do not be afraid to seek outside help for your problems. Your mental and physical health directly affects your job performance. If your problems are bogging you down, then you cannot be effective. Becoming involved in a good program of recovery will make you a better counselor and a better person. One of the best ways of learning about good therapy is to go to a good therapist. Make sure that this therapist is highly qualified in his or her field.

A good clinical staff does not "subgroup" against each other. This is where a smaller group of staff members gets together and talks about the other members. This is very common, and it is a disaster for the clinical team. If you are having problems with a staff member, then go to that staff member first and try to work the issue through. If you are unable to resolve the problem, then go to your supervisor and get him or her to help you. If you and the supervisor cannot handle the problem, then it needs to be addressed before the clinical staff as a whole. Do not let problems fester. The only way of resolving problems is to get everyone together and have each person share how he or she feels. Any problem can be solved in an atmosphere of love and truth. The staff needs to practice what it preaches to the clients.

The following guidelines are excellent for maintaining productive staff interaction.

Commitment to Coworkers

As your coworker with a shared goal of providing excellent care to our clients, I commit myself to the following:

1. I will accept responsibility for establishing and maintaining healthy interpersonal relationships with you and every member of this staff. I will talk to you promptly if I am having a problem with you. The only time I will discuss it with another person is when I need advice or help in deciding how to communicate to you appropriately.

2. I will establish and maintain a relationship of functional trust with you and every member of this staff. My relationships with each of you will be equally respectful, regardless of job titles or levels of educational preparation.

3. I will not engage in the "3 Bs" (bickering, back-stabbing, and bitching) and will ask you not to do [so] as well.

4. I will not complain about another team member and ask you not to do [so] as well. If I hear you doing so, I will ask you to talk to that person.

5. I will accept you as you are today, forgiving past problems, and ask you to do the same with me.

6. I will be committed to finding solutions to problems, rather than complaining about them, and ask you to do the same.

7. I will affirm your contribution to quality client care.

8. I will remember that neither of us is perfect and that human errors are opportunities, not for shame or guilt but rather for forgiveness and growth. (Manthey, 1991)

_____

Signature and date

Boundaries

Everyone on the clinical team needs to know and respect each other's professional boundaries. You need to know what each person's function is in treatment. Once you know that a part of treatment is not in your area of expertise, stay out of that area. Everyone on the staff wants to hear what you think—that is helpful—but do not concern yourself with client care outside of your area of specialization. You are an addiction counselor, not a physician or a nurse. You should not concern yourself with who gets certain medications, but you should express your concern about your client's signs and symptoms. Many counselors spend long hours worrying about whether or not their clients are being properly treated by the medical staff. If you worry that your medical staff is inadequate, then work somewhere else. Never accept a job in an institution that gives substandard care. Once you decide to accept a position, act as if your staff is the greatest. Be grateful for all of the good work the staff is doing.

Most staff problems are attitude problems, and attitudes can change. You need to keep a positive attitude about you and your coworkers. This will go a long way toward making your day more pleasant and enjoyable. If you see your attitude slipping, then talk about this with your supervisor. Check your own life. How are you doing? Many times, a negative attitude flags personal problems that need to be addressed outside of the treatment center. Remember that if you do not take good care of yourself you are not going to be very helpful to others. If you are suffering, your staff and clients will suffer. Do not hesitate to get help from your supervisor or an outside counselor. Most treatment centers have an employment assistant professional (EAP) who will see you a few times and, if you need it, will help you get a referral to the right professional.

Staff–Client Problems

The staff and the clients will constantly have problems with each other. It is the nature of transference and countertransference that there will be conflict. As the clients' maladaptive attitudes and behaviors come into play, the staff can teach new methods of dealing with problems.

Never agree that a client has been treated unfairly by a staff member until you first talk with the staff member. Clients will attempt to use you in a manipulative way against someone else. Remember the staff comes first. You must not subgroup with clients against staff. This decreases the effectiveness of the entire facility. You must prevent clients from using their old manipulative skills. If a client is having a problem with a staff member, then arrange for the staff member and the client to meet to see whether they can resolve the issue together. You are teaching the client how to resolve interpersonal problems. If the client has a problem with someone, then he or she has to go to that person to resolve the issue.

Certain clients will try to pit the staff members against each other. This is common for borderline and antisocial clients. This must be resolved by the staff as a whole. A client usually attempts this by telling different staff members different things. The only way of making this manipulation stop is to call everyone together at the same time. This way, the client cannot continue to manipulate. Any other means of trying to solve this problem will not work because the lies will continue to operate. Once everyone gets together with the client at the same time, you will have a more accurate picture of what the problem is and how to resolve it.

What to Do When a Client Does Not Like a Counselor

Sometimes a client will want to change counselors. This client needs to share how he or she feels with the current counselor often with a supervisor present. Something might be going wrong with the therapeutic alliance. This matter needs to be discussed with the counselor and the client who are having the problem.

Source: ©iStockphoto.com/slobo.

It should be rare for a client to change primary counselors while in treatment. Most of these problems revolve around lack of trust, and this is a common problem for chemically dependent persons.

Many staff–client problems result from miscommunication. It is common for two people to misinterpret each other's behavior. Only by bringing the parties together and having them check out their interpretations will the problems be resolved. Each person needs to ask for—and listen to—the other person's thoughts and feelings.

Sometimes clients will want the counselor to do too much. It is as though the clients want the counselor to do all of the work for them. When the counselor balks at this, the clients feel resentful. These clients need to accept the responsibility for their own behavior. They cannot count on someone else to work the program for them. They must work it for themselves.

A client who is having a problem with a staff member might need more time in individual sessions. The client needs to get his or her thinking accurate. Trust issues are of paramount importance in recovery. Trust is essential for the development of a good therapeutic alliance. If a client is having trust problems with the staff, you can bet that the client has this same problem outside of the treatment setting. The client might need to track his or her lack of trust to earlier situations, perhaps during childhood. Things that happened early can convince a client to trust no one. Keep asking the client if he or she ever felt these feelings at an earlier time. These situations will have to be explored in depth and worked through. The client needs to see that the situation has changed. The client is not in the original situation anymore. He or she is in a new situation that demands a new level of trust. What about the new situation makes the client feel that he or she cannot trust someone? What is the most rational decision for the client to make? Trust issues must be resolved for the client to move forward in treatment. The client will remain stuck until he or she can trust someone. Once the client trusts one person, the client can transfer the trust to someone else, the group, and then the Higher Power.

What to Do When a Client Complains About a Rule

Many staff–client problems revolve around rule violations. Clients will say that they did not break the rule, and they may have a very good story to tell about the situation. You must support other staff members in the things they direct the clients to do. Support their consequences. They were there, and you were not there. Talk about how to do it next time if you need to but do not change the consequence. If you do this, your staff members will be unable to discipline the clients. If the clients learn that the rules can be manipulated, then all of the rules become meaningless. Bring all members involved in the situation together, and talk the issue through. In very rare instances, the person who leveled the consequence may remove the consequence or change it to something more appropriate. This should be done only by the person who leveled the consequence.

No chemically dependent persons want to obey the rules, but the rules exist to protect them from harm. Once they understand that the rules are for them rather than against them, they will be more likely to obey the rules. Clients who are breaking the rules need to see how this tendency feeds into their addiction. If they learn how to follow the rules—particularly the rule of the 12-step program—then this is recovery.

The Work Environment

A treatment center should be a fun place to work. People who come into recovery at their worst are at their best in a few short weeks. This is an extremely rewarding environment. It is a place full of great joy. Real love abounds in a good treatment center. Clients and staff alike enjoy their days. If you do not genuinely enjoy your work, then you are at the wrong place or you are in the wrong business. Chemically dependent persons are a lot of fun to work with. They laugh and have a good time. They have been the life of the party. The staff can learn how to have fun at work. If the staff members work together and love each other, then they can grow from each work day.

Good treatment must be done in an atmosphere of love and trust. Staff members must support each other through the good times as well as the bad times. The old saying applies: "When the going gets tough, the tough get going." Even during periods of stress, the well-functioning staff pulls together and works things out. Humor often saves the day, and a genuine caring for each other smoothes the rough spots for staff members. Remember that you are in this field not only for your clients but also for yourself. You are actively involved in your own individual growth.

15 Discharge Summary and Continuing Care

Source: ©iStockphoto.com/Hohenhaus.

This is where there rubber hits the road, and it's where most addiction programs fall far short. Most programs advise the client to continue to work his or her 12-step program. The theory is if clients continue to work the 12 steps they will stay clean and sober. This is true, but most clients do not go to many 12-step meetings after treatment; some only go to one or two, and then they drop out. This is why two thirds of clients relapse in the first year of recovery. Work with physicians and airline pilots show that the case manager must follow the clients for 5 years after treatment. At the 5-year point, the relapse rate falls to around zero (Earley, 2009; Vaillant, 2003).

What the client needs is a contract negotiated with the continuing care case manager where they agree to all of the following:

• Submit to up to three random drug screens a week for the first 6 months and up to one random drug screen per week for the next 5 years. The client makes a phone call to the medical review officer, family member, or professional each day to see if this is the day for a drug test. If the test is refused, it is considered a positive sign of addiction. If this does not work, the client can wear a mechanical device that tests for alcohol in the blood and gives the GPS position of the client. Often a drug test failure means going directly to jail or into treatment.

• Send in a 12-step log sent to the case manager every month. This is a list of all meetings attended signed at the end of each meeting by the group leader.

• Get a sponsor, mentor, coach, school advocate, and community associate, and make contact with him or her at least once a week. For the first 90 days, the sponsor needs to be contacted with a daily telephone call.

• Attend all therapy recommended by the initial treatment team. This would include things such as anger management, marriage counseling, probation officer visits, school counselor sessions, etc. The more that people help and the less the client isolates, the more likely that he or she is to stay in recovery.

- Take all medications as ordered.

- Agree to several painful outlined consequences if the client does not follow recommendations or becomes involved in their addiction again. Here you must outline what will happen if the client fails to follow his or her continuing care plan. These consequences have to be unwanted events such as transferring the case to the judge, medical board, drug court, employer, spouse, family, significant other, sponsor, school advocate, probation officer, etc. These consequences have to be people who are prepared as a group to arrange for further assessment, inpatient or outpatient treatment if necessary.

Discharge planning begins at admission. You need to be constantly aware of what the client might need in continuing care. The discharge summary is the document that tells the client's story from the beginning to the end of treatment, and it details what the client is going to do in continuing care. It includes the initial assessment, diagnosis, course of treatment, final diagnosis, and continuing care plan. It summarizes the significant findings at the time of admission including the primary and secondary diagnoses. Significant findings that led to each diagnosis must be included. What were the problems, how were the problems treated, and what was the result of treatment?

Source: ©iStockphoto.com/tomeng.

The course of treatment includes detoxification and withdrawal, any medical treatment, and all treatment provided by the clinical team. You will follow each problem on the problem list, detailing what the problem is and how the problem was treated. You will discuss how the treatment affected the problem. Make sure that you concentrate on client behaviors, not your opinion. Include any changes in the treatment plan and the reasons for those changes as well as the family's response to treatment.

The final assessment of the client's current condition must include how the client is functioning at discharge compared to how he or she was functioning before treatment and during treatment. The changes in feelings, thoughts, and behaviors should be detailed. The continuing care plan should be laid out, and the client must agree to follow the continuing care plan. If the client needs to see someone for further treatment in continuing care, then this person must be named along with his or her address, e-mail address, and phone number in the discharge summary. If the client is on any medication at discharge, then this medication should be listed along with a follow-up plan for continuing or discontinuing this medication.

All clients must meet the discharge criteria developed by the American Society of Addiction Medicine (ASAM) (Mee-Lee, 2001).

Outpatient Discharge Criteria

For adult and adolescent outpatient discharge, the client must meet one of the following conditions:

I. The client is assessed, postadmission, as not having met the *Diagnostic and Statistical Manual of Mental Disorders (DSM)* criteria for a substance use disorder (American Psychiatric Association, 2000); or

II. The client must meet at least one of the following criteria:

1. The client must meet all of the following:

a. The client is not intoxicated or in withdrawal.

      b. The client does not manifest symptoms of protracted withdrawal syndrome.

      c. The client does not meet any of the Level I continued stay criteria.

2. The client must meet one of the following:

      a. The client's medical problems, if any, have diminished or stabilized to the point where they can be managed through outpatient appointments.

      b. There is a biomedical condition that is interfering with treatment and requires treatment at another setting.

3. The client must meet one of the following:

      a. The client's emotional behavioral problems have diminished or stabilized to the point where they can be managed through outpatient appointments.

4. The client must meet one of the following:

      a. The client's awareness and acceptance of an addiction problem and commitment to recovery are sufficient to expect maintenance of a self-directed recovery plan as evidenced by the following:

        (1) The client is able to recognize the severity of his or her relationship with alcohol or drugs.

        (2) The client has an understanding of his or her self-defeating relationship with alcohol or drugs.

        (3) The client is applying the essential skills necessary to maintain sobriety in a self-help fellowship and/or with further post treatment care.

      b. The client has consistently failed to achieve treatment goals, and no further progress is likely to be made.

5. The client must meet one of the following:

      a. The client's therapeutic gains that address cravings and relapse issues have been learned and internalized.

      b. The client is experiencing an exacerbation in drug-seeking behavior or craving that necessitates treatment in a more intense treatment setting.

6. The client must meet one of the following:

      a. The client's social system and significant others are supportive of recovery to the point where the client can be expected to adhere to a self-directed treatment plan.

      b. The client is functioning adequately in assessed deficiencies in life areas of work, social functioning, or primary relationships.

      c. The client's social system remains non-supportive or has deteriorated, and the client is at risk for relapse. The client needs placement in a higher level of care to prevent relapse.

Inpatient Discharge Criteria

Adults and adolescents in inpatient treatment are ready for discharge if they do not meet the *DSM* criteria for substance use disorder or when they meet the specifications in one of the following six dimensions:

1. The client must meet one of the following:

      a. The client is not intoxicated or in withdrawal or the symptoms have diminished to the point where the client can be managed in a less intense level of care.

      b. The client has protracted withdrawal symptoms that no longer require 24-hour monitoring.

      c. The client meets criteria for a more intensive level of treatment.

2. The client must meet one of the following:

   a. The client's biomedical problems, if any, have diminished or stabilized to the extent where daily availability of a 24-hour medical staff no longer is necessary.

   b. There is a biomedical condition that needs treatment in another setting.

3. The client must meet one of the following:

   a. The client's emotional/behavioral problems have diminished or stabilized to the point where a 24-hour staff no longer is necessary.

   b. An emotional/behavioral problem exists that needs treatment in another setting.

4. The client must meet one of the following:

   a. The client's awareness and acceptance of an addiction problem and commitment to treatment are sufficient to expect compliance in a less intensive setting as evidenced by the following:

      (1) The client is able to recognize the severity of his or her addictive problem.

      (2) The client understands his or her self-defeating relationship with alcohol and other drugs and also understands their triggers that lead to use.

      (3) The client accepts continued care and has participated in the development of a continuing care plan.

      (4) The client does not meet any of the Level III continuing care dimensions.

   b. The client has consistently failed to meet treatment goals even with changes in the treatment plan, and no further progress is expected.

5. The client must meet one of the following:

   a. The client is capable of following and completing a continuing care plan, and the client is not at substantial risk for relapse.

   b. The client is not committed to continuing care and has achieved the maximum benefit from all attempts to have the client see that he or she needs a continuing care plan.

6. The client must meet one of the following:

   a. Problem aspects of the client's social and interpersonal environment are responding to treatment, and the environment is now supportive enough to transfer the client to a less intense level of care.

   b. The social and interpersonal environment has not changed or has deteriorated, but the client has learned skills necessary to cope with the situation or has secured an alternative environment.

   c. The social environment has deteriorated, and the client has not learned the skills necessary to cope. An extended care environment has been secured, but the client is unwilling to be transferred.

How to Develop a Discharge Summary

The discharge summary must be entered into the client record within 15 days following discharge. It must summarize the following things about the client's treatment:

1. The significant findings of the clinical staff including the problem list and the initial primary and secondary diagnoses

2. The course of treatment through each identified problem

3. The final assessment of the client's current condition

4. The recommendations and arrangements for further treatment and continuing care

5. The final primary and secondary diagnoses

The continuing care plan details how the client is going to continue treatment after he or she leaves the treatment center. Each client will have a written continuing care plan that will list the specific arrangements for continuing care.

Each client will need a 12-step contact person/mentor/coach. It is this person's job to see to it that the client gets to the new 12-step group and is introduced to members. The contact person stays close to the client until the client chooses a sponsor. You will want to carefully build up your 12-step contact list over the years and get the other counselors to help you. Try to match the client and the contact person/mentor/coach carefully. Some clients will need this person to be hard and pushy, and some will need just the opposite. The contact person is an important link from you to the new group. This contact will keep you informed if anything goes wrong.

The continuing care plan is developed in accordance with the client's identified needs at the time of discharge. The plan is developed with the full participation of the client. The client must agree and sign a contract that agrees to abide by the continuing care plan. There is no use in developing a great continuing care plan if the client does not intend to follow it.

Clients will need a variety of care following treatment, and you need to find the least restrictive environment for the clients. Each of the following methods of continuing treatment needs to be considered in developing a continuing care plan:

1. *Inpatient treatment.* If clients' recovery is still shaky and they have serious medical or psychological problems, then the clients might need further inpatient care.

2. *Halfway house.* Some clients will need the structure of a halfway house to help them stay clean and sober. These clients will not function well on their own. They might have poor social skills, or they might need someone else to be in control of their environment. A good halfway house will structure the clients' days and usually will have 12-step meetings held at the house. Everyone eats together and shares the responsibilities of cooking and cleaning. This is a good alternative for many clients who are shaky in early recovery. If you feel uncomfortable about a client's ability to maintain a recovery program, then this is something you should encourage.

3. *Outpatient treatment.* Some clients need further treatment, but they can handle treatment in an outpatient setting. Outpatient programs usually offer 1 to 3 days of structured treatment per week. The clients come in and move through an individualized outpatient program. This is much like inpatient treatment, but it is not nearly as intensive or as structured. These clients must be able to stay abstinent between appointments.

4. *Continuing care.* All clients who come through treatment will need an extended care program to make sure that they are following through with their recovery plan. Ideally, a program should offer continuing care so long as it is necessary to stabilize recovery.

The Personal Recovery Plan (see Appendix 27) describes the client's goals in recovery. It is another treatment plan developed with client's is input. If the client still has problems that need to be addressed in continuing care, then each of these problems will need a treatment plan. You cannot send a client out of treatment with an unstable psychiatric or family problem without arranging for the client to receive treatment for this problem.

The Discharge Summary

You have collected the data necessary, and you are ready to do your discharge summary. You have the client's record before you. Remember that this is a summary. You do not have to put in everything, just the significant findings and the course of treatment. You will keep the personal recovery plan in the chart and give a copy to the client to take home. A sample discharge summary is given in Appendix 28.

After you have completed the discharge summary, write a letter to each of the people to whom you are referring the client. These letters are important to maintain good communication between your facility and the other professionals in the community. You will need to telephone all of these professionals and tell them about the client. You might want to send each of them a copy of the discharge summary.

The client's employer may request an exit interview. You should call the employer and let him or her know that the client is getting out of treatment and tell the employer how the client is doing. Employers are an important referral source for your facility, and they have an interest in the client's recovery.

Saying Good-Bye

Source: John Foxx/Thinkstock.

When your clients walk down that hallway for the last time, they are going to have mixed feelings. Probably for the first time in their lives, the clients have had a group of people consistently act on their behalf. The clients will not want to leave a good program. They will be feeling some fear of what is going to happen on the outside. For the first time in weeks, they are going to be on their own. It will be easy to get back to the old self-destructive behaviors, and the clients should know this. Alcohol and drugs will be easily accessible. The clients do not know whether they are going to make it. It is a long walk out that front door.

You need to be smiling and offering your clients encouragement all the way. Tell them that you are available if they have difficulty. Explain that you want to see them at the alumni functions that your center will be sponsoring. Tell the clients that they can make it and that you have faith in them. Tell them that no matter what happens out there, you care for them. You will be there for them if they need you. If they have trouble, they can call you or come back to the treatment center. Most of all, you need to give these clients a hug. You have walked with them through one of the most difficult and rewarding periods of their lives.

16

The Good Counselor

Source: Comstock Images/Thinkstock.

If you were to ask people in the field what makes a good substance abuse counselor, you would get many answers. This is a complicated question. Sometimes good counselors seem to be born rather than made. Clinical skills can be learned, but some characteristics a counselor has to have naturally developed from a variety of genetic and environmental factors.

Good Counselors Are Caring

Good counselors are, first of all, caring. They are interested and actively involved in other people's individual growth. They care for how people feel, and they care for what people want. They feel this not only at work but in their social lives as well. They instinctively believe that their clients have great worth. They help their clients to grow by gently guiding them. They do not hammer their clients; hurting their clients would deeply hurt them. They do not constantly confront clients with their faults; rather, they praise clients for their strengths.

Source: ©iStockphoto.com/track5.

They build on clients' strengths rather than concentrating on clients' weaknesses. They focus their attention on helping their clients grow in the way that they want to grow. They never push their own values and moral beliefs on their clients. They constantly encourage their clients to see the truth about themselves and others. They want their clients to be fully themselves and to reach for their full potential.

Good Counselors Love Their Work

Counselors do not feel burdened by their work. They feel that their work is a great privilege. It is an honor to have people share the intimate details of their lives with them. By caring for others in this program, the counselors will have love turned back on them. They will feel loved and important. Thomas Merton said, "Happiness is unselfishly giving to others." Caring counselors give freely of themselves and expect nothing in return.

Good Counselors Do Not Become Overly Involved

Good counselors do not become overly involved with their clients because to do so would not be helpful; it would be self-serving. To be caring, you have to be healthy in your life. You have to be reasonably comfortable with who you are, where you are, what you do, and whom you are with. If you have unmet needs, these will be a roadblock to you in becoming a good counselor. It is not that you have to be completely problem free—no one ever is—but you have to have a strong support system within yourself and outside of the treatment center. You have to be able to meet your own needs. If you ever think that clients can meet your needs, then you are in for trouble. Counselors who are in the field to heal their own problems will feel angry and frustrated. Clients are too sick to help you. They need to concentrate on their own recovery.

Good Counselors Do Not Lie

Good counselors never lie. Love necessitates action in truth. Without truth, love cannot occur. You can tell a client that you do not want to talk about an issue, but you never should make up a story, even if you think it is for the client's own good. It never is good to lie to a client. Lies cut the client off from reality and destroy their trust in you. Without trust, good treatment becomes impossible.

Good Counselors Are Gentle

Good counselors are gentle, tender, and kind. They are sensitive to their clients' pain. To cause unnecessary pain is inexcusable. The truth also may cause clients some pain, but without the truth, the clients never will recover. Good counselors can give consequences because they know that it is for the clients' own good.

Gentle means that you encourage the client to see the truth. Tender means you never yell or call the client names. You may get angry—that is normal—but try to use your anger appropriately. The client might have a very difficult time in dealing with your anger. It can permanently damage the therapeutic relationship. When you are angry, it is useful to be angry at the illness rather than at the client. If the client understands this, then he or she can join you in feeling angry at the disease. It might hurt the client some to give him or her a consequence, but it will feel good in the long run. You are doing the right thing by helping the client to learn from his or her maladaptive behavior.

Good Counselors Like Themselves

Good counselors like themselves. They nourish themselves. They cultivate stable relationships with family and friends. They spend quality time alone. If they are in recovery, then they work a daily program of recovery. Good counselors do not overwork, and they do not become overly involved. When they leave work, they do not bring the problems home.

Good Counselors Are Supersensitive

Good counselors must be supersensitive to other people's feelings. This seems to be an inborn trait rather than something learned. Some people have this sensitivity from birth or early environmental experiences, and other people do not. Some sensitivity can be learned, but the sensitivity that counselors need cannot. You need a hypersensitive autonomic nervous system for this. To be sensitive, you need to feel other people's pain almost as if it is your pain. When they hurt, you hurt. When they feel joy, you feel joy. This is called empathy. With empathy, you perceive, feel, and understand other people's experiences. Empathy means you concentrate on the other person so hard that every sense becomes involved. You have to be so concentrated that your feelings, wishes, wants, and judgments are placed in the background. The best way to tell if you understand the client is to repeat or rephrase what they just said until they agree you understand.

Good Counselors Have a Sixth Sense

The more sensitive you are, the better counselor you are going to be. The sensitivity will enable you to know where a client is emotionally. This gives you accurate information about your clients' motivation. The clients might not know how they feel. They may be cut off from their feelings. In a sense, you need to be ahead of the clients. You will feel the feelings as they are feeling them, but you will feel the feelings before they have processed them. There will be those few seconds when you know where they are going. You know because that sixth sense of yours has picked it up. This is your clinical thermometer, and it can get hot or cold, each temperature telling you something more about your client. Remember, feelings give us energy and direction for movement. If you know how other people feel, then you can predict what they are going to do.

You can learn sensitivity to some degree by trial and error. Constantly ask clients how they are feeling to check yourself for accuracy. Most clients will correct you if you are wrong. As you reflect or rephrase their people and they correct you, you will develop more sensitivity. This skill will develop and become more accurate over the years of your career. Practice this skill when you are away from work. Talk to the checkout person until you trigger them to feel like you see them as a person not a machine. Do this with every waiter, bell person, cab driver, neighbor, or family member. As you learn what people want and how they feel, you will be able to help them to move forward more quickly. You will make mistakes, but you will learn many things about people. You will learn that no one really wants to do a bad thing. People do bad things because they see the good in them. If you understand this, then you will be able to understand your clients. Child abuse can occur simply because the parent wanted the child to be quiet. The parent did not want to hurt the child for the joy of seeing someone in pain.

Your supersensitivity will help you to know what motivates clients. Borderline or schizophrenic clients are very difficult to understand unless you understand how they are feeling and what they are thinking. These are clients whom you have to explore until you understand their worldview.

Good Counselors Do Not Become Overly Emotional

Some counselors become overly emotional. This is countertransference. These counselors weep openly with most clients and at family sessions. They encourage their clients to call them at home, anytime. They call clients after they leave treatment just to see how they are doing. They encourage clients to drop by their homes, give them rides, and lend them money. These counselors have a great need to be liked, and they are transferring their unmet needs to their clients. Some of these counselors have unresolved psychological problems that are driving them. Their desire to help, please, and take care of others is out of control. These counselors get hurt, frustrated, and angry because they learn that the clients do not want a friend; they want a counselor. Many of these counselors burn out and eventually leave the profession. They never seek the professional help that they need to get their work in perspective.

You cannot be too sensitive if you use your sensitivity correctly. This supersensitivity will give you accurate direction. You will be able to say the right thing at the right time. You will just know what to say. You will know what you would want to hear. Best of all, this supersensitivity will give you great timing. You will be able to say the right thing at the right time. This is almost a magical experience. It will happen to you more and more as you grow in your counseling career.

Good Counselors Are Active Listeners

Good counselors actively listen. They know when to be quiet and focus on what their clients are saying. They are interested in how the clients perceive things. They want to know what the clients are thinking and how they are feeling. They desire to become a part of the clients' world. Counselors who are good listeners will have clients tell them that they are good. Good counselors are constantly pulling for more information and not only the facts but how the client feels about the facts. Good counselors make their clients feel understood.

Good Counselors Do Not Talk Too Much

A common mistake of new counselors is to talk too much. If they recorded themselves in group or in individual sessions, then they would see that they do most of the talking. They think that they have a lot to say, and the clients have a lot to learn, so why not just teach them. Counseling with these individuals is more like going to a lecture. Good counselors ask many questions, and they listen carefully for the answers. They are attentive to the clients' verbal and nonverbal behavior. If they see the clients saying one thing with their words and another thing with their behavior, they believe the behavior.

Active listeners will reflect how the clients are feeling and wait for feedback. Even with supersensitivity, you never know exactly what other people are experiencing. You have to ask and listen. Nothing helps clients feel more understood than to be listened to attentively. As you focus your attention on the clients, they feel important. They feel as though someone cares for them and knows them. Active listening takes a lot of energy. It is not easy. You have to listen with every fiber of your being. If you do not listen, then your clients never will feel loved. Counselors with poor listening skills hear their clients say, "You do not understand me."

Good counselors rarely hear these words. If clients do not feel understood, then they will be frustrated, their treatment will suffer, the therapeutic alliance will be shaky, and the clients will not trust. To trust you, the clients must feel known.

Good Counselors Maintain Boundaries

Good counselors know their boundaries. They know who they are as people, and they will not allow other people to violate them. You will have clients in treatment who will try to threaten you or throw their weight around. You will use the group with these clients to give you the support you need. Angry clients are using the only skill that they know how to use. It is your job to teach them how to get what they want in some other way.

You must know your professional boundaries and not cross them. You must use only techniques that you have learned through professional training and experience. You never should use a technique if you have only heard about it. Watch a skilled person use the technique a few times, and then have that person watch you. Use only the skills that you have been trained to use. You must be able to demonstrate, through professional education and experience, that you know what you are doing.

If you feel comfortable with yourself and your training, it allows the rest of the staff members to do their own thing. You do not have to question their skills. The professional staff organization will accept that responsibility. You can relax and enjoy your role as the counselor. That is plenty of work. You do not have to do everyone's job, just your own.

Boundaries include keeping your relationships with your clients professional. Good counselors never take advantage of their relationships with clients. They never act on romantic feelings or become involved in business dealings with their clients. If you do these things, it will be confusing to you and your clients. The clients are in a vulnerable situation, and you are their confidant—their hero. If you use these relationships for your own gain, then you are going to hurt your clients. The relationships with your clients are special. Do not take advantage of them.

Good Counselors Are Client-Centered

Good counselors are client-centered, not counselor-centered. They treat chemically dependent people at those individuals' own pace. They know that different clients come into treatment with different levels of readiness for treatment. Some clients are ready to disclose the truth very fast—the first day—and some clients will be reluctant to share the truth. It never helps to threaten or push clients to disclose information. All you can do is to give the clients the opportunity to share in a supportive environment. You teach the clients the consequences of not sharing. If the clients understand and see unconditional positive regard, then they will share. If they cannot share with you, then they can share in their Fifth Step. If they cannot share the truth there, then encourage them to share later. You cannot make people talk. If you try, you will be in trouble. People will view you as abusive and harmful. Your job is to provide a safe atmosphere in which people want to talk.

You need to give the clients the chance to grow at their own pace. You must take them through treatment at a pace that they can follow and understand. The clients must recognize the severity of their illness, understand their self-defeating relationship with substances, and apply the tools of recovery. They must see their new behaviors work.

Some clients will not do written work well, or they will not get things if they read them. Learning disabilities can handicap some clients. These clients have to be treated differently. If you try to push them to do something that they cannot do, then you will fail. Many people have physical, emotional, or social roadblocks to learning. You must recognize when clients are struggling and intervene as soon as possible. You must do something differently to make the program more understandable.

Good Counselors Have Effective Relationship Skills

Good counselors have good interpersonal relationship skills. They are good communicators. They tell people how they feel and what they think. They do not keep their feelings to themselves. They use their feelings appropriately to help them solve problems. They are trustworthy and reliable. If they tell the clients that they are going to do something, then they do it. They are there for the clients when they are needed. If a client asks for help, then good counselors stop what they are doing and focus on the client. This might take only a few minutes. If the discussion is going to take longer, then they can make an appointment to see the client later.

Good counselors never manipulate to get their way. They never say one thing and mean another. They never plot or plan against a client or against a member of the professional staff. Manipulation necessitates lies, and this is a program of rigorous honesty. Good counselors will not become involved in dishonest communication.

Good counselors are assertive, not aggressive. They do not use the power of their positions or their personalities to make the clients do things. They share with the clients how they feel and ask for what they want. If the clients have broken the rules and consequences are required, then the consequences are leveled without excessive guilt or remorse. Good counselors never attack, assault, abuse, yell, scream, chastise, torment, scold, assail, batter, shame, berate, condemn, lie into, insult, tongue-lash, intimidate, threaten, terrorize, force, violate, oppress, sneak, defame, or belittle. They treat the clients the same way in which they would want to be treated.

Good counselors suspect when clients are transferring energy from a previous relationship to the therapeutic relationship. They help the clients to understand and work through the transference. Good counselors always keep clients informed about what they are thinking and how they are feeling. The clients never feel left in the dark.

Good counselors treat clients with honor and respect. They believe that it is a privilege to work with all clients no matter who they are. If they have a client who they cannot work with, then they refer the client to someone else. They care for how clients feel and for what clients want. They want to help clients to feel comfortable.

Good counselors are constantly reinforcing. They are fun to be around. They enjoy life. They like giving people praise. They look for things to reinforce. These counselors try to see the good in everything. They always are reaching for the positive. They praise people for the little things. They notice when someone does something right, and they point it out. Good counselors rarely are punitive; they do not like to punish. When they are giving good things to others, they feel the best about themselves.

Good Counselors Have a Sound Code of Ethics

Good counselors have a good code of ethics (National Association of Alcohol and Drug Abuse Counselors [NAADAC] Code of Ethics, Appendix 67). This is what you need to do to maintain the highest in ethical principles:

1. You respect the dignity and worth of each client and strive to protect individual human rights.

2. You are committed to clients understanding themselves and reaching their full potential.

3. You protect the welfare of those who seek your services as a professional.

4. You do not permit clients' skills to be misused.

5. You accept the responsibility for the consequences of your actions. When you are wrong, you promptly admit it.

6. You make sure that your services are used appropriately.

7. You avoid relationships that may create a conflict of interest.

8. You try to prevent distortion or misuse of your findings.

9. You present material objectively, fully, and accurately.

10. You know that your work bears a heavy responsibility because your recommendations and actions may alter the lives of others.

11. You accurately represent your competence, education, training, and experience.

12. You recognize the need for continuing education and are open to new procedures and changes.

13. You recognize the differences among people of different races, sexes, cultures, creeds, ethnic backgrounds, and socioeconomic statuses. When necessary, you are willing to obtain special training in how to deal effectively with such persons.

14. If you use assessment tools, then you are responsible for knowing the reliability and validity of such instruments.

15. You recognize that personal problems may interfere with your professional effectiveness. You refrain from becoming engaged in an activity where your personal problems may have an influence. If you have serious problems, then you have a responsibility to seek appropriate professional assistance.

16. You obey the law.

17. You do not condone practices that you perceive as being inhumane or unjust.

18. When announcing professional services, you do not make claims that cannot be demonstrated by sound research.

19. You present yourself accurately, avoiding misrepresentation of you or your findings.

20. You respect the confidentiality of all information obtained within the context of your work.

21. You reveal such information only with the written permission of the client or the client's legal representative, except when the client is a clear danger to self or others.

22. When appropriate, you inform the client of the legal limits of confidentiality.

23. You discuss information obtained in professional relationships only for professional purposes and only with persons clearly concerned with the case.

24. You ensure that appropriate provisions are made for maintaining confidentiality in the storage and disposal of the client record.

25. You recognize your own needs and are cognizant of your potential to influence clients and subordinates.

26. You make every effort to avoid relationships that could impair your professional judgment or increase the risk of exploitation. This includes, but is not limited to, treatment of employees, close friends, or relatives.

27. You understand that sexual intimacies with clients are unethical.

28. You arrange for payment of services that safeguard the best interest of the client.

29. You terminate your services when it is reasonably clear that the client is not benefiting.

30. You understand the areas of your competence and make full use of other professionals who will serve the best interests of your client.

31. You cooperate fully with other professionals.

32. If a person is receiving a similar service from another professional, then you carefully consider that relationship and proceed cautiously, protecting the other professional and the client.

33. If you employ or supervise other professionals or professionals in training, then you accept the obligation to facilitate the professional development of these individuals. You provide appropriate working conditions, timely evaluations, constructive consultation, and continuing education.

34. You do not exploit your professional relationships with clients, supervisees, students, or employees sexually or otherwise. You do not condone or participate in any form of sexual harassment.

35. When you know of an ethical violation by another counselor, if it seems appropriate, you bring this violation to the attention of the counselor. If this behavior is not corrected, then you bring the information to the appropriate local, state, or national board.

Are you a good counselor? I hope so. If you are, you have chosen a field that will give you indescribable joy. You will see people at their worst and at their best. You will see them crying, and you will see them laughing. You will help people to change for the better. You will be there to help put broken families back together again. You will see, in the eyes of your clients, the love and appreciation that they will feel for you. You will experience a deep love for others. You will learn to appreciate people for their uniqueness. You will savor the fact that no two people are the same. You will travel with men and women who are addicted as they struggle toward new hope and new lives. Their hope is in you because you are the chemical dependency counselor.

Appendix 1

Cognitive Capacity Screening

Examination

Examiner   Date

Instructions: Check items answered correctly. Write incorrect or unusual answers in the space provided. If necessary, urge the client once to complete task.

Introduction to client: "I would like to ask you a few questions. Some you will find very easy, and others may be very hard. Just do your best."

1. What day of the week is this?

2. What month?

3. What day of the month?

4. What year?

5. What place is this?

6. Repeat the numbers 8 7 2.

7. Say them backward.

8. Repeat the numbers 6 3 7 1.

9. Listen to the numbers 6 9 4. Count 1 through 10 out loud, then repeat 6 9 4.

(Help if needed. The use numbers 5 7 3.)

10. Listen to the numbers 8 1 4 3. Count 1 through 10 out loud, then repeat 8 1 4 3.

11. Beginning with Sunday, say the days of the week backward.

12. 9 plus 3 is

13. Add 6 (to the previous answer or to 12).

14. Take away 5 (from 18).

Source: Reproduced, with permission, from Jacobs, J. W., Bernhard, M. R., Delgado, A., & Strain, J. J. (1977). Screening for organic mental syndromes in the medically ill. *Annals of Internal Medicine, 86*, 40–46.

Repeat these words after me and remember them. I will ask for them later: *hat, car, tree, twenty-six.*

15. The opposite of fast is slow. The opposite of up is

16. The opposite of large is

17. The opposite of hard is

18. An orange and a banana are both fruits. Red and blue are both

19. A penny and a dame are both

20. What are those words I asked you to remember? (*hat*)

21. (*car*)

22. (*tree*)

23. (*twenty-six*)

24. Take away 7 from 100, then take away 7 from what is left and keep going: 100 minus 7 is

25. Minus 7

26. Minus 7 (Write down the answer. Check correct subtraction of 7.)

27. Minus 7

28. Minus 7

29. Minus 7

30. Minus 7

Total Correct

Client was:

Cooperative

Uncooperative

Depressed

Lethargic

Other

If the client's score is less than 20, then some diminished cognitive capacity is present. Therefore, an organic mental syndrome should be suspected, and the medical staff should be notified.

Appendix 2

Short Michigan Alcoholism Screening Test

1. Do you feel you are a normal drinker? (By normal, we mean you drink less than or as much as most other people?) (No)

2. Does your wife, husband, a parent or other near relative ever worry or complain about your drinking? (Yes)

3. Do you ever feel guilty about your drinking? (Yes)

4. Do friends or relatives think you are a normal drinker? (No)

5. Are you able to stop drinking when you want to? (No)

6. Have you ever attended a meeting of Alcoholics Anonymous? (Yes)

7. Has drinking ever created problems between you and your wife, husband, a parent or other near relative? (Yes)

8. Have you ever gotten into trouble at work because of your drinking? (Yes)

9. Have you ever neglected your obligations, your family or your work for two or more days in a row? Because you were drinking? (Yes)

10. Have you ever gone to anyone for help about your drinking? (Yes)

11. Have you ever been in a hospital because of drinking? (Yes)

12. Have you ever been arrested for drunken driving, driving while intoxicated, or driving under the influence of alcoholic beverages? (Yes)

13. Have you ever been arrested, even for a few hours, because of other drunken behavior? (Yes)

Answers related to alcoholism are given in parentheses after each question. Three or more of these answers indicate probable alcoholism; two answers indicate the possibility of alcoholism; less than two answers indicate that alcoholism is not likely.

Source: Reprinted with permission from Short Michigan Alcoholism Screening Test. (1975). *Journal of Studies on Alcohol, 36,* 117–126. Copyright by Journal of Studies on Alcohol, Inc., Rutgers Center of Alcohol Studies, New Brunswick, NJ 08903.

Appendix 3

DSM–IV–TR Psychoactive Substance Use Disorder

I. Diagnostic Criteria for Psychoactive Substance Abuse

    A. A maladaptive pattern of substance use leading to clinically significant impairment or distress, as manifested by one (or more) of the following occurring within a 12-month period:

        1. Recurrent substance use resulting in a failure to fulfill major role obligations at work, school, or home (e.g., repeated absences or poor work performance related to substance use; substance-related absences, suspensions, or expulsions from school; neglect of children or household)

        2. Recurrent use in situations in which it is physically hazardous (e.g., driving while intoxicated or operating a machine when impaired by substance use)

        3. Recurrent substance-related legal problems (e.g., arrests for substance-related disorderly conduct)

        4. Continued use despite knowledge of having persistent or recurrent social or interpersonal problems caused or made worse by the effects of the substance (e.g., arguments with spouse about consequences of intoxication, physical fights)

    B. Never met the criteria for psychoactive substance dependence for this substance

II. Diagnostic Criteria for Psychoactive Substance Dependence

    A. A maladaptive pattern of substance use leading to clinically significant impairment or distress, as manifested by three (or more) of the following occurring at any time in the same 12-month period:

        1. Tolerance, as defined by either of the following:

            a. A need for markedly increased amounts of the substance to achieve intoxication or desired effect

            b. Markedly diminished effect with continued use of the same amount of the substance

        2. Withdrawal, as manifested by either of the following:

            a. Characteristic withdrawal syndrome of the substance

            b. The same (or a closely related) substance taken to relieve or avoid withdrawal symptoms

Source: Used with permission. American Psychiatric Association. (2000). *Diagnostic and statistical manual of mental disorders* (text revision). Washington, DC: Author.

3. Substance often taken in larger amounts or over a longer period of time than was intended

4. A persistent desire or unsuccessful efforts to cut down on or control substance use

5. A great deal of time spent in activities necessary to get the substance (e.g., visiting multiple doctors, driving long distances), use the substance (e.g., chain smoking), or recover from its effects

6. Important social, occupational, or recreational activities given up or reduced because of substance use

7. Substance use continued despite knowledge of having a persistent or recurrent social, psychological, or physical problem that is likely to have been caused or were made worse by the use of the substance (e.g., keeps using heroin despite family arguments about it, cocaine-induced depression, having an ulcer made worse by drinking)

Specify if:

With physiological dependence: Evidence of tolerance or withdrawal

Without physiological dependence: No evidence of tolerance or withdrawal

Appendix 4

Alcohol Withdrawal Scale

Client   Date   Time

Pulse or heart rate taken for 1 minute

Blood pressure   /

Nausea and Vomiting
Ask, "Do you feel sick to your stomach? Have you vomited?"

Observation:

0 No nausea and no vomiting
1 Mild nausea with no vomiting
2
3
4 Intermittent nausea with dry heaves
5
6
7 Constant nausea, frequent dry heaves, and vomiting

Tremor
Arms extended and fingers spread apart

Observation:

0 No tremor
1 Not visible but can be felt fingertip to fingertip
2
3
4 Moderate, with arms extended
5
6
7 Severe, even with arms not extended

Proximal Sweats

Observation:

0 No sweat visible
1 Barely perceptible sweating, palms moist
2

3
4 Beads of sweat obvious on forehead
5
6
7 Drenching sweats

Anxiety
Ask, "Do you feel nervous?"

Observation:

0 No anxiety, at ease
1 Mildly anxious
2
3
4 Moderately anxious or guarded, so anxiety is inferred
5
6
7 Equivalent to acute panic states, as seen in severe delirium or acute schizophrenic reactions

Agitation

Observation:

0 Normal activity
1 Somewhat more than normal activity
2
3
4 Moderately fidgety and restless
5
6
7 Paces back and forth during most of the interview or constantly thrashes about

Tactile Disturbances
Ask, "Have you had any itching, pins and needles sensations, burning, or numbness? Do you feel bugs crawling on or under your skin?"

Observation:

0 None
1 Very mild itching, pins and needles, burning, or numbness
2 Mild itching, pins and needles, burning, or numbness
3 Moderate itching, pins and needles, burning, or numbness
4 Moderately severe hallucinations
5 Severe hallucinations
6 Extremely severe hallucinations
7 Continuous hallucinations

Auditory Disturbances
Ask, "Are you more aware of sounds around you? Are they harsh? Do they frighten you? Are you hearing anything that is disturbing to you? Are you hearing things that you know are not there?"

Observation:

0 Not present
1 Very mild harshness or ability to frighten

2   Mild harshness or ability to frighten
3   Moderate harshness or ability to frighten
4   Moderately severe hallucinations
5   Severe hallucinations
6   Extremely severe hallucinations
7   Continuous hallucinations

Visual Disturbances

Ask, "Does the light appear to be too bright? Is the color different? Does it hurt your eyes? Are you seeing anything that is disturbing to you? Are you seeing things that you know are not there?"

Observation:

0   Not present
1   Very mild sensitivity
2   Mild sensitivity
3   Moderate sensitivity
4   Moderately severe hallucinations
5   Severe hallucinations
6   Extremely severe hallucinations
7   Continuous hallucinations

Headache, Fullness in Head

Ask, "Does your head feel different? Does it feel like there is a band around your head?" Do not rate dizziness or lightheadedness. Otherwise, rate severity.

Observation:

0   Not present
1   Very mild
2   Mild
3   Moderate
4   Moderately severe
5   Severe
6   Very severe
7   Extremely severe

Orientation and Clouding of Sensorium

Ask, "What day is this? Where are you? Who am I?"

Observation:

0   Oriented and can do serial additions
1   Cannot do serial additions or is uncertain about date
2   Disoriented about date by no more than 2 calendar days
3   Disoriented about date by more than 2 calendar days
4   Disoriented about place and/or person

Total Score

Rater's Initials

Maximum Possible Score = 67

A score higher than 25 indicates severe withdrawal (impending delirium tremens). If score is lower than 10 after two 8-hour reviews, then monitoring can stop. If score is higher than 20, then the client should be assessed hourly until the symptoms are under control.

Appendix 5

Narcotic Withdrawal Scale

There are four major stages in narcotics withdrawal:

Grade I: Lacrimation (teary eyes)
　　Rhinorrhea (runny nose)
　　Diaphoresis (sweating)
　　Yawning
　　Restlessness
　　Insomnia (difficulty sleeping)

Grade II: Dilated Pupils
　　Piloerection (goosebumps on skin)
　　Muscle twitching
　　Myalgia (muscle pain)
　　Arthralgia (joint pain)
　　Abdominal pain

Grade III: Tachycardia (pulse or heart rate higher than 100)
　　Hypertension (high blood pressure)
　　Tachypnea (rapid breathing)
　　Fever
　　Anorexia (loss of appetite)
　　Nausea
　　Extreme restlessness

Grade IV: Diarrhea
　　Vomiting
　　Dehydration
　　Hyperglycemia (high blood sugar)
　　Hypotension (low blood pressure)
　　Curled-up position

Source: Used with permission. Fultz, J. M., & Senay, E. C. (1975). Guidelines for the management of hospitalized narcotics addicts. *Annals of Internal Medicine, 82,* 815–818.

Appendix 6

Sample Biopsychosocial Interview

DATE: 2-2-11

CLIENT NAME: Jane Roberts

DEMOGRAPHIC DATA: This is a 28-year-old single white female. She is childless. She lives in Sioux, South Dakota, by herself. She has lived in Watertown for the past 5 years. She has a high school education. She is self-employed as a beautician at The Cut Above.

CHIEF COMPLAINT: "I could not go on drinking the way I was."

HISTORY OF THE PRESENT ILLNESS: This client's father died when she was very young. She was raised by an overly demanding alcoholic mother. Her mother had strict rules and made the client work hard to keep the house clean. The client never made an emotional connection with her mother. "I grew up feeling left out, abandoned, lost, and alone. I think I was loved, but I was not shown it." In school, she continued to feel isolated from her peers. She began drinking during her early teens. In high school, the client did not date a lot, but when she did, she fell immediately in love. She began a series of addictive relationships with men. In these relationships, she was able to experience the affection she had always longed for. The client was "devastated" when her boyfriends would go out with someone else. She would frantically "keep grasping" to hold on to these relationships. After high school, the client had an affair with a married man. This man was demonstrative in his affection, and this fooled the client into thinking that he "really loved me." The client was unable to disengage from this relationship, even though the man was married and emotionally and physically abusive. The client's drinking began to increase. Her tolerance to alcohol increased. She had blackouts. The client began to use Valium for sleep. Her dose of Valium has more than doubled. She currently is drinking at least a six-pack of beer and taking 30 milligrams of Valium every night. The client currently is suffering from acute alcohol and anxiolytic withdrawal. Her withdrawal will probably be protracted because she has been on Valium for 5 years. In withdrawal, she reports that she feels restless and is sleeping poorly. The client has few assertive skills and can be excessively dependent. She enjoys men who are powerful and controlling. The client has few healthy relationship skills, and she is dishonest. The client is accepting of treatment and has a strong desire to get help for her chemical dependency.

PAST HISTORY: This client was born in Livingston, South Dakota, on June 28, 1983. She reports a normal birth and normal developmental milestones. She was raised with her mother and two younger sisters. Her father died when she was too young to know him. Her ethnic heritage is Irish. She describes her home of origin as "I did not like it. I felt alone." In grade school, "I was timid, not very outgoing." In high school, "I was scared to relate." The client denies ever serving in the military. Her occupational history includes a 5-year stint as a secretary. She has held her current job as a beautician for 5 years. She is happily employed. Sexually, the client is heterosexual. She has a complex history of addictive relationships with men who have been abusive both verbally and physically. The client currently is involved with a new boyfriend. She has been seeing him for the past few months. She reports that this relationship is going well. Her friends and family support her coming into treatment. Spiritually, the client believes in God. She was raised in the

Lutheran faith. She attends church regularly. She denies any legal difficulties. For strengths, the client identifies that "I am caring. I get along with people real well. I think that I am intelligent." For weakness, the client states, "I have a drinking problem." For leisure activities, the client enjoys biking and jogging. Her leisure activities have been only mildly affected by her chemical use.

MEDICAL HISTORY:

- Illnesses: Measles, mumps, chicken pox
- Hospitalizations: None
- Allergies: None
- Medications at present: 5 milligrams of Valium three times a day for withdrawal

FAMILY HISTORY:

- Father: Age of death, "in his 20s"; cause of death, unknown; client does not remember her father
- Mother: Age 53, in good health; history of alcoholism; described as "quiet, demanding"
- Other relatives with significant psychopathology: None

MENTAL STATUS: This is a tall, thin, 28-year-old white female. She has short, curly light brown hair and blue eyes. She has a broad smile and a freckled face. She was dressed in white jeans and a white sweatshirt. Her sensorium was clear. She was oriented to person, place, and time. Her attitude toward the examiner was cooperative, friendly, and pleasant. Her motor behavior was mildly restless. The client fidgeted in her chair. She made good eye contact. Her speech was spontaneous and without errors. Her affect was mildly anxious. Her range of affect was within normal limits. Her mood was mildly anxious. Her thought processes were productive and goal directed. Suicidal ideation was denied. Homicidal ideation was denied. Disorders of perception were denied. Delusions were denied. Obsessions and compulsions were denied. The client exhibited an above average level of intellectual functioning. She could concentrate well. Her immediate, recent, and remote memories were intact. She exhibited fair impulse control. Her judgment was fair. She is insightful about her alcohol problem and is in minimal denial about her drinking. She is in more denial about her problem with Valium.

Diagnostic Summary

DATE: 2-10-11

CLIENT NAME: Jane Roberts

This is a 28-year-old single white female. She is childless. She lives in Watertown, South Dakota, by herself. She has lived in Sioux Falls for the past 5 years. She has a high school education. She currently is self-employed as a beautician. She comes to treatment with a chief complaint of a drinking problem. The client's father died when she was very young. She was raised by an emotionally distant alcoholic mother. Patty grew up feeling a profound sense of abandonment. All her life, she has felt empty and lost. She could gain her mother's approval only by being a hard worker. In grade school, the client was timid and shy. In high school, she began a series of addictive relationships with men. Patty gets love and sex mixed up. She is starved for attention and affection. She is vulnerable to manipulation. She had an affair with a married man. Her relationships with men have been dysfunctional and abusive. The client has few assertive skills. She cannot ask people for what she wants or share how she feels. She is dishonest. She lies to get what she wants. Patty began drinking during her early teens. After high school, her drinking began to increase. Her tolerance to alcohol increased. She has had multiple blackouts and has suffered withdrawal symptoms. She is drinking at least a six-pack of beer per day. Patty has been taking Valium for sleep for the past 5 years. She has increased her tolerance to Valium, and she has more than doubled her bedtime dose. The client currently is experiencing symptoms of alcohol and Valium withdrawal. She has been anemic for the past several years. She is being treated with vitamins. She has cold symptoms and is taking aspirin and an antihistamine. She has a history of arthritis, but she exhibits no current symptoms. She has a history of a heart murmur. The client is highly motivated for treatment, and her relapse potential is low. She is psychologically minded and is opening up well in group. She shows minimal resistance to treatment. Her current recovery environment is poor. She has no social support system except for her boyfriend of the past 2 months. The psychological testing shows that Patty is emotionally unstable and manipulative. She will break the rules of society to get her own way. She will openly defy authority. She is suffering from mild depressive symptoms, and she is experiencing significant daily anxiety. These symptoms seem to relate to the client's chemical dependency.

DIAGNOSIS:

Axis I: 303.90 Alcohol dependence

             304.10 Anxiolytic dependence

             291.80 Alcohol withdrawal

             292.00 Anxiolytic withdrawal

Axis II: V 71.09 No diagnosis Axis II

Axis III: Anemia, mild cold symptoms

Axis IV: Severity of psychosocial stressors, personal illness, Severity 3 (moderate)

Axis V: Current global assessment of functioning: 50

Highest global assessment of functioning past year: 70

PROBLEM LIST AND RECOMMENDATIONS:

Problem 1:   Extended withdrawal from alcohol and Valium, as evidenced by autonomic arousal and elevated vital signs

Problem 2:   Inability to maintain sobriety outside a structured program of recovery, as evidenced by client having tried to quit using chemicals many times unsuccessfully

Problem 3:   Anemia, as evidenced by a chronic history of low red cell counts

Problem 4:   Upper respiratory infection, as evidenced by sore throat and rhinitis

Problem 5:   Fear of rejection and abandonment, as evidenced by client feeling abandoned by both her mother and her father and now clinging to relationships even when abusive

Problem 6:   Poor relationship skills, as evidenced by client not sharing the truth about how she feels or asking for what she wants, leaving her unable to establish and maintain intimate relationships

Problem 7:   Dishonesty, as evidenced by client chronically lying about her chemical use history

Problem 8:   Poor assertiveness skills, as evidenced by client allowing other people to make important decisions for her, inhibiting her from developing a self-directed program of recovery

Treatment Plan

Problem 1: Inability to maintain sobriety outside a structured program of recovery, as evidenced by repeated unsuccessful attempts to remain abstinent as well as increased tolerance and withdrawal symptoms

Goal A: Acquire the skills necessary to achieve and maintain a sober lifestyle.

Objective 1: Patty will discuss three times when she unsuccessfully attempted to stop drug and alcohol use with her counselor by 2-15-11.

Intervention: Assign the client to list three times when she unsuccessfully attempted to stop or cut down on her drug and alcohol use, and have her discuss this in a one-to-one session.

*Responsible professional: Carla Smith, C.C.D.C., Level II

Objective 2: Patty will verbalize her powerlessness and unmanageability in group by 2-15-11.

Intervention: Encourage the client to share her powerlessness and unmanageability in group.

*Responsible professional: Carla Smith, C.C.D.C., Level II

Objective 3: Patty will verbalize her understanding of her chemical dependency with her group by 2-15-11.

Intervention: Assign the client to complete her chemical use history, and encourage her to share her story in group.

*Responsible professional: Robert Johnson, C.C.D.C., Level III

Objective 4: Patty will share her understanding of how to use Step Two in recovery with her counselor by 2-20-11.

Intervention: Assign the client to meet with her clergy person to discuss how to use a Higher Power in recovery.

*Responsible professional: Father Larry Jackson

Objective 5: Patty will log her meditation daily and will discuss how she plans to use the Third Step in sobriety with her clergy person by 2-25-11.

Intervention: The staff will administer medications as ordered and monitor for side effects.

*Responsible professional: Margaret Roth, RN

Objective 6: Patty will develop a written relapse prevention plan by 2-30-11.

Intervention: Help the client to develop a written relapse prevention plan.

*Responsible professional: Carla Smith, C.C.D.C., Level II

Objective 7: Patty will develop a continuing care plan with her counselor by 3-5-11.

Intervention: Have the continuing care coordinator help the client to develop a continuing care program.

*Responsible professional: Martha Riggs, C.C.D.C., Level I

Problem 2:   Chronic fear of abandonment, as evidenced by fear of losing all interpersonal relationships

Goal B: To alleviate the fear of abandonment by connecting the client to her Higher Power and her Alcoholics Anonymous (AA)/Narcotics Anonymous (NA) support group

Objective 1: In one-to-one counseling, Patty will share her feelings of abandonment by her parents and how this relates to her chemical dependency by 2-15-11.

Intervention: In a one-to-one session, encourage the client to share her feelings of abandonment by her parents, and help her to connect this to her chemical dependency.

*Responsible professional: Carla Smith, C.C.D.C., Level II

Objective 2: Patty will share her feelings of fear, loneliness, and isolation with her group by 2-20-11.

Intervention: Assign the client to share her feelings of fear, loneliness, and isolation in group.

*Responsible professional: Carla Smith, C.C.D.C., Level II

Objective 3: Patty will discuss her fear that the group will abandon her and receive feedback from the group by 2-25-11.

Intervention: In group, encourage the client to share her fears that the members of the group will abandon her.

*Responsible professional: Carla Smith, C.C.D.C., Level II

Objective 4: In one-to-one counseling, the client will discuss accepting her AA/NA group as her new support system by 2-28-11.

Intervention: Teach the client about how her recovery group can be her new support system.

*Responsible professional: Carla Smith, C.C.D.C., Level II

Objective 5: Patty will write a letter to her father and mother telling them how she felt as a child, and she will share this letter with her counselor and in group by 2-20-11.

Intervention: Assign the client to write a letter to her father and mother telling them about the abandonment she felt as a child, and have her read this letter to her primary counselor and the group.

*Responsible professional: Carla Smith, C.C.D.C., Level II

Problem 3:   Poor interpersonal relationship skills, as evidenced by inability to share emotions, wishes, and wants with others

Goal C: To develop healthy interpersonal relationship skills

Objective 1: Patty will verbalize an identification of her problem with relationships with her counselor by 2-15-11.

Intervention: Teach the client about interpersonal relationship skills and how her addiction affected her ability to have healthy relationships.

*Responsible professional: Carla Smith, C.C.D.C., Level II

Objective 2: Patty will ask five treatment peers for something she wants and share with them how she feels, keeping a log of each conversation and sharing this with her counselor by 2-15-11.

Intervention: Assign the client to ask five treatment peers for something she wants and share how she feels, and have her log each event and share in a one-to-one session.

*Responsible professional: Carla Smith, C.C.D.C., Level II

Objective 3: Patty will complete the Addictive Relationships exercise (see Appendix 12) and share her understanding of the differences in addictive and healthy relationships with her counselor by 2-20-11.

Intervention: Assign the client to complete the Addictive Relationships exercise, and teach her the difference between addictive and healthy relationships.

*Responsible professional: Carla Smith, C.C.D.C., Level II

Objective 4: Patty will use and log 10 "I feel" statements a day until the end of treatment, and she will share her daily feeling log with her counselor weekly by 2-25-11.

Intervention: Assign the client to log 10 feeling statements a day and to share in one-to-one sessions.

*Responsible professional: Carla Smith, C.C.D.C., Level II

Objective 5: Patty will discuss her normal and addictive relationships with her group by 2-30-11.

Intervention: In group, encourage the client to share her understanding of addictive relationships and the tools she can use to develop and maintain healthy relationships in recovery.

*Responsible professional: Carla Smith, C.C.D.C., Level II

Problem 4: Dishonesty, as evidenced by chronic lying about chemical use

Goal D: To develop a program of recovery based on rigorous honesty

Objective 1: Patty will complete the Honesty exercise (see Appendix 8) and verbalize in group 10 times when she was dishonest about her chemical use by 2-15-11.

Intervention: Assign the client to complete the Honesty exercise, and in group have her verbalize 10 times when she was dishonest about her addiction.

*Responsible professional: Bill Thompson, MSW

Objective 2: Patty will discuss in group how her alcohol use contributed to her dishonesty by 2-20-11.

Intervention: In group, have the client discuss the connection between addiction and dishonesty.

*Responsible professional: Bill Thompson, MSW

Objective 3: Patty will keep a daily log of the times when she lies in treatment and will share this log with her counselor weekly by 2-25-11.

Intervention: Help the client to keep a daily log of the lies she tells in treatment, and discuss with her how it feels to lie and how it feels to tell the truth.

*Responsible professional: Carla Smith, C.C.D.C., Level II

Objective 4: Patty will give a 20-minute speech to her group about why it is important to be honest in recovery by 2-25-11.

Intervention: Assign the client to write a 20-minute speech about why it is important for her to get honest, and then encourage her to read her paper in group.

*Responsible professional: Carla Smith, C.C.D.C., Level II

Objective 5: In a conjoint session with her mother, Patty will share her chemical use history by 2-30-11.

Intervention: In a family session, have the client share her chemical use history with her mother.

*Responsible professional: Ronda Vocal, L.M.F.T.

Objective 6: Patty will discuss how dishonesty separated her from her Higher Power with the clergy by 2-20-11.

Intervention: Have clergy meet with the client and discuss how her lies kept her away from her Higher Power.

*Responsible professional: Pastor Steve Schultz

Problem 5:   Poor assertiveness skills, as evidenced by being too passive and allowing other people to make important decisions

Goal E: To develop assertiveness skills

Objective 1:   In group, Patty will verbalize an identification of her problem of being passive and will directly relate her passivity to her chemical use by 2-20-11.

Intervention: The psychologist will help the client to understand passive traits and how this relates to addiction.

*Responsible professional: Frank Rockman, PhD

Objective 2:   Patty will verbalize an understanding of how her passive behaviors lead directly to increased chemical use with her group by 2-15-11.

Intervention: Assign the client to discuss in group how her passive traits lead to chemical use.

*Responsible professional: Carla Smith, C.C.D.C., Level II

Objective 3:   Patty will practice the assertiveness formula with two treatment peers per day, keeping a daily log of each interaction by 2-20-11.

Intervention: The psychologist will teach the client the assertiveness formula and, using behavior rehearsal, will role-play several assertiveness situations.

*Responsible professional: Frank Rockman, PhD

Objective 4:   Patty will have weekly individual sessions with the psychologist in which she will role-play assertiveness situations by 2-30-11.

Intervention: The psychologist will meet with the client weekly to role-play assertiveness situations.

*Responsible professional: Frank Rockman, PhD

Appendix 7

Chemical Use History

Robert R. Perkinson, PhD

This exercise will help you to become more aware of how chemicals have affected your life and the lives of those around you. Using alcohol, or any other mood-altering substance, is considered to be chemical use. Answer the questions as completely as you can. It is time to get completely honest with yourself. Write down exactly what happened.

1. How old were you when you had your first drink? Describe what happened and how you felt.

2. List all of the drugs you have ever used and the age at which you first used each drug.

3. What are your drug-using habits? Where do you use? With whom? Under what circumstances?

4. Was there ever a period in your life when you used too much or too often? Give at least five examples.

5. Has using chemicals ever caused a problem for you? Describe the problem or problems. Give at least five examples.

6. When you were using, did you find that you used more—or for a longer period of time—than you had originally intended? Give at least five examples.

7. Do you have to use more of the chemical now to get the same effect? How much more than when you first started?

8. Did you ever try to cut down on your use? Why did you try to cut down, and what happened to your attempt?

9. List at least five ways you tried to cut down. Did you change your beverage? Limit the amount ("I would only have three tonight")? Restrict your use to a certain time of day ("I would only drink after five o'clock")?

10. Did you ever stop completely? What happened? Why did you start again?

11. Did you spend a lot of time intoxicated or hungover?

12. Did you ever use while doing something dangerous such as driving a car? Give at least five examples.

13. Were you ever so high or hungover that you missed work or school? Give at least five examples.

14. Did you ever miss family events or recreation because you were high or hungover? Give at least five examples.

15. Did your use ever cause family problems? Give at least five examples.

16. Did you ever feel annoyed when someone talked to you about your drinking or use of drugs? Who was this person, and what did they say? Give at least five examples.

17. Did you ever feel bad or guilty about your use? Give at least five examples.

18. Did using ever cause you any psychological problems such as being depressed? Explain what happened.

19. Did using ever cause you any physical problems or make a physical problem worse? Give a few examples.

20. Did you ever have a blackout? How old were you when you had your first blackout? Give some examples of blackouts.

21. Did you ever get sick because you got too intoxicated? Give at least five examples.

22. Did you ever have a real bad hangover? Give at least five examples about how you felt.

23. Did you ever get the shakes or suffer withdrawal symptoms when you quit using? Describe what happened physically, mentally, and spiritually to you when you stopped using your drug of choice.

24. Did you ever use chemicals to avoid symptoms of withdrawal? Give at least five examples of when you used a substance to control withdrawal symptoms.

25. Have you ever sought help for your drug problem? When? Who did you see? Did the treatment help you? How?

26. Why do you continue to use? Give 5 to 10 reasons.

27. Why do you want to stop using? Give at least 10 reasons.

28. Has alcohol or drug use ever affected your reputation? Describe what happened and how you felt.

29. Describe the feelings of guilt you have about your use. How do you feel about yourself?

30. How has using affected you financially? Give at least five examples of how you wasted money in your addiction.

31. Has your ambition decreased due to your use? Give a few examples.

32. Has your addiction changed how you feel about yourself? How do you feel when you are seeking the addiction or in withdrawal?

33. Are you as self-confident as you were before? How has the addiction affected your faith in yourself?

34. List at least 10 reasons why you want treatment now.

35. List all of the chemicals you have used in the past 6 months.

36. List how often, and in what amounts, you have used each chemical in the past 6 months.

37. List the life events that have been affected by your chemical use (e.g., school, marriage, job, children).

38. Have you ever had legal problems because of your use? List each problem.

39. How has your addiction affected your relationship with your parents and other family members? List at least 10 reasons.

40. If you are in school, list at least five ways your addiction affected your schoolwork and relationships with teachers and school administrators.

41. Have you ever lost a job or been suspended or expelled from school because of your use? Describe each time.

42. Do you want treatment for your chemical problem? List at least 10 reasons why.

Appendix 8

Honesty

Robert R. Perkinson, PhD

This is an exercise to help you get honest with yourself. In recovery, it is essential to tell the truth. As you will hear at every 12-step meeting, this is a program of rigorous honesty. "Those who do not recover are people who cannot or will not completely give themselves to this simple program, usually men and women who are constitutionally incapable of being honest with themselves" (Alcoholics Anonymous [AA], 2001, p. 58).

Why is it so important to be honest? Because dishonesty to self and others distorts reality. "Rigorous honesty is the most important tool in learning to live for today" (Narcotics Anonymous [NA], 1988, p. 92). You never will solve problems if you lie. You need to live in the facts. In sobriety, you must commit yourself to reality. This means accepting everything that is real.

People who are chemically dependent think that they cannot tell the truth. They believe that if they do, they will be rejected. The facts are exactly the opposite; unless you tell the truth, no one can accept you. People have to know you to accept you. If you keep secrets, then you never will feel known or loved. An old AA saying states, "We are only as sick as our secrets." If you keep secrets from people, then you never will be close to them.

You cannot be a practicing alcoholic or drug addict without lying to yourself. You must not lie—and believe the lies—or else the illness cannot continue. The lies are attempts to protect you from the pain of the truth. If you had known the truth, then you would have known that you were sick and needed treatment. This would have been frightening, so you kept the truth from yourself and from others. "Let us face it; when we were using, we were not honest with ourselves" (NA, 1988, p. 27).

There are many ways you lied to yourself. This exercise will teach you exactly how you distorted reality, and it will start you toward a program of honesty. Answer each of the following questions as completely as you can.

1. *Denial:* You have told yourself or others, "I do not have a problem." Write down at least five examples of when you used this technique to avoid dealing with the truth.

    a.

    b.

    c.

    d.

    e.

2. *Minimizing:* This is making the problem smaller than it really was. You might have told yourself, or someone else, that your problem was not that bad. You might have told someone that you had a couple of beers when you really had six. Write down at least five examples of when you distorted reality by making it seem smaller than it actually was.

   a.

   b.

   c.

   d.

   e.

3. *Hostility:* You became angry or made threats when someone confronted you about your chemical use. Give at least five examples.

   a.

   b.

   c.

   d.

   e.

4. *Rationalization:* You have made an excuse. "I had a hard day. Things are bad. My relationship is bad. My financial situation is bad." Give at least 10 examples of when you thought that you had a good reason to use chemicals.

   a.

   b.

   c.

   d.

   e.

   f.

   g.

   h.

   i.

   j.

5. *Blaming:* You have shifted the responsibility to someone else. "The police were out to get me. My wife is overreacting." Give at least five examples of when you blamed someone else for a problem you caused.

   a.

   b.

   c.

   d.

   e.

6. *Intellectualizing:* You have overanalyzed and overthought about a problem. This avoids doing something about it. "Sure I drink some, but everyone I know drinks. I read this article, and it said that this is a drinking culture." Give at least five examples of how you use intellectual data and statistics to justify your use.

   a.

   b.

   c.

   d.

   e.

7. *Diversion:* You have brought up another topic of conversation to avoid the issue. Give at least five examples.

   a.

   b.

   c.

   d.

   e.

8. Make a list of five lies that you told to someone close to you about your drinking or drug use.

   a.

   b.

   c.

   d.

   e.

9. Make a list of five lies that you told yourself about your drug problem.

   a.

   b.

   c.

   d.

   e.

10. Make a list of 10 people you have lied to.

   a.

   b.

   c.

   d.

   e.

   f.

   g.

    h.

    i.

    j.

11. How do you feel about your lying? Describe at least five ways you feel about yourself when you lie.

    a.

    b.

    c.

    d.

    e.

12. List five things you think will change in your life if you begin to tell the truth.

    a.

    b.

    c.

    d.

    e.

13. List five ways you use lies in other areas of your life.

    a.

    b.

    c.

    d.

    e.

14. When are you the most likely to lie? Is it when you have been drinking or using addictive behavior?

15. Why do you lie? What does it get you? Give five reasons.

    a.

    b.

    c.

    d.

    e.

16. Common lies of addiction are listed here. Give a personal example of each. Be honest with yourself.

    a. Breaking promises:

    b. Pretending to be clean and sober when you are not:

    c. Pretending you remember things when you do not remember because of the addiction:

    d. Minimizing use: Telling someone you drink or use no more than others use:

    e. Telling yourself that you were in control when you were not:

    f. Telling someone that you never have been involved in addictive behavior:

   g. Hiding morning drinking:

   h. Hiding your supply:

   i. Substituting the addiction for food or things you or your family needs:

   j. Saying that you had the flu when you were really hungover or sick from the addiction:

   k. Having someone else call into work to say that you are too sick to come to work:

   l. Pretending not to care about your addiction:

People who are addicted lie to avoid facing the truth. Lying makes them feel more comfortable, but in the long run they end up feeling isolated and alone. Recovery demands living in the truth. "I am an alcoholic or an addict. My life is unmanageable. I am powerless over alcohol. I need help. I cannot do this alone." All of these are honest statements from someone who is living in reality.

Either you will get real and live in the real world, or you will live in a fantasy world of your own creation. If you get honest, then you will begin to solve real problems. You will be accepted for who you are.

Wake up tomorrow morning, and promise yourself that you are going to be honest for the next hour. Then try it for a half day and then a whole day. Stop and check your feelings, and write down five ways you feel different when you are honest.

Write down in a diary when you are tempted to lie. Watch your feelings when you lie. How does it feel? How do you feel about yourself? Keep a list of five ways you feel different about yourself when you lie. Keep a diary for 5 days and share it with your group or counselor. Tell them why you lied and how you felt about yourself when you lied. Then tell the group or counselor how it feels to be honest.

Take a piece of paper and write the word *truth* to place on your bathroom mirror. Commit yourself to rigorous honesty. You deserve to live a life filled with love and truth. You never need to lie again.

Appendix 9

Love, Trust, and Commitment

Robert R. Perkinson, PhD

It seems that going through life, we should be taught a few simple things about relationships. After all, we have a relationship first with ourselves and then, if we so choose, with others. How can we trust ourselves? How can we trust others? When are we committed? When do we love? This exercise will start you thinking about these essential parts of a relationship. Use this exercise to ask yourself some important questions.

The First Relationship

An infant learns about love, trust, and commitment from its primary caregiver. This usually is the mother. When the infant cries out, someone comes and addresses its needs. The baby cannot see very well, so this someone comes out of a haze, seemingly out of nowhere. Whenever the baby cries, this someone comes. This someone comes every time, and a great trust develops between the infant and its mother. As the infant grows older, it becomes aware that this someone has a particular sight, smell, sound, taste, and feel. Soon this someone has a name—mother.

The infant learns who he or she is by looking at the mother's face, particularly her eyes. Healthy mothers look at their children with a look that says, "You bring me joy." Therefore, a healthy child learns that he or she brings joy to the world. By mirroring the mother's facial expression, they learn that they are important, accepted, and loved. The mother always comes when the infant cries out, at all hours of the day or night, so in time a baby learns to trust that the caregiver will always come.

As infants grow older, they learn that the mother does not have to come; she chooses to come. Why does she come? Why, at all hours of the day or night, does she choose to come? She comes because she is bonded with her child. Her child's pain is her pain, and her child's joy is her joy. She cannot ignore her child's pain because when her child hurts, she hurts. In this bonding of mother and child, that builds a healthy brain where there is love, trust, and commitment. "The child knows mother will always be there for me." The child's very life depends on it. The mother has to be so in tune with her child that her loving gaze cannot last too long or the child will be overwhelmed. So she must look away every few seconds and instinctively know when to look back reassuring her baby. Later in childhood, the mother socializes the child by purposely looking away when the child does something wrong. But she does not look away too long or she will raise an anxious child—one who is unsure and uncomfortable about whether or not she or he can trust the mother. Unhealthy children are uncertain, anxious, or even angry in the mother's presence. Some babies who are abused have to look dead in order to make the abuse stop. Many of your clients will have a flat effect or look like they have no feelings. This person may have been abused as an infant or an adult (Schore, 2003).

Some children never learn to trust, and this is one of the primary characteristics of a child of an addict. Children from addicted homes never know what is going to happen, so they live in fear, uncertainty, and chaos. They learn to trust no one. They can love but have great difficulty feeling loved.

It is from this first relationship that we generalize what to expect from all of our other relationships. We expect relationships to have certain core characteristics. If the relationships are healthy, they will have love, trust, and commitment as essential building blocks.

Trust

List at least five ways you can show yourself that you can trust yourself.

List at least five things you are going to do to prove to yourself that you are trustworthy.

- You will need to develop consistency of action in your own behalf.
- If you act consistently in a manner that is in your best interest, then you have gone a long way toward learning how to trust yourself.
- You must be consistent even when times get rough.
- You need to learn that no matter what, you are going to do things that are good for you.
- You are trustworthy to someone else when you consistently act in that other person's interest.

Commitment

Commitment means that you are faithful and loyal for an extended period. It means that on a daily basis, you can count on yourself to follow through with your promises.

- You have plans to be good to yourself, and you are going to stick with these plans.
- You are going to hammer away at the things you want day by day.
- You are not going to give up.
- These same elements apply when you commit yourself to someone else.

Love

A good definition for love is that love is the interest in, and the active involvement in, a person's individual growth. Love for someone else needs trust and commitment, but it needs something more.

- Love needs empathy. You must feel the other person's feelings as if they were your own.
- Empathy is the feeling that you share with another person. It is being in harmony. "I feel your feelings."
- "When you feel sad, I feel sad. When you feel joy, I feel joy. To help you is to help myself."
- "To love you is to love myself."

Perhaps somewhere along the way you have lost the ability to experience normal relationships. Maybe you never developed a trustworthy, committed relationship with your primary caregiver. It could be that you never really felt accepted the way in which you needed to be. Children need a lot of encouragement when they try things, and they need a lot of praise. This makes them feel accepted, cherished, and loved. If you take children, sit on their beds every day of their lives, and tell them how wonderful they are, then maybe by the time they are 6 years old they will be ready for school. Children need a lot of encouragement to develop a sense of self-worth.

How to Be Caring to Yourself

To be caring to yourself, you must give yourself a lot of encouragement and a lot of praise. If you missed this as a child, then your challenge is to reinforce yourself.

- Treat yourself the way in which you wanted to be treated.
- Be your own healthy mother and your own healthy father.
- Give yourself all of the love you have always wanted.

Imagine for a moment that you are a very young child with a fragile and impressionable mind. Write down 10 things that you would need to see from your parents.

1.
2.
3.
4.
5.
6.
7.
8.
9.
10.

Only you know what you need. It is up to you to meet your needs. Give to yourself all of the love you need.

Relationship With Self

List the things that you need to see from yourself that will prove you can be trusted to act in your own best interests.

1.
2.
3.
4.
5.
6.
7.
8.

9.

10.

List the things that you need to see from yourself that will show you are committed to your own growth. This is a day-by-day commitment.

1.

2.

3.

4.

5.

6.

7.

8.

9.

10.

List the things that you will need to see from yourself that will show you love yourself.

1.

2.

3.

4.

5.

6.

7.

8.

9.

10.

How to Find Out the Good Things About Yourself

List the things about yourself that make you feel proud. Start with physical appearance. What are some of your good physical qualities? List as many as you can think of. Start with your hair, and move downward to the tips of your toes. Admire the color, size, shape, feel, smell, sound, or whatever you can think of. Do not let the old stinking thinking keep you feeling bad about yourself. Get accurate by asking your counselor or group to help you.

Physical appearance: What do you like about how you look?

1.

2.

3.

4.

5.

6.

7.

8.

9.

10.

Personality: List all of the personality characteristics that you like and admire about yourself. What do people seem to like about you? What do you like about yourself?

1.

2.

3.

4.

5.

6.

7.

8.

9.

10.

You need a lot of encouragement and praise. Now you have many accurate things to say to yourself that make you feel good about yourself.

Things you enjoy: List the things you enjoy doing. How do you play? What do you do for fun or entertainment? What would you like to start doing that will give you pleasure?

1.

2.

3.

4.

5.

6.

7.

8.

9.

10.

People you enjoy: List some of the people you enjoy being around. Write down what makes them feel special to you.

1.

2.

3.

4.

5.

6.

7.

8.

9.

10.

Take a long look at what you have written. See how wonderful you really are.

Say Good Things to Yourself

Now you have all of these good things to say to yourself. Start with 10 things, and write them down on note cards. Carry these cards with you, and read them to yourself periodically throughout the day. Look at yourself in the mirror, and say these things to yourself. Practice until you have these 10 memorized and then list 10 more. Constantly bombard yourself with positive self-talk. When you find yourself speaking harshly to yourself, stop and self-correct. Get out the note cards if you have to, but do not continue to treat yourself poorly.

Do Good Things for Yourself

You are saying good things to yourself. That is healing and treating yourself well. Now what can you do for yourself today that is really special?

- Maybe take a long, hot bath.
- Go for a relaxing walk.
- Spend some time with a friend you enjoy.
- Get some ice cream.
- Read something you enjoy.
- Take a nap.

- Come up with a few special things to do for yourself today. Write all of these things down and do them. When you are doing these things, think of why you are doing them because you are a person of great worth. Do this every day.
- Before you get up in the morning, commit yourself to treating yourself well and then get up and get busy, enjoy life, and feel the pleasure of being alive.
- You deserve it.

Relationship With Others

You have some things that you want from a significant other, a friend, or a lover. It is your responsibility to ask for what you want. Be specific and give that person a lot of encouragement when he or she tries to give these things to you. You know the secret.

- Be reinforcing.
- Give encouragement.
- Shower the person with praise—it is contagious.
- If you give more, you will get more often.
- Happiness is created when we unselfishly give to others.

How to Find Out If a Relationship Is Good for You

What are the things you need to see from someone that will show you he or she is trustworthy and committed to you?

1.

2.

3.

4.

5.

6.

7.

8.

9.

10.

How to Get What You Want in a Relationship

If you have a friend or partner, then you must be specific.

- Ask that person for what you want. The person cannot guess what you want or need; you must tell him or her.
- Remember to give the person a lot back when he or she gives you something.

- Ask the person for what he or she wants, and do your best to give it to this person.
- As you give to this other person, you will feel good about yourself and you will get more of your needs met in return.
- The more you give, the more you will get.

After completing this exercise, you should be treating yourself well. You should know what you need to see from yourself, and from others, to make you feel good. You have learned that you directly influence how you feel. You are not helpless to others or to your environment. You can love yourself. You are special. You are worth it. Others can love you. You can love others. You can feel whole, healthy, and complete. You have all of the skills that you need.

Appendix 10

Feelings

Robert R. Perkinson, PhD

Chemically dependent persons have a difficult time with their feelings. They never have learned how to use their feelings appropriately. They have been chemically altering their feelings for years. They do not know how they feel or what they want. They do not know what to do when they do feel. Many chemically dependent people were shamed for having normal feelings when they were children. When they were afraid, they were told that there was no reason to be afraid. When they were angry, they were told that there was no reason to be angry. Children who are taught these things learn that their feelings cannot be trusted. They learn that there is something wrong with their feelings. This exercise will help you to identify your feelings and use your feelings appropriately.

The Purpose of Feelings

Feelings or emotions are physiological states that motivate action. Each feeling gives you specific energy and direction for movement. This is how problems are solved.

- First, there is a situation that triggers thought.
- Thoughts create feelings.
- Feelings motivate action.

This is how all problems are solved. A person becomes involved in a problem, thinks about the problem, has feelings generated by the thoughts, acts on the feelings, and resolves the issue.

The Core Feelings

There are only a few core feelings. Feelings that are more complicated are various combinations of the primary ones. Plutchik (1980) studied feelings and found that there were eight primary emotions:

1. Joy

2. Acceptance

3. Anticipation

4. Surprise

5. Fear

6. Anger

7. Disgust

8. Sadness

Each of these feelings gives us specific energy and direction for movement. We need to discuss each feeling carefully and have you learn specifically what each feeling is like. Then you can recognize when the feeling occurs, and you will know what the feeling is telling you to do. You need practice in experiencing the subtle physiological changes that differentiate each feeling from the others.

Joy

Joy is that feeling we experience when we reach a goal. The harder we have been working for the goal, and the more important the goal is to us, the more joy we feel.

List at least five times when you felt joy in your life. As you write down each situation, take a moment to reexperience the feeling you had at that moment in your life. Feel the situation as if you were actually there.

1.

2.

3.

4.

5.

Joy gives us the energy and direction to celebrate, feel pleasure, and enjoy an activity. It directs us to seek more of whatever is giving us this pleasure.

Acceptance

Acceptance is the feeling we get when someone likes us or approves of us. List five times in your life when you felt accepted. Allow yourself to feel the feeling as you remember each situation.

1.

2.

3.

4.

5.

The feeling of acceptance gives us the energy and direction to stay involved, or become more intimately involved, with the person or group that is accepting. It is a feeling that bonds people together.

Anticipation

Anticipation is the feeling we get when we prepare ourselves for change. It mobilizes us for something new. We can anticipate something good or bad. List five times when you felt an intense sense of anticipation. Try to reexperience the feeling of each situation.

1.

2.

3.

4.

5.

Anticipation gives us the energy and direction to mobilize ourselves for change. We prepare ourselves for something new.

Surprise

Surprise is the feeling we get when something unexpected happens. Surprise gives us the energy to orient ourselves to a new situation. List five times when you felt surprised. Feel the feeling that you felt each time.

1.

2.

3.

4.

5.

Surprise mobilizes our bodies to take in the new situation as quickly as possible. The brain is very quickly deciding how to respond to the new stimuli.

Fear

Fear is the feeling we have when something is perceived as dangerous and to be avoided. List five times when you felt fear. Allow yourself to feel the feeling generated by each situation.

1.

2.

3.

4.

5.

Fear gives us the energy and direction to escape from a dangerous situation. It mobilizes us to get away from the offending stimuli.

Anger

Anger is the feeling we feel when we are violated. This violation may be real or imagined. You are hurt first and the anger is there to make the pain stop. List five times when you were angry. Feel the anger you felt in each situation. Concentrate on the physical changes in your body that occur when you get angry.

1.

2.

3.

4.

5.

Anger gives us the energy and direction to fight. It helps us to reestablish the boundaries around our-selves. Anger is necessary to prevent people from violating us.

Disgust

Disgust is the emotion we feel when something repels us. We loathe it; it is repugnant. List five times when something disgusted you. Allow yourself to reexperience the feeling of each situation.

1.

2.

3.

4.

5.

Disgust gives us the energy and direction to withdraw from the offending stimulation. We need to move away from the object that repels us.

Sadness

Sadness is the feeling we get when we have lost something. We can lose a love object or self-esteem. List five times when you felt sad. Allow yourself to reexperience the sad feeling. Sense the subtle physiological changes that occur when you feel sad.

1.

2.

3.

4.

5.

Sadness gives us the energy and direction to recover the lost object. If we are unable to recover the object, then the sadness can deepen. Sadness can immobilize an organism so that healing can begin to take place. The organism does not move or do new things. It stays still and recovers from the loss.

How to Use Feelings Appropriately

Feelings can be used appropriately or inappropriately. They can be based on accurate or inaccurate informa-tion. They can lead to adaptive behavior or maladaptive behavior. It is important to know how you feel and what to do when you feel. Feelings will help you to solve problems. Without using your feelings appropri-ately, you never will be able to solve problems well.

When you feel, you will be experiencing one or more of the eight primary feelings. Jealousy is feeling fear, anger, and sadness all at the same time. Each feeling needs to be addressed for full resolution of the problem.

If you feel confused, then you are feeling many feelings at the same time. Some of these feelings may be in conflict with each other, and you may be torn about what to do. When confused, you must separate each feeling and examine it carefully. What is each feeling telling you to do? What is the most rational thing to do?

When you have a feeling, you must decide how to act. The feeling is motivating you to take action. Feelings need to flow naturally and spontaneously into adaptive action. The actions must be appropriate to the situation. To always fight when you are angry is not appropriate. Most of the time, it is necessary to stop and think before you act. You want to use your feelings accurately. When you are having an intense feeling, always ask yourself two questions:

1. What is the best thing I can do for myself?

2. What is the best thing I can do for the others?

For the most part, you must practice thinking and planning before you act. Plan carefully how you are going to act when you have each feeling, and practice this action until it flows naturally. It will help you to role play each feeling with others in group. For example, one group member could play your father who is angry with you and you try to respond to his anger appropriately. Each person role-plays each feeling enough times that they automatically have the correct thoughts and the correct motor movements. One of the best things you can do for someone who is angry with you is to ask for more information about why they are hurt or angry. Then try to reflect to them how they are feeling and why.

Father: I am very upset with you for being late.

Client: Dad, I know I promised to be home on time, but I lost track of the time.

Father: That is the problem. You always lose track of time.

Client: It sounds like you are having trouble trusting me.

Father: That's right. You are always late.

Client: Dad, this is the only time I have been late this week, and I am willing to experience the consequence we discussed in the behavioral contract.

Tomorrow I will come home one hour earlier.

Father: How about two hours earlier and washing the car.

Client: I will gladly come home two hours earlier and wash the car. It is very important for me to know that you trust me, and I know I have to earn that trust.

Your feelings are important. They are great and wise counselors that need to be heard. You do not need to hide from your feelings. You need to listen and learn. Practice each feeling so you can get good at automatically knowing what to think and do when you have each feeling. You will blow it sometimes; everyone does, but the more you practice the better you will do, and you will have a more stable recovery.

Appendix 11

Relationship Skills

Robert R. Perkinson, PhD

There are certain skills that are necessary to establish and maintain close interpersonal relationships. The skills seem simple, but some of them can take great courage. Love is not a feeling; it is an action. We must love in action and in truth. To love someone, you must be actively involved in that other person's individual growth. Love is not self-oriented; it is other-oriented. There also is the love that you show yourself. This is when you are involved in your own growth.

How to Love

The first skill is love. Love is an action. You are interested in and actively involved in the other person's individual growth. You are there for that other person when he or she needs you. You respond to how the person feels and what he or she wants. You tell the truth all of the time. You are willing to spend your time and energy being involved in the other person's well-being.

List five times when, because of your addictive behavior, you were not there for someone when he or she needed you. Then list what you could have done, or should have done, to help that other person at that moment. Sometimes you might have been too intoxicated or hungover to be there for the other person. Sometimes you might have used your time or money for the addiction rather than for a family member.

1.

2.

3.

4.

5.

List five times when you lied to someone you loved. Love cannot exist where there are lies. Love necessitates truth. Without the truth, the other person does not know who you are.

1.

2.

3.

4.

5.

How to Commit

The second skill is commitment. You must commit yourself, on a daily basis, to work on building a close relationship. This means that you work to provide a safe atmosphere in which the relationship can grow. This is an atmosphere full of love and trust. You dedicate yourself to the other person and the relationship. You must take the time necessary to nourish yourself, the other person, and the relationship. You consistently ask yourself what you can do for the other person, and then you do it. Now make a plan. What do you think you need to do to make your relationship grow?

1.

2.

3.

4.

5.

How to Be Encouraging

The third skill is being encouraging. You must encourage the other person to reach his or her full potential in life. This takes a lot of reinforcement and praise. No one needs to be punished and criticized. This dampens the spirit and weakens interpersonal bonds. People need soothing, tender, and encouraging words. They need to know that you have faith in them, that you trust them, and that you will help them to grow. People need their good points praised. They need to hear what they are doing right. Encourage five people today. Write down each of their names and the situation. Watch their reactions, and make note of how they seem to feel and how you feel.

1.

2.

3.

4.

5.

How to Share

The fourth skill is sharing. Intimacy means "into-me-see." You must practice sharing how you feel and what you think. You must ask for what you want. You cannot keep these things to yourself. The relationship will falter if you withhold the truth. As children, we might have been taught that asking for what we want is self-ish. It is not selfish in a healthy relationship; it is necessary. Happiness occurs when you unselfishly give to others. How can your partner give to you if you do not tell him or her what you want? How can the other person be encouraged to grow and change unless you hold the person accountable for his or her actions? If you keep your feelings and wants to yourself, then your relationship will not work. Your partner cannot guess what you want. The other person is not capable of that. List 10 important things you want from your relationship, and decide how you are going to ask for these things.

1.

2.

3.

4.

5.

6.

7.

8.

9.

10.

Now list the feelings that you have difficulty sharing with your partner. What feelings do you tend to keep secret?

1.

2.

3.

4.

5.

Make yourself a promise: The next time you have a sharing time with someone, you are going to share how you feel and think. You are going to ask for what you want. Practice in a skills group or with your counselor. Play the role of yourself and your partner, and have another person play the other role. Then work through some problems you have had in the past and see if telling the truth, the whole truth, and nothing but the truth will help you solve problems. Practice rephrasing what the other person has said until he or she agrees that you understand. Then respond and have the other person rephrase what you said until you say he or she understands. Many problems occur because the people are not understanding each other and particularly understanding each other's needs. Most of the time you think you know what the other person needs but most of the time you will be wrong. You need to ask and rephrase until you understand.

How to Compromise

The fifth skill is compromise. No one is going to get everything he or she wants in a relationship. You have to create an atmosphere of give-and-take. You must be willing to respond to how the other person feels and what he or she wants. Always ask yourself what you would want if you were in the other person's position. Compromise creates an atmosphere of fairness and equality. List five areas in your life where you have stubbornly wanted to have things your own way. Then list what you are going to do to be more flexible in those situations.

1.

2.

3.

4.

5.

How to Show Respect

The sixth skill is establishing a relationship filled with respect. This means that you show the other person that he or she is important to you. You do things that make the person feel special, understood, and wanted. You care for how the person feels and for what he or she wants. This person matters to you. This person counts. You do not treat this person poorly; you love him or her too much for that. You want this person to be happy. When this person feels happy, you feel happy. List five ways in which you can show someone that he or she is special and important to you.

1.

2.

3.

4.

5.

These relationship skills need practice. They will not come easily. You need to work at telling the truth all of the time and role play in group and with your counselor a wide variety of situations that have given you difficulty in the past. You need to practice being encouraging. Practice sharing how you feel and asking for what you want. You need to develop the skill of commitment. You will struggle when you compromise. You need to work at showing someone that he or she is important.

Keep a log every day for the next week. Detail how you did on each skill and watch for the other person's reaction. Look carefully at how the other person's response changes how you feel about yourself.

The Daily Relationship Plan

1. Encourage someone today.

   a. Write down the situation. Exactly what happened?
   b. How did the person feel when you encouraged him or her?
   c. How did you feel?

2. Ask for something you want.

   a. How did it work?
   b. Did you get what you wanted?
   c. How did you feel about asking?
   d. How did the other person respond?

3. Share your feelings.

   a. What was the situation?
   b. How did you feel about yourself?
   c. What response did you get?

4. Tell someone that he or she is important to you.

   a. How did you feel about doing this?
   b. How did the other person feel?

5. Evaluate yourself on honesty.

   a. Did you lie or withhold truth today?
   b. How do you feel about what you did?

6. Help someone, and watch his or her reaction.

   a. How did the person respond?
   b. How did you feel?

7. Give something to someone without expecting anything in return.

   a. How did you feel about yourself?
   b. How was your gift accepted?

8. Compromise with someone.

   a. How did you feel?
   b. How did the other person feel?
   c. What was the result of your compromise?

The more you role-play and practice the skills, the more proficient you will become. If you hit all of the skills accurately, then your relationships will be stable. If you leave one of the skills out, then your relationships will be shaky and you will feel frightened. These skills are just like riding a bicycle. The first few times you try to ride, it feels awkward and clumsy; you may be worried about getting hurt. With practice, the skills get easy, and you will be able to relax and enjoy yourself.

Appendix 12

Addictive Relationships

Robert R. Perkinson, PhD

Relationships are our greatest challenge. Even the best relationships have periods of intense strain. It takes hard work to get along. You have to be willing to give and to think of the other person's needs first. This is not easy. Chemically dependent persons often are just as addicted to their sexual partners as they are to their drugs of choice. Sometimes that "love" feeling is the drug. This should not surprise you. Sexual feelings are created by powerful chemicals in the body called hormones. These pleasure chemicals can be just as addictive as any drug, and they can be just as destructive. The mesolimbic dopamine system that makes up the reptilian brain is only interested in three things:

- Eat.
- Do not be eaten.
- Procreate the species.

This center of the brain lies just over the brain stem, and it takes precedence over higher ordered function because it deals with survival. An addictive brain is a changed brain, and some people get addicted to a sexual partner. This relationship is seen as necessary for survival. In other words, if I lose this relationship I would die. This sets up an addictive relationship that is just as powerful as the strongest drug.

Addictive relationships are very different from normal ones. You need to be able to tell which is which. For stability and happiness, you want to get in and stay in a healthy relationship. You want to get out of or treat an addictive one.

The Cycle of Addictive Relationships

The addictive relationship begins with very powerful sexual feelings. These feelings may fool you because most of us taught that these feelings are love. They are not love; they are sexual motivators. These first feelings are extremely powerful, and they draw you, seemingly irresistibly, toward that other person. These are the "love at first sight" feelings. But do not be fooled; it is not love. We can feel these feelings with a movie star or even with someone's picture. Young teens are notorious for feeling madly in love with an entertainer. In an addictive relationship, you see someone across a crowded room. Your eyes are drawn to that person. Sexual acting out can occur quickly because these feelings are so powerful.

The feelings are so good that you will do anything to keep them. Here is where addictive relationships begin to get sick. You are so thrilled and enchanted with your new "love" that you begin to lie to keep the relationship going. You say things that you do not mean, and you do things that you do not want to do. You just want to keep these addictive hormones flowing in your system. This can be subtle, but it is the clearest difference between addictive and normal relationships. In addictive relationships, you lie. In normal relationships, you tell the truth.

People have an instinctive way of knowing when someone is being dishonest with them. It might take them a while to catch on but soon reality begins to sink in.

- Lies begin to show up.
- Fear begins to build.
- Fear feels uncomfortable, so the partners begin to test each other.
- Jealousy begins to rear its ugly head.
- The partners begin to accuse each other of being dishonest and unfaithful.
- They suspiciously keep track of each other. "Where were you? Who were you with? What did you do?"
- Repeatedly, the accusations fly back and forth.
- All of this fear, hurt, and anger gets its fuel from the lies. That is the problem. There are lies to uncover, and both people feel it and need to uncover the truth.

Eventually, there is an explosion. The fear, jealousy, and accusations reach a fever pitch, and the relationship shatters. There is a violent argument. This usually is verbally abusive and possibly physically abusive. The feelings are so intense—both the pleasure and the pain—that things explode. There usually is screaming and name calling. Demands are made as these two individuals try to reestablish their individual boundaries and resolve the aching fear.

After the explosion, there is a short cooling-off period, and then the two are back to the good feelings again. It is makeup time. The sex is just as good as it was before, maybe even better. "How could we have fought? We love each other so much. What could we have been thinking about?" This is the real thing. It feels so good.

This vicious cycle repeats itself over and over again. There is incredible pain in addictive relationships. You constantly feel desperately in love, scared, and angry. It feels like a roller-coaster relationship that is out of control. The intensity of the feelings and the lies are the primary factors that keep this sick relationship going—round and round the couple goes in a cycle of agony and ecstasy.

Normal Relationships

A normal relationship begins when you meet someone who interests you as a person. There is no intense sexual desire at first. You just want to spend time together because you enjoy each other's company. There is no reason to lie, so you tell each other the truth.

Sharing the truth, you gradually draw closer together. The intimacy begins to grow. The more you share, the closer you get. The closer you get, the more you share.

There is a genuine concern for each other. This relationship is based on trust and friendship. There is no reason to be afraid. In this safe atmosphere, surrounded by the truth, sexual feelings can begin and romance begins. This is not just a person with whom want to have sex. It is a person with whom you want to be and share your life. They make you feel safe and comfortable, not always on a sexual high.

Love

Love is an action. It is not a feeling. We must love in action and in truth. Love is the active involvement in someone's individual growth. If you love yourself, then you will be actively involved in your own growth. Similarly, if you love someone else, then you will be actively involved in that person's growth. It is time to find out where you are in your relationship. Is your relationship addictive or normal?

- List all of the lies you can think of that exist in your current relationship. Start with the big lies, such as infidelity, and work down from there. You will immediately get the idea if there are major lies in your relationship. A normal relationship cannot exist on a foundation of lies. Such a relationship will falter, crumble, and fail.

- Write down some things you are afraid of in your relationship. Are you afraid of infidelity? Why? Do you have any information that your partner has been unfaithful? If you do, what is it? Strong fears of infidelity are one of the core components in addictive relationships. These fears can be based on good evidence or can be groundless. It does not matter what causes the fear; it is the fear itself that is the damaging factor.

- Are you verbally or physically afraid of your partner? Abusive relationships are extremely damaging. Abusive relationships need treatment. Verbal and physical abuse is very common in addictive relationships.

- Describe three major fights you have had with your partner. Pick the worst ones that you can remember. What were the fights about? How did they progress? Were the problems resolved, or did you tend to fight about the same things repeatedly? How do you fight? What words are said? How does each of you act when you are very angry?

- Does your partner consistently care about how you feel? Does your partner change what he or she does because of how you feel?

- Is your partner interested and involved in what you want? Is your partner committed to your individual growth? Some individuals are so caught up in their own needs that they will not become involved in their partners' needs. These people may be incapable of love.

Now go over this information with your counselor or group. Do you believe that you are involved in an addictive relationship? If you are, then you must do one of two things: (1) You must get out of the relationship entirely or (2) get treatment. Both people must go to treatment. If you continue on the way you are going, then you are in for more misery. You now know what love is and what a normal relationship is like. You deserve a relationship filled with love. Do not settle for less.

Appendix 13

Communication Skills

Robert R. Perkinson, PhD

In developing good communication skills, you need to learn how to listen and how to share. You need to understand where the other person is coming from, and you need the ability to express yourself clearly. People communicate with words and actions. Tears or an angry voice can say a lot. You need to be sensitive to both verbal and nonverbal behavior.

Empathy

Empathy is the ability to mentally remove yourself from the situation and step into another person's world. Then you can see the world from that person's perspective. You can discover what the other person needs and understand how the person feels. You get in harmony. To develop empathy, you practice paraphrasing what the other person has said until you get the communication correct. The other person needs to be encouraged to correct your mistakes until you have the message correct. You need to practice communication skills in role playing with your group or counselor. Keep listening, asking, probing, and rephrasing what the other person said until you understand his or her needs. Once you understand the other person then and only then can you respond accurately.

Repeat what the other person said as exactly as you can—both the verbal and the nonverbal message. Continue to repeat the message until the person agrees that you have it right. This might take a few tries, but you will get better as you practice. Include the verbal and nonverbal parts of the message. You might have to ask questions as you go along. Try to be genuine, not sarcastic or punitive. Act as a mirror, reflecting exactly what the other person is saying and how he or she is saying it. Use the same tone of voice, facial expression, and body posture. Practice getting the total communication correct. As time goes on, you will need to ask for clarification less often—only when you are unsure of certain parts of the communication.

Validation

The other person has a right to his or her opinion, and that opinion always should be valuable to you. This is an essential element in healthy communication. The other person needs to know that you believe he or she is important and you will try to understand their point of view. People need to be validated often, particularly when they disagree with you. Not everything that a person says is wrong. Find the areas that you agree on and emphasize those areas. Always pick out the things you have in common and bring out those points for discussion.

How to Use "I Feel" Statements

Practice beginning many of your communications with "I feel." You might not know what is right or wrong in a given situation, but you always know how you feel. Start with your feelings, and then fill in what you think is creating those feelings. If you are feeling confused, then you are having many feelings at the same time. Try to break down the feelings and address each one separately. The "I feel" statements prevent you from concentrating on the other person. Communications that begin with "You" can be accusatory and punitive. Instead of pointing out what the other person is doing, concentrate on how you feel and what you think. Imagine that you are role-playing a discussion with your wife. One person in the group or the counselor plays your wife and you play yourself. Your wife has a problem and she is ready to discuss it.

Wife: I do not feel like you love me anymore.

Client: I do love you. I love you more each day. What makes you feel like I do not love you?

Wife: You never help me around the house, or with the children, then when we go to bed you want to have sex.

Counselor: (*The counselor steps in to help the client.*) So I am hearing that you need me to help you around the house and with the children.

Wife: That's right. You can help by cleaning up, washing the dishes once in a while, putting the children to bed, and reading them a story. You could at least pick up your own clothes and clean up after yourself.

Client: I can do all these things. I thought you wanted to do them all yourself.

Wife: Jack, I need you to help me. If you help me, I would feel like you love me.

Client: If you feel like I am loving you all day by helping out, you might even feel like having sex more often.

Wife: Yes, more often. Much more often. I need a husband that makes love to me all day. Then I would feel more like making love at night.

Be Positive

Always try to find something positive to say to the other person. Even when you are disagreeing, you need to show the other person that you are going to be reinforcing. This shows the other person that you respect and care about him or her. In the previous conversation, you could have said, "Honey, I really appreciate your doing all of this work, and I promise that I am going to help you a lot more from now on. I will show you that I love you by helping you. I would show the children that I love them by helping them. I see now what you mean. I am sorry, Joyce, I did not understand before, but I understand now, and you are going to see a new me."

Be genuine in your compliment; do not say something that is not true. Continue to be positive throughout your communications with others. Being positive is contagious; the more you look at the bright side of things, they better things actually become. A positive attitude can go a long way toward improving communication skills. People like being around someone who is positive. It gives them a lift, and they will want to be around you again.

How to Use Physical Proximity

One of the most important elements in whether a person will like you or not is physical proximity. People who you are around more often are more likely to be attracted to you. When you are talking with someone, stand or sit at a comfortable distance from that person. In the United States, this is a little more than an arm's length apart. In other countries, this distance can be different, so you must be up on the social norms. Do not have a piece of furniture or something else between you and the other person as you communicate; this increases interpersonal distance. Be conscious of how the other person is feeling. If the person seems uncomfortable, then back up a little.

How to Use Touch

Touch is a very powerful communication tool. It is hard to act angry with someone who you are touching. Touch increases intimacy and decreases fear. It shows the other person that you value him or her and the relationship. You often can touch someone during a conversation. Try to find that opportunity and take it. Even a simple touch on the arm is a powerful message that says "I care." If you ask for a hug, it is very likely that you are going to get one.

How to Use Eye Contact

Good communication necessitates good eye contact. If you do not look at the other person, then you will miss a good deal of what the person is saying. Focus on the person as if he or she is the most important person in the world. Eye contact is a lot like touch; it shows the person that you are interested. It also shows the person that he or she is important enough to warrant your full attention.

Be Reinforcing

Compliment the other person often. Say something nice. Tell the person how much you appreciate him or her. Point out how a color looks good on him or her. Say you love his or her new suit or dress. Try to be tender and kind. Give the person your full attention. Try to understand the person's point of view. Dress appropriately, and take good care of your appearance and personal hygiene. All of these make you a reinforcing person.

How to Practice Communication Skills

Find two people, and ask them to do the following exercise with you. Watch each of the communication skills in action as you go through the exercise. All of the information disclosed during your conversation should be kept confidential. Each person should have the opportunity to respond to each statement before continuing on to the next item.

Sit close to each other and make eye contact before you speak. Read the first part of the sentence and fill in the rest with your own words.

1. My name is . . .

2. My current hometown is . . .

3. My marital status is . . .

4. My occupation is . . .

5. The reason I am here is . . .

6. Right now, I am feeling . . .

Developing Empathy

1. When I think about the future, I see myself . . .

2. The second person repeats what the first person said until the first person agrees that he or she has been heard correctly.

3. When I am in a new group . . .

4. The second person repeats what the first person said until the first person agrees that he or she has been heard correctly.

5. When I enter a room full of people, I usually feel . . .

6. The second person repeats.

7. When I am feeling anxious in a new situation, I usually . . .

8. For the rest of the exercise, the second person will repeat or question only if he or she does not understand the communication.

9. In groups, I feel the most comfortable when . . .

10. When I am confused, I . . .

11. I am happiest when . . .

12. The thing that turns me on the most is . . .

13. Right now, I am feeling . . .

14. The thing that concerns me the most is . . .

15. When I am rejected, I usually . . .

16. I feel loved when . . .

17. A forceful person makes me feel . . .

18. When I break the rules . . .

19. The thing that turns me off the most is . . .

20. Toward you right now, I feel . . .

21. When I feel lonely, I usually . . .

22. Make a listening check. Have the second person repeat the last communication. "What I hear you saying is . . ."

23. I am rebellious when . . .

24. Take a few minutes to discuss the exercise so far. How do you feel you are doing? Is the level of sharing deep enough? How can you improve the level of sharing? Are you getting to know each other?

25. The emotion I find the most difficult to control is . . .

26. My most frequent daydreams are about . . .

27. My weakest point is . . .

28. I love . . .

29. When I feel jealous, I . . .

30. I am afraid of . . .

31. I believe in . . .

32. I am the most ashamed of . . .

33. Right now, I am the most afraid to discuss . . .

34. Reach out and touch the person on the arm.

35. When I touched you, I felt . . .

Take some time to evaluate each other's communication skills. Talk about what you did well and what you need to work on. Ask for help in developing your skills. Discuss one or two other issues together (e.g., politics, religion, sports, work, family).

Appendix 14

Self-Discipline

Robert R. Perkinson, PhD

Life is full of problems that need to be solved. We can reach our full potential in life only when we meet our problems head-on, accept the responsibility for them, and work toward resolution.

- Problems cause us to feel pain.
- This pain is not bad; it is good. It is a motivation for change.
- Pain gives us energy and direction for action.
- We can solve problems only if we learn how to endure pain and use it to grow.
- If we always seek immediate pain relief, then we never will stretch ourselves and grow stronger.
- If we can learn how to delay instant pleasure, then we can get higher quality and more enduring pleasure later.
- To get an A on an English test next week, we have to study this week. Studying hurts.
- We must learn how to endure the pain of work to get what we want later.
- This is the pathway to excellence.

Delayed Gratification

Self-discipline requires training and practice. Work does not feel good. If it did, then it would be called play. Work is the expenditure of energy. When we expend energy, things change.

We all want to be champions, but to be champions, we have to work. Professional athletes train every day. It is the only way of excelling. They cannot win a race every day, but they can train for a race every day. They must constantly keep in excellent physical and mental condition. They must be so practiced in their sport that they do things automatically. So it is with us. To do something well, we must practice and learn how to set long-term goals.

Take a piece of paper, and write down some things you wanted in your life that you did not get because you did not work hard enough. Perhaps you wanted to get on the football team, go to college, or get a certain job. Did you want a particular car or friend? Did you want to go out with someone special? Did you want to play a musical instrument? Find five things you wanted that you did not get. Write those down, and take a long look at each of them.

1.

2.

3.

4.

5.

What would it have taken for you to achieve each of these goals? What work needed to be done? Nothing reasonable is out of your grasp if you work hard enough. Write down the steps you needed to take to achieve that goal. Spend time thinking about exactly what needed to be done and think about why you did not do it.

Suppose that you wanted to be a mechanic. The first thing that you would need is training. You need the skills of a mechanic. Where would you get those? You could start with the Internet, or you could call an employment service and ask. Now this is work, and nobody likes it. You have to move and expend energy. It is not fun. It hurts. You want the job as a mechanic, and you will have to work to get it. It will happen one step at a time, not all at once. You cannot just wish it to be true. You need to be client and work hard. You need to delay pleasure and go through some pain to get what you want.

Okay, suppose that you look online and find a mechanics school. Now you have to get an application, fill it out, and mail or e-mail it in. This is getting to be hard work. It is not fun, but it will pay off. You will not get what you want if you do not work for it. If you quit, then you will get nothing, so do not quit. Keep trying. Stay committed for what you want. You deserve the best. Do not settle for less.

The Impulsive Temperament

Some people have a harder time with discipline because they have an impulsive temperament. They are born needing only a little bit of a feeling to initiate action.

- For example, they do not need to feel much anger before they act angry.
- Are you that kind of a person?
- Do you feel anger easily and act angry quickly?
- Do you do things impulsively that you feel sorry for later?
- Impulsive people respond too quickly to their feelings.
- This can be a problem because they do not naturally stop and think problems through.
- These individuals do not solve problems well, and they tend to have poor self-discipline.

What would you do if you came home and saw the person you love kissing someone else? "I would kill them," you might say. This is a typical impulsive response. It went immediately from feeling to action. Now stop and think about it. What good is it going to do you to kill two people? Is this going to help you? Are you going to feel better? Is your problem solved? You may get transient relief, but what is the long-term consequence? The result of a double homicide will be years of imprisonment. You will experience pain for a long time.

- If you are a person with an impulsive temperament, then you need to learn how to endure feelings before you act.
- You need to stop, think, and plan before you act. Until you do this, you will be helpless to circumstances.
- These new skills do not come easily. They take practice.
- When you feel a feeling, particularly an intense one, stop and think the problems through, consider your options, plan your response, and then act.

For the next week, keep a log of five situations that give you strong feelings. Write down the situation and the thoughts and feelings you had during the situation. Did you respond appropriately, or did you act impulsively? Learn from your mistakes. Practice.

1.

2.

3.

4.

5.

Rules

Rules do not exist to deny you pleasure. They exist to protect you from pain. If you break the rules, then you will hurt. It is as simple as that. Consistently obeying the rules takes self-discipline. You must decide that the rules are for your own good. The legislature did not make the speed laws to deny you the pleasure of driving fast. They made the rules to keep you safe.

Many of us who have a difficult time with self-discipline were raised in homes where the rules were inconsistent. This is confusing to children. Sometimes our parents would enforce the rules, and sometimes they would not. Sometimes we would be punished (even abusively punished), and sometimes we would get no punishment at all. Sometimes our parents would do the same things they told us not to do. For example, they would tell us not to hit others, and then they would hit us. This teaches children that rules are not important.

- A person without rules is a person with no self-respect.
- It is only when we respect ourselves that we set limits on what we will and will not do.
- Children know that people who love them set limits for them.
- There is no one more unhappy than a child with no rules.
- This child is the ruler of the home.
- This king or queen of the house will demand more and more until the child makes himself or herself miserable.
- Are you important enough to keep safe? If you are, then you need rules.

Get a piece of paper and write down some rules that you have broken. For example, write down three times when you lied or three times when you stole. Write down each situation as completely as you can. You had some good reasons for doing that thing, did you not? Why did you do it? What good came out of it?

1.

2.

3.

Now write down the consequences of breaking each of those rules. How did you feel about yourself? How did you feel about the other people? What happened?

1.

2.

3.

Now look at each situation, and ask yourself this question: Did breaking this rule help me to grow and reach my full potential as a person? Did I honor others, my Higher Power, and myself? You will find that breaking rules results in pain—your pain.

- Take lying as an example.
- We lie to avoid getting into trouble.
- In the short run this works, but in the end, it is interpersonal disaster.
- We want people to love us.
- If we lie, then people do not know us, so they cannot love us.
- In the end, if you lie, then you will be lonely.

To love, you must be self-disciplined. Love is an action, not a feeling. Love is work. Love takes time, energy, and commitment. To do unto others as you would have them do unto you is not always easy, but you will not experience joy unless you love like this. To love, you must be consistent. If you are selfish, and if you always come first, then you will hurt and you will be deprived of the joy of giving unselfishly to others.

Many parents love without discipline. They do not take time with their children, and they do not solve problems with their children. It is important for children to see their parents hurt with them when the children have a problem. The family members feel the pain together, and they buckle down to solve the problem together. In healthy homes, the family members have confidence that if they work together, they can solve problems.

How to Solve Problems

Life is an endless puzzle of problems that need to be solved. Problem solving is challenging, necessary, and fun. It needs to be practiced enough times that it gets to be automatic. Get a piece of paper and write down a problem of yours, and we will go through the problem solving steps together.

1. Write down the problem. What is the problem exactly? How do you feel about it? What do you want to see happen?

2. Make a list of options. What are all of the possible ways in which you can deal with this problem? Get input from others who you trust. Ask other people to give you alternatives of action. You will be surprised. Other people will come up with good ideas that you did not have.

3. Consider each option carefully and decide which choice will help you to grow into the person you want to be. If another person is involved, remember to treat that person the same way in which you would want to be treated.

4. Put the option you have chosen into action.

5. Evaluate the effect of your action on the original problem. This gives you information about how to solve future problems.

Problem → Options → Decision → Action → Evaluation

Work through several problems with your counselor or group. Get in the habit of writing down the problem and getting advice on options.

Responsibility

To solve a problem effectively, you must accept that problem as *your* problem. If you blame the problem on something else, then you are helpless. It is easy to feel this way, but it is self-defeating. "I would be okay if they would just leave me alone" is a common cry in treatment. This is the cry of someone who is defeated by life.

- Blaming other people for your problems never is effective.
- There always is something you can do to make things better.
- You have great power and influence over your own life.
- If you sit and do nothing, then nothing will change.

Take a piece of paper, and write down five times when you got into trouble. Maybe you were arrested or got into trouble at home or at school.

1.

2.

3.

4.

5.

- Think about all of your choices that led to this problem.
- What did you do that ended up getting you in trouble?
- Think about each choice you made along the way that led to the problem.
- Do not blame anyone else.
- Look at your own behavior.
- Use your counselor and group to help you.
- If you look closely, you will see that a series of choices—*your* choices—led to these events.
- Accidents do happen, but most of what happens to you is a result of your choices.
- Think of how scary the world would be if other people had the power to make you happy or unhappy.
- No one has that power but you.

Think of yourself as a gift to the world. There never has been anyone like you. There never will be anyone like you again. You owe the world only one thing—to be different. Only you can do this. Only you can be responsible for what you do. You will change the course of history because you were here. Maybe you will change things for the good, maybe for the bad. Maybe you will change things a little, maybe a lot, but you definitely will change things. Things will be different because you were here. You have a great responsibility to be yourself.

Appendix 15

Impulse Control

Robert R. Perkinson, PhD

You have problems controlling your impulses if you act too quickly on your feelings. You suffer negative consequences because you act without careful thought. If you had stopped to think, you would not have gotten into trouble. Maybe you ended up in jail, struck someone you cared for, were kicked out of school, or used drugs or alcohol. This set of exercises is for those people who lose control over their behavior too quickly. It outlines the skills necessary to overcome problems with impulse control.

- The first thing you have to understand is that you are held accountable in our society only for what you do.
- You are not held accountable for what you think or for how you feel.
- Your movements are what count. That is what people see. That is how people judge you.
- You can think about robbing a bank all day long, and you will not be arrested.
- If you rob a bank, then you have committed a crime and are in big trouble.
- To control your impulses, you must learn to control your movements.

How to Understand Your Feelings

To control your impulses, you need to understand your feelings.

- Feelings motivate action. They are a powerful force. They direct behavior.
- Each feeling is connected to a specific activity. Let us examine several feelings and the actions they stimulate. There are only a few basic feelings: fear, anger, sadness, surprise, joy, disgust, acceptance, and anticipation.

  1. Fear motivates you to run.

  2. Anger motivates you to make the pain stop.

  3. Sadness motivates you to recover a lost object.

  4. Surprise gets you ready to accept something new.

  5. Joy motivates you to enjoy something rewarding and special.

  6. Disgust motivates you to avoid the repulsive object.

7. Acceptance gives you the motivation to embrace something positive.

8. Anticipation gives you the energy and direction to understand and deal with a new situation.

- Examine each feeling and the movement to which it is attached. Learn that each feeling motivates a specific action, and learn what each feeling is and the action it initiates.

How to Develop Goals

Now it is time to take a close look at exactly what you want to change. Remembering that behavior is movement, take a piece of paper and write down five things you want to do differently. For example, someone who physically or mentally hurts people would want to write down something like this: "I want to stop hurting other people with my words and actions."

1.

2.

3.

4.

5.

Study each of your goals. Is it reasonable that you can attain this goal? Make sure that the goal is written in behavioral terms. It needs to be a movement you can see, hear, or touch.

Now that you have the specific behavior you want to change, we can look at exactly how you are going to change.

The Behavior Chain

Behavior can be analyzed by studying the behavior chain. This chain starts with a stimulus or trigger that initiates a thought, the thought initiates a feeling, and the feeling motivates action. All behavior results in a consequence. This consequence may be positive or negative. The behavior chain looks like this:

Trigger → Thought → Feeling → Behavior → Consequence

There are many points along a behavior chain where you can do things differently. Look at it like this: If you are on a train that is going to Kansas and stay on that train, then you are going to end up in Kansas. Likewise, if you initiate an old behavior chain and continue on that chain, then you are going to end up with the same consequence. Now maybe that behavior got you into a lot of trouble, and maybe you do not want to repeat the behavior. Next time, you want to do something different. The key word here is *doing*. You have to do something different if things are going to change.

Trigger

Let us take a close look at the behavior chain and see where you can change. Behavior will surface under certain situations or triggers. We can group relapse triggers into several categories.

- Negative emotions
- Social pressure

- Interpersonal conflict
- When something good happens
- When you feel powerless
- When your life seems unmanageable

Negative Feelings

Start by getting out a clean piece of paper and writing the heading "NEGATIVE FEELINGS" at the top of the page. Under this heading, write all of the negative feelings you can think of that lead to the behavior you want to change. Maybe you lapse into old behavior when you are angry, bored, lonely, happy, embarrassed, frustrated, irritable, or excited. Write down the feelings that seem to precede the action you want to change.

Social Pressure

Make the heading "SOCIAL PRESSURE," and list all of the social situations in which you are likely to lapse into the old behavior. Remember that social pressure can be direct (e.g., someone actively encouraging you to act in the old way) or indirect (e.g., a social situation in which the behavior might normally occur). Maybe you will be more likely to get back to the old behavior when you are with certain friends or at certain places or events. Write down every social situation in which you feel you will be vulnerable.

Interpersonal Conflict

The "INTERPERSONAL CONFLICT" heading comes next. Make that heading, and under it write every situation you can think of where a conflict with someone else leads to the behavior you want to change. Try to include the total situation. Who said what and how? What happened? When did you lose control? What preceded your behavior?

Positive Events

Now write "POSITIVE EVENTS" as a heading, and list the times when you acted in that old way when feeling good, to celebrate, or to increase the good feeling. Detail each situation and carefully study what you were after and what feelings you wanted to enhance.

Feeling Powerless

Write down "FEELING POWERLESS." Sometimes you feel powerless to resist the impulse to return to old behavior, but remember you always have many choices available to you when you are having a feeling. List five things you can do when you are craving the return to the addiction.

Feeling Like My Life Is Unmanageable

Write down "FEELING LIKE MY LIFE IS UNMANAGEABLE." You might be feeling like everything is going wrong, that everything you do makes things worse. Remember there are always many thoughts and behaviors available to you. There is never only one choice. When you feel like everything is going wrong, write down all the things that are going right. Make a list of all of the things you are grateful for such as family, friends, your pet, and your relationship with your Higher Power, the power of prayer, the clouds, trees, flowers, water, the sky, and a bird. Look around you, and find beauty in the world. It is always there if you look for it.

Thought

We will analyze thoughts next. These get a little tricky, so pay careful attention to them. Beck, Rush, Shaw, and Emery (1979) developed cognitive therapy for depression. Burns (1999) further developed this technique.

Many thoughts are very quick—so quick that they occur out of your awareness. These thoughts are called automatic thoughts because they do not come from anything you try to think. You think them automatically.

Take another piece of paper, and near the top write down a situation where you lost control. Write the specific situation in as much detail as you can.

Now explore how you were feeling in that situation. Remember that the eight primary feelings are (1) fear, (2) anger, (3) sadness, (4) surprise, (5) joy, (6) disgust, (7) acceptance, and (8) anticipation. Write down each feeling, and score the intensity of the feeling on a scale of 1 to 100 (1 = *as little of the feeling as possible*, 100 = *as much of the feeling as possible*).

Let us take an example. Frank came home, and his spouse angrily asked him where he had been. He was late coming home from work. Frank felt hurt at an intensity of 45, angry at 90, and frightened at 75.

Now it is your turn. You have the situation and all of the feelings you had during that situation. You have scored how intensely you were feeling each feeling.

- Now carefully process with your counselor what you were thinking between the situation and the feelings.
- This will take some time, so take it slow.
- Try to think of all the thoughts that came to mind between the event and the feelings.

Let us see how Frank did. "My wife asked me where I had been. I thought the following: 'Here we go again. She is mad. She thinks I have been drinking again. She is always mad at me. She never trusts me. She does not love me. She has never loved me.'"

Make as long a list of these thoughts as you can. You will be surprised at how many thoughts you can have in a short period of time.

Next, look at the thoughts and check them out for accuracy. Which thoughts are accurate, and which thoughts are inaccurate? Frank decided that his spouse was mad and that she was worried that he had been drinking again. Those thoughts were accurate, but she was not always mad at him and she trusted him plenty of times. She does love him, and she has loved him for a long time. These thoughts were inaccurate.

With your counselor or with your group, discover which thoughts are accurate and which thoughts are inaccurate.

On another sheet, write down the situation again. Write only the accurate thoughts you were having and then score all of the feelings you had listed on the previous page.

Frank did it like this. "My wife asked me where I had been. She was frightened that I had been drinking again and a little angry just at the thought of it. She is very concerned for me. She loves me very much, and she is afraid for my health. That does not hurt me at all, so I would put the hurt at 0. It still makes me a little mad, but much less, so I would put that at 20. That does not scare me at all, so I would rate the fear at 0."

Now add up your scores on each sheet, coming up with a total score of all the feelings when you were thinking inaccurately and when you were thinking accurately. This is Frank's sheet:

	Inaccurate Thinking	**Accurate Thinking**
Hurt	45	0
Angry	90	20
Fear	75	0
Total	210	20

You can now see what we are after.

- Many of your thoughts are automatic, are inaccurate, and lead to uncomfortable feelings.
- Some of these feelings are unnecessary because they are inaccurate assessments of reality.
- If you see a situation inaccurately, then you will react inaccurately.
- If you develop the skill of stopping and assessing the situation accurately, then you will feel more comfortable and be able to deal with the situation with more precision and skill.

For the next few days, keep a running account of any situation that makes you feel uncomfortable, and do this exercise again. After a few days, you will notice patterns in your thinking. You will see that you think the same inaccurate thoughts in many different situations. These are thoughts that need to be challenged repeatedly in treatment. Address them carefully with your group and your counselor, and begin to watch out for them. When they resurface, stop and correct yourself. Try to keep your thinking accurate. Write down 10 positive things about yourself, and carry this card around with you reading it to yourself many times a day. Soon you will memorize the accurate thoughts, and then come up with 10 more. Begin to say positive accurate things to yourself all day every day.

Feelings

All feelings are friendly, even the painful ones. They help us adapt to our environment and give us energy and direction for action.

- The skill necessary for dealing with feelings appropriately is to learn exactly what coping skills to use when having a particular feeling.
- Feelings should not be ignored; they should be acted on.
- Which action to take is the skill you want to learn.
- Spend some time with each feeling and learn coping skills for dealing with each one.
- Then practice the new skills until they become automatic. You cannot just learn what to do. You must practice the new behavior until it becomes second nature. This will take a lot of time and practice. Do not try to do this perfectly; just make progress.

Anger

Anger gives chemically dependent persons more problems than does any other feeling. You can relapse into old behavior when you feel angry and frustrated. Anger gives you the energy and direction to fight. Anger is there to make the pain stop. Anger is good, and acting angry can be good, so long as the actions are appropriate. The problems arise when we fight all the time or at inappropriate times.

Anger is friendly. It needs to be listened to and expressed. You need to learn how to use your anger assertively rather than aggressively. Much of this work is taken from *Your Perfect Right*, an assertive guide by Alberti and Emmons (1995).

- Physical aggression rarely is necessary and can even be harmful.
- Acting on your anger assertively is a much more effective means of getting what you want. Here is an assertive formula that you should memorize and practice until it becomes automatic.

I feel . . .

When you . . .

I would prefer it if . . .

When you feel angry with someone, you start by describing how you feel. Then, in behavioral terms, describe what the person did that led to your feelings. Then, again in behavioral terms, tell the person what you want him or her to do.

Let us try it in a situation to show how the assertive formula works.

The Aggressive Response

Bob comes home from work 1 hour late. Barbara, his spouse, is hurt and angry.

Barbara: Where have you been? You are such an incredible jerk!

How is Bob going to be feeling—attacked, hurt, angry, defensive? He might retaliate and say something like this:

Bob: What a nag! You are always mad at me!

The Assertive Response

Barbara: I feel hurt and angry when you are late. I would prefer it if you would call me and tell me when you are not going to be on time.

The assertive formula gives the other person accurate information that he or she can use to remedy the situation. The person knows what he or she did and knows what to do differently.

Try the assertive formula at least two times today. After each use, write down the situation and how it turned out. Notice the feelings that you have. If you are like most people, you will feel much more in control of your feelings. You also will get more of what you want. This will lead to less anger. Role-play several situations with your counselor or group. Role-play the situation acting too passive, too aggressive, and assertive. Being assertive just means you look at the other person in the eyes and tell them the truth in a normal tone of voice with a kind facial expression.

Fear

Fear is another difficult feeling for people.

- Fear motivates you to run or withdraw from a dangerous situation.
- Fear is friendly.
- Withdrawal is friendly, and it can be adaptive, but it also can be inappropriate.
- It is important to think accurately and consider the consequences before you withdraw.
- What are the pros and cons of withdrawing from the situation?
- It is not appropriate to run from all of your problems even if they are scary. If you did, then you would not solve many of them.
- You must learn to stand your ground even in a painful situation. That way, you can work a problem through to resolution.
- If you find that you always are running away, then you must find other coping skills to use when you feel frightened. The same assertive formula works here. "I feel, when you, I would prefer it if" works as well with fear as it does with anger.
- If people know you are frightened, they often will respond positively to your fear.
- It even helps to share your fear with someone who is not involved with the immediate situation.
- Remember to share your feelings. This is a major coping skill. It can be used with all feelings.

Behavior

Now you know that using the right behavior at the right time is the real secret to success when dealing with impulse control problems. It is the movements—the behavior—that people are responsible for, so you must practice not moving quickly.

- Practice delaying action until you have time to think and plan.
- Some people have to back away from the situation entirely to give them the time to think.
- They might have to go for a walk, a run, or a drive.
- They might have to leave the house, or the places of conflict, and give themselves some space.
- You know yourself the best, and you know beforehand when you are getting ready to lose control.
- Practice catching this increase in your feelings before you lose control. At this point, you must move away from the situation. You cannot stay there and hope to achieve control. That is too dangerous.
- Do not worry. You are going to come back to the problem and the situation is going to be addressed, but you need some time away from the problem. If you stay in a situation where you have lost control, then you are playing with fire. Do not do that to yourself.

Exactly what coping skills to use in a particular situation will take some planning. This planning must take place before the situation, and it must be practiced until it becomes automatic.

Get out another piece of paper, and write down the situation you are having difficulty with.

Now brainstorm with your counselor and your group. What else could you do in that situation? For example, Barbara is trying to control her tendency to yell at her children. She made this plan when she feels angry with them again:

When I am getting angry, I am going to do the following:

1. Recognize my anger.

2. Step back from the situation as far as necessary to feel the anger go down and then:
   a. Go in another room.
   b. Go for a walk.
   c. Go for a drive.
   d. Go to my mother's house.
   e. Go talk to a friend next door.
   f. Call my sponsor.

3. When I am thinking clearly, I will plan my response. I might have to do this with someone I trust.

4. Come back to my children and try my plan.

5. If I get too angry again, I will go back and repeat the whole procedure.

Consequence

It is important to take a careful look at the consequence of your behavior.

- You will not learn from your actions unless you see clearly what happens when you act in a certain manner.
- On another piece of paper, write briefly what happened each time you lost control of your actions. Under each situation, write down the negative consequence that resulted from that loss of control. This must be done in great detail. Take a lot of time and think.

- Do not blame anyone else for what happened. Concentrate on your own actions. Use every situation you can think of. The more clearly you can see the negative consequence of your behavior, the more you will tell yourself never to act that way again. You can learn from your behavior if you stop, think, and plan before you act.

We have looked carefully at the behavior you want to change. We have studied the trigger, thought, feeling, behavior, and consequence. Now let us go over what you are going to do when you are in a high-risk situation. What is your plan when you feel impulsively? First, think of the word *stop*.

S = *stop*: Stop and commit yourself to a rational response.

T = *think*:

1. What is the situation?

2. What is at stake?

3. Get your thinking accurate.

O = *options*:

1. What are the options?

2. What are the pros and cons of each option?

3. Choose the best option.

P = *plan*: Carry out the plan.

With your counselor and group, work through the situations and feelings that you are having the most difficulty with. If you are having a difficult time with anger, then discuss your anger carefully in individual sessions and in group. Role-play specific coping skills to deal with each feeling. Exactly what are you going to do? List options available to you, and carry them in your pocket or purse. Now practice, practice, practice. When you lapse into the old behavior, do not give up. Use the lapse as an education. What happened? What coping skill could you have used? How can you do things differently next time? You can do this. You no longer have to be a slave to your impulses. You can change your behavior. You have all of the necessary skills.

Appendix 16

Relapse Prevention

Robert R. Perkinson, PhD

There is some bad news and some good news about relapse. The bad news is that many clients have problems with relapse in early sobriety. About two thirds of clients coming out of addiction programs relapse within 3 months of leaving treatment (Hunt, Barnett, & Branch, 1971). The good news is that most people who go through treatment ultimately achieve a stable recovery (Frances, Bucky, & Alexopolos, 1984). Relapse does not have to happen to you, and even if it does, you can do something about it. Relapse prevention is a daily program that can help prevent relapse. It also can stop a lapse from becoming a disaster. This exercise has been developed using a combination of the models. This uses the disease concept model in combination with motivational enhancement, cognitive behavioral therapy, skills training, and 12-step facilitation.

Relapse Is a Process

Relapse is a process that begins long before you use drugs or alcohol. There are symptoms that precede the first use of chemicals. This exercise teaches you how to identify and control these symptoms before they lead to actual drug or alcohol use. If you allow these symptoms to go on without acting on them, then serious problems will result.

The Relapse Warning Signs

All relapse begins with warning signs that will signal for you that you are in trouble. If you do not recognize these signs, you will decompensate and finally use chemicals. All of the signs are a reaction to stress, and they are a reemergence of the disease. They are a means by which your body and mind are telling you that you are in trouble. You might not have all of these symptoms, but you will have some of them long before you actually use chemicals. You must determine which symptoms are the most characteristic of you, and you must come up with coping skills for dealing with each symptom.

Interpersonal Factors

- Self-efficacy is the degree you feel capable of performing a task like preventing relapse. Do you feel confident that you have the skills necessary to say no to the addiction when confronted with a high-risk situation including intense craving? Do you have the skills necessary to say no to alcohol, drugs, or addictive behavior?

- Make a list of 10 things you can do when you feel craving. There are people you can call, meetings you can attend, things you can read, a Higher Power you can pray to, family members, friends or people in the program you can share your feelings with, Alcoholics Anonymous (AA)/Narcotics Anonymous (NA)/Gamblers Anonymous (GA) hotlines you can call, physical exercise you can do, meditations you can perform, etc.

1. _____
2. _____
3. _____
4. _____
5. _____
6. _____
7. _____
8. _____
9. _____
10. _____

Practice each of these 10 things at least five times in group, with your counselor, your sponsor/mentor/coach. You need to get used to thinking and moving in a certain way when faced with craving. If these behaviors are not practiced in stills training sessions they are unlikely to be used when you get into trouble. Just knowing what to do is not enough; you need to practice the thoughts and motor movements to get good at the skill.

Think about the first time you learned how to ride a bike. Your teacher probably taught you all of the things you had to do to ride, but it was only after you practiced riding repeatedly that you began to trust yourself to ride a bike safely.

Make a list of five things in your life that you had to practice. Maybe it was basketball, baseball, soccer, or starting a conversation with someone you did not know.

1. _____
2. _____
3. _____
4. _____
5. _____

At first, you were terrible, making mostly mistakes, but after practicing thousands of times, you got better. Maybe you had to learn how to shoot a basket from the free throw line. The first times you tried, you missed most every shot. As you practiced, and particularly after you were coached, you got better. After thousands of shots, you got so you could make the shot most of the time. Then there came the big game and the score was tied and you had to shoot the final basket. If you made the shot your team won; if you missed, you lost. Now you need to go on automatic, athletes call this getting in the zone, where all of the fans and other players disappear and it is only you and that simple shot you have practiced so many times. If you miss the shot or relapse, it is not the end of the world; it just means you need more practice until the skill becomes automatic.

Higher levels of self-efficacy predict improved addiction treatment outcomes (Burling, Reilly, Molten, & Ziff, 1989; Greenfield et al., 2000).

What to Do When You Experience a Warning Sign

When you recognize you are in trouble, you need to take action. Make a list of the coping skills you can use when you experience a high-risk situation that is common for you. It might be interpersonal conflict, anger, boredom, certain music or parts of town, seeing old friends, social pressure, negative emotions, or a celebration. This will happen. You will have high-risk situations in recovery. Your task is to take affirmative action. Remember, craving is a danger signal. You are in trouble. Make a list of what you are going to do. Are you going to call your sponsor, go to a meeting, call your counselor, call someone in AA/NA, tell someone, exercise, read the "Big Book" (AA, 2002), pray, become involved in an activity you enjoy, turn it over, or go into treatment? List five telephone numbers of people you can call if you are in trouble. Remember what AA says: "What we cannot do alone, we can do together."

Plan 1.

Plan 2.

Plan 3.

Plan 4.

Plan 5.

Positive Outcome Expectations

This means the positive things we think will happen if we drink or use. These are dangerous thoughts, and if not corrected, they may lead to relapse. Write down five positive thoughts about what the addiction can do for you: things such as one drink will not hurt, I deserve to relax with a few drinks, I would only have one drink, I have had a hard day, I need to relax at the casino, nobody will know, I am going to show them, I am going to get even, I am going to make them sorry, I am under too much stress, I need a break, etc.

1. _____

2. _____

3. _____

4. _____

5. _____

Now write down 10 accurate thoughts that will keep you clean and sober, such as I cannot drink one drink I am an alcoholic; if I start gambling, I would never stop; I would use drugs again; I would go right back into that addiction misery again; I can go home and talk to my wife; I can go for a walk; I can meditate; I can go to a 12-step meeting; I can call my sponsor or spiritual leader and go out for a cup of coffee; I can read some AA/NA/GA material. I can cope with this feeling. If I just wait for 15 minutes, the craving will pass. If I move away from the high-risk situation, I would feel better soon.

1. _____

2. _____

3. _____

4. _____

5. _____

6. _____

7. _____

8. _____

9. _____

10. _____

Write down these 10 alternative behaviors and carry them with you. Remember that you have to practice these skills until they become automatic. Practice saying and doing these things with your group, counselor, sponsor, mentor, coach, spouse, friend, or 12-step member. Practice, practice, practice until you feel comfortable with the new skill.

You need to check warning signs daily in your personal inventory. You also need to have other people check you daily. You will not always pick up the symptoms in yourself. You might be denying the problem again. Your spouse, your sponsor, and/or a fellow 12-step member can warn you when they believe that you might be in trouble. Listen to these people. If they tell you that, they sense a problem, and then take action. You might need professional help in working the problem through. Do not hesitate to call and ask for help. Anything is better than relapsing. If you overreact to a warning sign, you are not going to be in trouble. If you underreact, you might be headed for real problems. Addiction is a deadly disease. Your life is at stake. Relapse is more likely to occur in certain situations. These situations can trigger relapse. People relapse when faced with high-risk situations that they could not cope with except by drinking or using. Your job in treatment is to develop coping skills for dealing with each high-risk situation.

Motivation

Motivation is the conscious or unconscious stimulus leading to the energy that gives you the power to act. Either you can act in an adaptive or a maladaptive way; both can be positive or negative reinforcers. You can have motivation to stay clean and sober, and you can have motivation to return to your addiction.

Prochaska and DiClemente (1984) proposed a model for motivation that goes through five stages, or readiness for change: (1) precontemplation, (2) contemplation, (3) preparation, (4) action, and (5) maintenance. Each stage characterizes a different level of motivational readiness for change.

- Interventions that cause ambivalence, evaluating the pros and cons of change may increase motivation by allowing clients to explore their own morals and values and how they may differ if they institute change. For example, people who are in the precontemplative stage have no interest in behavior change. If they explore the pros and cons of the addictive behavior, they might become more willing to think about the positive aspects of changing.
- This moves them into contemplation where you discuss all of the positive and negative aspects of using or stopping the addiction. Once the decision is made to try to stop the addictive behavior then we must concentrate on what needs to change to stop the addictive behavior.
- Then the action phase begins where we begin to change the thoughts and behaviors that cause addiction.
- Once the addiction stops, then we need skills to maintain this new lifestyle.

Negative Emotions

Many people relapse when feeling negative feelings that they cannot cope with. Most feel angry or frustrated, but some feel anxious, bored, lonely, or depressed. Almost any negative feeling can lead to relapse if you do not learn how to cope with the feeling. Feelings motivate you to take action. You must act to solve any problem.

Circle any of the following feelings that seem to lead you to use chemicals:

1. Loneliness
2. Anger
3. Rejection
4. Emptiness
5. Annoyance
6. Sadness
7. Exasperation
8. Betrayal
9. Cheated
10. Frustration
11. Envious
12. Exhaustion
13. Boredom
14. Anxious
15. Ashamed
16. Bitter
17. Burdened
18. Foolish
19. Jealous
20. Left out
21. Selfish
22. Restless
23. Weak
24. Sorrowful
25. Greediness
26. Aggravation
27. Miserable
28. Unloved
29. Worry

30. Scared

31. Spiteful

32. Sorrowful

33. Helpless

34. Neglected

35. Grief

36. Confusion

37. Crushed

38. Discontent

39. Restless

40. Irritation

41. Overwhelmed

42. Panicked

43. Trapped

44. Unsure

45. Intimidated

46. Distraught

47. Uneasy

48. Guilty

49. Threatened

50. Submissive

A Plan to Deal With Negative Emotions

These are just a few of the feeling words. Add more if you need to do so. Develop coping skills for dealing with each feeling that makes you vulnerable to relapse. Exactly what are you going to do when you have this feeling? Detail your specific plan of action. Some options are talking to your sponsor, calling a friend in the program, going to a meeting, calling your counselor, reading some recovery material, turning it over to your Higher Power, and getting some exercise. For each feeling, develop a specific plan of action.

Feeling _____

Plan 1. _____

Plan 2. _____

Plan 3. _____

Feeling _____

Plan 1. _____

Plan 2. _____

Plan 3. _____

Feeling _____

Plan 1. _____

Plan 2. _____

Plan 3. _____

Continue to fill out these feeling forms until you have all of the feelings that give you trouble and you have coping skills for dealing with each feeling.

Social Pressure

Social pressure can be direct (where someone directly encourages you to use chemicals) or indirect (a social situation where people are using). Both of these situations can trigger intense craving, and this can lead to relapse. More than 60% of alcoholics relapse in bars.

Certain friends are more likely to encourage you to use chemicals. These people do not want to hurt you. They want you to relax and have a good time. They want their old friend back. They do not understand the nature of your disease. Perhaps they are chemically dependent themselves and are in denial.

High-Risk Friends

Make a list of the friends who might encourage you to use drugs or alcohol.

1. _____

2. _____

3. _____

4. _____

5. _____

What are you going to do when they offer you drugs? What are you going to say? In group, set up a situation where the whole group encourages you to use chemicals. Look carefully at how you feel when the group members are encouraging you. Look at what you say. Have them help you to develop appropriate ways of saying no. The skills of saying no are the following:

- Look at the person and say, no thank you.
- Suggest another alternative behavior.
- If the person persists, tell him or her that you are trying to stop behavior that has been harming you. Then ask the person to help you by respecting your choice not to use.
- If the person persists, leave the situation. "Well, I have got to be going. Nice to see you."

High-Risk Social Situations

Certain social situations will trigger cravings. These are the situations where you have used chemicals in the past. Certain bars or restaurants, a particular part of town, certain music, athletic events, parties, weddings, and family events—all of these situations can trigger intense cravings. Make a list of five social situations where you will be vulnerable to relapse.

1. _____

2. _____

3. _____

4. _____

5. _____

In early sobriety, you will need to avoid these situations and friends. To put yourself in a high-risk situation is asking for trouble. If you have to attend a function where there will be people using chemicals, take someone with you who is in the program. Take someone with you who will support you in your sobriety. Make sure that you have a way to get home. You do not have to stay and torture yourself. You can leave if you feel uncomfortable. Avoid all situations where your sobriety feels shaky.

Interpersonal Conflict

Many addicts relapse when in a conflict with some other person. They have a problem with someone and have no idea of how to cope with conflict so they might revert to old behavior and use the addiction to deal with the uncomfortable feelings. The stress of the problem builds and leads to using. This conflict usually happens with someone who they are closely involved with—wife, husband, child, parent, sibling, friend, boss, and so on.

You can have a serious problem with anyone—even a stranger—so you must have a plan for dealing with interpersonal conflict. You will develop specific skills in treatment that will help you to communicate even when you are under stress.

You need to learn and practice the following interpersonal skills repeatedly.

1. Tell the truth all of the time.

2. Share how you feel.

3. Ask for what you want.

4. Find some truth in what the other person is saying.

5. Be willing to compromise.

If you can stay in the conflict and work it out, that is great. If you cannot, then you have to leave the situation and take care of yourself. You might have to go for a walk, a run, or a drive. You might need to cool down. You must stop the conflict. You cannot continue to try to deal with a situation that you believe is too much for you. Do not feel bad about this. Interpersonal relationships are the hardest challenge we face. Carry a card with you that lists the telephone numbers of people who you can contact. You might want to call your sponsor, minister, or counselor or a fellow AA/NA/GA member, friend, family member, doctor, or anyone else who may support you.

In an interpersonal conflict, you will fear abandonment. You need to get accurate and reassure yourself that people can disagree with you and still care about you. Remember that your Higher Power cares about you. A Higher Power created you and loves you. Remember the other people in your life who love you. This is one of the main reasons for talking with someone else. When the other person listens to you, that person gives you the feeling that you are accepted and loved.

If you still feel afraid or angry, then get with someone you trust and stay with that person until you feel safe. Do not struggle out there all by yourself. Any member of your 12-step group will understand how you are feeling. We all have had these problems. We all have felt lost, helpless, hopeless, and angry.

Make an emergency card that lists all of the people who you can call if you are having difficulty. Write down their phone numbers and carry this card with you at all times. Show this card to your counselor. Practice asking someone for help in treatment once each day. Write down the situation and show it to your counselor. Get into the habit of asking for help. When you get out of treatment, call someone every day just to stay in touch and keep the lines of communication open. Get used to it. Do not wait to ask for help at the last minute. This makes asking more difficult.

Positive Feelings

Some people relapse when they are feeling positive emotions. Think of all the times you used drugs and alcohol to celebrate. That has gotten to be such a habit that when something good happens, you will immediately think about using. You need to be ready when you feel like a winner. This may be at a wedding, birth, promotion, or any event where you feel good. How are you going to celebrate without drugs and alcohol? Make a celebration plan. You might have to take someone with you to a celebration, particularly in early recovery.

Positive feelings also can work when you are by yourself. A beautiful spring day can be enough to get you thinking about drinking or using. You need an action plan for when these thoughts pass through your mind. You must immediately get accurate and get real. In recovery, we are committed to reality. Do not sit there and recall how wonderful you will feel if you get high. Tell yourself the truth. Think about all of the pain that addiction has caused you. If you toy with positive feelings, then you ultimately will use chemicals.

Circle the positive feelings that may make you vulnerable to relapse.

1. Affection
2. Boldness
3. Bravery
4. Calmness
5. Capableness
6. Cheerful
7. Confident
8. Delightful
9. Desire
10. Enchanted
11. Joy
12. Free
13. Glad
14. Glee
15. Happy
16. Honored
17. Horny
18. Infatuated
19. Inspired
20. Kinky
21. Lazy
22. Loving
23. Peaceful
24. Pleasant
25. Pleased
26. Sexy
27. Wonderful

28. Cool

29. Relaxed

30. Reverent

31. Silly

32. Vivacious

33. Adequate

34. Efficient

35. Successful

36. Accomplished

37. Hopeful

38. Cheery

39. Elated

40. Merry

41. Ecstatic

42. Upbeat

43. Splendid

44. Yearning

45. Bliss

46. Excitement

47. Exhilaration

48. Proud

49. Aroused

50. Festive

A Plan to Cope With Positive Feelings

These are the feelings that may make you vulnerable to relapse. You must be careful when you are feeling good because pleasure triggers the same part of the brain that triggers addiction. Make an action plan for dealing with each positive emotion that makes you vulnerable to using chemicals.

Feeling _____

Plan 1. _____

Plan 2. _____

Plan 3. _____

Feeling _____

Plan 1. _____

Plan 2. _____

Plan 3. _____

Feeling _____

Plan 1. _____

Plan 2. _____

Plan 3. _____

Continue this planning until you develop a plan for each of the positive feelings that make you vulnerable. Practice what you are going to do when you experience positive feelings.

Test Control

Some people relapse to test whether they can use the addiction again. They fool themselves into thinking that they might be able to use normally. This time they will use only a little. This time they will be able to stay in control of themselves. People who fool themselves this way are in for big trouble. From the first use, most people are in full-blown relapse within 30 days.

Testing personal control begins with inaccurate thinking. It takes you back to Step One. You need to think accurately. You are powerless over mood-altering chemicals. If you use, then you will lose. It is as simple as that. You are physiologically, psychologically, and socially addicted. The cells in your body will not suddenly change no matter how long you are clean and sober. You are chemically dependent in your cells. This never will change.

How to See Through the First Use

You need to look at how the illness part of yourself will try to convince you that you are not chemically dependent. The illness will flash on the screen of your consciousness all the good things that the addiction did for you. Make a list of these things. In the first column, marked "Early Use," write down some of the good things that you were getting out of using chemicals. Why were you using? What good came out of it? Did it make you feel social, smart, pretty, intelligent, brave, popular, desirable, relaxed, or sexy? Did it help you to sleep? Did it make you feel confident? Did it help you to forget your problems? Make a long list. These are the good things that you were getting when you first started using. This is why you were using.

Early Use	Late Use
1.	1.
2.	2.
3.	3.
4.	4.
5.	5.
6.	6.
7.	7.
8.	8.
9.	9.
10.	10.

Now go back and place in the second column, marked "Late Use," how you were doing in that area once you became addicted. How were you doing in that same area right before you came into treatment? Did you still feel social, or did you feel alone? Did you still feel intelligent, or did you feel stupid? You will find that a great change has taken place. The very things that you were using for in early use, you get the opposite of in late use. If you were drinking for sleep, then you cannot sleep. If you were using to be more popular, then you are more isolated, insecure, and alone. If you were using to feel brave, then you are feeling more afraid. This is a major characteristic of addiction. The good things you got at first you get the opposite of in addiction. You can never go back to early use because your brain has permanently changed in chemistry, structure, and genetics.

Take a long look at both of these lists, and think about how the illness is going to try to work inside of your thinking. The addicted part of yourself will present to you all of the good things you got in early use. This is how the disease will encourage you to use. You must see through the first use to the consequences that are dead ahead.

Look at that second list. You must see the misery that is coming if you use chemicals. For most people who relapse, there are only a few days of controlled use before loss of control sets in. There usually is only a few hours or days before all of the bad stuff begins to click back into place. Relapse is terrible. It is the most intense misery that you can imagine.

Lapse and Relapse

A lapse is the use of any addictive substance or behavior. A relapse is continuing to use the behavior until the full biological, psychological, and social disease is present. All of the complex biological, psychological, and social components of the disease become evident very quickly.

The Lapse Plan

You must have a plan in case you lapse. It is foolish to think that you never will have a problem again. You must plan what you are going to do if you have a problem. Hunt and colleagues (1971), in a study of recovering addicts, found that 33% of clients lapsed within 2 weeks of leaving treatment, and 60% lapsed within 3 months. At the end of 8 months, 63% had used. At the end of 12 months, 67% had used.

The worst thing you can do when you have a lapse is to think that you have completely failed in recovery. This is inaccurate thinking. You are not a total failure. You have not lost everything. A lapse is a great learning opportunity. You have made a mistake, and you can learn from it. You let some part of your program go, and you are paying for it. You need to examine exactly what happened and get back into recovery.

A lapse is an emergency. It is a matter of life or death. You must take immediate action to prevent the lapse from becoming a full relapse. You must call someone in the program, preferably your sponsor, and tell that person what happened. You need to examine why you had a problem. You cannot use the addiction and the tools of recovery at the same time. Something went wrong. You did not use your new skills. You must make a plan of action to recover from your lapse. You cannot do this by yourself. You are in denial. You do not know the whole truth. If you did, you would not have relapsed.

Call your sponsor or a professional counselor, and have that person develop a new treatment plan for you. You may need to attend more meetings. You may need to see a counselor. You may need outpatient treatment. You may need inpatient treatment. You have to get honest with yourself. You need to develop a plan and follow it. You need someone else to agree to keep an eye on you for a while. Do not try to do this alone. What we cannot do alone, we can do together.

The Behavior Chain

All behavior occurs in a certain sequence. First, there is the *trigger*. This is the external event that starts the behavioral sequence. After the trigger, there comes *thinking*. Much of this thinking is very fast, and you will not consciously pick it up unless you stop and think about it. The thoughts trigger *feeling*, which gives you energy and direction for action. Next comes the *behavior*, or the action initiated by the trigger. Lastly, there always is a *consequence* for any action.

Diagrammed, the behavior chain looks like this:

Trigger → Thinking → Feeling → Behavior → Consequence

Let us go through a behavioral sequence and see how it works. On the way home from work, Bob, a recovering alcoholic, passes the local bar. (This is the trigger.) He thinks, "I have had a hard day. I need a couple of beers to unwind." (The trigger initiates thinking.) Bob craves a beer. (The thinking initiates feeling.) Bob turns into the bar and begins drinking. (The feeling initiates behavior.) Bob relapses. (The behavior has a consequence.)

Let us work through another example. It is 11:00 pm, and Bob is not asleep (trigger). He thinks, "I would never get to sleep tonight unless I have a few drinks" (thinking). He feels an increase in his anxiety about not sleeping (feeling). He gets up and consumes a few drinks (behavior). He gets drunk and wakes up hungover and unable to work the next morning (consequence).

How to Cope With Triggers

At every point along the behavior chain, you can work on preventing relapse. First, you need to carefully examine your triggers. What environmental events lead you to using chemicals? We went over some of these when we examined high-risk situations. Determine what people, places, or things make you vulnerable to relapse. Stay away from these triggers as much as possible. If a trigger occurs, then use your new coping skills.

Do not let the trigger initiate old behavior. Stop and think. Do not let your thinking get out of control. Challenge your thinking and get accurate about what is real. Let us look at some common inaccurate thoughts.

1. It is not going to hurt.

2. No one is going to know.

3. I need to relax.

4. I am just going to have a couple.

5. I have had a hard day.

6. My friends want me to drink.

7. I never had a problem with pot.

8. It is the only way I can sleep.

9. I can do anything I want to.

10. I am lonely.

All of these inaccurate thoughts can be used to fuel the craving that leads to relapse. You must stop and challenge your thinking until you are thinking accurately. You must replace inaccurate thoughts with accurate ones. You are chemically dependent. If you drink or use drugs, then you will die. That is the truth. Think through the first drink. Get honest with yourself.

How to Cope With Craving

If you think inaccurately, then you will begin craving. This is the powerful feeling that drives compulsive drug use. Craving is like an ocean wave; it will build and then wash over you. Craving does not last long if you move away from your drug of choice. If you move closer to the drug, then the craving will increase until you are compelled to use. Immediately on feeling a desire to use, think this thought:

"Drinking/using drugs/gambling is no longer an option for me."

Now drinking and using drugs no longer is an option. What are your options? You are in trouble. You are craving. What are you going to do to prevent relapse? You must move away from your drug of choice. Perhaps you need to call your sponsor, go to a meeting, turn it over, call the AA/NA/GA hotline, call the treatment center, call your counselor, go for a walk, run, or visit someone. You must do something else other than thinking about chemicals. Do not sit there and ponder using. You will lose that debate. This illness is called the great debater. If you leave it unchecked, it will seduce you into using chemicals.

Remember that the illness must lie to work. You must uncover the lie as quickly as possible and get back to the truth. You must take the appropriate action necessary to maintain your sobriety.

Develop a Daily Relapse Prevention Plan

If you work a daily program of recovery, then your chances of success increase greatly. You need to evaluate your recovery daily and keep a log. This is your daily inventory.

1. Assess all relapse warning signs.
    a. What symptoms did I see in myself today?
    b. What am I going to do about them?

2. Assess love of self.
    a. What did I do to love myself today?
    b. What am I going to do tomorrow?

3. Assess love of others.
    a. What did I do to love others today?
    b. What am I going to do tomorrow?

4. Assess love of God.
    a. What did I do to love God today?
    b. What am I going to do tomorrow?

5. Assess sleep pattern.
    a. How am I sleeping?

6. Assess exercise.
    a. Am I getting enough exercise?

7. Assess nutrition.
    a. Am I eating right?

8. Review total recovery program.
    a. How am I doing in recovery?
    b. What is the next step in my recovery program?

9. Read the *Twenty-Four Hours a Day* book (Walker, 1992).

10. Make conscious contact with God.
    a. Pray and meditate for a few minutes.
    b. Relax completely.

Social Support System

Every client needs to build a social support system. Positive social support is highly predictive of long-term abstinence rates across many addictive behaviors. You need to write down specifically who is going to be your advocate at home, work, community, and school. This person needs to talk to your counselor and understand exactly what being an advocate means. This person will have different tasks depending upon whether or not they are a school teacher, parent, spouse, pastor, sponsor, mentor, coach, community leader, school counselor, doctor, nurse, counselor, etc. You need to make a list of all of these people and decide who is going to do what. Someone needs to run up to three urine drug screens every week for the first 6 months and up to one drug screen a week for the next 5 years. This person who is best is the continuing care case manager. The client calls in every morning to see if this is one of their drug testing days or not. If so, the client goes to the clinic and gives a urine sample.

1. Case manager _____ phone _____

The continuing care case manager makes sure everyone on the team is working together to keep the client clean and sober. This person keeps a record of all therapy meetings, 12-step groups, and drug screens. They have a contract with the client that outlines exactly what is expected of the client and what the consequences are if the client does not follow through with the recovery program.

2. Parent or spouse _____ phone _____

The parent or spouse will be the person who knows what behavior is adaptive and maladaptive. What friends are to be avoided? If an adolescent develops the behavioral contract and is responsible for rewards and consequences

3. The teacher _____ phone _____
   or employer _____ phone _____

The teacher or employer knows about what behavior is to be expected and what is not to be tolerated. Members of the team often call each other to check up on the facts and make sure everyone is on the same team.

4. The sponsor/mentor/coach _____ phone _____

The sponsor, mentor, or coach guides the client through recovery. They have been or are in a 12-step program themselves and take the client to meetings and meet regularly to discuss the recovery process.

5. The physician _____ phone _____

The physician orders the medication and does history and physical examinations to maintain good health.

6. The spiritual guide _____ phone _____

The spiritual guide helps the patient discuss and grow in his or her spiritual journey. The client shares his or her spiritual journey and maybe keeps a spiritual prayer journal.

Fill out this inventory every day following treatment, and keep a journal about how you are doing. You will be amazed as you read back over your journal from time to time. You will be surprised at how much you have grown.

Make a list of 10 reasons why you want to stay clean and sober.

1. _____

2. _____

3. _____

4. _____

5. _____

6. _____

7. _____

8. _____

9. _____

10. _____

Never forget these reasons. Read this list over and over to yourself. Carry a copy with you and memorize them. If you are struggling in sobriety, then take it out and read it to yourself. You are important. No one has to live a life of misery. You can recover and live a clean and sober life.

Appendix 17

Step One

Robert R. Perkinson, PhD

> *We admitted that we were powerless over alcohol—that our lives had become unmanageable.*
>
> —Alcoholics Anonymous [AA] (2001, p. 59)

Before beginning this exercise, please read Step One in *Twelve Steps and Twelve Traditions* (AA, 2002b).

No one likes to admit defeat. Our minds rebel at the very thought that we have lost control. We are big, strong, intelligent, and capable. How can it be that we are powerless? How can it be that our lives are unmanageable? This exercise will help you to sort through your life and make some important decisions. Answer each question that applies to you as completely as you can. This is an opportunity for you to get accurate. You need to see the truth about yourself.

Let us pretend for a moment that you are the commander in a nuclear missile silo. You are in charge of a 10-megaton bomb. If you think about it, this is exactly the kind of control you want over your life. You want to be in control of your thinking, feeling, and behavior. You want to be in control all of the time, not just some of the time. If you do something by accident or do something foolishly, you might kill many people. You never want to be out of control of your behavior, not even for a second.

People who are powerless over alcohol or drugs occasionally will be under the influence of the chemical when they are doing something physically hazardous. They may be intoxicated or hungover when they are working, using dangerous equipment, or driving. Over 40,000 Americans are killed each year in alcohol-related accidents. If you have ever done anything like this, then you have been out of control. You have risked your own life and the lives of others. Surely you cannot drive better when you are intoxicated than when you are sober. Now it is time to get honest with yourself.

Powerlessness

- Have you ever been intoxicated when you were doing something dangerous? For example, have you ever driven a car when you were using? Give five examples.

    1.

    2.

    3.

    4.

    5.

- Did you think that you were placing your life and the lives of others in jeopardy? What were you thinking?

- Whose lives did you risk? Make a list of 10 people you endangered.

    1.

    2.

    3.

    4.

    5.

    6.

    7.

    8.

    9.

    10.

- How do you feel about putting all of those lives at risk?

People who are powerless occasionally will do things while intoxicated or hungover that they feel bad or guilty about later. They might act foolishly at a party, act out sexually, get angry, or say things they do not mean. Have you ever done anything while intoxicated that you felt guilty or bad about later? Make a list of five things that made you feel the most uncomfortable. Be specific about what happened.

    1.

    2.

    3.

    4.

    5.

People who are powerless gradually will lose respect for themselves. They will have difficulty in trusting themselves. In what ways have you lost respect for yourself due to drug or alcohol use?

    1.

    2.

    3.

    4.

    5.

People who are powerless will do things that they do not remember doing. If you drink enough or use enough drugs, you cannot remember things properly. You might have people come up to you after a party and tell you something you did that you do not remember doing. You might wake up and not know where you are. You might not remember how you got home. This is a blackout, and it is very scary. You could have done anything. Most blackouts last a few minutes, but some can go on for hours or days.

1. Describe any blackouts you have had. Be specific about what you were doing and what happened.

2. How does it feel to know that you did something that you do not remember?

3. Think for a minute of what you could have done. You could have done anything and forgotten it.

People who are powerless cannot keep promises that they make to themselves or others. They promise that they will cut down on their drinking, and they do not. They promise that they will not use, and they do. They promise to be home, to work, to be at the Cub Scout meeting, or to go to school, but they do not make it. They cannot always do what they want to do because sometimes they are too intoxicated or hungover. They disappoint themselves, and they lose trust in themselves. Other people lose trust in them. They can count on themselves some of the time, but they cannot count on themselves all of the time.

1. Did you ever promise yourself that you would cut down your drug or alcohol use?

   Yes   No

2. What happened to these promises?

3. Did you ever promise yourself that you would quit entirely?

   Yes   No

4. What happened to your promise?

5. Did you ever make a promise to someone that you did not keep because you were intoxicated or hungover? Give a few examples.

6. Are you reliable when you are intoxicated?

   Yes   No

People who are powerless have accidents. They fall down, or have accidents with their cars, when they are intoxicated. Evidence proves that drugs profoundly affect thinking, coordination, and reaction time. Have you ever had an accident while intoxicated? Describe each accident in detail.

People who are powerless lose control of their behavior. They do things that they would not normally do when they are clean and sober. They might get into fights. They might hit or yell at people they love—a spouse, child, parent, or friend. They might say things that they do not mean.

Have you ever gotten into a fight when you were intoxicated? Describe each instance, and describe what happened.

People who are powerless say things that they do not mean. They might say sexual or angry things that they feel bad about later. They might not remember everything they said, but the other people do remember. Have you ever said something you did not mean while intoxicated? What did you say? What did you do?

People are powerless when they have feelings that they cannot deal with. They might drink or use drugs because they feel frightened, angry, or sad. They medicate their feelings. Have you ever used drugs to cover up your feelings? Give a few examples.

What feelings do you have difficulty coping with?

People are powerless when they are not safe. List 10 reasons why you can no longer use drugs or alcohol.

1.

2.

3.

4.

5.

6.

7.

8.

9.

10.

People are powerless when they know that they should do something but they cannot do it. They may make a great effort, but they just cannot seem to finish what they started out to do.

1. Could you cut down on your drug or alcohol use every time you wanted and for as long as you wanted?

   Yes   No

2. Did being intoxicated or hungover ever keep you from doing something at home that you thought you should do? Give five examples.

3. Did being intoxicated or hungover ever keep you from going to work? Give a few examples.

4. Did you ever lose a job because of your drinking or drug use? Write down exactly what happened.

People are powerless when other people have to warn them that they are in trouble. You may have felt as if you were fine, but people close to you noticed that something was wrong. It probably was difficult for them to put their finger on just what was wrong, but they were worried about you. It is difficult to confront someone when the person is wrong, so people avoid doing so until they cannot stand the behavior anymore. When addicts are confronted with their behavior, they feel annoyed and irritated. They want to be left alone with the lies that they are telling themselves. Has anyone ever talked to you about your drinking or using drugs? Who? How did you feel?

People are powerless when they do not know the truth about themselves. Addicts lie to themselves about how much they are drinking or using. They lie to themselves about how often they use. They lie to themselves about their problems, even when the problems are obvious. They blame others for their problems. Here are some common lies they tell themselves:

"I can quit anytime I want to."

"I only had a couple."

"The police were out to get me."

"I only use when I need it."

"Everybody does it."

"I was drinking, but I was not drunk."

"Anybody can get arrested for drunk driving."

"My friends will not like me if I do not use."

"I never have problems when I drink beer."

"I will not drink until after 5:00 pm."

"From now on, I would only smoke pot."

"I am going to cut down to five pills a day."

Addicts continue to lie to themselves to the very end. They hold on to their delusional thinking, and they believe that their lies are the truth. They deliberately lie to those close to them. They hide their use. They make their problems seem smaller than they actually are. They make excuses for why they are using. They refuse to see the truth.

- Have you ever lied to yourself about your chemical use? List 10 lies you told yourself.

    1.

    2.

    3.

    4.

    5.

    6.

    7.

    8.

    9.

    10.

  1. List five ways in which you tried to convince yourself that you did not have a problem.

  2. List five ways in which you tried to convince others that you did not have a problem.

Unmanageability

Imagine that you are the manager of a large corporation. You are responsible for how everything runs. If you are not a good manager, then your business will fail. You must carefully plan everything and carry out those plans well. You must be alert. You must know exactly where you are and where you are going. These are the skills you need to manage your life effectively.

Chemically dependent persons are not good managers. They keep losing control. Their plans fall through. They cannot devise and stick to things long enough to see a solution. They are lying to themselves, so they do not know where they are and they are too confused to decide where they want to go next. Their feelings are being medicated, so they cannot use their feelings to give them energy and direction for problem solving. Problems are not solved; they escalate.

You do not have to be a bad manager all of the time to be a bad manager. It is worse to be a bad manager some of the time. It is very confusing. Most chemically dependent persons have flurries of productive activity when they work too much. They work themselves to the bone, and then they let things slide. It is like being on a roller-coaster. Sometimes things are in control; sometimes things are out of control. Things are up and down, and they never can predict which way things are going to be tomorrow.

People's lives are unmanageable when they have plans fall apart because they were too intoxicated or hungover to complete them. Make a list of the plans you failed to complete because of your chemical use.

People's lives are unmanageable when they cannot manage their finances consistently.

  1. List the money problems you are having.

  2. Are any of these problems the result of your addiction? Explain how chemicals have contributed to the problems.

People's lives are unmanageable when they cannot trust their own judgment.

1. Have you ever been so intoxicated that you did not know what was happening? Explain.

2. Did you ever lie to yourself about your chemical use? Explain how your lies contributed to your being unable to manage your life.

3. Have you ever made a decision while intoxicated that you were sorry about later? Explain.

People's lives are unmanageable if people cannot work or play normally. Addicts miss work and recreational activities because of their drug use. They make excuses, but the real reason that they missed these events was they were too intoxicated or hungover.

1. Have you ever missed work because you were too intoxicated or hungover? List at least five times.

2. Have you ever missed recreational or family activities because you were too drunk or hungover? List at least five times.

People's lives are unmanageable if they are in trouble with other people or society. Chemically dependent persons will break the rules to get their own way. They have problems with authority.

1. Have you ever been in legal trouble when you were drinking or using drugs? Describe the legal problems that you have had.

2. Have you ever had problems with your parents because of your drinking or using drugs? Explain.

3. Have you ever had problems in school because of your chemical use? Explain.

People's lives are unmanageable if people cannot consistently achieve their goals. Chemically dependent people reach out for what they want, but something keeps getting in the way. It does not seem fair. They keep falling short of their goals. Finally, they give up completely. They may have had the goal of going to school, getting a better job, improving their family problems, getting in good physical condition, or going on a diet. No matter what the goals are, something keeps going wrong. Chemically dependent people always will try to blame other people, but they cannot work hard enough or long enough to reach their goals. Alcoholics and drug addicts are good starters, but they are poor finishers.

List 10 goals that you had for yourself that you did not achieve due to the addiction.

1.

2.

3.

4.

5.

6.

7.

8.

9.

10.

People's lives are unmanageable if people cannot use their feelings appropriately. Feelings give us energy and direction for problem solving. Chemically dependent people medicate their feelings with drugs or alcohol. The substance gives them a different feeling—a chemically induced feeling. Chemically dependent people become very confused about how they feel.

1. What feelings have you tried to cope with addictive behavior?

2. What feelings are created by your drug of choice? How do you feel when you are intoxicated or hungover?

People's lives are unmanageable if they violate their own rules, morals, and values. Chemically dependent persons compromise their values to continue using chemicals. They have the value not to lie, but they lie anyway. They have the value not to steal, but they steal anyway. They have the value to be loyal to their spouses or friends, but when they are intoxicated or hungover, they do not remain loyal. Their values and morals fall away, one by one. They end up doing things that they do not believe in. They know that they are doing the wrong thing, but they do it anyway.

1. Did you ever lie to cover up your addictive behavior? How did you feel about yourself?

2. Were you ever disloyal to friends or family when using chemicals? List five times, and discuss exactly what happened and how you felt about yourself.

3. Did you ever steal to get your drugs? Explain what you did and how you felt about yourself later.

4. Did you ever break the law when intoxicated? Exactly what did you do?

5. Did you ever hit or hurt someone you loved while intoxicated or hungover. Explain each time in detail.

6. Did you treat yourself poorly by refusing to stop drinking or using drugs? Explain how you were feeling about yourself.

7. Did you stop going to church? How did that make you feel about yourself?

People's lives are unmanageable when they continue to do things that give them problems. Chemicals create physical problems, headaches, ulcers, nausea, vomiting, cirrhosis, and many other physical problems. Even if chemically dependent persons are aware of physical problems caused by chemicals, they keep on using anyway.

Chemicals cause psychological problems. They can make people feel depressed, fearful, anxious, or overly angry. Even if addicts are aware of these symptoms, they will continue to use.

Chemicals create relationship problems. They cause family problems such as family fights and verbal and physical abuse. They cause interpersonal conflicts at work, with family, and with friends. Chemically dependent persons withdraw and become more isolated and alone. Even if they believe that the problems are caused by the alcohol or drugs, they continue to use.

1. Did you have any persistent physical problems that were caused by your chemical use? Describe each problem.

2. Did you have any persistent psychological problems, such as anger, fear, hurt, depression, that were caused by your chemical use? Describe each problem in detail.

3. Did you have persistent interpersonal conflicts that were made worse by your chemical use? Describe each problem in detail.

You must have good reasons to work toward a clean and sober lifestyle. Look over this exercise, and list 10 reasons why you want to continue to remain clean and sober.

1.

2.

3.

4.

5.

6.

7.

8.

9.

10.

Make a list of these 10 things, and carry them around with you until you memorize them. Then when you think about becoming involved in the addiction again repeat the list over to yourself 10 times. After completing this exercise, take a long look at yourself.

1. I am powerless over my addiction.

    Yes   No

2. When I become involved in addictive behavior, my life becomes unmanageable.

    Yes   No

Appendix 18

Step Two

Robert R. Perkinson, PhD

[We] came to believe that a power greater than ourselves could restore us to sanity.

—Alcoholics Anonymous [AA] (2001, p. 59)

Before beginning this exercise, please read Step Two in the *Twelve Steps and Twelve Traditions* (AA, 2002b).

In Step One, you admitted that you were powerless over drugs or alcohol and that your life was unmanageable. In Step Two, you need to see the insanity of your disease and seek power to help you. If you are powerless, then you need power. If your life is unmanageable, then you need a manager. Step Two will help you to decide who that manager can be.

Most alcoholics and drug addicts who see the phrase *restore to sanity* revolt. They think that they may have a drinking or drug problem, but they do not feel as though they have a mental illness. They do not think that they have been insane.

In 12-step programs, the word *sanity* means being of sound mind. Someone with a sound mind knows what is real and knows how to adapt to reality. A sound mind feels stable, safe, and secure. Someone who is insane cannot see reality and is unable to adapt. A person does not have to have all of his or her reality distorted to be in trouble. If you miss a significant part of the journey ahead of you, then you will get lost. It only takes one wrong turn to end up in the ditch.

Going through life is like going on a long journey. You have a map given to you by your parents and significant others. The map shows the way to be happy and live your life in full. If you make significant wrong turns along the way, then you will end up unhappy and live an unfulfilling life. This is what happens in addiction. Searching for happiness, you make wrong turns. You think the addiction helps you to be and to feel better, but later you find out that this map is defective. Even if you followed your old map to perfection, you still would be lost. What you need is a new map. When you engage in addictive behavior the brain always says, "Good choice." Later you find the addiction has trapped you into a life full of incredible pain. Using this map, you have lost everything you wanted and broken every one of your own rules, morals, and values. The addiction has hijacked your brain, and you cannot say no to the addictive behavior or substance. Even in the face of profound negative consequences, you keep doing what you hate doing. You promise yourself that you will stop and get on a new road but every time you try, you find yourself back to the old road, the old map, the addiction. You are blocked in, lost, desperate, helpless, hopeless, and trapped. You find yourself in a muddy ditch, and the harder you try to get out the deeper you sink in.

Twelve-step programs give you a new map. It puts up 12 signposts to show the way. If you follow this map as millions of people have done, then you will find the joy and happiness that you have been seeking. You have reached and passed the first signpost, Step One. You have decided that your life is powerless and unmanageable. Now you need a new source of power. You need someone else to help you get out of the ditch. You need to find some other person that can manage your life.

This is a spiritual program, and it directs you toward a spiritual answer to your problems. It is not a religious program. Spirituality is the intimate relationship you have with yourself and all else. Religion is an organized system of faith and worship. Everyone has spirituality, but not everyone has religion.

You need to explore three relationships very carefully in Step Two: the relationships with yourself, with others, and with a Higher Power. This Higher Power can be any Higher Power of your choice. If you do not have a Higher Power right now, do not worry. Most of us started that way. Just be willing to consider that there is a power greater than yourself in the universe.

To explore these relationships, you need to see the truth about yourself. If you see the truth, then you can find the way. First, you must decide whether you were insane. Did you have a sound mind or not? Let us look at this issue carefully.

People do not have a sound mind when they cannot remember what they did. They have memory problems. They do not have to have memory problems all of the time, just some of the time. People who abuse chemicals might not remember what happened to them last night when they were intoxicated. Gamblers can lose hours of time without knowing the amount of time that has gone by. They can even gamble for 24 hours and think they just got to the casino. Alcoholics can wake up in another town or not know where they parked their car.

List any blackouts or memory problems you have had while being involved in your addictive behavior. You might have to think hard because you forgot but if you try you can remember when you lost time, money, or cannot remember some event. Try to list five times, and be as specific as you can.

1.

2.

3.

4.

5.

People who are insane lose control over their behavior. They do things when they are intoxicated or addicted that they never would do when they are sober.

List three times when you lost control over your behavior when intoxicated.

1.

2.

3.

List three times when you could not control your addictive behavior. You used more or longer than you intended.

1.

2.

3.

People who are insane consider self-destruction.

Did you ever consider hurting yourself when you were depressed about your addictive behavior?

Yes   No

Describe in detail what happened.

People who are insane feel emotionally unstable.

Have you ever thought that you were going crazy?

Yes   No

Describe this time.

Have you felt emotionally unstable recently?

Yes   No

Describe how you have been feeling about yourself and what you have done to those that have tried to love you.

People who are insane are so confused that they cannot get their lives in order. They may frantically try to fix things, but problems stay out of control.

List five personal, family, work, or school problems that you have not been able to control.

   1.

   2.

   3.

   4.

   5.

People who are insane cannot see the truth about what is happening to them. People who are addicted hide their addictive behavior from themselves and from others. They minimize, rationalize, and deny that there are problems.

Do you believe that you have been completely honest with yourself about your addiction?

Yes   No

List 10 lies that you have told yourself.

   1.

   2.

   3.

   4.

   5.

   6.

   7.

   8.

   9.

   10.

People who are insane cut themselves off from healthy relationships. They might find that they do not communicate with significant others as well as they used to. They do not see their friends as often. They feel uncomfortable answering the phone or a knock at the door, or opening the mail. More and more of their lives center on the addiction.

List three people who you have stopped seeing.

1.

2.

3.

As your drinking and drug use increased, did you go to church less often?

Yes   No

List five relationships you have damaged in your drinking and drug use.

1.

2.

3.

4.

5.

People who are insane cannot deal with their feelings. Alcoholics and drug addicts cannot deal with their feelings. They do not like how they feel, so they medicate their feelings. They may drink or use drugs to feel less afraid or sad. They may drink to feel more powerful or more social.

List five feelings that you tried to change by drinking or using drugs.

1.

2.

3.

4.

5.

Now look back over your responses. Get out your Step One exercise and read it. Look at the truth about yourself. Look carefully at how you were thinking, feeling, and behaving when you were drinking, gambling, or using drugs. Make a decision. Do you think when you were involved in your addictive behavior that you had a sound mind? If you were unsound at least some of the time, then AA and Narcotics Anonymous (NA) would say you were insane. If you believe this to be true, then say this to yourself: "I am powerless. My life is unmanageable. My mind is unsound. I have been insane."

A Power Greater Than Yourself

Consider a power greater than yourself. What exists in the world that has greater power than you do—a river, the wind, the universe, the sun?

List five things that have greater power than you do.

1.

2.

3.

4.

5.

The first Higher Power that you need to consider is the power of the group. The group is more powerful than you are. Ten hands are more powerful than two. Two heads are better than one. AA and NA operate in groups. The group works like a family. The group process is founded in love and trust. All members share their experiences, strengths, and hopes in an attempt to help themselves and others. There is an atmosphere of anonymity. What you hear in group is confidential.

The group acts as a mirror reflecting you to yourself. The group members will help you to discover the truth about who and what you are. You have been deceiving yourself for a long time. The group will help you to uncover the lies. You will come to understand the old AA saying: "What we cannot do alone, we can do together." In group, you will have greater power over the disease because the group will see the whole truth better than you can. They will give you a new map, and this map will lead you to a new life full of happiness, joy, and peace.

You were not lying to hurt yourself. You were lying to protect yourself. In the process of building your lies, you cut yourself off from others and reality. This is how addiction works. You cannot recover from addiction by yourself. You need power coming from somewhere else. Begin by trusting your group.

Keep an Open Mind

You need to share in your group. The more you share, the closer you will get and the closer you will get the more you can share. If you take risks and share your experience, strength, and hope then you will reap the rewards. You do not have to tell the group everything, but you need to share as much as you can. The group can help you to straighten out your thinking and can help restore you to sanity.

Many chemically dependent persons are afraid of a Higher Power. They believe that a Higher Power will punish them or treat them in the same way as their fathers did. They might fear losing control. List five fears that you have about connecting with a Higher Power.

1.

2.

3.

4.

5.

Some chemically dependent persons have difficulty in trusting anyone. They have been so hurt by others that they do not want to take the chance of being hurt again. List five things that have happened in your life that makes it difficult for you to trust others.

1.

2.

3.

4.

5.

What are at least five things that you will need to see from a Higher Power that will show you that the Higher Power can be trusted?

1.

2.

3.

4.

5.

Who was the most trustworthy person you ever knew?

Name:

How did this person treat you?

How did you learn to trust him or her?

List five things you hope to gain by accepting a Higher Power.

1.

2.

3.

4.

5.

AA wants you to come to believe in a power greater than yourself. You can accept any Higher Power that you feel can restore you to sanity. Your group, your counselor, your sponsor, and nature all can be used to give you this restoration. You must pick this Higher Power carefully. It is suggested that you use AA or NA as your Higher Power for now. Here is a group of millions of people who are recovering. They have found the way.

This program will direct you toward some sort of a God of your own understanding. The Big Book states, "That we were alcoholic and could not manage our own lives. That probably no human power could have removed our alcoholism. That God could and would if He were sought" (AA, 2001, p. 60).

Millions of chemically dependent persons have recovered because they were willing to reach out for God. AA makes it clear that nothing else will remove the obsession to use chemicals. Some of us have so glorified our own lives that we have shut out God. Now you have a new opportunity and a new need. You have a choice, and you need a manager. You are at a major turning point. You can try to open your heart and let God in, or you can try to keep God out.

Remember that this is the beginning of a new life. To be new, you have to do things differently. All that the program is asking you to do is to be open to the possibility that there is a power greater than you are. AA does not demand that you believe in anything. The 12 steps are but suggestions. You do not have to accept all of this now, but you need to be open-minded and willing. Most recovering persons take Step Two a piece at a time.

First, you need to learn how to trust yourself. You must learn how to treat yourself well. What are five things you need to see from yourself that will show you that you are trustworthy?

1.

2.

3.

4.

5.

Then you need to try to trust your group. See whether the group members act consistently in your interest. They will not always tell you what you want to hear. No real friend would do that. They will give you the opportunity and encourage you to grow. What are at least five things you need to see from the group members that will show you that they are trustworthy?

Every person has a unique spiritual journey. No one can start this journey with a closed mind. What is it going to take from God to show you that God exists? List as many as you can think of.

Step Two does not mean that we believe in God as God is presented in any religion. Remember that religion is an organized system of worship. Religion is created by humans. Worship means assigning worth to something. Many people have been so turned off by religion that the idea of God is unacceptable. Describe the religious environment of your childhood. What was it like? What did you learn about God from your parents, friends, or culture?

How did these early experiences influence the beliefs you have today?

What experiences have caused you to doubt God?

Your willingness is essential to your recovery. Give some examples of your willingness to trust in a Higher Power of your choice. What are you willing to do to try to be open-minded about a relationship with a Higher Power?

Describe your current religious beliefs.

Explain the God of your own understanding.

List five reasons why a Higher Power will be good for you.

1.

2.

3.

4.

5.

If you asked the people in your AA/NA group to describe a Higher Power, you would get a variety of answers. Each person has his or her own understanding of a Higher Power. It is this unique understanding that allows a Higher Power to work individually for each of us. God comes to each of us differently.

The God shown to us in scripture knows that love necessitates freedom. God created you and gave you the freedom to make your own decisions. You can do things that God does not want you to do. If God placed his face in the sky or was so obvious that everyone worshipped him, then no one would have a free choice. This is why God exists in a gentle whisper inside of your thoughts. You have to stop and listen to hear God. It is incredibly easy to keep God out, and it is incredibly easy to let God in. When you were abusing yourself, God was there encouraging you to love yourself. When you were lying to others and treating others poorly, God was there encouraging you to love others. God has loved you from the beginning.

It is difficult to deny God because God lives inside of you. To deny God is to deny an essential part of yourself. We all know instinctively what is right and what is wrong. We do not have to be taught these things. The rules are the same across every culture and group. No matter where or how you were raised, the moral laws are the same and everyone knows them. We know not to lie or steal. We know to help others. We know to love ourselves.

Bad things happen because God allows free will. People hurt each other when they make choices independent of God's will. They can break God's law, and when this happens, there is great suffering. You probably have done some things that make you feel ashamed. You never would have felt this shame if you had followed God's plan.

"Where was God when I needed God?" many people cry. "Where was God when all those bad things were happening to me?" Well, the answer to those questions is that God was right there encouraging you to see the truth. God never promises that life is not going to hurt. God promises that he is there, teaching you, educating you, and supporting you.

Do not be discouraged if you doubt God. Your doubt about God is not bad; it is good. It means that you think and reason. You should not blindly accept things without proof. That would be foolish. What you must know is this: Only God can overcome your doubt. There is nothing you can do to make doubt go away. You can only trust that if you seek God, then God will find you. Once God finds you, your doubt will be removed. Only by swimming in the sea of doubt can you learn how to swim with strong strokes. This is how your faith gets strong. No one is asking you to accept God blindly. Follow your AA/NA group. The group members know the way. Be willing to seek God. Open your heart and your mind in every way you know how. Seek the God of your understanding. Ask your clergy or your counselor for some reading. Go at your own rate. Follow God in your own way. Soon you will find a peace that will surpass your understanding. This is the peace that we call serenity.

Appendix 19

Step Three

Robert R. Perkinson, PhD

[We] made a decision to turn our will and our lives over to the care of God as we understood Him.

—Alcoholics Anonymous [AA] (2001, p. 59)

Before beginning this exercise, please read Step Three in the *Twelve Steps and Twelve Traditions* (AA, 2002b).

You have come a long way in the program, and you can feel proud of yourself. You have decided that you are powerless over mood-altering chemicals and that your life is unmanageable. You have decided that a Higher Power of some sort can restore you to sanity. In Step Three, you will reach toward God—the God of your own understanding. You will consider using God as your Higher Power. This is the miracle. It is the major focus of the 12-step program. This is a spiritual program that directs you toward the ultimate truth. It is important that you be open to the possibility that there is a God. It is vital that you give this concept room to blossom and grow. The "Big Book" says, "That probably no human power could have relieved our alcoholism. That God could and would if He were sought" (AA, 2001, p. 60).

Step Three should not confuse you. It calls for a decision to correct your character defects under spiritual supervision. You must make an honest effort to change your life and you are responsible for all of your choices. You have made some choices before that have hurt yourself and others. List 10 choices you made that hurt yourself or someone else.

1.

2.

3.

4.

5.

6.

7.

8.

9.

10.

Now it is time to make some different choices that will set you off on a new direction. Think about each choice carefully, and do not make a choice until you have carefully thought through the possible positive and negative consequences of your decision. The AA program is a spiritual program. About the Big Book, it states, "Its main object is to enable you to find a power greater than yourself that will solve your problem" (AA, 2001, p. 45). Both AA and Narcotics Anonymous (NA) clearly state that the God of your understanding is probably the answer to your problems. If you are willing to seek God, then you will find God. That is God's promise.

Understanding the Moral Law

All spirituality has, at its core, what is already inside of you. You do not have to look very far for God. Your Higher Power lives inside of you. Inside of all of us, there is inherent goodness. In all cultures, and in all lands, this goodness is expressed in what we call the moral law. God has put his law inside of everyone's mind, body, and spirit. The law asks you to love yourself, others, and God in action and in truth. It is simply stated as follows: Love God all you can, love others all you can, and love yourself all you can. This law is very powerful. If some stranger were drowning in a pool next to you, then this internal law would motivate you to help. Instinctively, you would feel driven to help, even if it put your own life at risk. The moral law is so important that it transcends our instinct for survival. You would try to save that drowning person. This moral law is exactly the same everywhere and in every culture. It exists inside of everyone. It is written on your heart. Even among thieves, honesty is valued.

When we survey religious thought, we come up with many different ideas about God, but if we look at the saints of the religions, they are living practically indistinguishable lives. They all are doing the same things with their lives. They do not lie, cheat, or steal; they believe in giving to others before giving to themselves; they are humble; and they try not to be envious of what other people have. They are content with their life, grateful for everything they have, and good to themselves and others. To believe in your Higher Power, you must believe that this good exists inside of you. You also must believe that there is more of this goodness at work outside of you. If you do not believe in a living and breathing God at this point, do not worry. Every one of us has started where you are.

All people have a basic problem: We break the moral law, even if we believe in it.

This fact means that there is something wrong with us. We are incapable of following the moral law as we want to. Even though we would consider it unfair for someone to lie to us, occasionally we lie to someone else. If we see someone dressed in clothes that make the person look terrible, we might tell that person that he or she looks good. This is a lie, and we would not want other people lying to us like that. In this and other situations, we do not obey the very moral law that we know is good.

You must ask yourself several questions. Where did we get this moral law? How did these laws of behavior get started? Did they just evolve over time, or were they set by someone? If it was set by someone, how did this someone set the same laws in every heart in every part of the world? The program of AA/NA believes that these good laws come from something good and that there is more of this good at work in the universe. People in the program believe that people can communicate with this good, and they call this good *God*.

Do you believe that there is something good in the Universe?

Yes   No

Do you believe that there is something good inside of you?

Yes   No

We do not know everything about the Higher Power. Much of God remains a mystery. If we look at science, we find the same thing: Most of science is a mystery. We know very little about the primary elements of science such as gravity or electromagnetic energy, but we can make judgments about these elements using our experience. No one has ever seen an electron, but we are sure that it exists because we have some experience of it. It is the same thing with the Higher Power. We can know that there is a power greater than we are if we have some experience of this power. Both science and spirituality necessitate a faith based on direct human experience.

There seems to emerge in people, as naturally as the ability to love, the ability to experience God. The experience cannot be taught. It is already there, and it must be awakened. It is primal, already planted, and awaiting growth. God is experienced as a force that is alive. This force is above and more capable than humans are. God is so good, pure, and perfect that God obeys the moral law all of the time. The experience of the Higher Power brings with it a feeling of great power and energy. This can be both attractive and frightening, but mainly you will find that God is loving. God has contacted humans through the ages and has said, "I am. I exist."

Do you believe that some sort of a supreme being exists?

Yes   No

Instinctively, people know that if they can get more of this goodness, then they will have better lives. Spirituality must be practical. It must make your life better or else you will discard it. If you open yourself up to the spiritual part of the program, then you will feel better immediately.

God knows that if you follow the law of love, then you will be happy. God makes love known to all people. It is born in everyone. The consequence for breaking the moral law is separation from God. This is experienced as deep emotional pain. We feel isolated, empty, frightened, and lonely.

Scripture tells us that God is hungry for your love. God desires a deep, personal relationship with you. All people have a similar instinctive hunger for God. By reading this exercise, you can begin to develop your relationship with God. You will find true joy here if you try. Without some sort of a Higher Power, your recovery will be more difficult. A Higher Power can relieve your addiction problem like nothing else can. Many people achieve stable recovery without calling their Higher Power *God*. That certainly is possible. There are many wonderful atheists and agnostics in our program, but the AA/NA way is to reach for some sort of a God of your own understanding.

You can change things in your life. You really can. You do not have to drown in despair any longer. No matter who you are, God loves you. God is willing to help you. Perhaps God has been waiting for you for a long time. Think of how wonderful it is. There is a God. God created you. God loves you. God has a purpose for your life and God will show you the way. God wants you to be happy. Try to open yourself up to this experience.

The Key to Step Three

The key to working Step Three is willingness—the willingness to turn your life over to the care of God as you understand God. This is difficult for many of us because we think that we are in control of everything and everyone. We are completely fooled by this delusion. We believe that we know the right thing to do. We believe that everything would be fine if others would just do things our way. This leads us to deep feelings of resentment and self-pity. People in our lives would not cooperate with all of our plans. No matter how hard we tried to control everything, things kept getting out of control. Sometimes the harder we worked, the nicer or meaner we acted, the worse things got.

You are not in control of the universe, and you never have been in control. Your Higher Power is in control. God is the only one that knows about everything. God created you and the universe. Chemically dependent persons, in many ways, are trying to be God. They want the universe to revolve around them. "Above everything, we alcoholics must be rid of this selfishness" (AA, 2001, p. 62).

How to Turn It Over

To arrest addiction, you have to stop playing God and let your Higher Power take control. If you sincerely want this and you try, it is easy to do so. Go to a quiet place and talk to your Higher Power about your addiction. Say something like this:

- "God I do not know if you are out there or not but if you are, come into my life and help me. I cannot do this by myself anymore."
- Then ask God this question, "God, what is the next step in my relationship with you?"
- Wait and tune your mind, body, and spirit. Do not be afraid. Wait for one word of phrase to come into your mind. This will not be audible but an inaudible, tender thought. You might get words inside of your mind or see an image.

Write down exactly what came into your mind.

_____

_____

This communication will be accompanied with a feeling of peace. The next time you have a problem, stop and turn the problem over to your Higher Power. Say something like this: "God, I cannot deal with this problem. You deal with it." Describe three times when this happened.

1.

2.

3.

As you ask for God's will to be done, you will find the right direction. God knows the way for you. If you follow your Higher Power, then you never will be lost again. God will encourage you to see the truth, and then God will leave the choices up to you. You always can decide. God wants you to be free. God wants you to make all of your own decisions, but God wants to have input into your decisions. Your Higher Power wants to show you the way. If you try to find the way by yourself, then you will ultimately slip off the path and find yourself lost. God promises that if you will follow God's plan, then God will see to it that you receive all of the desires of your heart. God knows exactly what you need.

Step Three offers no compromise. It calls for a decision. Exactly how you surrender and turn things over is not the point. The important thing is that you are willing to try.

Can you see that it is necessary to give up your self-centeredness?

Yes   No

Do you see that it is time to turn things over to a power greater than you are?

Yes   No

List 10 things that you have to gain by turning your will and your life over to a Higher Power. Get your group or counselor to help you.

1.

2.

3.

4.

5.

6.

7.

8.

9.

10.

List five reasons why you need to turn things over to a power greater than yourself.

1.

2.

3.

4.

5.

We should not confuse organized religion with spirituality. In Step Two, you learned that spirituality deals with your relationship with yourself, others, and God. Religion is an organized system of faith and worship. It is person-made, not God-made. It is humans' way of interpreting God's plan. Religion can be confusing or helpful. It can even drive people away from God. Are old, religious ideas keeping you away from trusting God? If so, then how?

A great barrier to your finding God may be impatience. You may want to find God right now. You must understand that your spiritual growth is set by God and not by you. You will grow spiritually when God knows you are ready. Remember that we are turning this whole thing over. Each person has his or her own unique spiritual journey. Each person must have his or her own individual walk. Spiritual growth, not perfection, is your goal. All you can do is seek the God of your understanding. When God knows that you are ready, God will find you. Finally, you will want to surrender to God's will for your life. If you are holding back, then you need to let go absolutely. Faith, willingness, and prayer will overcome all of the obstacles. Do not worry about your doubt. Just keep seeking in every way you know how.

List 10 ways in which you can seek God. Ask your friends or counselor to help you.

1.

2.

3.

4.

5.

6.

7.

8.

9.

10.

What does the AA saying "Let go and let God" mean to you?
List five ways in which you can put Step Three to work in your life.

1.

2.

3.

4.

5.

List the things in your life you still want to control.
How can these things be handled better by turning them over to your Higher Power?
List five ways in which you allowed chemicals to be the God in your life.

1.

2.

3.

4.

5.

List three ways your chemical use separated you from God.

1.

2.

3.

What changes have you noticed in yourself since you entered the program?
Of these changes, which of them occurred because you listened to someone else other than yourself?
Make a list of the things that are holding you back from turning things over.

1.

2.

3.

4.

5.

List five ways you see God taking care of you.

1.

2.

3.

4.

5.

Describe how you understand God now.

How to Pray

Pray by reading the Step Three prayer once each day for a week. Say the words carefully aloud, and listen to yourself as you speak. Feel God's presence with you, and when you are ready, begin to talk to God. Make prayer a dialogue, not a monologue. Talk to God, and then listen for God's answer to come to you inside of your mind.

God I offer myself to Thee—to build with me and to do with me as Thou wilt. Relieve me of the bondage of self, that I may better do Thy will. Take away my difficulties, that victory over them may bear witness to those I would help of Thy Power, Thy Love, and Thy Way of Life. May I do Thy will always! (AA, 2001, p. 63)

Listen for God in others. God may speak to you through them. Look for God's actions in the group, in the weather, and in nature. Read scripture, and seek God through your reading. Ask your counselor or your clergyperson for some suggestions.

How to Meditate

Take time to meditate each day. Sit in a quiet place for about 10 to 20 minutes, and pay attention to your breathing. Ask God this question: "God, what do you have to say to me today?" Then empty your mind. Do not be nervous if there is only silence for a while. Listen for God's message for you. Write down any words or images that come into your mind. Keep a log of each meditation for a week.

Day 1.

Day 2.

Day 3.

Day 4.

Day 5.

Day 6.

Day 7.

Make a list of what are you going to do on a daily basis to help your spiritual program grow.

Trust that if you seek God then God will find you—no matter who you are, no matter where you are. God loves you more than you can imagine. You are God's perfect child, created in God's image. God has great plans for you.

Appendix 20

Step Four

Robert R. Perkinson, PhD

[We] made a searching and fearless moral inventory of ourselves.

—Alcoholics Anonymous [AA] (2001, p. 59)

Before beginning this exercise, please read Step Four in *Twelve Steps and Twelve Traditions* (AA, 2002b).

Congratulations! You are doing well in the program. You have admitted your powerlessness over alcohol or drugs, and you have found a Higher Power that can restore you to sanity. Now you must up your maladaptive thoughts and behavior by taking a careful inventory of yourself. You must know exactly what resources you have available, and you must examine the exact nature of your wrongs. You need to be detailed about the good things about your choices and the bad choices you have made. Only by taking this inventory will you know exactly where you are. Then you can decide where you are going.

In taking this inventory, you must be detailed and specific. It is the only way of seeing the complete impact of your disease. A part of the truth might be, "I told lies to my children." The complete truth might be, "I told my children that I had cancer. They were terrified and cried for a long time." These two statements would be very different. Only the second statement tells the exact nature of the wrong, and the client felt the full impact of the disclosure. You can see how important it is to put the whole truth before you at one time.

Remember, the truth will set you free from the slavery to the addiction.

The Fourth Step is a long autobiography of your life. Read this exercise before you start, and underline things that pertain to you. You will want to come back and cover each of these issues in detail as you write your whole story down. If the problem does not relate to you, then leave it blank. Examine exactly what you did wrong. Look for your mistakes even though the situation was not totally your fault. Try to disregard what the other person did and to concentrate on what you did. It is also important to write down what you were thinking that lead to your bad choices. In time, you will realize that the person who hurt you was as spiritually sick as you were. You need to ask your Higher Power to help you forgive that person or to show that person the same forgiveness that you would want for yourself. You can honestly pray that the other person finds out the truth about what he or she did to you.

Review your natural desires carefully and think about how you acted on them. You will see that some of them became the Higher Powers of your life. Sex, food, money, relationships, power, influence, education, and many others can become the major focus of your life. The pursuit of these desires can take total control and can become the center of our existence. That is when we insult God. We say that these objects can make us happy and save us. Making good choices sets us free from the old behavior of the past. Once we begin to think, feel, and act accurately, we enjoy the positive consequences of our actions. If we continue to think inaccurately, we will feel and act in a way that hurts others and ourselves. We can always stop, think, and plan before we act. It helps to role-play difficulties in we have had in the past in skills group so we can learn new ways of thinking and acting. Many of us have one feeling that leads to one action. The truth is we can stop when we feel, get our thoughts and feelings accurate, and then find many ways we can cope with the situation.

In working through the Fourth Step inventory, you will experience pain. You will feel angry, sad, fearful, ashamed, embarrassed, guilty, and lonely. The Fourth Step is a grieving process. As you see clearly your inaccurate thoughts, feelings, and behaviors, you may feel that no one will ever love you again, but remember that God created you in perfection. You are God's perfect child: God's masterpiece, God's work of art. There is nothing wrong with you. You have everything that you need to be happy, joyous, and free. Sure, you made some mistakes. That is an essential part of life. We learn from our mistakes. Once you clean house, you can begin to purify yourself by shedding your defects of character. These are our old sick ways of thinking, feeling, and acting. These character defects will not go away easily, and you will feel the old behaviors fight for life. You have grown comfortable in the lies, and now you are walking into the truth. You are walking out of the darkness and into the light—out of the fear and into the peace that AA calls serenity.

Now let us take a basic look at right and wrong. We cover the following areas.

1. Did God come first in your life? Did you seek and follow God's will at all times?
   a. List your idols—money, fame, position, alcohol, drugs, sex, power, relationships.
   b. Have you always honored God with your language? List three ways you dishonored God with your actions or words.
   c. Have you always set aside a day to improve your relationship with God?
   d. Have you loved, honored, and respected your parents? List at least five ways you dishonored your mother and father.
   e. Make a list of your unresolved hate, anger, and resentments.
   f. List your adulterous acts or thoughts.
   g. List when you cheated, misrepresented yourself, made pressure deals, or had bad debts.
   h. List the times you slandered another person or spread gossip.
   i. List the times you lusted after something that belonged to someone else or felt envious or overly competitive.

2. Take a close look at any false pride.

   Egotistical vanity is having too great an admiration of yourself. Pride makes you your own law, moral judge, and Higher Power.

   a. List three times you boasted or self-glorified yourself with lies.

   b. Discuss your love of publicity.

   c. List five times you lied to pretend to be better than others are.

   d. List three times you refused to give up your will.

   e. List at least three times you resented someone who you thought crossed you.

   f. List three times when you quarreled when another person challenged your wishes.

   g. List five times when you knew you were disobeying or refusing to submit your will to the will of your superiors or to God.

3. Take a close look at any greed.

   Do you desire wealth, such as money or other things, as an end in itself rather than as a means to an end? In acquiring wealth in any form, do you disregard the rights of others? Do you give an honest day's work for an honest day's pay? How do you use what you have? Are you stingy with your friends and family? Do you love money and possessions for these things in themselves? How excessive is your love of luxury? Do you stoop to devices such as fraud, perjury, dishonesty, and sharp practices in dealing with others? Do you try to fool yourself in these regards? Do you call questionable business "Big Business"? Do you call unreasonable hoarding "security"? Will you do almost anything to attain these things and kid yourself by giving your methods innocent names?

4. Take a close look at any lust.

Lust is inordinate love and desire of the pleasures of the flesh. Are you guilty of lust in any of its forms? Do you tell yourself that improper or undue indulgence in sexual activities is okay? Do you treat people as objects of your desire other than as God's perfect creations? Do you use pornography or think unhealthy sexual thoughts? Do you treat other people sexually the same way in which you would want to be treated? Do you love others the same way in which you want them to love you?

5. Take a close look at any envy.

Do you dislike seeing others happy or successful, as though they had stolen something from you? Do you resent those who are smarter than you are? Do you criticize the good done by others because you secretly wish that you had done it yourself? Are you ever envious enough to try to lower another person's reputation by starting or engaging in gossip about that person? Do you call religious people "hypocrites" because they go to church and try to be religiously good even though they are subject to human failings? Do you ever accuse the educated, wise, or learned of being highbrow because you envy their advantages? Do you genuinely love other people, or do you find them distasteful because you envy them?

6. Take a close look at any anger.

Do you ever fly into a rage of temper, become revengeful, or entertain urges to "get even" or an "I would not let him get away with it" attitude? Do you ever resort to violence, clench your fists, or stomp about in a temper flare-up? Are you touchy, unduly sensitive, or impatient at the smallest slight? Do you ever murmur or grumble even in small matters? Do you ignore the fact that anger prevents development of personality and halts spiritual progress? Do you realize that anger often ruins good judgment? Do you permit anger to rule you when you know that it blinds you to the rights of others? Do you permit yourself to become angry when others are weak and become angry with you? Do you find yourself in a rage when someone criticizes you even for small things?

7. Take a close look at any overindulgence.

Do you weaken your moral and intellectual life by excessive use of food and drink? Do you generally eat to excess and, thus, enslave your soul and character to the pleasures of the body beyond the reasonable needs of the body? Did you ever, when drinking or using drugs, become nauseated and vomit, only to immediately return and drink or use some more? Did you use so much that your intellect and personality deteriorated? So much that memory, judgment, and concentration were affected? So much that personal pride and social judgment vanished? So much that you developed a spirit of despair?

8. Take a look at any laziness.

Are you finding yourself being lazy or given to idleness, procrastination, nonchalance, and indifference in material things? Are you lukewarm in prayer? Do you hold the self-discipline of others in contempt? Are you fainthearted in performance of those things that are morally or spiritually difficult? Are you ever listless with aversion to effort in any form? Are you easily distracted from things spiritual, quickly turning to things temporal?

Personality Defects

1. Selfishness

   This is taking care of one's own needs without regard for others.

   (1) Example: The family would like an outing. Dad would like drinking, golfing, or fishing, or he has a hangover. Who wins?

   (2) Example: Your child needs a new pair of shoes. You put it off until payday but get a fifth that same night.

   (3) You are afraid to dance because you might appear awkward.

2. Alibis

   This is the highly developed art of justifying our chemical use and behavior through excuses such as the following:

   (1) "A few will straighten me out."

   (2) "Starting tomorrow, I am going to change."

   (3) "If I did not have a wife and family . . ."

   (4) "If I could start all over again . . ."

   (5) "A drink will help me think."

   (6) "Nobody cares anyway."

   (7) "I had a hard day."

3. Dishonest thinking

   We take truths or facts and twist them to come up with the conclusions we need such as the following examples:

   (1) My secret love is going to raise the roof if I drop her. It is not fair to burden my wife with that sort of knowledge. Therefore, I will hang on to my girlfriend. This mess is not her fault.

   (2) If I tell my family about the $500 bonus, it will all go for bills. I have got to have some drinking money. Why start a family argument? I would leave well enough alone.

   (3) My spouse dresses well and eats well, and the kids are getting a good education. What more do they want from me?

4. Shame

   This is the feeling that something irreparable is wrong with us.

   (1) No matter how many people tell you that it is okay, you continue to berate yourself. List the things you cannot forgive yourself for doing.

   (2) You keep going over and over your mistakes, wallowing in what a terrible person you are.

5. Resentment

   a. This is displeasure aroused by a real or imagined wrong or injury accompanied by irritation.

      (1) You are fired from work. You hate the boss.

      (2) Your sister warns you about excessive drinking. You get fighting mad at her.

(3)   A coworker is doing a good job and gets accolades. You have a drug record and fear that this coworker might have been promoted over you. You hate his guts.

(4)   You may have resentment toward a person or a group of people, or you may resent an institution, a religion, and so on.

b. Anger and resentment lead to bickering, friction, hatred, and unjust revenge. It brings out the worst in our immaturity and produces misery for ourselves and all concerned.

6. Intolerance

This is the refusal to put up with beliefs, practices, customs, or habits that differ from our own.

(1)   Do you hate other people because they are of another race, come from a different country, or have a different religion?

(2)   Did you have any choice in being born a particular color or nationality?

(3)   Isn't our religion usually "inherited"?

7. Impatience

This is an unwillingness to calmly bear delay, opposition, pain, or bother.

(1)   A chemically dependent person is someone who jumps on a horse and gallops off madly in all directions at the same time.

(2)   Do you blow your stack when someone keeps you waiting over the "allotted time" you gave that person?

(3)   Did anyone ever have to wait for you?

8. Phoniness

This is a manifestation of our false pride or the old false front.

(1)   I present my love with a present as evidence of my love. Just by pure coincidence, it helps to smooth over my last binge.

(2)   I buy new clothes because my business position demands it. Meanwhile, the family also could use food and clothes.

9. Procrastination

This is putting off or postponing things that need to be done—the familiar "I would do it tomorrow."

(1)   Did little jobs that were put off become big and almost impossible later?

(2)   Do you pamper yourself by doing things "my way"?

(3)   Can you handle little jobs that you are asked to take care of, or do you feel picked on?

(4)   Little things, done for God, make them great. Are you doing the little things for God?

10. Self-pity

a. These people at the party are having fun with their drinking. Why can't I be like that? This is the "woe is me" syndrome.
b. If I had that person's money, then I would not have any problems. This is a similar attitude.

11. Feelings too easily hurt

a. I walk down the street and say hello to someone. The person does not answer. I am hurt and furious.
b. I am expecting my turn at the AA meeting, but the time runs out. I feel rejected.

12. Fear

This is an inner foreboding, whether real or imagined, of doom ahead. We suspect that our use of chemicals, behavior, negligence, and so on are catching up with us. We fear the worst.

When we learn to accept our powerlessness, ask our Higher Power for help, and face ourselves with honesty, the nightmare will be gone.

13. Depression

This is feeling sad or down most of the day.

(1) You keep going over all of the things that are going wrong.

(2) You tend to think the worst.

14. Feelings of inadequacy

This is feeling as though you cannot do it.

You hold on to a negative self-image even when you succeed.

15. Perfectionism

You have to do everything perfect all of the time.

(1) Even when you have done a good job, you find something wrong with it.

(2) Someone compliments you on something. You feel terrible because it could have been better.

Physical Liabilities

1. Diseases, disabilities, and other physical limitations about how you look or how your body functions

2. Sexual problems or hang-ups

3. Negative feelings about your appearance

4. Negative feelings about your age

5. Negative feelings about your sex

Time-Out

If you have gone through the exercise to this point without coming up for air—it figures. We did our drinking and drugging the same way. Whoa! Easy does it! Take this in reasonable stages. Assimilate each portion of the exercise thoughtfully. The reading of this is important, but the application of it is even more important. Take some time to think and rest, and let this entire exercise settle in. Develop some sort of a workable daily plan. Include plenty of rest.

When chemically dependent people stop using, part of their lives is taken away from them. This is a terrible loss to sustain unless it is replaced by something else. We cannot just boot the chemicals out the window. They meant too much to us. They were how we faced life, the key to escape, and the tool for solving life's problems. In approaching a new way of life, a new set of tools is substituted. These are the 12 steps and the AA/Narcotics Anonymous (NA) way of life.

The same principle applies when we eliminate our character defects. We replace them by substituting assets that are better adapted to a healthy lifestyle. As with substance use, you do not fight a defect. You replace it with something that works better. Use what follows for further character analysis and as a guide for character building. These are the new tools. The objective is not perfection but rather progress. You will be happy with the type of living that produces self-respect, respect and love for others, and security from the nightmare of addiction.

The Way to Recovery

1. Faith

    This is the act of leaving that part of our lives to the care of a power greater than ourselves with assurance that it will work out. This will be shaky at first, but with it comes a deep spiritual connection.

    (1) Faith is acquired through application—acceptance, daily prayer, and meditation.

    (2) We depend on faith. We have faith that the lights will come on, that the car will start, and that our coworkers will handle their end of things.

    (3) Spiritual faith is the acceptance of our gifts, limitations, problems, and trials with equal gratitude, knowing that God has a plan for us. With "Thy will be done" as our daily guide, we will lose our fear and find ourselves.

2. Hope

    Faith suggests reliance. We came to believe that a power greater than ourselves would restore us to sanity. We hope to stay clean and sober, regain our self-respect, and love our families. Hope resolves itself into a driving force. It gives purpose to our daily living.

    (1) Faith gives us direction, and hope gives us the steam to take action.

    (2) Hope reflects a positive attitude. Things are going to work out for us if we work the program.

3. Love

    This is the active involvement in someone's individual growth.

    (1) Love must occur in action and in truth.

    (2) "Love is patient, love is kind."

    (3) In its deeper sense, love is the art of living realistically and fully, guided by spiritual awareness of our responsibilities and our debt of gratitude to God and to others.

Analysis. Have you used the qualities of faith, hope, and love in your past? How will they apply to your new way of life?

We Stay on Track Through Action

1. *Courtesy:* Some of us are actually afraid to be gentle persons.

2. *Cheerfulness:* Circumstances do not determine our frame of mind; we do. "Today I will be cheerful. I will look for the beauty in life."

3. *Order:* Live today only. Organize one day at a time.

4. *Loyalty:* Be faithful to whom you believe in.

5. *Use of time:* Use your time wisely.

6. *Punctuality:* This includes self-discipline, order, and consideration for others.

7. *Sincerity:* This is the mark of self-respect and genuineness. Sincerity carries conviction and generates enthusiasm. It is contagious.

8. *Caution in speech:* Watch your tongue. We can be vicious and thoughtless. Too often, the damage is irreparable.

9. *Kindness:* This is one of life's great satisfactions. We do not have real happiness until we have given of ourselves. Practice this daily.

10. *Patience:* This is the antidote to resentments, self-pity, and impulsiveness.

11. *Tolerance:* This requires common courtesy, courage, and a "live and let live" attitude.

12. *Integrity:* This includes the ultimate qualifications of a person—honesty, loyalty, and sincerity.

13. *Balance:* Do not take yourself too seriously. We get a better perspective when we can laugh at ourselves.

14. *Gratitude:* The person without gratitude is filled with false pride. Gratitude is the honest recognition of help received. Use it often.

Analysis. In considering the little virtues, where did I fail and how did that contribute to my accumulated problem? What virtues should I pay attention to in this rebuilding program?

Physical Assets

1. *Physical health:* How healthy am I despite any ailments?

2. *Talents:* What am I good at?

3. *Age:* At my age, what can I offer to others?

4. *Sexuality:* How can I use my sexuality to express my love?

5. *Knowledge:* How can I use my knowledge and experience to help myself and others?

Mental Assets

1. Despite your problems, how healthy are you emotionally?

2. Do you care for others? Make a list of the ways you can share your experience, strength, and hope.

3. Are you kind?

4. Can you be patient? List some ways you can give others the time to think, plan, and act.

5. Are you basically a good person? In detail, describe the person you want to be.

6. Do you want to help others? List five ways you can help other people.

7. Do you try to tell the truth?

8. Do you try to be forgiving? List the people you are still having trouble forgiving, and turn them over to God.

9. Can you be enthusiastic?

10. Are you sensitive to the needs of others?

11. Can you be serene? Make plans to meditate every day by reading AA/NA material, scripture, or other recovery reading.

12. *Sincerity:* How are you going to try to be sincere?

13. *Self-discipline:* List the ways you are going to try to bring order and self-control into your life.

14. Are you going to accept the responsibility for your own behavior and stop blaming others?

15. How are you going to use your intelligence?

16. Are you going to seek the will of God?

17. *Education:* How might you improve your mind in furthering your education?

18. Are you going to be grateful for what you have?

19. *Integrity:* How can you improve your honesty and reliability?

20. *Joy:* In what areas of your life do you find happiness?

21. Are you humble and working on your false pride?

22. Are you seeking the Higher Power of your own understanding?

23. *Acceptance:* In what ways can you better accept your own limitations and the limitations of others?

24. *Courage:* Are you willing to trust and follow the God of your understanding?

The Autobiography

Using this exercise, write the story of your life. Cover your experiences in 5-year intervals. Be brief, but try not to miss anything. Tell the whole truth. Write down exactly what you thought and did. Consider all of the things that you marked during the exercise. Read the exercise again if you need to do so. Make an exhaustive and honest consideration of your past and present. Cover both assets and liabilities carefully. You will rebuild your life on the solid building blocks of your assets. These are the tools of recovery. Omit nothing because of shame, embarrassment, or fear. Determine the thoughts, feelings, and actions that plagued you. You want to meet these problems face-to-face and see them in writing. If you wish, you may destroy your inventory after completing the Fifth Step. Many clients hold a ceremony in which they burn the Fourth Step inventory. This symbolizes that they are leaving the old life behind. They are starting a new life free of the past.

Appendix 21

Step Five

Robert R. Perkinson, PhD

[We] admitted to God, ourselves, and to another human being the exact nature of our wrongs.

—Alcoholics Anonymous [AA] (2001, p. 57)

Before beginning this exercise, please read Step Five in *Twelve Steps and Twelve Traditions* (AA, 2002b).

With Steps One to Four behind you, it is now time to clean house and start over. You must free yourself of the guilt and shame and go forward in a new life full of faith and hope. The Fifth Step is meant to right the wrongs with your Higher Power, yourself, and others. You will develop a new attitude and a new relationship, particularly with yourself. You have admitted your powerlessness, and you have identified your liabilities and assets in the personal inventory. Now it is time to get right with your Higher Power. You will do this by admitting to God, to yourself, and to another person the exact nature of your wrongs. You are going to cover all of your assets and liabilities in the Fifth Step. You are going to tell someone the whole truth at one time. This person is important because he or she is a symbol of God and everyone else. You must watch this person's face. The illness has been telling you that if you tell anyone the whole truth about you, people will not like you. That is a lie, and you are going to prove that it is a lie. The truth is this: Unless you tell people the truth, they cannot like you because they do not know you. You must see yourself tell someone the truth and watch that person's reaction.

It is very difficult to discuss your faults with someone. It is hard enough just thinking about them yourself, but this is a necessary step. It will help to free you from the shame and guilt of the addictive behavior. You must tell this person everything, the whole story, all of the things that you are afraid to share. If you withhold anything, then you will not get the relief you need to start over. You will be carrying around excess baggage. You do not need to do this to yourself. God loves you and wants you to be free of guilt, shame, and hurt. God wants you to be happy and to reach your full potential.

Time after time, newcomers have tried to keep to themselves certain facts about their lives. Trying to avoid this humbling experience, they have turned to easier methods. Almost invariably, they got drunk. Having persevered with the rest of the program, they wondered why they fell. We think the reason is that they never completed their housecleaning. They took inventory all right but hung on to some of the worst items in stock. They only *thought* they had lost their egotism and fear; they only *thought* they had humbled themselves. But they had not learned enough of humility, fearlessness, and honesty, in the sense we find necessary, until they told someone else *all* their life story. (AA, 2001, pp. 72–73)

By finally telling someone the whole truth, you will rid yourself of that terrible sense of isolation and loneliness. You will feel a new sense of belonging, acceptance, and freedom. If you do not immediately feel relief, do not worry. If you have been completely honest, then the relief will come. "The dammed-up emotions of years break out of their confinement and miraculously vanish when they are exposed" (AA, 2001, p. 62). You can be forgiven, no matter what you have done. You are God's child, and he wants to make you into a new person who is dedicated to helping others.

The Fifth Step will develop within you a new humbleness of character that is necessary for normal living. You will come to recognize who and what you are. When you are honest with another person, it confirms that you have been honest with yourself and with God.

The person with whom you will share your Fifth Step has been chosen carefully for you. You will meet with this person several times before you do the step. You need to decide whether you can trust this person. Do you believe that this person is confidential? Do you feel comfortable with this person? Do you believe that this person will understand?

Once you have chosen that person, put your false pride aside and go for it. Tell this person everything about yourself. Do not leave one dark act untold. Tell this person about all of the good things as well as all of the bad things you have done. Share the details, and do not leave anything out. If it troubles you even a little, then share it. Let it all hang out to be examined by God, by you, and by that other person. Every good and bad part needs to be revealed. When you are finished, say a prayer to your Higher Power. Tell God that you are sorry for what you have done wrong, and commit yourself to a new way of life following the God of your understanding. Many clients like to say the Seventh Step prayer.

My Creator, I am now willing that you should have all of me, good and bad. I pray that you now remove from me every single defect of character, which stands in the way of my usefulness to you and my fellows. Grant me strength, as I go out from here, to do your bidding. (AA, 2001, p. 76)

Appendix 22
Adolescent Unit Level System

The adolescent unit uses the level system as a way to earn privileges and trust here. There are four levels. Each has its own set of criteria and privileges. You will be assigned the level the staff sees you meeting. Your level is entirely up to your willingness to work. The higher the level, the more freedom you will get, as well as responsibility.

Level 1: To move to the next level, you will need to do the following:

- Complete at least the first 7 days of treatment.
- Read and review the client handbook, and come to an understanding of the rights, rules, and expectations of the treatment program.
- Finish all assessments.
- Undergo lab work, have a physical examination, and complete detoxification (if needed).
- Participate in two sessions, including an initial interview with a primary counselor.
- Attend all groups as scheduled, and participate appropriately.
- Fulfill any additional criteria set for you by the clinical staff.

Possible privileges: At this level, you may . . .

- Earn up to 1,000 points per day.
- Go to the Point Store two times a week and get up to two food items, two drink items, and one other item.
- Attend off-campus spiritual activities if you have completed at least 7 days of treatment and the clinical staff has given approval.
- Use points to make one 10-minute phone call home (on speakerphone) each week.

Level 2: To move to the next level, you will need to do the following:

- Complete the following assignments or their equivalents (Why Am I Here? Are Alcohol and Drugs Causing My Problems, Honesty, and Step One), and discuss them in individual and group sessions.
- Participate in individual sessions with your primary counselor, two times per week.
- Attend groups as scheduled, and participate without staff always telling you to do so.
- Be in control of your behaviors, such as no physically or verbally aggressive behaviors.
- Accept consequences and feedback from staff and peers, taking responsibility for your actions.
- Consistently follow unit rules.
- Understand addiction in terms of the disease concept, and apply it to your life.
- Begin using healthy coping skills (journaling, time-outs, pushups, talking, etc.).
- Fulfill any additional criteria set for you by the clinical staff.

Possible privileges: At this level, you may . . .

- Earn up to 1,500 points per day.
- Go to the Point Store two times a week and get up to two food items, two drink items, and one other item.
- Attend off-campus activities at staff discretion.
- Use points to make two 10-minute or one 20-minute phone call home each week.
- Have approved free reading and drawing materials in the room at noon study time (and return them).
- Get a haircut with your own money.

Level 3: To move to the next level, you will need to do the following:

- Complete Steps Two, Three, Four, and Five as assigned, in a complete and timely manner, and discuss them in individual and group sessions as assigned.
- Participate in individual sessions with your primary counselor two times per week.
- Attend groups as scheduled and be an active participant on your own without staff having to ask.
- Accept consequences without talking back, fighting, or getting angry beyond control.
- Give honest and assertive feedback to peers.
- Behave in a manner consistent with what you say.
- Demonstrate willingness to help others, be an ally to others, and still work on self.
- Consistently use healthy coping skills (I feel statements, journaling, time-outs, etc.).
- Fulfill any additional criteria set by the clinical staff.

Possible privileges: At this level, you may . . .

- Earn up to 2,000 points per day
- Go to the Point Store two times a week and get up to two food items, two drink items, and one other item.
- Attend all off-campus activities.
- Use points to make two 10-minute or one 20-minute phone call home each week.
- Watch television during community time (based on staff availability).
- Have approved free reading and drawing materials in the room.
- Play a musical instrument or listen to music (approved by staff) in our serenity room for 30 minutes during noon self-time.
- Study at your desk in your room for last hour of study time.
- Add an extended family member to call and visitor list (must be approved by staff).

Level 4: To keep this level, you will need to do the following:

- Complete Steps Two, Three, Four, and Five as assigned, in a complete and timely manner, and discuss them in individual and group sessions as assigned.
- Complete additional treatment plan assignments as given.
- Be open-minded to aftercare and discharge plans, including behavior contract.
- Participate in individual sessions with your primary counselor two times per week.
- Attend groups as scheduled, taking a leadership role, showing by example how groups are done well.
- Take your own time-outs, not being placed there by staff direction.
- Give honest and assertive feedback to peers; help peers make positive choices.
- Be welcoming and positive to new peers, encouraging them to be positive about treatment.
- Demonstrate willingness to help others, be an ally to peers, and still work on self.

- Consistently use healthy coping skills (I feel statements, journaling, time-outs, etc.).
- Fulfill any additional criteria set by the clinical staff.

Possible privileges: At this level, you may . . .

- Earn up to 2,500 points per day.
- Go to the Point Store three times a week and get up to two food items, two drink items, and one other item.
- Attend all off-campus activities.
- Use points to make two 10-minute or one 20-minute phone call home each week.
- Use points to eat a meal at a local restaurant with staff.
- Watch television during community time (based on staff availability).
- Have approved free reading and drawing materials in the room.
- Play a musical instrument or listen to music (approved by staff) in our serenity room for 30 minutes during noon self-time.
- Study at the desk in your room for the entire study time.
- Have supervised time on the computer—no e-mail or chatting.
- Be a peer leader, helping other peers learn rules and feel welcomed here.
- When possible, attend an outside Alcoholics Anonymous (AA) or Narcotics Anonymous (NA) meeting with staff.
- Add a second extended family member to call and visitor list (must be approved by staff).
- Request other privileges that can be worked out with staff.
- Use the STOP level—a special level used to help you look at poor choices you may be making while here.

You may be placed on the STOP level due to the following:

- Major rule violations (such as smoking, engaging in physical or verbal aggression, and running away)
- Continued violation of rules
- Refusing to do what is asked of you by staff on several different occasions
- Hurting others' treatment program

While on the STOP level, you will . . .

- Earn no privileges or points for the time you are on the level.
- Work at completing the requirements for this level at the think table, or in the serenity room.

General criteria: At this level, you will . . .

- Identify the behaviors that led to you being placed on the STOP level.
- Complete assignments given by the staff and present those assignments to staff and/or peers.
- Accept consequences for your behavior without losing control of your behaviors.
- Make a plan to do things differently next time.
- Fulfill any additional criteria set for you by the clinical staff.

When criteria for the STOP Level are met, you will . . .

- Be placed at the level that staff will decide.
- Resume regular participation in the treatment program.
- Be able to earn privileges again as normal.

Level One Daily Point Card

Goal for the Day:

To move to the next level, you will need to do the following:

- Complete at least the first 7 days of treatment.
- Read and review the client handbook, and come to an understanding of the rights, rules, and expectations of the treatment program.
- Finish all assessments.
- Undergo lab work, have a physical examination, and complete detoxification (if needed).
- Participate in two sessions including an initial interview with the primary counselor.
- Attend all groups as scheduled and participate appropriately.
- Fulfill any additional criteria set for you by the clinical staff.

Possible privileges: At this level, you may . . .

- Earn up to 1,000 points per day.
- Go to the Point Store two times a week and get up to two food items, two drink items, and one other item.
- Attend off-campus spiritual activities (such as church and Inipi) if you have completed at least 7 days of treatment and the clinical staff has given approval.
- Use points to make one 10-minute phone call home (on speakerphone) each week.

Total Points to Begin the Day:

Points Awarded (1,000 point maximum)	Points Deducted (standard deduction of 100 points)
+ 500 (daily allowance)	
Total Awarded:	Total Deducted:

Total Points for the Day:

Level Two Daily Point Card

Goal for the Day:

To move to the next level, you will need to do the following:

- Complete the following assignments or their equivalents (Why Am I Here? Are Alcohol and Drugs Causing My Problems, Honesty, and Step 1), and discuss them in individual and group sessions.
- Participate in individual sessions with your primary counselor two times per week.
- Attend groups as scheduled, and participate without staff always telling you to do so.
- Be in control of your behaviors, such as no physically or verbally aggressive behaviors.
- Accept consequences and feedback from staff and peers, taking responsibility for your actions.
- Consistently follow unit rules.
- Understand addiction in terms of the disease concept, and apply it to your life.
- Begin using healthy coping skills (journaling, time outs, pushups, talking, etc.).
- Fulfill any additional criteria set for you by the clinical staff.

Possible privileges: At this level, you may . . .

- Earn up to 1,500 points per day.
- Go to the Point Store two times a week and get up to two food items, two drink items, and one other item.
- Attend off-campus activities at staff discretion.
- Use points to make two 10-minute or one 20-minute phone call home each week.
- Have approved free reading and drawing materials in room at noon self-time (they must be returned).
- Get a haircut with your own money.

Total Points to Begin the Day:

Points Awarded (1,500 point maximum)	Points Deducted (standard deduction of 300 points)
+ 1,000 (daily allowance)	
Total Awarded:	Total Deducted:

Total Points for the Day:

Level Three Daily Point Card

Goal for the Day:

To move to the next level, you will need to do the following:

- Complete Steps Two, Three, Four, and Five as assigned, in a complete and timely manner, and discuss them in individual and group sessions as assigned.
- Participate in individual sessions with your primary counselor two times per week.
- Attend groups as scheduled, and be an active participant on your own without staff having to ask.
- Accept consequences without talking back, fighting, or getting angry beyond control.
- Give honest and assertive feedback to peers.
- Behave in a manner consistent with what you say.
- Demonstrate willingness to help others, be an ally to others, and still work on self.
- Consistently use healthy coping skills (I feel statements, journaling, time-outs, etc.).
- Fulfill any additional criteria set by the clinical staff.
  Possible privileges: At this level, you may . . .
- Earn up to 2,000 points per day
- Go to the Point Store two times a week and get up to two food items, two drink items, and one other item.
- Attend all off-campus activities.
- Use points to make two 10-minute or one 20-minute phone call home each week.
- Watch television during community time (based on staff availability).
- Have approved free reading and drawing materials in room.
- Play a musical instrument or listen to music (approved by staff) in our serenity room for 30 minutes during noon self-time.
- Study at your desk in your room for the last hour of study time.
- Add an extended family member to call and visitor list (must be approved by staff).

Total Points to Begin the Day:

Points Awarded (2,000 point maximum)	Points Deducted (standard deduction of 500 points)
+ 1,500 (daily allowance)	
Total Awarded:	Total Deducted:

Total Points for the Day:

Level Four Daily Point Card

Goal for the Day:

To maintain this level, you will need to do the following:

- Complete Steps Two, Three, Four, and Five as assigned, in a complete and timely manner, and discuss them in individual and group sessions as assigned.
- Complete additional treatment plan assignments as given.
- Be open-minded to aftercare and discharge plans, including behavior contract.
- Participate in individual sessions with your primary counselor two times per week.
- Attend groups as scheduled, taking a leadership role, showing by example how groups are done well.
- Take your own time-outs, not being placed there by staff direction.
- Give honest and assertive feedback to peers, and help peers make positive choices.
- Be welcoming and positive to new peers, encouraging them to be positive about treatment.
- Demonstrate willingness to help others, be an ally to peers, and still work on self.
- Consistently use healthy coping skills (I feel statements, journaling, time-outs, etc.).
- Fulfill any additional criteria set by the clinical staff.
  Possible privileges: At this level, you may . . .
- Earn up to 2,500 points per day.
- Go to the Point Store three times a week and get up to two food items, two drink items, and one other item.
- Attend all off-campus activities.
- Use points to make two 10-minute or one 20-minute phone call home each week.
- Use points to eat a meal at a local restaurant with staff.
- Watch television during community time (based on staff availability).
- Have approved free reading and drawing materials in the room.
- Play a musical instrument or listen to music (approved by staff) in the serenity room for 30 minutes during noon self-time.
- Study at a desk in your room for the entire study time.
- Have supervised time on the computer—no e-mail or chatting.
- Be a peer leader, helping other peers learn rules and feel welcomed here.
- When possible, attend an outside AA or NA meeting with staff.
- Add a second extended family member to call and visitor list (must be approved by staff).
- Request other privileges that can be worked out with staff.

Total Points to Begin the Day:

Points Awarded (2,500 point maximum)	Points Deducted (standard deduction of 500 points)
+ 2,000 (daily allowance)	
Total Awarded:	Total Deducted:

Total Points for the Day:

Appendix 23

Peer Pressure

Robert R. Perkinson, PhD

You want your friends to accept you. Sure you do. That is normal. You want to be liked. You want to be loved and accepted by your peers. In treatment, it is important to learn about peer pressure, where it comes from, what is good about it, and what can be dangerous about it. There are things that you need to watch out for in recovery. If you are not careful, then the pressure of your peer group can get you back to drinking or using drugs. Your friends are not trying to hurt you. They just want their old friend back. These friends may have a chemical problem themselves. They may see your recovery as a threat to them.

How Peer Pressure Evolved

The roots of peer pressure evolved in the birds. Birds learned that they were safer if they gathered together in flocks. They could warn others of danger more easily if they stuck together. In a group, they were less likely to be singled out as prey. Birds learned how to stay together for safety. Because this worked so well, over thousands of years, birds developed a feeling of wanting to be together. They developed social skills used to keep together. They began to make social noises and movements to keep together. Anyone who has heard a flock of geese fly overhead will testify to the active communication patterns of these birds. Communications became more complicated over the years. The birds developed a particular sound for relaxation and a particular sound for danger. They developed the feeling of wanting to be together in groups. It felt better to be together. These feelings are what we now call emotions.

Higher ordered social activity continued to evolve in mammals. Baboons, for example, have very complicated social rituals. These animals groom each other to keep the troop together. The grooming serves to rid them of irritating insects, and it helps them to feel closer together. It is like a back scratch; it says, If you scratch my back, then I would scratch yours. These social rituals hold a group of animals together. When you go to the zoo, you will see animals rubbing and stroking each other. You will see mothers holding and licking their babies. As such, the species becomes bonded together. A touch says, I will help you carry the load.

Acceptance is a very important feeling because animals depend on acceptance by the group for survival. If they are rejected by the herd, then they have a higher chance of being killed by predators. All animals are safer if they are in a group.

As we move up the evolutionary scale, we finally get to humans. Early people, as we know them, were social creatures. They gathered together in groups or tribes for safety. A tribe could function better with people together. Tribe members could specialize and reap the benefits of other people's expertise. It was easier to hunt, fish, and gather food if the tribe members worked together. Some would do the hunting, and some would make tools. Each tribe member specialized in a particular function. It was very important for early people to be accepted by their tribes. If they were banished, then they would have to fend for themselves. Being alone in the world would put individuals at great risk. Humans developed a deep desire, a wish, or a need to be accepted. This was essential for survival.

The Importance of Peer Pressure

You are beginning to see why peer pressure is so important. If you are rejected by the group, you fear death. Without the acceptance of the group, people feel more vulnerable to the world. Now you can see why we try so hard to get our friends to like us. We need our friends so that we can survive.

It is very clear that being liked and being accepted by the group is important and good. It is important for all of us to learn the skills necessary to establish and maintain close interpersonal relationships. These are the skills that keep the group together.

There often are symbols or gestures that identify groups. Groups may have flags or jesters, or they may wear certain colors or uniforms. Group members all may ride a certain kind of motorcycle or wear a particular hat. Every group has a particular language that is unique to that group. Medical doctors do not use the same words as do auto mechanics.

How Peer Pressure Can Risk Your Sobriety

There are a few things about peer pressure that can get you into trouble. Groups can get you to do things that you would not normally do. They might talk you into doing something that you do not want to do—things such as stealing, drinking, and even playing a practical joke on someone. If we always follow the group, then we can be led into behavior that we know is wrong.

List five times when you were talked into doing something that you did not really want to do because of peer pressure.

1.

2.

3.

4.

5.

How the Group Uses Peer Pressure

The group will have a means of pressuring you into cooperating. In formal society, there are laws that govern group behavior. In most groups, members are subject to ridicule or even group expulsion if they do not cooperate. "Do not be chicken! What are you scared of?" There is any number of ways of encouraging individuals to do what the group wants them to do. In some gangs, it is blood in and blood out. This may mean you must kill or injure someone to join a gang, and the gang will hurt or kill you if you decide to leave.

List five ways your friends try to get you to cooperate with them.

1.

2.

3.

4.

5.

Today peers may use verbal, physical, or Internet bullying to control the behavior of others. This can be extremely painful, and surprisingly enough, the bully usually suffers the most. Bullies end up getting rejected by peers and failing in school and career achievement. They are avoided because people are afraid of them. Bullies harm others out of fear, and they tend to have good leadership skills that can be positively directed through treatment.

How to Cope With Peer Pressure

It is important to stay in the group, but it also is important for you to make your own decisions. If you do not make all of your decisions, then you will be held accountable for the decisions of others.

Here is a new concept for you to ponder in your heart.

The only thing that you owe anyone else is to be different.

You must be different from anyone that ever was or anyone that ever will be. You were created to be unique. The only way in which you can reach your full potential in life is to make all of your own decisions and be responsible for them. If you always follow a group, then you cannot be yourself. It is important for you to have the skill to say no. You need to be able to go against the group sometimes. If you are going to be responsible, then you have to make all of you own decisions and live with the consequences. That is the only way in which you can take your own direction. You must think about every choice you make. You cannot let other people make your decisions for you.

When you decide to do something that is different from what the group wants, the group will apply peer pressure. The group will try to get you to conform. The group members may threaten you or make fun of you. They may get angry with you. Remember that it is your responsibility to yourself, and to everyone else, to be different. Once you make a decision and you believe in it, you must be able to stick to it. If you cannot do this, then the group always will manipulate your choices and you will be their slave. You need to develop the skill of going your own way, even in the face of group opposition.

You do not have to have a good reason for not doing what the group wants. It can just be your choice. You do not have to explain yourself or your opinions to anybody. You do not need an excuse. You can simply say "because I want to." This is reason enough. Practice in skills group or with your counselor three times when the group or counselor is encouraging you to do one thing but you decide to do another. Discuss each role play and how you felt during the peer pressure and after you decided to stick to your own decision.

1.

2.

3.

You must keep the group informed about how you are feeling if it tries to pressure you. This holds the group members accountable for their behavior.

- If the group members are causing you to feel uncomfortable, then you must express this feeling. This will keep their behavior in line: "It makes me feel uncomfortable when you ask me to drink when you know that I am recovering from addiction."

- Honest statements usually will bring people under control. You must constantly keep people informed about how you are feeling and what you want from them: "I do not want any pot. I would prefer it if you would stop asking me."
- A simple no or no thank you is enough in most circumstances. Say no and stand your ground. You do not have to explain yourself further.
- If the group continues to coerce you even after you have said no, then you might have to leave the situation.
- If the group members do not respect your wishes, you do not want to be with those people anyway.
- Just excuse yourself and go home. You have not lost anything. If the group does not care for how you feel, then it is not the group for you.

People always can get you to feel a certain way if they try. They can get you to feel angry or guilty if they work at it, but even if they have some control over your feelings, they cannot control your actions. That is up to you. If they can get control over your actions by controlling your feelings, then you are their slave. They can get you to do anything. Group members often will try to lay guilt on you if you do not cooperate with them, but they cannot make you do anything with this guilt. You are in control of your actions.

Make a Plan to Say No

List 10 ways in which you are going to say no to alcohol and drugs.

1.

2.

3.

4.

5.

6.

7.

8.

9.

10.

Here are some important points to remember. The desire to be accepted by the group is normal and very powerful. The feeling of wanting to be accepted exists deep inside all of us, and this feeling helps us to gather together in groups for everyone's mutual gain. Being a part of a group feels good, but our primary responsibility to ourselves and to everyone else is to be different—to be one of a kind. Therefore, it is crucially important that you take your own direction, make all of your own decisions, and be yourself.

Appendix 24

The Behavioral Contract

Robert R. Perkinson, PhD

Behavioral contracting has been found to be a powerful means of directly influencing behavior (Stuart, 1971). Developing a behavioral contract and living within its limits will create a stable family situation for you and your child. Behavior is defined as any movement. When anyone acts or speaks, it is behavior. Counselors often are asked by frustrated parents, Why doesn't my child cooperate? The answer to this question is simple: No behavior exists, nor does it continue to exist, without reward. Children get good things for their behavior. They might get more freedom by arguing than they do by behaving in a more sociable manner. Many children have been reinforced for antisocial behavior. Parents do not mean to do this. It seems to happen on its own. Psychological laws are at play in all learning.

Reward and Punishment

A reward is anything that increases the frequency of a behavior. Behavior is reinforced when it gets children something they want or removes something they do not want. A reward might be money, praise, or free time. You cannot always tell what is reinforcing to children. You have to watch the behavior to determine this. If the behavior increases, then you can assume that what you have done is reinforcing. To most children, a hug is reinforcing. To some children, it is not reinforcing and might even be punitive.

A punishment decreases the frequency of a behavior. You can punish children by giving them something they do not want or taking away something they do want. You can verbally reprimand them, send them to their room, or take away their use of the family car. Again, you have to watch the behavior to see what a punishment is. If the behavior decreases, then you can assume that you have punished it. The problem with punishment is that you cannot teach children anything new and that you get the children's minds off what they did and onto what you are doing to them. If you want to change children, reinforcement is much more powerful.

Habits

If children are reinforced for a behavior over a period of time, then the behavior will get to be a habit. It will develop a life of its own. This behavior will not go away easily. It will stick like glue. It will take time for new behavior to replace it. In behavioral contracting, you teach children new behavior by carefully scheduling when they are reinforced. You want to think before you act. Give the children good things when they are acting the way in which you want them to act. This means that your behavior must change as well as theirs.

The family is a powerful force in teaching children new behavior. All children want to be loved, and you can use this desire to develop the behavior you want. A behavioral contract is a means by which you control the exchange of positive reinforcement. The contract specifies who is going to do what, for whom, and under what circumstances. The contract makes explicit the expectations of each party. It gives the parent and the child the opportunity to get the things they want. It clarifies the benefits of cooperation by making each person's role in the family clear. The contract makes it more likely that each person will live up to his or her responsibilities. This leads to family harmony and stability.

Love

Love is the active involvement in someone's individual growth. To love, you must be actively involved in your children reaching their full potential. Rewards must be earned. They should not be given randomly. If you give your children good things just because they exist, then you give them no direction and you do not teach them what works in life. They will think that the world owes them things. This is not fair to the children, and it is not an accurate view of the world.

Each member in a family has rights and duties to each other, and rewards must be exchanged equally. Many times, parents feel that they are doing all of the giving and the children are doing all of the taking. This is a mistake. Happiness comes from giving to others. If parents do not teach their children to give, then the children will not be happy.

In a healthy family, if you give something, then you get something in return. The more you give, the more you get. Each member of a family should want to give all that he or she can. In the behavioral contract, if children act responsible, they earn specific rewards. Some examples of rewards include free time, time with friends, television time, spending money, and use of the family car. Each child will have a different set of rewards, and the child should actively ask for what he or she wants.

How to Develop a Behavioral Contract

The behavioral contract details the behavior necessary for earning each reward. Let us say that you are having problems with your child coming home from school on time. For a variety of reasons, the child is late and you worry about him or her. You decide to put this behavior into the behavioral contract. If the child gets home from school every day on time, then he or she earns a certain amount of television time. If the child misses coming home, then he or she does not earn that privilege. Behaviors of interest might include minimum school attendance and performance, curfew hours, and completion of household chores. The responsibilities required must be monitored. You must be able to see whether the behavior is occurring. It would be useless for you to forbid your child from seeing a person at school because you could not monitor the behavior. If you want your child to be at school on time and to cooperate with school authorities, then you can have the teacher keep track for you. You could check with the teacher each week to be sure of compliance. You could send a school performance chart with your child to give to the teacher each day. It might look something like this:

The School Performance Chart

Name of Student   Date

To keep my parents informed about my school progress, I am asking all of my teachers to complete this form at the end of each class period. Thank you.

Subject:

Teachers, please place a check mark beside each point in the contract to indicate yes or no.

1. Student was on time for class	Yes	No
2. Student completed homework assignment (mark only if applicable)	Yes	No
3. Student obeyed class rules	Yes	No
4. Student was attentive to task	Yes	No
5. Student was cooperative with teacher	Yes	No

You must be sure that you are giving your child enough rewards to keep him or her cooperating with the contract. If the child believes that the contract is not good for him or her, then the child will resist the whole idea. All parties in the contract must have a full say about what they want, and everyone must be willing to compromise. All parties must agree to the contract and sign it. You must include the consequences that will occur if the child does not comply with the terms of the contract.

Get together with your child and come up with 10 ways to reinforce him or her.

1.

2.

3.

4.

5.

6.

7.

8.

9.

10.

Make sure that you verbally reinforce your child as he or she complies. We are striving for progress, not perfection. Statements such as "Good job! You are doing great! I am proud of you!" go a long way toward getting your child to cooperate cheerfully.

Detailing What Each Party Wants

The first thing you need to do is determine what all parties want from the family. The child might want to go out on weekend nights and stay out until 11:00 pm. The child might want to use the family car. The child might want to go out without explaining where he or she is going. The child might want a new bike. The child might want to choose his or her own clothes or hairstyle without your input. Brainstorm with your child about what he or she wants from you. Then decide what you want from your child. You might want the child to improve in school. You might want the child to come home on time. You might want the child to keep you informed about where he or she is. You might want the child to help out with the household chores.

Write down all of these things. With the counselor, work out what each person is willing to give to get what he or she wants from each other. It is important that each person get the reasonable things that they want from the contract. All parties mutually exchange things that they want from each other. The contract might look something like this.

A Sample Contract

Privilege	Responsibility
In exchange for the privilege of going out one weekend night of the week at 7:00 pm and coming home by 11:00 pm . . .	Robert agrees to maintain a weekly B average in school.
In exchange for going out one weeknight at 7:00 pm and returning by 10:00 pm . . .	Robert agrees to wash the family car once a week.
In exchange for the privilege of using the family car once a week . . .	Robert agrees to wash the dishes at dinner and take out the garbage.
In exchange for the privilege of having Robert cut the grass . . .	Mr. and Mrs. Jones agree to pay him $5 each week.
Consequence	
If Robert is 1 to 10 minutes late coming home . . .	Robert agrees to come home 30 minutes earlier the next time he goes out.
If Robert is 10 to 30 minutes late coming home . . .	Robert will lose the privilege of going out one weekend night.

In this contract, the parents will need to keep a written record of when Robert comes home, and Robert will have to provide the parents with a school performance chart each day.

The contract can include anything you want so long as everyone agrees to it. Let the primary counselor help you. If you have any problems with the contract, then you can discuss the issues in the continuing care group.

Appendix 25

Family Questionnaire

Robert R. Perkinson, PhD

Your name   *Date*

Client name   *Relationship*

Address

Home phone

Work phone

Best time for you to be contacted by the family program counselor

Addiction affects everyone it touches. Chemically dependent persons and everyone close to them are adversely affected. No one wants a loved one to be sick, so the family members pretend that the disease is not there. The average chemically dependent person has been ill for years before the family finally realizes that there is a problem. After the problem has been identified, there are even more years before the average chemically dependent person receives treatment.

The person you care for is in treatment. That is great! You can relax and know that this person is safe. This person stands at the turning point, and there is an excellent chance that he or she will achieve a stable sobriety. The person might have further problems, but this is a major step in the right direction. You have done the right thing, and you can feel good about it.

The client might not feel good about coming to treatment right now. The client might feel angry or rejected. The client might still believe that he or she does not have a problem. This is denial. It is very common, and it is one of the best signs that the disease is present. Addiction demands that these people lie to themselves. They are fooled into believing that they are okay even when their lives are falling apart.

It is important for you to understand that it is not only the chemically dependent person who is having problems. If you have lived close to a chemically dependent person, then you are having problems, too. All of these problems have, at their source, subtle distortions of reality. Family members change reality into something that does not make them so nervous. Trying to keep the reality of addiction hidden is like hiding an elephant in your living room. The problem is there, and it is big. It takes large distortions of reality to keep it hidden. The family tries to pretend that there is not a problem. As the problem gets bigger, it takes distortions of reality to keep it secret.

The distorting begins with minimizing. Family members pretend that the problem is not so bad. They believe that other people have more problems than they do. They think that the drinking is not that bad. It could be worse. They minimize to the point where they cannot see the real effect of the illness on themselves and on the other family members. The problem is big. They focus on the chemically dependent person and they become cut off from their own feelings. They have no time for themselves. This sinks the family deeper into an unreal world.

The next lie that families tell themselves is that there is a good excuse for the problem. This is called rationalization. It is not the drugs. It is the job, the boss, or maybe even me. The family members, even the children, may feel responsible for the chemically dependent person's drinking or drug use. They blame themselves, other people, institutions, and money—whatever it takes to take their minds off the real problem. The family actually believes that it is these other things that are the problem. It is not the chemicals.

The last distortion of reality is called denial. This is where the family members do not experience the full impact of their lives. They have developed such a tolerance for the craziness that they think it is normal. Their lives may be coming apart, but they still think that things are under control.

Now is the time for the client to get honest with himself or herself. Do not make things seem smaller than they were. Do not make excuses. Write down exactly what happened.

Why did the client decide to seek treatment at this time?

What mood altering chemicals does the client currently use? Mark all that apply.

Chemical	Amount Used per Day
Alcohol	
Tranquilizers	
"Sleeping pills"	
Marijuana (pot)	
Cocaine	
Amphetamines (speed)	
Pain medications	
Hallucinogens (LSD)	
Inhalants (e.g., gas, paint, glue)	
Over-the-counter medications	
Narcotics	
What is the pattern of use?	
Continuous (daily)	
Periodic (fairly regular pattern)	
Sporadic (off and on with no pattern)	
What is the problem as you see it?	
Alcohol	
Illegal/Street drugs	
Prescription drugs	
Combination of alcohol and drugs	
Emotional problems	

Chemical	Amount Used per Day
Family problems	
What is the problem as the client sees it?	
Alcohol	
Prescription drugs	
Illegal/street drugs	
Combination of alcohol and drugs	
Emotional problems	
Family problems	

What is the client's awareness of the problem?

No awareness: "I do not have a problem. It is no worse than anyone else."

Minimal awareness: "Sure I have had a problem, but I can take it or leave it."

Moderate awareness: "I have a problem, but I can handle it on my own."

Admits to a problem and accepts the responsibility for change.

What is the duration of the problem?

0 to 6 months

6 months to 1 year

1 to 2 years

2 to 5 years

More than 5 years (specify number of years:)

What is the longest period of abstinence?

Days

Weeks

A month at a time

6 to 12 months at a time

When the client was abstinent, what was the reason why he or she stopped using?

Which of the following symptoms of dependency apply to the client?

Blackouts (cannot remember what he or she did while drinking)

Hides or protects supply of drugs or alcohol

Cannot stop once he or she starts

Makes excuses for using alcohol or drugs

Has a physical problem associated with use (e.g., tremors, nausea, headache)

Personality changes while using

Other (explain):

Which of the following behaviors has the client demonstrated?

Violent, aggressive, or abusive behavior

Unreasonable resentments (e.g., holds grudges)

Changing type of friends (e.g., changing to friends who use)

Poor school or work performance

Unable to join in family activities

Unable to do things that he or she should do (e.g., unable to keep appointments or to get things done at home or at work)

How does the client obtain money to buy alcohol or other drugs?
How much do you think the client spends on alcohol or other drugs? Has this created a problem for you, your family, or the client?
How has the chemical use changed family activities?
What does the client think about Alcoholics Anonymous (AA)/Narcotics Anonymous (NA)?

Critical of AA/NA members

"Good program, but it is not for me"

AA/NA is the answer to the problem

Has no knowledge of AA/NA

Previous treatment: Has the client participated in any of the following treatments for addiction?

Attended a few AA/NA meetings

Participated regularly for a brief period

General hospital

Psychiatric treatment

Outpatient treatment

Inpatient treatment

Give a brief history of treatment dates.
Are there any other problems in connection with or related to the chemical problem?

Not to my knowledge

School problems

Work problems

Legal problems

Financial problems

Family problems

Psychiatric problems

Explain:

Have you or other family members experienced any of the following?

Health problems

School/work problems

Legal problems

Financial problems

Difficulty in expressing feelings

Explain:

What treatment have you sought for yourself and your family?

AA/NA

Al-Anon/Alateen

Counseling

Psychiatric visits

Explain:

Have any of your children been referred to the following?

Social services

Juvenile detention center

Court services

Psychological services

Addiction treatment

Explain:

Can you see anything that might interfere with the evaluation or treatment of your family member(s)?
What do you believe are the problem areas that need to be addressed while the client is in treatment?
In addition to the questions that have already been covered, is there any other information that we
should know about the client?
Which types of abuse have occurred in your current family?

Emotional

Verbal

Physical

Sexual

Explain:

Did any of the following types of abuse occur in the family where you were growing up?

Emotional

Verbal

Physical

Sexual

Explain:

Do you believe that addiction is a disease?

Yes   No

Explain how the chemical problem has affected your relationship with the client.

Write down the names of all members of your family and rate them on how they use mood-altering chemicals.

No Use = 0; Infrequent Use = 2; Social Use = 3; Misuse/Abuse = 4; Dependency = 5

Family Member	Chemical Used	Rating
Yourself		
Present spouse		
Former spouse		
Children		
Your father		
Your mother		
Your brothers and sisters		
Other family members		

Appendix 26

Codependency

Robert R. Perkinson, PhD

Codependency is what happens to someone who is trying to control someone who is addicted. If your loved one is an addict, then you probably have tried to help him or her. You have attempted to fix the problem. But you could not fix it any more than you could fix your loved one if he or she had cancer. Addiction is a disease for which no one is to blame. The causes of addiction are so varied and complex that no one has been able to figure it all out. It is too complicated.

In your love for the client, you might have done some things that were not good for you. It is very common for codependent persons to take better care of addict than they do of themselves. You may have been so concentrated on the other person's problems that you had no time for your own. This is a mistake. This is your turn to stop and concentrate on yourself. What has happened to you in your struggle against this disease? Our experience shows us that the family member who looks at his or her own life will immeasurably help the client to achieve a stable recovery. If only the client is treated, then the chance of success is reduced.

There are variety of codependent traits. These are maladaptive thoughts and behaviors that have been learned in response to the addiction. It is important that you take a look at each of these traits because they inhibit you from being able to live a normal life. You cannot solve problems accurately when these traits are at work. They distract you. They keep you from seeing the truth.

Defense Mechanisms

Defense mechanisms are mental states where we refuse to see reality. We cut ourselves off from reality because the real world is too painful for us. We need to live in a fantasy world of our own creation. The more · we use defense mechanisms, the more cut off from reality we are. We feel lonely and helpless because no one can reach us in our self-deceived world.

Minimization

It begins with minimization. When we minimize, we take reality and make it smaller than it really is. We pretend that the problem is not bad when it is bad. We may have become so deluded that we think that drinking a six pack of beer every night is normal. Doesn't everyone drink like this? We may minimize about the financial problems. They do not seem so bad either. Doesn't everyone struggle like this? We minimize about verbal and physical abuse. This person was just mad, out of control, or drunk. That was not really him or her. This person is not really like that. We may minimize by telling ourselves that the addicted person just overdid it at the party. This individual is really a good person. He or she did not mean it. When we minimize, we tell ourselves that we have no reason to feel afraid or angry. If the problem were bad, then we would have to feel bad and do something about it. It is not so bad, so we can relax.

List five times when you told yourself that things were not bad when they really were.

1.

2.

3.

4.

5.

Rationalization

The next defense mechanism we use is rationalization. This is where we make an excuse for the client. The client is addicted because he or she has had a hard life, had a fight with his or her mother, had a bad childhood, was fired, has financial problems, has problems with a sibling, or just is not understood. Codependents can think of a million reasons why the person is acting strangely, but the real reason is that the person is an addict. The person is sick and needs help. We do not want to see this truth because it is frightening. We do not want to believe that our loved one is ill. We want to believe that this person is just fine or is only having temporary difficulty.

A rationalization is a lie. It is an excuse for the real problem. Did you ever make an excuse for the chemically dependent person? Did you ever tell the boss that this person was sick or tell the children that the person was not feeling well when you knew that he or she was intoxicated or too hung over to function? If you did, you may have believed some of this yourself.

List five times when you made an excuse for the client's addictive behavior.

1.

2.

3.

4.

5.

You can see what is happening to the family. By minimizing and rationalizing, family members get more and more cut off from reality. They cannot accurately see what is going on anymore. They are using the defense mechanisms to cut themselves off from the painful truth.

Denial

The most characteristic form of defense used in addiction is denial. This is where the mind refuses to experience the full emotional impact of what is happening. Your life is falling apart. Your relationship is shot. You cannot talk to your family anymore. You are in severe financial trouble, and you still think that you can fix these things. You still think that all of these problems are something else other than addiction. You might even be so fooled that you think that the problems are your fault. If you were a better wife, husband, child, or parent, then the addict would not be having problems.

List five of the worst things that have happened during the past few years with the addicted person.

1.

2.

3.

4.

5.

In each of these situations, what were you telling yourself that convinced you that things were all right?

1.

2.

3.

4.

5.

Caretaking

Codependent people focus on the other person. They are obsessed with taking care of the addicted person to the point where they lose contact with reality. They actually think that everything will be all right if they do the right things. They plan everything for everyone. They scold and control. They read self-help books. They feel responsible for everyone's feelings. They go to extraordinary lengths to help. They feel much drained, as if there is not enough time in the day. They threaten, cry, lie, scream, blame, and shame. They seek counseling, pray, and manipulate. All of these behaviors, and many more, are designed to bring control to an out-of-control situation. Codependent people think that they can fix things if they just work hard enough. The fact of the matter is that they cannot control someone else's behavior, no matter how much they try. The more they try, the more frustrating it becomes.

List five ways in which you tried to control the addicted person.

1.

2.

3.

4.

5.

Enabling

In treatment, you must understand that you cannot control anyone but yourself. You are responsible for only your own actions. If you keep the addicted person out of trouble, then you keep that person from suffering the natural consequences of his or her behavior. If you call the boss and make excuses, then the client does not learn from his or her mistakes. This is called enabling. By protecting the client from the consequences of his or her addiction, you help the client stay sick. You must stop protecting the client from his or her maladaptive behavior. You must not pay the client's bad checks or debts, make excuses, or smooth over ruffled feathers. You must let the client be responsible.

By caretaking and enabling, codependent people constantly get the chemically dependent person out of trouble. They protect the client from the consequences of his or her actions. They may call the boss and say that the client is sick when, if fact, the client is too intoxicated, hungover, or busy gambling to come to work. They may tell the children that their dad or mom needs to rest when, in fact, the client has passed out on the couch. They may pay the bail or the bad checks. They may call the creditors who are clamoring for payment. They may comfort abused family members and try to make everything better.

List five times when you got the addicted person out of trouble.

1.

2.

3.

4.

5.

You were taking the responsibility for someone else's behavior. By protecting the client from the logical consequences of his or her own actions, you helped the client avoid the pain of the disease. This prevented the client from learning that he or she was sick and needed help. You enabled the illness to stay hidden. You helped the client to avoid reality. By protecting the client from pain, you prevented him or her from seeing the severity of the problem. This has to stop. Each person in a family has to accept the responsibility for his or her own behavior. Everyone must make his or her own decisions and live with the consequences.

Inability to Know Feelings

People who are codependent do not know how they feel. They are so focused on the other person's feelings that they ignore their own. They know how the other person is doing, but they do not know much about themselves. For the most part, codependent people think that they are fine, but what they are really feeling is frustrated, frightened, and depressed. They are desperately trying to bring order to disorder and confusion.

People who live in an addicted home do not trust how they feel. They feel as though something is wrong with them. They try to block out the reality of the nightmare that they are living. They might even make up what their family is like. Bradshaw (1988, 1990) described this as a fantasy bond. Children or family members create an idealized family in their minds. They might feel that their father is warm when, in fact, he is actually abusive. They might feel their mother is a good mother when, in fact, she always is away drinking at the bar.

In addicted homes, family members learn that feelings are dangerous. If they share how they feel, then bad things will happen. They keep their fear, sadness, anger, disgust, and hurt to themselves. They keep the secrets, sharing them with no one.

List some situations where you kept your real feelings to yourself. Whom were you trying to protect by keeping these feelings secret?

1.

2.

3.

4.

5.

Inability to Know What You Want

Codependent people are so obsessed with the wants and wishes of the addicted person that they lose what they want for themselves. They become experts at manipulating the family to get the sick person what he or she wants, but they become less and less skilled at getting what they themselves want. They believe that they have no wants. They are trying so desperately to control the situation that they have no time for their own needs.

Stop and think for a minute. What do you want out of life? List five things that you want.

1.

2.

3.

4.

5.

Now write a letter to the chemically dependent person telling him or her how you feel and share what you want. Be thorough. Do not leave out any of your feelings, wishes, hopes, dreams, or wants. Be completely honest with yourself and the other person. When you have the letter written, put it aside. We will use it later.

Lack of Trust

Family members from an addicted home have been living in a situation where they could not trust anything or anyone. They did not know what was going to happen. Family rules changed when the addicted person was using addictive behavior. A father who was once loving could turn into a monster. A mother who was quiet could turn loud, aggressive, and pushy. Someone who usually was happy could sob hopelessly. There was nothing that the family could trust. Addiction could change any rule at any time. This is an atmosphere permeated by fear. The family members live in a constant state of tension. When they come home, they do not know what to expect. When the car drives up in the driveway, they do not know what is going to happen. Things can get out of control in a hurry, and the behaviors can be life threatening. The addicted person and the people around that person constantly lie about what the addicted person is doing. They hide how much the addicted person is behaving. They lie about what the addicted person is doing. No one in the home can be trusted. No one knows the truth.

This lack of trust builds an atmosphere heavy with fear. The family members are constantly worried about what is going to happen next. What makes this even worse is that they try to hide the family secret from everyone. This increases their feelings of isolation and helplessness.

List five things that happened in your family that convinced you that you could not trust your family members.

1.

2.

3.

4.

5.

People Pleasing

Codependent people are people pleasers. They will do virtually anything to keep everyone happy. They feel personally responsible for other people's feelings. People pleasers never are interested in what they themselves want. They are interested in what the other person wants. They want to keep the other person happy. They do not care about how they themselves feel. People pleasers will go to incredible lengths to keep the other person feeling comfortable. They tell people that they are feeling fine when, in fact, they are coming apart at the seams. They have a smile for everybody. They are nice, nice, and nice. They rarely, if ever, go against the flow of things. They are almost incapable of saying no. If they say no, then they feel guilty. They will allow people to violate their boundaries. They never rock the boat.

List five times when you did something you did not want to do just to please some other person.

1.

2.

3.

4.

5.

Feelings of Worthlessness

Codependent persons feel worthless compared to other people. They do not feel as though they deserve the good stuff. They have been treated so badly, been taken advantage of so many times, and given of themselves without getting anything back so often that they have given up. They are tired. They feel burdened. It is like carrying the world around on their shoulders. Somewhere, deep down in a secret part of their minds, they fear that they deserve to be treated poorly. They feel like they are small persons of little worth. They feel like they do not matter. They are not important. These codependent people think that they are stupid, unattractive, inadequate, and incompetent. They do not feel capable of dealing with the world. They feel vulnerable, lost, and alone.

When you look at yourself in the mirror, what do you see? Circle all that apply.

1. I am stupid.

2. I am ugly.

3. I am old.

4. Other people are smarter than I am.

5. I never get the breaks.

6. I hate myself.

7. No one loves me.

8. No one knows me.

9. God made a mistake when God made me.

10. I am inadequate.

We could go on with the negative self-statements, but you get the idea. Codependent people constantly bombard themselves with negative self-talk. The talk is inaccurate and extremely self-damaging. If you use any of the preceding statements, you must feel terrible about yourself.

Treatment is a time to get accurate. You must learn to live in the real world and to see the positive as well as the negative. List 10 positive things about yourself. If you have difficulty, then ask your counselor or group to help you.

1.

2.

3.

4.

5.

6.

7.

8.

9.

10.

Write these down on a piece of paper, and tape it to your mirror. Read them to yourself at least once a day.

Dependent

Codependent persons are overly dependent. They feel incapable of making good decisions. They do not trust themselves. They get their self-worth from someone else. They may coerce and threaten to leave an addicted significant other, but the thought of leaving fills them with panic. They feel overly vulnerable to the world and everything in it. They do not feel as though they can do things on their own. Even if a spouse is incapacitated from the disease, a codependent person can still feel dependent on the spouse. "What would I do on my own? What would happen to the children? How would I support myself?" These all are serious questions, and it leaves codependent persons stuck in an intolerable situation. They cannot stay, and they cannot leave. Dependency is fueled by deep-seated feelings of inadequacy and shame. Codependent persons do not feel capable of doing anything other than holding on.

Do you feel competent to handle life on your own? Yes _____ No _____

Poor Communication Skills

Codependent people have poor communication skills. They cannot ask for what they want or share how they feel. This leaves them incapable of communicating effectively. They are so concerned with how the other person feels and with what the other person wants that they do not even think about their own needs. Closeness in interpersonal relationships depends on the ability to share the whole truth with someone. You have to be able to tell that person how you feel and ask him or her for what you want. To be a good communicator, you have to be a good listener. You have to probe and question the other person to bring out the whole truth. Codependents do not want to know the truth. The truth is too painful. They are busy keeping the truth from themselves and from everyone else. If they knew the whole truth, then they would be terrified.

Codependents feel lonely because they feel as though no one knows them. They feel as though no one understands them. They try to communicate but feel as though the message never really gets across. They feel isolated and trapped.

When is the last time you felt really understood by anybody? Describe the time, person, and what it meant to you.

Do you believe that the client understands you? Yes _____ No _____

Explain in detail your answer:
List five roadblocks in the way of your communicating openly with others.

1.

2.

3.

4.

5.

The Tools of Recovery

In treatment, you will learn the tools of recovery. The first of these tools is honesty. Without rigorous honesty, this program will not work for you. You must tell the truth all of the time. You will need to hold family members accountable by constantly sharing your feelings. This takes practice. In treatment, you must accept your powerlessness over the disease. If you still think that you can figure it out or work it out, then you are still acting codependent.

Alcoholics Anonymous (AA) says that probably no human power can remove this disease. The second tool of recovery is going to meetings. You must attend regular Al-Anon meetings to continue your recovery. If you think that it is only the chemically dependent person who needs to attend meetings, then you are off track. You have problems, too. You need treatment to get back on track. Al-Anon groups will give you the support, encouragement, and education that you need for continued recovery.

The third tool of recovery is a Higher Power. You must turn the problem over to a power greater than yourself. If you continue to try to handle the problem by yourself, then you will fail. If you turn the problem over to God, then you will succeed. Practice whenever you are faced with a problem. Stop and seek God's will in that matter. Do not try to figure it out for yourself. Ask for God's guidance.

The fourth tool of recovery is using good interpersonal relationship skills. This means that you have to share how you feel and ask for what you want. You have to listen and take the time that is necessary to develop healthy communication skills. This will not come easily. You have many habits to overcome. You no longer can just do what the other person wants. You no longer can live to please the other person in your life. You must accept the responsibility for your own behavior and allow the other person to accept the responsibility for his or her own behavior. You must allow the person to suffer the consequences for his or her actions. You have to stop living for the other person and start living for yourself.

Many of you are thinking, How selfish! You were taught to let the other person come first. You were taught that it is not right to ask for what you wanted. You have to love yourself to be happy. If you leave yourself out, then you will suffer. God says to love God all you can, love yourself all you can, and love others all you can. That is all that we are asking you to do. Bring this exercise and the letter to your family member to the family program.

Appendix 27

Personal Recovery Plan

Robert R. Perkinson, PhD

Name: *Home phone:*

Admission date: *Work phone:*

Discharge date: *Phone:*

Name of significant other:

I t is important to your recovery to continue to work through your problems on discharge. Your recovery never can stand still. You must be constantly moving forward in your program. Working with your counselor, you must detail exactly what you need to do following inpatient treatment. Each psychological problem or family problem will need a specific plan of action. You must commit yourself to following this recovery plan to the letter. Do not think that just because you have completed treatment, your problems are over. Your recovery is just beginning, and you need to work diligently to stay clean and sober.

Make a list of the problems that you need to address in continuing care. Any emotional, family, legal, social, physical, leisure, work, spiritual, or school problem will have to have a plan. How are you going to address that problem in recovery? What is the goal? What do you want to achieve? Develop your personal recovery plan with your counselor's assistance.

A. Treatment plan for continued sobriety

   1. Problem 1:

      Goal:

      Plan:

   2. Problem 2:

      Goal:

      Plan:

   3. Problem 3:

      Goal:

      Plan:

4. Problem 4:

    Goal:

    Plan:

5. Problem 5:

    Goal:

    Plan:

B. Relapse

In the event of a relapse, list five steps that you will take to deal with the problem.

1.

2.

3.

4.

5.

C. Support in recovery

Indicate the 12-step meetings that you will attend each week after discharge. We recommend that you attend 90 meetings in 90 days at first and at least three to five meetings per week for the remainder of that year, and then you can attend once a week for at least the next 5 years.

Day:

Time:

Location:

D. Indicate when you will attend continuing care group.

Day:

Time:

Location:

E. Who are three 12-step contact persons who can provide you with support in early recovery?

Name: Phone:

Name: Phone:

Name: Phone:

F. If you have any problems or concerns in sobriety, you always can call the treatment center staff at the following number:

Counselor:

Phone:

G. If you and your counselor have arranged for further counseling or treatment following discharge, then complete the following:

Name of agency:

Address: Phone:

First appointment:

Day:

Time:

H. List 10 things that you are going to do daily to stay clean and sober.

   1.

   2.

   3.

   4.

   5.

   6.

   7.

   8.

   9.

  10.

I. You are changing your lifestyle. It will be important to avoid certain people and situations that will put you at high risk. List 10 people and places you need to avoid in early recovery.

   1.

   2.

   3.

   4.

   5.

   6.

   7.

   8.

   9.

  10.

You will need a series of advocates that know your story and commitment to stay clean and sober. You sign a release with each of these people so they can talk to each other about your recovery. It helps to have someone at home, work, school, and community. List their names and numbers, contact them, and ask them to be an advocate for you in your community.

- Home advocate: person phone address
- School advocate: person phone address

- Work advocate: name   phone   address
- Community advocate: name   phone   address
- Case manager: name   phone   address

You will call the case manager every day to see if this is a day for you to come in for drug testing. You will get up to three drug tests per week for the first 6 months and up to one drug test for the next 5 years. You will send in a monthly log of 12-step meetings to your case manager by the 10th of each month. Each meeting has to be dated and signed by the meeting leader. The case manager will receive reports from all of the treatment that was recommended by the treatment center, such as anger management, marriage counseling, etc. You will sign a contract with the case manager that gives consequences if you do not follow the continuing care program. This will mean the manager will contact your boss, probation officer, family members, licensing board, or another person or agency that is dedicated to your successful treatment.

Statement of Commitment

I understand that the success of my recovery depends on adherence to my recovery plan. The continuing care program has been explained to me, and I understand fully what I must do in recovery. I commit to myself that I will follow this plan.

With your continuing care manager write out your continuing care plan and then have all mentors/sponsors/ coaches and advocates sign it.

Client's signature:

Physician signature:

Sponsor signature:

Employer signature:

Significant other signature:

Licensing board signature:

Community advocate signature:

School advocate signature:

Case manager signature:

Counselor signature:

Date:

Appendix 28

Sample Discharge Summary

IDENTIFYING INFORMATION: Mary Louise Roberts is a 45-year-old, married white female. She has two children. She lives in Thomas, Maryland, with her husband, Mark, and her two daughters. She has lived in Thomas for the past 5 years. She is currently employed as a secretary for Morton Electronics. She was admitted to Keystone Treatment Center on 9-9-01. She was referred by Marcie Frankle, a counselor at the Mandel Mental Health Clinic.

CHIEF COMPLAINT: "Drinking."

ASSESSMENT OF PROBLEM AREAS: The following problems were identified by the clinical staff as needing to be addressed in treatment.

Problem 1: Pathological relationship to alcohol

Problem 2: Depression

Problem 3: Poor interpersonal relationship skills

Problem 4: Unresolved grief

Problem 5: Borderline personality disorder

The following problems were identified and treated by the medical staff.

Problem 2: Depression

Problem 6: Fractured finger

MEDICAL REPORT (this report is completed by the medical staff): Mary's admission lab work and urinalysis were within normal limits. An admission physical was completed with no significant findings noted. While in treatment, Mary hit a door with her right hand. An X-ray was taken on 9-15-01, and it found evidence of a transverse hairline fracture on the radial side of the distal neck of the right fifth metacarpal. No specific treatment was needed. At discharge, Mary voiced no physical complaints. Her hand was observed to be healing. In treatment, the client received a daily multivitamin. We have recommended that the client continue her multivitamin therapy for at least 6 months following discharge.

Problem 2: Depression

Progress notes: For her major depression, Mary was started on Prozac (20 mg q.d.) on 9-22-01. No side effects were noted. The medication was reviewed with the client prior to discharge, and a 1-week supply of

Prozac was sent home with her. We have recommended that the client continue to take the medication daily and to see Dr. Frank Smith of the Mandel Mental Health Clinic in Thomas, Maryland. She has an appointment on 10-5-01 at 3:45 pm for a follow-up visit.

TREATMENT PLAN AND PROGRESS NOTES:

Goal 1: Begin a program of recovery congruent to a sober lifestyle.

Progress notes: When Mary first entered treatment, she minimized her drinking behavior and denied the need to be in treatment. She stated that she did not have a problem with alcohol that was severe enough to require treatment. She completed the Honesty exercise (see Appendix 8), and she began to see how she was deceiving herself about the extent of her alcohol problem. She was able to trace the family problems that were a direct cause of her drinking behavior. The client was able to see that the DWI she received last year was directly related to her drinking. In her first step, Mary was able to share her powerlessness to quit drinking on her own and the unmanageability of her life. Mary began to accept her alcoholism during the second week of treatment. She recognized that she would have to change her attitudes and behaviors if she was going to be able to maintain a sober lifestyle. A major obstacle to Mary's treatment was her lack of trust. It was difficult for her to trust her interpersonal group for the first few weeks of treatment. As Mary was able to share more in group, she was able to see that the group could be trusted. This was a great relief to the client, and this was a significant move forward in her treatment program. Mary struggled with the same trust issue when she worked through her Second Step and Third Step. She began to practice prayer and meditation in treatment, and this convinced her that there was a Higher Power called God. She completed a Fifth Step with the staff clergy, and this significantly relieved her. She stated that this was the first time that she had ever told anyone the whole truth. Mary was able to assess high-risk situations for relapse by working through the Relapse Prevention exercise (see Appendix 16). Her situation of greatest risk appears to be her tendency to become depressed, and this leads her to further drinking. The client has committed herself to call this treatment center, her sponsor, or her therapist if she begins to feel depressed in continuing care. Mary does state a sincere desire to maintain a sober lifestyle and to live a happy life without alcohol.

Goal 2: Alleviate symptoms of depression.

Progress notes: Mary stated on admission that she had been feeling severely depressed for the past 6 months. She had experienced suicidal ideation and had made two suicide attempts before coming into treatment. While in treatment, she visited with the staff psychologist and took the Hamilton Depression Rating Scale weekly. She read *Coping With Depression* (Beck & Greenberg, 1974) and logged her dysfunctional thoughts. The client's negative thinking centered on thinking that she was ugly, stupid, and inadequate. Once these thoughts were challenged for accuracy, the client could see that she was pretty; bright; and a capable wife, mother, and secretary. The client was placed on medication for her depression. Mary is aware that she has to stay on this medication for at least 6 months. Two weeks after starting the medication and working on correcting her thinking her Hamilton Depression Rating Scale scores began to improve. Her score dropped from severe depression to mild depression over her 4 weeks of treatment. Mary still shows some excessive sadness, and she continues to feel overly tired and fatigued. She is sleeping through the night.

Goal 3: Learn and practice healthy interpersonal relationship skills.

Progress notes: Mary has been unable to establish and maintain healthy interpersonal relationships. Her relationship with her husband has been dysfunctional for a number of years. Mary tends to become quickly attracted to men and to think that they are the answer to her problems. When she gets closer to them, she realizes that they have as many problems as she does. She has been involved in several extramarital affairs. In one-to-one counseling, Mary was able to see how alcohol played a significant role in her relationship problems. When she was drunk, she usually fought with her husband and became involved with other men at the bar. The client was able to see how her parents taught her to keep her feelings to herself. She learned never to ask for anything. The client completed the Relationship Skills exercise (see Appendix 11) and began to use these skills with her treatment peers. Mary was able to share her feelings with her interpersonal group. Again, the trust issue was a hurdle for her. Gradually, she was able to ask for what she wanted without feeling guilty. She found out that other people in the program were trustworthy and loyal to her; they could keep information in confidence. Mary was able to work though the Communication Skills exercise (see Appendix 13) and was able to improve her active listening skills. She began to stop manipulating to get what she wanted and began to ask for what she wanted. She worked on developing assertiveness skills and was able to confront people in group about behavior that troubled her. Mary was able to establish many meaningful relationships while in treatment.

Goal 4: Identify losses and share feelings with others. Develop an understanding of the grief process, and learn healthy ways of coping with her grief.

Progress notes: Mary lost her mother to cancer 2 years ago and lost her brother to an automobile accident last March. It became clear to the clinical staff that Mary had not appropriately grieved through these losses in her life. The pain was still very evident in Mary's behavior whenever she would talk about her mother or brother. She would cry for long periods of time whenever these issues were discussed in group. Mary talked about her grief and began to share her feelings in one-to-one counseling and in interpersonal group. Several of her treatment peers had similar losses to report, and Mary began to take an active role in getting them to talk about their losses. As she was able to share her pain with the group, Mary's grief began to ease. She wrote letters of closure to her mother and brother and read these letters to several treatment peers. Mary spoke on several occasions with the staff clergy about the deaths, and she began to turn the situation over to the care of God. She began to believe that God was taking good care of her mother and brother and that she would see them again. Mary stated that she felt that her mother and brother would want her to continue with her life and to let go of the grief she was feeling. At the end of treatment, Mary was able to talk about the deaths in her family without crying and with new hope about her dependence on God.

Goal 5: Learn coping skills for dealing with symptoms of borderline personality disorder.

Progress notes: Mary has had a persistent affective problem all of her life. She experiences rapid extreme shifts in her feelings, from feeling relatively normal to feeling severely angry, depressed, or frightened. The client had been drinking to relieve herself of these uncomfortable feelings. Her interpersonal relationships have been severely dysfunctional, and the client has felt chronically empty and bored. Mary becomes suicidal and has cut her wrists and arms to relieve herself of her pain. During treatment, Mary met regularly with the staff psychologist. She learned to identify her feelings and learned what action to take when she was feeling intense feelings. The client practiced talking to a staff member or a treatment peer when she was angry or frightened. She learned to get some exercise when she was feeling intense feelings. The client worked through the Relationship Skills exercise (see Appendix 11) and the Communication Skills exercise (see Appendix 13). She learned how to communicate with others. The client met with her husband once a week with her primary counselor to work on her marital problems. The client was referred to Dr. Frank Smith, a psychiatrist who will follow the client once a week in continuing care.

FAMILY PROGRAM: Mary's husband, Mark, and her two children, Kathy and Tina, attended the family program. Mary participated in all of the family sessions. Mark shared that he has been very frightened by Mary's drinking behavior. He tends to keep his feelings to himself and to not share what he wants from his wife. Mark expressed that he thought that Mary would come around if he could get her to address her alcohol problem. Mark was able to make significant progress in sharing his feelings in the family program. He was able to tell Mary of the hurt and fear that he had been feeling when she would go out and stay out all night. He expressed how angry he was at the extramarital affairs, one of which was with his best friend. Mark often openly wept as he shared his feelings. Kathy, the oldest child (age 10), was able to share how she had to take care of her younger sister when Mary was passed out on the couch. She explained how frightening it was to see her mother intoxicated and out of control. Kathy had witnessed one of her mother's suicide attempts and had to call the police to get Mary under control. This child had been more of a mother to Mary than Mary had been to her. It was obvious in the family sessions that this was a very responsible little girl. The youngest child, Tina (age 6), was very quiet during the sessions. She was able to express how frightened she was seeing her father and mother fight. She also had witnessed the suicide attempt. The family had problems severe enough that these family members were referred to the Mandel Mental Health Clinic for further family counseling. They have an appointment with Marcie Frankle, a marriage and family counselor, on 10-31-01 at 4:00 pm.

SUMMARY: While in treatment, Mary completed the Steps One to Five of the Alcoholics Anonymous (AA) 12-step program. She has been introduced to Steps Six to Twelve. She has worked a daily program of recovery while in treatment, and she understands what she needs to do to stay sober. Mary has developed a good understanding of her disease and has made significant changes in her attitudes and behaviors that can be used in a sober lifestyle. She is more honest with herself and with others, and she has learned good problem solving skills. Mary can now use her feelings to help her solve problems. Mary has begun to resolve her depression and will continue to work on her psychological problems in continuing care with Dr. Margaret Fine. Her marriage is more stable, and she is going to continue marriage counseling with Mel Thompson, licensed marriage and family therapist. She will be followed by Laurie Johnson as her continuing care manager who will arrange for random drug screening and regular attendance at 12-step meetings. She knows how to cope with her feelings without drinking. She has worked though her grief issues and has established conscious contact with her Higher Power. Mary is willing to take the responsibility for her own life and behavior.

PROGNOSIS: The client's prognosis is good. Mary has a positive attitude toward recovery. She made progress in treatment in many areas, and she worked hard. She has shown that she is willing to work to maintain her sobriety. She established many supportive relationships in treatment, and she plans to build on these friendships in recovery. She has plans to attend AA meetings with a good friend of hers who has 12 solid years of sobriety. Mary will need positive reinforcement in recovery, and she will have to address her depression until it clears. She will need to continue family counseling to stabilize her relationship with her husband and children. She is aware that she will need to stick close to AA to stay in recovery.

CONTINUING CARE:

1. Maintain complete abstinence from all mood-altering chemicals.

2. Attend AA meetings on a regular basis and get an AA sponsor who makes her feel comfortable. Mary does have an AA contact person: Cheryl M., 336-2281.

3. Attend continuing care group for a minimum of 12 months on Monday evenings at 7:00 pm at the Thompson Alcohol and Drug Center, 303 Fuller Lane, Thomas, Maryland. Her first appointment has been set with Charlene Schultz on 10-25-01 at 1:00 pm.

4. Continue to work on a daily spiritual program that she began in treatment. Mary will attend church at the Good Faith Lutheran Church. Reverend Bob Luce is the pastor.

5. Continue to check the relapse symptoms daily and work a daily program of relapse prevention.

6. Develop honest and open relationships with others who can aid her in recovery.

7. Avoid people and places that could trigger relapse symptoms.

8. Continue Prozac therapy and continue to see Dr. Frank Smith for psychotherapy for her depression. Her first appointment is on 10-22-01 at 2:30 pm at the Mandel Mental Health Clinic, 12 Tigar Street, Thomas, Maryland.

9. Continue family counseling with Marcie Frankle of the Mandel Mental Health Clinic, 12 Tigar Street, Thomas, Maryland. The first appointment is on 10-22-01 at 1:30 pm.

10. Continue to trust and praise herself in recovery. Practice self-affirmations daily.

11. Work her continuing care program with her case manager, submitting to up to three random drug screens per week for the first 6 months and up to one random drug screen for the next 5 years.

12. Meet regularly with each advocate and keep the advocacy group informed about her recovery asking for help when needed.

DIAGNOSTIC AND STATISTICAL MANUAL OF MENTAL DISORDERS (DSM–IV–TR) DIAGNOSIS:

Axis I: 303.90 Alcohol dependence, severe

             296.25 Major depression, single episode in partial remission

Axis II: 301.83 Borderline personality disorder

Axis III: Asthma

Axis IV: Severity of psychosocial stressors: Personal illness, death in the family, Severity 4 (severe)

Axis V: Current global assessment of functioning: 70

Appendix 29

Stress Management

Robert R. Perkinson, PhD

Unresolved stress fuels addiction. Addicted individuals deal with stress by using chemicals or addictive behavior rather than using other more appropriate coping skills. Everyone has stress, and everyone needs to learn how to cope with stress in daily life. Stress is the generalized physiological response to a stressor. A stressor is any demand made on the body.

A stressor can be anything that mobilizes the body for change. This can include psychological or physiological loss, absence of stimulation, excessive stimulation, frustration of an anticipated reward, conflict, and presentation or anticipation of painful events (Zegans, 1982).

The stress response is good and adaptive. It activates the body for problem solving. Stress is destructive only when it is chronic. The overly stressed body produces harmful chemicals such as cortisol that triggers inflammation, and soon the person gets sick. Initially, the body produces certain chemicals to handle the stressful situation. Initially, these chemical changes are adaptive. In the end, they are destructive. Severe or chronic stress has been linked to irreversible disease including kidney impairment, hypertension, arteriosclerosis, type 2 diabetes, ulcers, and a compromised immune system that can result in increased infections and cancer (Selye, 1956).

When animals encounter an unsolvable problem, they ultimately get sick. They fall victim to a wide variety of physical and mental disorders. Under chronic stress, these organisms ultimately die.

It seems that everyone has a genetic predisposition to break down in a certain organ system when under chronic stress. Some people get depressed; there are ulcers, heart attacks, strokes; and some become chemically dependent.

In treatment, you must learn how to deal with stress in ways other than by using your addiction. You must learn to use the stress signals that your body gives you to help you solve problems. If you cannot solve the problem yourself, then you need to get some help.

Most people who are addicted are dealing with unresolved pain. They begin drinking, gambling, or using chemicals to ease the pain, and soon they become dependent. Addiction is a primary disease. It takes over people's lives and makes everything worse.

Stress management techniques help addicted individuals to regain the control they have lost in their lives. By establishing and maintaining a daily program of recovery, they learn how to cope with stress. If you are dealing with stress better, then you are not as likely to relapse. There are three elements necessary to reduce your overall stress level: (1) a regular exercise program, (2) regular relaxation, and (3) creating a more rewarding lifestyle.

Relaxation

For centuries, people have relaxed or used meditation to quiet their minds and reach a state of peace. When animals have enough to eat and they are safe, they lay down. People do not do that because humans are the only animals that worry about the future. Humans fear that if they relax today, then they will be in trouble tomorrow.

Benson (1975, 2000) showed that when people relax twice a day for 10 to 20 minutes, it has a major impact on their overall stress levels. People who do this have fewer illnesses, feel better, and are healthier. Illness such as high blood pressure, ulcers, and headaches can go away completely with a regular relaxation program.

Benson maintained that the relaxation technique is simple.

1. Sit or lie down in a quiet place.

2. Pay attention to your breathing.

3. Every time you exhale, say the word *one* over quietly to yourself. It is normal for other ideas to come, but when they do, just return to the word or words you have chosen.

4. Do this for 10 to 20 minutes twice a day.

You do not have to use the word *one*. You can use any other word or phrase of your choice, but it has to be the same word or phrase repeated repeatedly. You can get some relaxation tapes or music that you find

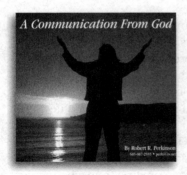

relaxing. You can pray or meditate. The most important thing is to relax as completely as you can. If you do this, then your stress level will be lower and you will be better able to mobilize yourself to deal with stress when it occurs. I have created a meditation exercise CD that you might find helpful. You can find this at www.cdbaby.com/cd/godtalks2. This tape has two tracks. Track 1 is a 20-minute spiritual exercise followed by relaxing music. Track 2 is a 12-minute meditation exercise followed by relaxing music. Many of our clients find this to be the turning point in their spiritual connection because it is the first time they experience the presence of God.

Progressive relaxation is tightening each muscle group and then relaxing them. For example, you tighten your right arm and feel the tension. Then let the muscle go and feel it deeply relax. Concentrate on the feeling of tension and relaxation. Soon you will not have to tighten the muscle group as often you will just have to concentrate on it relaxing. As you practice relaxation, you will learn how it feels to be relaxed. Try to keep this feeling all day long.

- When you feel stressed, stop and take two deep breaths.
- Breathe in through your nose and out through your mouth.
- As you exhale, feel a warm wave of relaxation flow down your body.
- Once you have regained your state of relaxation, return to your day and move a little slower this time.
- Remember, nothing is ever done too well or too slowly. You do not have to do things quickly to succeed.

When you come to some new task that you think you have to complete, ask yourself several important questions.

1. Do I have to do this?

2. Do I have to do it now?

3. Is this going to make a difference in 5 years?

If the new stressor is not that important, perhaps you should not do it at all. Do not overly stress yourself. That does not make any sense. Know your limits. Achieve a state of relaxation in the morning, and listen to your body all day long. If anything threatens your serenity, turn it over and let God deal with it.

For the next week, set aside two times a day for relaxation. Go through the meditation exercise we discussed or some other relaxation exercise. Score the level of relaxation you achieved from 1 (*as little as possible*) to 100 (*as much as possible*). Then score your general stress level during the day in the same way. Write down any comments about your stress. List the situations when you felt the most tension.

Day 1

Relaxation Score

Daily Stress Score

Comments

Day 2

Relaxation Score

Daily Stress Score

Comments

Day 3

Relaxation Score

Daily Stress Score

Comments

Day 4

Relaxation Score

Daily Stress Score

Comments

Day 5

Relaxation Score

Daily Stress Score

Comments

Day 6

Relaxation Score

Daily Stress Score

Comments

Day 7

Relaxation Score

Daily Stress Score

Comments

Exercise

The role of exercise in the treatment of addiction has been well established. Significant improvements in physical fitness can occur in as short a period as 20 days. People who maintain a regular exercise program feel less depressed and less anxious, improve their self-concepts, and enhance the quality of their lives (Folkins & Sime, 1981).

Most addicted people come into treatment in poor physical and mental shape. They gave up on exercise a long time ago. Even if they were in good physical condition at one time in their lives, the addiction has taken its toll. These people are unable to maintain a consistent level of physical fitness. The mind and body cannot maintain a regular exercise program when a person chronically abuses drugs, alcohol, or other addictive behaviors.

An exercise program, although difficult to develop, can be fun. You get a natural high from exercise that you do not get in any other way. It feels good, and it feels good all day.

A good exercise program includes three elements: (1) stretching, (2) strength, and (3) cardiovascular fitness. The recreational therapist or personal trainer will assist you in developing an individualized program specific to you.

Stretching means that you increase a muscle's range of motion until you become supple and flexible. Never stretch your muscles to the point of pain. The body will warn you well before you go too far. Let the exercise therapist show you how to stretch each major muscle group. Get into a habit of stretching before all exercise.

In a strength program, you gradually lift more weight until you become stronger. Do not lift more often than every other day. The muscles need a full day of rest to repair them. Soon you can increase the load. Three sets of 8 to 12 repetitions each is a standard exercise for each muscle group. The exercise therapist will show you how to complete each exercise. Correct technique is very important.

Endurance training means that you exercise at a training heart rate for an extended period of time. This is where the cardiovascular system gets stronger. Your training heart rate is calculated by taking your age, minus the number 220, multiplied by .75.

Cardiovascular fitness is attained when you exercise at a training heart rate, for 20 to 30 minutes, at least three times a week. Have the exercise therapist help you to determine your training heart rate and develop a program in which you gradually increase your cardiovascular fitness. Usually, you will be increasing your exercise by 10% each week.

Many forms of exercise can be beneficial for cardiovascular training. The key point is this: It must be sustained exercise for at least 20 to 30 minutes. Walking is probably the best exercise to start with. It is easy to do, and you do not need any specialized equipment. The exercise cannot be a stop–start exercise such as tennis or golf. It must be something that you can sustain. These include exercises such as walking, jogging, swimming, and biking.

After you have worked out your exercise program, keep a daily log of your exercise. Reinforce yourself when you reach one of your goals. You might have a goal of running a mile by the end of the month. If you reach your goal, then buy yourself something you want or treat yourself to a movie to celebrate. Write down your exercise schedule for the next month.

Exercise Program

Date   *Training Heart Rate*

Strength

Stretching

Cardiovascular fitness

Changing Your Lifestyle

Along with maintaining a regular relaxation and exercise time, you must change other aspects of your life to improve your stress management skills.

Problem Solving Skills

You need to be able to identify and respond to the problems in your life. Unsolved problems increase your stress level. Problems are a normal part of life, and you need specific skills to deal with them effectively. For each problem that you encounter, work through the following steps:

1. Identify the problem.

2. Clarify your goals. What do you want?

3. Consider all the alternatives of action.

4. Think through each alternative, eliminating one at a time, until you have the best alternative.

5. Act on the problem.

6. Evaluate the effect of your action.

Work through several problems with your counselor or group while in treatment. See how effective it is to seek the advice and counsel of others. You need to ask for help.

Developing Pleasurable Activities

One of the things that chemically dependent people fear the most is not being able to have fun when clean and sober. Chemicals have been involved in pleasurable activities for so long that they are directly equated with all pleasure. To look forward to a life without being able to have fun is intolerable.

You do not give up fun in sobriety. You change the way in which you have fun. You cannot use chemicals for pleasure anymore. This is not good for you. You can enjoy many pleasant activities without drugs or alcohol. If you think about it, this is real fun anyway. The fun you are missing is based on a false chemically created feeling. Once you see how much fun you can have when clean and sober, you will be amazed.

Increasing pleasurable activities will elevate your mood and decrease your overall stress level. If you are not feeling well in recovery, it is likely that you are not involved in enough pleasurable activities. If you increase the level of pleasure, then you will feel better and be less vulnerable to relapse.

First, identify the things that you might enjoy doing, and then make a list of the things that you are going to do more often. Make a list of the activities that you plan to do for yourself each day. Write down your plan. The more pleasurable things you do, the better you will feel.

1. Being in the country

2. Wearing expensive clothes

3. Talking about sports

4. Meeting someone new

5. Going to a concert

6. Playing baseball or softball

7. Planning trips or vacations

8. Buying things for yourself

9. Going to the beach

10. Doing artwork

11. Rock climbing or mountaineering

12. Playing golf

13. Reading

14. Rearranging or redecorating your room or house

15. Playing basketball or volleyball

16. Going to a lecture

17. Breathing the clean air

18. Writing a song

19. Boating

20. Pleasing your parents

21. Watching television

22. Thinking quietly

23. Camping

24. Working on machines (e.g., cars, bikes, motors)

25. Working in politics

26. Thinking about something good in the future

27. Playing cards

28. Laughing

29. Working puzzles or crosswords

30. Having lunch with a friend or an associate

31. Playing tennis

32. Taking a bath

33. Going for a drive

34. Woodworking

35. Writing a letter

36. Being with animals

37. Riding in an airplane

38. Walking in the woods

39. Having a conversation with someone

40. Working at your job

41. Going to a party

42. Going to church functions

43. Visiting relatives

44. Going to a meeting

45. Playing a musical instrument

46. Having a snack

47. Taking a nap

48. Singing

49. Acting

50. Working on crafts

51. Being with your children

52. Playing a game of chess or checkers

53. Putting on makeup or fixing your hair

54. Visiting people who are sick or shut in

55. Bowling

56. Talking with your sponsor

57. Gardening or doing lawn work

58. Dancing

59. Sitting in the sun

60. Sitting and thinking

61. Praying

62. Meditating

63. Listening to the sounds of nature

64. Going on a date

65. Listening to the radio

66. Giving a gift

67. Reaching out to someone who is suffering

68. Getting or giving a message or back rub

69. Talking to your spouse

70. Talking to a friend

71. Watching the clouds

72. Lying in the grass

73. Helping someone

74. Hearing or telling jokes

75. Going to church

76. Eating a good meal

77. Hunting

78. Fishing

79. Looking at the scenery

80. Working on improving your health

81. Going downtown

82. Watching a sporting event

83. Going to a health club

84. Learning something new

85. Horseback riding

86. Going out to eat

87. Talking on the telephone

88. Daydreaming

89. Going to the movies

90. Being alone

91. Feeling the presence of God

92. Smelling a flower

93. Looking at a sunrise

94. Doing a favor for a friend

95. Meeting a stranger

96. Reading the newspaper

97. Swimming

98. Walking barefoot

99. Playing catch or with a Frisbee

100. Cleaning your house or room

101. Listening to music

102. Knitting or crocheting

103. Having house guests

104. Being with someone you love

105. Having sexual relations

106. Going to the library

107. Watching people

108. Repairing something

109. Bicycling

110. Smiling at people

111. Caring for houseplants

112. Collecting things

113. Sewing

114. Going to garage sales

115. Water skiing

116. Surfing

117. Traveling

118. Teaching someone

119. Washing your car

120. Eating ice cream

Social Skills

What you do socially can turn people off or turn them on. If you do any of the following, you might be turning people off.

1. Not smiling

2. Failing to make eye contact

3. Not talking

4. Complaining

5. Telling everyone your troubles

6. Not responding to people

7. Whining

8. Being critical

9. Poor grooming

10. Not showing interest in people

11. Ignoring people

12. Having an angry look

13. Using nervous gestures

14. Feeling sorry for yourself

15. Always talking about the negative

You are turning people on if you do the following:

1. Smiling

2. Looking at people in the eyes

3. Expressing your concern

4. Talking about pleasant things

5. Being reinforcing

6. Telling people how nice they look

7. Being appreciative

8. Telling people that you care

9. Listening

10. Touching

11. Asking people to do something with you

12. Acting interested

13. Using people's names

14. Talking about the positive

15. Grooming yourself well

To have good social skills, you have to be assertive. You cannot be passive or aggressive. This means that you have to tell people the truth about how you feel and ask for what you want. You must tell the truth at all times. If you withhold or distort information, then you never will be close to anyone.

Do not tell other people what to do; instead, ask them what they want to do. Do not let other people tell you what to do; instead, negotiate. Do not yell; instead, explain. Do not throw your weight around. When you are wrong, promptly admit it. Happiness is giving to others. The more you give, the more you get.

In a 12-step program, you never have to be alone. Your Higher Power always is with you. Learn to enjoy the presence of God, and communicate with God as if God were standing right beside you. Call someone in the program every day. Go to many meetings. Reach out to those who are still suffering. There are many people in jails or hospitals who need your help. Volunteer to work on the 12-step hotline. Ask people out for coffee after meetings. Do not worry if you are doing all of the asking at first. The reason you are doing this is for you. Most people, particularly men, feel very uncomfortable asking others to go out with them. Do not let that stop you. If you do not ask, then you will not have the experience of someone saying yes.

Using the pleasant activities list, make a plan for how you are going to increase your social interaction this month. Write all of it down, and reward yourself when you make progress. Here are a few hints to get you going:

1. Read the activities and entertainment section of your local newspaper. Mark down events that fit into your schedule and attend them.

2. Offer to become more involved in your 12-step group.

3. Ask the local chamber of commerce for information about groups and activities in the area.

4. Spend your weekends exploring new parts of town.

5. Smile.

6. Join another self-help support group such as an Adult Children of Alcoholics group or a singles group.

7. Join a church and get involved. Tell the pastor that you want to do something to help.

8. Volunteer your services with a local charity or hospital. Help others and share your experiences, strengths, and hopes.

9. Join a group that does interesting things in the area—hiking, skydiving, hunting, bird watching, acting, playing sports, joining a senior center, and so on. Check the local library for a list of such clubs and activities.

10. Ask someone in the program for interesting things to do in the area.

11. Go to an intergroup dance.

12. Go to an Alcoholics Anonymous (AA)/Narcotics Anonymous (NA) conference.

The most important thing to remember is that you are in recovery. You are starting a new life. To do this, you must take risks. You must reach out as you have never done before.

Appendix 30

Hamilton Depression Rating Scale

The total Hamilton Depression Rating Scale (HAM-D) provides an indication of depression and, over time, provides a valuable guide to progress.

- Classification of symptoms that may be difficult to obtain can be scored as follows:

  0 = absent; 1 = doubtful or trivial; 2 = present

- Classification of symptoms where more detail can be obtained can be expanded to the following:

  0 = absent; 1 = mild; 2 = moderate; 3 = severe; 4 = incapacitating

In general, the higher the total score, the more severe the depression.

- HAM-D score level of depression as follows:

  10−13 = mild; 14−17 = mild to moderate; >17 = moderate to severe

Assessment is recommended at 2 weekly intervals.

HAM-D Rating Scale		Pretreatment	1st Follow-Up	2nd Follow-Up
Symptoms		Date	Date	Date
1.	Depressed mood	0 1 2 3 4	0 1 2 3 4	0 1 2 3 4
2.	Guilt feelings	0 1 2 3 4	0 1 2 3 4	0 1 2 3 4
3.	Suicide	0 1 2 3 4	0 1 2 3 4	0 1 2 3 4
4.	Insomnia—early	0 1 2 3 4	0 1 2 3 4	0 1 2 3 4
5.	Insomnia—middle	0 1 2 3 4	0 1 2 3 4	0 1 2 3 4
6.	Insomnia—late	0 1 2 3 4	0 1 2 3 4	0 1 2 3 4
7.	Work and activities	0 1 2 3 4	0 1 2 3 4	0 1 2 3 4

(Continued)

Source: Hamilton, M. (1979). The Hamilton rating scale for depression. *Journal of Operational Psychiatry, 10*(2): 149–165.

(Continued)

HAM-D Rating Scale		Pretreatment	1st Follow-Up	2nd Follow-Up
Symptoms		Date	Date	Date
8.	Retardation—psychomotor	0 1 2 3 4	0 1 2 3 4	0 1 2 3 4
9.	Agitation	0 1 2 3 4	0 1 2 3 4	0 1 2 3 4
10.	Anxiety—psychological	0 1 2 3 4	0 1 2 3 4	0 1 2 3 4
11.	Anxiety—somatic	0 1 2 3 4	0 1 2 3 4	0 1 2 3 4
12.	Somatic symptoms—GI	0 1 2 3 4	0 1 2 3 4	0 1 2 3 4
13.	Somatic symptoms—General	0 1 2 3 4	0 1 2 3 4	0 1 2 3 4
14.	Sexual dysfunction—menstrual disturbance	0 1 2 3 4	0 1 2 3 4	0 1 2 3 4
15.	Hypochondriasis	0 1 2 3 4	0 1 2 3 4	0 1 2 3 4
16.	Weight loss—by history —by scales	0 1 2 3 4 0 1 2 3 4	0 1 2 3 4 0 1 2 3 4	0 1 2 3 4 0 1 2 3 4
17.	Insight	0 1 2 3 4	0 1 2 3 4	0 1 2 3 4
Total Score:				

Appendix 31

Biopsychosocial Assessment

Robert R. Perkinson, PhD

DATE:

CLIENT NAME:

DEMOGRAPHIC DATA:

Age   Marital status   Race   Sex   Children

Others in residence:

Length of residence:

Education:

- ☐ Less than sixth grade
- ☐ Sixth grade
- ☐ Seventh grade
- ☐ Eighth grade
- ☐ Some high school

- ☐ High school graduate
- ☐ Some college
- ☐ College graduate
- ☐ Postgraduate work
- ☐ Postgraduate degree

Occupation:

Characteristics of informant:

- ☐ Reliable
- ☐ Unreliable

CHIEF COMPLAINT:

BIOPSYCHOSOCIAL ASSESSMENT:

HISTORY OF THE PRESENT ILLNESS (age of onset, duration, patterns and consequences of use, current use, last use, previous treatments, tolerance, blackouts, and symptoms of abuse or dependence):

PAST HISTORY

Place of birth: Date of birth:

Developmental milestones:

☐ Normal   ☐ Reading
☐ Walking   ☐ Spelling
☐ Talking   ☐ Arithmetic
☐ Toilet training

Specific disabilities:

Raised with:

☐ Mother   ☐ Brothers
☐ Father   ☐ Sisters

Birth order:

Significant others:

Ethnic/cultural heritage:

Description of home life:

Grade school:

High school:

College:

Military history:

Branch

Highest rank

Discharge status

Problems

Occupational history:

Longest job held

Length of time at current job

Employment satisfaction

Work problems

Financial history:

☐ Good   ☐ Fair   ☐ Poor

Current annual income:

Gambling history:

☐ None   ☐ Gambling problems (Explain)

Sexual history:

Sexual orientation

Physical abuse

Sexual abuse

Current sexual history

Relationship history

Recovery environment: ☐ Family   ☐ Friends

Spiritual history:

   ☐ Believes in God   ☐ Agnostic

   ☐ Higher Power   ☐ Atheist

Religious activities:

Church   Denomination

Attends:

   ☐ Weekly   ☐ Rarely

   ☐ Occasionally   ☐ Never

Legal history:

  Arrests

  Pending litigation

Self-identified strengths:

Self-identified weaknesses:

Self-identified needs:

Self-identified abilities:

Self-identified personal preferences:

Leisure activities:

Depression:

Mania:

Anxiety:

Panic attacks:

Agoraphobia:

Phobias:

Eating disorder:

MEDICAL HISTORY

Illnesses:

   ☐ Measles   ☐ Pneumonia

   ☐ Mumps   ☐ Tonsillitis

   ☐ Chicken pox   ☐ Appendicitis

   ☐ Whooping cough   ☐ Others

Hospitalizations:

   ☐ Tonsillectomy and adenoidectomy   ☐ Appendectomy

   ☐ Chemical dependency

Allergies   Environmental allergens

Medications at present:

<u>FAMILY HISTORY</u>

Father:

  Age

  Health:

    ☐ Good   ☐ Fair   ☐ Poor

  Description

Mother:

  Age

  Health:

    ☐ Good   ☐ Fair   ☐ Poor

  Description

Other relatives with significant psychopathology

<u>MENTAL STATUS EXAMINATION</u>

Description:

    ☐ Well developed and well nourished   ☐ Thin

    ☐ Obese   ☐ Underweight

Age   Race   Sex   Hair   Eyes

Distinguishing marks or characteristics

Appearance:

    ☐ Same as stated age   ☐ Older than stated age

    ☐ Younger than stated age

Dress:

    ☐ Casual   ☐ Meticulously neat

    ☐ Appropriate   ☐ Seductive

    ☐ Disheveled   ☐ Eccentric

    ☐ Other

Personal hygiene:

    ☐ Good   ☐ Fair   ☐ Poor

Sensorium:

    ☐ Clear   ☐ Lethargic

    ☐ Alert   ☐ Drowsy

    ☐ Vigilant   ☐ Other

Factors affecting sensorium:

☐ Alcohol   ☐ Medications

☐ Drugs   ☐ Withdrawal symptoms

☐ Other

Orientation:

Person

Place

Time

Situation

Attitude toward the examiner:

☐ Cooperative   ☐ Distant

☐ Friendly   ☐ Aloof

☐ Pleasant   ☐ Casual

☐ Suspicious   ☐ Overly intellectual

☐ Hostile   ☐ Neutral

☐ Passive   ☐ Apprehensive

☐ Dependent   ☐ Seductive

☐ Withdrawn

Motor behavior:

☐ Normal   ☐ Physical agitation

☐ Continuous movements or restlessness   ☐ Tremor

Unusual and inappropriate movements:

☐ Slow or retarded   ☐ Inappropriate

☐ Tics   ☐ Hand wringing

☐ Tearful   ☐ Pacing

☐ Rigid   ☐ Apprehensive

☐ Tense   ☐ Angry

☐ Slouched

Eye contact:

☐ Appropriate   ☐ Poor

Gait:

☐ Normal   ☐ Wide based

☐ Shuffling   ☐ Unsteady

☐ Other

Primary facial expression during interview:

☐ Normal and responsive   ☐ Hostile

☐ Sad   ☐ Worried

☐ Neutral   ☐ Other

Speech quantity:

- ☐ Normal
- ☐ Talkative
- ☐ Garrulous
- ☐ Unspontaneous
- ☐ Spontaneous
- ☐ Minimally responsive

Speech quality:

- ☐ Normal
- ☐ Slow
- ☐ Rapid
- ☐ Pressured
- ☐ Hesitant
- ☐ Emotional
- ☐ Monotonous
- ☐ Soft
- ☐ Loud
- ☐ Slurred
- ☐ Mumbled

Speech impairment:

- ☐ None
- ☐ Stuttering
- ☐ Other
- ☐ Marked by accent
- ☐ Articulation problem

Mood:

- ☐ Calm
- ☐ Cheerful
- ☐ Anxious
- ☐ Depressed
- ☐ Fearful
- ☐ Tearful
- ☐ Pessimistic
- ☐ Neutral
- ☐ Optimistic
- ☐ Elated
- ☐ Euphoric
- ☐ Irritable
- ☐ Angry
- ☐ Other

Client report of depression:

- ☐ None
- ☐ Mild
- ☐ Moderate
- ☐ Severe

Episodes of depression:

- ☐ None
- ☐ One or two episodes during past 6 months
- ☐ Frequently during past 6 months
- ☐ Continuously during past 6 months

Client report of symptoms of depression:

- ☐ None
- ☐ Poor appetite
- ☐ Loss of interests
- ☐ Guilt
- ☐ Motor retardation
- ☐ Sleep disturbance
- ☐ Fatigue
- ☐ Weight loss
- ☐ Loss of interest in sex
- ☐ Other

Observed signs of anxiety during interview:

- ☐ None
- ☐ Physical indications
- ☐ Other
- ☐ Apprehensive manner
- ☐ Problems in attention

Client report of anxiety:

☐ None   ☐ Moderate

☐ Mild   ☐ Severe

Episodes of anxiety:

☐ None   ☐ Frequently during past 6 months

☐ One or two episodes during past 6 months   ☐ Continuously during past 6 months

Client report of symptoms of anxiety:

☐ None   ☐ Paresthesias

☐ Shortness of breath   ☐ Muscle aches

☐ Palpitations   ☐ Cold hands

☐ Chest pain   ☐ Gastrointestinal symptoms

☐ Dizziness   ☐ Muscle twitching

☐ Faintness   ☐ Dry mouth

☐ Sweating   ☐ Other

Range of affect:

☐ Appropriate   ☐ Labile

☐ Blunted   ☐ Dramatized

☐ Restricted   ☐ Flat

☐ Contradictory   ☐ Other

Thought processes:

☐ Logical and coherent   ☐ Neologisms

☐ Blocking   ☐ Preservation

☐ Circumstantial   ☐ Evasive

☐ Tangential   ☐ Distracted

☐ Flight of ideas   ☐ Loose associations

☐ Incoherent   ☐ Clang associations

☐ Other

Thought content—preoccupations:

☐ None   ☐ Violent acts

☐ Presenting problem   ☐ Somatic symptoms

☐ Obsessions   ☐ Guilt

☐ Compulsions   ☐ Worthlessness

☐ Phobias   ☐ Religious issues

☐ Suicide   ☐ Sex

☐ Other

Thought content—delusions:

☐ None   ☐ Jealousy

☐ Persecution   ☐ Grandiosity

☐ Somatic   ☐ Religious

☐ Ideas of reference   ☐ Influence by others

☐ Thought broadcasting   ☐ Control

☐ Other

Description of delusional material

Quality of delusional material:

☐ Systematized   ☐ Poorly organized

Disorders of perception:

☐ None   ☐ Tactile hallucinations

☐ Auditory hallucinations   ☐ Gustatory hallucinations incorporated into delusions

☐ Visual hallucinations   ☐ Fragmented and not incorporated into delusions

☐ Olfactory hallucinations

Suicidal ideation:

☐ None   ☐ Ideation   ☐ Plan

Details of current plans

History of suicidal acts

Homicidal ideation:

☐ None   ☐ Ideation   ☐ Plan

Details of current plans

History of violent acts

Obsessions:

☐ None   ☐ Death

☐ Illness   ☐ Contamination

☐ Violence   ☐ Doubt

☐ Other

Compulsions:

☐ None   ☐ Checking

☐ Hand washing   ☐ Touching

☐ Counting   ☐ Other

Phobias:

☐ None   ☐ Insects

☐ Public places   ☐ Dogs

☐ Closed spaces   ☐ Social security

☐ Heights   ☐ Rodents

☐ Snakes   ☐ Travel

☐ Flying   ☐ Other

Estimated range of intellectual ability:

☐ Normal ☐ Below average

☐ Above average ☐ Borderline retarded

☐ Superior ☐ Retarded

Abstracting ability:

☐ Normal ☐ Impaired

Disturbances in consciousness:

☐ No recent disturbances ☐ Recent history of seizures

☐ Recent history of loss of consciousness ☐ Recent history of blackouts

Concentration:

☐ Normal ☐ Moderately impaired

☐ Mildly impaired ☐ Severely impaired

Memory functions:

☐ Intact ☐ Recent memory deficit

☐ Immediate memory deficit ☐ Remote memory deficit

Confabulations:

☐ None ☐ Suspected ☐ Definite

Amnesia:

☐ None ☐ Less than 1 month

☐ Less than 1 day ☐ Several months

☐ Less than 1 week ☐ Years

Impulse control:

☐ Good ☐ Fair ☐ Poor

Judgment:

☐ Good ☐ Fair ☐ Poor

Insight:

☐ Minimal: No understanding of problem or acceptance of personal responsibility

☐ Insightful: Accepts personal responsibility and desires professional assistance

Appendix 32

Anger Management

Robert R. Perkinson, PhD

Anger is a feeling that helps you to adapt to your environment. It is designed to make stress stop. It helps you to establish and maintain boundaries around yourself. It gives you the energy and direction to defend yourself from a physical attack.

Chronic anger is painful. It results in broken relationships. It does not help; it hurts. Studies show that people who are chronically angry die years earlier than they should. They have more colds and bouts with the flu as well as more mental and physical illnesses. Chronic anger has many painful consequences.

The reason why you are reading this exercise is that your anger sometimes gets out of control. When you are angry, you do things that you feel guilty about later. Chronic anger is a shameful cycle of pain. You do not want to hurt others, but you find yourself doing it anyway—repeatedly.

A lot of this exercise was taken from *When Anger Hurts* (McKay, Rogers, & McKay, 1989). When you get the opportunity, get that book and read it. This exercise will help you to manage your anger. This will not be easy, and you will have to work very hard. Learning new behaviors takes a lot of practice. You have had years of training in how to act angry. Now you need to learn new skills to deal with problems. Using the techniques described here, you will feel angry less often. When you feel angry, you will be able to solve problems rather then make them worse.

Anger Journal

Keep an anger journal every day. Write down every time that you feel angry. Write down exactly what happened in detail, and rate your angry feelings on a scale from 1 (*as little anger as possible*) to 100 (*as much anger as possible*). Rate your aggressiveness, angry words or actions, from 1 to 100. The more you look at each situation, the more you will learn about yourself and the more you will learn to control your behavior. Your journal might look something like this:

December 4: 8:00 am—Kathy asked me to take out the garbage three times while I was watching TV. I felt like she was trying to drive me crazy. She knew I had had a hard day and needed some time alone. At the same time, the kids were fighting in the other room.

Intensity of anger felt: 100

Aggressiveness: 90. I told her to shut up and leave me alone. I threw a pillow against the wall.

December 4: The sales meeting ended before I got a chance to share my concerns with the boss. I needed to talk to him and reassure him about my work. I know my sales have been falling off a bit lately. I felt more hurt than anything else did.

Intensity of anger felt: 75

Aggressiveness: 0. I did not do anything, but boy was I fuming.

By monitoring your anger, you will be able to observe your progress. You will feel successful as you see yourself handling your anger better.

The Anger Myth

There is a myth that anger has to be expressed or else you will explode into a violent rage. The anger will build up like water behind a dam. If you do not express it, then it will come bursting out all at once and destroy everything in the process. Research strongly disagrees with this myth. The research shows that anger does not help. The more you act angry or think angry thoughts, the more you feel angry. Anger feeds on itself. It never helps to hit walls or pillows or to yell. It just makes you act angrier.

What Does Anger Do to People?

1. Anger stuns and frightens people.

2. Anger makes people feel bad about themselves.

3. The more anger you express, the less effective your anger becomes. People get used to your anger and shrug it off.

4. People distance themselves from you.

5. Anger cuts you off from genuine closeness.

6. The more you act aggressively, the more you want to continue the attack and really rub people's noses in it.

7. Anger causes continued aggression from both parties.

8. Anger does not stop. It goes on and on, fueling itself in the process.

9. You resort to anger repeatedly. Each episode gets worse.

10. Anger leads to rigidity. Both parties become stuck and inflexible.

11. Anger breeds the desire for revenge.

12. Anger is trying to control the other person, but inevitably you lose control.

13. Anger causes the other person to act defensive and resistive.

14. People shield themselves from your anger by avoiding you.

15. People who are aggressive overestimate other people's aggression. Every word or action can seem like a threat. They also underestimate their own aggressive behavior.

16. To manage your anger, you have to get accurate in your thinking and learn other coping skills to use when you feel hurt or angry.

Angry people feel like victims caught in a trap. They desire closeness but have a fear of abandonment. Their friends seem selfish and insensitive, their employers seem cheap and uncaring, and their lovers seem unappreciative and withholding. Life is no fun.

Anger leads to helplessness in four steps:

1. You think that something is wrong with you.

2. You think that the other person should fix you, but he or she will not.

3. You blow up at that person.

4. The other person withdraws even further.

Anger Is a Choice

You do not have to act angry. You can solve your problems in other ways. Until now, anger has been automatic. It has been a decision made without thinking or a choice made out of habit. You spent years thinking that anger was saving you or helping you, while all the time it was hurting you. You want to be loved and accepted. Anger never will get you that. You can feel angry and act in a way that is more productive. Remember that the function of anger is to stop stress. Your problem is stress, not anger.

Anger helps you to cope with stress in several ways:

1. Anger blocks the awareness of pain.

2. Anger discharges high levels of fear, hurt, guilt, and sadness.

3. Anger discharges the pain that develops when your needs are frustrated.

4. Anger erases guilt.

5. Anger places the blame on someone else.

There are many ways of discharging stress other than acting angry. You can cry, exercise, work, make a joke, write in your journal, exercise, meditate, verbalize your feelings, talk to your counselor/sponsor/mentor/ coach or friend, ask for what you want, problem solve, listen to music, and do many other things.

Anger Is a Two-Step Process

1. You become aware of stress.

2. You blame someone else.

What will not help you is blaming someone or thinking about what he or she should have done differently.

To *blame,* you have to believe the following: The other person purposely did something wrong that hurt me. To *should,* you have to believe the following: The other person should have known better than to do what he or she did.

The should and blame are inaccurate thinking. The truth is that if the person had known better, he or she would not have done it. The other person was not trying to hurt you. The other person was trying to meet his or her own needs. If you will slow situations down and look at them closely, you will find out this is true.

To rid yourself of anger, you must stop blaming others.

The only thing that always is true when you are angry is that you are in pain. The trigger thoughts that fuel your anger usually are false. Your anger may have no legitimate basis. If you use inaccurate thinking, then you will generate a storm of inaccurate feelings. Armed with the real facts, you might not get angry at all.

It is not that anger builds; it is stress that builds. You need coping skills to deal with stress.

What Is Stressing You?

Go back to your anger journal, and look at each anger-producing situation.

1. Figure out what was stressing you before you got angry. What was the emotional pain, physical pain, frustration, or threat that preceded the anger? Prior to feeling angry, were you aware of any internal feeling of hurt, fear, sadness, or guilt? Did you feel uncomfortable physically or psychologically? Write down these things, and ask your counselor or group to help you uncover your automatic thinking.

2. Try to figure out the trigger thoughts. What were you thinking between the situation and the anger? Did you use the blame or should? Write down exactly what you were thinking.

Bob came home from work to find several soda cans lying in the middle of the living room floor. He thought, The kids know better than this. They only think about themselves. Nobody appreciates what I do around here. They do not care if I come home to a dirty house. Bob rated his anger at 100. He yelled at the kids and scored himself aggressively at 85. Later he felt guilty about yelling at the children and had to apologize.

Look at how Bob's inaccurate thinking inflamed his anger:

The kids should know better.

They only think about themselves.

They do not care about me.

Nobody appreciates what I do around here.

I live in a dirty house.

Thinking like that, it is no wonder Bob got angry. He was not thinking accurately. His angry feelings came from inaccurate thinking. He ended up feeling angry because of how he interpreted the actions of others.

Blaming

The impulse to assign blame lies at the root of all chronic anger. When you decide who is responsible for your pain, you feel justified in acting aggressively. You see yourself threatened, and you need to protect yourself. You are the helpless victim of another person's stupidity or selfishness.

There is pleasure in blaming. You can escape the responsibility for your own problems by blaming someone else. You can turn the focus off your mistakes and concentrate on the other person's mistakes. The problem with blaming is that it is not true. The truth is that other people are not responsible for your life; you are.

1. You are the only one who understands what you need.

2. Other people need to focus on their own needs.

3. People's needs occasionally will come into conflict with yours.

4. Your satisfaction in life depends on how well *you* meet your needs.

Strategies for Getting Your Needs Met

You must develop new skills for meeting your needs better. With your counselor's help, develop the following coping skills and practice them often.

1. Learn to give people rewards when they do something that you want them to do. Reinforce each person often. The more reinforcing you act toward others, the more reinforcing they will act toward you. List five times when you did this.

2. Learn to take care of your needs yourself. Do not count on others to meet your needs.

3. Develop new sources for support, nourishment, and appreciation. Join that Alcoholics Anonymous (AA)/Narcotics Anonymous (NA) group and go often. Take someone out for coffee. Call your sponsor. List 10 things you are going to do to support, nourish, and appreciate yourself.

4. Learn to say no. Practice in skills group a situation where you had a difficult time saying no to someone. Have other people in the group play the parts of the other people in the situation. Then act out the situation as if it happened. Then brainstorm with the group many other ways you could have responded. Then practice this situation using the other coping skills. Describe your saying no skills group and the other coping skills you learned.

5. Learn how to share how you feel and to ask for what you want. Practice in skills group three times when you kept your feelings to yourself. Set up the situations and role-play them in group. Get feedback from your counselor or group about why you need to share your feelings and the various ways you can share them. Practice sharing your feelings too passively, too aggressively, and assertively. Describe what happened in group and what you learned.

6. Learn to let go and let God. Set up an argument in skills group; when you are feeling angry, take two deep breaths. As you exhale, relax your body, have it go loose and limp, and then say over to yourself, "Let go and let God." Then practice removing yourself from the situation in a relaxed, comfortable manner. Describe your skills group in detail.

Taking Back the Responsibility

Go to your journal and examine your anger-generating situations. Ask for help from your counselor or group. Use them to help you to get accurate and uncover your automatic thoughts that lead to anger. Make a list of eight anger-generating situations, and process them with your group or counselor.

1. What was stressing you at the time?

2. What were your trigger thoughts?

3. What could you have done differently?

4. How could you have met your own needs?

5. How could you have found other sources of support?

6. What limits did you fail to set? Were you unable to say no?

7. How could you have negotiated better for what you wanted?

8. How could you have let go and let God?

Combating Trigger Thoughts

Inaccurate thinking leads you to feel inaccurate pain. If you blame, then you judge people all day by your own rules. Someone cuts in front of you in traffic and you fume, "That idiot knows better than that!" The fact is that many drivers think it is fine to cut in line. The problem with blaming is that people rarely agree with you. People all have their own sets of rules and judge themselves by their own standards. People often do not do what they think they should do; they do what works for them.

The Entitlement Fallacy

The entitlement fallacy is the belief that you deserve things because you want them very badly. Your need justifies the demand that someone give you what you want. The feeling of entitlement engulfs you. How can the other person say no? The truth is that people will give you what they want to give you and nothing more. They are trying to meet their own needs, not yours.

The Fallacy of Fairness

The idea here is that there is an absolute standard of conduct that everyone has to follow. Everyone should know these rules and follow them. If they do not, then they are bad and deserve to be punished. The problem with this thinking is that there is no absolute right and wrong standard of conduct. What is fair is very subjective. The other person could be functioning from an entirely different set of values.

Blame

Assigning blame lets you escape the responsibility of handing your problems. Blaming triggers anger by making your pain other people's fault. Blaming labels people as bad when they are doing all that they can with the coping skills they have at their disposal. By blaming, you punish people for doing things that they could not help from doing.

Mind Reading

Sometimes you get angry when you try to read someone's mind. You think that you know what a person did and why he or she did it. You think that you have the person all figured out. You assume that the person did something deliberately to harm you. This rarely is true. The other person almost always is trying to meet his or her own needs.

Changing Your Trigger Thoughts

Go back to your anger journal, and determine what you were thinking between each situation and the anger. Pull out as many of these trigger thoughts as you can and write them down. Let your counselor or group help you. This is uncovering your automatic thinking.

Once you have a list of the trigger thoughts, go back and develop thoughts that are accurate. What thinking would have been appropriate for each situation?

You will be amazed at how your inaccurate thinking fuels your anger. Keep a record of anger situations and your thinking for at least 12 weeks. In time, you will be able to catch yourself in the old thinking and correct yourself. Once you are thinking accurately, you will act appropriately. Soon the old thinking will not sound so convincing and so right. You will not feel like a victim anymore.

Stopping Escalation

Gerald Patterson of the Oregon Social Learning Center found that anger between people depends on *aversive chains* of behavior where people attempt to influence each other through a rapid exchange of punishing communications. These chains are more likely to occur when the people have relatively equal power such as like husband and wife, parents and children, peers, friends and coworkers. Aversive chains usually begin with small events and develop along predictable lines. Early exchanges often are overlooked because they seem unimportant.

Aversive chains are the building blocks to violence.

Most aversive chains never pass beyond the first link. Someone teases or insults another, and there is no response. Because no one reacts to the provocation, the problem stops after a few seconds. Three- or four-link chains usually last no longer than a half minute and exist even in healthy homes and relationships. If an aversive chain lasts longer than a half minute, then yelling, threatening, or hitting may occur. The longer a chain lasts, the more likely it is that things are going to get out of control.

Stop an aversive chain at the earliest possible moment.

The last link in an aversive chain is a trigger behavior. These behaviors usually precede violence. Triggers are verbal or nonverbal behaviors that bring up feelings of *abandonment* or *rejection*. These feelings are too painful to deal with, and the person feeling them needs them to stop right now.

A variety of statements can put the last link in an aversive chain. These are the responses that you need to eliminate, replacing them with your new coping skills.

Verbal Trigger Behaviors

1. Giving sarcastic advice: "Tell them to give you a raise. We need the money."

2. Engaging in global labeling: "All women are like that."

3. Criticizing: "You did not shovel the walk. You made a little path."

4. Blaming: "If you'd just do some work around here . . ."

5. Setting abrupt limits: "That's it. I am out of here."

6. Threatening: "If you do not like it, then get out."

7. Cursing: "Shut the hell up."

8. Complaining: "Ever since I married you, I have been unhappy."

9. Mind reading: "You are trying to drive me crazy."

10. Stonewalling: "There's nothing more to talk about."

11. Making sarcastic observations: "Did you dump the trash in your room?"

12. Making humiliating statements: "When we got married, you were better looking."

13. Giving dismissing statements: "Get out."

14. Giving put-downs: "Is this what you call clean?"

15. Accusing: "You did it again, didn't you?"

16. Laying on the guilt: "You know I cannot stand that."

17. Giving ultimatums: "If you do not shape up, I am leaving."

Nonverbal Trigger Sounds

1. Groaning: "I have had it with you."

2. Sighing: "You are such a burden."

3. Making a fist: "If you do not shut up, I am going to knock your head off."

4. Getting in a person's face: "You are going to get hurt if you keep this up!"

Voice Quality Triggers

1. Whining (irritating tone)

2. Flatness in voice (as though you checked out a long time ago)

3. Cold tone (the other person will never reach you)

4. Throaty constriction (barely controlled rage)

5. Loud and harsh tone (threatening)

6. Mocking and contemptuous tone (shaming)

7. Mumbling under your breath (the other person has to guess what you said)

8. Snickering (laughing at the other person)

9. Snarling (you had better back off)

Trigger Gestures

1. Finger-pointing

2. Shaking a fist

3. Flipping the bird

4. Folding arms

5. Waving away

Trigger Facial Expressions

1. Looking away

2. Rolling the eyes

3. Narrowing the eyes

4. Opening eyes wide

5. Grimacing

6. Sneering

7. Frowning

8. Tightening the lips

9. Raising an eyebrow

10. Scowling

Trigger Body Movements

1. Shaking the head

2. Shrugging the shoulders

3. Tapping a foot or finger

4. Leaning forward (intimidating)

5. Turning away

6. Putting hands on hips

7. Making quick and sudden movements

8. Kicking or throwing an object

9. Pushing or grabbing

Spend time each evening reviewing your anger journal. Write down your verbal and nonverbal trigger behaviors. In time, you will be able to recognize your patterns. Begin eliminating your trigger behaviors and using your new coping skills instead.

Example of an Aversive Chain

Bob comes home from the office and sees his spouse, Patty, sitting quietly on the couch. The boss got on his case again today, and Bob needs some support. Rather than asking Patty for what he needs, here is how the conversation goes:

Bob: I can see you had a hard day in front of the television.

Patty: I have been working my tail off. (Patty is instantly defensive.)

Bob: I know what you do. You lay around all day. (Bob crosses his arms sarcastically.)

Patty: I work every bit as hard as you do. (Patty looks at him angrily.)

Bob: Do I have to cook dinner, too? (Bob walks into the kitchen.)

Patty: What is wrong with you today? (Patty gets up and follows him.)

Bob: Don't yell at me!

Patty: Nothing I do pleases you anymore. (Patty begins to cry.)

Bob: If you don't like it, then get the hell out! (Bob is out of control, shaking in fury.)

Bob will not get Patty's support this way. He needed his wife to help him, but he got the exact opposite of what he wanted. Now his needs are more frustrated. He fumes and primes himself for the next battle.

At every point along this aversive chain, Bob and Patty could have de-escalated the conflict. Remember that anger is a choice.

Breaking Aversive Chains

Time-Out

The best thing you can do when you find yourself in an aversive chain is to call a time-out. This is a contract that two people make when they are not angry. The first party to recognize an aversive chain makes a time-out sign (a *T* made with both hands in front of the body). This person says, "Time-out." The other person only returns the gesture and says, "Okay, time-out." The person who called time-out then leaves the aversive situation for a predetermined amount of time, usually an hour. The person who leaves agrees to return and work on the problem after the time is up or to make an appointment to work on it later. Time-out never should be used to avoid a problem. Time-out is meant to avoid escalating stress. Time-out says, "It is time to separate. I will be right back."

Each person should know exactly what is going to happen after a time-out has been called. They need to be certain that the other person is going to return. Abandonment and rejection issues are involved here, and they create a lot of fear. A time-out contract needs to be written and signed by both parties. The couple needs to role-play using the time out several times in a nonthreatening situation.

After a called time out, wait for your feelings to cool down and then try to get accurate in your thinking. Take out these coping statements and read them to yourself.

"Do not blame."

"Do not try to fix the other person."

"What can I do differently?"

"The other person is not trying to hurt me. The other person is meeting his or her own needs."

"The other person is doing the only thing that he or she knows how to do at the moment."

"If I want the situation to change, then I need to change my behavior."

"What can I say to start the conversation off on a positive note?"

"I need to relax and stay relaxed."

Rechannel

If you see yourself in an aversive chain, rechannel the conversation to a subject that is nonthreatening. The earlier in the aversive chain this is done, the more effective it will be. Sometimes you can just keep quiet and that is enough. Do not fuel the anger with your old trigger behaviors. Defuse it with your new coping statements.

"There is no absolutely right or wrong answer here."

"We both are partially right."

"It is time to rechannel this discussion."

"Let us go over this later."

"Can we talk about this in an hour?"

Inquiry

When you see yourself in an aversive chain, pull information from the other person. This makes the other person feel important and loved. Remember that anger is a response to pain. Ask the person about how he or she is feeling and thinking.

"What is hurting you?"

"I am concerned about you."

"Tell me what is causing you to feel bad."

"What do you think we need to do to solve this problem?"

Old Road Map

An old road map takes events from our past and places it unrealistically over the present. We expect people to respond to us in the same way as others have in the past. If our parents were not trustworthy, then we assume that other people are not trustworthy. If we got hurt by a past relationship, then we expect the same thing from the next relationship.

The key to preventing mind reading is to check it out with the other person. Do not assume that you know what the other person is thinking. Ask the other person.

Once you begin asking the other person how he or she feels and what he or she thinks, you will learn a lot about yourself. You will learn about your old maps and how they are inaccurate.

"How do you feel?"

"What do you want me to do?"

"Tell me more about what you are thinking."

"What do you suggest we do to resolve the problem?"

Improving Self-Talk

You need to develop many positive things to say to yourself. Make a list of 10 positive self-statements and keep them with you. When you are feeling uncomfortable, take them out and read them over to yourself. Some work better than others do. Memorize the ones that work for you.

"I am a good person."

"I am smart and capable."

"I am God's child and he loves me."

"No matter what happens, I am going to be all right."

"I can take care of myself."

Reassure Yourself

You may have to reassure yourself that you are going to be able to get through an aversive chain.

"I can handle this."

"I can call a time out if I need to."

"If I find myself getting angry, I can deal with it."

"I can find the appropriate coping strategy."

"I believe in myself."

Stop Trigger Thoughts

Do not allow yourself to fall back into old thinking. You are not a victim. You always have a choice.

"I am responsible for what happens to me."

"I am never a victim. I have a choice."

"I can take care of my own needs."

"Do not blame."

"People never do what they should do."

"I am free to do anything I want."

"There is no right or wrong answer."

"The amount of support that I am getting is all I can get at the moment."

"Anger never will get me what I want."

"Do not mind read."

Physiological Coping

Monitor your physiological functioning. If you feel uptight, then tell yourself to relax. This reduces your stress and makes you deal with the situation more accurately.

"Take a deep breath."

"Relax."

"Feel your arms and legs become loose and limp."

"Stay calm."

"Visualize one of your favorite places."

"Meditate or relax for 20 to 30 minutes. Get in a quiet place, sit or lie down, and pay attention to your breathing. Each time you exhale, say the word *one* over to yourself. When other ideas come, just return to the number one."

Problem Solving

When you have a problem, use these problem solving skills. Continue to process through the options until everyone agrees to try a solution.

1. Write down the problem.

2. Communicate your feelings.

3. Ask for what you want.

4. Acknowledge the other person's point of view.

5. Develop a list of options.

6. Discuss the pros and cons of each option.

7. Keep working until you reach a consensus.

Coping Script

Prepare for an angry situation with a set of coping statements. Pick the coping statements that seem to work best for you. You might have to change them from time to time and from situation to situation. What are you going to say to yourself the next time you find yourself getting angry?

List five ways to reassure yourself:

1.

2.

3.

4.

5.

List five ways to stop the trigger thoughts:

1.

2.

3.

4.

5.

List five ways to cope physiologically:

1.

2.

3.

4.

5.

List five ways to move to problem solving:

1.

2.

3.

4.

5.

List five accurate sentences. When you find yourself in an aversive chain, say them over to yourself.

1.

2.

3.

4.

5.

Motivating Yourself

Each morning, go over the costs of your anger. Explore its toll on you and on those you love. Review the consequences of your last anger episode. Make a contract with your significant other to work on practicing the new coping skills and practice them often. You can do it.

The Time-Out Contract

When I realize that my (or my partner's) anger is rising, I will give a "T" time-out sign and leave at once. I will not hit or kick anything, and I will not slam the door.

I will return in no more than 1 hour. I will take a walk to use up the energy, and I will not drink or use drugs while I am away. I will try not to focus on resentments.

When I return, I will start the conversation with the following: "I know that I was partly wrong and partly right." I will then admit to a mistake that I made.

If my partner gives a "T" sign and leaves, then I will return the sign and let my partner go without a hassle no matter what is going on. I will not drink or use drugs while my partner is away. I will try to avoid focusing on resentments. When my partner returns, I will start the conversation with the following: "I know that I was partly wrong and partly right." I will then admit to a mistake that I made.

Signature _____ *Date* _____

Signature _____ *Date* _____

Appendix 33

Narcissism

Robert R. Perkinson, PhD

This might be a difficult exercise for you to read, so you need to be open-minded and willing to learn something new about yourself. You seem to have some narcissistic traits that get you into trouble and lead you to addiction. For example, you tend to be too sensitive to criticism. Whenever someone criticizes you even a little, you get very hurt and sometimes retaliate: "How dare you criticize me?" Underneath the anger, you feel wounded. You think that to be loved, you have to be the best, the brightest, the most beautiful, or the most successful. You do not know how to be genuinely close to others, but you have a great need for people to love you. The real problem is that, underneath it all, you do not feel good about yourself. You feel ashamed of who you are and what you have done. You fear that other people are better than you are.

Narcissus was a beautiful man in Greek mythology that refused to love others. As punishment for his indifference, the gods made him fall in love with himself. He became so enamored with himself that he could not stop gazing at his reflection in a pool of water. Finally, he fell into the water and drowned. Narcissism is a term for people who have an exaggerated need to be admired. Because of this need, they develop an exaggerated sense of their own importance. They exaggerate their talents, accomplishments, and achievements so as to be respected. They stretch the truth to build their fragile self-images. Narcissistic individuals develop an overwhelming need to feel special, and they expect to be treated in special ways. They become excessively concerned with themselves and their needs, losing the capacity to be sensitive to the needs of others. Their relationships start out in great hope and pleasure but end up in disaster. At first, everything seems fine, and the love is wonderful. When the other person begins to have his or her own needs and make demands, the anger gets going.

Alcoholics Anonymous (AA) (2002a) says that this self-centeredness is at the root of our addiction:

Each person is like an actor who wants to run the whole show [and] is forever trying to arrange the lights, the ballet, the scenery, and the rest of the players in his own way. If his arrangements would only stay put, if only people would do as he wished, the show would be great. Everybody, including himself, would be pleased. Life would be wonderful. In trying to make these arrangements, our actor may sometimes be quite virtuous. He may be kind, considerate, patent, generous, even modest and self-sacrificing. On the other hand, he may be mean, egotistical, selfish, and dishonest. As with most humans, he is more likely to have varied traits.

What usually happens? The show does not come off very well. He begins to think life does not treat him right. He decides to exert himself more. He becomes, on the next occasion, still more demanding or gracious, as the case may be. Still, the play does not suit him. Admitting he may be somewhat at fault, he is sure that other people are more to blame. He becomes angry, indignant, [and] self-pitying. What is his basic trouble? Is he not really a self-seeker even when trying to be kind? Is he not a victim of the delusion that he can wrest satisfaction and happiness of this world if he only managed well? (p. 61)

As you read this exercise, you might not think that you are self-centered. The very idea may make you feel angry. To have any flaw would dent that perfect image you have of yourself. That is the problem. So long as you need to be perfect, criticism sends you tumbling into shame. If you need to be right all of the time, others never seem to respect you. This is what happens. You think that you need to be the best at everything, and then someone comes along who is as good as, or better than, you are. Then you feel humiliated. Critical comments by others send you off the edge of sanity. You fume, you rage, and you get even. You cannot stand the suggestion that you are not perfect in every way.

To understand the trap of narcissism, you need to understand the narcissistic traits. Let us look at a few and circle any of them that fit you.

1. Do you often desire to be the center of attention?

2. Do you want to be the life of the party?

3. Do you feel resentful when your friends achieve something?

4. Do you feel unappreciated?

5. Do you want a beautiful woman or man to hang all over you so that other people can see how wonderful you are?

6. Do you think that you are more intelligent than most?

7. Do you tend to brag about and exaggerate your accomplishments?

8. Do you make a good first impression but have difficulty following through?

9. Do you think people would be better off if they would follow your direction?

10. Do you tend to resent authority figures?

11. Do you try to control people close to you?

12. Do you have difficulty accepting criticism?

13. Do you tend to be unsatisfied in interpersonal relationships?

14. Are you obsessed with money and material things?

15. Are you good at charming others to get what you want?

16. Do you fantasize about big plans and schemes?

17. Do you relish being the big shot?

18. Do you feel that you do not get the respect you deserve?

19. Do you believe that the rules and laws are made for other people?

20. Do you want to be God?

If you circled any of these statements, you have some narcissism. These are the immature narcissistic needs, or the infantile needs, of an individual who wants to be in control. They are the needs of someone who is desperate for attention. No amount of love would be enough for you. You always would need more and more love. Other people have tried to love you, and they always have fallen short, haven't they? Then you blame them without looking at yourself. It is always the other person's fault and never your own. If the other person would just recognize you for the great person that you are and do what you want him or her to do, then things would go fine.

Narcissistic traits are why you are spiritually bankrupt. This is why you have been feeling so empty. This is why you never fit in and you used the addiction to ease the pain.

Now let us look at the crux of the issue. When you look at these characteristics carefully, you can see that you have been trying to be God. You are not God, and you never will be God, so as long as you try being God, you will feel like a failure.

A Feeling of Worthlessness

Underneath your need to be in control is the feeling of worthlessness you learned as a small child. Somewhere in development, you learned you were a totally worthless person who is incapable of loving others like you should. These thoughts are intolerable, so you began to cover them with a false front. You are not worthless; you are the king, leader, star, director, best friend, and lover of all. With these two conflicting ideas in your mind, you vacillate between being the greatest person and the worst person. There is no middle ground. You are either on the top or on the bottom—never in between, never normal. The reason why you need constant reassurance from others is that you do not feel good about yourself. You feel inadequate. To counteract this feeling, you exaggerate your talents and accomplishments. This is a vain attempt to get people to love you. Give 10 examples of when you lied about your accomplishments or talents to get someone to like you.

1.

2.

3.

4.

5.

6.

7.

8.

9.

10.

Because you feel worthless, you have a difficult time hearing the word *no*. When someone says no, you feel that you are bad. Either you are the best or the worst. When someone says no, you get angry and go into a rage. That makes everything worse.

Give five examples of when someone told you no and you got furious.

1.

2.

3.

4.

5.

Because of your feelings of worthlessness, you need to feel special and other people need to recognize your unique abilities. You believe that only special people of high status can really understand you. Because you have a need to be perfect, you routinely overestimate your capabilities. For example, you think that you are going to make all As in your classes and get angry at the teacher when you get lower grades. It is always the teacher's fault, or the boss's fault, or the spouse's fault—never your own fault. You need to be admired and respected even when you have not worked for it. You expect to start at the top rather than work your way up like other people must do.

Give five examples of when you expected to be loved and respected and you did not deserve it.

1.

2.

3.

4.

5.

It is important for you to see how these unrealistic ideals set you up to fail. No one is perfect, so when you expect this of yourself, you always fail. When you think that your work has to be perfect, you end up feeling humiliated when someone points out that you did something wrong.

Give five examples of when someone criticized you and you felt hurt and angry.

1.

2.

3.

4.

5.

Because of your feelings of worthlessness, you spend a lot of time fantasizing about success, power, brilliance, and/or ideal love. You thought how wonderful this new job will be, or this new love, or this new ability. This immature need for unlimited success sets you up to fail. You end up feeling more miserable.

Discuss the last romance you had and what happened. Describe how perfect you thought it was at first and how it actually turned out. Concentrate on how you judged the relationship unrealistically from the beginning and see how you unrealistically judged the relationship in the end. Have your counselor or group help you. Both of these judgments were inaccurate.

Love and sex put you at high risk because you put unrealistic expectations on the relationship. You expect the other person to meet your needs to feel important, special, loved, powerful, brilliant, and beautiful. There is no way in which a person can make you feel like that, so the relationship fails and you sink into despair.

Give five examples of how relationship problems lead to addictive behavior.

1.

2.

3.

4.

5.

A narcissistic person feels jealous of others and their accomplishments. By constantly comparing yourself to others, you end up feeling bad.

List five people who you are envious of, and write down exactly what they have that you want.

1.

2.

3.

4.

5.

It is important for you to recognize how you constantly compare yourself to others and how you end up feeling either superior or inferior to them. Either way, you have separated yourself from the truth and made love impossible. Intimacy necessitates truth, commitment, love, trust, and openness. Both partners need to come into a relationship feeling good about themselves. Love is the active involvement in the other person's growth.

To Loosen the Narcissistic Bonds

These narcissistic traits enslave you. You never will be perfect. You never will be the most brilliant, or the most beautiful, or the most powerful, or the most loved, or the most wonderful, or the most special. Not everyone will worship you. You believe that to be accepted, you have to be the greatest, but you do not. Narcissism is a life built on lies.

You Must Get Honest

Honesty is a wonderful thing. You cannot solve problems without the facts. If you make up the facts, then the problems never will be solved and you will be back to the misery. You never will feel loved if you make up who you are. Even if you fool the other person, you know that the person does not love you. You never will feel known until you tell the truth.

• The first thing that you need to do is not tell the old lies—you know, as if you are someone special with special talents. If you never worked for the CIA, then do not tell people that you did. If you did not make a lot of money, then do not tell people that you did. If you did not save a person from drowning, then do not say that you did. You get what I mean. You have a million stories that are not true. You have to stop lying. If you do not stop lying, then you will be unhappy.

List 10 lies you tell to get people to like you.

1.

2.

3.

4.

5.

6.

7.

8.

9.

10.

Promise yourself that you never will tell these lies again. Wake up every morning, and be grateful that you have not lied that day. Then try to get through the next hour without lying. If you make it, then congratulate yourself. That is a victory. Check out how you feel. You will be feeling good about yourself. When you lie, check out how you feel. You will be feeling fear and shame. Dishonesty is the main reason why you have been isolated. Only by being honest will you ever feel accepted and loved.

You Must Go to Meetings

To loosen the bonds of narcissism, you must go to meetings and trust others to help you. This is very difficult because the only person you trust is yourself. In this illness, if you rely only on yourself, then you will die. You need to turn your will and your life over to someone who can manage your life. Start with anyone you can such as your counselor, group, or sponsor. Lay your trust in that person, and whatever you do, do not trust yourself. Your best judgment got you into this mess. You do not know the way out. Someone else is going to have to show you the way. Name the person(s) who you are going to try to trust.

Name: _____ Phone: _____

Name: _____ Phone: _____

Name: _____ Phone: _____

When you feel like taking the controls back again, do not do so. When someone makes a suggestion, try it.

You Must Seek a Higher Power

You need to seek a Higher Power of your own understanding. There is only one you, and you are special. You are not better than everyone; everyone is equal. This makes life better, not worse. This alone gives you the opportunity to love rather than rule. Everyone has his or her unique place in God's plan. Whatever you do, God will be there for you, supporting you, educating you, and caring for you. Take a risk, and ask God to come into your life. Say something like this: "God, I do not know if you are out there or not, but if you are, please come into my life and help me." Then ask God a question: "God, what is the next step in my relationship with you?" Now be quiet. Do not be afraid. Wait. A word or phrase will come through your mind. It will be something like this: "Trust me" or "Pray." That is God speaking to you inside of your thinking.

Write down what word, phrase, image, or feeling came to mind and what this means to your relationship with God.

If you take that step, then you will feel the peace that AA calls serenity. God will tell you the next step, not the second or the third step. If you follow God's plan systematically, then you are free.

Appendix 34

Honesty for Gamblers

Robert R. Perkinson, PhD

This is an exercise to help you get honest with yourself. In recovery, it is essential to tell the truth. As you will hear at every Gamblers Anonymous (GA) meeting, this is a program of rigorous honesty. Those who do not recover are people who cannot, or will not, completely give themselves to this simple program.

Dishonesty to self and others distorts reality. You never will solve problems if you lie. You need to live in the facts. You must commit yourself to reality. This means accepting everything that is real.

Gamblers lie to themselves when they think they can beat a game of chance. Chance means you cannot manipulate the outcome of a game. Gamblers constantly think they can figure a game out, which machine will win, which numbers will come up, which horse will win, which card they will draw, or which number will come up in roulette or bingo. The actual odds are this: The house gets 6% of every dollar you bet, so if you continue to gamble, you will lose every penny you have. Gambling establishments are not fancy because of the winners; they are fancy because they can predict that the odds are always in their favor. The casino will always win. All of the games are stacked in their favor, and there is no way you can predict a game of chance. Each time you play each game, the odds are exactly the same. There is no way to predict which horse, number, color, or machine will win. The odds are exactly the same each time you play. Gamblers constantly think they can figure a game out and increase the odds of winning, but this is never true. Memorize this sentence, and say it over and over to yourself: "If I continue to gamble, there is a 100% chance that I will lose everything."

A video lottery machine has a random number generator that randomly generates the next numbers. Let us say the odds on one machine are 200 to 1 big win. So imagine that you have 200 white marbles in a bin and one red marble. You spin the bin and draw out one marble. The odds of choosing the red marble are 200 to 1. Now you put the marble back in the bin, spin the bin, and draw out a marble. The odds are exactly the same 200 to 1. All gambling is a game of chance, and there is no way to predict when the machine, game, or player is going to change the odds. In the marble game, there will always be a 200 to 1 chance that you will win. The real odds are that if you continue to gamble you will be penniless. A casino only offers games of chance— never games of skill. The house would not let you play a game of skill because you could learn the skill and increase your odds of winning. The house never makes this mistake. The odds are always in favor of the casino. If you continue to gamble, the casino will always win. If you continue to gamble, you will always lose everything.

Here is a list of 10 statements you may have said to yourself that gave you the illusion that you could figure out a game of chance.

1. This machine has not paid out all day; it is ready to pay. No, the odds are always the same.

2. This horse always wins on a muddy track. No, the odds of one horse winning are always the same.

3. This blackjack dealer is unlucky; this is the table to play. I would win here. No, with every deal the odds are always the same.

4. If I keep playing this color it has to win soon. No, the odds are always random.

5. This roulette dealer spins too fast, the ball runs too fast, and this makes it more likely that the ball will fall on number 22. No, the odds are random and always the same. If you continue to gamble, you will be penniless.

6. If I keep count of the numbers, I can figure this game out and increase my odds of winning. No, games of chance are not games of skill. The odds are the same every time you play the game.

7. I always use this machine. It pays out the best. No, a machine has a random number generator, and each time you play you have the same odds of winning.

8. If I keep playing the numbers of my birthday, I will win every time. No, the odds are if you continue to gamble you will lose every cent you have.

9. If I do not want to win, I win every time. No, the odds are always the same.

10. This is my lucky day. I cannot lose. No, the odds are random; you cannot predict or use a skill to change the odds at a game of chance.

People who are pathological gamblers think that they cannot tell the truth. They believe that if they do, then they will be rejected. The facts, however, are exactly the opposite. Unless you tell the truth, no one can accept you. People have to know you to accept you. If you keep secrets, then you never will feel known or loved. You are only as sick as your secrets. If you keep secrets from people, then you never will be close to them.

You cannot be a practicing gambling addict without lying to yourself. You must lie and believe the lies or else the illness cannot operate. All of the lies are attempts to protect you from the truth. If you had known the truth, then you would have known that you were sick and needed treatment. This would have been frightening, so you kept the truth from yourself and from others. Let us face it. When we were gambling, we were not honest with ourselves.

There are many ways in which you lied to yourself. This exercise will teach you exactly how you distorted reality, and it will start you toward a program of honesty. Respond to each of the following as completely as you can.

1. *Denying:* This is telling yourself or others, "I do not have a problem." Write down five examples of when you used this technique to avoid the anxiety of the truth.

2. *Minimizing:* This is making the problem smaller than it really is. You may have told yourself, or someone else, that your problem was not that bad. You may have told someone that you lost a little money when, in fact, you lost a lot. Write down five examples of when you distorted reality by making the problem seem smaller than it actually was.

3. *Being Hosile:* This is getting angry, shutting people out, or making threats when someone confronts you about your gambling. Give five examples of when you expressed such hostility.

4. *Rationalizing:* This is making an excuse. "I had a hard day. Things are bad. My relationship is bad. My financial situation is bad. The only way I can recover my losses is to gamble." Give five examples of when you thought that you had a good reason to gamble.

5. *Blaming:* This is shifting the responsibility to someone else. "The police were out to get me. My wife is overreacting, my boss is a pain." Give five examples of when you blamed someone else for a problem that you caused by gambling.

6. *Intellectualizing:* This is overanalyzing and thinking to excess about a problem. This avoids doing something about it. "Sure, I gamble some, but everyone I know gambles. I read this article that said this is a gambling culture. I know this machine is ready to pay out." Give five examples of how you use intellectual data and statistics to justify your gambling.

7. *Diverting:* This is bringing up another topic of conversation to avoid being confronted with your gambling. Give five examples.

Make a list of five lies about your gambling problem that you told to someone close to you.

1.

2.

3.

4.

5.

Make a list of five lies about your gambling problem that you told to yourself.

1.

2.

3.

4.

5.

Make a list of 10 people to whom you have lied.

1.

2.

3.

4.

5.

6.

7.

8.

9.

10.

How do you feel about your lying? Describe how you feel about yourself when you lie.

List five things you think will change in your life if you stop gambling and tell the truth.

1.

2.

3.

4.

5.

How do you use lies in other areas of your life?

When are you the most likely to lie? Is it when you have been gambling?

Why do you lie? What does it get you? Give five reasons.

1.

2.

3.

4.

5.

Common lies of gamblers are listed here. Give a personal example of each.

1. Breaking promises:

2. Pretending you have not gambled when, in fact, you have:

3. Pretending that you remember how long you had been gambling when, in fact, you lost all track of time:

4. Telling someone that you gamble no more than others do:

5. Telling yourself that you were in control of your gambling:

6. Telling someone that you rarely gamble:

7. Hiding your gambling:

8. Hiding money for gambling:

9. Substituting gambling for other activities and then telling someone that you were not interested in doing what that person wanted to do:

10. Saying that you were too sick to do something when, in fact, you really wanted to gamble:

11. Pretending not to care about your gambling problem:

People who are pathological gamblers lie to avoid facing the pain of the truth. Lying makes them feel more comfortable, but in the end they end up feeling isolated and alone. Recovery demands living in the truth. "I am a pathological gambler. My life is unmanageable. I am powerless over gambling. I need help. I cannot do this alone." All of these are honest statements from someone who is living in reality.

You can either get real and live in the real world or live in a fantasy world of your own creation. If you get honest, then you will begin to solve real problems. You will be accepted for who you are.

Wake up tomorrow morning, and promise yourself that you are going to be honest all day. Write down in a diary when you are tempted to lie. Watch your emotions when you lie. How does it feel? How do you feel about yourself? Write it all down. Keep a diary for 5 days, and then share it with your group. Tell the group members how it feels to be honest.

Write the word *truth* on a piece of paper and hang it on your bathroom mirror. Commit yourself to rigorous honesty. You deserve to live a life filled with love and truth. You never need to lie again.

List 10 reasons you want to stop gambling.

1.

2.

3.

4.

5.

6.

7.

8.

9.

10.

Appendix 35

Step One for Gamblers

Robert R. Perkinson, PhD

We admitted we were powerless over gambling—that our lives had become unmanageable.

—Gamblers Anonymous (GA) (1989b, p. 38)

Before beginning this exercise, please read Step One in *G.A.: A New Beginning* (GA, 1989b).

No one likes to admit defeat. Our minds rebel at the very thought that we have lost control. We are big, strong, intelligent, and capable. How can it be that we are powerless? How can our lives be unmanageable? This exercise will help you to sort through your life and to make some important decisions. Answer as completely as you can each question that applies to you. This is an opportunity for you to get accurate. You need to see the truth about yourself.

Let us pretend for a moment that you are the commander in a nuclear missile silo. You are in charge of a bomb. If you think about it, this is exactly the kind of control that you want over your life. You want to be in control of your thinking, feeling, and behavior. You want to be in control all of the time, not just some of the time. If you do something by accident, or if you do something foolishly, then you might kill many people.

> What is the first thing a compulsive gambler ought to do in order to stop gambling? The compulsive gambler needs to accept the fact that he or she is in the grip of a progressive illness and has a desire to get well. (GA, 1989a, p. 8)

To accept powerlessness and unmanageability, a gambler must look at the truth. People who are powerless over gambling do things that are harmful to themselves and others. They do most anything to stay in action—to keep gambling. Gamblers do not consider the consequences of their behavior, and they keep gambling until they are on the verge of death.

Gamblers are *in action* when they plan a bet, make a bet, or wait for a bet to come in. Once the bet is in, they are out of action. Being in action is a primary goal of compulsive gamblers. By staying in action, gamblers feel how they want to feel. They escape reality. They live in a fantasy world of their own creation. Some gamblers gamble for the thrill and some to escape. Now it is time to get honest with yourself.

Powerlessness

People who are powerless do things that they feel bad or guilty about later. To gamble, they may lie, cheat, steal, hurt their family members, or do poor work. Make a list of five things that made you feel the most uncomfortable about gambling in the past.

1.

2.

3.

4.

5.

People who are powerless gradually lose respect for themselves. They will have difficulty in trusting themselves. List five ways have you lost respect for yourself due to gambling.

1.

2.

3.

4.

5.

People who are powerless will do things that they do not remember doing. When gamblers gamble, they can lose all track of time. They might think that they have been gambling for only a few minutes when, in fact, they have been gambling for many hours. If you gamble enough, you cannot remember things properly. Describe five situations when you lost track of time while you were gambling.

1.

2.

3.

4.

5.

People who are powerless cannot keep promises they make to themselves or others. They promise that they will cut down on their gambling, and they do not. They promise that they will not gamble, and they do. They promise to be home, to be at work, to be at the Cub Scout meeting, or to go to school, but they do not make it. They cannot always do what they want to do. They disappoint themselves, and they lose trust in themselves. Other people lose trust in them. Gamblers can count on themselves some of the time, but they cannot count on themselves all of the time.

1. List five times you promised yourself that you would cut down on your gambling.

2. What happened to each of these promises?

3. Did you ever promise yourself that you would quit entirely?

   Yes   No

4. What happened to your promise?

5. Did you ever make a promise to someone that you did not keep because you were gambling? Give five examples.

6. Are you reliable when you are gambling?

   Yes   No

People who are powerless lose control of their behavior. They do things that they would not normally do when not in action. They might get into fights. They might yell at people they love—their spouses, children, parents, or friends. They might say things that they do not mean.

Have you ever gotten into an argument with someone because you were gambling? Describe five times.

1.

2.

3.

4.

5.

The desire to gamble is very powerful. It makes a gambler feel irritable and impatient. People who are powerless say things that they do not mean. They say things that they feel guilty about later. We might not remember everything we said, but the other person does remember. List five times when you said something or did something that you did not mean when gambling or craving gambling? What did you say? What did you do?

1.

2.

3.

4.

5.

People are powerless when they cannot deal with their feelings. They may gamble because they feel frightened, angry, or sad. They medicate their feelings with gambling.

1. Have you ever gambled to cover up your feelings? Give three examples.

   a.
   b.
   c.

2. List the feelings that you have difficulty dealing with.

People are powerless when they are not safe. What convinces you that you no longer can gamble safely?

People are powerless when they know that they should do something, but they cannot make themselves do it. They might make a great effort to do the right thing, but they keep doing the wrong thing.

1. Could you cut down on your gambling every time you wanted for as long as you wanted?

   Yes   No

2. Did gambling ever keep you from doing something at home that you thought you should do? Give five examples.

    a.

    b.

    c.

    d.

    e.

3. Did gambling ever keep you from going to work? Give five examples.

    a.

    b.

    c.

    d.

    e.

4. Did you ever lose a job because of your gambling? Write down what happened.

People are powerless when other people have to warn them that they are in trouble. You may have felt as though you were fine, but people close to you noticed that something was wrong. It probably was difficult for them to define just what was wrong, but they worried about you. It is difficult to confront people when they are wrong, so most people avoid the problem until they cannot stand the behavior anymore. When gamblers are confronted with their behavior, they feel annoyed and irritated. They want to be left alone with the lies that they are telling themselves. Has anyone ever talked to you about your gambling? Who was this? How did you feel?

People are powerless when they do not know the truth about themselves. Gamblers lie to themselves about how much they are gambling. They lie to themselves about how often they gamble. They lie to themselves about the amount of money they are losing, even when the losses are obvious. They blame others for their problems. Some common lies that they tell themselves include the following:

"I can quit anytime I want to."

"I only gamble a little."

"The police are out to get me."

"I only gamble when I want to."

"Everybody does it."

"I gamble, but I do not have a problem."

"Anybody can have financial problems."

"My friends will not like me if I do not gamble."

"I never have problems when I gamble."

"I can pay the money back later."

"From now on, I would just gamble a little."

"When I win, I am going to buy a present for my family."

Gamblers continue to lie to themselves to the very end. They hold on to their delusional thinking, and they believe that their lies are the truth. They deliberately lie to those close to them. They hide their gambling. They make their problems seem smaller than they actually are. They make excuses for why they are gambling. They refuse to see the truth.

1. Have you ever lied to yourself about your gambling? List five lies that you told yourself.

2. List five ways in which you tried to convince yourself that you did not have a problem.

3. List five ways in which you tried to convince others that you did not have a problem.

Therefore, it is not surprising that our gambling careers have been characterized by countless vain attempts to prove we could gamble like other people. The idea that somehow, someday, we will control our gambling is the great obsession of every compulsive gambler. The persistence of this illusion is astonishing. Many pursue it to the gates of prison, insanity, or death (GA, 1989a, p. 2).

Unmanageability

Imagine that you are the manager of a large corporation. You are responsible for how everything runs. If you are not a good manager, then the business will fail. You must carefully plan everything and carry out those plans well. You must be alert. You must know exactly where you are and where you are going. These are the skills that you need to manage your life effectively.

Gamblers are not good managers. They keep losing control. Their plans fall through. They cannot devise and stick to things long enough to see a solution. They are lying to themselves, so they do not know who they are. They feel confused. Their feelings are being changed by gambling, so they cannot use their feelings to give them energy and direction for problem solving.

You do not have to be a bad manager all of the time. It is worse to be a bad manager some of the time. It is very confusing. Most gamblers have flurries of productive activity during which they work too much. They work themselves to the bone, and then they let things slide. It is like being on a roller coaster. Sometimes things are in control, and sometimes things are out of control. Things are up and down, and gamblers never can predict which way things are going to be tomorrow.

People's lives are unmanageable when they have plans fall apart because they are gambling. Make a list of 5 plans that you failed to complete because of your gambling.

1.

2.

3.

4.

5.

People's lives are unmanageable when they cannot manage their finances consistently.

1. List the money problems that you are having.

2. Explain how gambling has contributed to these problems.

People's lives are unmanageable when they cannot trust their own judgments.

1. Have you ever been so absorbed in your gambling that you did not know what was happening around you? Explain.

2. Did you ever lie to yourself about your gambling? Explain how your lies contributed to your being unable to manage your life.

3. Have you ever made a decision while gambling that you were sorry about later? List five times.

People's lives are unmanageable when they cannot work or play normally. Gamblers miss work and recreational activities because of their gambling.

List five times when you missed work because you were gambling.

1.

2.

3.

4.

5.

List five recreational or family activities you missed because you were gambling.

1.

2.

3.

4.

5.

People's lives are unmanageable when they are in trouble with other people or society. Gamblers break the rules of society to get their own way. They have problems with authority.

1. Have you ever been in legal trouble when you were gambling? Explain the legal problems you have had.

2. Have you ever had problems with your parents because of your gambling? Explain.

3. Have you ever had problems in school because of your gambling? Explain.

People's lives are unmanageable when they cannot consistently achieve goals. Gamblers reach out for what they want, but something keeps getting in the way. It does not seem fair. They keep falling short of their goals. Finally, they give up completely. They may have had the goals of going to school, getting a better job, working on family problems, getting in good physical condition, and/or going on a diet. No matter what the goals are, something keeps going wrong with the plans. Gamblers constantly try to blame someone else, but they cannot work long enough to reach their goals. Gamblers are good starters, but they are poor finishers.

List five goals that you had for yourself that you did not achieve because of gambling.

1.

2.

3.

4.

5.

People's lives are unmanageable when they cannot use their feelings appropriately. Feelings give us energy and direction for problem solving. Gamblers change their feelings by staying in action. Gambling gives them a different feeling. Gamblers become very confused about how they feel.

1. What feelings have you tried to alter with gambling?

2. How do you feel when you are gambling? Describe them in detail.

People's lives are unmanageable when they violate their own rules by violating their own morals and values. Gamblers compromise their values to continue gambling. They have the value not to lie, but they lie anyway. They have the value not to steal, but they steal anyway. They have the value to be loyal to spouses or friends, but when they are gambling they do not remain loyal. Their values and morals fall away, one by one. They end up doing things that they do not believe in. They know that they are doing the wrong things, but they do them anyway.

1. Did you ever lie to cover up your gambling? How did you feel about yourself?

2. Were you ever disloyal when gambling? Explain.

3. Did you ever steal or write bad checks to gamble? Explain what you did and how you felt about yourself later.

4. Did you ever break the law when gambling? What did you do?

5. Did you ever hurt someone you loved while gambling? Explain.

6. Did you treat yourself poorly by refusing to stop gambling when you knew that it was bad for you? Explain how you were feeling about yourself.

7. Did you stop going to church? How did this make you feel about yourself?

People's lives are unmanageable when they continue to do something that gives them problems. Gambling creates severe financial problems. Even if gamblers are aware of the problems, they gamble anyway. They see gambling as the solution.

Gambling causes psychological problems. Compulsive gambling makes people feel depressed, fearful, anxious, and/or angry. Even when gamblers are aware of these symptoms, they continue to gamble.

Gambling creates relationship problems. It causes family problems in the form of family fights as well as verbal and physical abuse. It causes interpersonal conflict at work, with family, and with friends. Gamblers withdraw and become isolated and alone.

1. Did you have any persistent physical problems caused by, or made worse by, gambling? Describe the problems.

2. Did you have any persistent psychological problems, such as depression, that were caused by your gambling? Describe the problems.

3. Did you have persistent interpersonal conflicts that were made worse by gambling? Describe the problems.

We know that no real compulsive gambler ever regains control. All of us felt at times we were regaining control, but such intervals—usually brief—were inevitably followed by still less control, which led in time to pitiful and incomprehensible demoralization. We are convinced that gamblers of our type are in the grip of a progressive illness. Over any considerable period of time, we get worse, never better. (GA, 1989a, p. 3)

You must have good reasons to work toward a new life free from gambling. Look over this exercise, and list 10 reasons why you want to stop gambling.

1.

2.

3.

4.

5.

6.

7.

8.

9.

10.

After completing this exercise, take a long look at yourself. What is the truth?

1. Have there been times when you were powerless over gambling?
    Yes   No

2. Have there been times when your life was unmanageable?
    Yes   No

Appendix 36

Step Two for Gamblers

Robert R. Perkinson, PhD

[We] came to believe that a power greater than ourselves could restore us to a normal way of thinking and living.

—Gamblers Anonymous (GA) (1989b, p. 39)

Before beginning this exercise, please read Step Two in *G.A.: A New Beginning* (GA, 1989b).

In Step One, you admitted that you were powerless over gambling and that your life was unmanageable. In Step Two, you need to see the insanity of your disease and seek a power greater than yourself. If you are powerless, then you need power. If your life is unmanageable, then you need a manager. Step Two will help you to decide who that manager can be.

Most gamblers revolt at the implications of the phrase "restore to a normal way of thinking and living." They think that they may have a gambling problem, but they do not feel as though they have been abnormal.

In GA, the word *normal* means being of sound mind. Someone with a sound mind knows what is real and knows how to adapt to reality. A sound mind feels stable, safe, and secure. Someone who is abnormal cannot see reality and is unable to adapt. A person does not have to have all of reality distorted to be in trouble. If you miss some reality, then you ultimately will get lost. One wrong turn is all that it takes to end up in a ditch.

Going through life is like a long journey. You have a map given to you by your parents. The map shows the way in which to be happy. If you make some wrong turns along the way, then you will end up unhappy. This is what happens in gambling. Searching for happiness, we make wrong turns. We find out that our map is defective. Even if we followed our map to perfection, we still would be lost. What we need is a new map.

GA gives us this new map. It puts up 12 signposts to show us the way. If you follow this map as millions of people have, then you will find the joy and happiness that you have been seeking. You have reached and passed the first signpost, Step One. You have decided that your life is powerless and unmanageable over gambling. Now you need a new power source. You need to find someone else who can manage your life.

GA is a spiritual program, and it directs you toward a spiritual solution. It is not a religious program. Spirituality is defined as the relationship you have with yourself and all else. Religion is an organized system of faith and worship. Everyone has spirituality, but not everyone has religion.

You need to explore three relationships very carefully in Step Two: the relationships with yourself, with others, and with a Higher Power. This Higher Power can be any Higher Power of your choice. If you do not have a Higher Power right now, do not worry. Most of us started that way. Just be willing to consider that there is a power greater than you in the universe.

471

To explore these three relationships, you need to see the truth about yourself. If you see the truth, then you can find the way. First you must decide whether you were abnormal. Did you have a sound mind or not? Let us look at this issue carefully.

People are abnormal when they cannot remember what they did. They have memory problems. To be abnormal, they do not have to have memory problems all of the time; they just need to have them some of the time. People who gamble might not remember what happened to them when they were gambling. Long periods of time can pass during which gamblers are relatively unaware of their environment.

List any memory problems that you have had while gambling. Did you ever find that you had spent more time gambling that you remembered?

People who are abnormal lose control over their behavior. They do things when they are gambling that they never would do otherwise.

List three times when you lost control over your behavior while gambling.

1.

2.

3.

List three times when you could not control your gambling—when you told yourself to stop but you could not.

1.

2.

3.

People who are abnormal consider self-destruction.
Did you ever consider hurting yourself when you were gambling or suffering from gambling losses?

Yes   No

Describe what happened.

People who are abnormal feel emotionally unstable.
Have you ever thought that you were going crazy because of your gambling?

Yes   No

Describe some of these times.
Have you recently felt emotionally unstable?

Yes   No

Describe how you have been feeling.

People who are abnormal are so confused that they cannot get their lives in order. They frantically try to fix things, but problems remain out of control.

List 10 personal, family, work, or school problems that you have not been able to control.

1.

2.

3.

4.

5.

6.

7.

8.

9.

10.

People who are abnormal cannot see the truth about what is happening to them. People who are gambling hide their gambling from themselves and from others. They minimize, rationalize, and deny that there are problems.

Do you feel that you have been completely honest with yourself?

Yes   No

List five lies that you told yourself so you could continue gambling.

1.

2.

3.

4.

5.

People who are abnormal cut themselves off from healthy relationships. You might find that you cannot communicate with your spouse as well as you used to. You might not see your friends as often. More and more of your life centers around gambling.

List three people you do not see anymore because of your gambling.

1.

2.

3.

As your gambling increased, did you go to church less often?

Yes   No

List five relationships that you have damaged in your gambling.

1.

2.

3.

4.

5.

People who are abnormal cannot deal with their feelings. Problem gamblers cannot deal with their feelings. They do not like how they feel, so they gamble to control their feelings. Some people gamble to feel excited and some people gamble to escape.

List the feelings that you wanted to change by gambling.

Now look back over your responses. Get out your Step One exercise and read it. Look at the truth about yourself. Look carefully at how you were thinking, feeling, and behaving when you were gambling. Make a decision. Do you think that you had a sound mind? If you were unsound at least some of the time, then you were abnormal. If you believe this to be true, then say this to yourself: "I am powerless. My life is unmanageable. My mind is unsound. I have been abnormal in thinking and living."

A Power Greater Than Ourselves

Consider a power greater than yourself. What exists in the world that has greater power than you do—a river, the wind, the universe, the sun?

List five things that have greater power than you do.

1.

2.

3.

4.

5.

The first Higher Power that you need to consider is the power of the GA group. The group is more powerful than you are. Ten hands are more powerful than two are. Two heads are better than one. GA operates in groups. The group works like a family. The group process is founded in love and trust. Each member shares his or her experiences, strengths, and hopes in an attempt to help him or her and others. There is an atmosphere of anonymity. What you hear in group is confidential.

The group acts as a mirror reflecting you to yourself. The group members will help you to discover the truth about whom and what you are. You have been deceiving yourself for a long time. The group will help you to uncover the lies. You will come to understand the old GA saying, What we cannot do alone, we can do together. In group, you will have greater power over the disease because the group will see the whole truth better than you can.

You were not lying to hurt yourself; you were lying to protect yourself. In the process of building your lies, you cut yourself off from reality. This is how compulsive gambling works. You cannot recover from addiction by yourself. You need power coming from somewhere else. Begin by trusting your group. Keep an open mind.

You need to share in your group. The more you share, the closer you will get and the more trust you will develop. If you take risks, then you will reap the rewards. You do not have to tell the group everything, but you need to share as much as you can. The group can help you to straighten out your thinking and restore you to sanity.

Many gamblers are afraid of a Higher Power. They fear that a Higher Power will punish them or treat them in the same way that their fathers or mothers did. They might fear losing control. List some of the fears that you have about a Higher Power.

Some gamblers have difficulty in trusting anyone. They have been so hurt by others that they do not want to take the chance of being hurt again. What has happened in your life that makes it difficult for you to trust?

What are some of the things you will need to see from a Higher Power that will show you that the Higher Power can be trusted?

Who was the most trustworthy person you ever knew?

How did this person treat you?

What do you hope to gain by accepting a Higher Power?

GA wants you to come to believe in a power greater than yourself. You can accept any Higher Power that you feel can restore you to sanity. Your group, nature, your counselor, and your sponsor all can be used to give you this restoration. You must pick this Higher Power carefully. We suggest that you use GA as your Higher Power for now. Here is a group of people who are recovering. They have found the way. This program ultimately will direct you toward a God of your own understanding.

Millions of gamblers have recovered because they were willing to reach out for God. GA makes it clear that nothing else will remove the obsession to gamble. Some of us have so glorified our own lives that we have shut out God. Now is your opportunity. You are at a major turning point. You can begin to open your heart and let God in, or you can keep God out. God tells us that all who seek will find.

Remember that this is the beginning of a new life. To be new, you have to do things differently. All that the program is asking you to do is be open to the possibility that there is a power greater than you are. GA does not demand that you believe in anything. The 12 steps are simply suggestions. You do not have to swallow all of this now, but you need to be open. Most recovering persons take the Second Step a piece at a time.

First you need to learn how to trust yourself. You must learn how to treat yourself well. What do you need to see from yourself that will show you that you are trustworthy?

Then you need to begin to trust your group. See whether the group members act consistently in your interest. They will not always tell you what you want to hear. No real friend would do that. They will give you the opportunity and encouragement to grow. What will you need to see from the group members that will show you that they are trustworthy?

Every person has a unique spiritual journey. No one can start this journey with a closed mind. What is it going to take to show you that God exists?

Step Two does not mean that we believe in God as God is presented in any religion. Remember that religion is an organized system of worship. It is human-made. Worship is a means of assigning worth to something. Many people have been so turned off by religion that the idea of God is unacceptable. "We found that some of the obstacles preventing us from attempting to believe were pride, ego, fear, self-centeredness, defiance, and grandiosity" (GA, 1989b, p. 40).

Describe the religious environment of your childhood. What was it like? What did you learn about God?

How did these early experiences influence the beliefs that you have today?

What experiences have caused you to doubt God?

Your willingness is essential to your recovery. Give some examples of your willingness to trust in a Higher Power of your choice. What are you willing to do?

Describe your current religious beliefs.

Explain the God of your own understanding.

List five reasons why a Higher Power will be good for you.

1.

2.

3.

4.

5.

If you asked the people in your GA group to describe God, you would get a variety of answers. Each person has his or her own understanding of God. It is this unique understanding that allows God to work individually for each of us. God comes to each of us differently.

Appendix 37

Step Three for Gamblers

Robert R. Perkinson, PhD

[We] made a decision to turn our will and our lives over to the care of this power of our own understanding.

—Gamblers Anonymous (GA) (1989b, p. 40)

Before beginning this exercise, please read Step Three in *G.A.: A New Beginning* (GA, 1989b).

You have come a long way in the program, and you can feel proud of yourself. You have decided that you are powerless over gambling and that your life is unmanageable. You have decided that a Higher Power of some sort can restore you to normal thinking and living.

In Step Three, you will reach toward a Higher Power of your own understanding. This is the miracle. It is the major focus of the GA program. This is a spiritual program that directs you toward the ultimate in truth. It is important that you be open to the possibility that there is a God. It is vital that you give this concept room to blossom and grow.

> Many of us used our sponsor, other members, or the fellowship as this Higher Power, but eventually, as we proceeded with the work required in these steps, we came to believe this Higher Power to be a God of our own understanding. (GA, 1989b, p. 40)

Step Three should not confuse you. It calls for a decision to correct your character defects under spiritual supervision. You must make an honest effort to change your life.

The GA program is a spiritual one. Gamblers in recovery must have the honesty to look at their illness, the open-mindedness to apply the solution being told to themselves, and the willingness to apply this solution by proceeding on with the recovery process. If you are willing to seek God, then you will find God. That is GA's promise.

Understanding the Moral Law

All spirituality has, at its core, what is already inside of you. Your Higher Power lives inside of you. Inside of all of us, there is inherent goodness. In all cultures, and in all lands, this goodness is expressed in what we call the moral law. Morality demands love in action and in truth. It is simply stated as follows: Love God all you can, love others all you can, and love yourself all you can. This law is very powerful. If some stranger were drowning in a pool next to you, then this law would motivate you to help. Instinctively, you would feel driven to help, even if it put your own life at risk. The moral law is so important that it transcends our instinct for survival. You would try to save that drowning person at your own risk. This moral law is exactly the same everywhere—in every culture. It exists inside of everyone. It is written on our hearts. Even among thieves, honesty is valued.

When we survey religious thought, we come up with many different ideas about God and about how to worship God. When we look at saints of the various religions, we see that they are living practically indistinguishable lives. They all are doing the same things. They do not lie, cheat, or steal. They believe in giving to others before they give to themselves. They try not to be envious of others. To believe in a Higher Power, you must believe that this good exists inside of you. You also must believe that there is more of this good outside of you. If you do not believe in a living, breathing God at this point, do not worry. Every one of us has started where you are.

All people have a basic problem: We break the moral law, even if we believe in it. This fact means that something is wrong with us. We are incapable of following the moral law. Even though we would deem it unfair for someone to lie to us, occasionally we lie to someone else. If we see someone dressed in clothes that look terrible, then we might tell the person that he or she looks good. This is a lie. We would not want other people lying to us like that. In this and other situations, we do not obey the very moral law that we know is good.

You must ask yourself several questions. Where did we get this moral law? How did this law of behavior get started? Did it just evolve? The GA program believes that these good laws come from something good. People in the program believe that you can communicate with this goodness.

Much of God remains a mystery. If we look at science, we find the same thing; most of science is a mystery. We know very little about the primary elements of science such as gravity, but we make judgments about these elements using our experience. No one has ever seen an electron, but we are sure that it exists because we have some experience of it. It is the same with the Higher Power. We can know that there is a power greater than we are if we have some experience of this power. Both science and spirituality necessitate a faith based on experience.

Instinctively, people know that if they can get more goodness, they will have better lives. Spirituality must be practical. It must make your life better, or you will discard it. If you open yourself up to the spiritual part of the program, then you will feel better immediately.

By reading this exercise, you can begin to develop your relationship with a Higher Power. You will find true joy here if you try. Without some sort of a Higher Power, your recovery will be more difficult. A Higher Power can relieve your gambling problem as nothing else can. Many people achieve stable recovery without calling their Higher Power "God." That certainly is possible. There are many wonderful atheists and agnostics in our program. The GA way is to reach for a God of your own understanding.

You can change things in your life. You really can. You do not have to drown in despair any longer.

The Key to Step Three

The key to working Step Three is willingness. You must have the willingness to turn your life over to the care of God as you understand God. This is difficult for many of us because we think that we are still in control. We are completely fooled by this delusion. We feel as though we know the right thing to do. We feel that everything would be fine if others would just do things our way. This leads us to deep feelings of resentment and self-pity. People would not cooperate with our plan. No matter how hard we tried to control everything, things kept getting out of control. Sometimes the harder we worked, the worse things got.

How to Turn It Over

To arrest gambling, you have to stop playing God and let the God of your own understanding take control. If you sincerely want this and you try, then it is easy. Go to a quiet place, and talk to your Higher Power about your gambling. Say something like this: "God, I am lost. I cannot do this anymore. I turn this situation over to you." Watch how you feel when you say this prayer. The next time you have a problem, stop and turn the problem over to your Higher Power. Say something like this: "God, I cannot deal with this problem. You deal with it." See what happens.

Your Higher Power wants to show you the way. If you try to find the way yourself, you will be constantly lost.

Step Three offers no compromise. It calls for a decision. Exactly how we surrender and turn things over is not the point. The important thing is that you be willing to try. Can you see that it is necessary to give up your self-centeredness? Do you feel that it is time to turn things over to a power greater than you are?

List five things you have to gain by turning your will and your life over to a Higher Power.

1.

2.

3.

4.

5.

Why do you need to turn things over to a Higher Power?

We should not confuse organized religion with spirituality. In Step Two, you learned that spirituality deals with your relationships with yourself, with others, and with your Higher Power. Religion is an organized system of faith and worship. It is human-made, not God-made. It is humans' way of interpreting God. Religion can be very confusing, and it can drive people away from God. Are old religious ideas keeping you from God? If so, then how?

A great barrier to finding your Higher Power may be impatience. You may want to find God right now. You must understand that your spiritual growth is not set by you. You will grow spiritually when God feels that you are ready. Remember that we are turning this whole thing over. Each person has his or her unique spiritual journey. Each individual must have his or her own walk. Spiritual growth, not perfection, is your goal. All that you can do is seek the God of your understanding. When God knows that you are ready, God will find you.

Total surrender is necessary. If you are holding back, then you need to let go absolutely. Faith, willingness, and prayer will overcome all of the obstacles. Do not worry about your doubt. Just keep seeking.

List 10 ways in which you can seek God. Ask someone in the program, a clergyperson, or your counselor to help you.

1.

2.

3.

4.

5.

6.

7.

8.

9.

10.

What does the saying, "Let go and let God," mean to you?

What are five ways in which you can put Step Three to work in your life?

1.

2.

3.

4.

5.

What things in your life do you still want to control?

How can these things be handled better by turning them over to your Higher Power?

List five ways in which you allowed gambling to be the God in your life.

1.

2.

3.

4.

5.

How did gambling separate you from God?

What changes have you noticed in yourself since you entered the program?

Of these changes, which of them occurred because you listened to someone other than yourself?

Make a list of five things that are holding you back from turning things over to God.

1.

2.

3.

4.

5.

How do you see God caring for you?

How do you understand God now?

Write down your spiritual plan. What are five things are you going to do on a daily basis to help your spiritual program grow?

1.

2.

3.

4.

5.

Appendix 38

Step Four for Gamblers

Robert R. Perkinson, PhD

[We] made a searching and fearless moral and financial inventory of ourselves.

—Gamblers Anonymous (GA) (1989b, p. 68)

Before beginning this exercise, please read Step Four in *G.A.: A New Beginning* (GA, 1989b).

You are doing well in the program. You have admitted your powerlessness over gambling, and you have found a Higher Power that can restore you to normal thinking and living. Now you must take an inventory of yourself. You must know exactly what resources you have available, and you must examine the exact nature of your wrongs. You need to be detailed about the good things about you as well as the bad things about you. Only by taking this inventory will you know exactly where you are. Then you can decide where you are going.

In taking this inventory, you must be detailed and specific. It is the only way of seeing the complete impact of your disease. A part of the truth might be, "I told lies to my children." The complete truth might be, "I told my children that I had cancer. They were terrified and cried for a long time." These two statements would be very different. Only the second statement tells the exact nature of the wrong, and the client felt the full impact of the disclosure. You can see how important it is to put the whole truth before you at one time—the truth that will set you free.

The Fourth Step is a long autobiography. You can write it down carefully. Read this exercise before you start, and underline things that pertain to you. You will want to come back and cover each of these issues in detail as you write it down. If the problem does not relate to you, then leave it blank. Examine exactly what you did wrong. Look for your mistakes, even where the situations were not totally your fault. Try to disregard what the other person did, and concentrate on yourself instead. In time, you will realize that the person who hurt you was spiritually sick. You need to ask God to help you forgive that person and to show that person the same understanding that you would want for yourself. You can pray that this person finds out the truth about himself or herself.

Review your natural desires carefully, and think about how you acted on them. You will see that some of them became the God of your life. Sex, food, money, relationships, sleep, power, and influence all can become the major focus of our lives. The pursuit of these desires can take total control and can become the center of our existence.

Review your sexuality as you move through the inventory. Did you ever use someone else selfishly? Did you ever lie to get what you wanted? Did you coerce or force someone into doing something that he or she did not want to do? Whom did you hurt, and exactly what did you do?

In working through the inventory, you will experience some pain. You will feel angry, sad, afraid, ashamed, embarrassed, guilty, and lonely. The Fourth Step is a grieving process. As you see your wrongs clearly, you may feel that no one will ever love you again. Remember that God created you in perfection. You are God's masterpiece. There is nothing wrong with you. You just made some mistakes.

Now let us take a basic look at right and wrong.

1. *Pride:* Too great an admiration of yourself

Pride makes you your own law, your own moral judge, and your own God. Pride produces criticism, backstabbing, slander, barbed words, and character assassinations that elevate your own ego. Pride makes you condemn as fools those who criticize you. Pride gives you excuses. It produces the following:

 a. Boasting or self-glorification
 b. Love of publicity
 c. Hypocrisy or pretending to be better than you are
 d. Hardheadedness or refusing to give up your will
 e. Discord or resenting anyone who crosses you
 f. Quarrelsomeness or quarreling whenever another person challenges your wishes
 g. Disobedience or refusing to submit your will to the will of superiors or to God

2. *Covetousness or avarice:* Perversion of humans' God-given right to own things

Do you desire wealth in the form of money or other things as an end in itself rather than as a means to an end such as taking care of the soul and body? In acquiring wealth in any form, do you disregard the rights of others? Are you dishonest? If so, then to what degree and in what fashion? Do you give an honest day's work for an honest day's pay? How do you use what you have? Are you stingy with your family? Do you love money and possessions for these things in themselves? How excessive is your love of luxury? How do you preserve your wealth or increase it? Do you stoop to devices such as fraud, perjury, dishonesty, and sharp practices in dealing with others? Do you try to fool yourself in these regards? Do you call stinginess "thrift"? Do you call questionable business "big business" or "drive"? Do you call unreasonable hoarding "security"? If you currently have no money and little other wealth, then how and by what practice will you go about getting it later? Will you do almost anything to attain these things and kid yourself by giving your methods innocent names?

3. *Lust:* Inordinate love and desires of the pleasures of the flesh

Are you guilty of lust in any of its forms? Do you tell yourself that improper or undue indulgence in sexual activities is required? Do you treat people as objects of your desire rather than as God's perfect creations? Do you use pornography or think unhealthy sexual thoughts? Do you treat other people sexually the same way in which you want to be treated?

4. *Envy:* Sadness at another person's good

How envious are you? Do you dislike seeing others happy or successful, almost as though they have taken from you? Do you resent those who are smarter than you are? Do you ever criticize the good done by others because you secretly wish you had done it yourself for the honor or prestige to be gained? Are you ever envious enough to try to lower another person's reputation by starting, or engaging in, gossip about that person? Being envious includes calling religious people "hypocrites" because they go to church and try to be religiously good even though they are subject to human failings. Do you depreciate well-bred people by saying or feeling that they put on airs? Do you ever accuse educated, wise, or learned people of being conceited because you envy their advantages? Do you genuinely love other people, or do you find them distasteful because you envy them?

5. *Anger:* A violent desire to punish others

Do you ever fly into rages of temper, become revengeful, entertain urges to "get even," or express an "I will not let him get away with it" attitude? Do you ever resort to violence, clench your fists, or stomp about in a temper flare-up? Are you touchy, unduly sensitive, or impatient at the smallest slight? Do you ever murmur or grumble, even regarding small matters? Do you ignore the fact that anger prevents development of personality and halts spiritual progress? Do you realize at all times that anger disrupts mental poise and often ruins good judgment? Do you permit anger to rule you when you know that it blinds you to the rights of others? How can you excuse even small tantrums of temper when anger destroys the spirit of recollection that you need for compliance with the inspirations of God? Do you permit yourself to become angry when others are weak and become angry with you? Can you hope to entertain the serene spirit of God within your soul when you often are beset by angry flare-ups of even minor importance?

6. *Gluttony:* Abuse of lawful pleasures that God attached to eating and drinking of foods required for self-preservation

Do you weaken your moral and intellectual life by excessive use of food and drink? Do you generally eat to excess and, thus, enslave your soul and character to the pleasures of the body beyond its reasonable needs? Do you kid yourself that you can be a "hog" without affecting your moral life? When gambling, did you ever win big, only to return and immediately gamble to win more? Did you gamble so much that your intellect and personality deteriorated? So much that memory, judgment, and concentration were affected? So much that personal pride and social judgment vanished? So much that you developed a spirit of despair?

7. *Sloth:* Laziness of the will that causes a neglect of duty

Are you lazy or given to idleness, procrastination, nonchalance, and indifference in material things? Are you lukewarm in prayer? Do you hold self-discipline in contempt? Would you rather read a novel than study something requiring brain work such as the GA (1989b) book? Are you fainthearted in performance of those things that are morally or spiritually difficult? Are you ever listless with aversion to effort in any form? Are you easily distracted from things spiritual, quickly turning to things temporal? Are you ever indolent to the extent where you perform work carelessly?

Personality Defects

1. *Selfishness:* Taking care of your own needs without regard for others
   a. The family would like an outing. Dad would like gambling, golfing, and fishing. Who wins?
   b. Your child needs a new pair of shoes. You put it off until payday but then gamble away the paycheck.
   c. You are afraid to dance because you might appear awkward. You fear any new venture because it might injure the false front that you put on.

2. *Alibis:* The highly developed art of justifying gambling and behavior through mental gymnastics
   a. "A few dollars will not hurt anything."
   b. "Starting tomorrow, I am going to change."
   c. "If I did not have a wife and family . . ."
   d. "If I could start all over again."
   e. "A little gambling will help me to relax."

    f. "Nobody cares anyway."

    g. "I had a hard day."

3. *Dishonest thinking:* Another way of lying

We may even take truths or facts and, through some phony hopscotch, come up with exactly the conclusions that we had planned to arrive at. Boy, we are great at that business.

    a. "My secret love is going to raise the roof if I drop her. It is not fair to burden my wife with that sort of knowledge. Therefore, I will hang on to my girlfriend. This mess isn't her fault." (good, solid con)

    b. "If I tell my family about the $500 bonus, then it will all go for bills, clothes, the dentist, and so on. I have to have some gambling money. Why start a family argument? I would leave well enough alone."

    c. "My husband dresses well, he eats well, and the kids are getting a good education. What more do they want from me?"

4. *Shame:* The feeling that something irreparable is wrong with you

    a. No matter how many people tell you it is okay, you continue to berate yourself.

    b. You keep going over and over your mistakes, wallowing in what a terrible person you are.

5. *Resentment:* Displeasure aroused by a real or imagined wrong or injury accompanied by irritation, exasperation, and/or hate

    a. You are fired from your job. Therefore, you hate the boss.

    b. Your sister warns you about excessive gambling. You get fighting mad at her.

    c. A coworker is doing a good job and gets accolades. You have a legal record and suspect that he might have been promoted over you. You hate his guts.

    d. You may have resentment toward a person or a group of people, or you may resent institutions, religions, and so on. Anger and resentment lead to bickering, friction, hatred, and unjust revenge. They bring out the worst of our immaturity and produce misery to ourselves.

6. *Intolerance:* Refusal to put up with beliefs, practices, customs, or habits that differ from our own

    a. Do you hate other people because they are of another race, come from a different country, or have a different religion? What would you do if you were one of those other persons? Kill yourself?

    b. Did you have any choice in being born a particular color or nationality?

    c. Isn't our religion usually "inherited"?

7. *Impatience:* Unwillingness to bear delay, opposition, pain, or bother

    a. A pathological gambler is someone who jumps on a horse and gallops off madly in all directions at the same time.

    b. Do you blow your stack when someone keeps you waiting over the "allotted time" that you gave that person?

    c. Did anyone ever have to wait for you?

8. *Phoniness:* A manifestation of our great false pride; a form of lying; rank and brash dishonesty; the old false front

    a. "I give to my love a present as evidence of my love. Just by pure coincidence, it helps to smooth over my last binge."

    b. "I buy new clothes because my business position demands it. Meanwhile, the family also could use food and clothes."

    c. A joker may enthrall a GA audience with profound wisdom but not give the time of day to his or her spouse or children.

9. *Procrastination:* Putting off or postponing things that need to be done; the familiar "I would do it tomorrow"

    a. Did little jobs, when put off, become big and almost impossible later? Did problems piling up contribute to gambling?

    b. Do you pamper yourself by doing things "my way," or do you attempt to put order and discipline into your life?

    c. Can you handle little jobs that you are asked to take care of, or do you feel picked on? Are you just too lazy or proud?

10. *Self-pity:* An insidious personality defect and a danger signal to look for

Stop self-pity in a hurry. It is the buildup to trouble.

    a. "These people at the party are having fun with their gambling. Why can't I be like that?" This is the "woe is me" syndrome.

    b. "If I had that guy's money, I would not have any problems." When you feel this way, visit a cancer ward or children's hospital and then count your blessings.

11. *Feelings easily hurt:* Overly sensitive to the slightest criticism

    a. "I walk down the street and say hello to someone. They do not answer. I am hurt and mad."

    b. "I am expecting my turn at the GA meeting, but the time runs out. I feel as though that is a dirty trick."

    c. "I feel as though they are talking about me at meetings when they're really not."

12. *Fear:* An inner foreboding, real or imagined, of doom ahead

We suspect that our use of gambling, behavior, negligence, and so on is catching up with us. We fear the worst.

When we learn to accept our powerlessness, ask God for help, and face ourselves with honesty, the nightmare will be over.

13. *Depression:* Feeling sad or down most of the day
    a. You keep going over all of the things that are going wrong.
    b. You tend to think that the worst is going to happen.

14. *Feelings of inadequacy:* Feeling as though you cannot do something
    a. You hold on to a negative self-image, even when you succeed.
    b. Feelings of failure will not go away.

15. *Perfectionism:* The need to do everything perfect all of the time
    a. Even when you have done a good job, you find something wrong with it.
    b. Someone compliments you on something. You feel terrible because it could have been better.
    c. You let your expectations get too high.

Physical Liabilities

1. Diseases, disabilities, and other physical limitations about how you look or how your body functions

2. Sexual problems or hang-ups

3. Negative feelings about your appearance

4. Negative feelings about your age

5. Negative feelings about your gender

Time-Out

If you have gone through the exercise to this point without coming up for air, it figures. We did our gambling the same way. Whoa! Easy does it! Take this in reasonable stages. Assimilate each portion of the exercise thoughtfully. The reading of this is important, but the application of it is even more important. Take some time to think and rest, and let this settle in. Develop some sort of a workable daily plan. Include plenty of rest.

When compulsive gamblers stop gambling, a part of their lives is taken away from them. This is a terrible loss to sustain unless it is replaced by something else. We cannot just boot gambling out the window. It meant too much to us. It was how we faced life, the key to escape, and the tool for solving life's problems. In approaching a new way of life, a new set of tools is substituted. These are the 12 steps and the GA way of life.

The same principle applies when we eliminate our character defects. We replace them by substituting assets that are better adapted to a healthy lifestyle. As with substance use, you do not fight a defect; you replace it with something that works better. Use what follows for further character analysis and as a guide for character building. These are the new tools. The objective is not perfection; it is progress. You will be happy with the type of living that produces self-respect, respect and love for others, and security from the nightmare of gambling.

Virtues

1. *Faith:* The act of leaving the part of our lives that we cannot control (i.e., the future) to the care of a power greater than ourselves, with the assurance that it will work out for our well-being

This will be shaky at first, but with it comes a deep conviction.

   a. Faith is acquired through application—acceptance, daily prayer, and meditation.
   b. We depend on faith. We have faith that the lights will come on, the car will start, and our coworkers will handle their end of things. If we had no faith, then we would come apart at the seams.
   c. Spiritual faith is the acceptance of our gifts, limitations, problems, and trials with equal gratitude, knowing that God has a plan for us. With "Thy will be done" as our daily guide, we will lose our fear and find ourselves.

2. *Hope:* The feeling that what is desired also is possible

Faith suggests reliance. We came to believe that a power greater than ourselves would restore us to sanity. We hope to stay free of gambling, regain our self-respect, and love our families. Hope resolves itself into a driving force. It gives purpose to our daily living.

   a. Faith gives us direction, hope, and stamina to take action.
   b. Hope reflects a positive attitude. Things are going to work out for us if we work the program.

3. *Love:* The active involvement in someone's individual growth
   a. Love must occur in action and in truth.
   b. Love is gentle and kind.
   c. In its deeper sense, love is the art of living realistically and fully, guided by spiritual awareness of our responsibilities and our debt of gratitude to God and to others.

Analysis. Have you used the qualities of faith, hope, and love in your past? How will they apply to your new way of life?

The Little Virtues

1. *Courtesy:* Some of us are actually afraid to be gentle persons. We would rather be boors or self-pampering types.

2. *Cheerfulness:* Circumstances do not determine our frames of mind. We do. "Today I will be cheerful. I will look for the beauty in life."

3. *Order:* Live today only. Organize one day at a time.

4. *Loyalty:* Be faithful to who you believe in.

5. *Use of time:* "I will use my time wisely."

6. *Punctuality:* This involves self-discipline, order, and consideration for others.

7. *Sincerity:* This is the mark of self-respect and genuineness. Sincerity carries conviction and generates enthusiasm. It is contagious.

8. *Caution in speech:* Watch your tongue. We can be vicious and thoughtless. Too often, the damage is irreparable.

9. *Kindness:* This is one of life's great satisfactions. We do not have real happiness until we have given of ourselves. Practice this daily.

10. *Patience:* This is the antidote to resentments, self-pity, and impulsiveness.

11. *Tolerance:* This requires common courtesy, courage, and a "live and let live" attitude.

12. *Integrity:* This involves the ultimate qualifications of a human—honesty, loyalty, sincerity.

13. *Balance:* Do not take yourself too seriously. You get a better perspective when you can laugh at yourself.

14. *Gratitude:* The person without gratitude is filled with false pride. Gratitude is the honest recognition of help received. Use it often.

Analysis. In considering the little virtues, ask where you failed and how that contributed to your accumulated problem. Ask what virtues you should pay attention to in this rebuilding program.

Physical Assets

1. *Physical health:* How healthy am I despite any ailments?

2. *Talents:* What do I do that is good?

3. *Age:* At my age, what can I offer to others?

4. *Sexuality:* How can I use my sexuality to express my love?

5. *Knowledge:* How can I use my knowledge and experience to help others and myself?

Mental Assets

1. Despite your problems, how healthy are you emotionally?

2. Do you care for others?

3. Are you kind?

4. Can you be patient?

5. Are you basically a good person?

6. Do you try to tell the truth?

7. Do you try to be forgiving?

8. Can you be enthusiastic?

9. Are you sensitive to the needs of others?

10. Can you be serene?

11. Are you going to try to be sincere?

12. Are you going to try to bring order and self-control into your life?

13. Are you going to accept the responsibility for your own behavior and stop blaming others for everything?

14. How are you going to use your intelligence?

15. Are you going to seek God?

16. How might you improve your mind furthering your education?

17. Are you going to be grateful for what you have?

18. How can you improve your honesty, reliability, and integrity?

19. In what areas of your life do you find joy and happiness?

20. Are you humble and working on your false pride?

21. Are you seeking the God of your own understanding?

22. In what ways can you better accept your own limitations and the limitations of others?

23. Are you willing to trust and follow the Higher Power of your own understanding?

The Autobiography

Using this exercise, write your autobiography. Cover your life in 5-year intervals. Be brief, but try not to miss anything. Tell the whole truth. Write down exactly what you did. Consider all of the things you marked during the exercise. Read the exercise again if you need to do so. Make an exhaustive and honest consideration of your past and present. Make a complete financial inventory. Mark down all debts. Exactly who do you owe, and what amount do you owe? Do not leave out relatives or friends. List all persons or institutions that you harmed with your gambling, and detail exactly how you were unfair. Cover both assets and liabilities carefully. You will rebuild your life on the solid building blocks of your assets. These are the tools of recovery. Omit nothing because of shame, embarrassment, or fear. Determine the thoughts, feelings, and actions that plagued you. You want to meet these problems face to face and see them in writing. If you wish, you may destroy your inventory after completing the Fifth Step. Many people hold a ceremony in which they burn their Fourth Step inventories. This symbolizes that they are leaving the old life behind. They are starting a new life free of the past.

Appendix 39

Step Five for Gamblers

Robert R. Perkinson, PhD

[We] admitted to ourselves and to another human being the exact nature of our wrongs.

—Gamblers Anonymous (GA) (1989b, p. 69)

Before beginning this exercise, please read Step Five in *G.A.: A New Beginning* (GA, 1989b).

With Steps One to Four behind you, it is now time to clean house and start over. You must free yourself of all the guilt and shame and go forward in faith. The Fifth Step is meant to right the wrongs with others and the Higher Power. You will develop new attitudes and a new relationship with yourself, others, and the Higher Power of your own understanding. You have admitted your powerlessness, and you have identified your liabilities and assets in the personal inventory. Now it is time to get right with yourself.

You will do this by admitting to yourself, and to another person, the exact nature of your wrongs. In your Fifth Step, you are going to cover all of your assets and liabilities detailed in the Fourth Step. You are going to tell one person the whole truth at one time. This person is important because he or she is a symbol of the Higher Power and all humankind. You must watch this person's face. The illness has been telling you that if you tell anyone the whole truth about you, then that person will not like you. That is a lie, and you are going to prove that it is a lie. The truth is this: Unless you tell people the whole truth, they cannot like you. You must actually see yourself tell someone the whole truth at one time and watch that individual's reaction.

It is very difficult to discuss your faults with someone. It is hard enough just thinking about them yourself. This is a necessary step. It will help to free you from the disease. You must tell this person everything, the whole story, all of the things that you are afraid to share. If you withhold anything, then you will not get the relief you need to start over. You will be carrying around excess baggage. You do not need to do this to yourself. Time after time, newcomers have tried to keep to themselves certain facts about their lives. Trying to avoid this humbling experience, they have turned to easier methods. Almost invariably, they wound up gambling again. Having persevered with the rest of the program, they wondered why they failed. The reason is that they never completed their housecleaning. They took inventory all right, but they hung on to some of the worst items in stock. They only *thought* that they had lost their egotism. They only *thought* that they had humbled themselves. They had not learned enough of humility and honesty in the sense necessary until they told someone their whole life stories.

By finally telling someone the whole truth, you will rid yourself of that terrible sense of isolation and loneliness. You will feel a new sense of belonging, acceptance, and freedom. If you do not feel relief immediately, do not worry. If you have been completely honest, then the relief will come. The dammed-up emotions of years will break out of their confinement and, miraculously, will vanish as soon as they are exposed.

The Fifth Step will develop within you a new humbleness of character that is necessary for normal living. You will come to recognize clearly who and what you are. When you are honest with another person, it confirms that you can be honest with yourself, others, and your Higher Power.

The person who you will share your Fifth Step with should be chosen carefully. Many of us find a clergyperson, experienced in hearing Fifth Steps, to be a good option. Someone further along in the GA program might also be a good choice. It is recommended that you meet with this person several times before you do the step. You need to decide whether you can trust this person. Do you feel that this person is confidential? Do you feel comfortable with this person? Do you feel that this person will understand?

Once you have chosen the person, put your false pride aside and go for it. Tell the individual everything about yourself. Do not leave one rock unturned. Tell about all of the good things and about all of the bad things that you have done. Share the details, and do not leave anything out. If it troubles you even a little, then share it. Let it all hang out to be examined by that other person. Every good and bad part needs to be revealed. After you are done, you will be free of the slavery to lies. The truth will set you free.

Appendix 40

Relapse Prevention for Gamblers

Robert R. Perkinson, PhD

There is some bad news and some good news about relapse. The bad news is that many clients have problems with relapse in early recovery. About two thirds of clients coming out of addiction programs relapse within 3 months of leaving treatment (Hunt, Barnett, & Branch, 1971). The good news is that most people who go through treatment ultimately achieve a stable recovery (Frances, Bucky, & Alexopolos, 1984). Relapse does not have to happen to you, and even if it does, you can do something about it. Relapse prevention is a daily program that can help prevent relapse. It also can stop a lapse from becoming a disaster. This exercise has been developed using a combination of the models. This uses the disease concept model in combination with motivational enhancement, cognitive behavioral therapy, skills training, and 12-step facilitation.

Relapse Is a Process

Relapse is a process that begins long before you gamble. There are symptoms that precede the first gambling episode. This exercise teaches you how to identify and control these symptoms before they lead to gambling. If you allow these symptoms to go on without acting on them, then serious problems will result.

The Relapse Warning Signs

All relapse begins with warning signs that will signal for you that you are in trouble. If you do not recognize these signs, you will decompensate and finally gamble. All of the signs are a reaction to stress, and they are a reemergence of the disease. They are a means by which your body and mind are telling you that you are in trouble. You might not have all of these symptoms, but you will have some of them long before you actually gamble. You must determine which symptoms are the most characteristic of you, and you must come up with coping skills for dealing with each symptom.

Interpersonal Factors

- Self-efficacy is the degree you feel capable of performing a task like preventing relapse. Do you feel confident that you have the skills necessary to say no to the addiction when confronted with a high-risk situation including intense craving? Do you have the skills necessary to say no to gambling?

- Make a list of 10 things you can do when you feel the urge to gamble. There are people you can call, meetings you can attend, things you can read, a Higher Power you can pray to, family members, friends or people in the program you can share your feelings with, the Gamblers Anonymous (GA) hotline, you can call someone in the program, physical exercise you can do, meditations you can perform, etc.

1.

2.

3.

4.

5.

6.

7.

8.

9.

10.

Practice each of these 10 things at least a five times in group with your counselor/sponsor/mentor/coach. You need to get used to thinking and moving in a certain way when faced with craving. If these behaviors are not practiced in skills training sessions, they are unlikely to be used when you get into trouble. Just knowing what do is not enough; you need to practice the thoughts and motor movements to get good at the skill.

Think about the first time you learned how to ride a bike. Your teacher probably taught you all of the things you had to do to ride, but it was only after you practiced riding repeatedly that you began to trust yourself to ride a bike safely.

Make a list of five things in your life that you had to practice. Maybe it was basketball, baseball, soccer, or starting a conversation with someone you did not know.

1.

2.

3.

4.

5.

At first you were terrible, making mostly mistakes, but after practicing thousands of times you got better. Maybe you had to learn how to shoot a basket from the free throw line. The first times you tried you missed most every shot. As you practiced, and particularly after you were coached, you got better. After thousands of shots, you got so you could make the shot most of the time. Then there came the big game, and the score was tied and you had to shoot the final basket. If you made the shot your team won; if you missed, you lost. Now you need to practice so much that you go on automatic—athletes call this getting in the zone—where all of the fans and other players disappear and it is only you and that simple shot you have practiced so many times. If you miss the shot or lapse, it is not the end of the world; it just means you need more practice until the skill becomes automatic.

Higher levels of self-efficacy predict improved addiction treatment outcomes (Burling, Reilly, Molten, & Ziff, 1989; Greenfield et al., 2000).

What to Do When You Experience a Warning Sign

When you recognize you are in trouble, you need to take action. Make a list of the coping skills you can use when you experience a high-risk situation that is common for you. It might be interpersonal conflict, anger, boredom, certain music or parts of town, seeing old friends, social pressure, negative emotions or a celebration. This will happen. You will have high-risk situations in recovery. Your task is to take affirmative action. Remember, craving is a danger signal. You are in trouble. Make a list of what you are going to do. Are you going to call your sponsor, go to a meeting, call your counselor, call someone in GA, tell someone, exercise, read the problem gambling material, pray, become involved in an activity you enjoy, turn it over, or go into treatment? List five telephone numbers of people you can call if you are in trouble. Remember what GA says, "What we cannot do alone, we can do together."

Plan 1.

Plan 2.

Plan 3.

Plan 4.

Plan 5.

Positive Outcome Expectations

This means the positive things we think will happen if we gamble. These are dangerous thoughts, and if not corrected, they may lead to relapse. Write down five positive thoughts about what gambling can do for you— things such as the following: One bet will not hurt. I deserve to relax. I would only bet one time. I have had a hard day. I need to relax at the casino; nobody will know. I am going to show them. I am going to get even. I am going to make them sorry. I am under too much stress. I need a break.

1.

2.

3.

4.

5.

Now write down 10 accurate thoughts that will keep you from gambling, such as the following: I cannot make one bet; I am a pathological gambler. If I start gambling, I would never stop; I would go right back into that addiction misery again. I can go home and talk to my wife. I can go for a walk. I can meditate. I can go to a 12-step meeting. I can call my sponsor or spiritual leader and go out for a cup of coffee. I can cope with this feeling. If I just wait for 15 minutes, the craving will pass. If I move away from the high-risk situation, I would feel better soon.

1.

2.

3.

4.

5.

6.

7.

8.

9.

10.

Write down these 10 alternative behaviors, and carry them with you. Remember that you have to practice these skills until they become automatic. Practice saying and doing these things with your group, counselor, sponsor, mentor, coach, spouse, friend, or 12-step member. Practice, practice, practice until you feel comfortable with the new skill.

You need to check warning signs daily in your personal inventory. You also need to have other people check you daily. You will not always pick up the symptoms in yourself. You might be denying the problem again. Your spouse, your sponsor, and/or a fellow 12-step member can warn you when they believe that you might be in trouble. Listen to these people. If they tell you that they sense a problem, then they take action. You might need professional help in working the problem through. Do not hesitate to call and ask for help. Anything is better than relapsing. If you overreact to a warning sign, you are not going to be in trouble. If you underreact, you might be headed for real problems. Addiction is a deadly disease. Your life is at stake.

High-Risk Situations

Relapse is more likely to occur in certain situations. These situations can trigger relapse. People relapse when faced with high-risk situations that they could not cope with except by gambling. Your job in treatment is to develop coping skills for dealing with each high-risk situation.

Motivation

Motivation is the conscious or unconscious stimulus leading to the energy that gives you the power to act. Either you can act in an adaptive or a maladaptive way; both can be positive or negative reinforcers. You can have motivation to stay clean and sober and you can have motivation to return to your addiction.

Prochaska and DiClemente (1984) proposed a model for motivation that goes through five stages or readiness for change: (1) precontemplation, (2) contemplation, (3) preparation, (4) action, and (5) maintenance. Each stage characterizes a different level of motivational readiness for change.

- Interventions that cause ambivalence, evaluating the pros and cons of change may increase motivation by allowing clients to explore their own morals and values and how they may differ if they institute change. For example, people who are in the precontemplative stage have no interest in behavior change. If they explore the pros and cons of the addictive behavior, they might become more willing to think about the positive aspects of changing.

- This moves them into contemplation where you discuss all of the positive and negative aspects of using or stopping the addiction. Once the decision is made to try to stop the addictive behavior, then we must concentrate on what needs to change to stop the addictive behavior.
- Then the action phase begins where we begin to change the thoughts and behaviors that cause addiction.
- Once the addiction stops, then we need skills to maintain this new lifestyle.

Negative Emotions

Many people relapse when feeling negative feelings that they cannot cope with. Most feel angry or frustrated, but some feel anxious, bored, lonely, or depressed. Almost any negative feeling can lead to relapse if you do not learn how to cope with the feeling. Feelings motivate you to take action. You must act to solve any problem.

Circle any of the following feelings that seem to lead you to use chemicals.

1. Loneliness
2. Anger
3. Rejection
4. Emptiness
5. Annoyed
6. Sad
7. Exasperated
8. Betrayed
9. Cheated
10. Frustrated
11. Envious
12. Exhausted
13. Bored
14. Anxious
15. Ashamed
16. Bitter
17. Burdened
18. Foolish
19. Jealous
20. Left out
21. Selfish
22. Restless
23. Weak
24. Sorrowful
25. Greedy

26. Aggravated

27. Exasperated

28. Miserable

29. Unloved

30. Worried

31. Scared

32. Spiteful

33. Sorrowful

34. Helpless

35. Neglected

36. Grief

37. Confused

38. Crushed

39. Discontented

40. Restless

41. Irritated

42. Overwhelmed

43. Panicked

44. Trapped

45. Unsure

46. Intimidated

47. Distraught

48. Uneasy

49. Guilty

50. Threatened

A Plan to Deal With Negative Emotions

These are just a few of the feeling words. Add more if you need to do so. Develop coping skills for dealing with each feeling that makes you vulnerable to relapse. Exactly what are you going to do when you have this feeling? Detail your specific plan of action. Some options are talking to your sponsor, calling a friend in the program, going to a meeting, calling your counselor, reading some recovery material, turning it over to your Higher Power, and getting some exercise. For each feeling, develop a specific plan of action.

Feeling _____

    Plan 1. _____

    Plan 2. _____

    Plan 3. _____

Feeling _____

   Plan 1. _____

   Plan 2. _____

   Plan 3. _____

Feeling _____

   Plan 1. _____

   Plan 2. _____

   Plan 3. _____

Continue to fill out these feeling forms until you have all of the feelings that give you trouble and you have coping skills for dealing with each feeling.

Social Pressure

Social pressure can be direct (where someone directly encourages you to gamble) or indirect (a social situation where people are gambling). Both of these situations can trigger intense craving, and this can lead to relapse.

Certain friends are more likely to encourage you to gamble. These people do not want to hurt you. They want you to relax and have a good time. They want their old friend back. They do not understand the nature of your disease. Perhaps they are problem gamblers themselves and are in denial.

High-Risk Friends

Make a list of the friends who might encourage you to gamble.

   1.

   2.

   3.

   4.

   5.

What are you going to do when they ask you to come with them to gamble? What are you going to say? In skills group, set up a situation where the whole group encourages you to gamble. Look carefully at how you feel when the group members are encouraging you. Look at what you say. Have them help you to develop appropriate ways of saying no. The skills of saying no are the following:

- Look at the person and say no thank you.
- Suggest another alternative behavior.
- If the person persists, tell him or her that you are trying to stop behavior that has been harming you. Then ask the person to help you by respecting your choice not to use.
- If the person persists, leave the situation. "Well, I have got to be going. Nice to see you."

High-Risk Social Situations

Certain social situations will trigger craving. These are the situations where you have gambled in the past. Certain casinos, bars, or restaurants with video lottery machines, service stations with video lottery terminals, a particular part of town, certain music, athletic events, parties, weddings, family events—all of these situations can trigger intense cravings. Make a list of five social situations where you will be vulnerable to relapse.

1.

2.

3.

4.

5.

In early sobriety, you will need to avoid these situations and friends. To put yourself in a high-risk situation is asking for trouble. If you have to attend a function where there will be people gambling, then take someone with you who is in the program. Take someone with you who will support you in your recovery. Make sure that you have a way to get home. You do not have to stay and torture yourself. You can leave if you feel uncomfortable. Avoid all situations where your sobriety feels shaky.

Interpersonal Conflict

Many addicts relapse when in a conflict with some other person. They have a problem with someone and have no idea of how to cope with conflict so they might revert to old behavior and use the addiction to deal with the uncomfortable feelings. The stress of the problem builds and leads to gambling. This conflict usually happens with someone who they are closely involved with—wife, husband, child, parent, sibling, friend, boss, and so on.

You can have a serious problem with anyone—even a stranger—so you must have a plan for dealing with interpersonal conflict. You will develop specific skills in treatment that will help you to communicate even when you are under stress.

You need to learn and practice the following interpersonal skills repeatedly.

1. Tell the truth all of the time.

2. Share how you feel.

3. Ask for what you want.

4. Find some truth in what the other person is saying.

5. Be willing to compromise.

If you can stay in the conflict and work it out, that is great. If you cannot, then you have to leave the situation and take care of yourself. You might have to go for a walk, a run, or a drive. You might need to cool down. You must stop the conflict. You cannot continue to try to deal with a situation that you believe is too much for you. Do not feel bad about this. Interpersonal relationships are the hardest challenge we face. Carry a card with you that lists the telephone numbers of people who you can contact. You might want to call your sponsor, minister, or counselor or a fellow GA member, friend, family member, doctor, or anyone else who may support you.

In an interpersonal conflict, you will fear abandonment. You need to get accurate and reassure yourself that people can disagree with you and still care about you. Remember that your Higher Power cares about you. A Higher Power created you and loves you. Remember the other people in your life who love you. This is one of the main reasons for talking with someone else. When the other person listens to you, that person gives you the feeling that you are accepted and loved.

If you still feel afraid or angry, then get with someone you trust and stay with that person until you feel safe. Do not struggle out there all by yourself. Any member of your 12-step group will understand how you are feeling. We all have had these problems. We all have felt lost, helpless, hopeless, and angry.

Make an emergency card that lists all of the people who you can call if you are having difficulty. Write down their phone numbers and carry this card with you at all times. Show this card to your counselor. Practice asking someone for help in treatment once each day. Write down the situation, and show it to your counselor. Get into the habit of asking for help. When you get out of treatment, call someone every day just to stay in touch and keep the lines of communication open. Get used to it. Do not wait to ask for help at the last minute. This makes asking more difficult.

Positive Feelings

Some people relapse when they are feeling positive emotions. Think of all the times you used gambling to celebrate. That has gotten to be such a habit that when something good happens, you will immediately think about gambling. You need to be ready when you feel like a winner. This may be at a wedding, birth, promotion, or any event where you feel good. How are you going to celebrate without gambling? Make a celebration plan. You might have to take someone with you to a celebration, particularly in early recovery.

Positive feelings also can work when you are by yourself. A beautiful spring day can be enough to get you thinking about gambling. You need an action plan for when these thoughts pass through your mind. You must immediately get accurate and get real. In recovery, we are committed to reality. Do not sit there and recall how wonderful you will feel if you get high. Tell yourself the truth. Think about all of the pain that addiction has caused you. If you toy with positive feelings, then you ultimately will gamble.

Circle the positive feelings that may make you vulnerable to relapse.

1. Affection

2. Boldness

3. Braveness

4. Calmness

5. Capableness

6. Cheerful

7. Confident

8. Delightful

9. Desire

10. Enchanted

11. Joy

12. Free

13. Gladness

14. Glee

15. Happy

16. Honored

17. Horny

18. Infatuated

19. Inspired
20. Kinky
21. Lazy
22. Loving
23. Peaceful
24. Pleasant
25. Pleased
26. Sexy
27. Wonderful
28. Cool
29. Relaxed
30. Reverent
31. Silly
32. Vivacious
33. Adequate
34. Efficient
35. Successful
36. Accomplished
37. Hopeful
38. Cheery
39. Elated
40. Merry
41. Ecstatic
42. Upbeat
43. Splendid
44. Yearning
45. Bliss
46. Excitement
47. Exhilaration
48. Proud
49. Arousal
50. Festive

A Plan to Cope With Positive Feelings

These are the feelings that may make you vulnerable to relapse. You must be careful when you are feeling good because pleasure triggers the same part of the brain that triggers addiction. Make an action plan for dealing with each positive emotion that makes you vulnerable to gambling.

Feeling _____

    Plan 1. _____

    Plan 2. _____

    Plan 3. _____

Feeling _____

    Plan 1. _____

    Plan 2. _____

    Plan 3. _____

Feeling _____

    Plan 1. _____

    Plan 2. _____

    Plan 3. _____

Continue this planning until you develop a plan for each of the positive feelings that make you vulnerable. Practice what you are going to do when you experience positive feelings.

Test Control

Some people gamble to test whether they can gamble safely again. They fool themselves into thinking that they might be able to gamble normally. This time they will gamble only a little. This time they will be able to stay in control of themselves. People who fool themselves this way are in for big trouble. From the first use, most people are in full-blown relapse within 30 days.

Testing personal control begins with inaccurate thinking. It takes you back to Step One. You need to think accurately. You are powerless over gambling. If you use, then you will lose. It is as simple as that. You are physiologically, psychologically, and socially addicted. The cells in your body will not suddenly change no matter how long you are in recovery. You are addicted in your cells. There are physical highways in the brain that will always think inaccurately that you can gamble safely.

How to See Through the First Use

You need to look at how the illness part of yourself will try to convince you that you are not a pathological gambler. The illness will flash on the screen of your consciousness all the good things that the addiction did for you. Make a list of these things. In the first column, marked "Early Gambling," write down some of the good things that you were getting out of gambling. Why were you using? What good came out of it? Did it make you feel social, smart, pretty, intelligent, brave, popular, desirable, relaxed, or sexy? Did it help you to sleep? Did it make you feel confident? Did it help you to forget your problems? Make a long list. These are the good things that you were getting when you first started using. This is why you were using.

Now go back and place in the second column, marked "Late Gambling," how you were doing in that area once you became addicted. How were you doing in that same area right before you came into treatment? Did you still feel social, or did you feel alone? Did you still feel intelligent, or did you feel stupid? You will find that a great change has taken place. The very things that you were using for in early use, you get the opposite of in late use. If you were gambling for relaxation, then you cannot relax. If you were gambling to be more popular, then you are more isolated, insecure, and alone. If you were gambling to feel powerful, then you are feeling more afraid. This is a major characteristic of addiction. The good things you got at first

Early Gambling	Late Gambling
1.	1.
2.	2.
3.	3.
4.	4.
5.	5.
6.	6.
7.	7.
8.	8.
9.	9.
10.	10.

you get the opposite of in addiction. You can never go back to early use because your brain has permanently changed in chemistry, structure, and genetics.

Take a long look at both of these lists, and think about how the illness is going to try to work inside of your thinking. The addicted part of yourself will present to you all of the good things you got in early gambling. This is how the disease will encourage you to gamble. You must see through the first gambling to the consequences that are dead ahead.

Look at that second list. You must see the misery that is coming if you gamble. For most people who relapse, there are only a few days of controlled use before loss of control sets in. There usually are only a few hours or days before all of the bad stuff begins to click back into place. Relapse is terrible. It is the most intense misery that you can imagine.

Lapse and Relapse

A lapse is the use of any addictive behavior. A relapse is continuing to use the behavior until the full biological, psychological, and social disease is present. All of the complex biological, psychological, and social components of the disease become evident very quickly.

The Lapse Plan

You must have a plan in case you lapse. It is foolish to think that you never will have a problem again. You must plan what you are going to do if you have a problem. Hunt et al. (1971), in a study of recovering addicts, found that 33% of clients lapsed within 2 weeks of leaving treatment and 60% lapsed within 3 months. At the end of 8 months, 63% had lapsed. At the end of 12 months, 67% had lapsed.

The worst thing you can do when you have a lapse is to think that you have completely failed in recovery. This is inaccurate thinking. You are not a total failure. You have not lost everything. A lapse is a great learning opportunity. You have made a mistake, and you can learn from it. You let some part of your program go, and you are paying for it. You need to examine exactly what happened and get back into recovery.

A lapse is an emergency. It is a matter of life or death. You must take immediate action to prevent the lapse from becoming a full relapse. You must call someone in the program, preferably your sponsor, and tell that person what happened. You need to examine why you had a problem. You cannot use the addiction and the tools of recovery at the same time. Something went wrong. You did not use your new skills. You must make a plan of action to recover from your lapse. You cannot do this by yourself. You are in denial. You do not know the whole truth. If you did, you would not have relapsed.

Call your sponsor or a professional counselor, and have that person develop a new treatment plan for you. You may need to attend more meetings. You may need to see a counselor. You may need outpatient treatment. You may need inpatient treatment. You have to get honest with yourself. You need to develop a plan and follow it. You need someone else to agree to keep an eye on you for a while. Do not try to do this alone. What we cannot do alone, we can do together.

The Behavior Chain

All behavior occurs in a certain sequence. First there is the *trigger*. This is the external event that starts the behavioral sequence. After the trigger, there comes *thinking*. Much of this thinking is very fast, and you will not consciously pick it up unless you stop and think about it. The thoughts trigger *feeling*, which gives you energy and direction for action. Next comes the *behavior* or the action initiated by the trigger. Lastly, there always is a *consequence* for any action.

Diagrammed, the behavior chain looks like this:

Trigger → Thinking → Feeling → Behavior → Consequence

Let's go through a behavioral sequence and see how it works. On the way home from work, Mark, a recovering gambler, passes a local casino. (This is the trigger.) He thinks, "I have had a hard day. I would make a couple of bets to unwind." (The trigger initiates thinking.) Mark craves gambling. (The thinking initiates feeling.) Mark turns into the bar and begins gambling. (The feeling initiates behavior.) Mark loses all of his money, including his next month's mortgage payment. (The behavior has a consequence.)

Let us work through another example. It is 11:00 pm, and Mark is not asleep (trigger). He thinks, "I would never get to sleep tonight unless I make a few bets on the Internet" (thinking). He feels an increase in his anxiety about not sleeping (feeling). He gets up and gambles online. He goes to sleep after going into debt on all of his credit cards and wakes up unable to work the next morning (consequence).

How to Cope With Triggers

At every point along the behavior chain, you can work on preventing relapse. First you need to examine your triggers. What environmental events lead you to using chemicals? We went over some of these when we examined high-risk situations. Determine what people, places, or things make you vulnerable to relapse. Stay away from these triggers as much as possible. If a trigger occurs, then use your new coping skills.

Do not let the trigger initiate old behavior. Stop and think. Do not let your thinking get out of control. Challenge your thinking, and get accurate about what is real. Let us look at some common inaccurate thoughts.

1. One bet is not going to hurt.

2. No one is going to know.

3. I need to relax.

4. I am just going to have a couple.

5. I have had a hard day.

6. My friends want me to gamble; it is fun.

7. I never had a problem with poker.

8. It is the only way I can sleep.

9. I can do anything I want to.

10. I am lonely.

All of these inaccurate thoughts can be used to fuel the craving that leads to relapse. You must stop and challenge your thinking until you are thinking accurately. You must replace inaccurate thoughts with accurate ones. You are a pathological gambler. If you gamble, you will lose everything. Think through the first gambling episode. Get honest with yourself.

How to Cope With Craving

If you think inaccurately, then you will begin craving. This is the powerful feeling that drives compulsive gambling. Craving is like an ocean wave; it will build and then wash over you. Craving does not last long if you move away from your addiction. If you move closer to the addiction, then the craving will increase until you are compelled to gamble. Immediately on feeling a desire to gamble, think this thought:

"Gambling is no longer an option for me."

Now gambling is no longer is an option. What are your options? You are in trouble. You are craving. What are you going to do to prevent relapse? You must move away from gambling thoughts and behaviors and choose what is accurate. Perhaps you need to call your sponsor; go to a meeting; turn it over; call the GA hotline; call the treatment center; call your counselor; go for a walk, run, or visit someone. You must do something else other than thinking about chemicals. Do not sit there and ponder gambling. You will lose that debate. This illness is called the great debater. If you leave it unchecked, it will seduce you into gambling.

Remember that the illness must lie to work. You must uncover the lie as quickly as possible and get back to the truth. You must take the appropriate action necessary to maintain your recovery.

Develop a Daily Relapse Prevention Plan

If you work a daily program of recovery, then your chances of success increase greatly. You need to evaluate your recovery daily and keep a log. This is your daily inventory.

1. Assess all relapse warning signs.
    a. What symptoms did I see in myself today?
    b. What am I going to do about them?

2. Assess love of self.
    a. What did I do to love myself today?
    b. What am I going to do tomorrow?

3. Assess love of others.
    a. What did I do to love others today?
    b. What am I going to do tomorrow?

4. Assess love of God.
    a. What did I do to love God today?
    b. What am I going to do tomorrow?

5. Assess sleep pattern.
    How am I sleeping?

6. Assess exercise.
    Am I getting enough exercise?

7. Assess nutrition.
    Am I eating right?

8. Review total recovery program.
    a. How am I doing in recovery?
    b. What is the next step in my recovery program?

9. Read GA material.

10. Make conscious contact with God.
     a. Pray and meditate for a few minutes.
     b. Relax completely.

Social Support System

Every client needs to build a social support system. Positive social support is highly predictive of long-term abstinence rates across many addictive behaviors. You need to write down specifically who is going to be your advocate at home, work, community, and school. This person needs to talk to your counselor and understand exactly what being an advocate means. This person will have different tasks depending upon whether or not he or she is a schoolteacher, parent, spouse, pastor, sponsor, mentor, coach, community leader, school counselor, doctor, nurse, counselor, etc. You need to make a list of all of these people and decide who is going to do what. Someone needs to check up on you every day. You will need to cancel all credit cards and give all of your extra money to someone you trust. Limit your ability to write a check by having to have a cosigner to write checks. Many gambling casinos have a self-exclusion program where you can sign a contract that will allow them to prevent you from gambling in their establishment. You will have to talk to security; they will take your picture and sign the no gambling contract with you. The contract can last as long as you like, but 5 years is a good length.

People Who Can Help You in Recovery

1. Case manager: _____ Phone: _____

The continuing care case manager makes sure everyone on the team is working together to keep the client free from gambling. This person keeps a record of all therapy meetings and 12-step groups. He or she has a contract with the client that outlines exactly what is expected of the client and what the consequences are if the client does not follow through with the recovery program.

2. Parent or spouse: _____ Phone: _____

The parent or spouse will be the person who knows what behavior is adaptive and maladaptive. What friends are to be avoided? If an adolescent develops the behavioral contract, he or she is responsible for rewards and consequences.

3. The teacher: _____ Phone: _____ or
    Employer: _____ Phone: _____

The teacher or employer knows about what behavior is to be expected and what is not to be tolerated. Members of the team often call each other to check up on the facts and make sure everyone is on the same team.

4. The sponsor/mentor/coach: _____ Phone: _____

The sponsor/mentor/coach is the person who guides the client through recovery. They are in a 12-step program themselves and take the client to meetings and meet regularly to discuss the recovery process.

5. The physician: _____ Phone: _____

The physician orders the medication and does history and physical examinations to maintain good health.

6. The spiritual guide: _____ Phone: _____

The spiritual guide helps the patent discuss and grow in his or her spiritual journey. The client shares his or her spiritual journey and maybe keeps a spiritual prayer journal.

Fill out this inventory every day following treatment, and keep a journal about how you are doing. You will be amazed as you read back over your journal from time to time. You will be surprised at how much you have grown.

Make a list of 10 reasons why you want to stop gambling.

1.

2.

3.

4.

5.

6.

7.

8.

9.

10.

Never forget these reasons. Read this list over and over to yourself. Carry a copy with you and memorize them. If you are struggling in sobriety, then take it out and read it to yourself. You are important. No one has to live a life of misery. You can recover and live a clean and sober life.

Appendix 41

Adolescent Unit Point System

Adolescents will carry a report card with them during the day for the staff to add and subtract points. Clients will count up their points each day and place the total on a chart that they keep in their room or in the hallway. The most important part of the program is that staff members need to catch the clients displaying appropriate behavior and reward them. Clients can be rewarded for any behavior that staff members want to see them increase such as being quiet in their room, making a positive recovery statement, being cooperative with the staff, and getting along with each other. The more points staff members hand out, the better and more quickly the maladaptive behavior will come under control. Clients will work for points if they can turn the points in for reinforcers that they want to earn. Points need to be taken away by the staff, or by the group, only if the behavior is bad enough to warrant a consequence. The best way in which to take away points is by the group process or a trial. For the first few days that clients are in treatment, all of the reinforcers need to be positive. Later, a staff member might need to tell a client something like this: "I am going to fine you occasionally. That does not mean I am mad at you, and you should not get mad at me. After all, these are just points, and you can earn them back." Clients need to be taught how to receive criticism. After a consequence, the staff member might say, "That is good. You looked me in the eye, did not mumble anything under your breath, and took the points off your card. Good job."

Points will be routinely given for the following behaviors:

Clients will get up in the morning.	100 points
Clients will shower.	100 points
Clients will dress.	100 points
Clients will clean their room.	100 points
Clients will be ready for breakfast on time.	100 points
Clients will remember to carry around the point system card.	100 points
Clients will complete chores by 10:00 am.	100 points
Clients will be on time for each group activity.	100 points
Clients will participate in each group.	100 points
Clients will complete Feelings sheets.	Up to 1,000 points
Clients will complete all assignments given to them by the group manager.	100 points

(Continued)

(Continued)

Clients will complete each assignment given to them by their counselor.	100 points
Clients will cooperate with the teacher and will study during study time.	100 points
Clients will go to bed at 11:00 pm and be quiet after lights out.	100 points
The counselor or staff will grade clients on daily participation in recovery.	Up to 100 points
Clients will assist the staff with duties such as filling water tank and leading Alcoholics Anonymous (AA) meetings.	Up to 1,000 points

Clients can turn in their points for the following rewards:

Xbox	500 points per 15 minutes for each player
One 5-minute telephone call	1,000 points
One call to parents or from parents	No charge
Store items	As marked
A meal out with a staff member	20,000 points
Saturday sleep until 11:00 am group (must get up for breakfast)	5,000 points
Sunday sleep until lunch (must get up for breakfast)	5,000 points
CDs	Charge or use as reward? (ability to check out being considered)
Special privileges—anything the client wants that is appropriate	Points negotiable
Special trip to a store or shopping	Under consideration

Clients can lose points for the following misbehaviors:

All contraband such as cigarettes, lighters, and CDs	Contraband will be taken away (discharge also is possible)
Being disrespectful to the staff	−1,500 points
Physical aggression	−5,000 points
Verbal aggression	−1,500 points
Violation of unit rules (e.g., doors not open at all times in opposite sex rooms, being out of room after staff advised to be in room)	−1,500 points

Violation of *group* rules	−1,500 points
Being late for groups and activities or leaving during groups	−2,000 points
Smell of smoke in room	−1,000 points
Caught with cigarette lit	−2,000 points

All large fines (more than 10,000 points), unless set, need to be adjudicated by the community group. The group will vote by secret ballot as to the guilt or innocence of the individual and set a consequence by a majority secret ballot. The person accused and the staff will not vote, but the staff will retain the right to veto any ruling.

Additional Guidelines

Phone Calls

1. Phone calls will cost 1,000 points for 5 minutes.

2. All phone calls will be dialed by the on-duty staff.

3. All phone calls will be placed on the hallway phone.

4. Outgoing phone calls will be allowed from 8:00 pm to 9:30 pm.

5. Incoming phone calls will be allowed from 4:30 pm to 9:30 pm.

Radios

1. No radios will be allowed in the hallway.

2. If radios are left on in a client's room and no one is in the room, then the radio will be taken away for 24 hours.

3. If a client is asked to turn down the volume of the radio and he or she refuses, then the radio will be taken away for 24 hours.

Smoking

1. Clients on the adolescent unit who are 18 years old will be given two cigarettes at a time by the on-duty staff.

2. If lighters and cigarettes are found on the adolescent unit, then these will be taken away and destroyed.

Doors

1. Doors are to remain open at all times.

Point Card

Room Checks	Group	Activities of Daily Living	Behavior/Attitude
100	100	100	100
200	200	200	200

Name:

Date:

Morning

Room Checks	Group	Activities of Daily Living	Behavior/Attitude
100	100	100	100
200	200	200	200
300	300	300	300
400	400	400	400

Morning total:

Afternoon

Room Checks	Group	Activities of Daily Living	Behavior/Attitude
100	100	100	100
200	200	200	200
300	300	300	300
400	400	400	400

Afternoon total:

Evening

Room Checks	Group	Activities of Daily Living	Behavior/Attitude
100	100	100	100
200	200	200	200
300	300	300	300
400	400	400	400

Evening total:

Extra points given (up to 1,500):

Total points given:

Points deducted:

Total points deducted:

Today's total:

Appendix 42

Results From the 2008 National Survey on Drug Use and Health

National Findings

U.S. DEPARTMENT OF HEALTH AND HUMAN SERVICES
Substance Abuse and Mental Health Services Administration Office of Applied Studies

Acknowledgments
This report was prepared by the Office of Applied Studies (OAS), Substance Abuse and Mental Health Services Administration (SAMHSA), U.S. Department of Health and Human Services (HHS), and by RTI International (a trade name of Research Triangle Institute), Research Triangle Park, North Carolina. Work by RTI was performed under Contract No. 283-2004-00022.

Recommended Citation
Substance Abuse and Mental Health Services Administration. (2009a). Results from the 2008 National Survey on Drug Use and Health: National Findings (Office of Applied Studies, NSDUH Series H-36, HHS Publication No. SMA 09-4434). Rockville, MD.

Electronic Access and Copies of Publication
This publication may be downloaded from http://www.oas.samhsa.gov. Hard copies may be obtained from http://www.oas.samhsa.gov/copies.cfm. Or please call SAMHSA's Health Information Network at 1-877-SAMHSA-7 (1-877-726-4727) (English and Español).

Originating Office
Substance Abuse and Mental Health Services Administration
Office of Applied Studies
Division of Population Surveys
1 Choke Cherry Road, Room 7-1044
Rockville, MD 20857
September 2009

Highlights

This report presents the first information from the 2008 National Survey on Drug Use and Health (NSDUH), an annual survey sponsored by the Substance Abuse and Mental Health Services Administration (SAMHSA). The survey is the primary source of information on the use of illicit drugs, alcohol, and tobacco in the civilian, noninstitutionalized population of the United States aged 12 years old or older. The survey interviews approximately 67,500 persons each year. Unless otherwise noted, all comparisons in this report described using terms such as "increased," "decreased," or "more than" are statistically significant at the .05 level.

Illicit Drug Use

- In 2008, an estimated 20.1 million Americans aged 12 or older were current (past month) illicit drug users, meaning they had used an illicit drug during the month prior to the survey interview. This estimate represents 8.0 percent of the population aged 12 years old or older. Illicit drugs include marijuana/hashish, cocaine (including crack), heroin, hallucinogens, inhalants, or prescription-type psychotherapeutics used nonmedically.
- The rate of current illicit drug use among persons aged 12 or older in 2008 (8.0 percent) was the same as the rate in 2007 (8.0 percent).
- Marijuana was the most commonly used illicit drug (15.2 million past month users). Among persons aged 12 or older, the rate of past month marijuana use in 2008 (6.1 percent) was similar to the rate in 2007 (5.8 percent).
- In 2008, there were 1.9 million current cocaine users aged 12 or older, comprising 0.7 percent of the population. These estimates were similar to the number and rate in 2007 (2.1 million or 0.8 percent), but lower than the estimates in 2006 (2.4 million or 1.0 percent).
- Hallucinogens were used in the past month by 1.1 million persons (0.4 percent) aged 12 or older in 2008, including 555,000 (0.2 percent) who had used Ecstasy. These estimates were similar to the corresponding estimates for 2007.
- There were 6.2 million (2.5 percent) persons aged 12 or older who used prescription-type psychotherapeutic drugs nonmedically in the past month. These estimates were lower than in 2007 (6.9 million or 2.8 percent).
- The number of past month methamphetamine users decreased by over half between 2006 and 2008. The numbers were 731,000 in 2006, 529,000 in 2007, and 314,000 in 2008.
- Among youths aged 12 to 17, the current illicit drug use rate remained stable from 2007 (9.5 percent) to 2008 (9.3 percent). Between 2002 and 2008, youth rates declined significantly for illicit drugs in general (from 11.6 to 9.3 percent) and for marijuana (8.2 to 6.7 percent), cocaine (0.6 to 0.4 percent), prescription-type drugs used nonmedically (4.0 to 2.9 percent), pain relievers (3.2 to 2.3 percent), stimulants (0.8 to 0.5 percent), and methamphetamine (0.3 to 0.1 percent).
- The rate of current marijuana use among youths aged 12 to 17 decreased from 8.2 percent in 2002 to 6.7 percent in 2006 and remained unchanged at 6.7 percent in 2007 and 2008.
- The rate of current hallucinogen use among youths aged 12 to 17 increased from 0.7 percent in 2007 to 1.0 percent in 2008.
- Rates of current use of illicit drugs in 2008 were higher among young adults aged 18 to 25 (19.6 percent) than for youths aged 12 to 17 (9.3 percent) and adults aged 26 or older (5.9 percent). Among young adults, there were no changes from 2007 to 2008 in the rate of current use of marijuana (16.5 percent in 2008), psychotherapeutics (5.9 percent), and hallucinogens (1.7 percent). The rate of cocaine use in this age group declined from 2.6 percent in 2005 to 1.5 percent in 2008.
- From 2002 to 2008, there was an increase among young adults aged 18 to 25 in the rate of current nonmedical use of prescription pain relievers (from 4.1 to 4.6 percent) and in LSD (from 0.1 to 0.3 percent). There were decreases in the use of inhalants (from 0.5 to 0.3 percent) and methamphetamine (from 0.6 to 0.2 percent).

- Among those aged 50 to 59, the rate of past month illicit drug use increased from 2.7 percent in 2002 to 4.6 percent in 2008. This trend may partially reflect the aging into this age group of the baby boom cohort, whose lifetime rate of illicit drug use is higher than those of older cohorts.

- Among persons aged 12 or older in 2007-2008 who used pain relievers nonmedically in the past 12 months, 55.9 percent got the drug they most recently used from a friend or relative for free. Another 18.0 percent reported they got the drug from one doctor. Only 4.3 percent got pain relievers from a drug dealer or other stranger, and 0.4 percent bought them on the Internet. Among those who reported getting the pain reliever from a friend or relative for free, 81.7 percent reported in a follow-up question that the friend or relative had obtained the drugs from just one doctor.

- Among unemployed adults aged 18 or older in 2008, 19.6 percent were current illicit drug users, which was higher than the 8.0 percent of those employed full time and 10.2 percent of those employed part time. However, most illicit drug users were employed. Of the 17.8 million current illicit drug users aged 18 or older in 2008, 12.9 million (72.7 percent) were employed either full or part time. The number of unemployed illicit drug users increased from 1.3 million in 2007 to 1.8 million in 2008, primarily because of an overall increase in the number of unemployed persons.

- In 2008, 10.0 million persons aged 12 or older reported driving under the influence of illicit drugs during the past year. This corresponds to 4.0 percent of the population aged 12 or older, the same as the rate in 2007 (4.0 percent), but lower than the rate in 2002 (4.7 percent). In 2008, the rate was highest among young adults aged 18 to 25 (12.3 percent).

Alcohol Use

- Slightly more than half of Americans aged 12 or older reported being current drinkers of alcohol in the 2008 survey (51.6 percent). This translates to an estimated 129.0 million people, which was similar to the 2007 estimate of 126.8 million people (51.1 percent).

- In 2008, more than one fifth (23.3 percent) of persons aged 12 or older participated in binge drinking. This translates to about 58.1 million people, similar to the estimate in 2007. Binge drinking is defined as having five or more drinks on the same occasion on at least 1 day in the 30 days prior to the survey.

- In 2008, heavy drinking was reported by 6.9 percent of the population aged 12 or older, or 17.3 million people. This rate was the same as the rate of heavy drinking in 2007. Heavy drinking is defined as binge drinking on at least 5 days in the past 30 days.

- Among young adults aged 18 to 25 in 2008, the rate of binge drinking was 41.0 percent, and the rate of heavy drinking was 14.5 percent. These rates were similar to the rates in 2007.

- The rate of current alcohol use among youths aged 12 to 17 was 14.6 percent in 2008, which is lower than the 2007 rate (15.9 percent). Youth binge and heavy drinking rates in 2008 were 8.8 percent (lower than the 9.7 percent rate in 2007) and 2.0 percent, respectively.

- Past month and binge drinking rates among underage persons (aged 12 to 20) declined between 2002 and 2008. The rate of past month underage drinking declined from 28.8 to 26.4 percent, and the rate of past month binge drinking declined from 19.3 to 17.4 percent.

- Past month alcohol use rates declined between 2002 and 2008 for those aged 12 or 13 (4.3 to 3.4 percent), 14 or 15 (16.6 to 13.1 percent), 16 or 17 (32.6 to 26.2 percent), and 18 to 20 (51.0 to 48.7 percent).

- Among persons aged 12 to 20, past month alcohol use rates in 2008 were 17.2 percent among Asians, 19.0 percent among blacks, 22.9 percent among those reporting two or more races, 23.1 percent among Hispanics, 26.4 percent among American Indians or Alaska Natives, and 30.1 percent among whites.

- In 2008, 56.2 percent of current drinkers aged 12 to 20 reported that their last use of alcohol in the past month occurred in someone else's home, and 29.6 percent reported that it had occurred in their own home. About one third (30.8 percent) paid for the alcohol the last time they drank, including 8.3 percent who purchased the alcohol themselves and 22.3 percent who gave money to someone else to purchase it. Among those who did not pay for the alcohol they last drank, 37.4 percent got it from an unrelated person aged 21 or older, 21.1 percent from another person under 21 years of age, and 21.0 percent from a parent, guardian, or other adult family member.

- In 2008, an estimated 12.4 percent of persons aged 12 or older drove under the influence of alcohol at least once in the past year. This percentage has dropped since 2002, when it was 14.2 percent. The rate of driving under the influence of alcohol was highest among persons aged 21 to 25 (26.1 percent).

Tobacco Use

- In 2008, an estimated 70.9 million Americans aged 12 or older were current (past month) users of a tobacco product. This represents 28.4 percent of the population in that age range. In addition, 59.8 million persons (23.9 percent of the population) were current cigarette smokers; 13.1 million (5.3 percent) smoked cigars; 8.7 million (3.5 percent) used smokeless tobacco; and 1.9 million (0.8 percent) smoked tobacco in pipes.
- The rate of current use of any tobacco product among persons aged 12 or older remained steady from 2007 to 2008 (28.6 and 28.4 percent, respectively). Rates of current use of cigarettes, smokeless tobacco, cigars, and pipe tobacco also did not change significantly over that period. However, between 2002 and 2008, past month use of any tobacco product decreased from 30.4 to 28.4 percent, and past month cigarette use declined from 26.0 to 23.9 percent. Rates of past month use of cigars, smokeless tobacco, and pipe tobacco in 2008 were similar to corresponding rates in 2002.
- The rate of past month cigarette use among 12 to 17 year olds declined from 9.8 percent in 2007 to 9.1 percent in 2008, continuing a decline since 2002 when the rate was 13.0 percent. However, past month smokeless tobacco use did not decline over this period (2.0 percent in 2002 and 2.2 percent in 2008).
- Among pregnant women aged 15 to 44, combined data for 2007 and 2008 indicated that the rate of past month cigarette use was 16.4 percent. The rate was higher among women in that age group who were not pregnant (27.3 percent).

Initiation of Substance Use (Incidence, or First-Time Use) Within the Past 12 Months

- In 2008, an estimated 2.9 million persons aged 12 or older used an illicit drug for the first time within the past 12 months. This averages to almost 8,000 initiates per day and is similar to the estimate for 2007. A majority of these past year illicit drug initiates reported that their first drug was marijuana (56.6 percent). Nearly one third initiated with psychotherapeutics (29.6 percent, including 22.5 percent with pain relievers, 3.2 percent with tranquilizers, 3.0 percent with stimulants, and 0.8 percent with sedatives). A sizable proportion reported inhalants (9.7 percent) as their first illicit drug, and a small proportion used hallucinogens as their first drug (3.2 percent).
- In 2008, the illicit drug categories with the largest number of past year initiates among persons aged 12 or older were marijuana use (2.2 million) and nonmedical use of pain relievers (2.2 million). These estimates were not significantly different from the numbers in 2007.
- In 2008, there were 729,000 persons aged 12 or older who had used inhalants for the first time within the past 12 months; 70.4 percent were under age 18 when they first used. There was no significant change in the number of inhalant initiates from 2007 to 2008, but the number in 2008 was significantly lower than the estimate in 2005 (877,000).
- The number of past year initiates of methamphetamine among persons aged 12 or older was 95,000 in 2008. This estimate was significantly lower than the estimate in 2007 (157,000) and was less than one third of the number estimated in 2004 (318,000).
- Following substantial drops in initiation between 2002 and 2003, estimates of initiation of Ecstasy and LSD among persons aged 12 or older have increased significantly. Between 2003 and 2008, the

number of Ecstasy initiates increased from 642,000 to 894,000, and the number of LSD initiates increased from 200,000 to 394,000.

- Most (84.6 percent) of the 4.5 million past year alcohol initiates were younger than age 21 at the time of initiation.

- The number of persons aged 12 or older who smoked cigarettes for the first time within the past 12 months was 2.4 million in 2008, similar to the estimate in 2007 (2.2 million) but significantly higher than the estimate for 2002 (1.9 million). Most new smokers in 2008 were under age 18 when they first smoked cigarettes (58.8 percent); however, the number of persons initiating smoking at age 18 or older increased from about 600,000 in 2002 to 1 million in 2008.

Youth Prevention-Related Measures

- Perceived risk is measured by NSDUH as the percentage reporting that there is great risk in the substance use behavior. The percentage of youths aged 12 to 17 perceiving great risk in smoking marijuana once or twice a week increased from 51.5 percent in 2002 to 55.0 percent in 2005, but dropped to 53.1 percent in 2008. A decline from 2005 to 2008 also was observed for using LSD once or twice a week (76.2 percent in 2002, 76.1 percent in 2005, and 73.9 percent in 2008). Between 2002 and 2008, the percentages who reported great risk in using alcohol and cigarettes increased. In 2002, 63.1 percent of youths reported great risk in smoking one or more packs of cigarettes per day, and in 2008 the percentage increased to 69.7 percent. In 2002, 38.2 percent reported great risk in binge drinking once or twice a week, and in 2008 the percentage increased to 40.5 percent.

- Almost half (49.2 percent) of youths aged 12 to 17 reported in 2008 that it would be "fairly easy" or "very easy" for them to obtain marijuana if they wanted some. Around one quarter reported it would be easy to get cocaine (22.1 percent). About one in seven (13.8 percent) indicated that LSD would be "fairly" or "very" easily available, and 13.0 percent reported easy availability for heroin. Between 2002 and 2008, there were declines in the perceived availability for all four drugs.

- A majority of youths aged 12 to 17 (90.8 percent) in 2008 reported that their parents would strongly disapprove of their trying marijuana or hashish once or twice. Current marijuana use was much less prevalent among youths who perceived strong parental disapproval for trying marijuana or hashish once or twice than for those who did not (4.3 vs. 29.8 percent).

- In 2008, 11.1 percent of youths aged 12 to 17 reported that they had participated in substance use prevention programs outside of school within the past year. This was lower than the percentage reported in 2002 (12.7 percent). Almost four fifths (78.0 percent) reported having seen or heard drug or alcohol prevention messages from sources outside of school, lower than in 2002 when the percentage was 83.2 percent. The percentage of school-enrolled youths reporting that they had seen or heard prevention messages at school also declined during this period, from 78.8 to 75.9 percent.

Substance Dependence, Abuse, and Treatment

- In 2008, an estimated 22.2 million persons (8.9 percent of the population aged 12 or older) were classified with substance dependence or abuse in the past year based on criteria specified in the Diagnostic and Statistical Manual of Mental Disorders, 4th edition (DSM-IV). Of these, 3.1 million were classified with dependence on or abuse of both alcohol and illicit drugs, 3.9 million were dependent on or abused illicit drugs but not alcohol, and 15.2 million were dependent on or abused alcohol but not illicit drugs.

- Between 2002 and 2008, there was no change in the number of persons with substance dependence or abuse (22.0 million in 2002 and 22.2 million in 2008).

- The specific illicit drugs that had the highest levels of past year dependence or abuse in 2008 were marijuana (4.2 million), followed by pain relievers (1.7 million) and cocaine (1.4 million).

- In 2008, adults aged 21 or older who had first used alcohol at age 14 or younger were more than 5 times as likely to be classified with alcohol dependence or abuse than adults who had their first drink at age 21 or older (15.1 vs. 2.6 percent).

- The rate of substance dependence or abuse for males aged 12 or older in 2008 was nearly twice as high as the rate for females (11.5 vs. 6.4 percent). Among youths aged 12 to 17, however, the rate of substance dependence or abuse was higher among females than males (8.2 vs. 7.0 percent).

- Between 2002 and 2008, the percentage of youths aged 12 to 17 with substance dependence or abuse declined from 8.9 to 7.6 percent.

- Treatment need is defined as having a substance use disorder or receiving treatment at a specialty facility (hospital inpatient, drug or alcohol rehabilitation, or mental health centers) within the past 12 months. In 2008, 23.1 million persons aged 12 or older needed treatment for an illicit drug or alcohol use problem (9.2 percent of persons aged 12 or older). Of these, 2.3 million (0.9 percent of persons aged 12 or older and 9.9 percent of those who needed treatment) received treatment at a specialty facility. Thus, 20.8 million persons (8.3 percent of the population aged 12 or older) needed treatment for an illicit drug or alcohol use problem but did not receive treatment at a specialty substance abuse facility in the past year.

- Of the 20.8 million people in 2008 who were classified as needing substance use treatment but did not receive treatment at a specialty facility in the past year, 1.0 million persons (4.8 percent) reported that they felt they needed treatment for their illicit drug or alcohol use problem. Of these 1.0 million persons who felt they needed treatment, 233,000 (23.3 percent) reported that they made an effort to get treatment, and 766,000 (76.7 percent) reported making no effort to get treatment.

Mental Health

- Serious mental illness (SMI) among adults is defined in Public Law 102-321 as persons aged 18 or older who currently or at any time in the past year have had a diagnosable mental, behavioral, or emotional disorder (excluding developmental and substance use disorders) of sufficient duration to meet diagnostic criteria specified within DSM-IV that has resulted in functional impairment, which substantially interferes with or limits one or more major life activities. In 2008, there were an estimated 9.8 million adults with SMI, representing 4.4 percent of adults.

- Rates of SMI in 2008 were highest for adults aged 18 to 25 (7.4 percent) and lowest for adults aged 50 or older (2.3 percent).

- The prevalence of SMI among women aged 18 or older (5.6 percent) was higher than that among men in that age group (3.0 percent).

- The rate of SMI was higher among adults who were unemployed (8.0 percent) than among those who were employed full time (3.5 percent) or part time (4.8 percent).

- SMI in the past year was associated with past year substance dependence or abuse. Among adults aged 18 or older with SMI in 2008, 25.2 percent (2.5 million) were dependent on or abused illicit drugs or alcohol. The rate among adults without SMI was 8.3 percent (17.9 million).

- Among the 9.8 million adults with SMI in 2008, 5.7 million (58.7 percent) used mental health services in the past year. Among all adults with SMI, 52.6 percent received a prescription medication, 40.5 percent received outpatient services, and 7.5 percent received inpatient services for a mental health problem in the past year.

- Among the 2.5 million adults with both SMI and substance dependence or abuse (i.e., a substance use disorder) in 2008, more than half (60.5 percent) received mental health care or substance use treatment at a specialty facility; 11.4 percent received both mental health care and specialty substance use treatment, 45.2 percent received only mental health care, and 3.7 percent received only specialty substance use treatment.

- In 2008, an estimated 8.3 million adults (3.7 percent) had serious thoughts of suicide in the past year. The rate was 3.9 percent among women and 3.4 percent among men. The rate was highest among young adults aged 18 to 25 (6.7 percent) compared with adults 26 to 49 (3.9 percent) and adults aged 50 or older (2.3 percent).

- Among adults aged 18 or older in 2008, 2.3 million (1.0 percent) made suicide plans in the past year, and 1.1 million (0.5 percent) reported attempting suicide. A half million adults reported staying overnight in a hospital as a result of their suicide attempt in the past year.

- In 2008, 6.4 percent of persons aged 18 or older (14.3 million persons) had at least one major depressive episode (MDE) in the past year. Over 1 in 25 adults (4.2 percent or 9.5 million persons) had past year MDE with severe impairment.

- In 2008, adults with past year MDE were more likely than those without MDE to be dependent on or abuse illicit drugs or alcohol (20.3 vs. 7.8 percent).

- Among adults aged 18 or older who had MDE in the past year in 2008, 71.0 percent received treatment (i.e., saw or talked to a medical doctor or other professional or used prescription medication) for depression in the same time period.

- Among adults aged 18 or older with MDE in the past year in 2008, women were more likely than men to receive treatment for depression in the past year (74.2 vs. 65.0 percent).

- In 2008, there were 2.0 million youths (8.3 percent of the population aged 12 to 17) who had MDE during the past year. An estimated 1.5 million (6.0 percent) had MDE with severe impairment in one or more role domains (chores at home; school or work; close relationships with family; or social life).

- The rate of MDE in the past year was higher for adolescent females (12.4 percent) than for adolescent males (4.3 percent). The prevalence of MDE with severe impairment was 9.2 percent for females and 2.9 percent for males.

- Among 12 to 17 year olds who had past year MDE in 2008, 37.4 percent had used illicit drugs during the same period. This was higher than the rate of 17.2 percent among youths who did not have past year MDE. Similarly, the rates of past month daily cigarette use and heavy alcohol use were higher for youths with MDE (3.6 and 3.4 percent, respectively) than for youths who did not have MDE (1.8 and 1.8 percent, respectively).

- In 2008, 37.7 percent of youths aged 12 to 17 with past year MDE received treatment for depression (saw or talked to a medical doctor or other professional or used prescription medication). Among youths with past year MDE, 21.7 percent saw or talked to a medical doctor or other professional only, 2.9 percent used prescription medication only, and 13.1 percent received treatment from both sources for depression in the past year.

- In 2008, 3.1 million youths aged 12 to 17 (12.7 percent) received treatment or counseling for problems with behavior or emotions in the specialty mental health setting (inpatient or outpatient care). Additionally, 11.8 percent of youths received services in the education setting, and 2.9 percent received mental health services in the general medical setting in the past 12 months. Mental health services were received in both the specialty setting and either the education or general medical settings (i.e., care from multiple settings) by 5.3 percent of youths.

1. Introduction

This report presents a first look at results from the 2008 National Survey on Drug Use and Health (NSDUH), an annual survey of the civilian, noninstitutionalized population of the United States aged 12 years old or older. The report presents national estimates of rates of use, numbers of users, and other measures related to illicit drugs, alcohol, and tobacco products. Measures related to mental health problems also are presented, including data on serious mental illness, depression, and the co-occurrence of substance use and mental health problems. The report focuses on trends between 2007 and 2008 and from 2002 to 2008, as well as differences across population subgroups in 2008. Estimates from NSDUH for States and areas within States will be presented in separate reports.

1.1. Summary of NSDUH

NSDUH is the primary source of statistical information on the use of illegal drugs by the U.S. population. Conducted by the Federal Government since 1971, the survey collects data by administering questionnaires to a representative sample of the population through face-to-face interviews at the respondent's place of residence. The survey is sponsored by the Substance Abuse and Mental Health Services Administration (SAMHSA), U.S. Department of Health and Human Services, and is planned and managed by SAMHSA's Office of Applied Studies (OAS). Data collection and analysis are conducted under contract with RTI International, Research Triangle Park, North Carolina.[1] This section briefly describes the survey methodology; a more complete description is provided in Appendix A.

NSDUH collects information from residents of households and noninstitutional group quarters (e.g., shelters, rooming houses, dormitories) and from civilians living on military bases. The survey excludes homeless persons who do not use shelters, military personnel on active duty, and residents of institutional group quarters, such as jails and hospitals. Appendix D describes surveys that cover populations outside the NSDUH target population.

From 1971 through 1998, the survey employed paper and pencil data collection. Since 1999, the NSDUH interview has been carried out using computer-assisted interviewing (CAI). Most of the questions are administered with audio computer-assisted self-interviewing (ACASI). ACASI is designed to provide the respondent with a highly private and confidential mode for responding to questions in order to increase the level of honest reporting of illicit drug use and other sensitive behaviors. Less sensitive items are administered by interviewers using computer-assisted personal interviewing (CAPI).

The 2008 NSDUH employed a State-based design with an independent, multistage area probability sample within each State and the District of Columbia. The eight States with the largest population (which together account for about half of the total U.S. population aged 12 or older) were designated as large sample States (California, Florida, Illinois, Michigan, New York, Ohio, Pennsylvania, and Texas) and had a sample size of about 3,600 each. For the remaining 42 States and the District of Columbia, the sample size was about 900 per State. The design oversampled youths and young adults, so that each State's sample was approximately equally distributed among three age groups: 12 to 17 years, 18 to 25 years, and 26 years or older.

Nationally, screening was completed at 142,938 addresses, and 68,736 completed interviews were obtained. The survey was conducted from January through December 2008. Weighted response rates for household screening and for interviewing were 89.0 and 74.4 percent, respectively. See Appendix B for more information on NSDUH response rates.

1.2. Limitations on Trend Measurement

Because of the shift in interviewing method in 1999, the estimates from the pre-1999 surveys are not comparable with estimates from the current CAI-based surveys. Although the design of the 2002 through 2008 NSDUHs is similar to the design of the 1999 through 2001 surveys, there are also important methodological differences that affect the comparability of the 2002 to 2008 estimates with estimates from prior surveys. The most important change was the incentive payment started in 2002 and continuing in subsequent surveys. Each NSDUH respondent completing the interview is given $30. Also, the name of the survey was changed in 2002, from the National Household Survey on Drug Abuse (NHSDA) to the current name. Improved data collection quality control procedures were introduced in the survey starting in 2001, and updated population data from the 2000 decennial census were incorporated into the sample weights starting with the 2002 estimates. Analyses of the effects of these factors on NSDUH estimates have shown that 2002 and later data should not be compared with 2001 and earlier data from the survey series to assess changes over time. Appendix C of the 2004 NSDUH report on national findings discusses this in more detail (see OAS, 2005).

Because of changes in the questionnaire, estimates for methamphetamine, stimulants, and psychotherapeutics in this report should not be compared with corresponding estimates in OAS reports for data years prior to 2007. Estimates for 2002 to 2006 for these drug categories in this report, as well as in the 2007 report, incorporate statistical adjustments to enable year-to-year comparisons to be made over the period from 2002 to 2008.

The next section describes questionnaire changes that affect trend measurement for serious psychological distress and major depressive episode.

1.3. New Data on Mental Health

Several important changes were made to the adult mental health section in the 2008 NSDUH questionnaire. These changes provide valuable new data on mental health, but they also affect some of the measures that have been collected in NSDUH since 2004. A brief summary of the changes and their impact is provided below.

From 2004 to 2007, NSDUH collected data for adults aged 18 or older on lifetime and past year major depressive episode (MDE). The survey also included the K6 distress scale with a past 12 month time frame. SAMHSA used the K6 data to generate estimates of serious psychological distress (SPD) in the past 12 months. To address SAMHSA's need for estimates of serious mental illness (SMI), as well as data on suicidal ideation and behavior, OAS modified the NSDUH adult mental health module in 2008 to obtain these data. Scales were added that assessed impairment caused by mental problems. OAS also expanded the K6 questions to ask about the past 30 days (the time frame for which the K6 was originally designed). A Mental Health Surveillance Study (MHSS) was initiated in which a subsample of adults (about 1,500 in 2008) who had completed the NSDUH interview was administered a standard clinical interview by mental health clinicians via paper and pencil over the telephone to determine their SMI status. Using both clinical interview and computer-assisted interview data for the respondents who completed the clinical interview, statistical models were developed that then were applied to the full NSDUH adult sample to produce SMI estimates. See Section B.4.6 in Appendix B for a more complete discussion.

The first estimates from the expanded mental health module, including those for SMI, 30-day SPD, and suicidal thoughts and behavior, are included in Chapter 8 of this report. However, the questionnaire changes caused discontinuities in trends for MDE and 12-month SPD. Analyses of these data have determined that the 2008 data for MDE and 12-month SPD are not comparable with 2007 and earlier data (see Section B.4.4 in Appendix B). Thus, no 12-month SPD data are discussed in the report, and MDE data are presented only for 2008.

No questionnaire changes were made in 2008 that affected MDE items for youths aged 12 to 17 or for the youth and adult mental health service utilization questions. The discussion of estimates for these measures in this report includes comparisons with prior years' data.

1.4. Format of Report and Explanation of Tables

This report has separate chapters that discuss the national findings on seven topics: use of illicit drugs; use of alcohol; use of tobacco products; initiation of substance use; prevention-related issues; substance dependence, abuse, and treatment; and mental health problems and treatment. A final chapter summarizes the results and discusses key findings in relation to other research and survey results. Technical appendices describe the survey (Appendix A), provide technical details on the statistical methods and measurement (Appendix B), offer key NSDUH definitions (Appendix C), discuss other sources of related data (Appendix D), list the references cited in the report (Appendix E), and present selected tabulations of estimates (Appendices F and G). A list of contributors to the production of this report also is provided (Appendix H).

Tables, text, and figures present prevalence measures for the population in terms of both the number of persons and the percentage of the population. Substance use tables show prevalence estimates by lifetime (i.e., ever used), past year, and past month use. Analyses focus primarily on past month use, which also is referred to as "current use." Tables and figures in which estimates are presented by year have footnotes indicating whether the 2008 estimates are significantly different from 2007 or earlier estimates. In some tables and figures, estimates are presented based on data combined from two or more survey years to increase precision of the estimates; those estimates are annual averages based on multiple years of data.

Statistical tests have been conducted for all statements appearing in the text of the report that compare estimates between years or subgroups of the population. Unless explicitly stated that a difference is not statistically significant, all statements that describe differences are significant at the .05 level. Statistically significant differences are described using terms such as "higher," "lower," "increased," and "decreased." Statements that use terms such as "similar," "no difference," "same," or "remained steady" to describe the relationship between estimates denote that a difference is not statistically significant. In addition, a set of estimates for survey years or population subgroups may be presented without a statement of comparison, in which case a statistically significant difference between these estimates is not implied and testing was not conducted.

All estimates presented in the report have met the criteria for statistical reliability (see Section B.2.2 in Appendix B). Estimates that do not meet these criteria are suppressed and do not appear in tables, figures, or text. Subgroups with suppressed estimates are not included in statistical tests of comparisons. For example, a statement that "whites had the highest prevalence" means that the rate among whites was higher than the rate among all nonsuppressed racial/ethnic subgroups, but not necessarily higher than the rate among a subgroup for which the estimate was suppressed.

Data are presented for racial/ethnic groups based on current guidelines for collecting and reporting race and ethnicity data (Office of Management and Budget [OMB], 1997). Because respondents were allowed to choose more than one racial group, a "two or more races" category is presented that includes persons who reported more than one category among the basic groups listed in the survey question (white, black or African American, American Indian or Alaska Native, Native Hawaiian, Other Pacific Islander, Asian, Other). Respondents choosing both Native Hawaiian and Other Pacific Islander but no other categories mentioned above are classified in the combined "Native Hawaiian or Other Pacific Islander" category instead of the "two or more race" category. It should be noted that, except for the "Hispanic or Latino" group, the racial/ethnic groups discussed in this report include only non-Hispanics. The category "Hispanic or Latino" includes Hispanics of any race.

Data also are presented for four U.S. geographic regions and nine geographic divisions within these regions. These regions and divisions, defined by the U.S. Census Bureau, consist of the following groups of States:

Northeast Region—New England Division: Connecticut, Maine, Massachusetts, New Hampshire, Rhode Island, Vermont; Middle Atlantic Division: New Jersey, New York, Pennsylvania.

Midwest Region—East North Central Division: Illinois, Indiana, Michigan, Ohio, Wisconsin; West North Central Division: Iowa, Kansas, Minnesota, Missouri, Nebraska, North Dakota, South Dakota.

South Region—South Atlantic Division: Delaware, District of Columbia, Florida, Georgia, Maryland, North Carolina, South Carolina, Virginia, West Virginia; East South Central Division: Alabama, Kentucky, Mississippi, Tennessee; West South Central Division: Arkansas, Louisiana, Oklahoma, Texas.

West Region—Mountain Division: Arizona, Colorado, Idaho, Montana, Nevada, New Mexico, Utah, Wyoming; Pacific Division: Alaska, California, Hawaii, Oregon, Washington.

Geographic comparisons also are made based on county type, a variable that reflects different levels of urbanicity and metropolitan area inclusion of counties, based on metropolitan area definitions issued by the OMB in June 2003 (OMB, 2003). For this purpose, counties are grouped based on the 2003 rural-urban continuum codes. These codes were originally developed by the U.S. Department of Agriculture (Butler & Beale, 1994). Each county is either inside or outside a metropolitan statistical area (MSA), as defined by the OMB.

Large metropolitan areas have a population of 1 million or more. Small metropolitan areas have a population of fewer than 1 million. Small metropolitan areas are further classified based on whether they have a population of 250,000 or more. Nonmetropolitan areas are outside of MSAs. Counties in nonmetropolitan areas are further classified based on the number of people in the county who live in an urbanized area, as defined by the Census Bureau at the subcounty level. "Urbanized" counties have a population of 20,000 or more in urbanized areas, "less urbanized" counties have at least 2,500 but fewer than 20,000 population in urbanized areas, and "completely rural" counties have populations of fewer than 2,500 in urbanized areas.

1.5. Other NSDUH Reports and Data

Other reports focusing on specific topics of interest will be produced using the 2008 NSDUH data and made available on SAMHSA's website. A report on State-level estimates for 2007-2008 will be available in early 2010.

A comprehensive set of tables, referred to as "detailed tables," is available through the Internet at http://oas.samhsa.gov. The tables are organized into sections based primarily on the topic. Most tables are provided in several parts, showing population estimates (e.g., numbers of drug users), rates (e.g., percentages of population using drugs), and standard errors of all nonsuppressed estimates. A small subset of these detailed tables has been selected for inclusion in Appendices F and G of this report. The appendix tables can be mapped back to the detailed tables by using the table number in parentheses in the upper left corner of each table (e.g., Table G.1 in Appendix G is Table 8.1A in the detailed tables). Additional methodological information on NSDUH, including the questionnaire, is available electronically at the same web address.

Brief descriptive reports and in-depth analytic reports focusing on specific issues or population groups also are produced by OAS. A complete listing of previously published reports from NSDUH and other data sources is available from OAS. Most of these reports also are available through the Internet (http://oas.samhsa .gov). In addition, OAS makes public use data files available to researchers through the Substance Abuse and Mental Health Data Archive (SAMHDA, 2009) at http://www.datafiles.samhsa.gov. Currently, files are available from the 1979 to 2007 surveys.[2] The 2008 NSDUH public use file will be available by the end of 2009.

2. Illicit Drug Use

The National Survey on Drug Use and Health (NSDUH) obtains information on nine categories of illicit drug use: use of marijuana, cocaine, heroin, hallucinogens, and inhalants; and the nonmedical use of prescription-type pain relievers, tranquilizers, stimulants, and sedatives. In these categories, hashish is included with marijuana, and crack is considered a form of cocaine. Several drugs are grouped under the hallucinogens category, including LSD, PCP, peyote, mescaline, psilocybin mushrooms, and "Ecstasy" (MDMA). Inhalants include a variety of substances, such as nitrous oxide, amyl nitrite, cleaning fluids, gasoline, spray paint, other aerosol sprays, and glue. The four categories of prescription-type drugs (pain relievers, tranquilizers, stimulants, and sedatives) cover numerous medications available by prescription. They also include drugs within these groupings that originally were prescription medications but currently may be manufactured and distributed illegally, such as methamphetamine, which is included under stimulants. Respondents are asked to report only "nonmedical" use of these drugs, defined as use without a prescription of the individual's own or simply for the experience or feeling the drugs caused. Use of over-the-counter drugs and legitimate use of prescription drugs are not included. NSDUH reports combine the four prescription-type drug groups into a category referred to as "psychotherapeutics."

Estimates of "illicit drug use" reported from NSDUH reflect the use of any of the nine drug categories listed above. Use of alcohol and tobacco products, while illegal for youths, is not included in these estimates, but is discussed in Chapters 3 and 4.

This chapter includes estimates of the nonmedical use of prescription psychotherapeutic drugs and prescription stimulants that take into account data on methamphetamine use based on information obtained from survey items added to NSDUH beginning in 2005. Estimates for these drugs for earlier years when these items were not collected have been adjusted to be comparable with the current estimates. For further information, see Section B.4.6 of the 2007 NSDUH national findings report (Office of Applied Studies [OAS], 2008). The estimates for the nonmedical use of stimulants and psychotherapeutic drugs in this report are not comparable with corresponding estimates in NSDUH reports prior to the 2007 data year, and the methamphetamine use estimates in this report also are not comparable with those in NSDUH reports for survey years prior to 2006.

- In 2008, an estimated 20.1 million Americans aged 12 or older were current (past month) illicit drug users, meaning they had used an illicit drug during the month prior to the survey interview (Figure 2.1). This estimate represents 8.0 percent of the population aged 12 or older.
- The overall rate of current illicit drug use among persons aged 12 or older in 2008 (8.0 percent) was the same as the rate in 2007 and has remained stable since 2002 (8.3 percent) (Figure 2.2).
- Marijuana was the most commonly used illicit drug (15.2 million past month users). In 2008, marijuana was used by 75.7 percent of current illicit drug users and was the only drug used by 57.3 percent of them. Illicit drugs other than marijuana were used by 8.6 million persons or 42.7 percent of illicit drug users aged 12 or older. Current use of other drugs but not marijuana was reported by 24.3 percent of illicit drug users, and 18.4 percent used both marijuana and other drugs.
- Among persons aged 12 or older, the overall rate of past month marijuana use in 2008 (6.1 percent) was similar to the rate in 2007 and the rates in earlier years going back to 2002 (Figure 2.2).
- An estimated 8.6 million people aged 12 or older (3.4 percent) were current users of illicit drugs other than marijuana in 2008. The majority of these (6.2 million persons or 2.5 percent of the population) used psychotherapeutic drugs nonmedically. An estimated 4.7 million persons used pain relievers nonmedically in the past month in 2008, 1.8 million used tranquilizers, 904,000 used stimulants, and 234,000 used sedatives.
- The number and percentage of current nonmedical users of psychotherapeutic drugs in 2008 (6.2 million or 2.5 percent) were lower than in 2007 (6.9 million or 2.8 percent) (Figure 2.2). A small decline in the percentage of pain reliever users between 2007 (2.1 percent) and 2008 (1.9 percent), although not statistically significant, partly contributed to the lower rate for current use of psychotherapeutic drugs (Figure 2.3).

Figure 2.1   Past Month Illicit Drug Use Among Persons Aged 12 or Older: 2008

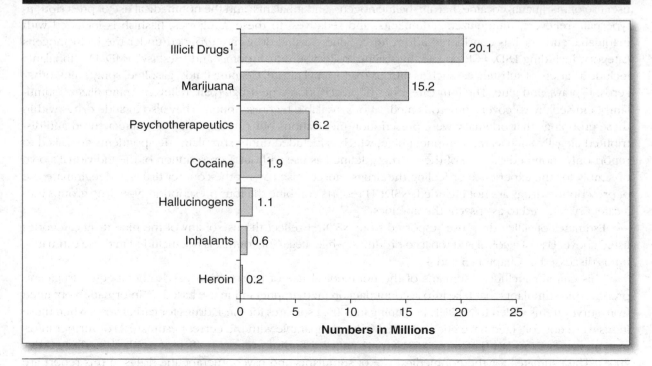

[1]Illicit Drugs include marijuana/hashish, cocaine (including crack), heroin, hallucinogens, inhalants, or prescription-type psychotherapeutics used nonmedically.

Figure 2.2   Past Month Use of Selected Illicit Drugs Among Persons Aged 12 or Older: 2002–2008

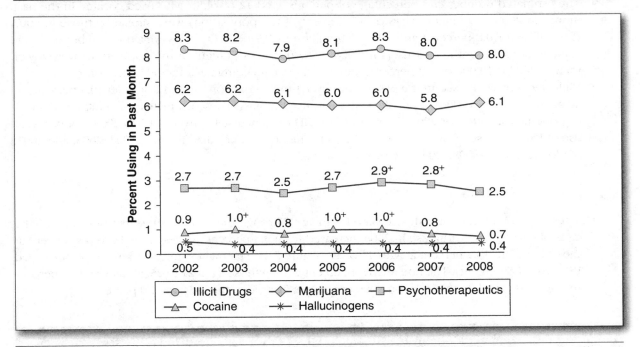

⁺Difference between this estimate and the 2008 estimate is statistically significant at the .05 level.

Figure 2.3   Past Month Nonmedical Use of Types of Psychotherapeutic Drugs Among Persons Aged 12 or Older: 2002–2008

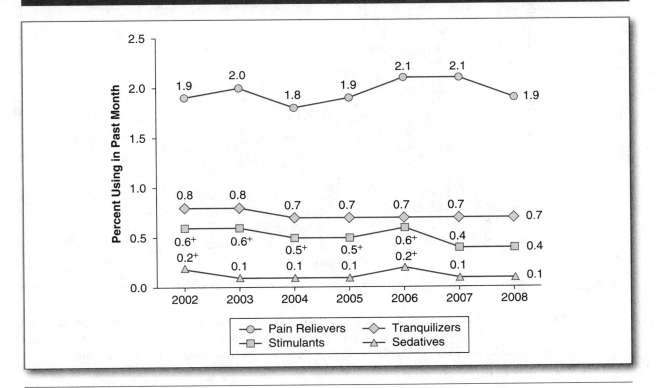

⁺Difference between this estimate and the 2008 estimate is statistically significant at the .05 level.

- The number of past month methamphetamine users decreased by over half between 2006 and 2008. The numbers were 731,000 in 2006, 529,000 in 2007, and 314,000 in 2008.
- The estimated number and percentage of persons aged 12 or older who used cocaine in the past month in 2008 (1.9 million users or 0.7 percent of the population) were similar to those in 2007 (2.1 million or 0.8 percent) and 2002 (2.0 million or 0.9 percent). However, the number and percentage of past month crack users in 2008 (359,000 or 0.1 percent of the population) were lower than in 2007 (610,000 or 0.2 percent) and all other years going back to 2002 except for 2004.
- Hallucinogens were used in the past month by 1.1 million persons aged 12 or older (0.4 percent) in 2008, including 555,000 (0.2 percent) who had used Ecstasy. These estimates are similar to the corresponding estimates for 2007. Current use of LSD remained stable from 2007 to 2008, but past year use of LSD increased from 620,000 to 802,000, a higher number than in 2003, 2004, 2005, and 2007, but lower than the 999,000 past year users in 2002.

Age

- Rates of past month illicit drug use varied with age. Through the adolescent years from 12 to 17, the rates of current illicit drug use in 2008 increased from 3.3 percent at ages 12 or 13 to 8.6 percent at ages 14 or 15 to 15.2 percent at ages 16 or 17 (Figure 2.4). The highest rate was among persons aged 18 to 20 (21.5 percent). The rate was 18.4 percent among those aged 21 to 25, and it was 13.0 percent among those aged 26 to 29. Among persons aged 65 or older, the rate was 1.0 percent.

Figure 2.4 Past Month Illicit Drug Use Among Persons Aged 12 or Older, by Age: 2008

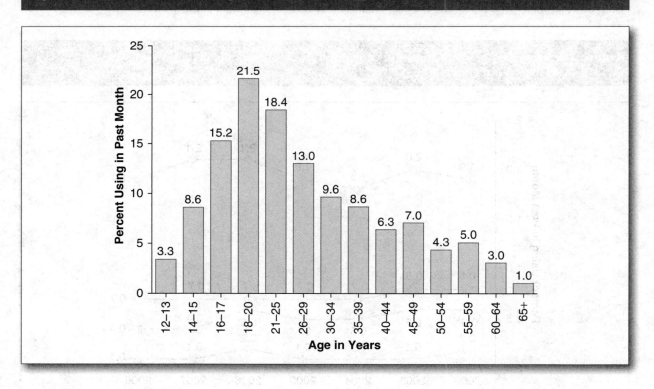

- In 2008, adults aged 26 or older were less likely to be current drug users than youths aged 12 to 17 or young adults aged 18 to 25 (5.9 vs. 9.3 and 19.6 percent, respectively). However, there were more drug users aged 26 or older (11.3 million) than users in the 12-to-17-year age group (2.3 million) and 18-to-25-year age group (6.5 million) combined.

- Current illicit drug use remained stable from 2007 to 2008 among youths aged 12 to 17, young adults aged 18 to 25, and adults aged 26 or older. From 2002 to 2008, however, the rate of current illicit drug use among 12 to 17 year olds decreased from 11.6 to 9.3 percent (Figure 2.5).

Figure 2.5   Past Month Use of Selected Illicit Drugs Among Youths Aged 12 to 17: 2002–2008

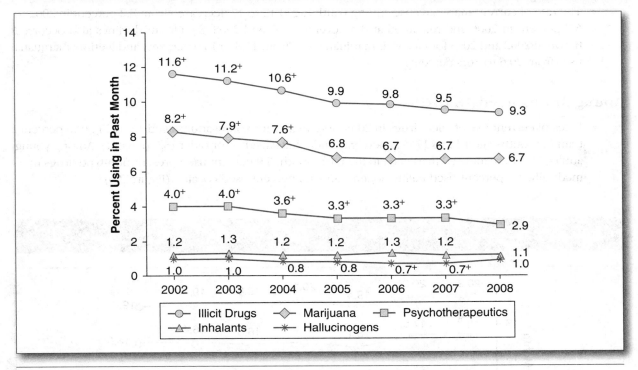

[+]Difference between this estimate and the 2008 estimate is statistically significant at the .05 level.

Youths Aged 12 to 17

- In 2008, 9.3 percent of youths aged 12 to 17 were current illicit drug users: 6.7 percent used marijuana, 2.9 percent engaged in nonmedical use of prescription-type psychotherapeutics, 1.1 percent used inhalants, 1.0 percent used hallucinogens, and 0.4 percent used cocaine.
- Among youths aged 12 to 17, the types of drugs used in the past month varied by age group. Among 12 or 13 year olds, 1.5 percent used prescription-type drugs nonmedically, 1.2 percent used inhalants, and 1.0 percent used marijuana. Among 14 or 15 year olds, marijuana was the most commonly used drug (5.7 percent), followed by prescription-type drugs used nonmedically (3.0 percent), inhalants (1.3 percent), and hallucinogens (1.0 percent). Marijuana also was the most commonly used drug among 16 or 17 year olds (12.7 percent); it was followed by prescription-type drugs used nonmedically (4.0 percent), hallucinogens (1.6 percent), cocaine (0.7 percent), and inhalants (0.7 percent).
- The overall rate of current illicit drug use remained stable from 2007 to 2008 among youths aged 12 to 17, as did the rates for most specific drugs, except for hallucinogens and the nonmedical use of psychotherapeutics. An increase was seen in the rate of past month hallucinogen use, which went from 0.7 percent in 2007 to 1.0 percent in 2008, driven in part by an increase in Ecstasy use from 0.3 to 0.4 percent. However, the rate of nonmedical use of prescription psychotherapeutic drugs among youths declined from 3.3 percent in 2007 to 2.9 percent in 2008, driven largely by a decrease in the misuse of pain relievers from 2.7 to 2.3 percent (Figure 2.5).

- From 2002 to 2008, rates of current use among youths aged 12 to 17 declined significantly for illicit drugs overall and for several specific drugs, including marijuana (from 8.2 to 6.7 percent), cocaine (from 0.6 to 0.4 percent), prescription-type drugs used nonmedically (from 4.0 to 2.9 percent), pain relievers (from 3.2 to 2.3 percent), stimulants (from 0.8 to 0.5 percent), and methamphetamine (from 0.3 to 0.1 percent) (Figure 2.5). For illicit drug use overall, the rates were 11.6 percent in 2002, 11.2 percent in 2003, 10.6 percent in 2004, 9.9 percent in 2005, 9.8 percent in 2006, 9.5 percent in 2007, and 9.3 percent in 2008.
- The rate of current marijuana use among youths aged 12 to 17 decreased from 8.2 percent in 2002 to 6.7 percent in 2006 and remained at that level in 2007 and 2008. Significant declines also occurred between 2002 and 2008 for past year marijuana use (from 15.8 to 13.0 percent) and lifetime marijuana use (from 20.6 to 16.5 percent).

Young Adults Aged 18 to 25

- Rates of current use of illicit drugs in 2008 were higher for young adults aged 18 to 25 (19.6 percent) than for youths aged 12 to 17 (9.3 percent) and adults aged 26 or older (5.9 percent). Among young adults, 16.5 percent used marijuana in the past month, 5.9 percent used prescription-type drugs nonmedically, 1.7 percent used hallucinogens, and 1.5 percent used cocaine (Figure 2.6).

Figure 2.6   Past Month Use of Selected Illicit Drugs Among Young Adults Aged 18 to 25: 2002–2008

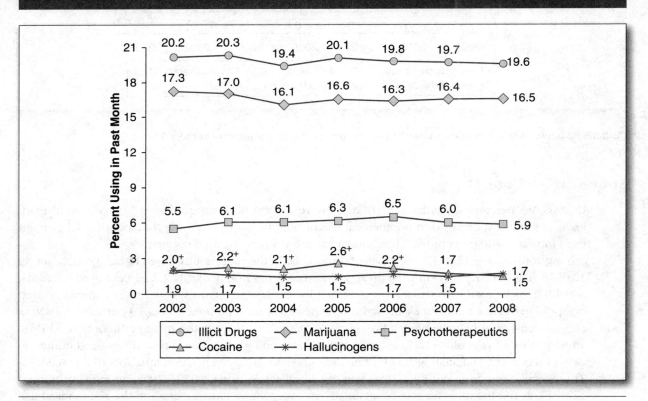

[+] Difference between this estimate and the 2008 estimate is statistically significant at the .05 level.

- From 2007 to 2008, rates of current use among young adults aged 18 to 25 remained stable for illicit drugs overall and each specific drug.

- From 2002 to 2008, there were declines in young adults' past month cocaine use (from 2.0 to 1.5 percent), inhalant use (from 0.5 to 0.3 percent), nonmedical use of stimulants (from 1.3 to 1.1 percent), and methamphetamine use (from 0.6 to 0.2 percent). Over the 7-year period, there were increases in the current use of pain relievers (from 4.1 to 4.6 percent) and LSD (from 0.1 to 0.3 percent).

Adults Aged 26 or Older

- Among adults aged 26 or older, 5.9 percent were current illicit drug users in 2008. In this age group, 4.2 percent used marijuana, and 1.9 percent used prescription-type drugs nonmedically. Less than 1 percent used cocaine (0.7 percent), hallucinogens (0.1 percent), heroin (0.1 percent), and inhalants (0.1 percent). The only significant change between 2007 and 2008 in the rates of past month use among adults in this age group involved crack, which decreased from 0.3 to 0.2 percent. In addition, the rates of past year nonmedical use declined for psychotherapeutic drugs overall (from 4.9 percent in 2007 to 4.4 percent in 2008), sedatives (from 0.3 to 0.2 percent), and methamphetamine (from 0.4 to 0.3 percent). However, increases occurred in lifetime use of hallucinogens (from 14.2 percent in 2007 to 15.2 percent in 2008) and lifetime nonmedical use of pain relievers (from 11.8 to 12.7 percent).

- Among adults aged 50 to 59, the rate of current illicit drug use increased from 2.7 to 4.6 percent between 2002 and 2008 (Figure 2.7). For those aged 50 to 54, the rate increased from 3.4 percent in 2002 to 6.0 percent in 2006, then dropped to 4.3 percent in 2008, not significantly different from the rate in either 2002 or 2006. Among those aged 55 to 59, current illicit drug use showed an increase from 1.9 percent in 2002 to 5.0 percent in 2008. These patterns and trends may partially reflect the aging into these age groups of members of the baby boom cohort, whose rates of illicit drug use have been higher than those of older cohorts.

Figure 2.7   Past Month Illicit Drug Use Among Adults Aged 50 to 59: 2002–2008

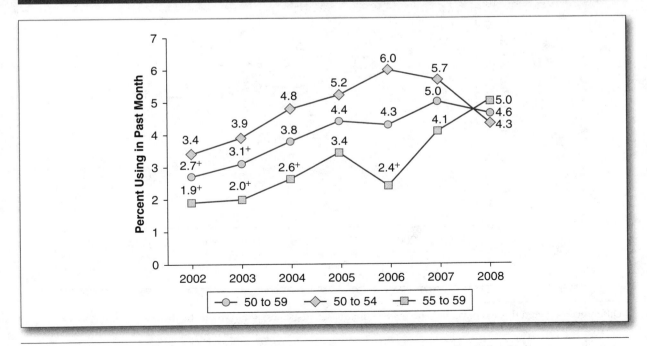

+Difference between this estimate and the 2008 estimate is statistically significant at the .05 level.

Gender

- In 2008, as in prior years, the rate of current illicit drug use among persons aged 12 or older was higher for males than for females (9.9 vs. 6.3 percent, respectively). Males were more likely than females to be past month users of marijuana (7.9 vs. 4.4 percent). However, males and females had similar rates of past month nonmedical use of psychotherapeutic drugs (2.6 and 2.4 percent, respectively), pain relievers (2.0 and 1.8 percent), tranquilizers (0.7 and 0.8 percent), stimulants (0.4 percent for both), methamphetamine (0.1 percent for both), and sedatives (0.1 percent for both).

- Although males were more likely than females to be current illicit drug users in 2008, the rate of current illicit drug use among females aged 12 or older increased from 5.8 percent in 2007 to 6.3 percent in 2008. However, the rate did not change significantly for males (10.4 and 9.9 percent for 2007 and 2008, respectively). Current marijuana use also increased from 3.8 to 4.4 percent among females, but for males there was no significant change (8.0 and 7.9 percent, respectively).

- For males, current nonmedical use of psychotherapeutics declined from 3.2 percent in 2007 to 2.6 percent in 2008, driven in part by a decline in pain reliever misuse from 2.6 to 2.0 percent. Current use of crack by males also decreased in this time period from 0.4 to 0.2 percent. There were no significant changes in the use of these drugs among females.

- Among youths aged 12 to 17 in 2008, males and females had similar rates of current use of illicit drugs (9.5 percent for males and 9.1 percent for females), cocaine (0.5 and 0.3 percent, respectively), hallucinogens (1.1 and 0.8 percent), and inhalants (1.1 percent for both). However, current marijuana use was more prevalent among male youths (7.3 percent) than female youths (6.0 percent) (Figure 2.8). Nonmedical use of psychotherapeutic drugs among 12 to 17 year olds, on the other hand, was more prevalent among females (3.3 percent) than males (2.5 percent), as was nonmedical use of pain relievers (2.6 and 2.0 percent, respectively).

Figure 2.8   Past Month Marijuana Use Among Youths Aged 12 to 17, by Gender: 2002–2008

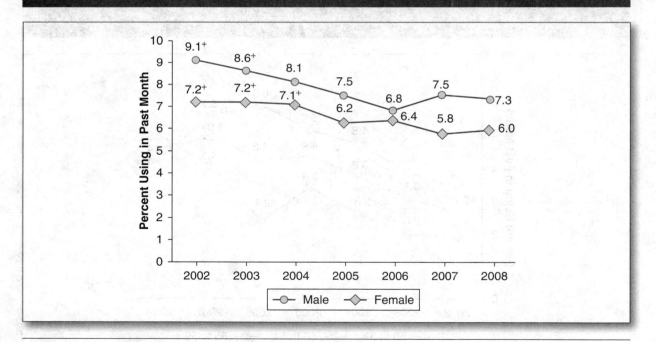

+Difference between this estimate and the 2008 estimate is statistically significant at the .05 level.

- Past month marijuana use among males aged 12 to 17 declined from 9.1 percent in 2002 to 6.8 percent in 2006 (Figure 2.8). In 2008, the rate was 7.3 percent, which was not significantly different from the rate in 2006 and was lower than the rate in 2002. Among female youths, little change in current marijuana use occurred from 2002 to 2004, but rates subsequently declined and the percentage in 2008 (6.0 percent) was lower than that in 2002 (7.2 percent).

Pregnant Women

- Among pregnant women aged 15 to 44 years, 5.1 percent used illicit drugs in the past month based on data averaged for 2007 and 2008. This rate was significantly lower than the rate among women in this age group who were not pregnant (9.8 percent). Among pregnant women, the average rate of current illicit drug use in 2007-2008 (5.1 percent) did not change significantly from 2005-2006 (4.0 percent) and was similar to the rate observed in 2003-2004 (4.6 percent).
- The rate of current illicit drug use in the combined 2007-2008 data was lower for pregnant women than for nonpregnant women among those aged 18 to 25 (7.1 vs. 16.2 percent, respectively) and among those aged 26 to 44 (3.0 vs. 6.7 percent). Among women aged 15 to 17, however, those who were pregnant had a higher rate of use than those who were not pregnant (21.6 vs. 12.9 percent).

Race/Ethnicity

- Current illicit drug use among persons aged 12 or older varied by race/ethnicity in 2008, with the lowest rate among Asians (3.6 percent) (Figure 2.9). Rates were 14.7 percent for persons reporting two or more races, 10.1 percent for blacks, 9.5 percent for American Indians or Alaska Natives, 8.2 percent for whites, 7.3 percent of Native Hawaiians or Other Pacific Islanders, and 6.2 percent for Hispanics.
- There were no statistically significant changes between 2007 and 2008 in the rate of current illicit drug use for any racial/ethnic group among persons aged 12 or older.
- Below is a bar graph.

Figure 2.9 Past Month Illicit Drug Use Among Persons Aged 12 or Older, by Race/Ethnicity: 2008

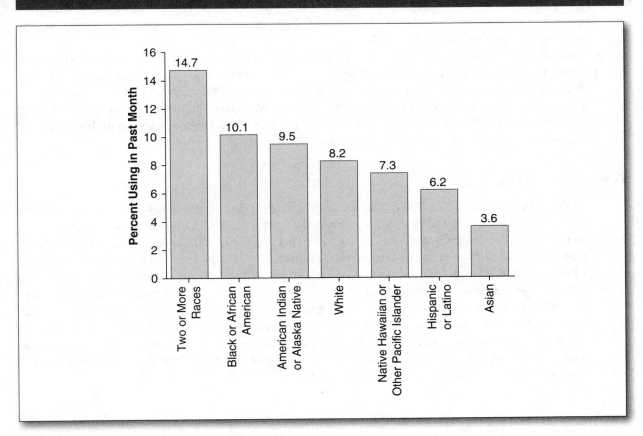

Education

- Illicit drug use in 2008 varied by educational status. Among adults aged 18 or older, the rate of current illicit drug use was lower for college graduates (5.7 percent) than for those who did not graduate from high school (8.1 percent), high school graduates (8.6 percent), and those with some college (9.4 percent). However, adults who had graduated from college were more likely to have tried illicit drugs in their lifetime when compared with adults who had not completed high school (51.8 vs. 37.7 percent). The rate of current illicit drug use declined from 9.3 percent in 2007 to 8.1 percent in 2008 among adults who had not completed high school.

College Students

- Among persons aged 18 to 22 years old, the rate of current use of illicit drugs in 2008 among full-time college students (20.2 percent) was similar to the rate among other persons in that age group (21.9 percent), which includes part-time college students, students in other grades or types of institutions, and nonstudents. The rate of current use of illicit drugs overall among 18 to 22 year olds did not change significantly from 2007 to 2008 among either full-time college students or others in this age group.
- Among full-time college students aged 18 to 22, there were increases from 2007 to 2008 in the current rate of use of hallucinogens (from 1.0 to 2.1 percent). Increases were seen for the specific hallucinogens Ecstasy (from 0.5 to 1.2 percent) and LSD (from 0.3 to 0.6 percent). There were no significant changes in the rates of current use for any drugs among persons aged 18 to 22 who were not full-time college students.

Employment

- Current illicit drug use differed by employment status in 2008. Among adults aged 18 or older, the rate of illicit drug use was higher for unemployed persons (19.6 percent) than for those who were employed full time (8.0 percent) or part time (10.2 percent) (Figure 2.10). These rates were all similar to the corresponding rates in 2007.
- Although the rate of past month illicit drug use was higher among unemployed persons compared with those from other employment groups, most drug users in 2008 were employed. Of the estimated 17.8 million current illicit drug users aged 18 or older in 2008, 12.9 million (72.7 percent) were employed either full or part time. The number of unemployed illicit drug users increased from 1.3 million in 2007 to 1.8 million in 2008, primarily because of an overall increase in the number of unemployed persons between 2007 and 2008 (Figure 2.10).

Geographic Area

- Among persons aged 12 or older, the rate of current illicit drug use in 2008 was 9.8 percent in the West, 7.6 percent in the Midwest, 8.2 percent in the Northeast, and 7.1 percent in the South.
- In the South, current illicit drug use declined from 9.3 percent in 2007 to 8.0 percent in 2008 among youths aged 12 to 17, and use of crack decreased from 0.3 to 0.2 percent among persons aged 12 or older. Also in the South, current nonmedical use of prescription psychotherapeutics declined from 3.0 to 2.4 percent among persons aged 12 or older, from 3.8 to 2.8 percent among youths aged 12 to 17, and from 2.3 to 1.7 percent among adults aged 26 or older. These decreases were driven in part by decreases in the rates of nonmedical use of pain relievers for youths aged 12 to 17 and adults aged 26 or older, although the decrease among adults aged 26 or older was not significant. There were no significant changes in the rates of current use in any of the nine illicit drug categories for the Northeast, Midwest, and West between 2007 and 2008.

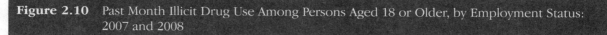

Figure 2.10   Past Month Illicit Drug Use Among Persons Aged 18 or Older, by Employment Status: 2007 and 2008

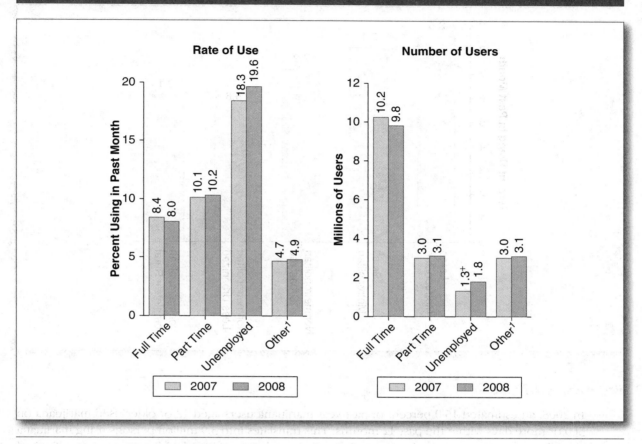

[+]Difference between this estimate and the 2008 estimate is statistically significant at the .05 level.

[1]The Other Employment category includes retired persons, disabled persons, homemakers, students, or other persons not in the labor force.

- In 2008, the rate of current illicit drug use among persons aged 12 or older was higher in metropolitan areas than in nonmetropolitan areas. The rates were 8.5 percent in large metropolitan counties, 8.1 percent in small metropolitan counties, and 6.3 percent in nonmetropolitan counties as a group (Figure 2.11). Within nonmetropolitan areas, the rate was 7.2 percent in urbanized counties, 5.6 percent in less urbanized counties, and 6.1 percent in completely rural counties.

Criminal Justice Populations

- In 2008, an estimated 1.6 million adults aged 18 or older were on parole or other supervised release from prison at some time during the past year. Almost one fifth of these (18.3 percent) were current illicit drug users, which was higher than the rate of 7.8 percent among adults not on parole or supervised release.
- Among the 5.2 million adults on probation at some time in the past year, 23.9 percent reported current illicit drug use in 2008. This was higher than the rate of 7.5 percent among adults not on probation in 2008.

Figure 2.11 Past Month Illicit Drug Use Among Persons Aged 12 or Older, by County Type: 2008

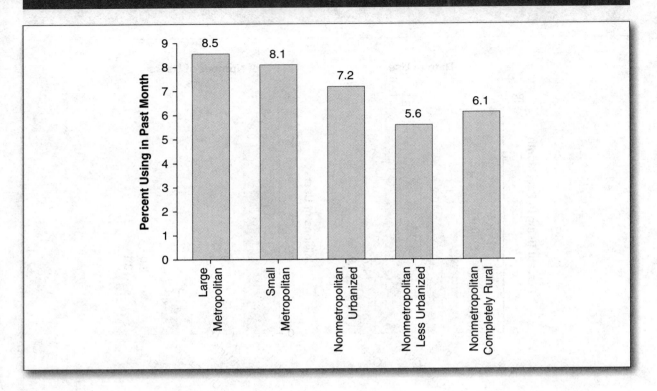

Frequency of Use

- In 2008, an estimated 15.0 percent of past year marijuana users aged 12 or older used marijuana on 300 or more days within the past 12 months. This translates into 3.9 million persons using marijuana on a daily or almost daily basis over a 12-month period. An estimated 35.7 percent (5.4 million) of past month marijuana users aged 12 or older used the drug on 20 or more days in the past month.

Association With Cigarette and Alcohol Use

- In 2008, the rate of current illicit drug use was more than 9 times higher among youths aged 12 to 17 who smoked cigarettes in the past month (49.0 percent) than it was among youths who did not smoke cigarettes in the past month (5.3 percent).
- Past month illicit drug use also was associated with the level of past month alcohol use. Among youths aged 12 to 17 in 2008 who were heavy drinkers (i.e., consumed five or more drinks on the same occasion on each of 5 or more days in the past 30 days), 68.5 percent also were current illicit drug users, which was higher than the rate among nondrinkers (4.3 percent). The rate of current illicit drug use among youths reporting heavy drinking in the past month increased from 60.1 percent in 2007 to 68.5 percent in 2008, and a similar increase in illicit drug use (from 37.9 to 42.6 percent) was seen among youths who engaged in binge drinking (i.e., consumption of five or more drinks on the same occasion on at least 1 day in the past month).

Driving Under the Influence of Illicit Drugs

- In 2008, 10.0 million persons aged 12 or older reported driving under the influence of illicit drugs during the past year. This corresponds to 4.0 percent of the population aged 12 or older, the same as the rate in 2007, but lower than the rate in 2002 (4.7 percent). Across age groups, the rate of driving under the influence of illicit drugs in 2008 was highest among young adults aged 18 to 25 (12.3 percent).

Source of Prescription Drugs

- Past year nonmedical users of prescription-type psychotherapeutic drugs are asked how they obtained the drugs they recently used nonmedically. Rates averaged for 2007 and 2008 show that over half of the nonmedical users of prescription-type pain relievers, tranquilizers, stimulants, and sedatives aged 12 or older said they got the drugs they used most recently "from a friend or relative for free." In a follow-up question, the majority of these respondents indicated that their friend or relative had obtained the drugs from one doctor.

- Among persons aged 12 or older in 2007-2008 who used pain relievers nonmedically in the past 12 months, 55.9 percent got the pain relievers they most recently used from a friend or relative for free. Another 8.9 percent bought them from a friend or relative, and 5.4 percent took them from a friend or relative without asking. Nearly one fifth (18.0 percent) indicated that they got the drugs they most recently used through a prescription from one doctor. About 1 in 20 users (4.3 percent) got pain relievers from a drug dealer or other stranger, and 0.4 percent bought them on the Internet. These percentages are similar to those reported in 2006-2007.

- In 81.7 percent of the instances in 2007-2008 where nonmedical users of prescription pain relievers aged 12 or older obtained the drugs from a friend or relative for free, the individuals indicated that their friend or relative had obtained the drugs from just one doctor. Only 1.6 percent reported that the friend or relative had bought the drugs from a drug dealer or other stranger.

- In 2007-2008, 42.8 percent of past year methamphetamine users aged 12 or older reported that they obtained the methamphetamine they used most recently from a friend or relative for free, lower than the 49.7 percent reported in 2006-2007. In contrast, the percentage of past year methamphetamine users who bought it from a friend or relative increased from 25.1 percent in 2006-2007 to 30.1 percent in 2007-2008. About one in five users (21.7 percent) in 2007-2008 bought the methamphetamine they used most recently from a drug dealer or other stranger, which was comparable with the rate for 2006-2007 (20.5 percent).

3. Alcohol Use

The National Survey on Drug Use and Health (NSDUH) includes questions about the recency and frequency of consumption of alcoholic beverages, such as beer, wine, whiskey, brandy, and mixed drinks. An extensive list of examples of the kinds of beverages covered is given to respondents prior to the question administration. A "drink" is defined as a can or bottle of beer, a glass of wine or a wine cooler, a shot of liquor, or a mixed drink with liquor in it. Times when the respondent only had a sip or two from a drink are not considered to be consumption. For this report, estimates for the prevalence of alcohol use are reported primarily at three levels defined for both males and females and for all ages as follows:

Current (past month) use—At least one drink in the past 30 days.

Binge use—Five or more drinks on the same occasion (i.e., at the same time or within a couple of hours of each other) on at least 1 day in the past 30 days.

Heavy use—Five or more drinks on the same occasion on each of 5 or more days in the past 30 days.

These levels are not mutually exclusive categories of use; heavy use is included in estimates of binge and current use, and binge use is included in estimates of current use.

This chapter is divided into two main sections. Section 3.1 describes trends and patterns of alcohol use among the population aged 12 or older. Section 3.2 is particularly concerned with the use of alcohol by persons aged 12 to 20. These persons are under the legal drinking age in all 50 States and the District of Columbia.

3.1. Alcohol Use Among Persons Aged 12 or Older

- Slightly more than half of Americans aged 12 or older reported being current drinkers of alcohol in the 2008 survey (51.6 percent). This translates to an estimated 129.0 million people, which is similar to the 2007 estimate of 126.8 million people (51.1 percent).
- More than one fifth (23.3 percent) of persons aged 12 or older participated in binge drinking at least once in the 30 days prior to the survey in 2008. This translates to about 58.1 million people. The rate in 2008 is the same as the rate in 2007 (23.3 percent).
- In 2008, heavy drinking was reported by 6.9 percent of the population aged 12 or older, or 17.3 million people. This percentage is the same as the rate of heavy drinking in 2007 (6.9 percent).

Age

- In 2008, rates of current alcohol use were 3.4 percent among persons aged 12 or 13, 13.1 percent of persons aged 14 or 15, 26.2 percent of 16 or 17 year olds, 48.7 percent of those aged 18 to 20, and 69.5 percent of 21 to 25 year olds (Figure 3.1). These estimates showed significant declines from 2007 for the 14 or 15 year olds (from 14.7 to 13.1 percent) and for the 16 or 17 year olds (from 29.0 to 26.2 percent).

Figure 3.1   Current, Binge, and Heavy Alcohol Use Among Persons Aged 12 or Older, by Age: 2008

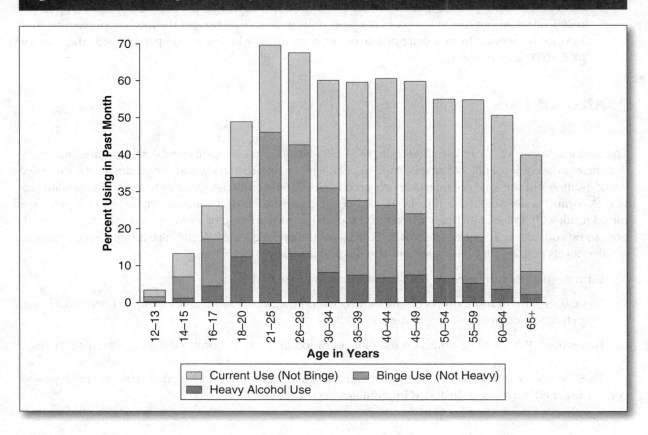

- Among older age groups, the prevalence of current alcohol use decreased with increasing age, from 67.4 percent among 26 to 29 year olds to 50.3 percent among 60 to 64 year olds and 39.7 percent among people aged 65 or older.
- Rates of binge alcohol use in 2008 were 1.5 percent among 12 or 13 year olds, 6.9 percent among 14 or 15 year olds, 17.2 percent among 16 or 17 year olds, 33.7 percent among persons aged 18 to 20, and peaked among those aged 21 to 25 at 46.0 percent. The 2008 binge drinking rate for 16 or 17 year olds showed a decrease from 2007, when it was 19.4 percent.
- The binge drinking rate decreased beyond young adulthood from 36.4 percent of 26 to 34 year olds to 18.8 percent of persons aged 35 or older.
- The rate of binge drinking was 41.0 percent for young adults aged 18 to 25. Heavy alcohol use was reported by 14.5 percent of persons aged 18 to 25. These rates are similar to the rates in 2007 (41.8 and 14.7 percent, respectively).
- Persons aged 65 or older had lower rates of binge drinking (8.2 percent) than adults in other age groups. The rate of heavy drinking among persons aged 65 or older was 2.2 percent.
- The rate of current alcohol use among youths aged 12 to 17 was 14.6 percent in 2008, which is lower than it was in 2007, when it was 15.9 percent. Youth binge and heavy drinking rates were 8.8 and 2.0 percent, respectively. The 2008 rate for youth binge drinking is also lower than the 2007 rate, which was 9.7 percent.

Gender

- In 2008, 57.7 percent of males aged 12 or older were current drinkers, higher than the rate for females (45.9 percent). However, among youths aged 12 to 17, the percentage of males who were current drinkers (14.2 percent) was similar to the rate for females (15.0 percent).
- Among adults aged 18 to 25, an estimated 58.0 percent of females and 64.3 percent of males reported current drinking in 2008. These rates are similar to those reported in 2007 (57.1 and 65.3 percent, respectively).

Pregnant Women

- Among pregnant women aged 15 to 44, an estimated 10.6 percent reported current alcohol use, 4.5 percent reported binge drinking, and 0.8 percent reported heavy drinking. These rates were significantly lower than the rates for nonpregnant women in the same age group (54.0, 24.2, and 5.5 percent, respectively). Binge drinking during the first trimester of pregnancy was reported by 10.3 percent of pregnant women aged 15 to 44. All of these estimates by pregnancy status are based on data averaged over 2007 and 2008. The 2007-2008 estimate for first-trimester binge drinking is higher than in 2005-2006, when it was 4.6 percent.

Race/Ethnicity

- Among persons aged 12 or older, whites in 2008 were more likely than other racial/ethnic groups to report current use of alcohol (56.2 percent) (Figure 3.2). The rates were 47.5 percent for persons reporting two or more races, 43.3 percent for American Indians or Alaska Natives, 43.2 percent for Hispanics, 41.9 percent for blacks, and 37.0 percent for Asians.
- The rate of binge alcohol use was lowest among Asians (11.9 percent). Rates for other racial/ethnic groups were 20.4 percent for blacks, 22.0 percent for persons reporting two or more races, 24.0 percent for whites, 24.4 percent for American Indians or Alaska Natives, and 25.6 percent for Hispanics.
- Among youths aged 12 to 17 in 2008, Asians had lower rates of current alcohol use than any other racial/ethnic group (5.7 percent), while 10.1 percent of black youths, 13.6 percent of those reporting two or more races, 14.8 percent of Hispanic youths, and 16.3 percent of white youths were current drinkers.

Figure 3.2   Current, Binge, and Heavy Alcohol Use Among Persons Aged 12 or Older, by Race/Ethnicity: 2008

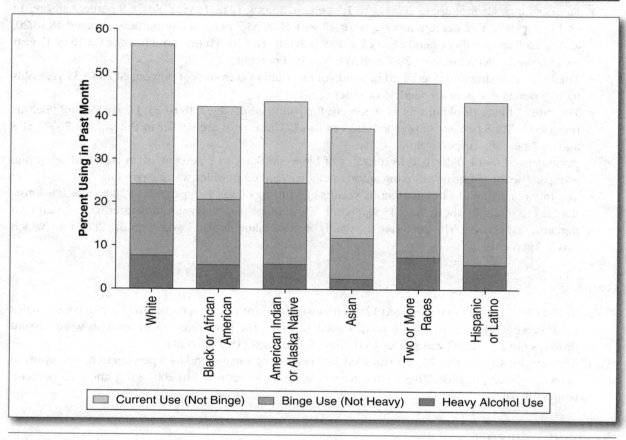

Note: Due to low precision, estimates for Native Hawaiians or Other Pacific Islanders are not shown.

Education

- Among adults aged 18 or older, the rate of past month alcohol use increased with increasing levels of education. Among adults with less than a high school education, 36.8 percent were current drinkers in 2008, significantly lower than the 67.9 percent of college graduates who were current drinkers. However, among adults aged 26 or older, binge and heavy alcohol use rates were lower among college graduates (19.5 and 4.6 percent, respectively) than among those who had not completed college (23.2 vs. 7.0 percent, respectively).

College Students

- Young adults aged 18 to 22 enrolled full time in college were more likely than their peers not enrolled full time (i.e., part-time college students and persons not currently enrolled in college) to use alcohol in the past month, binge drink, and drink heavily. Among full-time college students in 2008, 61.0 percent were current drinkers, 40.5 percent binge drank, and 16.3 percent were heavy drinkers. Among those not enrolled full time in college, these rates were 54.2, 38.1, and 13.0 percent, respectively. Rates of current alcohol use and binge use for full-time college students decreased from 2007, when they were 63.7 and 43.6 percent, respectively.
- The pattern of higher rates of current alcohol use, binge alcohol use, and heavy alcohol use among full-time college students compared with rates for others aged 18 to 22 has remained consistent since 2002 (Figure 3.3).

Figure 3.3 Heavy Alcohol Use Among Adults Aged 18 to 22, by College Enrollment: 2002–2008

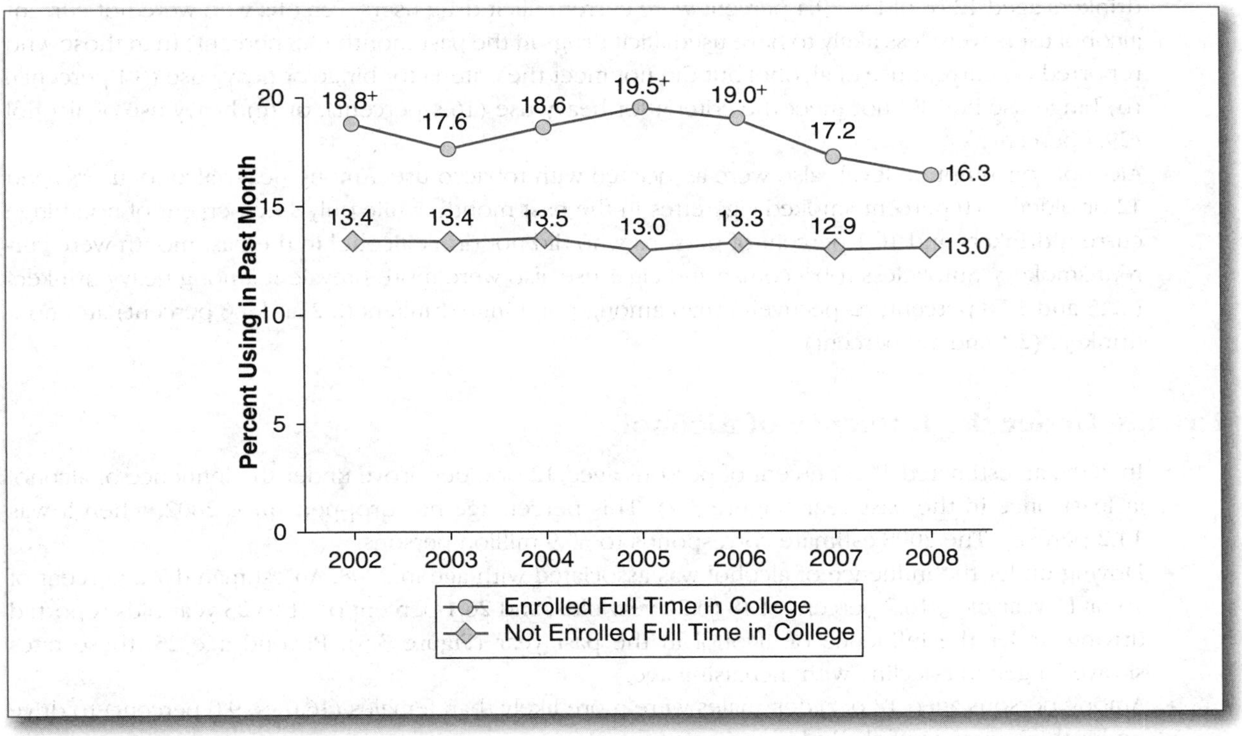

+Difference between this estimate and the 2008 estimate is statistically significant at the .05 level.

Employment

- The rate of current alcohol use was 63.0 percent for full-time employed adults aged 18 or older in 2008, higher than the rate for unemployed adults (55.5 percent). However, the rate of heavy use for unemployed persons was 12.8 percent, which was higher than the rate of 8.8 percent for full-time employed persons. There was no significant difference in binge alcohol use rates between full-time employed adults (30.3 percent) and unemployed adults (33.4 percent).
- Most binge and heavy alcohol users were employed in 2008. Among 55.9 million adult binge drinkers, 44.6 million (79.7 percent) were employed either full or part time. Among 16.8 million heavy drinkers, 13.1 million (78.0 percent) were employed.
- Rates of binge and heavy alcohol use did not change significantly between 2007 and 2008 for full-time employed or unemployed adults. However, the number of unemployed binge and heavy drinkers did increase (from 2.3 million to 3.0 million for binge use and from 851,000 to 1.2 million for heavy use).

Geographic Area

- The rate of past month alcohol use for people aged 12 or older in 2008 was lower in the South (47.3 percent) than in the Northeast (56.8 percent), Midwest (54.2 percent), or West (51.8 percent).
- Among people aged 12 or older, the rate of past month alcohol use in large metropolitan areas (53.6 percent) was higher than the 51.3 percent in small metropolitan areas and 45.8 percent in nonmetropolitan areas. Binge drinking was equally prevalent in small metropolitan areas (22.5 percent), large metropolitan areas (23.9 percent), and nonmetropolitan areas (22.8 percent).
- The rates of binge alcohol use among youths aged 12 to 17 were 9.8 percent in nonmetropolitan areas, 9.0 percent in small metropolitan areas, and 8.4 percent in large metropolitan areas.

Association With Illicit Drug and Tobacco Use

- The level of alcohol use was associated with illicit drug use in 2008. Among the 17.3 million heavy drinkers aged 12 or older, 29.4 percent were current illicit drug users. Persons who were not current alcohol users were less likely to have used illicit drugs in the past month (3.3 percent) than those who reported (a) current use of alcohol but did not meet the criteria for binge or heavy use (6.1 percent), (b) binge use but did not meet the criteria for heavy use (16.4 percent), or (c) heavy use of alcohol (29.4 percent).
- Alcohol consumption levels also were associated with tobacco use. Among heavy alcohol users aged 12 or older, 58.0 percent smoked cigarettes in the past month, while only 19.2 percent of non-binge current drinkers and 16.1 percent of persons who did not drink alcohol in the past month were current smokers. Smokeless tobacco use and cigar use also were more prevalent among heavy drinkers (12.5 and 17.8 percent, respectively) than among non-binge drinkers (2.2 and 4.6 percent) and non-drinkers (2.1 and 2.0 percent).

Driving Under the Influence of Alcohol

- In 2008, an estimated 12.4 percent of persons aged 12 or older drove under the influence of alcohol at least once in the past year (Figure 3.4). This percentage has dropped since 2002, when it was 14.2 percent. The 2008 estimate corresponds to 30.9 million persons.
- Driving under the influence of alcohol was associated with age in 2008. An estimated 7.2 percent of 16 or 17 year olds, 16.7 percent of 18 to 20 year olds, and 26.1 percent of 21 to 25 year olds reported driving under the influence of alcohol in the past year (Figure 3.5). Beyond age 25, these rates showed a general decline with increasing age.
- Among persons aged 12 or older, males were more likely than females (16.0 vs. 9.0 percent) to drive under the influence of alcohol in the past year.

Figure 3.4   Driving Under the Influence of Alcohol in the Past Year Among Persons Aged 12 or Older: 2002–2008

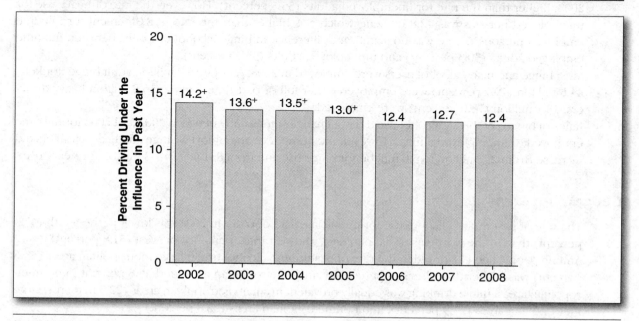

[+]Difference between this estimate and the 2008 estimate is statistically significant at the .05 level.

Figure 3.5   Driving Under the Influence of Alcohol in the Past Year Among Persons Aged 16 or Older, by Age: 2008

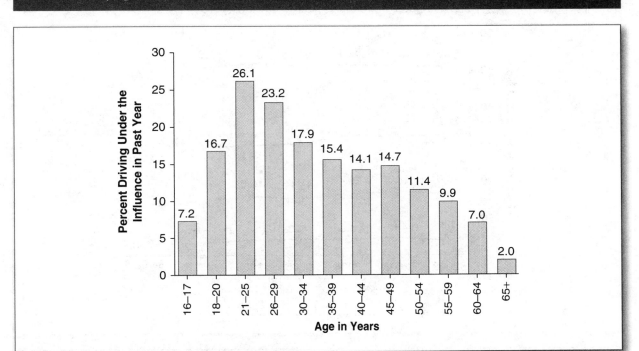

3.2. Underage Alcohol Use

- In 2008, about 10.1 million persons aged 12 to 20 (26.4 percent of this age group) reported drinking alcohol in the past month. Approximately 6.6 million (17.4 percent) were binge drinkers, and 2.1 million (5.5 percent) were heavy drinkers. The rates for current and binge alcohol use are lower than they were in 2007, when they were 27.9 and 18.6 percent, respectively.

- Rates of current, binge, and heavy alcohol use among underage persons declined between 2002 and 2008. Current use dropped from 28.8 to 26.4 percent; binge use declined from 19.3 to 17.4 percent; and heavy use declined from 6.2 to 5.5 percent.

- Past month underage alcohol use rates declined between 2002 and 2008 for specific age categories (12 or 13, 14 or 15, 16 or 17, and 18 to 20) (Figure 3.6).

- Rates of current alcohol use increased with increasing age among underage persons. In 2008, 3.4 percent of persons aged 12 or 13, 13.1 percent of persons aged 14 or 15, 26.2 percent of 16 or 17 year olds, and 48.7 percent of 18 to 20 year olds drank alcohol during the 30 days before they were surveyed. This pattern has remained stable since 2002 (Figure 3.6).

- More males than females aged 12 to 20 reported binge drinking (19.2 vs. 15.5 percent) and heavy drinking (7.0 vs. 4.0 percent) in 2008 (Figure 3.7). However, rates of current alcohol use were similar by gender (27.1 percent for males and 25.8 percent for females).

- Among persons aged 12 to 20, past month alcohol use rates in 2008 were 17.2 percent among Asians, 19.0 percent among blacks, 22.9 percent among those reporting two or more races, 23.1 percent among Hispanics, 26.4 percent among American Indians or Alaska Natives, and 30.1 percent among whites.

- In 2008, among persons aged 12 to 20, binge drinking was reported by 20.8 percent of whites, followed by 15.1 percent of Hispanics and 15.0 percent of persons reporting two or more races, but only by 9.4 percent of Asians and 9.3 percent of blacks.

Figure 3.6   Current Alcohol Use Among Persons Aged 12 to 20, by Age: 2002–2008

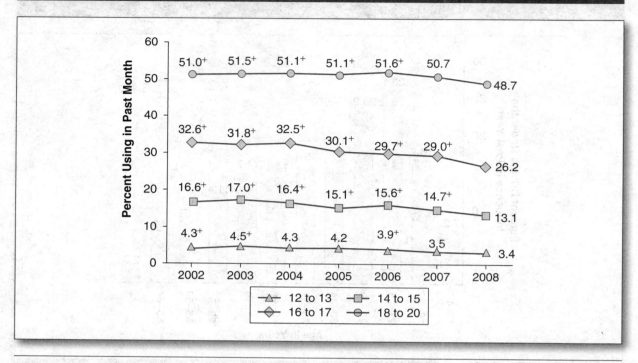

[+]Difference between this estimate and the 2008 estimate is statistically significant at the .05 level.

Figure 3.7   Current, Binge, and Heavy Alcohol Use Among Persons Aged 12 to 20, by Gender: 2008

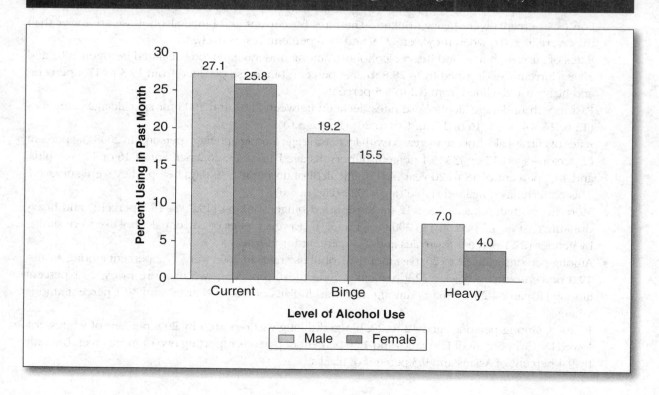

- Across geographic regions in 2008, underage current alcohol use rates were higher in the Northeast (30.0 percent) than in the Midwest (27.1 percent), and both rates were higher than in the South (24.7 percent). The rate in the West (25.8 percent) was similar to rates in the South and Midwest regions, but was significantly lower than the rate in the Northeast.
- In 2008, underage current alcohol use rates were higher in small metropolitan areas (27.9 percent) compared with large metropolitan areas (25.9 percent) and similar in large metropolitan areas and nonmetropolitan areas (25.3 percent). The rate in nonmetropolitan areas decreased from 2007, when it was 28.8 percent.
- In 2008, 81.7 percent of current drinkers aged 12 to 20 were with two or more other people the last time they drank alcohol, 13.6 percent were with one other person the last time they drank, and 4.7 percent were alone.
- A majority of underage current drinkers in 2008 reported that their last use of alcohol in the past month occurred either in someone else's home (56.2 percent) or their own home (29.6 percent). Underage males were more likely than females to have been at a concert or sports game on their last drinking occasion (2.5 vs. 1.1 percent), whereas females were more likely than males to have been in a restaurant, bar, or club on their last drinking occasion (10.3 vs. 7.0 percent).
- Among underage current drinkers in 2008, 30.8 percent paid for the alcohol the last time they drank, including 8.3 percent who purchased the alcohol themselves and 22.3 percent who gave money to someone else to purchase it.
- Among underage drinkers who did not pay for the alcohol the last time they drank, the most common source was an unrelated person aged 21 or older (37.4 percent). Other underage persons provided the alcohol on the last occasion 21.1 percent of the time. Parents, guardians, or other adult family members provided the alcohol 21.0 percent of the time. Other sources of alcohol for underage drinkers included (a) took the alcohol from home (5.8 percent), (b) took it from someone else's home (3.2 percent), and (c) got it some other way (6.9 percent).
- Underage drinkers were more likely than persons aged 21 or older to use illicit drugs within 2 hours of alcohol use on their last reported drinking occasion (17.4 vs. 4.6 percent, respectively). The most commonly reported illicit drug used by underage drinkers in combination with alcohol was marijuana, which was used within 2 hours of alcohol use by 16.5 percent of current underage drinkers (1.6 million persons) on their last drinking occasion.

4. Tobacco Use

The National Survey on Drug Use and Health (NSDUH) includes a series of questions about the use of tobacco products, including cigarettes, chewing tobacco, snuff, cigars, and pipe tobacco. Cigarette use is defined as smoking "part or all of a cigarette." For analytic purposes, data for chewing tobacco and snuff are combined as "smokeless tobacco."

- In 2008, an estimated 70.9 million Americans aged 12 or older were current (past month) users of a tobacco product. This represents 28.4 percent of the population in that age range. In addition, 59.8 million persons (23.9 percent of the population) were current cigarette smokers; 13.1 million (5.3 percent) smoked cigars; 8.7 million (3.5 percent) used smokeless tobacco; and 1.9 million (0.8 percent) smoked tobacco in pipes (Figure 4.1).
- The rate of current use of any tobacco product among persons aged 12 or older remained steady from 2007 to 2008 (28.6 and 28.4 percent, respectively). The rates of current use of cigarettes, smokeless tobacco, cigars, and pipe tobacco also did not change significantly over that period. Between 2002 and 2008, past month use of any tobacco product decreased from 30.4 to 28.4 percent, and past month cigarette use declined from 26.0 to 23.9 percent. Rates of past month use of cigars, smokeless tobacco, and pipe tobacco were similar in 2002 and 2008.

Figure 4.1 Past Month Tobacco Use Among Persons Aged 12 or Older: 2002–2008

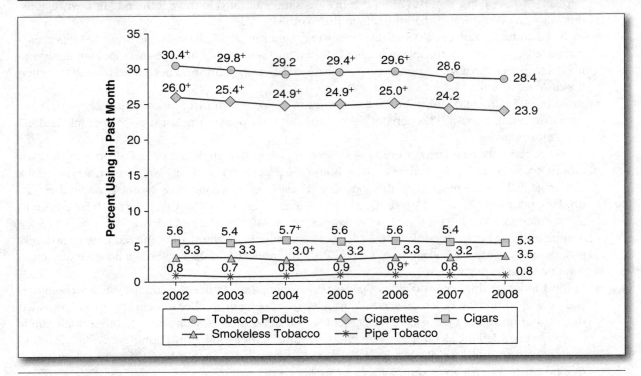

+Difference between this estimate and the 2008 estimate is statistically significant at the .05 level.

Age

- In 2008, young adults aged 18 to 25 had the highest rate of current use of a tobacco product (41.4 percent) compared with youths aged 12 to 17 and adults aged 26 or older (11.4 and 28.3 percent, respectively). Young adults had the highest usage rates of each of the specific tobacco products as well. In 2008, the rates of past month use among young adults were 35.7 percent for cigarettes, 11.3 percent for cigars, 5.4 percent for smokeless tobacco, and 1.4 percent for pipe tobacco. The rate of current use of a tobacco product by young adults was similar in 2007 and 2008 (41.8 and 41.4 percent, respectively), as was the rate of cigarette use between 2007 and 2008 (36.2 and 35.7 percent, respectively). Between 2002 and 2008, there was a significant decrease in the rates for current use of tobacco products and cigarettes among young adults; in 2002, the rates were 45.3 and 40.8 percent, respectively.

- The rate of past month tobacco use among youths aged 12 to 17 decreased from 12.4 percent in 2007 to 11.4 percent in 2008 (Figure 4.2). This decrease was driven by a decline in the rate of past month cigarette use that was statistically significant (9.8 to 9.1 percent) and a decline in past month cigar use that was not statistically significant (4.2 to 3.8 percent). The rate of past month cigarette use among 12 to 17 year olds declined from 13.0 percent in 2002 to 9.1 percent in 2008. One-half million or 2.2 percent of youths aged 12 to 17 used smokeless tobacco in 2008 compared with 2.0 percent in 2002; this slight increase was not statistically significant.

- In 2008, 2.1 percent of 12 or 13 year olds and 7.6 percent of 14 or 15 year olds were current cigarette smokers (Figure 4.3). The percentage of current cigarette smokers among 16 or 17 year olds dropped from 18.9 percent in 2007 to 16.8 percent in 2008. Across age groups, current cigarette use peaked at 37.1 percent among persons aged 21 to 25 and those aged 26 to 29. About one third of 18 to 20 year olds and one third of 26 to 34 year olds (33.5 and 33.6 percent, respectively) smoked cigarettes in the past month. Less than a quarter (21.6 percent) of persons aged 35 or older in 2008 smoked cigarettes in the past month.

Figure 4.2   Past Month Tobacco Use Among Youths Aged 12 to 17: 2002–2008

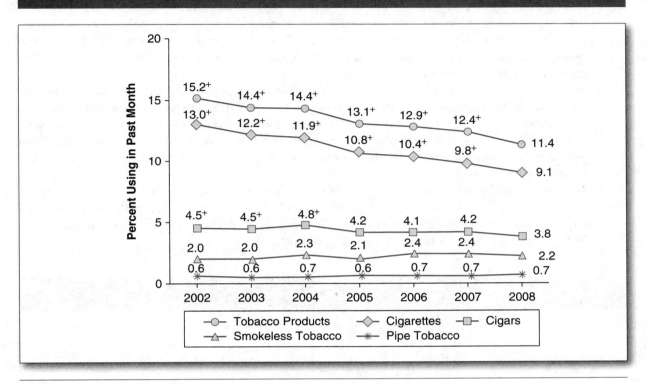

[+]Difference between this estimate and the 2008 estimate is statistically significant at the .05 level.

Figure 4.3   Past Month Cigarette Use Among Persons Aged 12 or Older, by Age: 2008

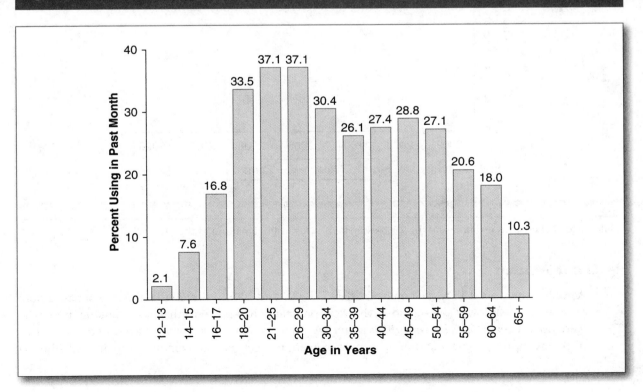

Gender

- In 2008, current use of a tobacco product among persons aged 12 or older was reported by a higher percentage of males (34.5 percent) than females (22.5 percent). Males also had higher rates of past month use than females of each specific tobacco product: cigarettes (26.3 percent of males vs. 21.7 percent of females), cigars (9.0 vs. 1.7 percent), smokeless tobacco (6.8 vs. 0.4 percent), and pipe tobacco (1.2 vs. 0.3 percent).

- Among youths aged 12 to 17, the rate of current cigarette smoking in 2008 did not differ significantly by gender (9.0 percent for males vs. 9.2 percent for females). The rate declined for both males and females between 2007 and 2008 (10.0 vs. 9.0 percent for males and 9.7 vs. 9.2 percent for females), although the decline for females was not statistically significant. From 2002 to 2008, the rate of current cigarette smoking among youths decreased for both males (from 12.3 to 9.0 percent) and females (from 13.6 to 9.2 percent) (Figure 4.4).

- After dropping from 34.9 percent in 2006 to 31.8 percent in 2007, the rate of current cigarette smoking among female young adults aged 18 to 25 held steady at 31.8 percent in 2008. Between 2002 and 2008, the rate of cigarette use among young adults declined for both males (from 44.4 to 39.5 percent) and females (from 37.1 to 31.8 percent).

Figure 4.4 Past Month Cigarette Use Among Youths Aged 12 to 17, by Gender: 2002–2008

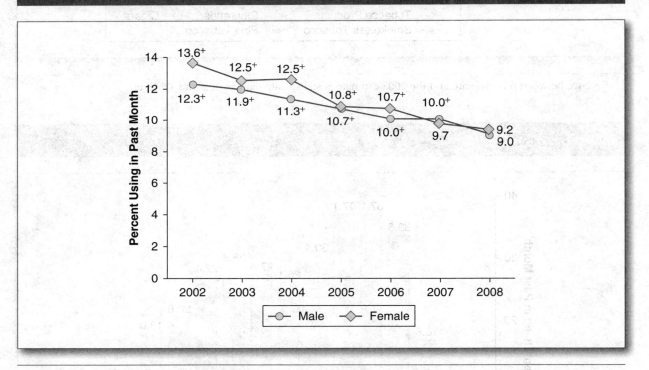

+Difference between this estimate and the 2008 estimate is statistically significant at the .05 level.

Pregnant Women

- Among women aged 15 to 44, combined data for 2007 and 2008 indicated that the rate of past month cigarette use was lower among those who were pregnant (16.4 percent) than it was among those who were not pregnant (27.3 percent). This pattern was also evident among women aged 18 to 25 (22.1 vs. 32.3 percent for pregnant and nonpregnant women, respectively) and among women aged 26 to 44

(12.6 vs. 27.4 percent, respectively). However, among those aged 15 to 17, the rate of cigarette smoking was higher for pregnant women than nonpregnant women (20.6 vs. 14.7 percent), although the difference was not statistically significant.

- Two-year moving average rates from 2002–2003 to 2007-2008 indicate that current cigarette use among women aged 15 to 44 decreased from 30.7 to 27.3 percent for those who were not pregnant and from 18.0 to 16.4 percent for those who were pregnant, although the latter difference was not statistically significant (Figure 4.5).

Figure 4.5   Past Month Cigarette Use Among Women Aged 15 to 44, by Pregnancy Status: Combined Years 2002–2003 to 2007–2008

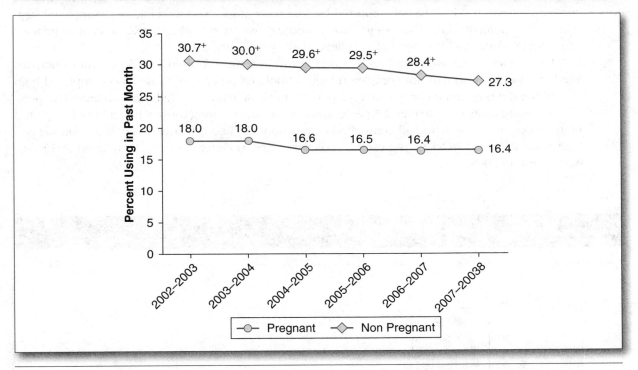

+Difference between this estimate and the 2007–2008 estimate is statistically significant at the .05 level.

Race/Ethnicity

- In 2008, the prevalence of current use of a tobacco product among persons aged 12 or older was 13.9 percent for Asians, 21.3 percent for Hispanics, 28.6 percent for blacks, 30.4 percent for whites, 37.3 percent for persons who reported two or more races, and 48.7 percent for American Indians or Alaska Natives. There were no statistically significant changes in past month use of a tobacco product between 2007 and 2008 for any of these racial/ethnic groups. Among the specific tobacco products, smokeless tobacco use in the past month among blacks increased from 0.7 percent in 2007 to 1.4 percent in 2008.
- In 2008, current cigarette smoking among youths aged 12 to 17 and young adults aged 18 to 25 was more prevalent among whites than blacks (10.6 vs. 5.0 percent for youths and 40.6 vs. 26.3 percent for young adults).
- The current smoking rates for Hispanics were 7.9 percent among youths aged 12 to 17, 30.0 percent among young adults aged 18 to 25, and 19.1 percent among those aged 26 or older.

- The smoking rate for Asian young adults aged 18 to 25 fell from 25.7 percent in 2007 to 18.0 percent in 2008. The rates for Asian youths aged 12 to 17 and adults aged 26 or older held steady between 2007 and 2008 (3.4 to 3.8 percent for youths and 13.5 to 11.8 percent for adults, respectively).
- The smoking prevalence rate declined for white youths aged 12 to 17 from 12.2 percent in 2007 to 10.6 percent in 2008. This decrease occurred for both male and female youths: 11.7 to 10.1 percent for white males, and 12.7 to 11.2 percent for white females.

Education

- As observed from 2002 onward, cigarette smoking in the past month was less prevalent among adults who were college graduates compared with those with less education. Among adults aged 18 or older, current cigarette use in 2008 was reported by 34.4 percent of those who had not completed high school, 30.6 percent of high school graduates who did not attend college, 26.6 percent of persons with some college, and 14.0 percent of college graduates (Figure 4.6).
- In 2008, the use of smokeless tobacco in the past month was reported by 4.3 percent of persons aged 18 or older who had not completed high school, 4.6 percent of those who completed high school but did not attend college, and 3.2 percent of those who attended some college. The prevalence among college graduates, 2.5 percent, was lower than among those who had not completed high school and those who had completed high school but had not attended college. Among college graduates aged 18 to 25, the use of smokeless tobacco increased from 2.9 percent in 2007 to 4.3 percent in 2008.

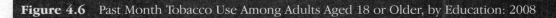

Figure 4.6   Past Month Tobacco Use Among Adults Aged 18 or Older, by Education: 2008

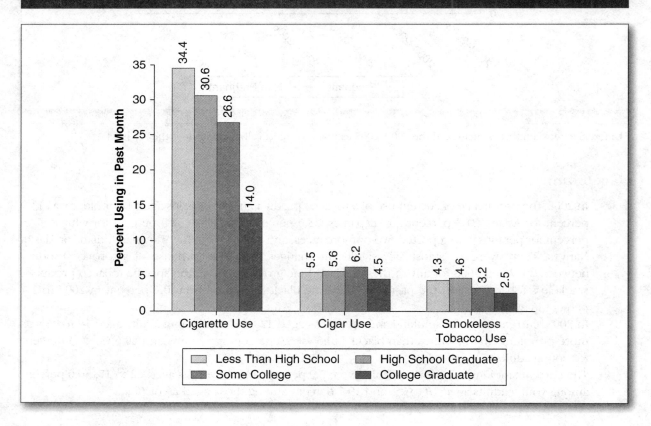

College Students

- Among young adults 18 to 22 years old, full-time college students were less likely to be current cigarette smokers than their peers who were not enrolled full time in college. Cigarette use in the past month in 2008 was reported by 27.2 percent of full-time college students, less than the rate of 40.6 percent for those not enrolled full time.
- Among males aged 18 to 22 in 2008, full-time college students and those not enrolled full time in college did not differ significantly in their rates of past month cigar smoking (18.0 and 18.5 percent, respectively). However, cigar use by males in this age range who were not enrolled full time in college declined from 2007 (21.7 percent) to 2008 (18.5 percent).

Employment

- In 2008, current cigarette smoking was more common among unemployed adults aged 18 or older than among adults who were working full time or part time (43.0 vs. 27.2 and 23.8 percent, respectively). Cigar smoking followed a similar pattern, with 9.8 percent of unemployed adults reporting past month use compared with 6.4 percent of full-time workers and 5.5 percent of part-time workers.
- Current use of smokeless tobacco in 2008 was higher among adults aged 18 or older who were employed full time (4.8 percent) and those who were unemployed (4.9 percent) than among adults who were employed part time (1.8 percent) and those in the "other" employment category, which includes persons not in the labor force (2.0 percent).

Geographic Area

- In 2008, current cigarette smoking among persons aged 12 or older was lower in the West (21.0 percent) and Northeast (22.2 percent) than in the South (25.5 percent) and Midwest (25.9 percent). Use of smokeless tobacco was also higher in the Midwest and South (3.9 and 4.4 percent, respectively) than in the West (2.8 percent), which in turn was higher than in the Northeast (2.1 percent).
- Among persons aged 12 or older, the rate of current cigarette use was associated with county type in 2008. The rates of cigarette smoking were 22.6 percent in large metropolitan areas, 23.6 percent in small metropolitan areas, and 28.7 percent in nonmetropolitan areas.
- Use of smokeless tobacco in the past month in 2008 among persons aged 12 or older was lowest in large metropolitan areas (2.1 percent). In small metropolitan areas, the rate was 4.0 percent; in nonmetropolitan areas, it was 6.9 percent.

Association With Illicit Drug and Alcohol Use

- Use of illicit drugs and alcohol was more common among current cigarette smokers than among nonsmokers in 2008, as in prior years since 2002. Among persons aged 12 or older, 20.4 percent of past month cigarette smokers reported current use of an illicit drug compared with 4.2 percent of persons who were not current cigarette smokers. Past month alcohol use was reported by 67.4 percent of current cigarette smokers compared with 46.7 percent of those who did not use cigarettes in the past month. The association also was found with binge drinking (44.6 percent of current cigarette smokers vs. 16.5 percent of current nonsmokers) and heavy drinking (16.8 vs. 3.8 percent, respectively).

Frequency of Cigarette Use

- Among the 59.8 million current cigarette smokers aged 12 or older in 2008, 36.9 million (61.7 percent) used cigarettes daily. The percentage of daily cigarette smokers increased with age, with 22.3

percent among past month cigarette users aged 12 to 17, 48.1 percent among those aged 18 to 25, and 67.1 percent among those aged 26 or older. Daily cigarette use among current smokers in the 12 to 17 year age group dropped from 26.3 percent in 2007 to 22.3 percent in 2008.

- About half (49.1 percent) of daily smokers aged 12 or older reported smoking 16 or more cigarettes per day; this is approximately one pack or more. The percentage of daily smokers who smoked at least one pack of cigarettes per day increased with age from 18.4 percent among those aged 12 to 17 to 32.1 percent among those aged 18 to 25 to 52.8 percent among those aged 26 or older.

5. Initiation of Substance Use

Information on substance use initiation, also known as incidence or first-time use, is important for policy-makers and researchers. Measures of initiation are often leading indicators of emerging patterns of substance use. They provide valuable information that can be used to assess the effectiveness of current prevention programs and to focus prevention efforts.

With its large sample size and oversampling of youths aged 12 to 17 and young adults aged 18 to 25, the National Survey on Drug Use and Health (NSDUH) provides a variety of estimates related to substance use (illicit drugs, cigarettes, and alcohol) initiation based on reported age and on year and month at first use. This chapter presents estimates of initiation occurring in the 12 months prior to the interview date. Individuals who initiated use within the past 12 months are referred to as recent or past year initiates. One caveat of this approach is that because the survey interviews persons aged 12 or older and asks about the past 12 months, the initiation estimates will represent some, but not all, of the initiation at age 11 and no initiation occurring at age 10 or younger. This underestimation problem primarily affects estimates of initiation for cigarettes, alcohol, and inhalants because they tend to be initiated at a younger age than other substances. See Section B.4.1 in Appendix B for further discussion of the methods and bias in initiation estimates.

This chapter includes estimates of the number and rate of past year initiation of illicit drug, cigarette, and alcohol use among the total population aged 12 or older and by age and gender categories from the 2002 to 2008 NSDUHs. Also included are initiation estimates that pertain to persons at risk for initiation (i.e., those who had never used as of 12 months prior to the interview date). Some analyses are based on the ages at the time of interview, and others focus on the age at the time of first substance use. Readers need to be aware of these alternative estimation approaches when interpreting NSDUH incidence estimates and pay close attention to the approach used in each situation. Titles and notes on figures and associated detailed tables document which method applies.

For trend measurement, initiation estimates for each year (2002 to 2008) are produced independently based on the data from the survey conducted that year. It should be mentioned that trend estimates of incidence based on long recall periods have not been considered because of concerns about their validity (Gfroerer, Hughes, Chromy, Heller, & Packer, 2004).

Regarding the age at first use estimates, means, as measures of central tendency, are heavily influenced by the presence of extreme values in the data. Thus, for the purposes of this report and unless specified otherwise, the mean age at initiation pertains to persons aged 12 to 49. This constraint was implemented so that the mean age estimates reported would not be influenced by those few respondents who were past year initiates at age 50 or older. Note that this constraint only affects estimates of mean age at initiation; other estimates in this chapter, including the number and prevalence of past year initiates, are among all persons aged 12 or older.

Another important consideration in examining incidence estimates across different drug categories is that substance users typically initiate use of different substances at different times in their lives. Thus, the estimates for past year initiation of specific illicit drugs cannot be added to obtain the overall number of illicit drug initiates because some of the initiates previously had used other drugs. The overall illicit drug initiation estimate only includes the past year initiation of specific drug use that was not preceded by use of other drugs. For example, a respondent who reported initiating marijuana use in the past 12 months is counted as a marijuana initiate. The same respondent also can be counted as an overall illicit drug initiate only if his or her marijuana use initiation was not preceded by use of any other drug (cocaine, heroin, hallucinogens, inhalants, pain relievers, tranquilizers, stimulants, or sedatives). To say it differently, the overall illicit drug initiation estimate only takes into account the first drug initiated. To help clarify this aspect of the incidence data, additional analyses have been generated to identify which specific illicit drug was used at the time of first use of any illicit drug. Furthermore, the overall illicit drug use initiation estimates in this chapter are based on data only from the core section of the questionnaire and do not take account of data from new items on the initiation of methamphetamine use that were added to the noncore section beginning in 2007. See Section B.4.8 in Appendix B of this report for details.

Initiation of Illicit Drug Use

- In 2008, an estimated 2.9 million persons aged 12 or older used an illicit drug for the first time within the past 12 months; this averages to almost 8,000 initiates per day. This estimate was not significantly different from the number in 2007 (2.7 million). About three fifths of initiates (56.7 percent) were younger than age 18 when they first used, and 54.9 percent of new users were female. The average age at initiation among persons aged 12 to 49 was 18.8 years.

- In 2008, of the 2.9 million persons aged 12 or older who used illicit drugs for the first time within the past 12 months, a majority reported that their first drug was marijuana (56.6 percent) (Figure 5.1). Nearly one third initiated with psychotherapeutics (29.6 percent, including 22.5 percent with pain relievers, 3.2 percent with tranquilizers, 3.0 percent with stimulants, and 0.8 percent with sedatives). A sizable proportion reported inhalants (9.7 percent) as their first drug, and a small proportion used hallucinogens as their first illicit drug (3.2 percent). Between 2007 and 2008, the percentage of past year illicit drug initiates whose first drug was tranquilizers decreased from 6.5 to 3.2 percent, while the percentage whose first drug was inhalants decreased between 2003 and 2008 from 12.9 to 9.7 percent.

Figure 5.1   Specific Drug Used When Initiating Illicit Drug Use Among Past Year Initiates of Illicit Drugs Aged 12 or Older: 2008

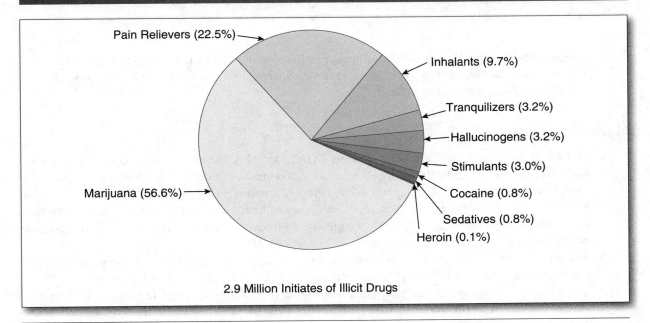

2.9 Million Initiates of Illicit Drugs

Note: The percentages do not add to 100 percent due to rounding or because a small number of respondents initiated multiple drugs on the same day.

Comparison, by Drug

- In 2008, the specific drug categories with the largest number of recent initiates among persons aged 12 or older were marijuana use (2.2 million) and nonmedical use of pain relievers (2.2 million), followed by nonmedical use of tranquilizers (1.1 million), Ecstasy (0.9 million), inhalants (0.7 million), cocaine (0.7 million), and stimulants (0.6 million) (Figure 5.2).

Figure 5.2   Past Year Initiates for Specific Illicit Drugs Among Persons Aged 12 or Older: 2008

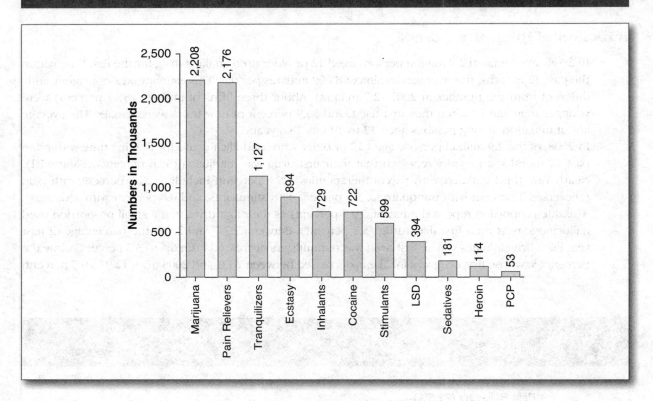

- Among persons aged 12 to 49, the average age at first use of inhalants in 2008 was 15.9 years; it was 17.8 years for marijuana, 19.8 years for cocaine, 20.3 years for Ecstasy, 21.2 years for pain relievers, and 24.4 years for tranquilizers (Figure 5.3).

Marijuana

- In 2008, there were 2.2 million persons aged 12 or older who had used marijuana for the first time within the past 12 months; this averages to about 6,000 initiates per day. This estimate was about the same as the estimate in 2007 (2.1 million) and 2002 (2.2 million) (Figure 5.4).
- Most (61.8 percent) of the 2.2 million recent marijuana initiates were younger than age 18 when they first used. Among youths aged 12 to 17, an estimated 5.0 percent had used marijuana for the first time within the past year, similar to the rate in 2007 (4.6 percent).
- As a percentage of those aged 12 to 17 who had not used marijuana prior to the past year, the youth marijuana initiation rate in 2008 (5.6 percent) was similar to the rate in 2007 (5.2 percent).
- In 2008, the average age at first marijuana use among recent initiates aged 12 to 49 was 17.8 years, which was similar to the average in 2007 (17.6 years) (Figure 5.4). However, the average age at first marijuana use has increased since 2003, when it was 16.8 years. Among recent initiates aged 12 or older who initiated use prior to the age of 21, the mean age at first use was 16.1 years in 2008, which was not significantly different from the estimate (16.2 years) in 2007.

Figure 5.3   Mean Age at First Use for Specific Illicit Drugs Among Past Year Initiates Aged 12 to 49: 2008

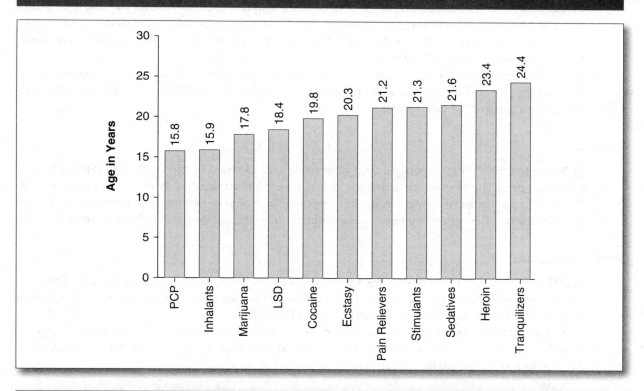

Figure 5.4   Past Year Marijuana Initiates Among Persons Aged 12 or Older and Mean Age at First Use of Marijuana Among Past Year Marijuana Initiates Aged 12 to 49: 2002–2008

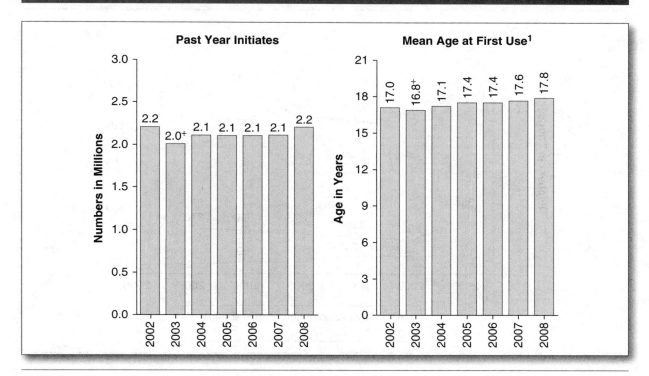

+Difference between this estimate and the 2008 estimate is statistically significant at the .05 level.

[1]Mean-age-at-first-use estimates are for recent initiates aged 12 to 49.

Cocaine

- In 2008, there were 722,000 persons aged 12 or older who had used cocaine for the first time within the past 12 months; this averages to approximately 2,000 initiates per day. This estimate was significantly lower than the number in 2007 (906,000). The annual number of cocaine initiates declined from 1.0 million in 2002 to 722,000 in 2008.
- Most (66.9 percent) of the 0.7 million recent cocaine initiates were 18 or older when they first used. The average age at first use among recent initiates aged 12 to 49 was 19.8 years, which was similar to the average age in 2007 (20.2 years).

Heroin

- In 2008, there were 114,000 persons aged 12 or older who had used heroin for the first time within the past 12 months. The average age at first use among recent initiates aged 12 to 49 was 23.4 years in 2008. There were no significant changes in the number of initiates or in the average age at first use from 2007 to 2008. The number of heroin initiates was not significantly different from the number in 2002 (117,000).

Hallucinogens

- In 2008, there were 1.1 million persons aged 12 or older who had used hallucinogens for the first time within the past 12 months (Figure 5.5). This estimate was not significantly different from the estimate in 2007, but was higher than the estimate for 2003 (886,000).
- Past year initiates of LSD aged 12 or older increased from 270,000 in 2007 to 394,000 in 2008, approximately doubling since 2003, when the estimate was 200,000. Past year initiates of PCP decreased from 123,000 in 2002 to 53,000 in 2008 (Figure 5.5).

Figure 5.5 Past Year Hallucinogen Initiates Among Persons Aged 12 or Older: 2002–2008

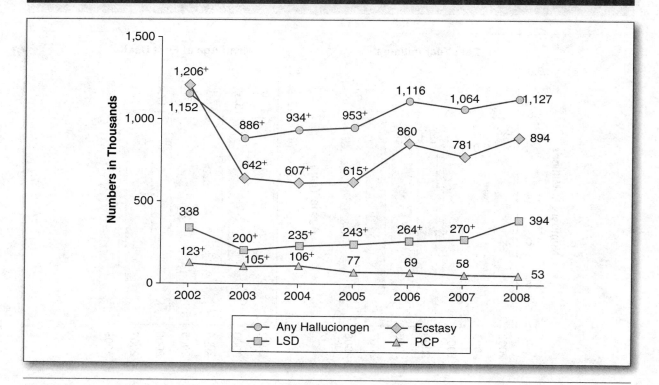

+Difference between this estimate and the 2008 estimate is statistically significant at the .05 level.

- There was no significant change in the number of past year initiates of Ecstasy between 2007 (781,000) and 2008 (894,000) (Figure 5.5). The number of past year Ecstasy initiates in 2008, however, was significantly higher than the estimates in 2003 (642,000), 2004 (607,000), and 2005 (615,000). The estimate had been 1.2 million in 2002, significantly higher than in 2008. Most (68.5 percent) of the recent Ecstasy initiates in 2008 were aged 18 or older at the time they first used Ecstasy. Among past year initiates aged 12 to 49, the average age at initiation of Ecstasy in 2008 was 20.3 years, similar to the average age in 2007 (20.2 years).

Inhalants

- In 2008, there were 729,000 persons aged 12 or older who had used inhalants for the first time within the past 12 months; 70.4 percent were under age 18 when they first used. There was no significant difference in the number of inhalant initiates between 2007 and 2008, but the 2008 estimate was significantly below the number in 2003 (871,000), 2004 (857,000), and 2005 (877,000). However, there was a significant decrease in the average age at first use among recent initiates aged 12 to 49 from 2007 (17.1 years) to 2008 (15.9 years).

Psychotherapeutics

- Psychotherapeutics include the nonmedical use of any prescription-type pain relievers, tranquilizers, stimulants, or sedatives. Over-the-counter substances are not included. In 2008, there were 2.5 million persons aged 12 or older who used psychotherapeutics nonmedically for the first time within the past year, which averages out to around 7,000 initiates per day. This annual estimate of the initiates of psychotherapeutics was significantly lower than the 2004 estimate (2.8 million). In 2008, the numbers of new users of specific classes of psychotherapeutics were 2.2 million for pain relievers, 1.1 million for tranquilizers, 599,000 for stimulants, and 181,000 for sedatives. There was a significant decrease in the number of past year initiates of stimulants from 2006 (845,000) to 2008 (599,000), but there were no significant changes in the estimates for the remaining psychotherapeutics between these years.
- In 2008, the average age at first nonmedical use of any psychotherapeutics among recent initiates aged 12 to 49 was 22.0 years. More specifically, it was 21.2 years for pain relievers, 24.4 years for tranquilizers, 21.3 years for stimulants, and 21.6 years for sedatives.
- In 2008, the number of new nonmedical users of OxyContin® aged 12 or older was 478,000, with an average age at first use of 21.8 years among those aged 12 to 49. These estimates are similar to those for 2007 (554,000 and 24.0 years, respectively). OxyContin® initiation declined between 2004 (615,000) and 2008.
- The number of recent new users of methamphetamine among persons aged 12 or older was 95,000 in 2008 (Figure 5.6). This estimate was significantly lower than the estimate in 2002 (299,000), 2003 (260,000), 2004 (318,000), 2005 (192,000), 2006 (259,000), and 2007 (157,000). The average age of new methamphetamine users aged 12 to 49 in 2008 was 19.2 years, which was not significantly different from the average ages between 2002 and 2007.

Alcohol

- In 2008, there were 4.5 million persons aged 12 or older who had used alcohol for the first time within the past 12 months; this averages to approximately 12,000 initiates per day.
- Most (84.6 percent) of the 4.5 million recent alcohol initiates were younger than age 21 at the time of initiation.
- In 2008, the average age at first alcohol use among recent initiates aged 12 to 49 was 17.0 years, similar to the corresponding 2007 estimate (16.8 years). The mean age at first use among recent initiates aged 12 or older who initiated use prior to the age of 21 was 15.9 years, which was similar to the 2007 estimate (15.8 years).

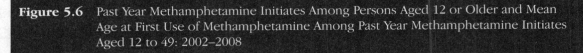

Figure 5.6   Past Year Methamphetamine Initiates Among Persons Aged 12 or Older and Mean Age at First Use of Methamphetamine Among Past Year Methamphetamine Initiates Aged 12 to 49: 2002–2008

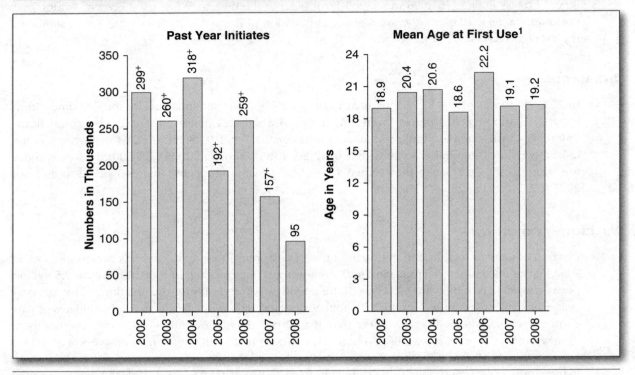

[+]Difference between this estimate and the 2008 estimate is statistically significant at the .05 level.

[1]Mean-age-at-first-use estimates are for recent initiates aged 12 to 49.

Tobacco

- The number of persons aged 12 or older who smoked cigarettes for the first time within the past 12 months was 2.4 million in 2008, which was similar to the estimate in 2007 (2.2 million) but significantly higher than the estimate for 2002 (1.9 million), 2003 (2.0 million), and 2004 (2.1 million) (Figure 5.7). The 2008 estimate averages out to approximately 6,600 new cigarette smokers every day. Most new cigarette smokers in 2008 were under age 18 when they first smoked cigarettes (58.8 percent).
- The increase in cigarette initiation was due primarily to an increase among persons initiating at age 18 or older. Between 2002 and 2008, the number of initiates under age 18 remained stable (1.3 million in 2002 and 1.4 million in 2008), but the number of initiates aged 18 or older increased from about 600,000 to 1 million.
- In 2008, among recent initiates aged 12 to 49, the average age of first cigarette use was 17.4 years, similar to the average in 2007 (16.9 years).
- Of those aged 12 or older who had not smoked cigarettes prior to the past year, the past year initiation rate for cigarettes was 2.7 percent in 2008, similar to the rate in 2007 (2.5 percent). Among youths aged 12 to 17 years who had not smoked cigarettes prior to the past year, the incidence rate showed no significant difference between 2007 (5.9 percent) and 2008 (6.2 percent). Among males aged 12 to 17 who had never smoked prior to the past year, the decrease in the past year initiation rate from 6.1 percent in 2002 to 5.7 percent in 2008 was not statistically significant (Figure 5.8). Similarly for females, the decrease from 7.4 percent in 2002 to 6.7 percent in 2008 was not statistically significant.

Figure 5.7   Past Year Cigarette Initiates Among Persons Aged 12 or Older, by Age at First Use: 2002–2008

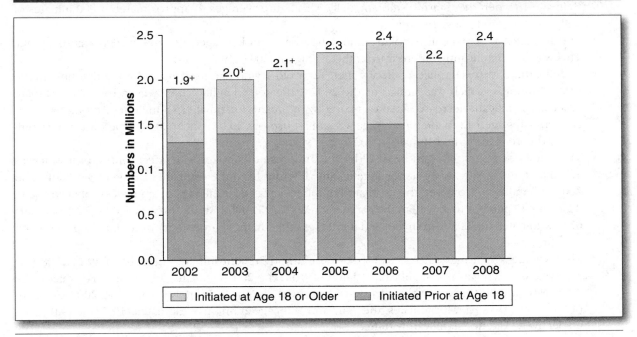

⁺Difference between this estimate and the 2008 estimate is statistically significant at the .05 level.

Figure 5.8   Past Year Cigarette Initiation Among Youths Aged 12 to 17 Who Had Never Smoked Prior to the Past Year, by Gender: 2002–2008

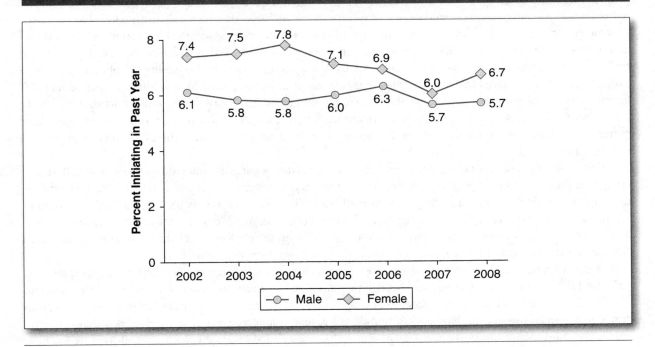

⁺Difference between this estimate and the 2008 estimate is statistically significant at the .05 level.

- In 2008, the number of persons aged 12 or older who had started smoking cigarettes daily within the past 12 months was 0.9 million. This estimate was similar to the estimates for 2002 (1.0 million) and 2007 (1.0 million). Of the new daily smokers in 2008, 37.2 percent, or 350,000 persons, were younger than age 18 when they started smoking daily. This figure averages to approximately 1,000 initiates of daily smoking under age 18 every day.
- The average age of first daily smoking among new daily smokers aged 12 to 49 in 2008 was 20.1 years. This was not significantly different from the average in 2007 (19.2 years).
- In 2008, there were 2.9 million persons aged 12 or older who had used cigars for the first time in the past 12 months, which was similar to the 2007 estimate (3.1 million). However, the 2008 estimate reflects a significant decrease when compared with the 2005 estimate (3.3 million). Among past year cigar initiates aged 12 to 49, the average age at first use was 20.0 years in 2008, which was not significantly different from the estimate in 2007 (20.5 years).
- The number of persons aged 12 or older initiating use of smokeless tobacco in the past year was 1.4 million in 2008, which was not significantly different from the estimate in 2006 (1.3 million) and 2007 (1.3 million). However, the estimated number of past year initiates of smokeless tobacco use in 2008 was 47 percent higher than the estimate in 2002 (951,000). About three quarters (72.5 percent) of new initiates in 2008 were male, and a little less than half (47.4 percent) were under age 18 when they first used.
- The average age at first smokeless tobacco use among recent initiates aged 12 to 49 in 2008 was 18.9 years, which was not significantly different from the 2007 estimate (18.0 years). For males, the 2008 estimate of this average age (18.8 years) was significantly higher than the 2007 estimate (17.4 years). However, for females, the 2007 and 2008 age at first use estimates (19.7 and 19.0 years, respectively) did not significantly differ.

6. Youth Prevention-Related Measures

The National Survey on Drug Use and Health (NSDUH) includes questions for youths aged 12 to 17 about a number of risk and protective factors that may affect the likelihood that they will engage in substance use. Risk factors are individual characteristics and environmental influences associated with an increased vulnerability to the initiation, continuation, or escalation of substance use. Protective factors include individual resilience and other circumstances that are associated with a reduction in the likelihood of substance use. Risk and protective factors include variables that operate at different stages of development and reflect different domains of influence, including the individual, family, peer, school, community, and societal levels (Hawkins, Catalano, & Miller, 1992; Robertson, David, & Rao, 2003). Interventions to prevent substance use generally are designed to ameliorate the influence of risk factors and enhance the effectiveness of protective factors.

This chapter presents findings for youth prevention-related measures collected in the 2008 NSDUH and compares these with findings from previous years. Included are measures of perceived risk from substance use (cigarettes, alcohol, and illicit drugs), perceived availability of substances, being approached by someone selling drugs, perceived parental disapproval of youth substance use, feelings about peer substance use, involvement in fighting and delinquent behavior, participation in religious and other activities, exposure to substance use prevention messages and programs, and parental involvement.

In this chapter, rates of substance use are compared for persons responding differently to questions reflecting risk or protective factors, such as the perceived risk of harm from using a substance. Because the NSDUH data for an individual are collected at only one point in time, it is not possible to determine causal connections from these data. However, a number of research studies of youths have shown that reducing risk factors and increasing protective factors can reduce rates of substance use (Botvin, Botvin, & Ruchlin, 1998). This report shows that marijuana, cigarette, and alcohol use among youths aged 12 to 17 decreased between 2002 and 2008, yet corresponding changes in individual risk and protective factors for the same period may or may not have occurred. There can be many reasons for this, such as the lack of or a weak causal connection, a lagged relationship between the occurrence of a risk factor and the change in drug use behavior, or that individual use is typically the result of multiple simultaneous risk factors rather than a single factor (Newcomb, Maddahian, & Bentler, 1986).

Perceptions of Risk

One factor that can influence whether youths will use tobacco, alcohol, or illicit drugs is the extent to which youths believe these substances might cause them harm. NSDUH respondents were asked how much they thought people risk harming themselves physically and in other ways when they use various substances in certain amounts or frequencies. Response choices for these items were "great risk," "moderate risk," "slight risk," or "no risk."

- The percentages of youths reporting binge alcohol use and use of cigarettes and marijuana in the past month were lower among those who perceived great risk in using these substances than among those who did not perceive great risk. For example, in 2008, 5.0 percent of youths aged 12 to 17 who perceived great risk from "having five or more drinks of an alcoholic beverage once or twice a week" reported binge drinking in the past month (consumption of five or more drinks of an alcoholic beverage on a single occasion on at least 1 day in the past 30 days); by contrast, past month binge drinking was reported by 11.5 percent of youths who saw moderate, slight, or no risk from having five or more drinks of an alcoholic beverage once or twice a week (Figure 6.1). Past month marijuana use was reported by 1.5 percent of youths who saw great risk in smoking marijuana once a month compared with 9.4 percent of youths who saw moderate, slight, or no risk.

Figure 6.1   Past Month Binge Drinking and Marijuana Use Among Youths Aged 12 to 17, by Perceptions of Risk: 2008

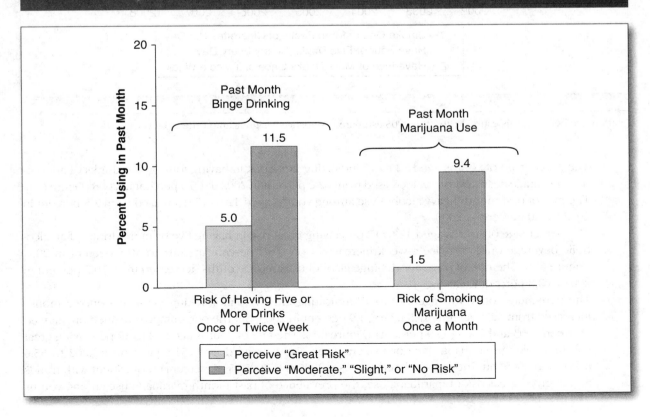

- Decreases in the rate of current use of a substance often occur when there are increases in the level of perceived risk of using that substance. Looking over the 7-year period, the proportion of youths aged 12 to 17 who reported perceiving great risk from smoking one or more packs of cigarettes per day increased from 63.1 percent in 2002 to 69.7 percent in 2008 (Figure 6.2). During the same period, the rate of past month cigarette smoking among youths aged 12 to 17 dropped from 13.0 to 9.1 percent.

Figure 6.2 Perceived Great Risk of Cigarette and Alcohol Use Among Youths Aged 12 to 17: 2002–2008

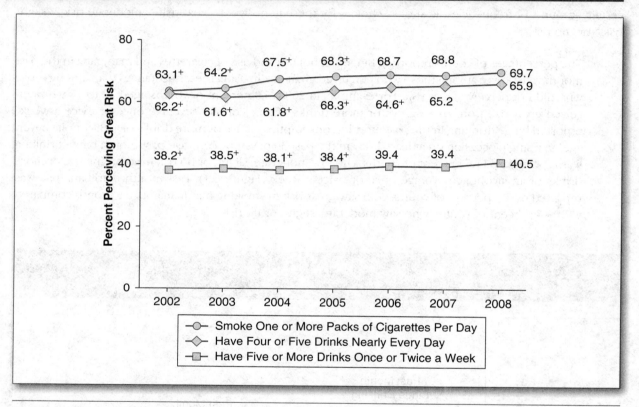

+Difference between this estimate and the 2008 estimate is statistically significant at the .05 level.

- The percentage of youths aged 12 to 17 indicating great risk in having four or five drinks of an alcoholic beverage nearly every day increased from 62.2 percent in 2002 to 65.9 percent in 2008 (Figure 6.2). The rate of past month heavy alcohol use among youths aged 12 to 17 decreased from 2.5 percent in 2002 to 2.0 percent in 2008.
- The percentage of youths aged 12 to 17 perceiving great risk in having five or more drinks of an alcoholic beverage once or twice a week increased from 38.2 percent in 2002 to 40.5 percent in 2008 (Figure 6.2). The rate of past month binge alcohol use among youths decreased from 10.7 percent in 2002 to 8.8 percent in 2008.
- The percentage of youths aged 12 to 17 indicating great risk in smoking marijuana once a month increased from 32.4 percent in 2002 to 34.9 percent in 2003, but the percentage remained unchanged between 2003 and 2008 (33.9 percent) (Figure 6.3). The rate of youths aged 12 to 17 perceiving great risk in smoking marijuana once or twice a week also increased from 51.5 percent in 2002 to 55.0 percent in 2005, but the rate declined between 2005 and 2008 (53.1 percent). Coincident with trends in perceived great risk of marijuana use, the prevalence of past month marijuana use among youths

aged 12 to 17 decreased between 2002 (8.2 percent) and 2005 (6.8 percent), then remained stable between 2005 and 2008 (6.7 percent).

Figure 6.3   Perceived Great Risk of Marijuana Use Among Youths Aged 12 to 17: 2002–2008

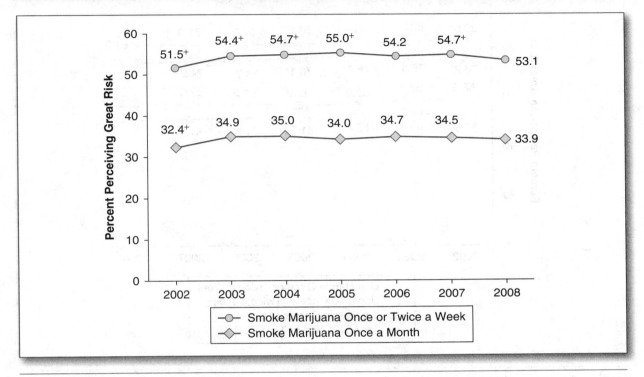

[+]Difference between this estimate and the 2008 estimate is statistically significant at the .05 level.

- Between 2002 and 2008, the percentage of youths aged 12 to 17 perceiving great risk declined for the following substance use patterns: using heroin once or twice a week (from 82.5 to 81.3 percent), trying LSD once or twice (from 52.6 to 50.5 percent), and using LSD once or twice a week (from 76.2 to 73.9 percent) (Figure 6.4). Over the same period, however, there were no statistically significant changes in the percentages of youths aged 12 to 17 indicating great risk for trying heroin once or twice (from 58.5 to 57.7 percent), using cocaine once a month (50.5 percent in 2002 and 49.7 percent in 2008), and using cocaine once or twice a week (79.8 percent in 2002 and 79.2 percent in 2008). Moreover, percentages for all of these perceptions of risk measures remained stable between 2007 and 2008.

Perceived Availability

- In 2008, about half (49.2 percent) of the youths aged 12 to 17 reported that it would be "fairly easy" or "very easy" for them to obtain marijuana if they wanted some (Figure 6.5). One in seven (13.0 percent) indicated that heroin would be "fairly" or "very" easily available, and 13.8 percent reported so for LSD. Between 2002 and 2008, there were decreases in the perceived easy availability of marijuana (from 55.0 to 49.2 percent), cocaine (from 25.0 to 22.1 percent), crack (from 26.5 to 23.2 percent), LSD (from 19.4 to 13.8 percent), and heroin (from 15.8 to 13.0 percent). The perceived availability of the following illicit drugs declined between 2007 and 2008: cocaine from 24.5 to 22.1 percent; crack from 25.3 to 23.2 percent; and heroin from 14.1 to 13.0 percent. However, the perceived availability of marijuana and LSD did not change significantly during the 2-year period.

Figure 6.4 Perceived Great Risk of Use of Selected Illicit Drugs Among Youths Aged 12 to 17: 2002–2008

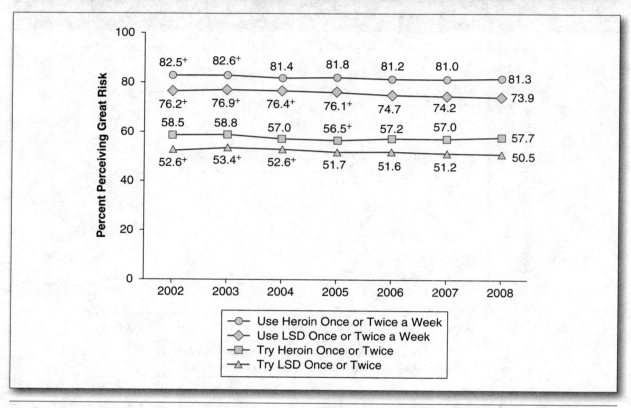

+Difference between this estimate and the 2008 estimate is statistically significant at the .05 level.

- The percentage of youths who reported that marijuana, cocaine, and LSD would be easy to obtain increased with age in 2008. For example, 20.5 percent of those aged 12 or 13 said it would be fairly or very easy to obtain marijuana compared with 52.2 percent of those aged 14 or 15 and 71.0 percent of those aged 16 or 17.
- In 2008, 13.7 percent of youths aged 12 to 17 indicated that they had been approached by someone selling drugs in the past month, which was down from the 16.7 percent reported in 2002 (Figure 6.6). The rate remained stable between 2007 (14.5 percent) and 2008.

Perceived Parental Disapproval of Substance Use

- Most youths aged 12 to 17 believed their parents would "strongly disapprove" of their using substances. In 2008, 90.8 percent of youths reported that their parents would strongly disapprove of their trying marijuana or hashish once or twice; this was similar to the 91.0 percent reported in 2007, but was higher than the 89.1 percent reported in 2002. Most (89.7 percent) reported that their parents would strongly disapprove of their having one or two drinks of an alcoholic beverage nearly every day, which was similar to the rates in 2007 (89.6 percent) and 2002 (89.0 percent). In 2008, 92.4 percent of youths reported that their parents would strongly disapprove of their smoking one or more packs of cigarettes per day, which was similar to the 92.1 percent reported in 2007, but was higher than the 89.5 percent reported in 2002.
- Youths aged 12 to 17 who believed their parents would strongly disapprove of their using substances were less likely to use that substance than were youths who believed their parents would somewhat

Figure 6.5   Perceived Availability of Selected Illicit Drugs Among Youths Aged 12 to 17: 2002–2008

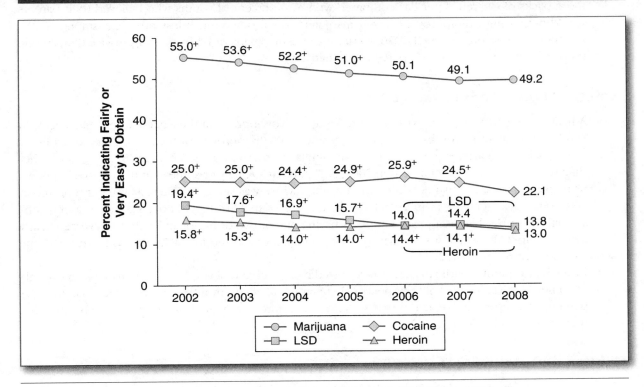

+Difference between this estimate and the 2008 estimate is statistically significant at the .05 level.

Figure 6.6   Approached in the Past Month by Someone Selling Drugs Among Youths Aged 12 to 17: 2002–2008

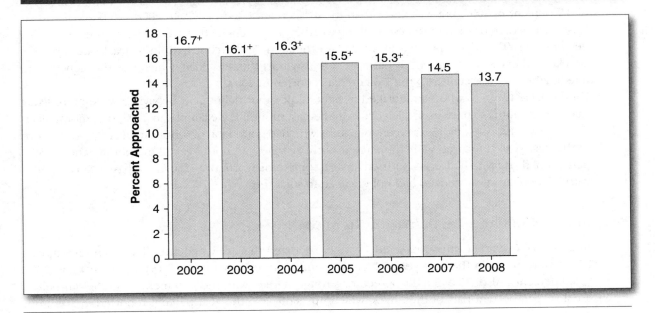

+Difference between this estimate and the 2008 estimate is statistically significant at the .05 level.

disapprove or neither approve nor disapprove. For example, in 2008, past month cigarette use was reported by 6.7 percent of youths who perceived strong parental disapproval of their smoking one or more packs of cigarettes per day compared with 37.3 percent of youths who believed their parents would not strongly disapprove. Current marijuana use also was much less prevalent among youths who perceived strong parental disapproval for trying marijuana or hashish once or twice than among those who did not (4.3 vs. 29.8 percent, respectively).

Feelings About Peer Substance Use

- A majority of youths aged 12 to 17 reported that they disapprove of their peers using substances. In 2008, 89.6 percent of youths "strongly" or "somewhat" disapproved of their peers smoking one or more packs of cigarettes per day, which was similar to the rate of 89.7 percent in 2007, but higher than the 87.1 percent in 2002. Also in 2008, 82.7 percent strongly or somewhat disapproved of peers using marijuana or hashish once a month or more, which was similar to the 82.9 percent reported in 2007, but was an increase from the 80.4 percent reported in 2002. In addition, 87.0 percent of youths strongly or somewhat disapproved of peers having one or two drinks of an alcoholic beverage nearly every day in 2008, which was similar to the 86.6 percent reported in 2007, but was higher than the 84.7 percent reported in 2002.

- In 2008, past month marijuana use was reported by 2.3 percent of youths aged 12 to 17 who strongly or somewhat disapproved of their peers using marijuana once a month or more, lower than the 27.1 percent of youths who reported that they neither approve nor disapprove of such behavior from their peers.

Fighting and Delinquent Behavior

- In 2008, 21.4 percent of youths aged 12 to 17 reported that, in the past year, they had gotten into a serious fight at school or at work; this was similar to the rates in 2007 (22.3 percent) and 2002 (20.6 percent). Almost one in six (14.5 percent) in 2008 had taken part in a group-against-group fight, which was lower than the rates in 2007 (15.4 percent) and 2002 (15.9 percent). About 1 in 30 (3.2 percent) had carried a handgun at least once, which was similar to the rates in 2007 and 2002 (both at 3.3 percent). An estimated 3.0 percent had sold illegal drugs, which was similar to the rate of 2.9 percent in 2007, but was lower than the 4.4 percent rate in 2002. In 2008, 4.6 percent had, at least once, stolen or tried to steal something worth more than $50; this was similar to the rates of 4.3 percent in 2007 and 4.9 percent in 2002. An estimated 7.3 percent had, in at least one instance, attacked others with the intent to harm or seriously hurt them in 2008, which was the same as the rate in 2007 and was similar to the 7.8 percent reported in 2002.

- Youths aged 12 to 17 who had engaged in fighting or other delinquent behaviors were more likely than other youths to have used illicit drugs in the past month. For example, in 2008, past month illicit drug use was reported by 15.9 percent of youths who had gotten into a serious fight at school or work in the past year compared with 7.3 percent of those who had not engaged in fighting, and by 39.8 percent of those who had stolen or tried to steal something worth over $50 in the past year compared with 7.7 percent of those who had not engaged in such theft.

Religious Beliefs and Participation in Activities

- In 2008, 31.7 percent of youths aged 12 to 17 reported that they had attended religious services 25 or more times in the past year, which was similar to the rates in 2007 (31.4 percent) and 2002 (33.0 percent). Also, 75.0 percent agreed or strongly agreed with the statement that religious beliefs are a very important part of their lives, which was similar to the 76.1 percent reported in 2007, but was lower than the 78.2 percent reported in 2002. In addition, 33.8 percent agreed or strongly agreed with the statement that it is important for their friends to share their religious beliefs, which was lower than the rates in 2007 (35.1 percent) and 2002 (35.8 percent).

- The rates of past month use of illicit drugs, cigarettes, and alcohol (including binge alcohol) were lower among youths aged 12 to 17 who agreed with these statements about religious beliefs than among those who disagreed. For example, in 2008, past month illicit drug use was reported by 6.8 percent of those who agreed that religious beliefs are a very important part of life compared with 16.2 percent of those who disagreed with that statement.

Exposure to Substance Use Prevention Messages and Programs

- In 2008, approximately one in nine youths aged 12 to 17 (11.1 percent) reported that they had participated in drug, tobacco, or alcohol prevention programs outside of school in the past year. This rate was similar to the 11.3 percent reported in 2007, but was lower than the rates reported in 2002 (12.7 percent) and 2003 (13.9 percent). The prevalence of past month use of illicit drugs, marijuana, cigarettes, or binge alcohol use among those who participated in these prevention programs outside of school was not significantly lower (8.9 percent, 5.6 percent, 8.0 percent, or 7.5 percent, respectively) than among those who did not (9.2 percent, 6.7 percent, 9.2 percent, or 8.9 percent, respectively).
- In 2008, 78.0 percent of youths aged 12 to 17 reported having seen or heard drug or alcohol prevention messages in the past year from sources outside of school, which was similar to the 77.9 percent reported in 2007, but was lower than the 83.2 percent reported in 2002 (Figure 6.7). The prevalence of past month use of illicit drugs was lower among those who reported having such exposure (8.9 percent) than among those who reported having no such exposure (10.2 percent).

Figure 6.7   Exposure to Substance Use Prevention Messages and Programs Among Youths Aged 12 to 17: 2002–2008

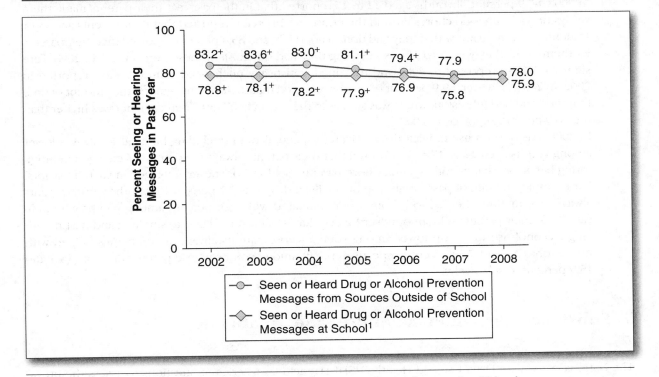

[+]Difference between this estimate and the 2008 estimate is statistically significant at the .05 level.

[1]Estimates are from youths aged 12 to 17 who were enrolled in school in the past year.

- In 2008, 75.9 percent of youths aged 12 to 17 enrolled in school in the past year reported having seen or heard drug or alcohol prevention messages at school, which was similar to the 75.8 percent reported in 2007, but was lower than the 78.8 percent reported in 2002 (Figure 6.7). The prevalence of past month use of illicit drugs or marijuana was lower among those who reported having such exposure (8.5 percent and 6.1 percent for illicit drugs and marijuana, respectively) than among those who reported having no such exposure (12.1 percent and 9.0 percent, respectively).

- In 2008, 58.7 percent of youths aged 12 to 17 reported that they had talked at least once in the past year with at least one of their parents about the dangers of drug, tobacco, or alcohol use, which was similar to rates reported in 2007 (59.6 percent) and 2002 (58.1 percent). The prevalence of past month use of illicit drugs or cigarettes among those who reported having had such conversations with their parents (8.6 percent and 8.5 percent, respectively) was lower than that among those who reported having no such conversations (10.0 percent and 9.8 percent, respectively). However, the prevalence of past month use of marijuana or binge alcohol among those who reported having had such conversations with their parents (6.5 percent and 8.7 percent, respectively) was similar to that among those who reported having no such conversations (6.8 percent and 8.9 percent, respectively).

Parental Involvement

- Youths aged 12 to 17 were asked a number of questions related to the extent of support, oversight, and control that they perceived their parents exercised over them in the year prior to the survey. In 2008, among youths aged 12 to 17 enrolled in school in the past year, 79.3 percent reported that in the past year their parents always or sometimes checked on whether or not they had completed their homework, and 70.2 percent reported that their parents limited the amount of time that they spent out with friends on school nights. Both of these rates reported in 2008 were similar to those reported in 2007 and remained statistically unchanged from the rates reported in 2002. However, in 2008, 80.0 percent reported that their parents always or sometimes provided help with their homework, which was similar to the rate in 2007 (80.9 percent) but was lower than the rate in 2002 (81.4 percent).

- In 2008, 87.9 percent of youths aged 12 to 17 reported that in the past year their parents made them always or sometimes do chores around the house, 86.1 percent reported that their parents always or sometimes let them know that they had done a good job, and 85.4 percent reported that their parents let them know they were proud of something they had done. All of these percentages in 2008 were similar to those reported in 2007 and remained statistically unchanged from the rates reported in 2002. In 2008, however, 39.9 percent of youths reported that their parents limited the amount of time that they watched television, which was similar to the rate in 2007 (39.7 percent), but was higher than the 36.9 percent reported in 2002.

- In 2008, past month use of illicit drugs, cigarettes, and alcohol (including binge alcohol) was lower among youths aged 12 to 17 who reported that their parents always or sometimes engaged in monitoring behaviors than among youths whose parents "seldom" or "never" engaged in such behaviors. For example, the rate of past month use of any illicit drug was 7.7 percent for youths whose parents always or sometimes helped with homework compared with 15.6 percent among youths who indicated that their parents seldom or never helped. Rates of current cigarette smoking and past month binge alcohol use were also lower among youths whose parents always or sometimes helped with homework (7.7 and 7.3 percent, respectively) than among youths whose parents did not (15.3 and 15.9 percent, respectively).

7. Substance Dependence, Abuse, and Treatment

The National Survey on Drug Use and Health (NSDUH) includes a series of questions to assess the prevalence of substance use disorders (i.e., dependence on or abuse of a substance) in the past 12 months. Substances include alcohol and illicit drugs, such as marijuana, cocaine, heroin, hallucinogens, inhalants, and the nonmedical use of prescription-type psychotherapeutic drugs. These questions are used to classify persons as dependent on or abusing specific substances based on criteria specified in the Diagnostic and Statistical Manual of Mental Disorders, 4th edition (DSM-IV) (American Psychiatric Association [APA], 1994).

The questions related to dependence ask about health and emotional problems associated with substance use, unsuccessful attempts to cut down on use, tolerance, withdrawal, reducing other activities to use substances, spending a lot of time engaging in activities related to substance use, or using the substance in greater quantities or for a longer time than intended. The questions on abuse ask about problems at work, home, and school; problems with family or friends; physical danger; and trouble with the law due to substance use. Dependence is considered to be a more severe substance use problem than abuse because it involves the psychological and physiological effects of tolerance and withdrawal. Although individuals may meet the criteria specified here for both dependence and abuse, persons meeting the criteria for both are classified as having dependence, but not abuse. Persons defined with abuse in this report do not meet the criteria for dependence.

This chapter provides estimates of the prevalence and patterns of substance use disorders occurring in the past year from the 2008 NSDUH and compares these estimates against the results from the 2002 through 2007 surveys. It also provides estimates of the prevalence and patterns of the receipt of treatment in the past year for problems related to substance use. This chapter concludes with a discussion of the need for and the receipt of treatment at specialty facilities for problems associated with substance use.

7.1. Substance Dependence or Abuse

- In 2008, an estimated 22.2 million persons aged 12 or older were classified with substance dependence or abuse in the past year (8.9 percent of the population aged 12 or older) (Figure 7.1). Of these, 3.1 million were classified with dependence on or abuse of both alcohol and illicit drugs, 3.9 million were dependent on or abused illicit drugs but not alcohol, and 15.2 million were dependent on or abused alcohol but not illicit drugs.

Figure 7.1   Substance Dependence or Abuse in the Past Year Among Persons Aged 12 or Older: 2002–2008

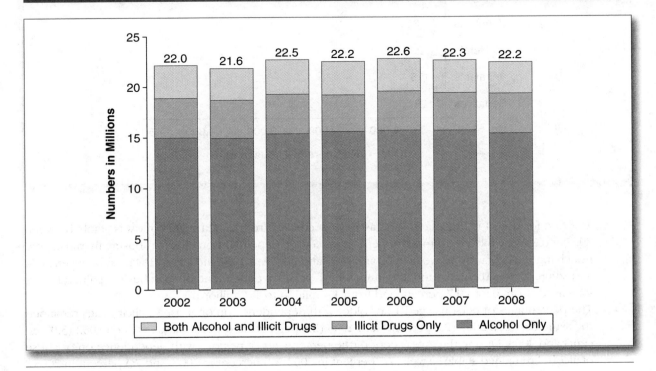

⁺Difference between this estimate and the 2008 estimate is statistically significant at the .05 level.

- The number of persons with substance dependence or abuse was stable between 2002 and 2008 (22.0 million in 2002, 21.6 million in 2003, 22.5 million in 2004, 22.2 million in 2005, 22.6 million in 2006, 22.3 million in 2007, and 22.2 million in 2008).
- In 2008, 18.3 million persons aged 12 or older were classified with dependence on or abuse of alcohol. This represents 7.3 percent of the population. The number and percentage have remained similar since 2002.
- Marijuana was the illicit drug with the highest rate of past year dependence or abuse in 2008, followed by pain relievers and cocaine. Of the 7.0 million persons aged 12 or older classified with dependence on or abuse of illicit drugs in 2008, 4.2 million were dependent on or abused marijuana or hashish (representing 1.7 percent of the total population aged 12 or older, and 60.1 percent of all those classified with illicit drug dependence or abuse), 1.7 million persons were classified with dependence on or abuse of pain relievers, and 1.4 million persons were classified with dependence on or abuse of cocaine (Figure 7.2). None of these estimates changed significantly between 2007 and 2008 or between 2002 and 2008 (Figure 7.3).

Figure 7.2 Dependence on or Abuse of Specific Illicit Drugs in the Past Year Among Persons Aged 12 or Older: 2008

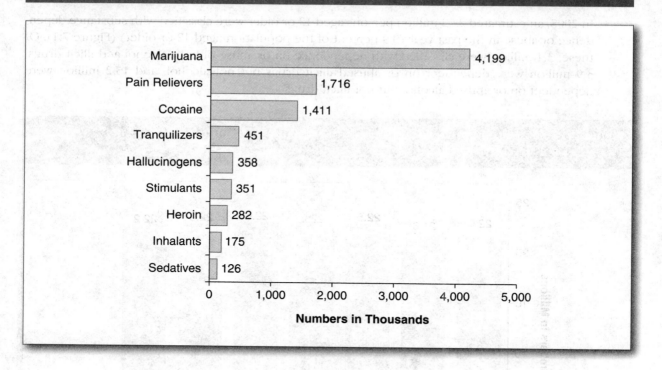

- The rate for use of marijuana in the past year decreased from 2002 to 2008 but was stable between 2007 and 2008, while the number of persons who were dependent on or were abusing marijuana did not change significantly between 2002 and 2008 and between 2007 and 2008. However, between 2004 and 2008, the percentage and the number of persons dependent on or abusing pain relievers increased (from 0.6 to 0.7 percent and from 1.4 million to 1.7 million).
- The percentages of persons aged 12 or older with dependence on or abuse of illicit drugs remained the same between 2007 (2.8 percent) and 2008 (2.8 percent) and were stable between 2002 (3.0 percent) and 2008. During the 7-year period, the percentages of persons with dependence on or abuse of alcohol remained stable as well (7.7 percent in 2002, 7.5 percent in 2007, and 7.3 percent in 2008).

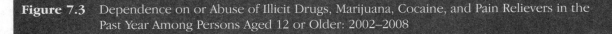

Figure 7.3   Dependence on or Abuse of Illicit Drugs, Marijuana, Cocaine, and Pain Relievers in the Past Year Among Persons Aged 12 or Older: 2002–2008

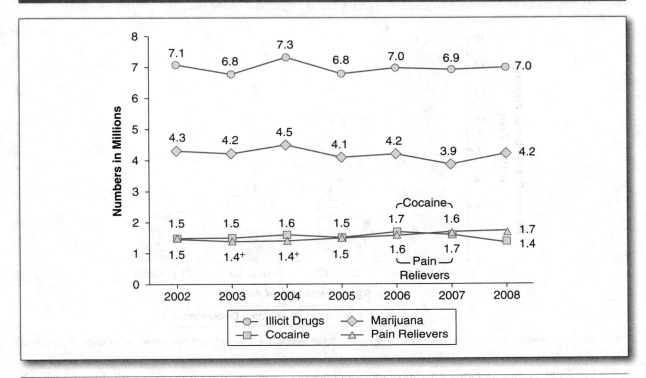

+ Difference between this estimate and the 2008 estimate is statistically significant at the .05 level.

Age at First Use

- In 2008, among adults aged 18 or older, age at first use of marijuana was associated with dependence on or abuse of marijuana. Among those who first tried marijuana at age 14 or younger, 13.5 percent were classified with illicit drug dependence or abuse, higher than the 2.2 percent of adults who had first used marijuana at age 18 or older.
- Among adults, age at first use of alcohol was associated with dependence on or abuse of alcohol. Among adults aged 18 or older who first tried alcohol at age 14 or younger, 16.5 percent were classified with alcohol dependence or abuse compared with only 3.9 percent of adults who had first used alcohol at age 18 or older. Adults aged 21 or older who had first used alcohol before age 21 were more likely than adults who had their first drink at age 21 or older to be classified with alcohol dependence or abuse (15.1, 9.3, and 4.7 percent for adults who first used alcohol at age 14 or younger, age 15 to 17, and age 18 to 20, respectively, vs. 2.6 percent for first use at age 21 or older) (Figure 7.4).

Age

- Rates of substance dependence or abuse were associated with age. In 2008, the rate of substance dependence or abuse among adults aged 18 to 25 (20.8 percent) was higher than that among youths aged 12 to 17 (7.6 percent) and among adults aged 26 or older (7.0 percent). None of these rates changed significantly between 2007 and 2008. For youths aged 12 to 17, the rate decreased from 8.9 percent in 2002 to 7.6 percent in 2008. For young adults aged 18 to 25 and adults aged 26 or older, these rates remained stable from 2002 to 2008.

Figure 7.4 Alcohol Dependence or Abuse in the Past Year Among Adults Aged 21 or Older, by Age at First Use of Alcohol: 2008

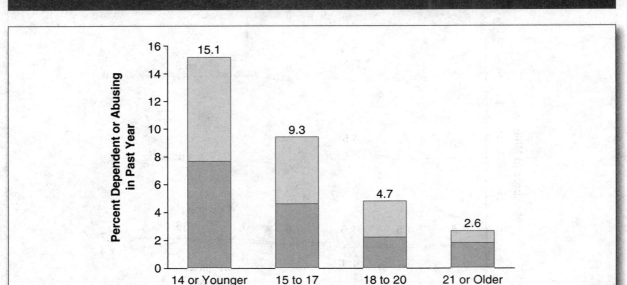

- In 2008, among persons with substance dependence or abuse, the proportion with dependence on or abuse of illicit drugs also was associated with age: 60.6 percent of youths aged 12 to 17 were dependent on or abused illicit drugs compared with 37.4 percent of young adults aged 18 to 25 and 24.3 percent of adults aged 26 or older.
- The rate of alcohol dependence or abuse among youths aged 12 to 17 was 4.9 percent in 2008, which was down from 5.4 percent in 2007 and from 5.9 percent in 2002 (Figure 7.5). Among adults aged 26 or older, the rate remained stable between 2007 (6.2 percent) and 2008 (6.0 percent) and between 2002 (6.2 percent) and 2008. Among young adults aged 18 to 25, the rate of alcohol dependence or abuse remained similar between 2007 (16.8 percent) and 2008 (17.2 percent) and between 2002 (17.7 percent) and 2008.

Gender

- As was the case from 2002 through 2007, the rate of substance dependence or abuse for males aged 12 or older in 2008 was about twice as high as the rate for females. For males in 2008, the rate was 11.5 percent, which was down from the 12.5 percent in 2007, while for females, it was 6.4 percent, which was higher than the 5.7 percent in 2007 (Figure 7.6). Among youths aged 12 to 17, however, the rate of substance dependence or abuse among males was lower than the rate among females in 2008 (7.0 vs. 8.2 percent).

Race/Ethnicity

- In 2008, among persons aged 12 or older, the rate of substance dependence or abuse was the lowest among Asians (4.2 percent). Racial/ethnic groups with similar rates included American Indians or Alaska Natives (11.1 percent), persons reporting two or more races (9.8 percent), whites (9.0 percent), blacks (8.8 percent), and Hispanics (9.5 percent). These rates in 2008 were similar to the rates in 2002 through 2007.

Figure 7.5 Dependence on or Abuse of Alcohol and Illicit Drugs Among Youths Aged 12 to 17: 2002–2008

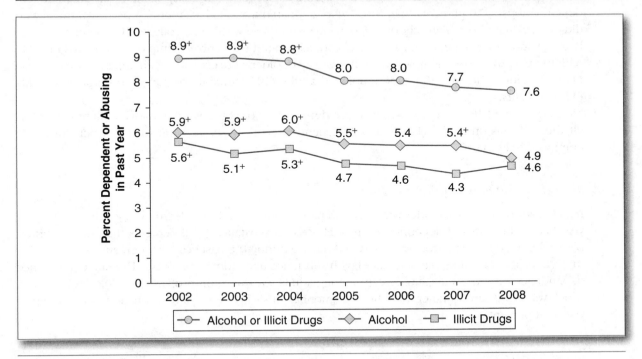

+Difference between this estimate and the 2008 estimate is statistically significant at the .05 level.

Figure 7.6 Substance Dependence or Abuse in the Past Year, by Age and Gender: 2008

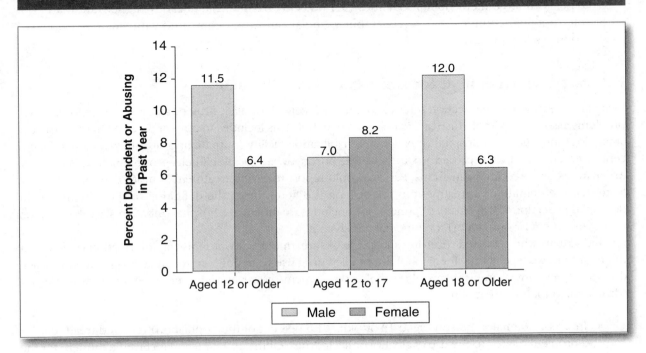

Education/Employment

- Rates of substance dependence or abuse were associated with level of education in 2008. Among adults aged 18 or older, those who graduated from a college or university had a lower rate of dependence or abuse (7.0 percent) than those who graduated from high school (9.4 percent), those who did not graduate from high school (9.5 percent), and those with some college (10.5 percent).
- Rates of substance dependence or abuse were associated with current employment status in 2008. A higher percentage of unemployed adults aged 18 or older were classified with dependence or abuse (19.0 percent) than were full-time employed adults (10.2 percent) or part-time employed adults (11.0 percent).
- Most adults aged 18 or older with substance dependence or abuse were employed full time in 2008. Of the 20.3 million adults classified with dependence or abuse, 12.5 million (61.5 percent) were employed full time.

Criminal Justice Populations

- In 2008, adults aged 18 or older who were on parole or a supervised release from jail during the past year had higher rates of dependence on or abuse of a substance (27.8 percent) than their counterparts who were not on parole or supervised release during the past year (8.9 percent).
- In 2008, probation status was associated with substance dependence or abuse. The rate of substance dependence or abuse was 34.0 percent among adults who were on probation during the past year, which was significantly higher than the rate among adults who were not on probation during the past year (8.4 percent).

Geographic Area

- In 2008, rates of substance dependence or abuse for persons aged 12 or older showed evidence of differences by region, with the West (9.6 percent) having a higher rate than the South (8.2 percent), but a similar rate to the Midwest (9.4 percent) and the Northeast (8.9 percent). Rates for substance dependence or abuse among persons aged 12 or older in 2008 also varied by county type, with large metropolitan counties (9.3 percent) having a significantly higher rate than nonmetropolitan counties (8.0 percent), but a similar rate when compared with small metropolitan counties (8.6 percent).

7.2. Past Year Treatment for a Substance Use Problem

Estimates described in this section refer to treatment received for illicit drug or alcohol use, or for medical problems associated with the use of illicit drugs or alcohol. This includes treatment received in the past year at any location, such as a hospital (inpatient), rehabilitation facility (outpatient or inpatient), mental health center, emergency room, private doctor's office, prison or jail, or a self-help group, such as Alcoholics Anonymous or Narcotics Anonymous. Persons could report receiving treatment at more than one location. Note that the definition of treatment in this section is different from the definition of specialty treatment described in Section 7.3. Specialty treatment only includes treatment at a hospital (inpatient), a rehabilitation facility (inpatient or outpatient), or a mental health center.

Individuals who reported receiving substance use treatment but were missing information on whether the treatment was specifically for alcohol use or illicit drug use were not counted in estimates of either illicit drug use treatment or in estimates of alcohol use treatment; however, they were counted in estimates for "drug or alcohol use" treatment.

- In 2008, 4.0 million persons aged 12 or older (1.6 percent of the population) received treatment for a problem related to the use of alcohol or illicit drugs. Of these, 1.3 million received treatment for the use of both alcohol and illicit drugs, 0.8 million received treatment for the use of illicit drugs but not alcohol, and 1.6 million received treatment for the use of alcohol but not illicit drugs. (Note that estimates by substance do not sum to the total number of persons receiving treatment because the total includes persons who reported receiving treatment but did not report for which substance the treatment was received.)

- The percentage of the population aged 12 or older receiving substance use treatment within the past year remained stable between 2007 and 2008 and between 2002 and 2008 (1.6 percent in 2008, 1.6 percent in 2007, and 1.5 percent in 2002). Although the number of persons receiving substance use treatment within the past year remained stable between 2007 and 2008, the number increased between 2002 (3.5 million) and 2008 (4.0 million).

- In 2008, among the 4.0 million persons aged 12 or older who received treatment for alcohol or illicit drug use in the past year, 2.2 million persons received treatment at a self-help group, and 1.5 million received treatment at a rehabilitation facility as an outpatient (Figure 7.7). There were 1.1 million persons who received treatment at a mental health center as an outpatient, 743,000 persons who received treatment at a rehabilitation facility as an inpatient, 675,000 at a hospital as an inpatient, 672,000 at a private doctor's office, 374,000 at an emergency room, and 343,000 at a prison or jail. None of these estimates changed significantly between 2007 and 2008 or between 2002 and 2008, except that the number of persons who received treatment at a rehabilitation facility as an inpatient in 2008 was lower than that in 2007 (1.0 million) and 2002 (1.1 million).

- In 2008, during their most recent treatment in the past year, 2.7 million persons aged 12 or older reported receiving treatment for alcohol use, and 947,000 persons reported receiving treatment for marijuana use (Figure 7.8). Accordingly, estimates on receiving treatment for the use of other drugs were 663,000 persons for cocaine, 601,000 for pain relievers, 341,000 for heroin, 336,000 for stimulants, 326,000 for tranquilizers, and 287,000 for hallucinogens. None of these estimates changed significantly between 2007 and 2008. Also, none of these estimates changed significantly between 2002 and 2008, except that the numbers who received treatment for the use of pain relievers and tranquilizers in 2008 were higher than the numbers in 2002 (360,000 and 197,000 persons, respectively) (Figure 7.9). (Note that respondents could indicate that they received treatment for more than one substance during their most recent treatment.)

Figure 7.7   Locations Where Past Year Substance Use Treatment Was Received Among Persons Aged 12 or Older: 2008

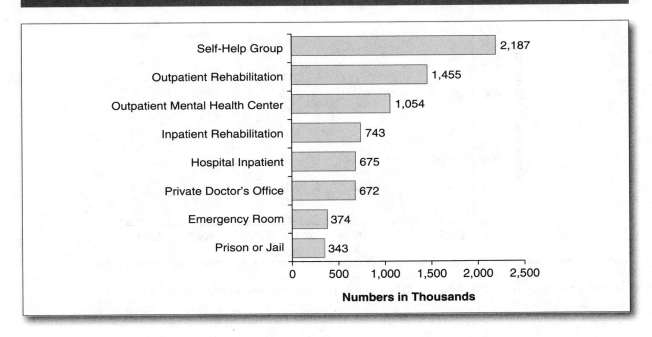

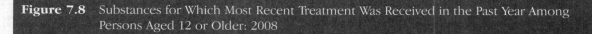

Figure 7.8 Substances for Which Most Recent Treatment Was Received in the Past Year Among Persons Aged 12 or Older: 2008

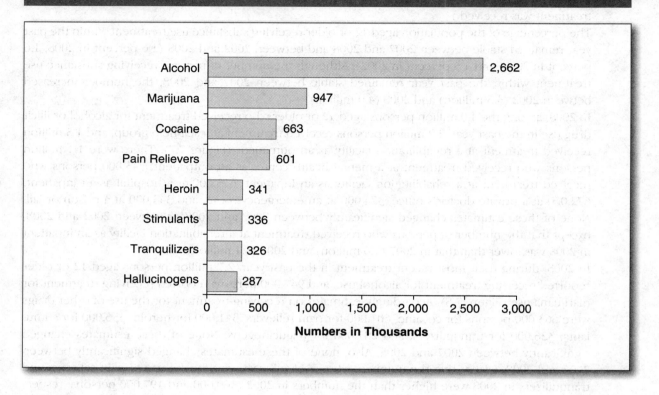

Figure 7.9 Received Most Recent Treatment in the Past Year for the Use of Pain Relievers Among Persons Aged 12 or Older: 2002–2008

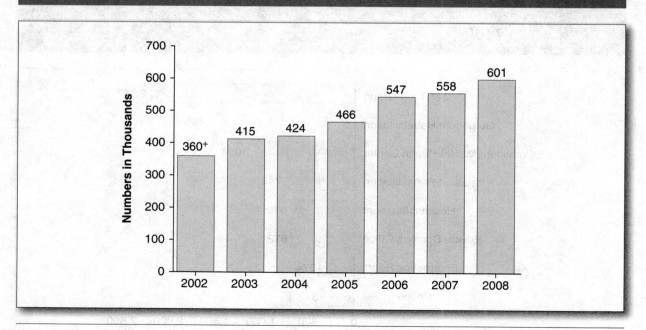

+Difference between this estimate and the 2008 estimate is statistically significant at the .05 level.

7.3. Need for and Receipt of Specialty Treatment

This section discusses the need for and receipt of treatment for a substance use problem at a "specialty" treatment facility. Specialty treatment is defined as treatment received at any of the following types of facilities: hospitals (inpatient only), drug or alcohol rehabilitation facilities (inpatient or outpatient), or mental health centers. It does not include treatment at an emergency room, private doctor's office, self-help group, prison or jail, or hospital as an outpatient. An individual is defined as needing treatment for an alcohol or drug use problem if he or she met the DSM-IV (APA, 1994) diagnostic criteria for dependence on or abuse of alcohol or illicit drugs in the past 12 months or if he or she received specialty treatment for alcohol use or illicit drug use in the past 12 months.

In this section, an individual needing treatment for an illicit drug use problem is defined as receiving treatment for his or her drug use problem only if he or she reported receiving specialty treatment for drug use in the past year. Thus, an individual who needed treatment for illicit drug use but only received specialty treatment for alcohol use in the past year or who received treatment for illicit drug use only at a facility not classified as a specialty facility was not counted as receiving treatment for drug use. Similarly, an individual who needed treatment for an alcohol use problem was only counted as receiving alcohol use treatment if the treatment was received for alcohol use at a specialty treatment facility. Individuals who reported receiving specialty substance use treatment but were missing information on whether the treatment was specifically for alcohol use or drug use were not counted in estimates of specialty drug use treatment or in estimates of specialty alcohol use treatment; however, they were counted in estimates for "drug or alcohol use" treatment.

In addition to questions about symptoms of substance use problems that are used to classify respondents' need for treatment based on DSM-IV criteria, NSDUH includes questions asking respondents about their perceived need for treatment (i.e., whether they felt they needed treatment or counseling for illicit drug use or alcohol use). In this report, estimates for perceived need for treatment are only discussed for persons who were classified as needing treatment (based on DSM-IV criteria) but did not receive treatment at a specialty facility. Similarly, estimates for whether a person made an effort to get treatment are only discussed for persons who felt the need for treatment.

Illicit Drug or Alcohol Use Treatment and Treatment Need

- In 2008, 23.1 million persons aged 12 or older needed treatment for an illicit drug or alcohol use problem (9.2 percent of the persons aged 12 or older). Of these, 2.3 million (0.9 percent of persons aged 12 or older and 9.9 percent of those who needed treatment) received treatment at a specialty facility. Thus, 20.8 million persons (8.3 percent of the population aged 12 or older) needed treatment for an illicit drug or alcohol use problem but did not receive treatment at a specialty substance abuse facility in the past year. These estimates are similar to the estimates for 2007 and for 2002.
- Of the 2.3 million people aged 12 or older who received specialty substance use treatment in 2008, 983,000 received treatment for alcohol use only, 632,000 received treatment for illicit drug use only, and 577,000 received treatment for both alcohol and illicit drug use. These estimates are similar to the estimates for 2007 and for 2002.
- In 2008, among persons who received their most recent substance use treatment at a specialty facility in the past year, 49.5 percent reported using their "own savings or earnings" as a source of payment for their most recent specialty treatment, 36.1 percent reported using private health insurance, 24.7 percent reported using Medicaid, 22.3 percent reported using public assistance other than Medicaid, 17.5 percent reported using Medicare, and 16.5 percent reported using funds from family members. None of these estimates changed significantly between 2007 and 2008 and between 2002 and 2008. (Note that persons could report more than one source of payment.)
- Of the 20.8 million persons in 2008 who were classified as needing substance use treatment but not receiving treatment at a specialty facility in the past year, 1.0 million persons (4.8 percent) reported that they perceived a need for treatment for their illicit drug or alcohol use problem (Figure 7.10).

Of these 1.0 million persons who felt they needed treatment but did not receive treatment in 2008, 233,000 (23.3 percent) reported that they made an effort to get treatment, and 766,000 (76.7 percent) reported making no effort to get treatment. These estimates remained stable between 2007 and 2008, except that the number of persons who felt they needed treatment, made an effort to get treatment, but did not receive treatment in 2008 decreased from 380,000 persons in 2007 to 233,000 persons in 2008, and the percentage of persons who felt they needed treatment among those who were classified as needing substance use treatment declined from 6.4 percent in 2007 to 4.8 percent in 2008.

Figure 7.10 Past Year Perceived Need for and Effort Made to Receive Specialty Treatment Among Persons Aged 12 or Older Needing But Not Receiving Treatment for Illicit Drug or Alcohol Use: 2008

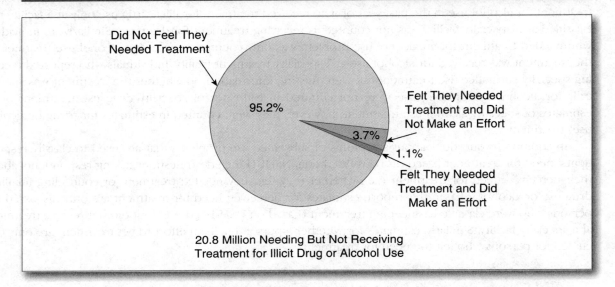

- The number and the percentage of youths aged 12 to 17 who needed treatment for an illicit drug or alcohol use problem remained unchanged between 2007 (2.0 million, 7.9 percent) and 2008 (1.9 million, 7.8 percent); however, there was a significant decrease between 2002 (2.3 million, 9.1 percent) and 2008. Of the 1.9 million youths who needed treatment in 2008, 143,000 received treatment at a specialty facility (about 7.4 percent of the youths who needed treatment), leaving 1.8 million who needed treatment for a substance use problem but did not receive it at a specialty facility.
- Based on 2005-2008 combined data, the five most often reported reasons for not receiving illicit drug or alcohol use treatment among persons aged 12 or older who needed but did not receive treatment at a specialty facility and perceived a need for treatment included (a) not ready to stop using (38.8 percent), (b) no health coverage and could not afford cost (32.1 percent), (c) possible negative effect on job (12.3 percent), (d) not knowing where to go for treatment (12.0 percent), and (e) concern that receiving treatment might cause neighbors/community to have negative opinion (11.8 percent).
- Based on 2005-2008 combined data, among persons aged 12 or older who needed but did not receive illicit drug or alcohol use treatment, felt a need for treatment, and made an effort to receive treatment, the most often reported reasons for not receiving treatment were (a) no health coverage and could not afford cost (37.4 percent), (b) not ready to stop using (29.3 percent), (c) able to handle the problem without treatment (13.0 percent), (d) no transportation/inconvenient (10.6 percent), (e) no program having type of treatment (8.3 percent), (f) did not feel need for treatment at the time (8.2 percent), (g) did not know where to go for treatment (8.1 percent), (h) might cause neighbors/community to have negative opinion (7.7 percent), and (i) might have negative effect on job (7.4 percent) (Figure 7.11).

Figure 7.11   Reasons for Not Receiving Substance Use Treatment Among Persons Aged 12 or Older Who Needed and Made an Effort to Get Treatment But Did Not Receive Treatment and Felt They Needed Treatment: 2005–2008 Combined

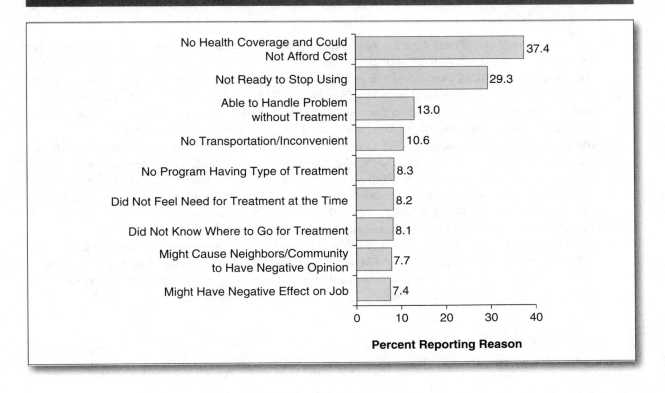

Illicit Drug Use Treatment and Treatment Need

- In 2008, the number of persons aged 12 or older needing treatment for an illicit drug use problem was 7.6 million (3.0 percent of the total population). Of these, 1.2 million (0.5 percent of the total population and 16.0 percent of the persons who needed treatment) received treatment at a specialty facility for an illicit drug use problem in the past year. Thus, there were 6.4 million persons (2.5 percent of the total population) who needed but did not receive treatment at a specialty facility for an illicit drug use problem in 2008. None of these estimates changed significantly between 2007 and 2008. The percentage of persons needing treatment for an illicit drug use problem decreased between 2002 (3.3 percent) and 2008 (3.0 percent).

- Of the 6.4 million people aged 12 or older who needed but did not receive specialty treatment for illicit drug use in 2008, 400,000 (6.3 percent) reported that they perceived a need for treatment for their illicit drug use problem. Of the 400,000 persons who felt a need for treatment in 2008, 99,000 (24.7 percent) reported that they made an effort (the number and percentage decreased from 205,000 persons and 37.5 percent in 2007), and 301,000 (75.3 percent) reported making no effort to get treatment (the number and percentage remained similar to those reported in 2007).

- Among youths aged 12 to 17, there were 1.2 million (4.8 percent) who needed treatment for an illicit drug use problem in 2008. Of this group, only 111,000 received treatment at a specialty facility (9.3 percent of youths aged 12 to 17 who needed treatment), leaving 1.1 million youths who needed treatment but did not receive it at a specialty facility.

- Among people aged 12 or older who needed but did not receive illicit drug use treatment and felt they needed treatment (based on 2005-2008 combined data), the most often reported reasons for not receiving treatment were (a) no health coverage and could not afford cost (37.2 percent), (b) not ready to stop using (29.5 percent), (c) concern that receiving treatment might cause neighbors/

community to have negative opinion (15.4 percent), (d) not knowing where to go for treatment (15.3 percent), (e) possible negative effect on job (13.0 percent), and (f) being able to handle the problem without treatment (12.0 percent).

Alcohol Use Treatment and Treatment Need

- In 2008, the number of persons aged 12 or older needing treatment for an alcohol use problem was 19.0 million (7.6 percent of the population aged 12 or older). Of these, 1.6 million (0.6 percent of the total population and 8.2 percent of the people who needed treatment for an alcohol use problem) received alcohol use treatment at a specialty facility. Thus, there were 17.4 million people who needed but did not receive treatment at a specialty facility for an alcohol use problem. None of these estimates changed significantly between 2007 and 2008 and between 2002 and 2008.
- Among the 17.4 million people aged 12 or older who needed but did not receive treatment for an alcohol use problem in 2008, there were 651,000 (3.7 percent) who felt they needed treatment for their alcohol use problem. The number and the percentage were similar to those reported in 2007 (859,000 persons and 4.8 percent, respectively) and 2002 (761,000 persons and 4.5 percent, respectively). Of these, 512,000 (78.6 percent) did not make an effort to get treatment, and 139,000 (21.4 percent) made an effort but were unable to get treatment in 2008.
- In 2008, there were 1.2 million youths (5.0 percent) aged 12 to 17 who needed treatment for an alcohol use problem. Of this group, only 77,000 received treatment at a specialty facility (0.3 percent of all youths and 6.2 percent of youths who needed treatment), leaving almost 1.2 million youths who needed but did not receive treatment.

8. Mental Health

This chapter presents findings on mental health problems in the United States, including the prevalence of serious mental illness (SMI), serious psychological distress (SPD), suicidal thoughts and behavior, and major depressive episode (MDE). The association of these problems with substance use and substance dependence or abuse (i.e., substance use disorder) is discussed. Also reported here are the rates of treatment for depression (among those with MDE) in the past year among adults aged 18 or older and youths aged 12 to 17, the percentages of adults and youths who received mental health care in the past year, and the percentage of adults who had an unmet need for mental health care in the past year.

Serious Mental Illness

Public Law No. 102-321, the Alcohol, Drug Abuse, and Mental Health Administration Reorganization Act of 1992, established a block grant for U.S. States to fund community mental health services for adults with SMI. The law required States to include prevalence estimates in their annual applications for block grant funds. This legislation also required the Substance Abuse and Mental Health Services Administration (SAMHSA) to develop an operational definition of SMI. SAMHSA defined SMI as persons aged 18 or older who currently or at any time in the past year have had diagnosable mental, behavioral, or emotional disorder (excluding developmental and substance use disorders) of sufficient duration to meet diagnostic criteria specified within the 4th edition of the Diagnostic and Statistical Manual of Mental Disorders (DSM-IV) (American Psychiatric Association [APA], 1994) that has resulted in serious functional impairment, which substantially interferes with or limits one or more major life activities.

To establish the means to generate estimates of SMI in the United States, SAMHSA conducted a methodological study—the Mental Health Surveillance Study (MHSS)—to calibrate mental health questionnaire items in the National Survey on Drug Use and Health (NSDUH) with a "gold standard" clinical psychiatric interview and assessment of functioning. A split-sample design was used to administer the 12-month K6 distress scale and either an abbreviated World Health Organization Disability Assessment Schedule (WHODAS) or the Sheehan Disability Scale (SDS) to each respondent aged 18 or older. A subsample of 1,502 adults selected from the main study participated in the calibration study by agreeing to undergo additional mental health assessment via a telephone interview. An analysis was conducted to determine the statistical models (using K6 plus WHODAS items or K6 plus SDS) that accurately predict SMI status as determined by the clinical interview and assessment of function. The analyses found that the WHODAS impairment measure performed slightly better than the SDS, so the WHODAS has been retained as the only impairment scale in the survey instrument for 2009 going forward. A description of the MHSS design and results may be found in Section B.4.6 in Appendix B.

Serious Psychological Distress

As a direct outcome of the MHSS, this report focuses on a past 30 day indicator of SPD rather than a past year reference period as has been reported in previous national findings reports. SPD is defined as having a score of 13 or higher on the 30-day K6 scale. Based on responses about symptoms (on the K6) in the past 30 days, this measure of SPD now more closely corresponds with SPD reference periods reported in other surveys, such as the National Health Interview Survey (NHIS) and the Behavioral Risk Factor Surveillance System (BRFSS). Although the differing modes and contexts of the other surveys prevent direct comparisons of SPD prevalence, there is utility in examining health and behavior correlates of SPD within each survey. Further description of the SPD measure may be found in Section B.4.5 in Appendix B.

Suicidal Thoughts and Behavior

Responding to a need for national data on the prevalence of suicidal thoughts and behavior, a brief module was added to the 2008 NSDUH questionnaire. Suicidality data have been (and continue to be) collected within the context of the MDE module; however, that approach did not capture respondents who screened out of the depression module before they were asked about suicide and did not specifically assess suicidal thoughts and behaviors in the past 12 months. The current module asks all adult respondents if they had serious thoughts of suicide, and if they had thoughts of suicide, whether they made suicide plans or attempts in the past year and further, if an attempt was made, whether the respondent received medical attention or hospitalization as a result of attempted suicide.

Major Depressive Episode (Depression)

A module of questions designed to obtain measures of lifetime and past year prevalence of MDE, the level of functional impairment caused by MDE in the past year, and treatment for depression has been administered to adults aged 18 or older and youths aged 12 to 17 since 2004. Some questions in the adolescent depression module differ slightly from the adult depression module to make them more appropriate for youths. Given these differences, adult and youth depression estimates are presented separately in this chapter.

MDE is defined as a period of at least 2 weeks when a person experienced a depressed mood or loss of interest or pleasure in daily activities and had at least four of seven additional symptoms reflecting the criteria as described in the DSM-IV. It should be noted that unlike the DSM-IV criteria for MDE, no exclusions were made in NSDUH for depressive symptoms caused by medical illness, bereavement, or substance use disorders. Impairment is defined by the level of role interference reported to be caused by MDE in the past 12 months. For adults aged 18 or older, the SDS role domains are (1) home management, (2) work, (3) close relationships with others, and (4) social life. The role domains are assessed on a 0 to 10 scale with impairment categories of "none" (0), "mild" (1-3), "moderate" (4-6), "severe" (7-9), and "very severe" (10). The role domains for youths aged 12 to 17 are slightly modified to be made age appropriate, but are assessed on the same 0 to 10 scale described for adults. The specific questions used to measure MDE and role impairment and the scoring algorithm for these responses are included in Section B.4.7 in Appendix B.

One consequence of the MHSS is that the measures inserted to accommodate it (i.e., the past 30 day K6 scale, the functional impairment scale[s], and the suicidal thoughts and behavior items) are suspected of having some impact on respondents' reporting of symptoms in the adult MDE module. As a result, direct comparison with previous years of data is compromised, requiring that a new MDE trend begin with the 2008 data. To facilitate comparison with the 2009 MDE estimates, only data from the sample of respondents receiving the WHODAS items are presented in this report.

Comparing the Measures

Although the populations classified with SMI, MDE, and SPD substantially overlap, the definitions used for the three measures differ distinctly. Meeting the criteria for SMI indicates that a respondent endorsed having symptoms and related functional impairment at a level that is predictive of having a clinically significant mental disorder and functional impairment as measured by a "gold standard" clinical interview. Meeting the criteria for past year MDE indicates that a respondent had the specific physical and emotional symptom profile indicative of MDE for 2 weeks or more in the past 12 months as described in the DSM-IV. (MDE is known to be a fairly common disorder that often includes significant impairment in a person's functioning at work, at home, and in his or her social life.) Meeting the criteria for past 30 day SPD indicates a respondent recently experienced heightened distress symptomatology that may be affecting health and behavior. This distress may be part of a chronic psychological disturbance (even SMI) or may represent a temporary disturbance (e.g., in reaction to an acute stressor) that could subside after a brief period of adjustment.

Mental Health Service Utilization

This chapter also presents data on mental health care among adults aged 18 or older and youths aged 12 to 17. Initiated in 2000, the mental health service utilization modules are asked of respondents regardless of SMI, MDE, or SPD status. In the adult module, respondents are asked whether they received treatment or counseling for any problem with emotions, "nerves," or mental health in the past year in any inpatient or outpatient setting or used prescription medication for a mental or emotional condition. The treatment questions in this module are generic in that they do not ask specifically about treatment for a particular disorder, as do the questions in the MDE module. Consequently, references to treatment or counseling for any problem with emotions, nerves, or mental health are described broadly as "mental health service use" or receiving/needing "mental health care." Of note, it is possible for a respondent to have indicated receipt of treatment for depression without having indicated that he or she received services for any problems with emotions, nerves, or mental health.

In NSDUH, questions designed to assess mental health service utilization asked of youths differ from those asked of adults. Youths aged 12 to 17 are asked whether they received any treatment or counseling within the 12 months prior to the interview for problems with behavior or emotions in the specialty mental health setting (outpatient or inpatient care), the general medical setting (pediatrician or family physician care for emotional or behavior problems), or the education setting (talked with a counselor, psychologist, or teacher; or received special education services while in a regular classroom; or placed in a special classroom, special program, or special school). Youths also are asked for the number of nights spent in overnight facilities, the number of visits they had to outpatient mental health providers, and the reason(s) for the most recent stay or visit. Both the youth and the adult mental health questions specifically exclude treatment for problems with substance use because substance use treatment is assessed in other interview modules.

Estimates of unmet need for mental health care are reported for adults. Unmet need is established using a question that asks whether a respondent perceived a need for, but did not receive mental health treatment or counseling at any time in the 12 months prior to the NSDUH interview. This measure also includes persons who received some type of mental health service in the past 12 months, but reported a perceived need for additional services they did not receive.

It is important to note that because the survey covers the U.S. civilian, noninstitutionalized population, persons residing in long-term psychiatric or other institutions continuously throughout the year were not included in the NSDUH sampling frame. Persons who were hospitalized or institutionalized for a period of time during 2008, but who resided in households during the rest of the year, were included in the sample.

8.1. Adults Aged 18 or Older

Prevalence of Serious Mental Illness Among Adults

- In 2008, there were an estimated 9.8 million adults aged 18 or older in the United States with SMI in the past year. This represents 4.4 percent of all adults in this country (Figure 8.1).

Figure 8.1   Serious Mental Illness in the Past Year Among Adults Aged 18 or Older, by Age and Gender: 2008

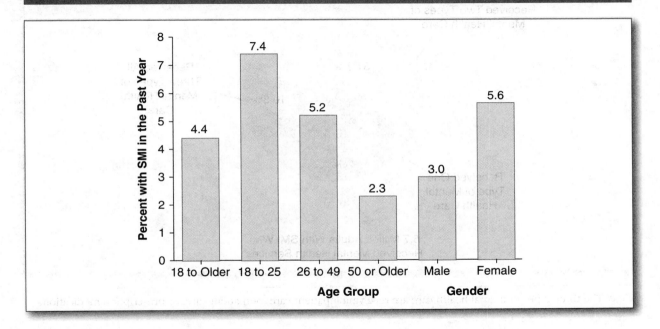

- Rates of SMI in 2008 were highest for adults aged 18 to 25 (7.4 percent) and lowest for adults aged 50 or older (2.3 percent).
- The prevalence of SMI in 2008 among women aged 18 or older (5.6 percent) was significantly higher than among men in that age group (3.0 percent).
- In 2008, the rate of past year SMI was lowest among Asians (2.9 percent) and blacks (3.5 percent). Rates for other racial/ethnic groups were 4.0 percent among Hispanics, 4.2 percent among American Indians or Alaska Natives, 4.7 percent among whites, and 5.6 percent among persons reporting two or more races. Estimates of SMI among Native Hawaiians or Other Pacific Islanders could not be reported due to low precision.
- The rate of SMI in 2008 was higher among adults who were unemployed (8.0 percent) than those who were employed full time (3.5 percent) or part time (4.8 percent).

Mental Health Service Use Among Adults With Serious Mental Illness

- Among the 9.8 million adults aged 18 or older with SMI in 2008, 5.7 million (58.7 percent) used mental health services in the past year. Service use was higher among adults with SMI who were aged 50 or older (70.9 percent) and aged 26 to 49 (62.2 percent) than among adults aged 18 to 25 (40.4 percent).

- Among all adults aged 18 or older with SMI, 52.6 percent received prescription medication, 40.5 percent received outpatient services, and 7.5 percent received inpatient services for a mental health problem in the past year. Respondents could report more than one type of service used.
- Among adults aged 18 or older with SMI who reported receiving mental health services in the past year, 38.5 percent received one type of care (inpatient, outpatient, or prescription medication), 51.2 percent received two types of care, and 10.3 percent received all three types of care (Figure 8.2).

Figure 8.2   Number of Types of Mental Health Services Received in the Past Year Among Persons Aged 18 or Older With Past Year Serious Mental Illness Who Received Mental Health Services in the Past Year: 2008

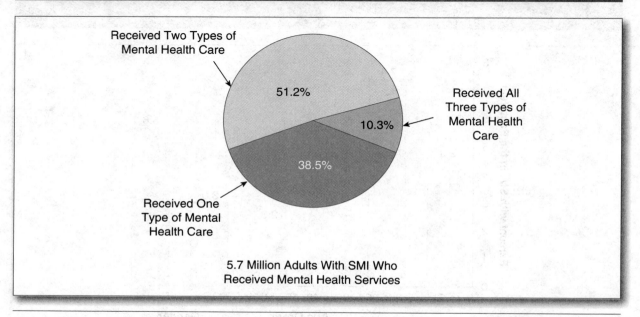

Received Two Types of Mental Health Care

51.2%

Received All Three Types of Mental Health Care

10.3%

38.5%

Received One Type of Mental Health Care

5.7 Million Adults With SMI Who Received Mental Health Services

Note: The three types of mental health care are receiving inpatient care, outpatient care, or prescription medication.

Serious Mental Illness and Substance Use and Dependence or Abuse Among Adults

- Past year illicit drug use in 2008 was higher among adults aged 18 or older with past year SMI (30.3 percent) than among adults without SMI (12.9 percent). Similarly, the rate of past year cigarette use was higher among adults with SMI (50.5 percent) than among adults without SMI (28.5 percent).
- Among adults aged 18 or older with past year SMI in 2008, the rate of binge alcohol use (drinking five or more drinks on the same occasion [i.e., at the same time or within a couple of hours of each other] on at least 1 day in the past 30 days) was 29.4 percent, which was higher than the 24.6 percent among adults who did not meet the criteria for SMI. Similarly, the rate of heavy alcohol use (drinking five or more drinks on the same occasion on each of 5 or more days in the past 30 days) among adults with SMI in the past year (11.6 percent) was higher than the rate reported among adults without SMI in the past year (7.3 percent).
- SMI in the past year was associated with past year substance dependence or abuse in 2008. Among adults aged 18 or older with SMI, 25.2 percent (2.5 million) were dependent on or abused illicit drugs or alcohol. The rate among adults without SMI was 8.3 percent (17.9 million).

Mental Health Care Among Adults With Co-Occurring Serious Mental Illness and Substance Use Disorders

- Among the 2.5 million adults aged 18 or older with both SMI and substance dependence or abuse (i.e., a substance use disorder) in 2008, 60.5 percent received mental health care or substance use treatment at a specialty facility; 11.4 percent received both mental health care and specialty substance use treatment, 45.2 percent received only mental health care, and 3.7 percent received only specialty substance use treatment (Figure 8.3).

Figure 8.3   Past Year Mental Health Care and Treatment for Substance Use Problems Among Adults Aged 18 or Older With Both Serious Mental Illness and a Substance Use Disorder: 2008

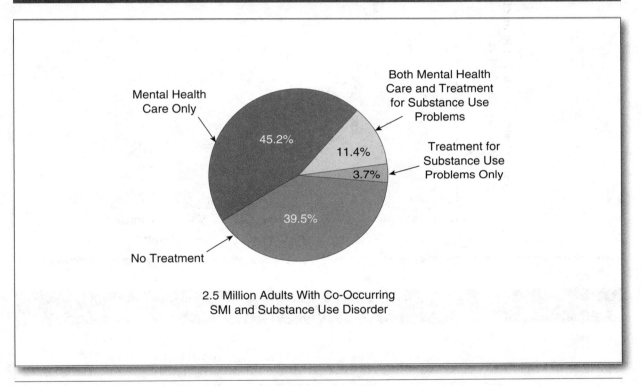

Note: The percentages add to less than 100 percent because of rounding.

Note: Mental health care is defined as having received inpatient care or outpatient care or having used prescription medication for problems with emotions, nerves, or mental health. Treatment for substance use problems refers to treatment at a hospital (inpatient), rehabilitation facility (inpatient or outpatient), or mental health center in order to reduce or stop drug or alcohol use, or for medical problems associated with drug or alcohol use.

Prevalence of Suicidal Thoughts and Behavior Among Adults

- In 2008, an estimated 8.3 million adults (3.7 percent) aged 18 or older had serious thoughts of suicide in the past year (Figure 8.4). The rate was 3.9 percent among women and 3.4 percent among men. Rates of serious thoughts of suicide were highest among young adults aged 18 to 25 (6.7 percent) compared with adults aged 26 to 49 (3.9 percent) and adults aged 50 or older (2.3 percent).
- Among adults 18 or older, 2.3 million (1.0 percent) made suicide plans in the past year (Figure 8.5). The rate was 1.1 percent among women and 0.9 percent among men. Rates of adults who made suicide plans were also highest among 18 to 25 year olds (1.9 percent), followed by 26 to 49 year olds (1.1 percent) and adults 50 years or older (0.7 percent).

• In 2008, 1.1 million adults (0.5 percent) aged 18 or older attempted suicide (Figure 8.5). Among those 1.1 million adults who attempted suicide, 0.9 million reported having made plans for suicide, while 0.2 million had not made suicide plans. Among adults, 678,000 (0.3 percent) received medical attention for their suicide attempt, and 500,000 (0.2 percent) stayed overnight or longer in a hospital as a result of their suicide attempt in the past year.

Figure 8.4   Suicidal Thoughts in the Past Year Among Adults Aged 18 or Older, by Age and Gender: 2008

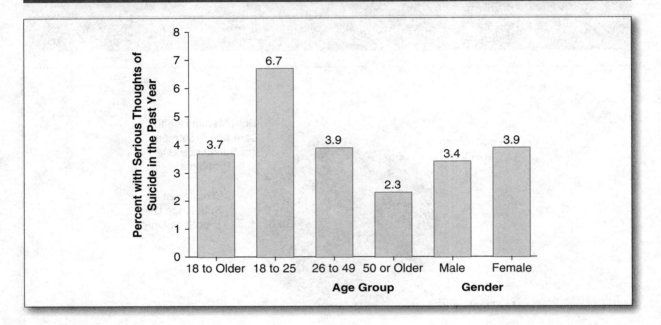

Figure 8.5   Suicidal Thoughts and Behavior in the Past Year Among Adults Aged 18 or Older: 2008

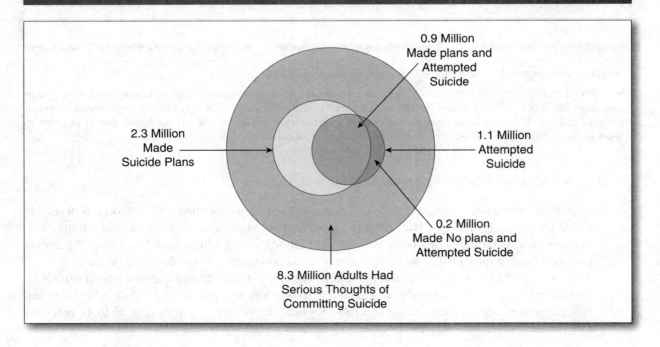

Prevalence of Major Depressive Episode Among Adults

- In 2008, 6.4 percent of adults aged 18 or older (14.3 million people) had at least one MDE in the past year (Figure 8.6). Over 1 in 25 adults (4.2 percent or 9.5 million people) had past year MDE with severe impairment.

Figure 8.6   Major Depressive Episode in the Past Year Among Adults Aged 18 or Older, by Severe Impairment, Age, and Gender: 2008

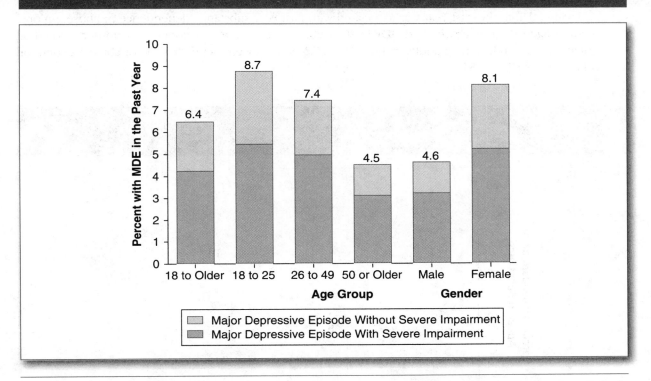

Note: Respondents with an unknown level of impairment were included in the estimates for Major Depressive Episode Without Severe Impairment.

- The past year prevalence of MDE in 2008 was lower for those aged 50 or older (4.5 percent) compared with rates among persons aged 18 to 25 (8.7 percent) and those aged 26 to 49 (7.4 percent).
- The past year prevalence of MDE was higher among adult females than among adult males (8.1 vs. 4.6 percent). Among women, past year MDE rates were higher in the younger age groups (12.1 percent for 18 to 25 year olds, 8.8 percent for 26 to 49 year olds) compared with those 50 or older (6.0 percent).
- Among adults aged 18 or older, past year prevalence of MDE varied by race/ethnicity in 2008. The rate of MDE was highest among persons reporting two or more races (12.7 percent), while rates for single race groups were 7.0 percent among whites, 5.2 percent among Hispanics, 4.9 percent among American Indians or Alaska Natives, 4.9 percent among blacks, and 3.6 percent among Asians. Estimates of past year MDE among Native Hawaiians or Other Pacific Islanders could not be reported due to low precision.
- Among adults aged 18 or older in 2008, past year prevalence of MDE with severe impairment was higher among unemployed persons (6.6 percent) than among persons employed full time (3.2 percent). Past year prevalence of MDE was 4.8 percent among persons employed part time and 5.7 percent among persons retired or otherwise not in the labor force.

Major Depressive Episode and Substance Use and Dependence or Abuse Among Adults

- In 2008, adults aged 18 or older with past year MDE had higher rates of past year illicit drug use than those without MDE (27.2 vs. 13.0 percent). A similar pattern was observed for specific types of past year illicit drug use, such as the use of marijuana, cocaine, heroin, or hallucinogens and the non-medical use of prescription-type psychotherapeutics.

- Among adults aged 18 or older with MDE in the past year, 9.6 percent were heavy alcohol users in the past month, higher than the 7.1 percent of heavy alcohol users without MDE in the past year. Similarly, among adults with past year MDE, the rate of daily cigarette use in the past month was 29.1 percent, while the rate was 15.2 percent among adults without past year MDE.

- Having MDE in the past year was associated with past year substance dependence or abuse. Among adults aged 18 or older who had MDE in 2008, 20.3 percent were dependent on or abused alcohol or illicit drugs, while among adults without MDE, 7.8 percent were dependent on or abused alcohol or illicit drugs (Figure 8.7).

Figure 8.7 Substance Dependence or Abuse Among Adults Aged 18 or Older, by Major Depressive Episode in the Past Year: 2008

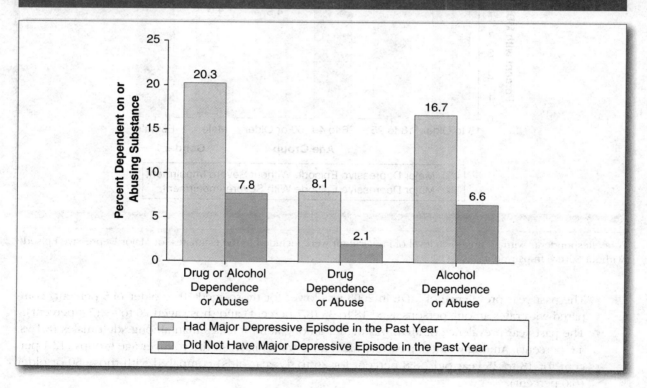

Treatment for Major Depressive Episode Among Adults

- Among adults aged 18 or older who had past year MDE in 2008, 71.0 percent received treatment (i.e., saw or talked to a medical doctor or other professional or used prescription medication) for depression in the same time period. The past year MDE treatment rate was highest among persons aged 50 or older (86.3 percent), followed by adults aged 26 to 49 (72.6 percent) and adults aged 18 to 25 (44.7 percent). Of all adults aged 18 or older who had past year MDE with severe impairment in 2008, 75.0 percent received treatment.

- In 2008, women aged 18 or older who had MDE in the past year were more likely than their male counterparts to have received treatment for depression in the past year (74.2 vs. 65.0 percent).
- Among adults aged 18 or older with past year MDE in 2008, about two thirds of those with no insurance (64.1 percent) and private insurance (69.8 percent) received treatment for depression in the past year compared with higher rates for those with Medicaid or CHIP (83.1 percent) and 83.5 percent of adults with other health insurance (including Medicare, CHAMPUS, TRICARE, CHAMPVA, VA, and other sources of health care or insurance).

Prevalence of Past 30 Day Serious Psychological Distress Among Adults

- In 2008, there were an estimated 10.2 million adults aged 18 or older in the United States with SPD in the past month. This represents 4.5 percent of all U.S. adults.
- Rates of SPD were highest for adults aged 18 to 25 (7.5 percent) and lowest for adults aged 50 or older (2.9 percent).
- In 2008, rates of past 30 day SPD were higher among unemployed adults (10.2 percent) than among adults employed full time (3.3 percent), part time (4.4 percent), or other persons not in the labor force (6.1 percent).

Serious Psychological Distress and Substance Use Among Adults

- Past 30 day illicit drug use in 2008 was higher among adults aged 18 or older with SPD (19.6 percent) than among adults without SPD (7.3 percent). Past 30 day use of illicit drugs other than marijuana in 2008 was higher among adults with SPD (12.3 percent) than among adults without SPD (2.9 percent).
- Among adults aged 18 or older with past month SPD in 2008, the rate of binge alcohol use (drinking five or more drinks on the same occasion [i.e., at the same time or within a couple of hours of each other] on at least 1 day in the past 30 days) was 30.9 percent, which was higher than the 24.6 percent rate among adults who did not meet the criteria for SPD. The rate of heavy alcohol use (drinking five or more drinks on the same occasion on each of 5 or more days in the past 30 days) among adults with SPD in the past month was higher (12.1 percent) than the rate reported among adults without SPD in the past month (7.3 percent). Similarly, the rate of past month use of cigarettes was higher among adults with SPD (47.6 percent) than among adults without SPD (24.5 percent).

Mental Health Service Use and Unmet Need for Mental Health Care Among Adults

- In 2008, 30 million adults (13.4 percent of the population 18 years or older) received mental health services during the past 12 months (Figure 8.8). This was similar to the rate in 2007 (13.2 percent).
- In 2008, the type of mental health services most often received by adults aged 18 or older was prescription medication (11.3 percent), followed by outpatient services (6.8 percent). Rates of prescription medication and outpatient service use in 2008 were similar to the rates in 2007 (11.1 and 6.9 percent, respectively). Note that respondents could report receiving more than one type of mental health care. Between 2002 and 2008, the percentage of adults receiving outpatient services declined from 7.4 to 6.8 percent, while the percentage receiving prescription medication increased from 10.5 to 11.3 percent.
- About 2.0 million adults (0.9 percent of the population aged 18 years or older) received inpatient care for mental health problems during the past year. This estimate was similar to the rate reported in 2007 (1.0 percent or 2.1 million adults).

Figure 8.8 Past Year Mental Health Service Use Among Adults Aged 18 or Older, by Type of Care: 2002–2008

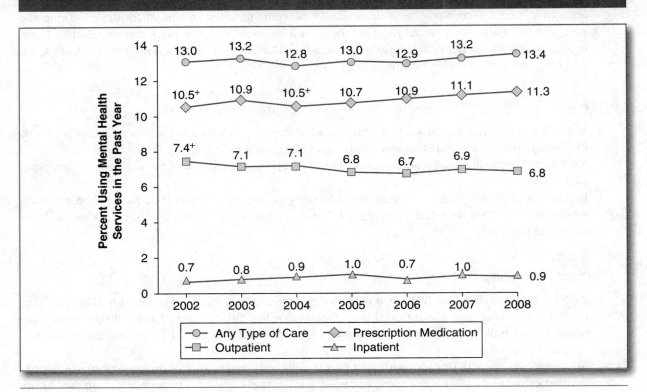

+Difference between this estimate and the 2008 estimate is statistically significant at the .05 level.

- Rates of mental health service use varied by age for adults aged 18 or older. Adults aged 18 to 25 had a lower rate of mental health service use (10.8 percent) than both adults aged 26 to 49 (14.0 percent) and adults aged 50 or older (13.6 percent).

- Men were less likely than women to receive outpatient mental health services (5.0 vs. 8.5 percent) and prescription medication (7.5 vs. 14.8 percent) for mental health problems in the past year.

- Among racial/ethnic groups, the rates of mental health service use for adults aged 18 or older in 2008 were 18.8 percent for persons reporting two or more races, 16.0 percent for whites, 13.2 percent for American Indians or Alaska Natives, 8.7 percent for blacks (up from 6.8 percent in 2007), 6.8 percent for Hispanics, and 4.5 percent for Asians. Estimates of mental health service use among Native Hawaiians or Other Pacific Islanders could not be reported due to low precision.

- In 2008, there were 10.6 million adults aged 18 or older (4.7 percent) who reported an unmet need for mental health care in the past year. This included 5.1 million adults who did not receive any mental health services in the past year. Among adults who did receive some type of mental health service in the past year, 17.9 percent (5.4 million) reported an unmet need for mental health care. (Unmet need among adults who received mental health services may reflect a delay in care or a perception of insufficient care.)

- Among the 5.1 million adults who reported an unmet need for mental health care and did not receive mental health services in the past year, several barriers to care were reported. These included an inability to afford care (42.7 percent), believing at the time that the problem could be handled without care (28.6 percent), not knowing where to go for care (19.8 percent), and not having the time to go for care (13.9 percent) (Figure 8.9).

Figure 8.9   Reasons for Not Receiving Mental Health Services in the Past Year Among Adults Aged 18 or Older With an Unmet Need for Mental Health Care Who Did Not Receive Mental Health Services: 2008

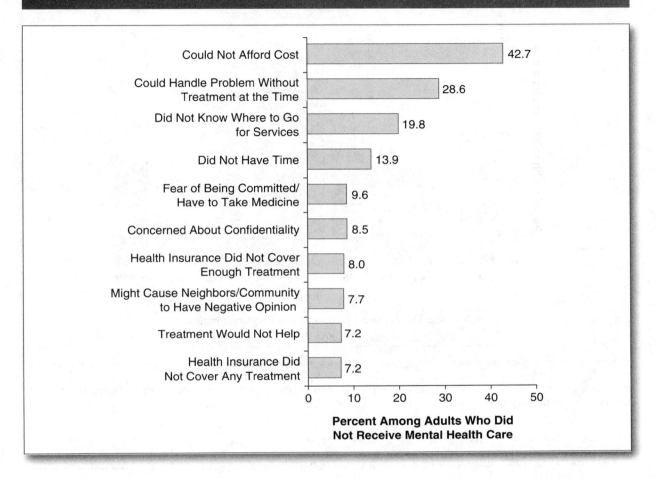

8.2. Youths Aged 12 to 17

Prevalence of Major Depressive Episode Among Youths

- In 2008, there were 2.0 million youths (8.3 percent of the population aged 12 to 17) who had major depressive episode (MDE) during the past year. An estimated 1.5 million (6.0 percent) had MDE with severe impairment in one or more role domains (chores at home; school or work; close relationships with family; or social life).
- Among youths aged 12 to 17 in 2008, the past year prevalence of MDE ranged from 3.9 percent among 12 year olds to 11.6 percent among those aged 16 and 10.6 percent among those aged 17 (Figure 8.10). Similarly, rates of past year MDE with severe impairment ranged from 2.5 percent among 12 years olds to 8.8 percent among 16 year olds and 7.9 percent among 17 year olds.
- Among youths aged 12 to 17 in 2008, the prevalence rates of MDE and MDE with severe impairment among females were higher than those of their male counterparts. Female youths had an MDE prevalence rate of 12.4 percent in 2008, almost 3 times the rate for males in the same age range (4.3 percent). The prevalence of MDE with severe impairment was 9.2 percent for females, which was over 3 times the rate for males (2.9 percent).

Figure 8.10   Major Depressive Episode in the Past Year Among Youths Aged 12 to 17, by Severe
Impairment, Age, and Gender: 2008

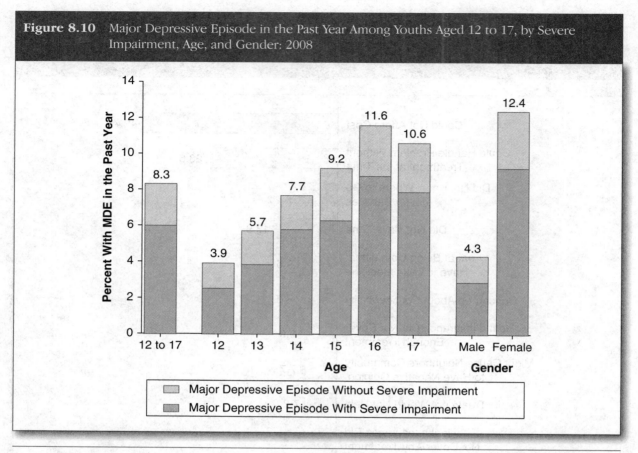

Note: Respondents with an unknown level of impairment were included in the estimates for Major Depressive Episode Without Severe Impairment.

Major Depressive Episode and Substance Use Among Youths

- Among 12 to 17 year olds who had past year MDE in 2008, 37.4 percent had used illicit drugs during the same period (Figure 8.11), which was higher than the rate of 17.2 percent among youths who did not have past year MDE. This pattern was similar for most specific types of illicit drug use, including the use of marijuana, cocaine, hallucinogens, or inhalants and the nonmedical use of prescription-type psychotherapeutics.

- In 2008, youths aged 12 to 17 who had MDE during the past year were more likely to report daily cigarette use in comparison with those who did not have MDE during the past year (3.6 vs. 1.8 percent). Similarly, youths who had past year MDE were more likely to report heavy use of alcohol than those who did not have MDE (3.4 vs. 1.8 percent).

- The occurrence of MDE in the past year among youths aged 12 to 17 was associated with a higher prevalence of illicit drug or alcohol dependence or abuse (21.3 percent). Among youths who did not report past year MDE, 6.4 percent had illicit drug or alcohol dependence or abuse during the same period.

Treatment for Major Depressive Episode Among Youths

- In 2008, 37.7 percent of youths aged 12 to 17 with past year MDE received treatment for depression (i.e., saw or talked to a medical doctor or other professional or used prescription medication).

- In 2008, among youths with past year MDE, 21.7 percent saw or talked to a medical doctor or other professional only, 2.9 percent used prescription medication only, and 13.1 percent received treatment from both sources for depression in the past year.

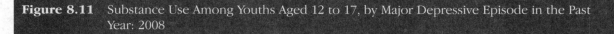

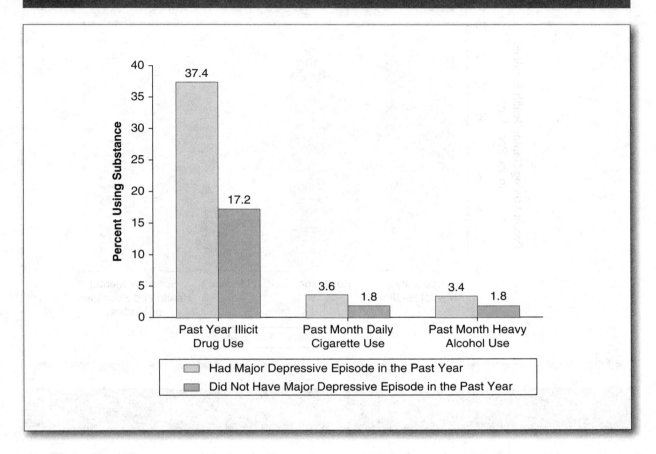

Figure 8.11   Substance Use Among Youths Aged 12 to 17, by Major Depressive Episode in the Past Year: 2008

Mental Health Service Use Among Youths

- In 2008, 3.1 million youths aged 12 to 17 (12.7 percent) received treatment or counseling for problems with behavior or emotions in a specialty mental health setting (inpatient or outpatient care). Additionally, 11.8 percent of youths received services in an education setting, and 2.9 percent received mental health services in a general medical setting in the past 12 months. Mental health services were received in both a specialty setting and either an education or a general medical setting (i.e., care from multiple settings) by 5.3 percent of youths.
- Female youths were more likely than male youths to report using outpatient specialty mental health services (13.6 vs. 9.3 percent), education services (13.0 vs. 10.5 percent), or general medical-based services (3.2 vs. 2.6 percent), but there was no significant gender difference in the use of inpatient specialty mental health services (Figure 8.12).
- Of the 2.8 million youths who received outpatient specialty mental health services in the past 12 months, 18.3 percent reported having 1 visit, 15.8 percent reported having 2 visits, 29.1 percent reported having 3 to 6 visits, 25.1 percent reported having 7 to 24 visits, and 11.8 percent reported having 25 or more visits (Figure 8.13).
- Of the 598,000 youths who received inpatient or residential specialty mental health services in the past 12 months, about one third (36.0 percent) reported staying overnight 1 night, 31.4 percent reported staying 2 to 6 nights, 19.6 percent reported staying 7 to 24 nights, and 13.0 percent reported staying 25 or more nights.

Figure 8.12 Past Year Mental Health Service Use Among Youths Aged 12 to 17, by Gender: 2008

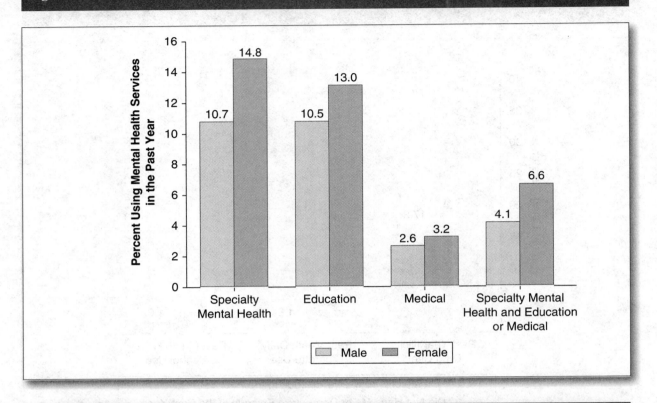

Figure 8.13 Number of Outpatient Visits in the Past Year Among Youths Aged 12 to 17 Who Received Outpatient Specialty Mental Health Services: 2008

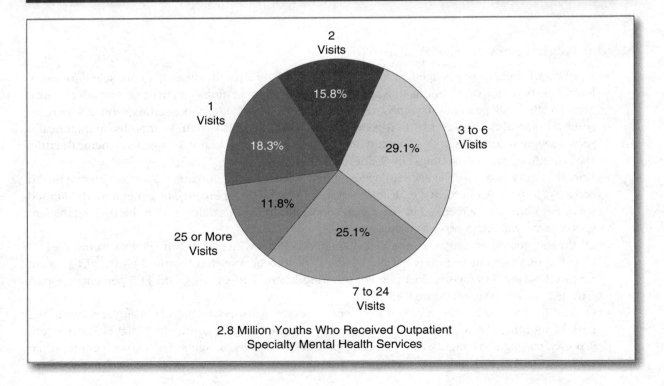

9. Discussion of Trends in Substance Use Among Youths and Young Adults

This report presents findings from the 2008 National Survey on Drug Use and Health (NSDUH). Conducted since 1971 and previously named the National Household Survey on Drug Abuse (NHSDA), the survey underwent several methodological improvements in 2002 that have affected prevalence estimates. As a result, the 2002 through 2008 estimates are not comparable with estimates from 2001 and earlier surveys. Therefore, the primary focus of the report is on comparisons of measures of substance use and mental health problems across subgroups of the U.S. population in 2008, changes between 2007 and 2008, and changes between 2002 and 2008. This chapter provides an additional discussion of the findings concerning a topic of great interest—trends in substance use among youths and young adults.

An important step in the analysis and interpretation of NSDUH or any other survey data is to compare the results with those from other data sources. This can be difficult sometimes because the other surveys typically have different purposes, definitions, and designs. Research has established that surveys of substance use and other sensitive topics often produce inconsistent results because of different methods used. Thus, it is important to understand that conflicting results often reflect differing methodologies, not incorrect results. Despite this limitation, comparisons can be very useful. Consistency across surveys can confirm or support conclusions about trends and patterns of use, and inconsistent results can point to areas for further study. Further discussion of this issue is included in Appendix D, along with descriptions of methods and results from other sources of substance use and mental health data.

Unfortunately, few additional data sources are available at this time to compare with NSDUH results. One established source is Monitoring the Future (MTF), a study sponsored by the National Institute on Drug Abuse (NIDA). MTF surveys students in the 8th, 10th, and 12th grades in classrooms during the spring of each year, and it also collects data by mail from a subsample of adults who had participated earlier in the study as 12th graders (Johnston, O'Malley, Bachman, & Schulenberg, 2008a, 2008b, 2009). Historically, NSDUH rates of substance use among youths have been lower than those of MTF, and occasionally the two surveys have shown different trends over a short time period. Nevertheless, the two sources have shown very similar long-term trends in prevalence. NSDUH and MTF rates of substance use generally have been similar among young adults, and the two sources also have shown similar trends.

A comparison of NSDUH and MTF estimates for 2002 to 2008 is shown in Tables 9.1 and 9.2 at the end of this chapter for several substances that are defined similarly in the two surveys. For comparison purposes, MTF data on 8th and 10th graders are combined to give an age range close to 12 to 17 years, the standard youth age group for NSDUH. Appendix D provides comparisons according to MTF definitions (8th, 10th, and 12th grades). MTF follow-up data on persons aged 19 to 24 provide the closest match on age to estimates for NSDUH young adults aged 18 to 25. The NSDUH results are remarkably consistent with MTF trends for both youths and young adults, as discussed below.

Both surveys generally show decreases between 2002 and 2008 in the percentages of youths who used marijuana, cocaine, Ecstasy, LSD, alcohol, and cigarettes in the lifetime, past year, and past month (Table 9.1). Exceptions were for the past month use of LSD in both NSDUH and MTF data and the past month use of Ecstasy in the NSDUH data. The hallucinogen trends are discussed in more detail below. Both surveys show no decrease in the rates of past year and past month inhalant use among youths between 2002 and 2008, and only NSDUH shows a significant decrease in lifetime use. The consistency between NSDUH and MTF trend data is found not only in terms of the specific drugs showing decreases, but also in terms of the magnitude of the decreases. Despite the higher levels of prevalence estimated from MTF, the two surveys show very similar rates of change in past month prevalence, especially for the three substances used most commonly by youths: alcohol, cigarettes, and marijuana. Between 2002 and 2008, the rate of current alcohol use among youths declined 17 percent according to NSDUH and 19 percent according to MTF, and between 2007 and 2008 the declines were 8 and 9 percent, respectively. Current cigarette use prevalence rates in 2008 were 30 percent lower in NSDUH and 32 percent lower in MTF compared with 2002 rates. For past month marijuana use, the NSDUH decline from 2002 to 2008 was 18 percent, and the MTF decline was 25 percent.

In both surveys, the decline in marijuana use among youths between 2002 and 2008 was driven by decreases early in the 7-year period, while in the most recent years, little change has occurred in the rate of use. Between 2006 and 2008, there was no significant change in rates of lifetime, past year, or past month marijuana use for youths in NSDUH (aged 12 to 17) or MTF (8th and 10th graders).

Data on young adults also show similar trends in the two surveys, although not as consistent as for the youth data (Table 9.2). Potential reasons for differences from the data for youths are the relatively smaller MTF sample size for young adults and possible bias in the MTF sample due to noncoverage of school drop-outs and a low overall response rate, considering nonresponse by schools, by students in the 12th grade survey, and in the follow-up mail survey.

Both surveys show declines between 2002 and 2008 for past year and past month cigarette and mari-juana use among young adults, although the decline in past month marijuana use in NSDUH was not sig-nificant. In addition, the extent of the declines in current cigarette and marijuana use for young adults in NSDUH from 2002 through 2008 were less than the corresponding declines for young adults in MTF. Past month marijuana prevalence among young adults declined 5 percent according to NSDUH and by 13 percent according to MTF. Similarly, the prevalence of past month cigarette use among young adults in NSDUH declined by 13 percent over this period and by 23 percent in MTF. Both surveys show no significant change between 2002 and 2008 in the rate of current alcohol use among young adults. A significant decline in past month cocaine use between 2006 and 2008 is seen in the NSDUH data. The MTF data show a similar drop in use between 2006 and 2008 (although not statistically significant).

Both NSDUH and MTF generally show decreases for both youths and young adults in the past year use of Ecstasy and LSD between 2002 and 2004, then a leveling in 2005. The 2006, 2007, and 2008 data from NSDUH show evidence of a possible resurgence in the use of these two hallucinogens among both youths and young adults. Between 2005 and 2008, there were increases in the use of Ecstasy in the lifetime among youths according to NSDUH (from 1.6 to 2.1 percent) and past year (from 1.0 to 1.4 percent); past month use among youths increased from 0.3 to 0.4 percent between 2007 and 2008. LSD use among youths also increased between 2007 and 2008 in the lifetime (0.8 to 1.1 percent) and in the past year (0.5 to 0.7 percent). Past year Ecstasy and LSD estimates among youths in MTF were higher in 2008 than in 2006, but these dif-ferences were not statistically significant (Figure 9.1). For young adults in NSDUH, past year Ecstasy use increased from 3.1 percent in 2005 to 3.9 percent in 2008, and LSD use increased from 1.0 to 1.5 percent during that same period. No significant changes were observed in the MTF data on past year Ecstasy use for young adults between 2004 and 2008. However, past year LSD use among young adults in MTF in 2008 was significantly greater than in 2004 and 2005.

Data on availability and perceived risk from NSDUH and MTF provide important context for these emerging trends. Both surveys indicate diminishing availability of these drugs in early years of the decade, but a plateau in recent years. In NSDUH, the percentage of youths aged 12 to 17 reporting that LSD is easy to get declined from 19.4 percent in 2002 to 14.0 percent in 2006, but the rate has not changed since then (13.8 percent in 2008). MTF (8th and 10th graders combined) has shown the same trend for per-ceived availability of LSD (21.0 percent in 2002, 15.0 percent in 2006, and 15.1 percent in 2008). Although NSDUH does not ask about availability of Ecstasy, MTF showed similar trends for perceived availability of Ecstasy (31.9 percent in 2002, 21.0 percent in 2006, and 20.4 percent in 2008). Measures of youths' percep-tions of risk in using these hallucinogens declined during the period from 2002 to 2008 in both surveys. Declining perceived risk could lead to more young people initiating use of these drugs and could be con-tributing to the increase from 2005 to 2008 in the number of past year initiates of Ecstasy (from 615,000 to 894,000) and LSD (from 243,000 to 394,000) among persons aged 12 or older.

Another source of data on trends in the use of drugs among youths is the Youth Risk Behavior Survey (YRBS), sponsored by the Centers for Disease Control and Prevention. YRBS surveys students in the 9th through 12th grades in classrooms every other year during the spring (Eaton et al., 2008). The most recent survey was completed in 2007. YRBS has generally shown higher prevalence rates but similar long-term

Figure 9.1 Past Year Ecstasy and LSD Use Among Youths in NSDUH and MTF: 2002–2008

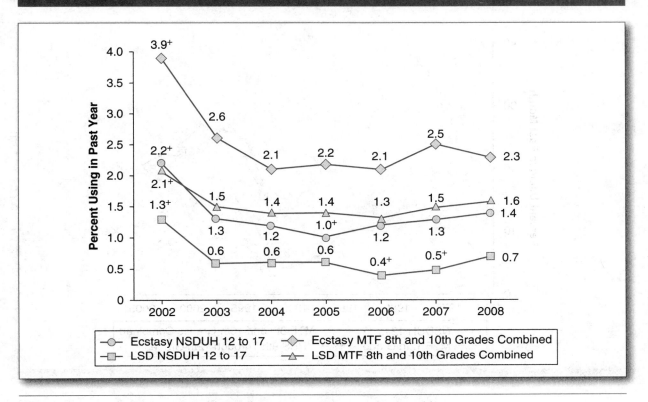

MTF = Monitoring the Future; NSDUH = National Survey on Drug Use and Health.

[+]Difference between this estimate and the 2008 estimate is statistically significant at the .05 level.

trends when compared with NSDUH and MTF. However, comparisons between YRBS and NSDUH or MTF are less straightforward because of the different periodicity (i.e., biennially instead of annually) and ages covered, the limited number of drug use questions, and smaller sample size in the YRBS. For the substances for which information on current use is collected in the YRBS, including alcohol, cigarettes, marijuana, and cocaine, the YRBS trend results between 2001 and 2007 are consistent with NSDUH and MTF (Eaton et al., 2008; Grunbaum et al., 2002). YRBS data for the combined grades 9 through 12 showed no significant change in current alcohol use (47.1 percent in 2001 and 44.7 percent in 2007), but decreases in cigarette use (28.5 percent in 2001, 20.0 percent in 2007), marijuana use (23.9 percent in 2001, 19.7 percent in 2007), and cocaine use (4.2 percent in 2001, 3.3 percent in 2007).

Although changes in NSDUH survey methodology preclude direct comparisons of recent estimates with estimates from before 2002, it is important to put the recent trends in context by reviewing longer term trends in use. NSDUH data (prior to the design changes in 1999 and 2002) on youths aged 12 to 17 and MTF data on high school seniors have shown substantial increases in youth illicit drug use during the 1970s, reaching a peak in the late 1970s. Both surveys then showed significant declines throughout the 1980s until about 1992, when rates reached a low point. These trends were driven by the trend in marijuana use. With the start of annual data collection in NSDUH in 1991, along with the biennial YRBS and the annual 8th and 10th grade samples in MTF, trends among youths are well documented since the low point that occurred in the early 1990s. Although they employ different survey designs and cover different age groups, the three surveys are consistent in showing increasing rates of marijuana use during the early to mid-1990s, reaching a peak in the late 1990s, although not as high as in the late 1970s, followed by declines in use after the turn of the 21st century and a leveling in the most recent years (Figure 9.2).

Figure 9.2   Past Month Marijuana Use Among Youths in NSDUH, MTF, and YRBS: 1971–2008

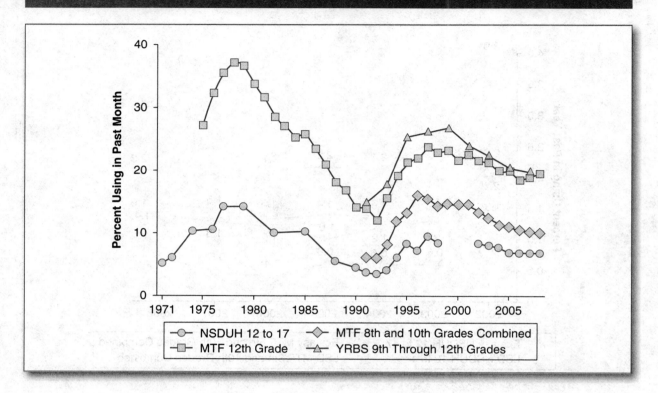

Appendix 43

Drug Categories for Substances of Abuse

To assist you in locating substances in this appendix, the following cross-reference by category is provided.

Narcotics
Alfentanil
Cocaine[a]
Codeine
Crack cocaine[a]
Fentanyl
Heroin
Hydromorphone
Ice
Meperidine
Methadone
Morphine
Nalorphine
Opium
Oxycodone
Propoxyphene

Depressants
Amobarbital
Benzodiazepine
Chloral hydrate
Chlordiazepoxide
Diazepam
Glutethimide
Meprobamate
Methaqualone
Nitrous Oxide
Pentobarbital
Phenobarbital
Secobarbital

Stimulants
Amphetamine
Benzedrine
Benzphetamine
Butyl nitrite
Dextroamphetamine
Methamphetamine
Methylphenidate
Phenmetrazine

Hallucinogens
Bufotenine
LSD
MDA
MDEA
MDMA
Mescaline
MMDA
Phencyclidine
Psilocybin

Cannabis
Lorazepam
Marijuana
Tetrahydrocannabinol

Alcohol
Ethyl alcohol
Steroids
Dianabol
Nandrolone

Source: U.S. Department of Labor. (1994). *America in jeopardy: The young employee and drugs in the workplace.* Washington, DC: U.S. Department of Labor, Office of the Assistant Secretary for Policy.

597

a. Cocaine, although classified under the Controlled Substances Act as a narcotic, also is discussed as a stimulant.

Drug Category Profiles

Narcotics

Drug	Dependence: Physical/Psychological	How Used	Duration (hours)
Opium	High/High	Oral, smoked	3–6
Morphine	High/High	Oral, smoked, injected	3–6
Codeine	Moderate/Moderate	Oral, injected	3–6
Heroin	High/High	Smoked, injected, sniffed	3–6
Hydromorphone	High/High	Oral, injected	3–6
Meperidine	High/High	Oral, injected	3–6
Methadone	High/High	Oral, injected	12–24

What are narcotics?	Drugs used medicinally to relieve pain
	High potential for abuse
	Cause relaxation with an immediate "rush"
	Initial unpleasant effects—restlessness, nausea
Possible effects	Euphoria
	Drowsiness, respiratory depression
	Constricted (pinpoint) pupils
Symptoms of overdose	Slow and shallow breathing, clammy skin
	Convulsions, coma, possible death
Withdrawal syndrome	Watery eyes, runny nose, yawning, cramps
	Loss of appetite, irritability, nausea
	Tremors, panic, chills, sweating
Indications of possible misuse	Scars (tracks) caused by injections
	Constricted (pinpoint) pupils
	Loss of appetite
	Sniffles, watery eyes, cough, nausea
	Lethargy, drowsiness, nodding
	Syringes, bent spoons, needles

Depressants

Drug	Dependence: Physical/Psychological	How Used	Duration (hours)
Barbiturates	High/Moderate	Oral	1–16
Methaqualone	High/High	Oral	4–8

Drug	Dependence: Physical/Psychological	How Used	Duration (hours)
Tranquilizers	High/High	Oral	4–8
Chloral hydrate	Moderate/Moderate	Oral	5–8
Glutethimide	High/Moderate	Oral	4–8

What are depressants?	Drugs used medicinally to relieve anxiety, irritability, tension High potential for abuse, development of tolerance Produce state of intoxication similar to that of alcohol Combined with alcohol, increase effects and multiply risks
Possible effects	Sensory alteration, anxiety reduction, intoxication Small amounts cause calmness, relaxed muscles Larger amounts cause slurred speech, impaired judgment, loss of motor coordination Very large doses may cause respiratory depression, coma, death Newborn babies of abusers may show dependence, withdrawal symptoms, behavioral problems, birth defects
Symptoms of overdose	Shallow respiration, clammy skin, dilated pupils Weak and rapid pulse, coma, death
Withdrawal syndrome	Anxiety, insomnia, muscle tremors, loss of appetite Abrupt cessation or reduced high dose may cause convulsions, delirium, death
Indications of possible misuse	Behavior similar to alcohol intoxication (without odor of alcohol on breath) Staggering, stumbling, lack of coordination, slurred speech Falling asleep while at work, difficulty concentrating Dilated pupils

Stimulants

Drug	Dependence: Physical/Psychological	How Used	Duration (hours)
Cocaine[a]	Possible/High	Sniffed, smoked, injected	1–2
Amphetamines	Possible/High	Oral, injected	2–4
Methamphetamine	Possible/High	Oral, injected	2–4
Phenmetrazine	Possible/High	Oral, injected	2–4
Methylphenidate	Possible/Moderate	Oral, injected	2–4
Other stimulants	Possible/High	Oral, injected	2–4
Ice	High/High	Smoked, oral, injected, inhaled	4–14

What are stimulants?	Drugs used to increase alertness, relieve fatigue, feel stronger and more decisive
	Used for euphoric effects or to counteract the "down" feeling of tranquilizers or alcohol
Possible effects	Increased heart and respiratory rates, elevated blood pressure, dilated pupils, and decreased appetite
	High doses may cause rapid or irregular heartbeat, loss of coordination, collapse
	May cause perspiration, blurred vision, dizziness, a feeling of restlessness, anxiety, delusions
Symptoms of overdose	Agitation, increase in body temperature, hallucinations, convulsions, possible death
Withdrawal syndrome	Apathy, long periods of sleep, irritability, depression, disorientation
Indications of possible misuse	Excessive activity, talkativeness, irritability, argumentativeness, or nervousness
	Increased blood pressure or pulse rate, dilated pupils
	Long periods without sleeping or eating
	Euphoria

a. Cocaine, although classified under the Controlled Substances Act as a narcotic, also is discussed as a stimulant.

Substances of Abuse: Brief Profiles

Cocaine

Also known as:

Coke, dust, snow, flake, blow, girl

You probably know why cocaine is abused:

- Carefree feeling
- Euphoria
- Relaxation
- In control

But did you know that:

- A cocaine "high" lasts only about 5 to 20 minutes.
- Cocaine use may cause severe "mood swings" and irritability.
- You need more and more cocaine each time you want a "high."
- Cocaine increases your blood pressure and heart rate, and this is particularly dangerous if you have a heart condition.

- One use can cause death.
- Possession and use are illegal and can result in fines and arrest.

Crack

Also known as:

Crack, crack cocaine, freebase rocks, rock

You probably know why crack is abused:

- Quick high
- Power
- Euphoria

But did you know that:

- Crack is almost instantly addictive.
- One use could cause a fatal heart attack.
- Repeated use may cause insomnia, hallucinations, seizures, and paranoia.
- The euphoric effects of crack last for only a few minutes.
- Possession and use are illegal in all 50 states.
- There are more hospitalizations per year resulting from crack and cocaine use than from the use of any other illicit substance.

Ice

Also known as:

Meth, crystal, crank, methamphetamine

You probably know why ice is abused:

- Temporary mood elevation
- Exhilaration (high)
- Increased mental alertness
- Upper—increase wakefulness

But did you know that:

- Ice is extremely addictive, sometimes with just one use.
- Ice can cause convulsions, heart irregularities, high blood pressure, depression, restlessness, tremors, and severe fatigue.
- An overdose can cause coma and death.
- When one stops using ice, one may experience a deep depression.
- Ice causes a very jittery high along with anxiety, insomnia, and sometimes paranoia.

Inhalants

Some of the substances that are abused:

- Butyl nitrite
- Amyl nitrite (gas in aerosol cans)
- Gasoline and toluene vapors (typewriter correction fluid, glue, marking pens)

You probably know why inhalants are abused:

- Cheap high
- Quick buzz
- Fun

But did you know that inhalants may cause:

- Loss of muscle control
- Slurred speech
- Drowsiness or loss of consciousness
- Excessive secretions from the nose and watery eyes
- Brain damage and damage to lung cells

Drug Category Profile

Hallucinogens

Drug	Dependence: Physical/Psychological	How Used	Duration
PCP Angel dust Loveboat	Unknown/High	Smoked, oral, injected	Up to days
LSD Acid Green/Red dragon	None/Unknown	Oral	8–12 hours
Mescaline, peyote	None/Unknown	Oral, injected	8–12 hours
Psilocybin	None/Unknown	Oral, injected, smoked, sniffed	Variable
Designer drugs[a] Ecstacy, PCE	Unknown/Unknown	Oral, injected, smoked	Variable

a. Phencyclidine analogs, amphetamine variants

What are hallucinogens?	Drugs that produce behavioral changes that often are multiple and dramatic
	No known medical use, but some block sensation to pain and use may result in self-inflicted injuries
	"Designer drugs," made to imitate certain illegal drugs, often are many times stronger than drugs they imitate

Possible effects	Rapidly changing feelings, immediately and long after use
	Chronic use may cause persistent problems, depression, violent behavior, anxiety, distorted perception of time
	Large doses may cause convulsions, coma, heart/lung failure, ruptured blood vessels in the brain
	May cause hallucinations, illusions, dizziness, confusion, suspicion, anxiety, loss of control
	Delayed effects—"flashbacks" may occur long after use
	Designer drugs—one use may cause irreversible brain damage
Symptoms of overdose	Longer, more intense "trip" episodes, psychosis, coma, death
Withdrawal syndrome	No known withdrawal syndrome
Indications of possible misuse	Extreme changes in behavior and mood
	Person may sit or recline in a trance-like state
	Person may appear fearful
	Chills, irregular breathing, sweating, trembling hands
	Changes in sense of light, hearing, touch, smell, time
	Increase in blood pressure, heart rate, blood sugar

Substances of Abuse: Brief Profile

Hallucinogens

Types:

- LSD (acid, red/green dragon)
- Ecstacy (designer drug)
- PCP (angel dust, loveboat)
- PCP and cocaine ("Beam me up, Scottie")
- Mescaline
- Psilocybin

You probably know why hallucinogens are abused:

- Fun
- Stimulation or depression
- Behavioral changes

But did you know that:

- One use of LSD or PCP may cause multiple and dramatic behavioral changes.
- Large doses of hallucinogens may cause convulsions, ruptured blood vessels in the brain, and irreversible brain damage.
- Many hallucinogens cause unpleasant and potentially dangerous "flashbacks" long after the drug was used.
- Most hallucinogens cause hallucinations—changes in perception of time, smell, touch, and so on.

Drug Category Profile

Cannabis

Drug	Dependence: Physical/ Psychological	How Used	Duration (hours)
Marijuana Pot Grass	Unknown/Moderate	Smoked, oral	2–4
Tetrahydro-cannabinol	Unknown/Moderate	Smoked, oral	2–4
Hashish	Unknown/Moderate	Smoked, oral	2–4
Hashish oil	Unknown/Moderate	Smoked, oral	2–4

What is cannabis?	Hemp plant from which marijuana and hashish are produced
	Hashish consists of resinous secretions of the cannabis plant
	Marijuana is a tobacco-like substance
Possible effects	Euphoria followed by relaxation; loss of appetite; impaired memory, concentration, knowledge retention; loss of coordination; more vivid sense of taste, sight, smell, hearing
	Stronger doses cause fluctuating emotions, fragmentary thoughts, disoriented behavior, psychosis
	May cause irritation to lungs, respiratory system
	May cause cancer
Symptoms of overdose	Fatigue, lack of coordination, paranoia, psychosis
Withdrawal syndrome	Insomnia, hyperactivity, sometimes decreased appetite
Indications of possible misuse	Animated behavior and loud talking followed by sleepiness
	Dilated pupils, bloodshot eyes
	Distortions in perception, hallucinations
	Distortions in depth and time perception, loss of coordination

Substances of Abuse: Brief Profile

Marijuana

Also known as:

Pot, grass, joints, roaches, reefer, weed, Mary Jane

You probably know why marijuana is abused:

- Relaxation
- Euphoria

But did you know that:

- Marijuana may cause impaired short-term memory, a shortened attention span, and delayed reflexes.
- During pregnancy, marijuana may cause birth defects.
- Marijuana may cause a fast heart rate and pulse.
- Repeated use of marijuana may cause breathing problems.
- Possession of marijuana is illegal in all 50 states.
- Marijuana may cause relaxed inhibitions and disoriented behavior.

Drug Category Profile

Alcohol

Drug	Dependence: Physical/Psychological	How Used	Duration (hours)
Ethyl alcohol	Possible/Possible	Oral	1–4
Ethanol	Possible/Possible	Oral	1–4

What is alcohol?	Liquid distilled product of fermented fruits, grains, vegetables Used as solvent, antiseptic, sedative Moderate potential for abuse
Possible effects	Intoxication Sensory alteration Anxiety reduction
Symptoms of overdose	Staggering Odor of alcohol on breath Loss of coordination Slurred speech, dilated pupils Fetal alcohol syndrome (in babies) Nerve and liver damage
Withdrawal syndrome	Sweating Tremors Altered perception Psychosis, fear, auditory hallucinations
Indications of possible misuse	Confusion, disorientation, loss of motor nerve control Convulsions, shock, shallow respiration Involuntary defecation, drowsiness Respiratory depression, possible death

Substances of Abuse: Brief Profile

Alcohol

Also known as:

Booze, juice, brew, vino, sauce

You probably know why alcohol is abused:

- Relaxation
- Sociability
- Cheap high

But did you know that:

- Alcohol is a depressant that decreases the responses of the central nervous system.
- Excessive drinking can cause liver damage and psychotic behavior.
- As little as two beers or drinks can impair coordination and thinking.
- Alcohol often is used by substance abusers to enhance the effects of other drugs.
- Alcohol continues to be the most frequently abused substance among young adults.

Drug Category Profile

Steroids

Drug	Dependence: Physical/Psychological	How Used	Duration
Dianabol	Possible/Possible	Oral	Days to weeks
Nandrolone	Possible/Possible	Oral	Days to weeks

What are steroids?	Synthetic compounds available legally and illegally
	Drugs that are closely related to the male sex hormone (testosterone)
	Moderate potential for abuse, particularly among young males
Possible effects	Increase in body weight
	Increase in muscle strength
	Enhance athletic performance
	Increase physical endurance
Symptoms of overdose	Quick weight and muscle gains
	Extremely aggressive behavior or "road rage"
	Severe skin rashes
	Impotence, withered testicles
	In females, development of irreversible masculine traits

Withdrawal syndrome	Significant weight loss
	Depression
	Behavioral changes
	Trembling
Indications of possible misuse	Increased combativeness and aggressiveness
	Jaundice
	Purple or red spots on body, unexplained darkness of skin
	Persistent unpleasant breath odor
	Swelling of feet or lower legs

Substances of Abuse: Brief Profile

Steroids

Types:

Anabolic (male hormone, steroids most frequently abused), cortical, estrogenic (female hormone)

You probably know why steroids are abused:

- Increase strength
- Increase muscle size
- Help muscles to recover

But did you know that abuse of steroids may cause:

- Severe acne, rashes, stunted growth
- Sexual function problems
- Women to take on masculine traits, develop hairiness
- Behavioral changes, aggressiveness ("paranoid rages")
- Long-term effects such as cholesterol increases, heart disease, liver tumors, cancer, cataracts, death

Appendix 44

Adult Inpatient Program Schedule

Time	Monday	Tuesday	Wednesday	Thursday	Friday	Saturday	Sunday
7:00 am	Wake-up call	Wake-up call	Wake-up call	Wake-up call	Wake-up call	Wake up Showers	Sleep in
7:00–7:45	Medications and blood pressure at the nurses' station	Medications and blood pressure at the nurses' station	Medications and blood pressure at the nurses' station	Medications and blood pressure at the nurses' station	Medications and blood pressure at the nurses' station	Room checks Goals	Sleep in
7:45–8:05	Breakfast	Breakfast	Breakfast	Breakfast	Breakfast	Breakfast	Wake up Showers
9:00–9:45	Lecture	Lecture	Lecture	Lecture	Lecture	Daily meditation	9:15 Breakfast
10:00–11:30	Interpersonal group	10:00–11:00 Spirituality group 11:00–11:45 Fifth Step review	Interpersonal group	Interpersonal group	Interpersonal group	Chores	Chores
11:45–12:05	Noon meal	Noon meal	Noon meal	Noon meal	Noon meal	Study time	Church
12:30–2:00 pm	Individual counseling 12:30–1:30 Gambling group	Individual counseling	Individual counseling	Free time	Individual counseling	Study time Interpersonal group	Church
1:00–2:00	Young adult group	1:30–3:00 Interpersonal group	Young adult group	Free time	Young adult group	Lunch	Lunch

(Continued)

(Continued)

Time	Monday	Tuesday	Wednesday	Thursday	Friday	Saturday	Sunday
2:00–3:00	Recovery skills group	3:00–3:30 Family conjoints (if scheduled) Free time	Recovery skills group	Video	Recovery skills group	Video	Free time
3:30–4:00	Lecture	Video	Topic group	Men's and women's groups	Lecture	Recreation	Visitors
4:30–5:00	Exercise time	Exercise time	Exercise time 4:30–5:15 Gambling group	Exercise time 4:30–5:15 Gambling group	Exercise time	Recreation	4:30 Visitors leave
5:15–5:35	Evening meal	Evening meal	Evening meal	Evening meal	Evening meal	Room checks Goals	Family process group
5:45–7:00	Free time	Free time	Free time	Free time 6:45 Outside continuing care (if scheduled)	Free time	Group	Room checks Goals
7:00–8:00	Alcoholics Anonymous (AA) speaker	AA speaker 7:30 Outside AA meeting (if scheduled)	AA speaker	Narcotics Anonymous (NA) speaker	AA speaker 7:00 Outside Gamblers Anonymous (GA) meeting	Dinner	Dinner
Following the AA meeting	Personal inventory group	Personal inventory group	Personal inventory group	Personal inventory group	Personal inventory group	Study time	Study time
Following the personal inventory group	Relaxation group	Relaxation group	Relaxation group	Relaxation group	Relaxation group	Topic group	Topic group
9:00	Free time	Free time	Free time	Free time	8:30 Talking circle	Recreation time Showers Phone	Recreation time Showers Phone
						In rooms	In rooms
						Lights out	Lights out

Appendix 45

Adolescent Inpatient Program Schedule

Time	Monday	Tuesday	Wednesday	Thursday	Friday	Saturday	Sunday
7:00 am	Wake up Showers	Wake up Showers	Wake up Showers	Wake up Showers	Wake up Showers	Wake up Showers	Sleep in
8:00	Room checks Goals	Room checks Goals	Room checks Goals	Room checks Goals	Room checks Goals	Room checks Goals	Sleep in
8:20	Breakfast	Breakfast	Breakfast	Breakfast	Breakfast	Breakfast	Wake up Showers
9:00	Lecture: Dr. Ron	Medical lecture	Daily meditation	Daily meditation	Community group	Daily meditation	9:15 Breakfast
9:30	Chores	Chores	Chores	Chores	Chores	Chores	Chores
10:00	Study time	Study time/Inipi	Study time	Study time	Study time/ Group	Study time	Church
11:00	Exercise	Exercise	Exercise	Exercise	Exercise	Study time Interpersonal group	Church
12:20 pm	Lunch	Lunch	Lunch	Lunch	Lunch	Lunch	Lunch
1:00	Study time	Study time	Arts/Crafts	Study time	Group	Video	Free time
2:00	Interpersonal group	Recreation	Study time	Recovery skills group	Recreation	Recreation	Visitors
3:00	Red road	Recovery skills group Conjoints	Talking circle	Leisure Education	Recreation	Recreation	4:30 Visitors leave
4:30	Room checks Goals	Room checks Goals	Room checks Goals	Room checks Goals	Room checks Goals	Room checks Goals	Family process group

(Continued)

(Continued)

Time	Monday	Tuesday	Wednesday	Thursday	Friday	Saturday	Sunday
5:00	Red road	Group	Spirituality group	Video	Video	Group	Room checks Goals
5:45	Dinner	Dinner	Dinner	Dinner	Dinner	Dinner	Dinner
6:30	Study time	Study time	Study time	Study time	Study time	Study time	Study time
7:00	Topic group Alcoholics Anonymous (AA)	Topic group AA	Topic group AA	Topic group AA	Corrective thinking	Topic group	Topic group
8:00	Recreation time Showers Phone	Recreation time Showers Phone	Recreation time Showers Phone	Recreation time Showers Phone	Recreation time Showers Phone	Recreation time Showers Phone	Recreation time Showers Phone
10:00	In rooms	In rooms	In rooms	In rooms	In rooms	In rooms	In rooms
10:30	Lights out	Lights out	Lights out	Lights out	Lights out	Lights out	Lights out

Appendix 46

Adult Outpatient Program Schedule

WEEK 1

Monday

    6:00 pm–6:30 pm   Open—Serenity Prayer

        Commitments

        Open discussion

        Group rules

    6:30–7:15   Interpersonal relationship group

    7:15–7:30   Break

    7:30–9:00   Continue interpersonal group

    9:00   Close—Lord's Prayer

Tuesday

    6:00 pm–6:30 pm   Open—Serenity Prayer

        Commitments

    6:30–7:15   Spirituality group

    7:15–7:30   Break

    7:30–9:00   Continue spirituality group

        Family interpersonal group

    9:00   Close—Lord's Prayer

Wednesday

    6:00 pm–6:30 pm   Open—Serenity Prayer

        Commitments

        Open discussion

    Hamilton Depression Rating Scale (HAM-D)

    6:30–7:15   Recovery skills group

    7:15–7:30   Break

    7:30–9:00   Continue recovery skills group

    9:00   Close—Lord's Prayer

Each week, the schedule stays the same on Mondays and Wednesdays. The following schedules are rotating schedules on Tuesdays for each additional week.

WEEK 2

Tuesday

    6:00 pm–6:30 pm   Open—Serenity Prayer
    Commitments

    6:30–7:15   Disease concept video and discussion

    7:15–7:30   Break

    7:30–9:00   Lecture and discussion on progression/Jellinek chart
    Family interpersonal group

    9:00   Close—Lord's Prayer

WEEK 3

Tuesday

    6:00 pm–6:30 pm   Open—Serenity Prayer
    Commitments

    6:30–7:15   *Recovery and the Family* video and discussion

    7:15–7:30   Break

    7:30–9:00   Lecture and discussion on family dynamics
    Family interpersonal group

    9:00   Close—Lord's Prayer

WEEK 4

Tuesday

    6:00 pm–6:30 pm   Open—Serenity Prayer
    Commitments

    6:30–7:15   *Chalk Talk* video and discussion

    7:15–7:30   Break

    7:30–9:00   Lecture and discussion on Steps One, Two, and Three
    Family interpersonal group

    9:00   Close—Lord's Prayer

WEEK 5

Tuesday

    6:00 pm–6:30 pm   Open—Serenity Prayer
    Commitments

    6:30–7:15   *Feelings* video and discussion

    7:15–7:30   Break

    7:30–9:00   Lecture and discussion on Steps Four, Five, Six, and Seven

Family interpersonal group

9:00   Close—Lord's Prayer

WEEK 6

Tuesday

6:00 pm–6:30 pm   Open—Serenity Prayer

    Commitments

6:30–7:15   *Medical Aspects* video and discussion

7:15–7:30   Break

7:30–9:00   Lecture and discussion on Steps Eight and Nine

    Family interpersonal group

9:00   Close—Lord's Prayer

WEEK 7

Tuesday

6:00 pm–6:30 pm   Open—Serenity Prayer

    Commitments

6:30–7:15   *HIV* video and discussion

7:15–7:30   Break

7:30–9:00   Lecture and discussion on Steps Ten, Eleven, and Twelve

    Family interpersonal group

9:00   Close—Lord's Prayer

WEEK 8

Tuesday

6:00 pm–6:30 pm   Open—Serenity Prayer

    Commitments

6:30–9:00   Social and recreational activities

9:00   Close—Lord's Prayer

Appendix 47

Adolescent Outpatient Program Schedule

WEEK 1

Monday

    4:30 pm   Open—Serenity Prayer

        Highs and lows

        Open discussion

    4:45   Interpersonal relationship group

    5:20   Break

    5:30   Continue interpersonal relationship group

    6:30   Close—Lord's Prayer

Wednesday

    4:30 pm   Open—Serenity Prayer

        Highs and lows

        Open discussion

    4:45   Recovery skills group

    5:20   Break

    5:30   Continue recovery skills group

    6:30   Close—Lord's Prayer

Thursday

    4:30 pm   Open—Serenity Prayer

        Highs and lows

        Open discussion

    4:45   *Pot* video

    5:20   Break

    5:30   Read, complete, and discuss *Pot* handout

    6:30   Close—Lord's Prayer

Each week, the schedule stays the same on Mondays and Wednesdays. The following schedules are rotating schedules on Thursdays for each additional week.

WEEK 2

Thursday

4:30 pm   Open—Serenity Prayer
Highs and lows
Open discussion

4:45   *Three-Headed Dragon* video

5:20   Break

5:30   Discuss video and handout

6:30   Close—Lord's Prayer

WEEK 3

Thursday

4:30 pm   Open—Serenity Prayer
Highs and lows
Open discussion

4:45   *Step One* video

5:20   Break

5:30   Facts about alcohol test and discussion

6:30   Close—Lord's Prayer

WEEK 4

Thursday

4:30 pm   Open—Serenity Prayer
Highs and lows
Open discussion

4:45   *Teens and AA* video and discussion

5:20   Break

5:30   Sponsorship role-playing

6:30   Close—Lord's Prayer

WEEK 5

Thursday

4:30 pm   Open—Serenity Prayer
Highs and lows
Open discussion

4:45   *Soft Is the Heart of a Child* video

5:20   Break

5:30   Discuss systems dynamics roles

6:30   Close—Lord's Prayer

WEEK 6

Thursday

4:30 pm   Open—Serenity Prayer

Highs and lows

Open discussion

4:45   *What Is Wrong With This Picture* video

5:20   Break

5:30   Values exercise and discussion

6:30   Close—Lord's Prayer

WEEK 7

Thursday

4:30 pm   Open—Serenity Prayer

Highs and lows

Open discussion

4:45   *Epitaph for a Drug User* video

5:20   Break

5:30   Lecture and discussion on HIV and AIDS

6:30   Close—Lord's Prayer

WEEK 8

Thursday

4:30 pm   Open—Serenity Prayer

Highs and lows

Open discussion

4:45   *Fetal Alcohol Syndrome* video

5:20   Break

5:30   Discussion regarding fetal alcohol syndrome and fetal alcohol effects

6:30   Close—Lord's Prayer

Appendix 48

Gambling Inpatient Program Schedule

WEEK 1		
Monday	12:30 pm–1:30 pm	Recovery skills
Tuesday	3:00 pm–4:00 pm 5:30 pm–6:30 pm	Conjoint with family (family program) Individual session
Wednesday	4:15 pm–5:15 pm	Interpersonal group—journaling
Thursday	2:00 pm–3:00 pm 6:00 pm–9:00 pm	*Hooked* video Gambling group—outreach
Friday	4:15 pm–5:15 pm 6:30 pm–7:30 pm	Group education (progression/characteristics) Outside Gamblers Anonymous (GA) meeting
Saturday	3:00 pm–5:00 pm	Individual sessions
WEEK 2		
Monday	12:30 pm–1:30 pm	Group—questions and recovery skills
Tuesday	3:00 pm–4:00 pm 5:30 pm–6:30 pm	Conjoint with family (family program) Individual session
Wednesday	4:15 pm–5:15 pm	Interpersonal group—journaling
Thursday	2:00 pm–3:00 pm 6:00 pm–9:00 pm	*Compulsive Gambling* (Part 1) video Gambling group—outreach
Friday	4:15 pm–5:15 pm 6:30 pm–7:30 pm	Group education (budgeting/financial) Outside GA meeting
Saturday	3:00 pm–5:00 pm	Individual sessions
WEEK 3		
Monday	12:30 pm–1:30 pm	Group—recovery skills and "Twenty Questions"
Tuesday	3:00 pm–4:00 pm 5:30 pm–6:30 pm	Conjoint with family (family program) Individual session

(Continued)

(Continued)

Wednesday	4:15 pm–5:15 pm	Interpersonal group—journaling
Thursday	2:00 pm–3:00 pm 6:00 pm–9:00 pm	*Compulsive Gambling* (Part 2) video Gambling group—outreach
Friday	4:15 pm–5:15 pm 6:30 pm–7:30 pm	Group (relapse prevention) Outside GA meeting
Saturday	3:00 pm–5:00 pm	Individual sessions
WEEK 4		
Monday	12:30 pm–1:30 pm	Group—recovery skills and "Twenty Questions"
Tuesday	3:00 pm–4:00 pm 5:30 pm–6:30 pm	Conjoint with family (family program) Individual session
Wednesday	4:15 pm–5:15 pm	Interpersonal group—journaling
Thursday	2:00 pm–3:00 pm 6:00 pm–9:00 pm	*Broken Circle* video Gambling group—outreach
Friday	4:15 pm–5:15 pm 6:30 pm–7:30 pm	Group (resentments/regrets) Outside GA meeting
Saturday	3:00 pm–5:00 pm	Individual sessions

Note: Individual sessions are to include assessments, evaluations, individual financial responsibility, and continuing care plans. Family conjoints are to be done during the week of the family program, or more as needed, and are to be assessed on an individual basis.

Aspects of the gambling program are combined with all addiction-based disorders.

Family dynamics: Family program scheduled for the first Monday and Tuesday following admission

Problem solving: Daily interpersonal groups

Relapse prevention: Weekly in a 4-week cycle (triggers, thoughts, feelings, and slips)

Cross-addiction: Lecture

Spirituality: Weekly sessions with clergy

Appendix 49

Gambling Outpatient Program Schedule

WEEK 1		
Monday	6:00 pm–9:00 pm	Open Introductions Commitments Meetings attended Interpersonal group—share problems, feelings, and concerns and apply problem solving skills
Wednesday	6:00 pm–9:00 pm	Open Introductions Commitments Educational/Family group Family dynamics—identifying roles in the family
Thursday	6:00 pm–9:00 pm	Open Introductions Commitments Recovery skills group—written exercises presented to the group
WEEK 2		
Monday	6:00 pm–9:00 pm	Open Introductions Commitments Meetings attended Interpersonal group—share problems, feelings, and concerns and apply problem solving skills
Wednesday	6:00 pm–9:00 pm	Open Introductions Commitments Educational/Family group Resolving conflicts—Communication Skills exercise (see Appendix 13)

(Continued)

(Continued)

Thursday	6:00 pm–9:00 pm	Open Introductions Commitments Recovery skills group—written exercises presented to the group
WEEK 3		
Monday	6:00 pm–9:00 pm	Open Introductions Commitments Meetings attended Interpersonal group—share problems, feelings, and concerns and apply problem solving skills
Wednesday	6:00 pm–9:00 pm	Open Introductions
		Commitments Educational/Family group Progression of gambling illness and characteristics of a compulsive gambler
Thursday	6:00 pm–9:00 pm	Open Introductions Commitments Recovery skills group—written exercises presented to the group
WEEK 4		
Monday	6:00 pm–9:00 pm	Open Introductions Commitments Meetings attended Interpersonal group—share problems, feelings, and concerns and apply problem solving skills
Wednesday	6:00 pm–9:00 pm	Open Introductions Commitments Educational/Family group Lecture and discussion—relapse triggers *Compulsive Gambling* (Part 1) video
Thursday	6:00 pm–9:00 pm	Open Introductions Commitments Recovery skills group—written exercises presented to the group

WEEK 5		
Monday	6:00 pm–9:00 pm	Open Introductions Commitments Meetings attended Interpersonal group—share problems, feelings, and concerns and apply problem solving skills
Wednesday	6:00 pm–9:00 pm	Open Introductions Commitments Educational/Family group Lecture—similarities of chemical addictions and compulsive gambling *Compulsive Gambling* (Part 2) video
Thursday	6:00 pm–9:00 pm	Open Introductions
		Commitments Recovery skills group—written exercises presented to the group
WEEK 6		
Monday	6:00 pm–9:00 pm	Open Introductions Commitments Meetings attended Interpersonal group—share problems, feelings, and concerns and apply problem solving skills
Wednesday	6:00 pm–9:00 pm	Open Introductions Commitments Educational/Family group Lecture—transition from treatment to Gamblers Anonymous (GA) and continuing care Discharge planning group and referrals—develop a long-term personal recovery plan
Thursday	6:00 pm–9:00 pm	Open Introductions Commitments Recovery skills group—written exercises presented to the group

Appendix 50

Day Treatment Program Schedule

Intensive Outpatient/Partial Care/Day Treatment Program Schedule		
WEEK 1		
Monday	9:00 am	Lecture—Jellinek chart
	10:00	Interpersonal group
	11:00	Gambling group—recovery skills
	12:00 pm	Lunch
	12:30	Topic group—relapse prevention
	1:30	Medical aspects of alcoholism I and II—video and discussion
	2:30	Reading group—Narcotics Anonymous (NA)
	3:00	Close for the day
Tuesday	9:00 am	Working a recovery program
	10:00	Interpersonal group
	11:00	Spiritual group—*Spiritual Aspects of Recovery* Father Martin video
	12:00 pm	Lunch
	12:30	Individual sessions and homework
	1:30	Personal inventory group
	2:30	Reading group—Gamblers Anonymous (GA)
	3:00	Close for the day
Wednesday	9:00 am	Lecture—Step One
	10:00	Interpersonal group
	11:00	Gambling group—budget
	12:00 pm	Lunch
	12:30	*Three-Headed Dragon* video and discussion
	1:30	Topic group—sexuality
	2:30	Reading group—Alcoholics Anonymous (AA)
	3:00	Close for the day

(Continued)

(Continued)

Thursday	9:00 am	Community group
	10:00	Interpersonal group
	11:00	*Big Steve* video and discussion
	12:00 pm	Lunch
	12:30	Recovery skills group—all clients
	1:30	Gambling group—journal
	2:30	Treatment progress review
	3:00	Close for the day
WEEK 2		
Monday	9:00 am	Lecture—Steps Two and Three
	10:00	Interpersonal group
	11:00	Gambling group—recovery skills
	12:00 pm	Lunch
	12:30	Topic group—spiritual assessment
	1:30	HIV/AIDS video and discussion
	2:30	Reading group—NA
	3:00	Close for the day
Tuesday	9:00 am	Lecture—stress management
	10:00	Interpersonal group
	11:00	Spiritual group—*Values* Father Martin video
	12:00 pm	Lunch
	12:30	Individual sessions and homework
	1:30	Personal inventory group
	2:30	Reading group—GA
	3:00	Close for the day
Wednesday	9:00 am	Lecture—Steps Four and Five
	10:00	Interpersonal group
	11:00	Gambling group—budget
	12:00 pm	Lunch
	12:30	*Everybody Wins* video and discussion
	1:30	Topic group—addictive relationships
	2:30	Reading group—AA
	3:00	Close for the day
Thursday	9:00 am	Community group
	10:00	Interpersonal group
	11:00	*Disease Concept* video and discussion
	12:00 pm	Lunch
	12:30	Recovery skills group—all clients
	1:30	Gambling group—journal
	2:30	Treatment progress review
	3:00	Close for the day

WEEK 3		
Monday	9:00 am	Lecture—Steps Six and Seven
	10:00	Interpersonal group
	11:00	Gambling group—recovery skills
	12:00 pm	Lunch
	12:30	Topic group—guilt
	1:30	*Back to Basics* Father Martin video and discussion
	2:30	Reading group—NA
	3:00	Close for the day
Tuesday	9:00 am	Lecture—cross-addiction
	10:00	Interpersonal group
	11:00	Spiritual group—*I Am My Brother's Keeper* Father Martin video
	12:00 pm	Lunch
	12:30	Individual sessions and homework
	1:30	Personal inventory group
	2:30	Reading group—GA
	3:00	Close for the day
Wednesday	9:00 am	Lecture—Steps Eight and Nine
	10:00	Interpersonal group
	11:00	Gambling group—journal
	12:00 pm	Lunch
	12:30	*Even Up the Odds* video and discussion
	1:30	Topic group—control
	2:30	Reading group—AA
	3:00	Close for the day
Thursday	9:00 am	Community group
	10:00	Interpersonal group
	11:00	*Recovery and the Family* video and discussion
	12:00 pm	Lunch
	12:30	Recovery skills group—all clients
	1:30	Gambling group—educational/interpersonal/budget
	2:30	Treatment progress review
	3:00	Close for the day
WEEK 4		
Monday	9:00 am	Lecture—Step Ten
	10:00	Interpersonal group
	11:00	Gambling group—recovery skills
	12:00 pm	Lunch
	12:30	Topic group—spiritual death
	1:30	*Bill W. Story* video and discussion
	2:30	Reading group—NA
	3:00	Close for the day

(Continued)

(Continued)

Tuesday	9:00 am	Lecture—denial
	10:00	Interpersonal group
	11:00	Spiritual group—*Feelings* Father Martin video
	12:00 pm	Lunch
	12:30	Individual sessions and homework
	1:30	Personal inventory group
	2:30	Reading group—GA
	3:00	Close for the day
Wednesday	9:00 am	Lecture—Step Eleven
	10:00	Interpersonal group
	11:00	Gambling group—journal
	12:00 pm	Lunch
	12:30	*Relapse Prevention: The Facts* video and discussion
	1:30	Topic group—frozen feelings
	2:30	Reading group—AA
	3:00	Close for the day
Thursday	9:00 am	Community group
	10:00	Interpersonal group
	11:00	*Medical Aspects of Mind-Altering Drugs* video and discussion
	12:00 pm	Lunch
	12:30	Recovery skills group—all clients
	1:30	Gambling group—educational/interpersonal/budget
	2:30	Treatment progress review
	3:00	Close for the day

Appendix 51

Pressure Relief Group Meeting and Budget Form

To the Gamblers Anonymous Group:

When a member attends his or her first meeting, it is important that a pressure relief meeting be explained to him or her and that a member will contact him or her within 30 days to arrange a pressure relief meeting.

The member should be told to contact all creditors and tell them that he or she will be back to them in 30 days. It should be emphasized that no payments should be made and also that no commitment of dollar amounts should be promised. Each member should be told to choose someone to take care of his or her money (spouse, if married). It is suggested that the member's name be removed from all items of value (e.g., house, cars, stocks, bonds, bank books, credit cards, checking accounts). The member should be told not to carry more money than he or she needs for daily essentials.

The pressure relief meeting should be given only by a Gamblers Anonymous (GA) member experienced in pressure relief procedures. There should be at least one other GA member and a Gam-Anon member present. The pressure relief meeting should not take place at a member's home; there could be too many distractions. Do not plan a pressure relief meeting at a GA meeting room prior to a regularly scheduled meeting.

One week prior to the pressure relief meeting, the member should be given copies of the budget forms.

The pressure relief committee should schedule a reevaluation date approximately 6 months after the pressure relief meeting.

Dear Gamblers Anonymous Member:

According to the standards set forth by your local GA chapter, you are now eligible for a pressure group.

An integral part of your recovery is that of making financial restitution. Considering the fact that your debts usually are much greater than those of the average individual, it is vitally important that great care be taken when planning a manageable budget. The key word is manageable. It is very difficult for anyone to live a normal life while being overburdened with financial pressures, especially for a compulsive gambler.

The main concepts behind a compulsive gambler's pressure relief meeting are to allow the gambler and his or her family to be able to lead a normal life and, at the same time, make financial restitution to his or her creditors.

The first step in planning a budget requires total honesty. If you have withheld any information pertaining to your debts, now is the time to become totally honest. Hopefully, by now you have followed the advice of your fellow GA members and have done the following:

1. Contact all creditors and ask for a 30- to 45-day moratorium on payments. Be sure not to pay anyone, and do not make any financial commitments.

2. Choose someone to handle your money (spouse, if married).

3. Turn all ownership of properties (e.g., home, car) over to someone else.

4. Remove your name from all bank books, checking accounts, and credit cards.

5. Turn over all paychecks uncashed with stubs attached to the individual who will manage your money.

The Choice Is Yours

The choice between paying over a long period of time, while functioning and living as a human being, or complete collapse due to immense financial pressures that cannot be met is, in reality, not a choice at all but rather the only avenue that will return you back to sanity and solvency. You have to be honest, forthright, and humble in regard to the debts that you owe and in your determination to repay them. GA experience has shown that our creditors, in a very human and helpful way, will respond to sincerity, honesty, and courage but will rightfully reject arrogance and self-pity. Everyone is willing to help a person who is down (and who wants to get back up), but much more important is the willingness to help yourself. This is the key. This is the quest. This is the never-ending endeavor.

Have faith in the GA program and follow the budget that will be set up for you. If you adhere to the budget and refrain from gambling, your financial pressures will soon be relieved, and this will greatly improve your chances for recovery. Remember that you have a gambling problem, not a financial problem. Go slow; take it *one day at a time*.

DIRECTIONS: Please complete these pages with the most accurate and up-to-date information that you have available. Do not leave anything out.

To the Creditor

Dear Creditor:

The attached budget has been prepared for   , who is a member of GA. He/she has admitted that he/she is a compulsive gambler and that his/her life has become unmanageable. An integral part of the compulsive gambler's recovery is to make restitution to all of his/her creditors. Due to the fact that the compulsive gambler has accumulated a large debt, it may be necessary to repay you over a long period of time. If a previous repayment schedule already exists, the compulsive gambler may have to give you smaller payments and, therefore, take longer to repay his/her debt.

As you can see by the prepared budget, the compulsive gambler must provide for all living expenses for himself/herself and his/her family before paying his/her debts. The repayment schedule has been prepared by experienced members of GA. The amount suggested for repayment of each debt was based on the amount originally borrowed, the balance due, and the original monthly payment.

The compulsive gambler is not claiming bankruptcy and is not running away. He/she wants to repay his/her debts. Your cooperation is greatly appreciated.

GA is not responsible for the information listed on this form, nor does it guarantee the compliance of the proposed financial arrangement on this form.

Signed:

Pressure Relief Chairperson

Name   Spouse's name   Date

GA group

Budget committee chairperson   Others

Member's phone   Chairperson's phone

Reevaluation date

Budget

Expenses	Per Month[a]	Per Week
Alimony		
Allowance (children)		
Allowance (member)		
Allowance (spouse)		
Auto insurance		
Auto license		
Auto payment		
Auto registration		
Auto repairs		
Auto taxes/tolls		
Babysitter		
Cable TV		
Car fare		
Child support/day care		
Children's activities		
Christmas/Hanukkah gifts		
Cigarettes		
Clothing		
Coal/wood/kerosene		
Dentist		
Doctor		
Donations (e.g., church, temple, GA, Gam-Anon)		

(Continued)

(Continued)

Expenses	Per Month[a]	Per Week
Drugs and toiletries		
Dry cleaning and laundry		
Electricity		
Emergencies (e.g., home repairs)		
Eyeglasses/contacts		
Family entertainment		
Film and developing		
Food		
GA conferences		
Garbage removal		
Gas (home)		
Gasoline (auto)		
Gifts (e.g., birthdays, anniversaries)		
Haircuts/beauty salon		
Homeowner's/renter's insurance		
Life insurance (term)		
Life-liner contribution		
Lunches (work)		
Medical insurance		
Mortgage (first)		
Mortgage (second)		
Mortgage (third)		
Music lessons		
Newspapers/magazines		
Oil heat		
Pet care		
Postage		
Rent		
Savings/retirement funds		

Expenses	Per Month[a]	Per Week
School tuition		
Taxes (income)		
Taxes (property)		
Telephone		
Therapy/counseling		
Union/club dues		
Vacation		
Water		
ITEMS NOT LISTED:		
TOTAL EXPENSES		

a. 4.33 weeks per month.

List of Creditors

Please list, in the following order, (1) bad checks or debts for which you may be prosecuted, (2) court-ordered judgments, (3) credit unions, (4) bank or finance company loans, (5) back taxes, (6) credit cards, (7) bookmakers and loan sharks, (8) family and friends, and (9) others.

Creditor's Name	Date of Debt	Original Amount	Present Balance	Monthly Payment	Months in Default	Cosigner

Repayment Schedule

Creditor's Name	Original Balance	Balance	Monthly Payment	Weekly Payment	Date of First Payment	Estimated Date of Last Payment

Financial Summary

Income	Per month		Child support		Property income	
	Per week		Alimony		Spouse's income available	
	Primary job					
	Secondary job				Other income	
	Pensions				TOTAL	

TOTAL INCOME:

SUBTRACT TOTAL EXPENSES:

AMOUNT AVAILABLE FOR REPAYMENT:

Note: GA is not responsible for the information listed on this form, nor does it guarantee the compliance of the proposed financial arrangement on this form.

Appendix 52

Heroin

What Are the Treatments for Heroin Addiction?

A variety of effective treatments are available for heroin addiction. Treatment tends to be more effective when heroin abuse is identified early. The treatments that follow vary depending on the individual, but methadone, a synthetic opiate that blocks the effects of heroin and eliminates withdrawal symptoms, has a proven record of success for people addicted to heroin. Other pharmaceutical approaches (e.g., LAAM [levo-alpha-acetyl-methadol], buprenorphine), as well as many behavioral therapies, also are used for treating heroin addiction.

Detoxification

The primary objective of detoxification is to relieve withdrawal symptoms while clients adjust to a drug-free state. Not in itself a treatment for addiction, detoxification is a useful step only when it leads to long-term treatment that either is drug free (residential or outpatient) or uses medications as part of the treatment. The best-documented drug-free treatments are the therapeutic community residential programs lasting at least 3 to 6 months.

Methadone Programs

Methadone treatment has been used effectively and safely to treat opioid addiction for more than 30 years. Properly prescribed methadone is not intoxicating or sedating, and its effects do not interfere with ordinary activities such as driving a car. The medication is taken orally, and it suppresses narcotic withdrawal for 24 to 36 hours. Clients are able to perceive pain and have emotional reactions. Most important, methadone relieves the craving associated with heroin addiction (craving is a major reason for relapse). Among methadone clients, it has been found that normal street doses of heroin are ineffective at producing euphoria, thereby making the use of heroin more easily extinguishable.

Methadone's effects last for about 24 hours—four to six times as long as those of heroin—so people in treatment need to take it only once a day. Also, methadone is medically safe even when used continuously for 10 years or more. Combined with behavioral therapies or counseling and other supportive services, methadone enables clients to stop using heroin (and other opiates) and return to more stable and productive lives.

Methadone doses must be monitored carefully in clients who are receiving antiviral therapy for HIV infection so as to avoid potential medication interactions.

Source: With the exception of the LAAM and Other Medications and Methadone Programs sections, all information is taken from National Institute on Drug Abuse. (2005, May). *Heroin abuse and addiction* (Rev. ed.). Bethesda, MD: Author.

LAAM and Other Medications

LAAM, like methadone, is a synthetic opiate that can be used to treat heroin addiction. LAAM can block the effects of heroin for up to 72 hours with minimal side effects when taken orally. In 1993, the Food and Drug Administration approved the use of LAAM for treating clients addicted to heroin. Its long duration of action permits dosing just three times per week, thereby eliminating the need for daily dosing and take-home doses for weekends. LAAM will be increasingly available in clinics that already dispense methadone. Naloxone and naltrexone are medications that also block the effects of morphine, heroin, and other opiates. As antagonists, they are especially useful as antidotes. Naltrexone has long-lasting effects, ranging from 1 to 3 days depending on the dose. Naltrexone blocks the pleasurable effects of heroin and is useful in treating some highly motivated individuals. Naltrexone also has been found to be successful in preventing relapse by former opiate addicts released from prison on probation.

Another medication to treat heroin addiction, buprenorphine, is a particularly attractive treatment because, compared to other medications such as methadone, it causes weaker opiate effects and is less likely to cause overdose problems. Buprenorphine also produces a lower level of physical dependence, so clients who discontinue the medication generally have fewer withdrawal symptoms than do those who stop taking methadone. Because of these advantages, buprenorphine may be appropriate for use in a wider variety of treatment settings than is the case with the currently available medications. Several other medications with potential for treating heroin overdose or addiction currently are under investigation by the National Institute on Drug Abuse.

Behavioral Therapies

Although behavioral and pharmacological treatments can be extremely useful when employed alone, science has taught us that integrating both types of treatments ultimately will be the most effective approach. There are many effective behavioral treatments available for heroin addiction. These can include residential and outpatient approaches. An important task is to match the best treatment approach to meet the particular needs of the client. Moreover, several new behavioral therapies, such as contingency management therapy and cognitive-behavioral interventions, show particular promise as treatments for heroin addiction. Contingency management therapy uses a voucher-based system, where the client earns points based on negative drug tests that the client can exchange for items that encourage healthy living. Cognitive-behavioral interventions are designed to help modify the client's thinking, expectancies, and behaviors and to increase skills in coping with various life stressors. Both behavioral and pharmacological treatments help to restore a degree of normalcy to brain function and behavior, with increased employment rates and lower risk of HIV and other diseases and criminal behavior.

What Are the Opioid Analogs and Their Dangers?

Drug analogs are chemical compounds that are similar to other drugs in their effects but differ slightly in their chemical structure. Some analogs are produced by pharmaceutical companies for legitimate medical reasons. Other analogs, sometimes referred to as "designer" drugs, can be produced in illegal laboratories and often are more dangerous and potent than the original drugs. Two of the most commonly known opioid analogs are fentanyl and meperidine (e.g., marketed under the brand name Demerol).

Fentanyl was introduced in 1968 by a Belgian pharmaceutical company as a synthetic narcotic to be used as an analgesic in surgical procedures because of its minimal effects on the heart. Fentanyl is particularly dangerous because it is 50 times more potent than heroin and can rapidly stop respiration. This is not a problem during surgical procedures because machines are used to help clients breathe. On the street, however, users have been found dead with the needles used to inject the drug still in their arms.

Methadone Programs

There are approximately 980,000 heroin addicts in the United States, and 20% receive methadone or LAAM. A client who comes into a methadone clinic first receives a complete physical, biopsychosocial, and treatment plan. The client is stabilized on liquid methadone (up to 100 milligrams per day). Then the counselor begins to talk to the client about treatment. Does the client want to be on methadone forever, or does the client want to work toward abstinence? All clients need to be encouraged to move toward abstinence as the ultimate goal.

The client needs to be stabilized on enough methadone to get his or her life back from abusing drugs on the street. Methadone levels are taken to verify compliance. When the time is right, methadone is tapered very slowly, as little as 2 milligrams per month or as much as the client can comfortably tolerate. At any point, the client may reach a level where he or she cannot decrease any further without going into uncomfortable withdrawal symptoms. The client is maintained at the lowest level until another decrease can be attempted.

All clients have a monthly drug screen, and if their urine is found to be positive for substances of abuse, then they discuss this with their counselors and make plans for abstaining. Clients should not be discharged from treatment just because they use. Recovery is a program of progress, not perfection.

Clients can earn take-home doses of methadone by having clean urine samples for a required period, usually one take-home dose for each month clean. They can get guest doses from another clinic if they travel.

Clients should get individual, group, or family therapy each month as needed. The extent of this counseling is negotiated between the clients and their counselors. All methadone clients need to be examined for chronic pain syndromes to meet the needs of this population. A pain management team is used to help these clients manage the pain and the addiction simultaneously. Clients need to be educated about pregnancy, parenting, reproductive health, and HIV/AIDS as they go through treatment.

More information on methadone can be obtained from the National Association of Methadone Advocates (www.methadone.org) and the National Institute on Drug Abuse (www.nida.nih.gov).

Appendix 53

South Oaks Gambling Screen

1. Indicate which of the following types of gambling you have done in your lifetime. For each type, mark one answer: *not at all, less than once a week,* or *once a week or more*

Not at All	Less Than Once a Week	Once a Week or More
a.	Played cards for money	
b.	Bet on horses, dogs, or other animals (in off-track betting, at the track, or with a bookie)	
c.	Bet on sports (parley cards, with a bookie, or at jai alai)	
d.	Played dice games (including craps, over and under, or other dice games) for money	
e.	Went to casino (legal or otherwise)	
f.	Played the numbers or bet on lotteries	
g.	Played Bingo	
h.	Played the stock and/or commodities market	
i.	Played slot machines, poker machines, or other gambling machines	
j.	Bowled, shot pool, played golf, or played some other game of skill for money	

2. What is the largest amount of money you have ever gambled with on any one day?

    Never have gambled

    $10 or less

    More than $100 up to $1,000

    More than $1,000 up to $10,000

    More than $10,000

Source: Reprinted with permission. Lesieur H. R., & Blume, S. D. (1987). The South Oaks Gambling Screen (SOGS): A new instrument for the identification of pathological gamblers. *American Journal of Psychiatry, 144,* 1184–1188. Copyright © 1987.

3. Do (Did) your parents have a gambling problem?

   Both my father and mother gamble (gambled) too much.

   My father gambles (gambled) too much.

   My mother gambles (gambled) too much.

   Neither parent gambles (gambled) too much.

4. When you gamble, how often do you go back another day to win back money you lost?
   Never

   Some of the time (less than half of the time) I lost

   Most of the time I lost

   Every time I lost

5. Have you ever claimed to be winning money gambling but were not really winning? In fact, you lost?
   Never (or never gamble)

   Yes, less than half of the time I lost

   Yes, most of the time

6. Do you feel that you have ever had a problem with gambling?
   No

   Yes, in the past, but not now

   Yes

Yes	No	
7.		Did you ever gamble more than you intended?
8.		Have people criticized your gambling?
9.		Have you ever felt guilty about the way in which you gamble or what happens when you gamble?
10.		Have you ever felt as though you would like to stop gambling but did not think that you could?
11.		Have you ever hidden betting slips, lottery tickets, gambling money, or other signs of gambling from your spouse, children, or other important people in you life?
12.		Have you ever argued with people you like over how you handle money?
13.		(If you answered *yes* to Question 12): Have money arguments ever centered on your gambling?
14.		Have you ever borrowed from someone and not paid the person back as a result of your gambling?
15.		Have you ever lost time from work (or school) due to gambling?
16.		If you borrowed money to gamble or to pay gambling debts, where did you borrow from? (Check *yes* or *no* for each.)
		a. From household money
		b. From your spouse
		c. From other relatives or in-laws
		d. From banks, loan companies, or credit unions
		e. From credit cards
		f. From loan sharks (shylocks)
		g. You cashed in stocks, bonds, or other securities
		h. You sold personal or family property
		i. You borrowed on your checking account (passed bad checks)
		j. You have (had) a credit line with a bookie
		k. You have (had) a credit line with a casino

Scores are determined by adding up the number of questions that show an "at risk" response, indicated as follows. If you answered the preceding questions with one of the following answers, then mark the space next to that question:

Questions 1 to 3 are not counted.

Question 4: Most of the time I lost *or* Every time I lost

Question 5: Yes, less than half of the time I lost *or* Yes, most of the time

Question 6: Yes, in the past, but not now *or* Yes

Question 7: Yes

Question 8: Yes

Question 9: Yes

Question 10: Yes

Question 11: Yes

Question 12 is not counted.

Question 13: Yes

Question 14: Yes

Question 15: Yes

Question 16a: Yes

Question 16b: Yes

Question 16c: Yes

Question 16d: Yes

Question 16e: Yes

Question 16f: Yes

Question 16g: Yes

Question 16h: Yes

Question 16i: Yes

Questions 16j and 16k are not counted.

TOTAL = (20 questions are counted)

3 or 4 = Potential pathological gambler (problem gambler)

5 or more = Probable pathological gambler

Appendix 54

Barriers in Thinking

Blueprint for Change

• Barriers in Thinking	➢ Appropriate Staff Responses	❖ Steps to Responsible Thinking

1. Closed Thinking
 	
• Non-receptive
• That is my business
• "He started it."
• Good at pointing out faults of others
• Little or no self-discipline
• Deceives by omitting facts
• Is not self-critical
• Disregards feedback from others
	➢ Require complete honesty
	➢ Point out lies
	➢ Point out contradictions
	➢ Check to see if the individual has understood what has been said.
	  • Avoid argument—stay focused by calmly repeating yourself
	  • "Can you and I have an agreement?"
	  • "What Thinking led you to choose . . ."
	  • "Let us look at what others who've succeeded have done."
	➢ Help the individual see his or her part in the situation
		1. Open Channels
		
		• Receptive to positive change
		• Is doing things differently
		• Communicates openly and honestly
		• Evaluates self honestly and critically

2. Victim Role • Sees self as victim (not victimizer) • "She started it." • "I could not Help it" • "He did not give me a chance"	➢ Accept no excuses ➢ Bring the focus back to the individual ➢ Emphasize reasons the individual cannot be trusted or has betrayed trust	**2. Personal Accountability** • Proves to be reliable, prompt, and prepared • Fulfills commitments and promises • Takes responsibility for choices and actions

Source: Spon, A.R. (1999). *Blueprint for change: Corrective thinking facilitator's guide.* Roscoe, IL: Truthought, LLC.

More information can be obtained by contacting Truthought Corrective Thinking Process, PO Box 22, Roscoe, IL 61073. 815-389-0127. Copyright © 2001. Used with permission.

(Continued)

(Continued)

• Barriers in Thinking	➤ Appropriate Staff Responses	❖ Steps to Responsible Thinking
• Blames others or authorities to make them feel it is their fault • Blames environment, poverty, race, etc. • States that others cannot be trusted	➤ Never let betrayal, rule-breaking, or crime go unnoticed/without consequences ➤ Insist on trust being earned • "What led you to choose . . . ?" • "What is your responsibility?" • "What will you do differently?"	• Works a changing destructive patterns
3. Superior Self-Image • Focuses only on positive traits • "I am a good guy" • "There's nothing wrong with me . . ." • "It is no big deal . . ." • Refuses to admit harm to others • Fails to acknowledge own destructive behavior	➤ Point out harm that has been done (use ripple chart) ➤ Do not allow minimizing, point to reality of his or her behavior ➤ Help the individual realize that good actions do not cancel out harmful actions • "Look inside yourself and decide." • "Ask yourself on the inside . . ." • "Only you can convince yourself." • "What effect have you had on others?"	**3. Self-Respect** • Shows gratitude • Earns others' respect • Explores alternatives before acting • Controls feelings and works toward positive solutions
4. Reckless Attitude • Says, "I cannot," when means "I will not" • No concept of obligation • Unwilling to do anything boring or disagreeable • Considers responsible living to be dull and unsatisfying • Complies only when immediate benefits exist • Exhibits self-pity • Psychosomatic aches and pains to avoid effort • Tires to prove inability when actually refusing to comply • Denies obligation by saying, "I forgot" • Lacks empathy for others	➤ Do not accept "I cannot," when it means "I will not" ➤ Give consequences for lack of effort ➤ Point out the energy the individuals have for activities they like ➤ Explain how to meet obligations ➤ Encourage individuals to stick with it until genuine interest develops ➤ Ask how they would feel if others did not meet obligations or "forgot," such as parents not feeding or providing for them ➤ Use a "victim script" to get the individual to develop empathy for others ➤ Emphasize consequences of failing to meet obligations or being irresponsible ➤ Emphasize consequences of crime or breaking rules	**4. Daily Effort** • Is considerate of others • Has healthy relationships • Works toward resolution • Balances time, work, and fun to achieve what is expected • Fulfills obligations to family, friends, teacher, employer, community • Realizes that interest and motivation follow effort and change

• **Barriers in Thinking**	➤ **Appropriate Staff Responses**	❖ **Steps to Responsible Thinking**

• Fails to put self in others' place
• Apathetic
• Gets excited doing the forbidden
• Does not look for alternatives
• Short attention span
• Gives up or quits early
	➤ Emphasize consequences of apathy and procrastination
	
	  • "What do you want to accomplish?"
	  • "What are your obligations to . . . ?"
	  • "What can you do to improve your relationship with . . . ?"	

5. Instant Gratification
 	
• "I want it now"
• Does not learn from past mistakes
• Demands an immediate response
• Makes decisions on feelings
• Fails to plan ahead except to accomplish the forbidden or to imagine getting away with it
• Believes success comes overnight
• Thinks failure is anything less than #1
• Easily slips into "O" State when tactics are interrupted
• Blames someone or something immediately. Does not suspend judgment for more information
	➤ Point out irresponsible decision-making based on feelings or assumptions
	➤ Help individuals examine faulty assumptions and find facts
	➤ Explain how some decisions cannot be made immediately or may not work out as planned
	➤ Emphasize that time and effort are necessary to gain benefits or payoffs from being responsible
	➤ Help individuals establish habits or thinking ahead at every step
	➤ Help them view things in stages or accomplishment
	➤ Aid them in building toward something important to them
	➤ Assist them in the process of learning from mistakes
	
	  • "What is important about . . . ?"
	  • "How will this affect your future?"
	  • "Have you done the same thing before?"
	  • "What are the facts?"
		5. Self-Discipline
		
		• Exhibits patience with others
		• Shows patience when facing problems
		• Plans and build toward the future
		• Makes decisions on facts, not feelings
		• Learns from the past and relies on guilt feelings to consider the effects on others

6. Fear of "Losing Face"
 	
• Profound fear of personal insults
• Has irrational fears but refused to admit them
• Feels put-down when things do not go his or her way
• Experiences "O" State–powerless when held accountable
	➤ Identify and challenge fears
	➤ Teach that criticism is something everyone needs when it is accurate
	➤ Address the individual's need to trust responsible others
	➤ Show where his or her expectations were unrealistic
	
	  • "What would it take for you to respect yourself?"
	  • "Who do you trust?"
	  • "If you could get help with something, what would that be?"
		6. Courage Over Fear
		
		• Sees criticism as helpful feedback
		• Acts on feedback from others
		• Trusts others and asks for advice or help on what to do or how to do things
		• Admits fears
		• Meets challenges without dodging

Appendix 55

Psychotherapeutic Medications 2008

What Every Counselor Should Know

About this Publication

Originally developed as a companion piece to the Mid-America ATTC systems change curriculum, *A Collaborative Response: Addressing the Needs of Consumers With Co-Occurring Substance Use and Mental Health Disorders*, this edition includes adaptations made for inclusion in CSAT's *TIP 42: Substance Abuse Treatment for Persons with Co-Occurring Disorders*. The language has been modified to increase readability for a larger audience and, in keeping with the goal of updating the publication biannually, several new medications are included.

Counselors' Use Of This Publication

A list of generic and brand names is included for the following medications:

Antipsychotics/Neuroleptics

Antiparkinsonian Medications

Antimanic Medications

Antidepressant Medications

Antianxiety Medications

Stimulant Medications

Narcotic and Opioid Analgesics

Hypnotics (Sleep Aids)

Addiction Treatment Medications

Alcohol

Opioids

Tobacco

Others

Source: Mid-America Addiction Technology Transfer Center. (2008). *Psychotherapeutic medications 2008: What every counselor should know* (7th ed.). Kansas City, MO: Author. Retrieved from http://www.narha.org/images/pdf/resources/PsychotherapeuticMedications2008.pdf

Each section includes the following topics for the different medication types:

Purpose: Describes typical uses of medications, including specific symptoms treated and positive treatment response expected.

Usual dose, frequency, and side effects: Discusses when and how medications are administered, typical side effects, and methods for monitoring side effects.

Potential side effects: Lists common side effects.

Potential for abuse or dependence: Elaborates upon those medications with potential for abuse and/or physical dependence. Discusses withdrawal reactions and management of withdrawal.

Emergency Conditions: Includes risks associated with overdose, withdrawal or other drug reactions.

Cautions: Describes risks associated with use of additional medications (i.e., over the counter), increasing or discontinuing use of medications, adverse consequences with concurrent use of alcohol and/or street drugs.

Special Considerations for Pregnant Women: Describes risks for pregnant women prescribed psychotherapeutic medications. References to research are included. The special role of the substance abuse counselor in encouraging discussion between clients and the prescribing physician is emphasized.

Important Notes Across Medication Types

Name brand medications have a limited patent. When the patent expires, the medication may be made as a generic. The generic name of a medication is the *actual name of the medication and never changes*. A generic medication may be made by many different manufacturers. Additionally, manufacturers can make several forms of a single medication with only slight variations. For instance, they may vary the color, size, or shape of the medication. If a person says his or her medication "looks different" AND he or she is experiencing new side effects, *contact the prescriber immediately*.

For ease of reading, some technical terms are defined in accompanying footnotes. All medications are listed in the index along with page numbers for quick reference. When specific brands are discussed in the accompanying text, the name of the medication is **bolded** to assist the reader in finding the reference.

This publication is available for free download via the Mid-America ATTC Web site at www.ATTC network.org.

Limitations of the Publication

This publication is designed as a quick "desk reference" for substance abuse and mental health treatment providers. It is not intended to be used as a complete reference for psychotherapeutic medications. The section, "Tips for Communicating with Physicians," is meant to be just that: tips for communicating. The publication assumes providers are knowledgeable about the Health Insurance Portability and Accountability Act (HIPAA) regulations, including issues related to privacy and confidentiality and will use these communication tips in accordance with those regulations. For more information about HIPAA, refer to the SAMHSA Web site "HIPAA: What It Means for Mental Health and Substance Abuse Services" at http://www.hipaa.samhsa.gov/hipaa.html.

The section, "Talking with Clients about their Medication," is a prompt designed to help the provider initiate conversation about medication management and adherence with clients who have co occurring mental health and substance use disorders. It is not intended as a complete guide to client education. For a more thorough discussion of these co occurring issues, see the current edition of the American Society of Addiction Medicine's (ASAM's) *Principles of Addiction Medicine*, Third Edition (ASAM 2003).

For physicians desiring a more in-depth discussion regarding the challenges of treating specific population groups with substance use disorders (e.g., homeless, older adults, people with HIV/AIDS or hepatitis, pregnant or nursing women, etc.), which include medication compliance, adverse drug interactions, and relapse with the use of potentially addictive medications, refer to the current edition of the American Society of Addiction Medicine's (ASAM's) *Principles of Addiction Medicine*, Third Edition (ASAM 2003), and CSAT's *TIP 42: Substance Abuse Treatment for Persons with Co Occurring Disorders* (CSAT 2005).

Antipsychotics/Neuroleptics

GENERIC	BRAND
Traditional antipsychotics	
chlorpromazine	Thorazine, Largactil
fluphenazine	Prolixin, Permitil, Anatensol
haloperidol	Haldol
loxapine	Loxitane, Daxolin
mesoridazine	Serentil
molindone	Moban, Lidone
perphenazine	Trilafon, Etrafon
pimozide	Orap
thioridazine	Mellaril
thiothixene	Navane
trifluoperazine	Stelazine
Novel or atypical antipsychotics	
aripiprazole	Abilify
clozapine	Clozaril
olanzapine	Zyprexa, Zyprexa Zydis
paliperidone	Invega
quetiapine fumarate	Seroquel
risperidone	Risperdal
risperidone long-acting injection	Risperdal Consta
ziprasidone	Geodon

Purpose

Antipsychotics (neuroleptics) are most frequently used for persons who experience psychotic symptoms as a result of having some form of schizophrenia, severe depression or bipolar disorder. They may be used to treat brief psychotic episodes caused by drugs of abuse. Psychotic symptoms may include being out of touch with reality, "hearing voices," and having false perceptions (e.g., thinking you are a famous person, thinking someone is out to hurt you). Antipsychotic medications can be effective in either minimizing or stopping these symptoms altogether. In some cases, these medications can shorten the course of the illness or prevent it from happening again.

Positive treatment response to antipsychotic medications allows many with severe and disabling mental disorders to live and function in the community, often relatively normally. This positive response may include thoughts that are more rational, decreased psychosis[1], paranoia and delusions, behavior that is more appropriate, and the ability to have relationships and work.

---

[1]*psychosis:* A mental disorder characterized by distinct distortions of a person's mental capacity, ability to recognize reality, and relationships to others to such a degree that it interferes with that person's ability to function in everyday life.

All of the older and newer antipsychotic medications are approved by the Food and Drug Administration (FDA) and are thus evidence-based treatments (EBT) for schizophrenia. The newest antipsychotic medications—**Risperdal, Zyprexa, Seroquel, Geodon**, and **Abilify**—are showing positive effects across a range of disorders. These medications stabilize mood and are also used to treat bipolar disorder. They are being added to antidepressants to treat severe depressions. Some have been shown to be effective at relieving anxiety in low doses, but the FDA does not approve this use. A growing number of the atypical antipsychotic medications have received FDA approval for treatment of manic episodes, and some for extended treatment of bipolar disorder.

Usual Dose, Frequency & Side Effects

All medications have specific doses and frequencies. The physician will specify the exact amount of medication and when it should be taken. This information is on the prescription bottle. Many medications are taken once a day, some at bedtime to take advantage of the drowsiness side effect of some antipsychotic medications. Several medications are taken in pill form or liquid form. Others are given by injection once or twice per month to ensure that the medication is taken reliably. It is important to take medications on schedule. It is also important that people talk to their doctor so they know about potential side effects and steps they need to take to monitor their health.

Novel or atypical antipsychotics are different from traditional antipsychotics. These medications are more powerful with treatmentresistant schizophrenia but may also be used with severe depression or other psychiatric illness. Because the atypical antipsychotics work in a slightly different way than traditional antipsychotics, they are less likely to produce serious side effects, such as tardive dyskinesia[2] or neuroleptic malignant syndrome[3]. The most common mild side effects are either sedation[4] or agitation, especially when starting the medications. The most worrisome side effects are weight gain and elevated blood sugar and lipids[5]. There is also some evidence that the use of atypical antipsychotics may lead to the development of diabetes mellitus[6] (Sernyak et al. 2002). Because diabetes is associated with obesity, it is unclear whether the diabetes is actually caused by certain atypical antipsychotic medications or obesity. These issues can be medically worrisome and can lead to medication noncompliance. Since effectiveness and side effects vary across medications and people, matching the right medication to the right person is the key.

Clozapine (**Clozaril**) can very rarely cause serious abnormalities or irregularities in the blood cells (blood dyscrasias[7]). Approximately 1 to 2 percent of people who take **Clozaril** develop a condition in which their white blood cell count drops drastically (agranulocytosis[8]). As a result, they are at high risk for infections due to a compromised immune system, and this could be fatal. However, most cases of agranulocytosis can be treated successfully by stopping **Clozaril** treatment. To maintain safety, white blood cell counts must be

---

[2] *tardive dyskinesia:* A central nervous system disorder characterized by twitching of the face and tongue, and involuntary motor movements of the trunk and limbs; occurring especially as a side effect of prolonged use of antipsychotic medications.

[3] *neuroleptic malignant syndrome:* A very rare but lifethreatening neurological disorder most often caused by a reaction to antipsychotic/neuroleptic medications. Typically developing within the first 2 weeks of treatment; but can develop at any time. The syndrome can also occur in people taking antiparkinsonian medications if discontinued abruptly.

[4] *sedation:* Inducing a relaxed easy state especially by the use of *sedatives* (drugs).

[5] *lipids:* Any of various substances including fats, waxes, and phosphatides that with proteins and carbohydrates make up the principal structural components of living cells.

[6] *diabetes mellitus:* An endocrine disorder in which insulin is inadequately secreted or used by the body.

[7] *blood dyscrasias:* A disease of the blood usually involving cellular abnormalities (i.e., poorly functioning or fewer than normal platelets, or loss of certain blood proteins called "clotting factors"; poorly functioning or decreased numbers of red and/or white blood cells.

[8] *agranulocytosis:* A condition in which there are too few of a specific type of white blood cell called neutrophils in the blood. Affected people are susceptible to infections.

checked each week for 6 months and every 2 weeks thereafter. The results must be sent to the person's pharmacy before he or she can pick up the next supply of medication.

Risperidone (**Risperdal**) and olanzapine (**Zyprexa**) came soon after clozapine. Both are strong and predictable antipsychotics. Risperidone may cause involuntary movements, tremors, muscular rigidity, and immobility without paralysis, and at higher doses and is moderately sedative. Olanzapine is highly sedative and has more tendency to cause weight gain and other metabolic changes.

Risperidone long-acting injections (**Risperdal Consta**) also a newly approved antipsychotic, is an injection of microencapsulated[9] medication that releases into the body at a constant level. An injection is usually given every 2 weeks. Side effects are similar to those for **Risperdal**.

Quetiapine (**Seroquel**) is antipsychotic only in higher doses, but is most used for non-psychotic conditions such as bipolar disorder, depression, and PTSD conditions. It is very sedative and calming at moderate to high doses. In some prison settings, there have been reports of "abuse" of both quetiapine and olanzapine, by prisoners feigning psychotic symptoms in order to obtain heavy sedation.

Ziprasidone (**Geodon**) and aripiprazole (**Abilify**) are newer agents and have only moderate sedative and few weight, diabetes, or lipid effects, but their antipsychotic response seems to be less predictable.

Paliperidone (**Invega**) is the newest of the antipsychotics and is related to risperidone but contained in a capsule which distributes the medicine over 24 hours.

Traditional antipsychotics are cheap, and the newer ones are expensive. In general, the newer antipsychotics, when taken in proper dosage, have fewer clinical side effects and a broader treatment response than traditional antipsychotics.

Potential Side Effects

Tardive Dyskinesia

- Involuntary movements of the tongue or mouth
- Jerky, purposeless movements of legs, arms or entire body
- More often seen in women
- Risk increases with age and length of time on medication
- Usually seen with long-term treatment using traditional antipsychotic medications; rarely seen with atypical antipsychotic medications

Symptoms of diabetes mellitus (associated with obesity)

- Excessive thirst and hunger
- Fatigue
- Frequent urination
- Headaches
- Slow healing cuts and/or blemishes
- Weight loss

Neuroleptic Malignant Syndrome (very rare)

- Blood pressure up and down
- Dazed and confused
- Difficulty breathing
- Muscle stiffness

---

[9] *microencapsulated:* To enclose in a tiny capsule material (as a medicine) that is released when the capsule is broken, melted, or dissolved.

- Rapid heart rate
- Sweating and shakiness
- Temperature above normal

Other

- Blurred vision
- Changes in sexual functioning
- Constipation
- Diminished enthusiasm
- Dizziness
- Drowsiness
- Dry mouth
- Lowered blood pressure
- Muscle rigidity
- Nasal congestion
- Restlessness
- Sensitivity to bright light
- Slowed heart rate
- Slurred speech
- Upset stomach
- Weight gain

Note: Any side effects that bother a person need to be reported and discussed with the prescribing physician. Anticholinergic/antiparkinsonian medications like **Cogentin** or **Artane** may be prescribed to control movement difficulties associated with the use of antipsychotic medications.

Emergency Conditions

Contact a physician and/or seek emergency medical assistance if the person experiences involuntary muscle movements, painful muscle spasms, difficulty urinating, eye pain, skin rash or any of the symptoms listed above under *tardive dyskinesia*, and *neuroleptic malignant syndrome*. An overdose is always considered an emergency and treatment should be sought immediately.

Cautions

- Doctors and pharmacists should be told about all medications being taken and dosage, including over the counter preparations, vitamins, minerals, and herbal supplements (i.e., St. John's wort, echinacea, ginkgo, and ginseng).
- People taking antipsychotic medications should not increase their dose unless this has been *checked with their physician and a change is ordered*.

Special Considerations for Pregnant Women

For women of childbearing age who may be or think they may be pregnant, the physician should discuss the safety of this medication before starting, continuing, or discontinuing medication treatment. Substance abuse counselors may have a role in encouraging this discussion by suggesting their clients talk with the prescribing physician.

Generally, the use of antipsychotic medications should be avoided in the first trimester unless the mother poses a danger to herself, to others, or to the unborn child, or if the mother shows signs of profound psychosis (Cohen 1989). Tapering and discontinuation of antipsychotic medication 10 days to 2 weeks before delivery is generally advised, though the way this is done varies by medication (Mortola 1989).

Antiparkinsonian Medications

GENERIC	**BRAND**
amantadine hydrochloride	Symmetrel, Symadine
benztropine mesylate	Cogentin
diphenhydramine hydrochloride	Benadryl
trihexyphenidyl hydrochloride	Artane

Purpose

Antiparkinsonian (anticholinergic) medications are used to control the side effects associated with antipsychotic medications. They are called antiparkinsonian because the neurological side effects of antipsychotic medications are similar to the symptoms of Parkinson's disease (i.e., tremors, stiff or rigid muscles, poor balance, and a distinctive unsteady walk).

Usual Dose & Frequency

All medications have specific doses and frequencies. The physician will specify the exact amount of medication and when it should be taken. This information is on the prescription bottle. These medications have very specific doses and taking too much can be harmful. A doctor must be consulted in order to safely change the dose in response to side effects of the antipsychotic medications.

Potential Side Effects

- Constipation
- Dizziness
- Dry mouth
- Heart failure
- Irritability
- Light headedness
- Stomach upset
- Tiredness

Emergency Conditions

Report immediately any overdose or changes in heart rate and/or rhythm to the doctor.

Potential for Abuse or Dependence

Despite their utility, these medications can be abused by some persons with severe mental illness who require neuroleptics. Survey research has found that many abusers of antiparkinsonians used these medications "to get high, to increase pleasure, to decrease depression, to increase energy and to relax" (Buhrich et al. 2000, p. 929). The survey also found that the misuse of other drugs accompanied the misuse of antiparkinsonian medications. Consequently, in the context of co-occurring mental health and substance use disorders, providers and consumers need to be aware of and openly communicate about the abuse potential of these medications.

Cautions

- Doctors and pharmacists should be told about all medications being taken and dosage, including over-the-counter preparations, vitamins, minerals, and herbal supplements (i.e., St. John's wort, echinacea, ginkgo, ginseng).
- People taking antiparkinsonian medications should not increase their dose unless this has been *checked with their physician and a change is ordered*.

Special Considerations for Pregnant Women

The risk of birth defects associated with **Cogentin**, **Artane**, and **Benadryl** is not clear, although there is some evidence to suggest that amantadine (**Symmetrel, Symadine**) may produce a deformed baby (Mortola 1989). For all women of childbearing age who may be or think they may be pregnant, the physician should discuss the safety of this medication before starting, continuing, or discontinuing medication treatment. Substance abuse counselors may have a role in encouraging this discussion by suggesting their clients talk with the prescribing physician.

Antimanic Medications

GENERIC	BRAND
Lithium products	
lithium carbonate	Eskalith, Eskalith CR, Lithane, Lithobid, Lithonate, Lithotabs
lithium citrate	Cibalith
Anticonvulsant products	
carbamazepine	Tegretol
divalproex sodium	Depakote, Depakote Sprinkle, Depakote ER
lamotrigine	Lamictal
Atypical antipsychotics	
(see Antipsychotics/Neuroleptics, p. 6 for side effects)	
aripiprazole	Abilify
olanzapine	Zyprexa, Zyprexa Zydis
olanzapine plus fluoxetine	Symbyax
quetiapine fumarate	Seroquel
risperidone	Risperdal
ziprasidone	Geodon
Other anticonvulsant products (not FDA approved for the treatment of mania)	
gabapentin	Neurontin
levetiracetam	Keppra
oxcarbazepine	Trileptal
tiagabine hydrochloride	Gabitril
topiramate	Topamax, Topamax Sprinkle
valproate sodium	Depakene, Depacon
valproic acid	Depakene

Purpose

Antimanic medications are used to control the mood swings of bipolar (manic–depressive) illness. Bipolar illness is characterized by cycling mood changes from severe highs (mania) to severe lows (depression). The "highs" and "lows" vary in intensity, frequency, and severity. Bipolar I conditions include full manic episodes. Bipolar II conditions, by definition do not include full mania, but are characterized more as depression plus a low level of mania (hypomania). Bipolar cycles that occur more often than 3 times a year are considered "rapid cycling," a condition often found in people with higher rates of substance abuse.

Positive treatment responses to antimanic medications include less hyperactivity, pressured speech and/or illogical thought. They improve the clients' ability to sleep, concentrate and allow the person to function more normally.

If bipolar disorder is left untreated, the associated mania may worsen into a psychotic state and depression may result in thoughts of suicide. By leveling mood swings with antimanic medications, some of the suicidal and other self-harming behaviors can be decreased. Additionally, appropriate treatment with antimanic medications can reduce a person's violent outbursts toward others or property.

All of the lithium products, **Tegretol**, **Depakote**, and those products listed under atypical antipsychotics qualify as evidence-based treatments (EBT) for Bipolar I disorder. **Lamictal** qualifies as an EBT for Bipolar II disorder.

Usual Dose, Frequency & Side Effects

All medications have specific doses and frequencies. The physician will specify the exact amount of medication and when it should be taken. This information is provided on the prescription bottle. Most medications in this class are given 2 to 4 times per day. Some extended release formulations[10] may be given every 12 hours. Dosage is determined by the active amount of medication found in the person's blood after taking the medication, and by his or her response to the medication. Expect a check of monthly blood levels until the person is at his or her optimal dose.

Lithium products: Most common side effects are tremor, acne, and weight gain. People taking these products may require more fluids than they did before taking the medication. However, too much fluid in a person's diet can "wash" the lithium out of his or her system, and too little fluid can allow the lithium to concentrate in the system. Additionally, anything that can decrease sodium in the body (i.e., decreased table salt intake, a lowsalt diet, excessive sweating during strenuous exercise, diarrhea, vomiting) could result in lithium toxicity[11]. People taking any antimanic medications should have blood levels tested regularly to check the concentration level of the medication in their bodies. Specifically, people taking lithium products, **Tegretol**, **Depakote**, and **Depakene** need their blood levels monitored.

Anticonvulsant products:[12] Most common side effects are sedation and weight gain. **Keppra** is noted for causing mood changes, primarily depression and anger in some people. This may limit its use as a mood stabilizer.

For the most common side effects of atypical antipsychotics, refer to *Antipsychotics/Neuroleptics,* p. 6. It is likely that all of the newer atypical antipsychotics mentioned in the previous section will soon be FDA approved for treatment of mania.

---

[10] *extended release formulations:* Medications that have been made so that they act over a long period of time and do not have to be taken as often; may be referred to as CR (controlled release), ER or XR (extended release), or SR (sustained release).

[11] *lithium toxicity:* The quality, state, or relative degree of being poisonous, in this instance because of the presence or concentration of too much of the drug lithium in the blood.

[12] *anticonvulsants:* Usually refers to an agent that prevents or stops *convulsions;* an abnormal violent, involuntary contraction or series of contractions of the muscles.

Potential Side Effects

- Blurred vision
- Coma*
- Diarrhea*
- Drowsiness
- Fatigue
- Hand tremor*
- Increased thirst and urination*
- Inflammation of the pancreas
- Irregular heart beats
- Kidney damage*
- Liver inflammation, hepatitis
- Nausea or vomiting
- Problems with the blood, both red and white cells
- Rash and skin changes
- Seizures
- Under or overactive thyroid*
- Weakness
- Weight gain

*These side effects are associated with lithium, anticonvulsants, and atypical antipsychotics only. Effects vary greatly between persons.

Emergency Conditions

Lithium overdose is a life-threatening emergency. Signs of lithium toxicity may include nausea, vomiting, diarrhea, drowsiness, mental dullness, slurred speech, confusion, dizziness, muscle twitching, irregular heartbeat and blurred vision. An overdose of any of the other antimanic medications is always considered an emergency and treatment should be sought immediately.

Cautions

- Doctors and pharmacists should be told about all medications being taken and dosage, including over-the-counter preparations, vitamins, minerals, and herbal supplements (i.e., St. John's wort, echinacea, ginkgo, ginseng).
- People taking antimanic medications should not increase their dose unless this has been *checked with their physician and a change is ordered*.
- Persons taking antimanic medications are particularly vulnerable to adverse medical consequences if they concurrently use alcohol and/or street drugs.
- Lithium can cause birth defects in the first 3 months of pregnancy.
- Thyroid function must be monitored if a person takes lithium.
- Heavy sweating or use of products that cause excessive urination (i.e., coffee, tea, some high caffeine sodas, use of diuretics) can lower the level of lithium in the blood.
- Blood tests for medication levels need to be checked every 1 to 2 months.
- Use of these medications will lower the effectiveness of birth control medications.

Special Considerations for Pregnant Women

Some antimanic medications, such as Depakene (valproic acid), are associated with several birth defects if taken during pregnancy. If this type of medication must be used during pregnancy, the woman must be told that there is substantial risk of malformations (Robert et al. 2001). Lithium is also a medication that may be harmful to an unborn child. Those exposed to lithium before week 12 of gestation are at increased risk of heart abnormalities. For women taking lithium, blood levels of the medication should be monitored every 2 weeks. Ultrasound examinations should be performed on the fetus to rule out the development of an enlarged thyroid (goiter) in the unborn child (Mortola 1989).

Generally, the use of antipsychotic medications should be avoided in the first trimester unless the mother poses a danger to herself, to others, or to the unborn child, or if the mother shows signs of profound psychosis (Cohen 1989). Tapering and discontinuation of antipsychotic medication 10 days to 2 weeks before delivery is generally advised, though the way this is done varies by medication (Mortola 1989).

For women of childbearing age who may be or think they may be pregnant, the physician should discuss the safety of these medications before starting, continuing, or discontinuing medication treatment. Substance abuse counselors may have a role in encouraging this discussion by suggesting their clients talk with the prescribing physician.

Antidepressant Medications

GENERIC	BRAND
SSRIs — Selective Serotonin Reuptake Inhibitors	
citalopram	Celexa
escitalopram oxalate	Lexapro
fluoxetine	Prozac, Prozac Weekly, Sarafem
fluvoxamine	Luvox
paroxetine	Paxil, Paxil CR
sertraline	Zoloft
Other new antidepressants	
bupropion	Wellbutrin, Wellbutrin SR
duloxetine	Cymbalta
mirtazapine	Remeron, Remeron SolTab
nefazodone	Serzone
trazodone	Desyrel
venlafaxine	Effexor, Effexor ER
Tricyclics & quatracyclics	
Amitriptyline	Elavil
Amoxapine	Asendin
Clomipramine	Anafranil
Desipramine	Nopramin, Pertofrane
Doxepin	Sinequan
Imipramine	Tofranil
Maprotiline	Ludiomil
Nortriptyline	Pamelor
Protriptyline	Vivactil
Monoamine Oxidase (MAO) Inhibitors	
Isocarboxazid	Marplan
Phenelzine	Nardil
Tranylcypromine	Parnate

Purpose

Antidepressant medications are used for moderate to serious depressions, but they can also be very helpful for milder depressions such as dysthymia. Most antidepressants must be taken for a period of 3 to 4 weeks to begin to reduce or take away the symptoms of depression but a full therapeutic effect may not be present for several months. Antidepressants are also the first line medications for certain anxiety disorders such as panic disorder, social phobia, and obsessive-compulsive disorders.

Positive early treatment responses to antidepressant medications include improved energy, concentration, and sleep. Later positive treatment responses include improved mood, attitude, and statements of "feeling better."

Treatment for a single episode of major depression should be continued for 2 years before discontinuing. Since major depression is a chronic recurrent illness for many people, long-term use of antidepressants is often indicated (much as one would take medication for high blood pressure or diabetes for a long period of time). Discontinuing antidepressant therapy before the depression is completely resolved may result in the person decompensating[13] and possibly becoming medication resistant. Untreated depression may result in suicide, especially with co-occurring substance use disorders. Therefore, treatment for depression must be taken as seriously as treatment for any other major life-threatening illness.

Types of Antidepressants

SSRIs are the most frequently prescribed class of antidepressants because of their broad effectiveness, low side effects, and safety. They are thought to affect the serotonin[14] system to reduce symptoms of depression. The extended release formula of fluoxetine (**Prozac Weekly**) can be dosed once per week. **Sarafem** is fluoxetine under another label used for treatment of Premenstrual Dysphoric Disorder. SSRIs include both less expensive generic medications (fluoxetine, citalopram, and paroxetine) and more expensive brand name only versions.

Other new antidepressants, such as venlafaxine (**Effexor**) work on both the serotonin and norepinephrine[15] levels. Bupropion (**Wellbutrin**) is an antidepressant unrelated to other antidepressants. It has more effect on norepinephrine and dopamine levels than on serotonin levels in the brain. In addition, bupropion (**Wellbutrin**) can be "activating" (as opposed to sedating). It is not associated with weight gain or sexual dysfunction like many other antidepressant medications. Bupropion (**Wellbutrin**) should, however, be avoided by people who are at risk for or who currently have a seizure disorder.

The MAO inhibitors and the tricyclic and quatracyclic antidepressants (named for their chemical structures) are older and less commonly used due to safety and side effects. MAOs are used for "atypical depressions," which produce symptoms like oversleeping, anxiety or panic attacks, and phobias. Also, they may be used when a person does not respond to other antidepressants. The older tricyclics may be preferred in spite of their common side effects because they are inexpensive.

Usual Dose, Frequency & Side Effects

All medications have specific doses and frequencies. The physician will specify the exact amount of medication and when it should be taken. This information is provided on the prescription bottle. Several factors are considered before an antidepressant is prescribed: the type of medication, the person's individual body

---

[13] *decompensate:* Loss of the body's ability to correct a defect by over development of or increased functioning of another organ or unimpaired parts of the same organ; loss of psychological ability to counterbalance feelings of inferiority, frustration, or failure in one area by achievement in another.

[14] *serotonin:* A type of neurotransmitter in the brain.

[15] *norepinephrine:* A hormone secreted by the adrenal gland, which (together with epinephrine) brings about changes in the body known as the "fight or flight" reaction. It works as a neurotransmitter in the brain.

chemistry, weight, and age. Generally, people are started on a low dose, and the dosage is slowly raised until the optimal effects are reached without troublesome side effects.

Both mild sedation and mild agitation sometimes occur with SSRI use. The most troubling SSRI side effect is decreased sexual performance, which may be difficult for many persons to discuss. Common side effects specific to both bupropion (**Wellbutrin**) and venlafaxine (**Effexor**) include sleeplessness and agitation. For the older tricyclics, side effects include dry mouth and sedation.

Potential Side Effects

SSRIs

- Anxiety, agitation or nervousness
- Change in appetite (lack of or increase)
- Change in sexual desire
- Confusion
- Decrease in sexual ability
- Diarrhea or loose stools
- Dizziness
- Dry mouth
- Headache
- Heart rhythm changes
- Increased sweating
- Insomnia or sleepiness
- Lack or increase of appetite
- Shakiness
- Stomach upset
- Taste disturbances (**Wellbutrin**)
- Weight loss or gain

Tricyclics & quatracyclics

- Allergic reactions
- Blood cell problems (both white and red cells)
- Blurred vision
- Change in sexual desire
- Changes in heartbeat and rhythm
- Constipation
- Decrease in sexual ability
- Difficulty with urination
- Dizziness when changing position
- Dry mouth
- Fatigue
- Heart block[16]
- Increased sweating
- Kidney failure (**Asendin**)
- Muscle twitches
- Neuroleptic Malignant Syndrome (**Asendin**)
- Seizures

---

[16] *heart block:* A condition where the heart beats irregularly or much more slowly than normal. Sometimes the heart may even stop for up to 20 seconds; caused by a delay or disruption of the electrical signals that usually control the heartbeat.

- Stroke
- Weakness
- Weight gain

MAO Inhibitors

- Blood cell problems (both white and red cells)
- Dizziness when changing position
- Fluid retention (swollen ankles, feet, legs or hands)
- Headache
- High blood pressure crisis[17]
- Insomnia
- Lack of appetite
- Rapid heart beat

Emergency Conditions

An overdose of any of the MAO inhibitors, tricyclics, quatracyclics, or other antidepressants is serious and potentially life threatening and *must be reported to a physician immediately*. Symptoms of tricyclic and quatracyclic overdose may include rapid heartbeat, dilated pupils, flushed face, agitation, loss of consciousness, seizures, irregular heart rhythm, heart and breathing stopping, and death.

The potential for a fatal outcome from an overdose with the SSRIs is much less. However, the possibility that a person has attempted suicide should be dealt with as an emergency situation that needs immediate intervention.

Cautions

- Doctors and pharmacists should be told about all medications being taken and dosage, including over-the-counter preparations, vitamins, minerals, and herbal supplements (i.e., St. John's wort, echinacea, ginkgo, ginseng).
- People taking antidepressant medications should not increase their dose unless this has been *checked with their physician and a change is ordered.*
- Withdrawal from SSRIs and other new antidepressants can cause flu-like symptoms. Discontinuing antidepressant therapy should be done gradually under a physician's care.
- People taking MAO inhibitors must avoid all foods with high levels of tryptophan or tyramine (e.g., aged cheese, wine, beer, chicken liver, chocolate, bananas, soy sauce, meat tenderizers, salami, bologna, and pickled fish). High levels of caffeine must also be avoided. If eaten, these foods may react with the MAO inhibitors to raise blood pressure to dangerous levels.
- Many medications interact with the MAO inhibitors. It is largely for this reason that they are rarely used. Other medications should not be taken unless the treating physician approves them. Even a simple over-the-counter cold medication can cause life-threatening side effects.
- People using MAO inhibitors should check all new medications with a physician or pharmacist before taking them.
- People taking antidepressant medications are particularly vulnerable to adverse medical consequences if they concurrently use alcohol and/or street drugs.
- If there is little to no change in symptoms after 3 to 4 weeks, talk to the doctor about raising the dose or changing the antidepressant.
- Treatment with antidepressants usually lasts a minimum of 9 to 12 months. Many patients are on long-term antidepressant therapy to avoid the frequency and severity of depressive episodes.

---

[17] *high blood pressure crisis:* A severe increase in blood pressure that can lead to stroke. Two types—emergency and urgent—require immediate medical attention.

Special Considerations for Pregnant Women

Using SSRIs is safer for the mother and fetus than using tricyclic antidepressants. Fluoxetine (**Prozac**) is the most studied SSRI in pregnancy and no increased incidence in birth defects has been noted, nor were developmental abnormalities of the nervous system observed in preschoolage children (Garbis and McElhatton 2001). However, possible withdrawal signs have been observed in the newborn. Fluoxetine (**Prozac**) is the recommended SSRI for use during pregnancy (Garbis and McElhatton 2001). MAO Inhibitor use is not advised in pregnancy, and its use should be discontinued immediately if a woman discovers she is pregnant (Mortola 1989).

The physician should discuss the safety of antidepressant medications before starting, continuing, or discontinuing medication treatment with all women of childbearing age who may be or think they may be pregnant. Substance abuse counselors may have a role in encouraging this discussion between their clients and the prescribing physician.

Antianxiety Medications

GENERIC	BRAND
See also SSRI Antidepressants (p. 17)	
Benzodiazepines	
Alprazolam	Xanax
Chlordiazepoxide	Librium, Libritabs, Librax
Clonazepam	Klonopin
Clorazepate	Tranxene
Diazepam	Valium
Lorazepam	Ativan
Oxazepam	Serax
Beta-blockers	
Propranolol	Inderal
Other	
Buspirone	BuSpar
Gabapentin	Neurontin
Hydroxyzine	Atarax, Vistaril
Olanzapine	Zyprexa, Zyprexa Zydis
Pregabalin	Lyrica
quetiapine fumarate	Seroquel
risperidone	Risperdal
tiagabine hydrochloride	Gabitril

Purpose

Antianxiety medications are used to help calm and relax the anxious person as well as remove troubling symptoms associated with generalized anxiety disorder, posttraumatic stress disorder (PTSD), panic, phobias, and obsessive-compulsive disorders (OCD). The most common antianxiety medications are the antidepressants and the benzodiazepines. Positive treatment response to antianxiety medications varies a great deal by medication class.

SSRI antidepressants have become first line medications for the treatment of panic, social phobia, obsessive-compulsive disorders (in higher doses) and, more recently, generalized anxiety disorder. Positive treatment response to antidepressant medications includes a gradual reduction in anxiety, panic, and PTSD or OCD symptoms over weeks to months.

Benzodiazepines have a depressant effect on the central nervous system. Positive treatment response to benzodiazepines occurs rapidly, within days. However, especially among persons with co-occurring substance use disorders, the response may be short-lived and tolerance develops leading to the need for increased doses. Additionally, benzodiazepines are cross tolerant[18] with alcohol and have a market as street drugs. For these reasons, most addiction medicine physicians only use them for a short time as alcohol withdrawal medicines, or as sedatives in acute[19] psychotic or manic episodes. If used in outpatient settings, careful monitoring for tolerance and abuse is needed.

Beta-blockers work on the central nervous system to reduce the flight or fight response. Propranolol (**Inderal**), occasionally prescribed for performance anxiety, is not addictive.

Buspirone (**BuSpar**) works through the serotonin system to induce calm. It takes 3 to 4 weeks for buspirone (**BuSpar**) to reach adequate levels in the brain to successfully combat anxiety. Hydroxyzine (**Atarax**, **Vistaril**) is an antihistamine that uses the drowsiness side effect of the antihistamine group to calm and relax. Hydroxyzine works within an hour of being taken. Buspirone (**BuSpar**) and hydroxyzine (**Atarax**, **Vistaril**) are not addictive.

Low doses of risperidone (**Risperdal**), quetiapine fumarate (**Seroquel**), olanzapine (**Zyprexa**), or other atypical antipsychotics are sometimes used "off label" as non-addictive antianxiety medications. They are usually used when several other medications have failed (though use of atypical antipsychotics is expensive and not FDA approved for treatment of anxiety disorders). Their special formulation works to reduce anxiety and help the person think more clearly, though the mechanism for this is unclear.

Gabapentin (**Neurontin**), tiagabine (**Gabitril**), and pregabalin (**Lyrica**) have all been used to treat anxiety (off label) especially in those persons with an addiction history and for whom antidepressants have been effective. These agents are all-mildly sedative, and do not cause a high dependence, or withdrawal. They are thought to enhance the effects of the body's own naturally produced calmative agent, gamma aminobutyric acid (GABA)[20]. None are FDA approved for treatment of anxiety disorders.

Usual Dose, Frequency & Side Effects

All medications have specific doses and frequencies. The physician will specify the exact amount of medication and when it should be taken. This information is provided on the prescription bottle. Usually, people are started on a low dose of medication, which is raised gradually until symptoms are removed or diminished. Major factors considered in establishing the correct dose are individual body chemistry, weight, and ability to tolerate the medication.

People taking benzodiazepines for longer than 4 to 8 weeks may develop physical tolerance to the medication. Benzodiazepines have a relatively low potential for abuse in those without addiction histories, but moderate or higher potential in those with addiction histories. Even when taken as directed, withdrawal symptoms may occur if regular use of benzodiazepines is abruptly stopped. Withdrawal from high dose abuse of benzodiazepines may be a life-threatening situation. For these reasons benzodiazepines are usually prescribed for brief periods of time—days or weeks—and sometimes intermittently for stressful situations or anxiety attacks. Except for treating alcohol or benzodiazepine withdrawal, or for acute sedation in manic or psychotic states, benzodiazepines are not recommended for most people with a past or current history of substance abuse or dependence.

---

[18] *cross tolerant*: Refers to a drug that produces a similar effect as the misused substance but does not produce the "high." Withdrawal symptoms can be minimized through use of *cross-tolerant* substances (i.e., alcohol withdrawal symptoms can be minimized through use of *cross-tolerant* sedatives, like benzodiazepines).

[19] *acute*: Marked by sharpness of severity (an *acute* pain). Having a sudden onset and short duration (*acute* disease). Urgent or critical condition.

[20] *gamma aminobutyric acid (GABA):* A type of neurotransmitter in the brain.

Beta-blockers act on the sympathetic nervous system and are not considered addictive. They also are used to treat high blood pressure, thus side effects might be low blood pressure or dizziness. Beta-blockers may enhance the effects of other psychotropic medications and are inexpensive. Propranolol (**Inderal**) is taken as needed for performance anxiety. It is taken regularly (as prescribed) for treatment of high blood pressure or other heart conditions.

Buspirone (**BuSpar**) is often used to control mild anxiety and is considered safe for long-term therapy but is expensive.

Hydroxyzine (**Atarax** and **Vistaril**) are safe, and nonaddictive medications used to reduce anxiety. They are inexpensive and may be used for longerterm therapy. Common side effects are dry mouth and sedation. A less common side effect is urinary retention in older men; this is a serious condition.

Potential Side Effects

- Blood cell irregularities
- Constipation
- Depression
- Drowsiness or lightheadedness
- Dry mouth
- Fatigue
- Heart collapse (weakened heart muscles)
- Loss of coordination
- Memory impairment (**Inderal**)
- Mental slowing or confusion
- Slowed heart beat (**Valium**)
- Stomach upset
- Suppressed breathing (restrained or inhibited)
- Weight gain

Potential for Abuse or Dependence

Between 11 and 15 percent of people in the U.S. take a form of antianxiety medication—including benzodiazepines—at least once each year. If antidepressants are included, this figure is doubled. Benzodiazepines may cause at least mild physical dependence in almost everyone who uses the medication for longer than 6 months (i.e., if the medicine is abruptly stopped, the person will experience anxiety, increased blood pressure, fast heart beat, and insomnia). However, becoming physically dependent on benzodiazepines does not necessarily mean a person will become psychologically dependent or addicted to the medication. Most people can be gradually withdrawn from the medication—when indicated—and will not develop psychological dependence.

In general, abuse and dependence occur at lower rates with long-acting antianxiety medications (e.g., **Klonopin**, **Serax**, and **Tranxene**). Abuse and dependence are more likely to occur with faster-acting, high-potency antianxiety medications (e.g., **Ativan**, **Valium**, and **Xanax**).

Risk Factors Related to Developing
Dependency on Antianxiety Medication:

Less than 1% of persons *who do not have a current substance abuse problem or a history of substance abuse* becomes dependent on antianxiety medications. These people are at ***little or no risk.*** They are more likely to skip doses, take lower doses than prescribed, or decrease their dose over time.

People with a prior history of substance abuse or dependence who are in recovery are at increased risk of becoming dependent on antianxiety medications. These people are at ***moderate risk.***

Those with a history of abusing antianxiety medications or those who are opiate users are at **_higher_** **_risk_** of becoming dependent on antianxiety medications. Some studies indicate there is a moderately higher risk for alcohol dependent persons to become dependent on antianxiety medications.

Emergency Conditions

High doses of diazepam (**Valium**) can cause slowed heartbeat, suppression of breathing, and stop the heart from beating. Overdose on the older tricyclic antidepressant medications, which are often used for combined anxiety depression disorders, can be life threatening and immediate referral to emergency care is indicated.

Withdrawal from regular use of any of the benzodiazepines and similar medications must be done slowly over a month's time. Abrupt withdrawal from these medications can cause hallucinations, delusions and delirium, disorientation, difficulty breathing, hyperactivity, and grand mal seizures. A protocol for decreasing or tapering off doses of benzodiazepines is needed.

Cautions

- Doctors and pharmacists should be told about all medications being taken and dosage, including over-the-counter preparations, vitamins, minerals, and herbal supplements (i.e., St. John's wort, echinacea, ginkgo, ginseng).
- People taking antianxiety medications should not increase their dose unless this has been *checked with their physician and a change is ordered.*
- People should not stop using these medications without talking to a doctor.
- People taking antianxiety medication are particularly vulnerable to adverse medical consequences if they concurrently use alcohol and/or street drugs.
- Using alcohol in combination with benzodiazepines may result in breathing failure and sudden death.

Special Considerations for Pregnant Women

The current state of knowledge suggests that benzodiazepine therapy in general does not pose as much risk of producing a deformed baby as compared to anticonvulsants (e.g., valproic acid) as long as they are given over a short time period. It appears that short-acting benzodiazepines, like those used to treat alcohol withdrawal (detoxification[21]), can be used in low doses even in the first trimester (Robert et al. 2001). Long-acting benzodiazepines should be avoided—their use during the third trimester or near delivery can result in a withdrawal syndrome in the baby (Garbis and McElhatton 2001). For use of the SSRIs in pregnancy, see page 21.

During pregnancy, the capacity of many drugs to bind to proteins[22] is decreased, including diazepam (a benzodiazepine) and **Methadone** (Adams and Wacher 1968; Dean et al. 1980; Ganrot 1972) with the greatest decrease noted during the third trimester (Perucca and Crema 1982). From a clinical standpoint, pregnant women could be at risk for developing greater toxicity[23] and side effects to these medications. Yet at the same time, increased metabolism of the medication may result, reducing the therapeutic effect (such as with methadone since many women seem to require an increase in their dose of methadone during the last trimester) (Pond et al. 1985). In addition, there is a documented withdrawal syndrome in newborns exposed to benzodiazepines in utero (Sutton and Hinderliter 1990). Onset of this syndrome may be delayed more so than that associated with other drugs.

---

[21] *detoxification:* A medical and biopsychosocial procedure that assists a person who is dependent on one or more substance to withdraw from dependence on all substances of abuse.

[22] *protein binding:* The affinity of a drug to attach (*bind*) to blood plasma proteins. The extent to which a drug is *bound* to plasma proteins can affect the distribution of the drug in the body. In most cases, *binding* to plasma proteins is reversible.

[23] *toxicity:* Poisonous nature; poisonous quality.

For all women of childbearing age who may be or think they may be pregnant, the physician should discuss the safety of this medication before starting, continuing, or discontinuing medication treatment. Substance abuse counselors may have a role in encouraging this discussion by suggesting their clients talk with the prescribing physician.

Stimulant Medications

GENERIC	BRAND
d-amphetamine	Dexedrine
l & d-amphetamine	Adderall, Adderall CII, Adderall XR
methamphetamine	Desoxyn
methylphenidate	Ritalin, Ritalin SR, Concerta, Metadate ER, Metadate CD, Methylin ER, Focalin
pemoline	Cylert
modafinil	Provigil

Non-stimulants for AD/HD[24]

atomoxetine hydrochloride	Strattera
bupropion	Wellbutrin
guanfacine	Tenex

Purpose

Stimulant medications are used to treat attention deficit/hyperactivity disorder (AD/HD), which is typically diagnosed in childhood but also occurs in adults. Symptoms consistent with AD/HD include short attention span, excessive activity (hyperactivity), impulsivity, and emotional development below the level expected for the person's age. The underlying manifestation of AD/HD is that it severely impacts and interferes with a person's daily functioning. Other conditions that may be treated with stimulants are narcolepsy[25], obesity, and sometimes depression.

Positive treatment responses to stimulant medications include increased attention, focus and/or ability to stay on task, less hyperactivity, and moderation of impulsive behavior. People with AD/HD generally report that they feel "normal" when taking stimulants.

Non-stimulant medications for AD/HD differ somewhat. Atomoxetine (**Strattera**) blocks the reuptake of norepinephrine, which helps reduce the symptoms of AD/HD. Guanfacine (**Tenex**) and bupropion (**Wellbutrin**) are non-stimulants that have been used successfully to treat symptoms of AD/HD. The advantage of these medications is that they are non-addictive, and do not cause a "high" even in larger doses. Atomoxetine (**Strattera**) is FDA approved. While studies have shown bupropion (**Wellbutrin**) to be effective, it is not FDA approved.

Usual Dose, Frequency & Side Effects

All medications have specific doses and frequencies. The physician will specify the exact amount of medication and when it should be taken. This information is provided on the prescription bottle. With stimulants, there may be periods when the medication is not to be taken. The most common side effects of the

---

[24] *AD/HD:* Refers to two types of disorders. Attention deficit disorder without hyperactivity (**ADD**), and attention deficit disorder with hyperactivity (**ADHD**). The terms are often used interchangeably.

[25] *narcolepsy:* A condition characterized by brief attacks of deep sleep.

stimulants are nervousness, sleeplessness, and loss of appetite. Some of these medications are expensive, but others are generic and quite inexpensive.

Potential Side Effects

Stimulants

- Blood disorders (**Ritalin** and **Cylert**)
- Change in heart rhythm
- Delayed growth
- Dilated pupils
- Elevated blood pressure
- Euphoria
- Excitability
- Increased pulse rate
- Insomnia
- Irritability
- Liver damage (**Cylert**)
- Loss of appetite
- Rash
- Seizures (**Ritalin** and **Cylert**)
- Tourette's syndrome (**Cylert**)
- Tremor

Non-stimulants for AD/HD

Strattera side effects include:

- High blood pressure
- Nervousness, and side effects similar to some antidepressants

Wellbutrin side effects include:

- Increased chance of seizure activity

Tenex side effects include:

- Constipation
- Dizziness
- Dry mouth
- Low blood pressure
- Sleepiness

Potential for Abuse or Dependence

Stimulant medications may be misused. Recreational or non-medically indicated uses have been reported for performance enhancement and/or weight loss. People with AD/HD or narcolepsy, however, rarely abuse or become dependent on stimulant medications unless they have an addiction problem with other substances. Most addiction medicine doctors use antidepressants or atomoxetine (**Strattera**) (both non-stimulants) to treat AD/HD in adults with co-occurring substance use disorders. Using stimulant medications to treat AD/HD in children has been shown to reduce the potential development of substance use disorders.

Emergency Conditions

Psychiatric symptoms including paranoid delusions, thought disorders, and hallucinations have been reported when stimulants are used for long periods or taken at high dosages. Overdose with stimulants is a medical emergency. Seek help immediately.

Cautions

- Doctors and pharmacists should be told about all medications being taken and dosage, including over-the-counter preparations, vitamins, minerals, and herbal supplements (i.e., St. John's wort, echinacea, ginkgo, ginseng).
- People taking stimulant medications should not increase their dose unless this has been *checked with their physician and a change is ordered.*
- People taking stimulant medications are particularly vulnerable to adverse medical consequences if they concurrently use alcohol and/or street drugs.
- With stimulants, there is the potential for development of tolerance and dependence on the medications with accompanying withdrawal. The potential for abuse and misuse is high, as is true with all Schedule II drugs[26].

Special Considerations for Pregnant Women

For women of childbearing age who may be or think they may be pregnant, the physician should discuss the safety of this medication before starting, continuing, or discontinuing medication treatment. Substance abuse counselors may have a role in encouraging this discussion by suggesting their clients talk with the prescribing physician.

Narcotic and Opioid-Analgesics

Natural opioids

Opium, morphine and codeine products

Pure, semi or totally synthetic derivatives

Heroin, Percodan, Demerol, Darvon, oxycodone, and others

GENERIC	BRAND
buprenorphine	Buprinex
buprenorphine	Subutex, Suboxone*
butorphanol tartarate	Stadol spray
codeine phosphate	Codeine tablets
codeine sulfate	Codeine tablets
dihydromorphone hydrochloride	Dilaudid-5, Dilaudid HP
fentanyl transdermal	Duragesic patches
fentanyl transmucosal	Fentanyl, Oraley
hypromorphone hydrochloride	Dilaudid
meperidine hydrochloride	Demerol
methadone hydrochloride	Methadone

---

[26] *Schedule II drugs:* Drugs classified in *Schedule II* of the Controlled Substances Act; have a high potential for abuse with severe liability to cause psychic or physical dependence, but have some approved medical use.

morphine hydrochloride	Morphine
morphine sulfate	Oramorph, Roxanol, Statex
oxycodone hydrochloride	Roxicodone, OxyContin
oxymorphone hydrochloride	Numorphan
pentazocine hydrochloride	Talwin
propoxyphene hydrochloride	Darvon
propoxyphene napsylate	Darvon-N
tramadol hydrochloride	Ultram

*Combined with naloxone[27] and taken under the tongue (sublingually).

The following products use a combination of an opioid or narcotic along with aspirin, **Tylenol**, or other pain reliever to treat mild to moderate pain.

Anesxia 5/50	Percocet
Capital with Codeine	Percodan
Darvocet N 100	Roxicet
Darvocet N 50	Roxicet oral solution (contains alcohol)
E-Lor or Wygesic	Roxiprin
Empirin or Phenaphen with Codeine #3	Talacen
Empirin or Phenaphen with Codeine #4	Talwin Compound
Endocet	Tylenol with Codeine
Fioricet with Codeine	Tylenol with Codeine syrup (contains alcohol)
Fiorinal with Codeine	Tylox
Lorcet Plus	Vicodin
Lortab	Vicodin ES

Purpose

Opiate medications are commonly used to control moderate to severe acute pain. They are typically used for a short time because they cause physiological tolerance (takes more to get the same analgesic effect) and physical dependence (get withdrawal symptoms if abruptly stopped) as amount and duration of doses increase. Longer-term use is indicated to alleviate the chronic pain associated with cancer and certain other conditions, and research has shown that abuse or addiction to these medications rarely occurs in such patients. Severe and chronic pain has long been under treated in the United States due to irrational fears that anyone prescribed opiates will become addicted. This has clearly been shown to be not the case. People with substance use disorders need pain management just like anyone else. Opioids are appropriately pre-scribed to manage chronic cancer pain—especially oxycodone (**OxyContin**) and methadone.

Methadone is a synthetic opioid used in heroin detoxification treatment programs to maintain sobriety from heroin addiction. Many people who have been addicted to heroin have returned to a productive life because of methadone treatment. **Methadone** is also frequently used to provide relief for specific types of pain, especially in pain clinics. The management of chronic pain in a person who has been opiate abusing and dependent is one of the most challenging tasks in addiction medicine.

Heroin is a drug of abuse.

Usual Dose & Frequency

All narcotic and opioid analgesics have specific doses and frequencies. The physician will specify the exact amount of medication and when it should be taken. This information is provided on the prescription bottle.

---

[27]*naloxone:* A narcotic antagonist used to reverse the effects of opioids.

Many narcotic or opioid medications are taken two or more times a day. Some medications are taken in pill or liquid form. A few are taken in a nasal spray or as transdermal patches. Injectable narcotics are not listed here because they are not often used outside a hospital setting.

Potential Side Effects

- Constipation
- Decreased ability to see clearly
- Decreased ability to think clearly
- Flushing and sweating
- Pupil constriction
- Respiratory depression (slowed breathing rate)
- Stomach upset
- Tolerance

Potential for Abuse or Dependence

With narcotic and opioid medications, there is a potential for the development of tolerance and dependence as well as the possibility of abuse and severe withdrawal reactions. There are many nonaddictive pain medications available for pain management that can be used after acute pain is reduced.

Emergency Conditions

Convulsions and/or cardiac arrest with high dosages.

Overdose may increase pulse rate, result in convulsions followed by coma or death.

Overdose may depress the breathing centers in the brain leading to inability to breathe.

An overdose is always considered an emergency and treatment should be sought immediately.

Cautions

- Doctors and pharmacists should be told about all medications being taken and dosage, including over-the-counter preparations, vitamins, minerals, and herbal supplements (i.e., St. John's wort, echinacea, ginkgo, ginseng).
- People taking narcotic and opioid analgesics should not increase their dose unless this has been *checked with their physician and a change is ordered.*
- Persons taking an opioid medication are particularly vulnerable to adverse medical consequences if they concurrently use alcohol and/or street drugs, because alcohol and street drugs can increase the sedation effects of the opioids.
- Potential for development of tolerance and dependence exists.

Special Considerations for Pregnant Women

For all women of childbearing age who may be or think they may be pregnant, the physician should discuss the safety of this medication before starting, continuing, or discontinuing medication treatment. Both pregnant women and their unborn infants can become tolerant and physically dependent on opioids. This dependence as well as possible withdrawal syndromes needs to be assessed. Substance abuse counselors may have a role in encouraging this discussion by suggesting their clients talk with the prescribing physician. See p. 45 for information about methadone use during pregnancy.

Hypnotics (Sleep-Aids)

GENERIC	BRAND
Barbiturates	
secobarbital	Seconal
Benzodiazepines	
clonazepam	Klonopin
diazepam	Valium
estazolam	ProSom
flurazepam	Dalmane
lorazepam	Ativan
oxazepam	Serax
quazepam	Doral
temazepam	Restoril
triazolam	Halcion
Non-benzodiazepines	
anticonvulsants	Neurontin*, Depakote*, Topamax*
sedating antidepressants	Desyrel, Remeron, Serzone, Sinequan
sedating antipsychotics	Seroquel*, Zyprexa*, Zyprexa Zydis*
zaleplon	Sonata
zolpidem	Ambien

*Use of these medications for sleep aid is "off-label."

Purpose

Hypnotics are used to help people with sleep disturbances get restful sleep. Lack of sleep is one of the greatest problems faced by those with chemical dependency and psychiatric illnesses. It can cause the symptoms of these disorders to worsen. For example, mood changes, psychosis and irritability increase with insomnia. Lack of sleep diminishes a person's ability to think clearly or process information. Sleep-wake cycles and the body's ability to heal itself also suffer when a person is sleep deprived. Older hypnotics, like barbiturates, cause the body to slow down and "pass out" or sleep. However, they also have a tendency to disturb sleep cycles. For this reason, and because of their potential for abuse and dependence, barbiturates are now rarely used.

Benzodiazepines enhance the body's natural calming agents, which induces sleep. Non-benzodiazepines such as zolpidem (**Ambien**) and zaleplon (**Sonata**) affect one of the body's receptors for the natural calming agent, GABA. These medications are short acting and do not disturb sleep-staging cycles. Rebound insomnia is a side effect of both, however, if the medications are used for more than two weeks and then abruptly stopped.

Sedating antidepressants work by using their sleep producing side effects to induce sleep. They are nonaddictive but have the capacity to produce all the side effects of their class of antidepressant. Sedating antipsychotics use their calming and sedation side effects to induce sleep. They are nonaddictive but have the capacity to produce all the side effects of atypical antipsychotics. Anticonvulsants may be used for sedation when treating acute or prolonged withdrawal symptoms from alcohol.

Paradoxically, those with addiction disorders can become rapidly tolerant and dependent on the most commonly used hypnotics, which are the benzodiazepines and even one of the non-benzodiazepines— zolpidem

(**Ambien**). Tolerance can lead to decreasing effectiveness, escalating doses, and an even worse sleep disorder when the agent is withdrawn. For this reason, most addiction medicine doctors use sedating antidepressants, anticonvulsants, or sedating antihistamines if the sleep problem continues past acute withdrawal symptoms.

Usual Dose & Frequency

All medications have specific doses and frequencies. The physician will specify the exact amount of medication and when it should be taken. This information is provided on the prescription bottle. All of these medications are generally used for limited periods (3 to 4 days for barbiturates or up to a month for others). All of these medications quickly develop tolerance and eventually the usual dose will no longer help the person sleep.

Potential Side Effects

- Breathing difficulty (**Seconal**)
- Dizziness
- Drowsiness
- Hangover feeling or daytime sleepiness
- Headache
- Lethargy
- Weakness

Potential for Abuse or Dependence

With hypnotics, there is the potential for development of tolerance and dependence on the medications with accompanying withdrawal. The potential for abuse and misuse is high. See *Potential for Abuse or Dependence* for benzodiazepines, p. 24. There are many drawbacks to long-term use of hypnotics such as damaged sleep staging and addiction. Even zolpidem (**Ambien**) and zaleplon (**Sonata**), if taken for longer than 7 to 14 days, can have a discontinuation rebound insomnia effect. Nonaddictive medications are available to treat insomnia.

Emergency Conditions

Overdose with any of these medications can be life threatening. Seek help immediately.

   Combinations of alcohol and barbiturates or alcohol and benzodiazepines can be deadly.

Cautions

- Doctors and pharmacists should be told about all medications being taken and dosage, including over-the-counter preparations, vitamins, minerals, and herbal supplements (i.e., St. John's wort, echinacea, ginkgo, ginseng).
- People taking hypnotic medications should not increase their dose unless this has been *checked with their physician and a change is ordered*.
- People taking hypnotic medications are particularly vulnerable to adverse medical consequences if they concurrently use alcohol and/or street drugs.
- There is potential for development of tolerance and dependence with accompanying withdrawal. Potential for abuse and misuse is high.

Special Considerations for Pregnant Women

Barbiturate use during pregnancy has been studied to some extent, but the risk of taking this medication should be discussed with the client (Robert et al. 2001). There also are reports of a withdrawal syndrome in newborns following prenatal exposure to some barbiturates (Kuhnz et al. 1988). For all women of childbearing age who may be or think they may be pregnant, the physician should discuss the safety of this medication before starting, continuing, or discontinuing medication treatment. Substance abuse counselors may have a role in encouraging this discussion by suggesting their clients talk with the prescribing physician.

Addiction Treatment Medications

ALCOHOL

GENERIC	BRAND
Alcohol withdrawal agents*	
benzodiazepines (e.g., lorazepam)	Ativan
anticonvulsants (e.g., carbamazepine,	
divalproex sodium, gabapentin)	Tegretol, Depakote, Neurontin
barbiturates (e.g., secobarbital)	Seconal

*For more information on benzodiazepines, anticonvulsants and barbiturates see Antimanic Medications, Antianxiety Medications and Hypnotics sections in this publication.

Alcohol relapse prevention agents	
disulfiram	Antabuse
naltrexone hydrochloride	ReVia
naltrexone extended-release injection	Vivitrol
acamprosate	Campral
nalmefene hydrochloride	Revex
topiramate	Topamax

Purpose

Medications involved in alcohol treatment include those used for acute alcohol withdrawal as well as a growing number used for alcohol relapse prevention. Alcohol relapse prevention medications are just starting to be accepted in the field. It is anticipated that within the next few years, medications like naltrexone (**ReVia**) and acamprosate (**Campral**) will be more widely used given the developing body of research indicating that these medications work.

Alcohol withdrawal: Though usually only treated for 1 to 5 days, signs and symptoms of alcohol withdrawal go on for weeks or months. Signs and symptoms especially include sleep disorder, anxiety, agitation, and craving alcohol, knowing that a few drinks may temporarily make the alcoholic with "protracted withdrawal" feel more normal.

Benzodiazepines are by far the most commonly used medications for acute withdrawal. If used longer than a few days, they induce tolerance and dependence. Anticonvulsants such as carbamazepine, divalproex sodium, and gabapentin are more commonly used in Europe. The advantage in using these medications is that they can be prescribed for weeks and months versus only days. A well-designed U.S. study (Malcolm et al. 2002) demonstrated that carbamazepine is much superior to lorazepam, a commonly used benzodiazepine, in treating alcohol withdrawal. Propranolol (**Inderal**), a beta-blocker, is sometimes used in alcohol withdrawal treatment along with either benzodiazepines or anticonvulsants to decrease anxiety, heart rate, sweating, and blood pressure. Antipsychotics may be used if the person develops severe alcohol withdrawal with hallucinations.

Alcohol relapse prevention: The oldest medication used in alcohol relapse prevention is disulfiram (**Antabuse**). It has been used for over 50 years. Disulfiram (**Antabuse**) blocks the breakdown of alcohol, resulting in toxic acetaldehyde[28] levels in the body. This in turn leads to severe nausea and vomiting. Research indicates disulfiram (**Antabuse**) works better than placebo only in persons motivated enough to take it regularly, or in those that receive it in a "monitored" fashion 3 to 5 times per week. It works by causing the person to rethink a move to impulsive drinking, since they know if they have disulfiram (**Antabuse**) on board, they will get sick.

Naltrexone (**ReVia**) was first developed as an opioid receptor blocker and used in monitored treatment programs for opioid dependence. Many opioid addicts, however, stopped taking it and returned to opioid use or they preferred methadone maintenance therapy. In spite of this, clinical observation of persons taking naltrexone showed that those who also used alcohol seemed to drink less and reported that alcohol use affected them less. Subsequent controlled, clinical trials comparing use of naltrexone to placebo condition have shown its effectiveness over placebo to decrease alcohol craving and relapse potential. Research with community populations (where persons are not monitored as closely for medication adherence) has not supported its effectiveness over a placebo condition to promote abstinence.

A new long-acting injectable form of naltrexone is now available. Use of this monthly treatment with even those persons who are less motivated about their recovery has led to a reduction in days drinking; and when drinking does occur, they consume less alcohol. Thus, naltrexone may be best seen as a "harm reduction" medicine versus a "complete abstinence" treatment enhancer.

Naltrexone is nonpsychoactive[29] and as an opioid receptor blocker, it can interfere with the use of opioids for treatment of acute pain. For more information on Naltrexone, see *TIP 28: Naltrexone and Alcoholism Treatment* (CSAT 1998).

Acamprosate (**Campral**) was FDA approved in early 2005. It has been available in Europe and other countries for over 10 years. Acamprosate appears to work through the GABA system and holds promise for alcohol craving and preventing relapse through a method different than naltrexone. It is reported to be nonpsychoactive, does not interact with most other medications, and does not cause any kind of tolerance or withdrawal symptoms even if the person uses alcohol when taking the medication.

Unlike the injectable naltrexone, acamprosate does not appear to be effective in persons who are less than moderately motivated to abstain from alcohol use. Because of the way the medication is absorbed in the body, it must be taken several times a day. Outcome studies indicate that acamprosate is best at increasing complete abstinence from alcohol, or increasing the time before the first drink (relapse). The profile of the person for whom acamprosate would be selected is one seeking complete abstinence and who is moderately to highly motivated to abstain from alcohol use.

Nalmefene (**Revex**) is beginning to be used in its oral form to reduce alcohol craving; it is also beginning to be used in gambling and nicotine addictions.

Topiramate (**Topamax**) is an anticonvulsant that at higher doses can cause sedation and confusion.

Opioids

GENERIC	BRAND
Opioid withdrawal agents	
buprenorphine	Subutex
buprenorphine and naloxone	Suboxone

---

[28] *acetaldehyde:* A chemical compound produced when the body metabolizes alcohol; the liver enzyme, alcohol dehydrogenase, converts ethanol into *acetaldehyde*, which is then further converted into the harmless acetic acid by *acetaldehyde* dehydrogenase.

[29] *psychoactive*: Substances or drugs that affect the mind, especially mood, thought, or perception.

clonidine   Catapres
methadone hydrochloride   Methadone
naltrexone hydrochloride   ReVia
naltrexone extended-release injection   Vivitrol
nalmefene hydrochloride   Revex

Opioid maintenance agents

buprenorphine   Subutex
buprenorphine and naloxone   Suboxone
methadone hydrochloride   Methadone

Purpose

Medications for opioid withdrawal and maintenance are a key component in the stabilization of persons addicted to opiates. These medications have shown marked ability to decrease illness, crime, and deaths in this population. **Methadone** maintenance treatment is extensively researched. See *TIP 19: Detoxification from Alcohol and Other Drugs* (CSAT 1995) and *TIP 20: Matching Treatment to Patient Needs in Opioid Substitution Therapy* (CSAT 1995).

Opioid withdrawal: Mild opioid withdrawal can be accomplished with clonidine, a medication for treatment of high blood pressure. Usually clonidine is used in combination with sedatives such as benzodiazepines, antihistamines or even phenobarbital. Major opioid withdrawal is usually treated with either an equivalent dose of methadone gradually decreased over time, or more recently, a single dose of 24 mg of buprenorphine. In pilot studies, buprenorphine appears superior to clonidine.

Opioid maintenance agents: **Methadone** has been used in the U.S. for maintenance treatment of opioid addiction since the 1960s. It is a synthetic, long-acting medication used in heroin detoxification programs to maintain abstinence from heroin use. When used in proper doses, methadone stops the cravings but does not create euphoria, sedation, or an analgesic[30] effect. Many people who have been addicted to heroin have returned to a productive life because of methadone treatment programs. **Methadone** also is occasionally used to provide relief for specific types of pain. (See also *Narcotic and Opioid Analgesics*, p. 30.)

Buprenorphine, or **Subutex**, is a prescription medication approved in 2002 for treating opioid addiction. It can be used for both opioid withdrawal and as a substitute for opioids in long-term treatment. Buprenorphine is the first medication available to doctors for use in their office-based practice. At low doses, it acts like methadone and satisfies the dependent person's need for an opioid to avoid painful withdrawal. It does not provide the user with the euphoria or rush typically associated with use of other opioids or narcotics. At moderate to high doses, it can precipitate withdrawal. It is, therefore, safer in overdose than methadone. **Suboxone** is buprenorphine combined with naloxone, a narcotic antagonist[31] used to reverse the effects of opioids. **Suboxone** is also approved for treating opioid addiction and offers the same benefits as those previously stated for buprenorphine.

Naltrexone and nalmefene completely block the pleasurable reinforcement that comes from opioids. They are beginning to be more widely used for alcohol relapse prevention (see pp. 36–37). Nalmefene is more commonly used in its injectable form to reverse the effects of opioids when used for anesthesia. It is beginning to be used in its oral form to reduce alcohol craving; it is also beginning to be used in gambling and nicotine addictions.

---

[30] *analgesic:* Producing relief or insensibility to pain without loss of consciousness.

[31] *antagonist:* A substance that blocks the normal physiological function of a receptor site in the brain.

Tobacco

GENERIC	BRAND
Nicotine Replacement Therapies (NRT)	
nicotine patch/transdermal nicotine	Nicoderm CQ, Nicotrol, Habitrol, Prostep
nicotine polacrilex gum	Nicorette
nicotine polacrilex lozenges	Commit
nicotine inhaler	Nicotrol Inhaler
nicotine nasal spray	Nicotrol NS
Pharmacotherapies for Smoking Cessation	
varenicline tartrate	Chantix
bupropion, bupropion SR	Wellbutrin, Wellbutrin SR, Zyban
nortriptyline	Aventyl, Pamelor
clonidine	Catapres

Purpose

Complete long-term abstinence from all nicotine-containing products is the goal of tobacco cessation therapies. Medications and products for tobacco cessation assist clients with nicotine dependence[32] to achieve abstinence by alleviating or reducing common nicotine withdrawal symptoms[33] and cravings. Numerous scientific studies have shown that is easier for individuals to quit tobacco when supported by a medical or a mental health clinician. For this reason, recommended treatment strategies incorporate both behavioral counseling and pharmacotherapy. Nonetheless, pharmacotherapy is contraindicated for some specific populations (i.e., pregnant women, smokeless tobacco users, light smokers, and adolescents). Empirically validated tobacco treatment strategies are available as cited in the *2008 Treating Tobacco Use and Dependence Guidelines* (DHHS 2008).

Nicotine, the addictive chemical in cigarettes and other forms of tobacco, crosses the blood-brain barrier and activates the brain's reward center. This causes the brain to release noradrenaline and dopamine, which act as stimulants (implicated in mood, memory, and a sense of well-being). Nicotine remains active for 20-40 minutes in the brain, and then withdrawal symptoms begin, leading to cravings for more nicotine.

Nicotine Replacement Therapies (**NRT**) such as transdermal nicotine patch, nicotine polacrilex gum and lozenge, nicotine nasal spray, and nicotine inhaler are FDA approved. These therapies reduce withdrawal symptoms and cravings by replacing nicotine that would be ingested through chewing tobacco or smoking cigarettes. Numerous clinical trials involving NRT have demonstrated the effectiveness of these products for smoking cessation.

Bupropion, as an antidepressant, can help with withdrawal anxiety and depression. Sustained-release bupropion (bupropion SR) is one of the few non-nicotine pharmaceutical aids that are FDA

---

[32] *nicotine dependence:* Nicotine dependence is a recognized mental health disorder that is often overlooked by counselors. This addiction significantly reduces the overall qualityoflife and is considered the deadliest yet most preventable disease to be treated. Cigarette smoking is a primary cause of cancers of the esophagus, lung, throat, mouth and is associated with the development of cancers of the bladder, cervix, kidneys, pancreas, stomach and some leukemias. Smoking is also a major cause of heart disease, bronchitis, emphysema, and stroke.

[33] *nicotine withdrawal symptoms:* Common nicotine withdrawal symptoms include irritability, anger, impatience, restlessness, difficulty concentrating, insomnia, increased appetite, anxiety, and depressed mood. The replacement of nicotine in the brain during withdrawal produces the sense of "relief" and "relaxation" commonly expressed by individuals when they readminister nicotine to the body.

approved for smoking cessation. This agent is thought to affect dopamine[34] and norepinephrine[35] levels, and blocks nicotinic acetylcholinergic receptors,[36] thereby decreasing cravings for cigarettes and symptoms of nicotine withdrawal. The use of bupropion roughly doubles cessation rates relative to placebo, and the combination of bupropion with the nicotine patch has shown higher quit rates than using the patch alone.

Varenicline (**Chantix**) is a more recently FDA approved smoking cessation medication and the first in its class targeting specifically the neurobiology of nicotine addiction. It reduces the smoker's craving for nicotine by binding to nicotine receptors in the brain and thereby reducing withdrawal symptoms as well as resulting in a less satisfying smoking experience. Smokers using varenicline have better rates of smoking cessation compared to those who use bupropion. **Chantix** offers a new option for those who cannot tolerate the adverse effects associated with **NRT** and bupropion, and represents an alternative for clients with contraindications to such therapies.

Others

Stimulant intoxication: Agitation, paranoia and psychosis are treated with antipsychotics, often combined with benzodiazepines. Both alcohol and stimulant intoxication together commonly appear to cause these symptoms.

Stimulant withdrawal: There are no standard effective agents to treat stimulant withdrawal, though dopamine-enhancing agents such as amantadine, bupropion (**Wellbutrin**), and desipramine have been tried with mixed results. This area has not been well researched.

Stimulant relapse prevention: Again, dopamine-enhancing agents such as bupropion (**Wellbutrin**) and desipramine have mixed results. The National Institute on Drug Abuse (NIDA) is researching agents that might alter how stimulants act on a person, including the development of "inoculation" agents that might inactivate stimulants.

Club Drugs: Little research has occurred in this area. There are reports that SSRI's may be protective of the damage caused to nerve cells by some of these drugs. Antipsychotics and sedatives are used to treat induced psychoses associated with club drug abuse.

Marijuana: Recently, a withdrawal syndrome to marijuana dependence has been described and validated. Medications for treating this syndrome have not been adequately tested. THC[37], the chief intoxicant in marijuana, is a strong anticholinergic agent and is sedating. Therefore some clinicians have used moderate doses of the older tricyclic antidepressants (e.g., **Elavil** or **Tofranil)** to treat withdrawal from marijuana as they also have anticholinergic and sedating qualities but do not cause a high, nor are they abused.

Usual Dose & Frequency

All medications have specific doses and frequencies. The physician will specify the exact amount of medication and when it should be taken; this information is provided on the prescription bottle. Disulfiram (**Antabuse**) should never be given to people without their full knowledge or when they are intoxicated. It should not be given until the person has abstained from alcohol for at least twelve hours. A daily, uninterrupted dose of disulfiram (**Antabuse**) is continued until the person is in full and mature recovery and has reorganized his or her life to maintain recovery. Maintenance therapy may be required for months or even years.

---

[34] *dopamine:* A type of neurotransmitter in the brain.

[35] *norepinephrine:* A type of neurotransmitter in the brain.

[36] *acetylcholinergic receptors:* A type of neurotransmitter receptor in the brain activated by the neurotransmitter acetylcholine.

[37] *THC: Te*trahydrocannabinol: an active chemical from hemp plant resin that is the chief intoxicant in marijuana.

Naltrexone (**ReVia**) in its oral form is usually taken once a day but can be taken at a higher dose every second or third day. It is usually started at full dose. The injectable form of naltrexone (**Vivitrol**) is taken once a month. Because of the way acamprosate (**Campral**) is absorbed, it must be taken as two pills three times a day with each dose separated by at least four hours.

Buprenorphine combined with naloxone (**Suboxone**) is given as a sublingual tablet (it is absorbed under the tongue). It is not absorbed if swallowed or chewed. If injected intravenously, **Suboxone** will cause opioid withdrawal. **Suboxone** and buprenorphine (**Subutex**) can be given by prescription and do not require daily attendance at a clinic. This is an advantage for persons who do not live near a methadone clinic.

People should continue to take naltrexone, acamprosate or **Suboxone** until they have reached full and mature recovery and have reorganized their life to maintain recovery.

Some Nicotine Replacement Therapy NRT medications can be obtained without a prescription, including the nicotine patch, gum, and lozenge. Specific information on how to use NRT products correctly, recommended dosing schedules, symptoms of overdose, and proper storage/disposal of the products are included on the product label or inside the package.

The nicotine patch is available in three strengths and a "step-down" approach is used: 21 mg for 6 weeks, then 14 mg for 2 weeks, then 7 mg for 2 weeks. For those who smoke less than one pack a day, consider starting at 14 mg dose. A new patch needs to be reapplied each day, at roughly the same time each day.

The nicotine polacrilex gum and lozenge are offered in 2 milligrams (mg) and 4 mg. Individuals who smoke fewer than 25 cigarettes per day should initiate therapy with the 2 mg strength, and heavier smokers should initiate with the 4 mg strength. During the initial 6 weeks of therapy, one piece of gum should be chewed every 1 to 2 hours while awake; at least nine pieces of gum daily. The gum should be used for up to 12 weeks and no more than 24 pieces should be chewed a day. A "chew and park" technique is necessary for nicotine to absorb correctly and food or beverages should be avoided 15 minutes before or after using the nicotine gum.

Unlike other forms of NRT, which are dosed based on the number of cigarettes smoked per day; the recommended dosage of the nicotine lozenge is based on the "time to first cigarette" of the day. Some studies suggest that the best indicator of nicotine dependence is having a strong desire or need to smoke soon after waking. Clients who smoke their first cigarette of the day within 30 minutes of waking are likely to be more highly dependent on nicotine and require higher dosages than those who delay smoking for more than 30 minutes after waking. During the initial 6 weeks of therapy, clients should use one lozenge every 1 to 2 hours while awake; at least nine lozenges daily. Clients can use additional lozenges (up to 5 lozenges in 6 hours or a maximum of 20 lozenges per day) if cravings occur between the scheduled doses. The lozenges should be used for up to 12 weeks with no more than 20 lozenges used a day. Lozenges should be allowed to dissolve in the mouth and food or beverages should be avoided 15 minutes before or after using the nicotine lozenge.

Bupropion should be started 7-14 days before a targeted smoking cessation date. Generally, for the first 3 days of treatment, individuals take 150 mg, then 150 mg twice a day for 7 to 12 weeks, and for some individuals, up to 6 months to increase the likelihood of long-term tobacco cessation.

The approved course of varenicline (**Chantix**) treatment is 12 weeks; however, an additional 12 weeks of treatment may increase the likelihood of long-term smoking cessation for some individuals. For the first 3 days of treatment, individuals take 0.5 mg once a day, followed by 0.5 mg twice a day for the next four days, and then 1 mg twice a day for the remainder of the treatment period.

For certain groups of smokers, it may be appropriate to continue NRT treatment or pharmacotherapies for periods longer than is usually recommended. In general, the more intense the treatment for tobacco cessation (e.g., combined use of NRT and pharmacotherapies), the higher the likelihood of successful cessation. Specific combinations of first line medications shown to be effective include the nicotine patch and bupropion SR, the nicotine patch and the inhaler, and long-term nicotine patch (greater than 14 weeks) and *ad libitum* NRT use. Chantix is not recommended for use in combination with NRT because of its nicotine antagonist properties.

Potential Side Effects

Potential side effects for disulfiram (**Antabuse**) (rare at lower doses mostly occur at higher doses > 500 mg day):

- Dark urine
- Drowsiness
- Eye pain
- Fatigue
- Impotence
- Indigestion
- Inflammation of optic nerve
- Jaundice
- Light colored stool
- Liver inflammation
- Loss of vision
- Psychotic reactions
- Skin rashes, itching
- Tingling sensation in arms and legs

Potential side effects for acamprosate (Campral) (Side effects on therapeutic doses of acamprosate are rare, other than mild transient gastrointestinal symptoms during the first week):

- Agitation
- Coma
- Confusion
- Decreased urine output
- Depression
- Dizziness
- Headache
- Irritability and hostility
- Lethargy
- Muscle twitching
- Nausea
- Rapid weight gain
- Seizures
- Swelling of face ankles or hands
- Unusual tiredness or weakness

Potential side effects for opioid treatment medications (See also Narcotic and Opioid Analgesics, p. 30):

- Abdominal cramps
- Body aches lasting 5–7 days
- Diarrhea
- Dizziness
- Fatigue
- Headache
- Insomnia
- Nausea
- Nervousness
- Opioid withdrawal (in some cases)
- Runny eyes and nose

- Severe anxiety
- Vomiting

Potential side effects for NRT and pharmacotherapies for smoking cessation*

Nicotine patch: Skin reactions (i.e., itching, burning, redness or rash at patch site) are usually mild and often resolved by rotating patch site. Other side effects include insomnia and/or vivid dreams.

Nicotine gum: Mouth soreness, hiccups, indigestion, jaw muscle aches. Most of these are mild and subside with continued use of the gum.

Nicotine lozenges: nausea, hiccups, heartburn. For 4mg. lozenge, increased rates of headaches and coughing reported.

Bupropion: dry mouth, insomnia.

Chantix: nausea, trouble sleeping, abnormal/vivid/strange dreams.

*See FDA package insert for each product for a more complete list of side effects.

Emergency Conditions

An overdose of any addiction treatment medication is always considered an emergency and treatment should be sought immediately.

Symptoms of a nicotine overdose may include nausea, vomiting, diarrhea, stomach pain, cold sweats, headache, dizziness, problems with hearing or vision, confusion, an irregular heartbeat, chest pain, seizures, and death.

Cautions

- Doctors and pharmacists should be told about all medications being taken and dosage, including over-the-counter preparations, vitamins, minerals, and herbal supplements (i.e., St. John's wort, echinacea, ginkgo, ginseng).
- People taking disulfiram (**Antabuse**) should be warned to avoid even small amounts of alcohol in other food products or "disguised forms" as this will cause a reaction (i.e., vanilla, sauces, vinegars, cold and cough medicines, aftershave lotions, liniments).
- People taking disulfiram (**Antabuse**) should be warned that consuming even small amounts of alcohol will produce flushing, throbbing in head and neck, headache, difficulty breathing, nausea, vomiting, sweating, thirst, chest pain, rapid heart rate, blurred vision, dizziness, and confusion.
- People taking opioid medications should not increase or decrease their dose unless this has been *checked with their physician and a change is ordered*.
- People taking opioid medications are particularly vulnerable to adverse medical consequences if they concurrently use alcohol and/or street drugs.
- People taking naltrexone or nalmefene should be warned that if they are dependent on opioids, taking these medications will cause opioid withdrawal for up to three days and block the effect of any opioids taken for up to three days.
- Smoking can have an effect on the way the body processes other prescribed medications. Substances found in tar in cigarettes stimulate enzymes in the liver, and fluctuations in an individual's smoking pattern can result in higher or lower doses of medications needed to reach therapeutic levels.
- Although studies have now documented the lack of association between the nicotine patch and acute cardiovascular events, even with individuals who continued to smoke while on the patch, all NRT products should be used with caution for individuals who had a recent (within 2 weeks) myocardial infarction (**MI**),[38] those with severe arrhythmias, or those with unstable angina pectoris.[39]

---

[38] *myocardial infarction (MI):* Myocardial Infarction more commonly known as a heart attack is a medical condition that occurs when the blood supply to a part of the heart is interrupted.

[39] *unstable angina pectoris:* commonly known as angina, is chest pain due to ischemia (a lack of blood and hence oxygen supply) of the heart muscle, generally due to obstruction or spasm of the coronary arteries (the heart's blood vessels).

- NRT products should be properly disposed of to insure safety of children and pets. Nicotine on hands can get into nose or eyes, causing stinging and redness. Wash hands with soap and water after handling the patch.
- Because seizures have been reported in 0.1% of patients, bupropion is contraindicated in individuals who have a history of seizure disorder, have a current or prior diagnosis of anorexia[40] or bulimia,[41] are currently using another form of bupropion, are currently using or have used a Monoamine Oxidase (MAO) Inhibitor within the past two weeks. Other factors that might increase the odds of seizure and are classified as warnings for this medication include a history of head trauma, central nervous system tumor, the presence of severe hepatic cirrhosis, and concomitant use of medications that lower the seizure threshold. Bupropion can be used safely in combination with NRT and may be beneficial for use in clients with underlying depression.
- Although varenicline (**Chantix**) is well tolerated in most individuals, recent case reports describe exacerbations of existing psychiatric illness in clients who took varenicline prompting the FDA to add a warning regarding the use of varenicline in February 2008. Specifically, the warning notes that depressed mood, agitation, changes in behavior, suicidal ideation, and suicide have been reported in clients attempting to quit smoking while using varenicline (**Chantix**).
- Because varenicline (**Chantix**) is eliminated almost entirely unchanged in the urine, it should be used with caution in clients with severe renal dysfunction.

Special Considerations for Pregnant Women

A National Institutes of Health consensus panel recommended methadone maintenance as the standard of care for pregnant women with opioid dependence. Pregnant women should be maintained on an adequate (i.e., therapeutic) methadone dose. An effective dose prevents the onset of withdrawal for 24 hours, reduces or eliminates drug craving, and blocks the euphoric effects of other narcotics. An effective dose usually is in the range of 50–150mg (Drozdick et al. 2002). Dosage must be individually determined, and some pregnant women may be able to be successfully maintained on less than 50mg while others may require much higher doses than 150mg. The dose often needs to be increased as a woman progresses through pregnancy, due to increases in blood volume and metabolic changes specific to pregnancy (Drozdick et al. 2002; Finnegan and Wapner 1988).

Generally, dosing of methadone is for a 24-hour period. However, because of metabolic changes during pregnancy it might not be possible to adequately manage a pregnant woman during a 24-hour period on a single dose. Split dosing (giving half the dose in the morning and half in the evening), particularly during the third trimester of pregnancy, may stabilize the woman's blood methadone levels and effectively treat withdrawal symptoms and craving.

Women who are on methadone may breastfeed their infant(s). Very little methadone comes through breast milk. The American Academy of Pediatrics (AAP) Committee on Drugs lists methadone as a "maternal medication usually compatible with breastfeeding" (AAP 2001, pp. 780–781).

The Federal government mandates that prenatal care be available for pregnant women on methadone. It is the responsibility of treatment providers to arrange this care. More than ever, there is need for collaboration involving obstetric, pediatric, and substance abuse treatment providers. Comprehensive care for the pregnant woman who is opioid dependent must include a combination of methadone maintenance, prenatal care, and substance abuse treatment. While it is not recommended that pregnant women who are maintained on methadone undergo detoxification, if these women require detoxification, the safest time is during the second trimester. In contrast, it is possible to detoxify women dependent on heroin who are abusing illicit opioids by using a methadone taper. For further information, consult the forthcoming.

---

[40] *anorexia:* An eating disorder marked by an extreme fear of becoming overweight that leads to excessive dieting to the point of serious ill-health and sometimes death.

[41] *bulimia:* A condition in which periods of overeating are followed by under-eating, use of laxatives, or self-induced vomiting. It is associated with depression and anxiety about putting on weight.

Buprenorphine has been examined in pregnancy and appears not to cause birth defects but it may be associated with a withdrawal syndrome in the newborn (Jones and Johnson 2001). Buprenorphine has not yet been approved for use with this population. More data are needed about the safety and effectiveness of buprenorphine with pregnant women.

Naloxone should not be given to a pregnant woman even as a last resort for severe opioid overdose. Withdrawal can result in spontaneous abortion, premature labor, or stillbirth (Weaver 2003).

Inderal, **Trandate**, and **Lopressor** are the beta-blockers of choice for treating high blood pressure during pregnancy (McElhatton 2001). However, the impact of using them for alcohol detoxification during pregnancy is unclear.

Nicotine replacement therapy (NRT) is contraindicated during pregnancy.

For all women of childbearing age who may be or think they may be pregnant, the physician should discuss the safety of these medications before starting, continuing, or discontinuing medication treatment. Substance abuse counselors may have a role in encouraging this discussion by suggesting their clients talk with the prescribing physician.

Tips for Communicating With Physicians About Clients and Medication

▶ Send a written report.

The goal is to get your concerns included in the client's medical record. When information is in a medical record, it is more likely to be acted on. Records of phone calls and letters may or may not be placed in the chart.

▶ Make it look like a report—and be brief.

Include date of report, client name and Social Security Number. Most medical consultation reports are one page. Longer reports are less likely to be read. Include and prominently label sections:

Presenting Problem

Assessment

Treatment and Progress

Recommendations and Questions

▶ Keep the tone neutral.

Provide details about the client's use or abuse of prescription medications. Avoid making direct recommendations about prescribed medications. Allow the physician to draw his or her own conclusions. This will enhance your alliance with the physician and makes it more likely that he or she will act on your input.

Do your best to become a "team."

▶ When the physician does not respond.

Professional duty dictates that a report should be updated whenever a client's condition or situation changes in a manner thought to affect the client's general health and/or medical care. Continue attempts to coordinate care when it is in the client's best interest even if the physician appears not to respond.

▶ Download The Substance Abuse Treatment Coordination Report (available in English and Spanish)—www.ATTCnetwork.org.

References

Adams, J.B., and Wacher, A. Specific changes in the glycoprotein components of seromucoid in pregnancy. *Clinica Chimica Acta: International Journal of Clinical Chemistry* 21(1):155-157, 1968.

American Academy of Pediatrics, Committee on Drugs. The transfer of drugs and other chemicals into human milk. *Pediatrics* 108(3):776-789, 2001.

Buhrich, N., Weller, A., and Kevans, P. Misuse of anticholinergic drugs by people with serious mental illness. *Psychiatric Services* 51(7):928-929, 2000.

Center for Substance Abuse Treatment. *Detoxification from Alcohol and Other Drugs.* Treatment Improvement Protocol (TIP) Series 19. DHHS Publication No. (SMA) 95-3046. Rockville, MD: Substance Abuse and Mental Health Services Administration, 1995.

Center for Substance Abuse Treatment. *Matching Treatment to Patient Needs in Opioid Substitution Therapy.* Treatment Improvement Protocol (TIP) Series 20. DHHS Publication No. (SMA) 95-3049. Rockville, MD: Substance Abuse and Mental Health Services Administration, 1995.

Center for Substance Abuse Treatment. *Naltrexone and Alcoholism Treatment.* Treatment Improvement Protocol (TIP) Series 28. DHHS Publication No. (SMA) 98-3206. Rockville, MD: Substance Abuse and Mental Health Services Administration, 1998.

Center for Substance Abuse Treatment. *Substance Abuse Treatment for Persons with Co-Occurring Disorders.* Treatment Improvement Protocol (TIP) Series 42. DHHS Publication No. (SMA) 05-3992. Rockville, MD: Substance Abuse and Mental Health Services Administration, 2005.

Cohen, L.S. Psychotropic drug use in pregnancy. *Hospital & Community Psychiatry* 40(6):566-567, 1989.

Dean, M., Stock, B., Patterson, R.J., and Levy, G. Serum protein binding of drugs during and after pregnancy in humans. *Clinical Pharmacology and Therapeutics* 28(2):253-261, 1980.

Drozdick, J., III, Berghella, V., Hill, M., and Kaltenbach, K. Methadone trough levels in pregnancy. *American Journal of Obstetrics and Gynecology* 187(5):1184-1188, 2002.

Finnegan, L.P., and Wapner, R.J. Narcotic addiction in pregnancy. In: Niebyl, J.R., ed. *Drug Use in Pregnancy.* 2d ed. Philadelphia: Lea and Febiger, 1988. pp. 203-222.

Fiore, M. C., Hatsukami, D. K., & Baker, T. B. Effective tobacco dependence treatment. *JAMA, 288*(14), 1768-1771, 2002.

Fiore, M. C., Jaén, C. R., Baker, T.B., et al. *Treating Tobacco Use and Dependence: 2008 Update.* Clinical Practice Guideline. Rockville, MD: U.S. Department of Health and Human Services. Public Health Service. May 2008.

Fiore, M. C., & Schroeder, L. L. Effective interventions for persons who use tobacco. Key findings from the United States public health service clinical practice guideline: Treating tobacco use and dependence. *Journal of Clinical Psychiatry Monographs, 18*(1), 64-73, 2003.

Ganrot, P.O. Variation of the concentrations of some plasma proteins in normal adults, in pregnant women and in newborns. *Scandinavian Journal of Clinical and Laboratory Investigation Supplementum* 124:83-88, 1972.

Garbis, H., and McElhatton, P.R. Psychotropic, sedative-hypnotic and Parkinson drugs. In: *Drugs During Pregnancy and Lactation: Handbook of Prescription Drugs and Comparative Risk Assessment: With Updated Information on Recreational Drugs.* New York: Elsevier, 2001. pp. 182-191.

Hudmon, K.S., Kroon, L.A., and Corelli R.L. Smoking Cessation. In: Handbook of nonprescription drugs: An interactive approach to self-care, 15th Edition. Washington DC: American Pharmacists Association, 2006. pp.1021-1044.

Jones, H.E., and Johnson, R.E. Pregnancy and substance abuse. *Current Opinion in Psychiatry* 14:187-193, 2001.

Kuhnz, W., Koch, S., Helge, H., and Nau, H. Primidone and phenobarbital during lactation period in epileptic women: Total and free drug serum levels in the nursed infants and their effects on neonatal behavior. *Developmental Pharmacology and Therapeutics* 11(3):147-154, 1988.

Malcolm, R., Myrick, H., Roberts, J., Wang, W., and Anton, R. The differential effects of medication on mood, sleep disturbance, and work ability in outpatient alcohol detoxification. *American Journal on Addictions* 11(2):141-150, 2002.

McElhatton, P. Heart and circulatory system drugs. In: Schaefer, C. *Drugs During Pregnancy and Lactation: Handbook of Prescription Drugs and Comparative Risk Assessment.* Amsterdam: Elsevier Science B.V., 2001. pp. 116-131.

Mortola, J.F. The use of psychotropic agents in pregnancy and lactation. *Psychiatric Clinics of North America* 12:69-88, 1989.

National Tobacco Cessation Collaborative (NTCC). *Key points to help dispel the myths about nicotine and NRT: For consumers, patients, quitline operators, and health care providers.* Retrieved on November 06, 2007, from: http://www.tobacco-cessation.org/PDFs/NicFactSheet-3-07.pdf

National Tobacco Cessation Collaborative (NTCC). NTCC news: March 2007. Retrieved on November 06, 2007, from: http://www.tobacco-cessation.org/news_march.htm

National Tobacco Cessation Collaborative (NTCC). Resources: Tobacco cessation medications (FDA approved). Retrieved on November 06, 2007, from: http://www.tobacco-cessation.org/resources.htm

Northwest Network Mental Illness Research and Education Center and Center for Excellence in Substance Abuse Treatment and Education of the VA Puget Sound Health Care System. *Brief Smoking Cessation Treatment for Substance Dependent Populations: Clinician Training Manual,* (n.d.).

Okuyemi, K. S., Nollen, N. L., & Ahluwalia, J. S. Interventions to facilitate smoking cessation. *American Family Physician,* 74, 262-271, 2006.

Perucca, E., and Crema, A. Plasma protein binding of drugs in pregnancy. *Clinical Pharmacokinetics* 7(4):336-352, 1982.

Pond, S.M., Kreek, M.J., Tong, T.G., Raghunath, J., and Benowitz, N.L. Altered methadone pharmacokinetics in methadone-maintained pregnant women. *Journal of Pharmacology and Experimental Therapeutics* 233(1):1-6, 1985.

Potts, L.A., Garwood, C.L. Varenicline: The newest agent for smoking cessation. *Am J Health Syst Pharm* **64**: 1381-4, 2007.

Robert, E., Reuvers, M., and Shaefer, C. Antiepileptics. In: Schaefer, C.H., ed. *Drugs During Pregnancy and Lactation: Handbook of Prescription Drugs and Comparative Risk Assessment: With Updated Information on Recreational Drugs.* Amsterdam: Elsevier, 2001. pp. 46-57.

Sernyak, M.J., Leslie, D.L., Alarcon, R.D., Losonczy, M.F., and Rosenheck, R. Association of diabetes mellitus with use of atypical neuroleptics in the treatment of schizophrenia. *American Journal of Psychiatry* 159(4):561-566, 2002.

Sutton, L.R., and Hinderliter, S.A. Diazepam abuse in pregnant women on methadone maintenance: Implications for the neonate. Clinical Pediatrics 29:108-111, 1990.

The Tobacco Use and Dependence Clinical Practice Guideline Panel, Staff, and Consortium Representatives. A clinical practice guideline for treating tobacco use and dependence: A US Public Health Service report. *The Journal of the American Medical Association, 283*(24), 3244-3254, 2000.

Tobacco Free Coalition of Oregon (TOFCO). *Make it your business: Insure a tobacco-free workforce.* Cessation fact sheet. Retrieved on November 02, 2007, from: http://www.tobaccofreeoregon.org/projects/miyb/pdf/cessation_fact_sheet.pdf

US Food and Drug Administration, Center for Drug Evaluation and Research. *FDA Patient Information Sheet for Varenicline (marketed as Chantix).* Retrieved on November 02, 2007, from: http://www.fda.gov/cder/drug/InfoSheets/patient/vareniclinePIS.htm

Weaver, M.F. Perinatal addiction. In: Graham, A.W., Schultz, T.K., Mayo-Smith, M.F., Ries, R.K., and Wilford, B.B., eds. *Principles of Addiction Medicine,* 3d ed. Chevy Chase, MD: American Society of Addiction Medicine, 2003. pp. 1231-1246.

Acknowledgments

This 2008 revision was made possible because of the dedication and commitment of many individuals and organizations. It includes an adaptation of the 2004 edition that was modified and enhanced by CSAT for inclusion in their *TIP 42: Substance Abuse Treatment for Persons with Co-Occurring Disorders.*

The Mid-America Addiction Technology Transfer Center gratefully acknowledges the following contributors:

Sally Baehni, MDiv

Jan Campbell, MD

Merritt Engel, MA

Joseph Parks, MD

Richard K. Ries, MD

Joyce Sasse, MS, APRN-BC, CARN

Pat Stilen, LCSW, CADAC

Main Editors for the 2008 edition:

Ignacio Alejandro Barajas Muñoz, MS, Project Manager of Evaluation at the Mid-America Addiction Technology Transfer Center, University of Missouri-Kansas City, Kansas City, MO

Alicia M. Wendler, PhD, VA Eastern Kansas Health Care System, Dwight D. Eisenhower VAMC, Leavenworth, KS

Talking With Clients About Their Medication

Untreated psychiatric problems are a common cause for treatment failure in substance abuse treatment programs. Supporting clients with mental illness in continuing to take their psychiatric medications can significantly improve substance abuse treatment outcomes.

Getting Started. Take 5-10 minutes every few sessions to go over these topics with your clients:

Remind them that taking care of their mental health will help prevent relapse.

Ask how their psychiatric medication is helpful.

Acknowledge that taking a pill every day is a hassle.

Acknowledge that everybody on medication misses taking it sometimes.

Do not ask *if* they have missed any doses, rather ask, *"How many doses have you missed?"*

Ask if they felt or acted different on days when they missed their medication.

Was missing the medication related to any substance use relapse?

Without judgment, ask *"Why did you miss the medication? Did you forget, or did you choose not to take it at that time?"*

For clients who forgot, ask them to consider the following strategies:
Keep medication where it cannot be missed: with the TV remote control, near the refrigerator, or taped to the handle of a toothbrush. Everyone has two or three things they do every day without fail. Put the medication in a place where it cannot be avoided when doing that activity, but always away from children.

Suggest they use an alarm clock set for the time of day they should take their medication. Reset the alarm as needed.

Suggest they use a Mediset: a small plastic box with places to keep medications for each day of the week, available at any pharmacy. The Mediset acts as a reminder and helps track whether or not medications were taken.

For clients who admit to choosing NOT to take their medication:
Acknowledge they have a right to choose NOT to use any medication.

Stress that they owe it to themselves to make sure their decision is well thought out. It is an important decision about their personal health and they need to discuss it with their prescribing physician.

Ask their reason for choosing not to take the medication.

Don't accept *"I just don't like pills."* Tell them you are sure they wouldn't make such an important decision without having a reason.

Offer as examples reasons others might choose not to take medication. For instance, they:

1. Don't believe they ever needed it; *never were mentally ill*

2. Don't believe they need it anymore; *cured*

3. Don't like the side effects

4. Fear the medication will harm them

5. Struggle with objections or ridicule of friends and family members

6. Feel taking medication means they're not personally in control

Transition to topics other than psychiatric medications. Ask what supports or techniques they use to assist with emotions and behaviors when they choose not to take the medication.

General Approach: The approach when talking with clients about psychiatric medication is exactly the same as when talking about their substance abuse decisions.

Explore the triggers or cues that led to the undesired behavior (either taking drugs of abuse or not taking prescribed psychiatric medications).

Review why the undesired behavior seemed like a good idea at the time.

Review the actual outcome resulting from their choice.

Ask if their choice got them what they were seeking.

Strategize with clients about what they could do differently in the future.

Brief Counselor Strategies for Tobacco Users—the Five A's*

▶ ASK about tobacco use and past quit efforts

Get the conversation started:

"Do you currently use any form of tobacco? Have you used it in the past? How old were you when you started? Tell me about your efforts to quit. What helped, what didn't help?"

▶ ADVISE abstinence

Advice should be:

Clear: "Quitting is the most important thing you can do for your health. Cutting down is not enough."
Strong: "You are more likely to die from smoking than from all other drugs and alcohol use combined."
Personalized: "You have powerful reasons to quit. For example..." [tie tobacco use in with current symptoms or health concerns].

▶ ASSESS willingness for a quit attempt during next 30 days

Determine motivation level to quit:

"On a scale from 1 to 10, with 1 being 'not at all motivated' to 10 being 'extremely motivated,' how ready are you to quit in the next 30 days?"

If willing to make a quit attempt:

Communicate research in quitting, "Research shows that quitting is possible for all populations. In fact, more people have quit than are still smoking and about 80% of all Americans are smoke free."

Discuss effective treatments available, such as nicotine replacement therapies (NRTs), medications, self-help resources (help lines or support groups), and counseling.

Initiate agreed upon treatment plan, "Let's come up with a plan."

If unwilling to make a quit attempt, provide motivational intervention (see Five R's section)

▶ ASSIST quit attempt effort

Develop a quit plan (STAR):

Set a specific quit date, ideally within two weeks, that has some meaning (e.g., anniversary, stress-free weekend)

Tell family, friends, coworkers others about quitting, request extra support and understanding; ask other smokers in the household to not smoke inside; identify at least one non-smoker to talk to when tempted to smoke

Anticipate challenges that will occur including withdrawal symptoms, cravings, and high-risk situations

Remove environmental triggers (e.g., ashtrays, lighters); avoid smoking in 'favorite' places (e.g., car, dinner table, easy chair); limit smoking to uncomfortable places (e.g., outside); recommend visiting only smoke-free establishments

Provide problem-solving strategies and skills training:

Track tobacco use patterns (e.g., time, circumstances) and identify high risk situations:

Internally—mood swings, negative self-talk, smoking urges

Externally—drinking coffee, taking a break, watching TV, driving, seeing other smokers

Identify substitute behaviors to smoking and other cognitive behavioral activities for coping (e.g., keep hands busy with a 'worry stone;' chew gum; exercise; engage in 'self-soothing' activities such as warm bath, listen to soothing music; imagine telling people you are a non-smoker, practice asking others to not smoke around you or leave cigarettes around; change daily routine)

Provide basic information about smoking and successful quitting (e.g., educate on the addictive nature of smoking; discuss that even a single puff increases the likelihood of a full relapse; withdrawal symptoms typically peak within 1–2 weeks after quitting but may persist for months)

Recommend use of NRTs, tobacco cessation medications:

Explain how these products increase smoking cessation rates and reduce withdrawal symptoms and cravings

Provide materials on dosages, contraindications, side effects, etc.

Assist in obtaining prescription

▶ ARRANGE follow-up help

Timing:

Schedule first follow-up within one week of quit date and a second within one month; schedule additional follow-ups as indicated, encouraging and allowing phone calls as needed

Make sure that NRTs, medications, and educational materials are received prior to quit date

If abstinent during follow-up:

Congratulate on success; consider giving a certificate or other reinforcement

Check on whether cravings increased for other substances (alcohol, other drugs)

Discuss relapse prevention

Start planning ahead for a smoke-free life

If slip or relapse occurred:

Normalize the difficulty in quitting

Reframe relapse as a learning experience and does not mean failure or necessitate a return to full tobacco use

Motivate to try to quit again immediately

Reassess and re-initiate quit plan

Brief Counselor Strategies for Tobacco Users Unwilling to Quit— the Five R's*

▶ RELEVANCE of quitting

Discuss the Relevance of quitting for health and economic concerns:

Encourage identifying why quitting is personally relevant to him/her (health status, family or social situation, age, gender, prior quitting experiences, etc.)

Write down personal incentives for quitting, rank order reasons, focus on them as often as possible, carry around on card in cigarette pack

▶ RISKS of continued use

Discuss short- and long-term impact to person and family:

Highlight risks specific to him/her and prioritize, "Spouses, children, and other people exposed to secondhand smoke are at higher risk to get colds, the flu, ear infections, and lung infections than people who are not around second-hand smoke"

Inform him/her that reducing number of cigarettes, using alternative tobacco products (cigars), or switching brands will not eliminate risks

Discuss acute (e.g., harm to pregnancy) and long-term (e.g., lung and other cancers) risks

▶ REWARDS of quitting

Discuss physical changes (some immediate) as a result of quitting and highlight those most relevant:

Pulmonary benefits:

Carbon monoxide and oxygen levels in the blood return to normal after 8 hours

Bronchial tubes relax, making it easier to breathe after 72 hours

Cilia re-grow in lungs, increasing ability to fight infection after 1-9 months

Coughing, sinus infection, and shortness of breath decrease after 1-9 months

Cardiac benefits:

Blood pressure and body temperature returns to normal after 20 minutes

Chance of heart attack decreases after only 24 hours

Risk of coronary heart disease is half that of a smoker within 1 year

Heart attack risk drops to near normal within 2 years

Stroke risk is reduced after 5 years

Risk of coronary heart disease is the same as non-smokers within 15 years

Reduced cancer risk benefits:

Lung cancer death rates for a former pack per day-smoker is cut in half after 5 years

Risk of throat, mouth, and esophageal cancers is cut in half after 5 years

Lung cancer death rate is similar to that of non-smokers within 10 years

Pre-cancerous cells are replaced within 10 years

Other benefits:

Expect to save $2000/year or more, list ideas for how to spend money saved

Improved taste and smell, improved smell of home and car, reduce aged appearance

Improved sleep, reduced anxiety, reduced depression, and improved sexual functioning after period of abstinence

Strengthened sobriety from other addictive substances (when sobriety from those substances is already established)

▶ Identify ROADBLOCKS to quitting

Encourage each individual to discuss his/her perceived barriers to quitting and offer strategies that address these challenges:

Examples of roadblocks could include fear of failure, weight gain, lack of support, mood or emotional problems, withdrawal symptoms, life circumstances, presence of another smoker in the household, enjoyment of tobacco, etc.

▶ Use REPETITION

Use motivational interventions each session:

Repeat the Relevance, Risks, and Rewards

*The Five As and Five Rs are available in the 2008 update of the Treating Tobacco Use and Dependence Guidelines (DHHS 2008).

Appendix 56

Drug Abuse Screening Test

Drug Abuse Screening Test (DAST)			
Name:			
Date:			
Score:			
1.	Have you used drugs other than those required for medical reasons?	Yes	No
2.	Have you abused prescription drugs?	Yes	No
3.	Do you abuse more than one drug at a time?	Yes	No
4.	Can you get through the week without using drugs (other than those required for medical reasons)?	Yes	No
5.	Are you always able to stop using drugs when you want to?		
6.	Do you abuse drugs on a continuous basis?	Yes	No
7.	Do you try to limit your drug use to certain situations?		
8.	Have you had "blackouts" or "flashbacks" as a result of drug use?	Yes	No
9.	Do you ever feel bad about your drug abuse?	Yes	No
10.	Does your spouse (or parents) ever complain about your involvement with drugs?	Yes	No
11.	Do your friends or relatives know or suspect you abuse drugs?	Yes	No
12.	Has drug abuse ever created problems between you and your spouse?	Yes	No
13.	Has any family member ever sought help for problems related to your drug use?	Yes	No
14.	Have you ever lost friends because of your use of drugs?	Yes	No
15.	Have you ever neglected your family or missed work due to your use of drugs?	Yes	No
16.	Have you ever been in trouble at work because of drug abuse?	Yes	No
17.	Have you ever lost a job because of drug abuse?	Yes	No

(Continued)

(Continued)

18.	Have you gotten into fights when under the influence of drugs?	Yes	No
19.	Have you ever been arrested because of unusual behavior while under the influence of drugs?	Yes	No
20.	Have you ever been arrested for driving while under the influence of drugs?	Yes	No
21.	Have you engaged in illegal activities to obtain drugs?	Yes	No

Each item is scored one point. Six or more points to a substance abuse problem.

Appendix 57

Clinical Opiate Withdrawal Scale

Resting Pulse Rate: Measured after client is sitting or lying for one minute

0 = pulse rate 80 or below

1 = pulse rate 81–100

2 = pulse rate 101–120

4 = pulse rate greater than 120

GI Upset: Over past half hour

0 = no GI symptoms

1 = stomach cramps

2 = nausea or loose stool

3 = vomiting or diarrhea

5 = multiple episodes of diarrhea or vomiting

Sweating: Over past half hour not accounted for by room temperature or client activity

0 = no report of chills or flushing

1 = subjective report of chills or flushing

2 = flushed or observable moistness on face

3 = beads of sweat on brow or face

4 = sweat streaming off face

Restlessness: Observation during assessment

0 = able to sit still

1 = reports difficulty sitting still, but is able to do so

3 = frequent shifting or extraneous movements of legs/arms

5 = Unable to sit still for more than a few seconds

Source: Wesson DR, Ling W. The Clinical Opiate Withdrawal Scale (COWS). *Journal of Psychoactive Drugs* 2003;35(2):253–59; http://www.drdave.org/Articles/Journal-Of-PsychedelicDrugs.htm

Pupil Size:

0 = pupils pinned or normal size for room light

1 = pupils possibly larger than normal for room light

2 = pupils moderately dilated

5 = pupils so dilated that only the rim of the iris is visible

Bone or Joint Aches: If client was having pain previously, only the additional component attributed to opiate withdrawal is scored

0 = not present

1 = mild diffuse discomfort

Tremor: Observation of outstretched hands

0 = no tremor

1 = tremor can be felt, but not observed

2 = slight tremor observable

4 = gross tremor or muscle twitching

Yawning: Observation during assessment

0 = no yawning

1 = yawning once or twice during assessment

2 = yawning three or more times during assessment

4 = yawning several times/minute

Anxiety or Irritability:

0 = none

1 = client reports increasing irritability or anxiousness

2 = client obviously irritable/anxious

4 = client so irritable/anxious that participation in the assessment is difficult

Gooseflesh skin: Score:

0 = skin is smooth; 5–12 = Mild Withdrawal

3 = piloerection of skin can be felt or hairs standing up on arms; 13–24 = Moderate Withdrawal

5 = prominent piloerection; 25–36 = Severe Withdrawal

Appendix 58

Adult Nurses Intake

Julie Braaten, RN, and Carol Regier, RN

Date: _____

What events precipitated your admission? _____

_____

Who referred you? _____

_____

CHEMICAL USE HISTORY

Have you ever had a previous treatment for chemical dependency?   Yes_____   No_____   (If yes, complete the following questions.)

When: Month & Year	Where: Name of Facility & Address	Did you complete treatment? Yes/No	Outpatient Treatment	Inpatient Treatment	Length of Sobriety After the Treatment

Please list any alcohol and/or drug education you may have had such as PPP/IPP classes. _____

_____

Do you have an alcohol and/or drug free environment to live in?   Yes_____   No_____   If no, why not?

_____

_____

Have you ever attended Alcoholics Anonymous (AA)/Narcotics Anonymous (NA) or Gamblers Anonymous (GA) meetings in the past?   Yes _____   No _____

ALCOHOL:

Diagnostic and Statistical Manual of Mental Disorders (DSM–IV) DIAGNOSIS: 303.00 Alcohol Intoxication; 291.80 Alcohol Withdrawal; 305.00 Alcohol Abuse; 303.90 Alcohol Dependence with or without Physiological Dependence

What was your age of first use of alcohol? _____

How old were you when you started drinking alcohol on a regular basis? _____
_____

How often are you drinking alcohol? (daily, number of times per week, or number of times per month)
_____

How long have you been drinking alcohol in this pattern? _____

How much alcohol do you usually drink at one time? _____

What is your maximum amount of alcohol that you can drink at one time? _____

When was your last drink of alcohol, and how much alcohol did you consume at that time? _____
_____

Do you feel you have a problem with alcohol? Yes _____   No _____   If yes, how long has your alcohol use been causing problems? _____

Do you require increased alcohol amounts to achieve intoxication or your desired effect?
Yes _____   No _____

Do you experience a diminished effect with continued use of the same amount of alcohol?
Yes _____   No _____

Have you ever had to go to an emergency room or physician's office for an alcohol related illness or accident?

Yes _____   No _____   If yes, explain: _____
_____

Have you ever experienced alcohol poisoning? Yes _____   No _____   If yes, explain: _____
_____
_____

Have you ever experienced the following withdrawal symptoms?

	YES	NO
Coarse tremors of hands, tongue, and/or eyelids		
Nausea and/or vomiting		
Malaise/weakness		
Autonomic hyperactivity (tachycardia, sweating, elevated blood pressure)		
Anxiety/nervousness		
Depressed mood		
Irritability		
Transient hallucinations and/or delusions		
Headache		
Insomnia		

Do you drink alcohol or use other drugs to relieve or avoid withdrawal symptoms?   Yes _____   No _____

Have you ever experienced blackouts?   Yes _____   No _____

Have you tried to quit drinking alcohol before?   Yes _____   No _____   If yes, explain: _____
_____

Have you ever tried to control your drinking before?   Yes _____   No _____   If yes, explain: _____
_____
_____

What was the longest period you went without drinking alcohol in the past 12 months? _____
_____

Why did you abstain from drinking alcohol during that time period? _____
_____

Has drinking created any problems with interpersonal relationships in the following areas:

	YES	**NO**	**If yes, explain**
With your spouse?			
With your children?			
With other members of your family?			
With your friends?			

When drinking alcohol, have you ever been involved in any of the following:

	YES	**NO**	**If yes, explain**
Physical and/or verbal fighting			
Motor vehicle accidents			
Injuries of any kind			

CANNABIS:

DSM–IV DIAGNOSIS: 305.20 Cannabis Abuse; 304.30 Cannabis Dependence with or without Physiological Dependence

Have you ever used cannabis, marijuana, pot, THC, hashish, weed, dope, green goddess, hydro, indo, KGB, locoweed, Mary Jane, sinsemilla, homegrown, etc.?   Yes _____   No _____   The following are not applicable if the previous question was answered no.

Name of Drug	Age of First Use	Method(s) of Use: Smoked; Oral	Past/Current Pattern/ Frequency of Use (daily, weekly, monthly— number of times)	How Long Have You Used in This Pattern	Past/Current Usual Consumption	Maximum Consumption	Date of Last Use

Have you ever experienced the following with use or after use of cannabis?

	YES	NO		YES	NO
Chronic cough			Bronchitis		
Headache			Irritability		
Muscle cramps			Sleep disturbances		
Decreased exercise tolerance			Increased heart rate		
Panic attacks					

COCAINE:

DSM–IV DIAGNOSIS 305.60 Cocaine Abuse; 304.20 Cocaine Dependence with or without Physiological Dependence

Have you ever used crack, coke, powder, white, snow, flake, devil's dandruff, fast white lady, uptown, white boy, white dragon, 24-7, cookies, glo, hard ball, rock, etc.?   Yes _____   No _____   The following are not applicable if the previous question was answered no.

Name of Drug	Age of First Use	Method(s) of Use: Smoked; Oral	Past/Current Pattern/ Frequency of Use (daily, weekly, monthly— number of times)	How Long Have You Used in This Pattern	Past/Current Usual Consumption	Maximum Consumption	Date of Last Use

Have you ever seen things that other people could not see, or heard things other people could not hear (hallucinations and/or delusions)?   Yes _____   No _____

Have you experienced the following withdrawal symptoms?

	YES	NO		YES	NO
Fatigue			Agitation		
Nausea/vomiting			Craving for cocaine		
Depression			Insomnia/hypersomnia		
Sweating/chills			Anxiety		
Irritability			Increased appetite		
Preoccupation with obtaining cocaine			Vivid/unpleasant dreams		

HALLUCINOGENS:

DSM–IV DIAGNOSIS: 305.30 Hallucinogen Abuse; 304.50 Hallucinogen Dependence with or without Physiological Dependence

Have you ever used LSD, acid, DMT, peyote, buttons, mushrooms, mescaline, psilocybin, battery acid, dots, zen, window pane, boomers, yellow sunshine, etc.? Yes _____ No _____ The following are not applicable if the previous answer was no.

Have you ever had a flashback? Yes _____ No _____

Name of Drug	Age of First Use	Method(s) of Use: Smoked; Oral; Sniffed; Injected; Inhaled	Past/Current Pattern/ Frequency of Use (daily, weekly, monthly— number of times)	How Long Have You Used in This Pattern	Past/Current Usual Consumption	Maximum Consumption	Date of Last Use

OPIOIDS & OTHER ANALGESICS (INCLUDING NARCOTICS):

DSM–IV DIAGNOSIS: 305.50 Opioid Abuse; 304.00 Opioid Dependence with or without Physiological Dependence

Have you ever used heroin, eigth, H, hell dust, horse, junk, poppy, smack, train, thunder, opium, Darvon (propoxyphene hydrochloride), Darvocet (propoxyphene napsylate), Lortab (hydrocodone bitartrate & acetaminophen), Lorcet, Percocet (oxycodone & acetaminophen), Percodan, Roxicet, Roxanol, Tylox, Codeine, Demerol (meperidine hydrochloride), Morphine, Oxycontin, Oxycodone, MS Contin, Oxy IR, Hydrocodone, Flexeril (cyclobenzaprine hydrochloride), Fioricet with Codeine, Fiorinal with Codeine, Fentanyl (Duragesic) patch, Sublimaze (fentanyl citrate), Dilaudid, Methadone, Vicodin, Stadol (butorphanol tartrate), Talwin (pentazocine hydrochloride), Ultram (tramadol hydrochloride)?

Yes _____ No _____ The following are not applicable if the previous question was answered no.

Name of Drug	Age of First Use	Method(s) of Use: Smoked; Oral; Sniffed; Injected	Past/Current Pattern/Frequency of Use (daily, weekly, monthly— number of times)	How Long Have You Used in This Pattern	Past/Current Usual Consumption	Maximum Consumption	Date of Last Use

Have you experienced the following withdrawal symptoms?

	YES	NO		YES	NO
Craving for an opioid			Nausea/vomiting		
Muscle aches/cramps			Pupillary dilation		
Fever			Goose bumps		
Tremors			Loss of appetite		
Increased heart rate			Lacrimation		
Diarrhea			Rhinorrhea		
Yawning			Sweating		

INHALANTS:

DSM–IV DIAGNOSIS: 305.90 Inhalant Abuse; 304.60 Inhalant Dependence with or without Physiological Dependence

Have you ever sniffed/inhaled aerosols, lighter fluid, gasoline, model cements, solvents, rush, white out, glue, paint, paint thinner, felt tip markers, nail polish, nail polish remover, rubber cement, ether, amyl nitrite, butyl nitrite, nitrous oxide, cooking sprays (like Pam), Freon, markers?   Yes _____   No _____
The following are not applicable if the previous question was answered no.

Name of Drug	Age of First Use	Method(s) of Use: Inhaled; Sniffing; Huffing; Bagging; Snappers; Poppers	Past/Current Pattern/ Frequency of Use (daily, weekly, monthly—number of times)	How Long Have You Used in This Pattern	Past/Current Usual Consumption	Maximum Consumption	Date of Last Use

Have you experienced the following?

	YES	NO		YES	NO
Sleep disturbances			Nausea/vomiting		
Shakes/Tremors			Sweating		
Abdominal discomfort			Chest discomfort		
Irritability			Being amotivational		
Dizziness			Hallucinations/delusions		
Belligerence			Apathy		
Impaired judgment			Weight loss		
Muscle weakness			Disorientation/confusion		
Lack of coordination			Depression		
Rapid pulse			Seizures		
Memory impairment			Slurred speech		

AMPHETAMINES (INCLUDING METHAMPHETAMINES) & STIMULANTS:

DSM–IV DIAGNOSIS: 305.70 Amphetamine Abuse; 304.40 Amphetamine Dependence with or without Physiological Dependence

Have you ever used speed, ecstasy, MDMA, speeders, methamphetamine, glass, ice, white crosses, ephedrine, crank, crystal, uppers, Adderall (dextroamphetamine sulfate), Ritalin (methylphenidate hydrochloride), Dexedrine (dextroamphetamine sulfate), Dexedrine Spansules, Cylert (pemoline)?   Yes _____   No _____
The following are not applicable if the previous question was answered no.

Name of Drug	Age of First Use	Method(s) of Use: Oral; Sniffed; Injected; Smoked	Past/Current Pattern/ Frequency of Use (daily, weekly, monthly— number of times)	How Long Have You Used in This Pattern	Past/Current Usual Consumption	Maximum Consumption	Date of Last Use

Have you experienced the following withdrawal symptoms?

	YES	NO		YES	NO
Depression			Anxiety		
Agitation			Irritability		
Insomnia/hypersomnia			Fatigue		
Vivid unpleasant dreams			Decreased or increased appetite		
Increased heart rate			Lacrimation (abnormal secretion of tears)		
Diarrhea			Rhinorrhea (excessive mucous secretion from the nose)		
Yawning			Sweating		

SEDATIVE, HYPNOTIC OR ANXIOLYTIC:

DSM–IV DIAGNOSIS: 305.40 Sedative, Hypnotic or Anxiolytic Abuse; 304.10 Sedative, Hypnotic or Anxiolytic Dependence with or without Physiological Dependence

Have you ever used a barbiturate, downer, sleeping medication, Valium (diazepam), chloral hydrate, Dalmane (flurazepam hydrochloride), Klonopin (clonazepam), Seconal (secobarbital sodium),Restoril (temazepam), Halcion (triazolam), Ambien (zolpidem tartrate), Ativan (Lorazepam), Xanax (alprazolam), Librium (chlordiazepoxide hydrochloride), Tranxene (clorazepate dipotassium), Atarax (hydroxyzine hydrochloride), Serax (oxazepam), etc.?   Yes _____   No _____

The following are not applicable if the previous question was answered no.

Name of Drug	Age of First Use	Method(s) of Use: Oral; Injected	Past/Current Pattern/ Frequency of Use (daily, weekly, monthly— number of times)	How Long Have You Used in This Pattern	Past/Current Usual Consumption	Maximum Consumption	Date of Last Use

Have you experienced the following withdrawal symptoms?

	YES	NO		YES	NO
Anxiety			Agitation		
Tremors			Insomnia		
Shakiness			Headaches		
Tinnitus (a sensation of noise, ringing, or roaring & can only be heard by the one affected)			Blurred vision		
Diarrhea			Seizures		
Nausea and/or vomiting			Muscle aching/twitching		
Dizziness			Concentration difficulties		

PHENCYCLIDINE:

DSM–IV DIAGNOSIS: 305.90 Phencyclidine Abuse; 304.90 Phencyclidine Dependence with or without Physiological Dependence

Have you ever used phencyclidine (PCP), angel dust, animal tranquilizer, embalming fluid, ozone, rocket fuel, wack, happy sticks, magic dust, Peter Pan, trank, etc.? Yes _____ No _____

The following are not applicable if the previous question was answered no.

Name of Drug	Age of First Use	Method(s) of Use: Oral; Injected; Sniffed; Smoked	Past/Current Pattern/ Frequency of Use (daily, weekly, monthly— number of times)	How Long Have You Used in This Pattern	Past/Current Usual Consumption	Maximum Consumption	Date of Last Use

Have you experienced the following?

	YES	NO		YES	NO
Rage/violence			Craving		
Compulsive PCP seeking behaviors			Seizures		
Coma			Accidental injury—related to the drug's effects		
Delusions			Paranoia		
Memory loss			Difficulty with speech		
Difficulty with thought			Depression		
Weight loss					

ANABOLIC ANDROGENIC STEROIDS (AAS):

DSM–IV DIAGNOSIS: (Other or Unknown Substance—Related Disorders) 305.90 Abuse; 304.90 Dependence—(You need to specify the individual substance that is being abused in relation to the previous abuse & dependence diagnosis. Example: 304.90 AAS Dependence)

Have you ever used steroids, roids, rage, anabolics, juicers, step ups, etc.?   Yes _____   No _____

The following are not applicable if the previous question was answered no.

Name of Drug	Age of First Use	Method(s) of Use: Oral; Injected	Past/Current Pattern/ Frequency of Use (daily, weekly, monthly— number of times)	How Long Have You Used in This Pattern	Past/Current Usual Consumption	Maximum Consumption	Date of Last Use

Have you experienced the following?

	YES	NO		YES	NO
Fatigue			Depression		
Muscle pain			Headache		
Craving			Irritability		
Aggressiveness			Changes in levels of energy		

GAMMA HYDROXYBUTYRATE (GHB) & ANALOGS:

DSM–IV DIAGNOSIS: (Other or Unknown Substance-Related Disorders) 305.90 Abuse; 304.90 Dependence (You need to specify the individual substance that is being abused in relation to the previous abuse & dependence diagnosis. Example: 304.90 GHB Dependence)

Have you ever used GHB, Georgia home boy, G, goop, liquid ecstasy, cherry meth, fantasy, G-riffic, jib, liquid E, liquid X, salty water, scoop, sleep, sleep – 500, soap, vita – G, etc.?   Yes _____   No _____

The following are not applicable if the previous question was answered no.

Name of Drug	Age of First Use	Method(s) of Use: Oral	Past/Current Pattern/ Frequency of Use (daily, weekly, monthly— number of times)	How Long Have You Used in This Pattern	Past/Current Usual Consumption	Maximum Consumption	Date of Last Use

Have you experienced the following?

	YES	NO		YES	NO
Nausea and/or vomiting			Delusions/hallucinations		
Depression			Seizures		
Respiratory distress			Loss of consciousness		
Slowed heart rate			Lowered blood pressure		
Amnesia			Coma		
Anxiety			Insomnia		
Tremors			Tachycardia		
Delirium			Agitation		

OVER-THE-COUNTER MEDICATION(S):

Do you use and/or abuse antihistamines, Nytol, Nyquil, laxatives, Primatene, diet pills, Mydol, Coricidin Cold & Cough, Robitussin, etc.?

Yes _____ No _____ The following are not applicable if the previous question was answered no.

Name of Drug	Age of First Use	Method(s) of Use: Oral	Current Pattern/ Frequency of Use (daily, weekly, monthly— number of times)	How Long Have You Used in This Pattern	Current Usual Consumption	Maximum Consumption	Date of Last Use

NICOTINE:

Do you smoke cigarettes?   Yes _____ No _____   If yes, age of first use of cigarettes?

_____

How many packs of cigarettes do you smoke per day? _____

Do you use smokeless tobacco?   Yes _____ No _____ How much do you use in one day? _____

Do you experience a chronic cough, possibly related to your tobacco use? Yes_____ No_____

Have you ever coughed up or expectorated blood, possibly related to your tobacco use?
Yes _____ No _____

Do you have any sores on the inside of your mouth?   Yes _____   No _____

Have you attempted to quit or control your use of nicotine?   Yes _____   No _____   If yes, how long were you able to quit your tobacco use and what were the reason(s) why you attempted to quit? _____

_____

****

Do you use drugs to relieve or avoid withdrawal symptoms?   Yes _____   No _____

Do you require increased amounts of your drugs/medications to achieve intoxication or your desired effect?
Yes _____   No _____

Do you experience a markedly diminished effect with continued use of the same amount of drugs/
medications?
Yes _____   No _____

Have you ever had to go to an emergency room or physician's office for a drug/medication related illness or accident?

Yes _____   No _____   If yes, explain: _____
_____

Have you ever experienced a drug/medication overdose?   Yes _____   No _____   If yes, explain: _____
_____
_____

Have you tried to quit your drug use before?   Yes _____   No _____   If yes, explain: _____
_____
_____

Have you ever tried to control your drug use before?   Yes _____   No _____   If yes, explain: _____
_____
_____

What was the longest period you went without using drugs in the past 12 months? _____
_____

Why did you abstain from using drugs during that time period? _____
_____
_____

Has your drug use created any problems with interpersonal relationships in the following areas:

	YES	**NO**	**If yes, explain**
With your spouse?			
With your children?			
With other members of your family?			
With your friends?			

When using drugs have you ever been involved in any of the following:

	YES	NO	If yes, explain
Physical and/or verbal fighting			
Motor vehicle accidents			
Injuries of any kind			

Additional Critical Life Areas

Yes_____ No_____ Have you ever used injectable drugs/drugs intravenously?

Yes_____ No_____ Have you stayed drunk and/or high for more than one day?

Yes_____ No_____ Have you ever drank alcohol and/or used drugs in dangerous situations (driving, swimming, etc.)?

GAMBLING HISTORY: (312.31 Pathological Gambling)

When was the last time you gambled? _____

Have you ever been assessed and/or had previous treatment for gambling? Yes _____ No _____ If yes, please answer the following questions in the table.

When: Month & Year	Where: Name of Facility & Address	Did you complete treatment? Yes/No	Outpatient Treatment	Inpatient Treatment	Length of Abstinence After Your Treatment

Have you ever had credit counseling? Yes_____ No_____ If yes, when and where was the credit counseling completed?_____

What forms of gambling do you participate in?

	YES	NO		YES	NO		YES	NO		YES	NO
Video lottery			Scratch tickets			Slot machines			Pull tabs		
Blackjack			Poker (Cards)			Powerball			Dog racing		
Bingo			Horse racing			Sports			Simulcasting		
Stock market			Table games			Internet			Other(s)		

What was the most dollar amount that you have ever won? _____

What was the most dollar amount that you have ever lost? _____

What was your age of your first gambling episode? _____

If "no" is answered on all of the previous questions, the following questions do not need to be asked.

Do you feel that you have a problem with gambling?   Yes _____   No _____   If yes, how long has gambling been a problem for you? _____

How much money do you spend on an average on gambling per month? _____

How often do you gamble (daily, weekly, monthly, yearly) and how much (number of times weekly and monthly, yearly)? _____

_____

What is your current gambling related debt? (weekly and monthly, yearly)? _____

Have you ever filed bankruptcy due to your gambling?   Yes _____   No _____   If yes, explain: _____

_____

_____

	YES	NO
Are you preoccupied with gambling (e.g., preoccupied with reliving past gambling experiences, handicapping or planning the next venture, or thinking of ways to obtain money with which to gamble)?		
Have you ever gambled with increasing amounts of money in order to achieve the desired excitement?		
Have you ever tried to control, cut back, or stop gambling?		
Have you ever felt restless or irritable when attempting to cut down or stop gambling?		
Have you ever gambled as a way of escaping from problems or of relieving a dysphoric mood (e.g., feelings of helplessness, guilt, anxiety, depression)?		
Have you ever gambled the next day to win back your losses (chasing losses)?		
Have you ever lied to family members, therapists, or others to conceal the extent of involvement with your gambling?		
Have you ever committed illegal acts such as forgery, fraud, theft, or embezzlement to finance your gambling?		
Have you ever been arrested because of your gambling, spent time in jail or prison?		
Have you ever jeopardized or lost a significant relationship, job, educational, or career opportunity because of your gambling?		
Have you relied on others to provide money to relieve a desperate financial situation caused by gambling?		
Have you used credit cards to obtain money for gambling?		
Did you ever write bad checks in order to gamble?		
Have you ever gotten behind on bills because of your gambling losses?		

(Continued)

(Continued)

Have you ever gone without necessities because of gambling losses?		
Have you ever sold or pawned anything to obtain money for gambling?		
After winning, have you ever gambled away your winnings or part of it?		
Have you ever felt remorseful after gambling?		

PHYSICAL ASSESSMENT:

Are you currently under the care of a physician(s)? Yes _____ No _____

When was the last time you saw a physician? _____

What was the reason for the visit? _____

Name and address of family physician: _____

_____

Name and address of other physicians you are seeing: _____

_____

Do you have any medical or physical problems for which you see a physician? Yes _____ No _____ If yes, what are your problems or concerns? _____

_____

How would you assess your health? Good (   ) Fair (   ) Poor (   )

Do you feel that your alcohol and/or drug use has affected your health? Yes _____ No _____ If yes, explain how your health has been affected? _____

Have you ever been told that the use of alcohol and/or drugs are a serious threat to your health? Yes _____ No _____ If yes, who told you and why? _____

TUBERCULOSIS:

Have you ever had tuberculosis (TB)? Yes _____ No_____ Have you ever had a BCG vaccination? Yes _____ No _____

Have you ever been exposed to someone else who has had TB? Yes _____ No _____

Have you ever experienced any of the following symptoms within the previous 3 months?

	YES	NO
Productive cough for a 2 to 3 week duration**		
Unexplained night sweats**		
Unexplained fevers**		
Unexplained weight loss**		

**If a client responds yes to any of the previous four questions, they shall be referred to the physician for a medical evaluation to determine the absence or presence of active disease. A Mantoux skin test may or may not be given during this evaluation based on the opinion of the evaluating physician.

Have you ever had a TB tine of Mantoux test?   Yes_____   No_____

Did you have a reaction to the test?   Yes_____   No_____

If you reacted, when was your last chest X-ray, and where did you have the chest X-ray taken? _____
_____

****

SEIZURES/CONVULSIONS:

Have you ever had a seizure/convulsion?   Yes _____   No _____   If yes, explain: _____
_____

_____

When was your last seizure activity? _____

Was your seizure activity directly related to your alcohol and/or drug use?   Yes _____   No _____

Did the seizure occur during your alcohol and/or drug use?   Yes _____   No _____

Did the seizure occur during withdrawal from alcohol and/or drug use?   Yes _____   No _____

Are you currently taking medication(s) for your seizure activity?   Yes _____   No _____

Have you taken medication(s) in the past to control your seizure activity?   Yes _____   No _____

****

Have you had any of the following?

	YES	NO		YES	NO
Whooping cough			Mumps		
Measles			Chicken pox		

Do you currently have any sores, cuts, bruises, or any injuries?   Yes _____   No _____   If yes, explain:
_____
_____

Do you have any of the following?

	YES	NO		YES	NO
1. Heart problems			8. Diabetes		
2. High blood pressure			9. Thyroid problems		
3. Stroke/CVA/TIA			10. Liver problems/hepatitis		
4. Lung problems/breathing problems COPD/emphysema/asthma			11. Numbness/Tingling of extremities		
5. Anemia			12. Medication allergies		
6. Arthritis/gout			13. Food allergies		
7. Back problems			14. Latex allergy		

(Continued)

(Continued)

15. Edema/swelling			22. Prostate problems (if male)		
16. Headaches			23. Cancer		
17. Skin problems			24. Eyes, ears, nose, and throat (EENT) problems		
18. Bowel problems/Constipation/ diarrhea/bloody bowel movements/ tarry bowel movements			25. Muscle cramps/weakness		
19. Ulcers/stomach problems/ hematemesis (Vomited Blood)			26. Surgical procedures		
20. Pancreatitis			27. Other medical issues not asked		
21. Urinary tract problems (frequency of voiding)					

If yes is answered to any of the previous questions, please write down the number and explain: _____

_____

_____

_____

_____

_____

_____

_____

List medications that the client has previously taken but not taking currently:

Name of Medication	Was Medication Effective?		Reason for Use of Medication
	Yes	No	
	Yes	No	
	Yes	No	

_____ Client unable to recall names of previous medications that he or she has taken.

****

FEMALES ONLY:

Do you experience any menstrual problems? Yes _____ No _____ If yes, explain: _____

_____

Date of your last menstrual period? _____

Date of your last Pap smear: _____

Are you currently pregnant? Yes _____ No _____ If yes, when is your estimated due date, and what physician are you seeing for this pregnancy? _____

_____

Have you ever been pregnant? Yes _____   No _____   If yes, number of pregnancies: _____

_____

Have you ever had a miscarriage? Yes _____   No _____

Have you ever had an abortion? Yes _____   No _____ If yes, give date(s): _____

_____

Describe any complications during your pregnancy(ies): _____

_____

* *

AUDITORY ASSESSMENT:

Do you have a hearing loss? Yes _____   No _____   If yes, which ear is affected? _____

_____

Do you wear any hearing aide devices? Yes _____   No _____

* *

VISUAL ASSESSMENT:

Do you wear contacts and/or glasses? Yes _____   No _____

Is your vision blurred or do you see double? Yes _____   No _____

Eye Chart Results: Both eyes: _____   Right eye: _____   Left eye: _____

* *

NUTRITIONAL ASSESSMENT:

How would you assess your eating habits?   Good (   )   Fair (   )   Poor (   )

	YES	NO	EXPLANATION TO A YES RESPONSE
1. Are you on a special diet?			If yes, what type of diet?
2. Have you had any recent weight changes in the past 6 months?			# of pounds lost _____ # of pounds gained _____ Reason for weight loss or gain:
3. Do you skip meals or go without food when you are drinking alcohol and/or using drugs?			
4. Have you ever induced vomiting after eating?			
5. Have you ever been diagnosed as anorexic or bulimic?			

If there is a yes response to questions 1, 2, 4, and/or 5, please inform the dietary staff so that the dietician may visit with the client.

* *

SEXUAL HISTORY:

Age of your first sexual experience: _____

Do you have any concerns about sex and/or your sexuality?   Yes _____   No _____   If yes, explain:
_____

_____

Does your alcohol and/or drug use affect your choices about sex?   Yes _____   No _____   If yes, explain:
_____

_____

Have you ever been in trouble because of sexual behavior(s)?   Yes _____   No _____   If yes, explain:
_____

_____

Do you currently have or ever have been treated for a sexually transmitted disease?   Yes _____   No _____
If yes, explain: _____

Do you use protection during sexual intercourse?   Yes _____   No _____

Have you had sexual intercourse with more than one partner?   Yes _____   No _____

* *

PAIN ASSESSMENT:

Pain Level: □ 0   □ 1   □ 2   □ 3   □ 4   □ 5   □ 6   □ 7   □ 8   □ 9   □ 10
(0 being no pain)

What is your acceptable level of pain? _____

Are you currently experiencing pain?   Yes _____   No _____   If yes, answer the following questions:

Location and description of pain: _____

What relief measures do you use to decrease your pain? _____

Pain Management Booklet given to the client: Yes _____   No _____   (In the Client Handbook)

* *

PSYCHOLOGICAL HISTORY/SCREENING/MENTAL HEALTH ISSUES:

Have you ever seen a counselor/psychologist/psychiatrist?   Yes _____   No _____   If yes, answer the following questions:

When was your last visit? _____

How long have you been seeing this therapist? _____

Have you ever been hospitalized for mental health issues?   Yes _____   No _____

Name of Person & Facility Name	Reason for Counseling/Hospitalization	Date(s)

Have you ever received treatment for any of the following mental health or psychiatric problems?

	YES	NO		YES	NO		YES	NO
Adjustment disorders			Anxiety disorders (Panic disorder, phobias, OCD, post-traumatic stress disorder [PTSD], etc.)			Sexual abuse or sexual assault		
Grief issues			Sleep disorders			Physical and/or emotional abuse		
Fetal alcohol syndrome disorder			Personality disorders (antisocial, avoidant, narcissistic, and/or borderline, schizoid, dependent, paranoid)			Impulse control disorders (intermittent explosive disorder)		
Fetal alcohol effects			Other psychotic disorders			Eating disorders		
Sleep disorders			Attention deficit & disruptive behavior disorders			Bipolar disorders		
Dementia			Depressive disorders			Dissociative disorders (amnesia and depersonalization)		
Schizophrenia & other psychotic disorders			Hyperactivity disorder			Learning disorders		

If yes, please explain:_____

_____

_____

_____

How would you assess your sleeping habits?   Good _____   Fair _____   Poor _____

How many hours of sleep do you get per night? _____

Do you have problems with falling asleep?   Yes _____   No _____   Do you have problems awakening frequently throughout the night?   Yes _____   No _____

Do you feel sad, down, and/or depressed?   Constantly _____   Often _____   Occasionally _____ Infrequently _____

   Explain: _____

Do you feel fearful, anxious and/or nervous?   Constantly _____   Often _____   Occasionally _____ Infrequently _____

   Explain: _____

Have you ever had a panic attack (suddenly fearful without cause)?   Yes _____   No _____   If yes, explain (when was your last panic attack, did you go to the hospital, etc.?): _____

Do you have feelings of uncontrollable anger, rage, or violence?   Yes _____   No _____   If yes, explain:

_____

_____

What do you do when you are angry? _____

Are you or have you been in the past physically abusive to others?   Yes _____   No _____

   When and explain:_____

   Was this abuse reported?   Yes _____   No _____

Have you ever been physically abused?   Yes _____   No _____

   When and explain: _____

_____

   Was this abuse reported?   Yes _____   No _____

   Did you ever tell anyone?   Yes _____   No _____

Do you ever physically abuse yourself?   Yes _____   No _____   If yes, explain: _____

_____

Are you or have you been in the past sexually abusive to others?   Yes _____   No _____

   When and explain: _____

   Was this abuse reported?   Yes _____   No _____

Have you ever been sexually abused?   Yes _____   No _____

   When and explain: _____

_____

Was this abuse reported?   Yes _____   No _____

Did you ever tell anyone?   Yes _____   No _____

Do you have thoughts of harming other people?   Yes _____   No _____   If yes, when and explain: _____
_____
_____

Have you ever been verbally aggressive toward others?   Yes _____   No _____   If yes, explain: _____
_____
_____

Have you ever been physically aggressive?   Yes _____   No _____   If yes, explain (when, where, how violent, was there property destruction, was a weapon involved?): _____
_____
_____

Was law enforcement involved when you were physically aggressive?   Yes _____   No _____   N/A _____   If yes, please explain: _____
_____

Have you ever had thoughts of harming yourself?   Yes _____   No _____   If yes, explain (when was the last time you had these thoughts, etc.?): _____
_____

Are you currently experiencing any thoughts of harming yourself?   Yes _____   No _____   If yes, explain:
_____
_____

Have you made plans for carrying out any of these thoughts?   Yes _____   No _____   If yes, explain:
_____
_____

Have you ever attempted suicide?   Yes _____   No _____   If yes, explain (when was last attempt, etc.?):
_____
_____

Has anyone in your family tried to hurt themselves?   Yes _____   No _____

Have you ever self-mutilated (cutting, burning, etc.)?   Yes _____   No _____   If yes, please explain (describe when, where on the body, with what, how long have you engaged in this behavior, and the date of your most recent behavior and if you required medical intervention): _____
_____
_____

Do you use alcohol and/or drugs to relieve or avoid your problems?   Yes _____   No _____

Do you feel unable to change things?   Yes _____   No _____

Do you use alcohol and/or drugs to escape?   Yes _____   No _____

Do you have plans for the future?   Yes _____   No _____

Briefly describe how you react when things do not go your way. _____

****

EDUCATIONAL:

What was your highest grade of education completed? _____
_____

Do you have a college degree? Yes _____ No _____ If yes, what degree and what major? _____
_____

What type of grades did you obtain in school? _____

Did you attend an individualized educational program (IEP/special education)? Yes _____ No _____

Did you drink alcohol and/or use drugs:

	YES	**NO**
Before school		
During school		
After school		

* *

VOCATIONAL:

Do you currently have a job? Yes _____ No _____ If yes, answer the following questions:

Do you work full-time? Yes _____ No _____ Do you work part-time? Yes _____ No _____

Name of your employer: _____

What is your position/title at work? _____

How long have you been employed with this company/business? _____

Have you ever been placed on probation or suspension at work due to your alcohol and/or drug use and/or gambling?

Yes _____ No _____ If yes, explain: _____
_____

If you are unemployed, how long have you been unemployed? _____

	YES	NO
Have you ever stolen alcohol and/or drugs and/or money from the workplace?		
Have you ever been fired from a job due to your alcohol and/or drug use and/or gambling?		
Have you ever used alcohol and/or drugs or gambled before going to work?		
Have you ever used alcohol and/or drugs or gambled while at work?		
Have you ever just quit going to work?		
Has alcohol and/or drugs caused changes in your performance at work?		
Have you ever called in sick for work due to your alcohol and/or drug use?		

* *

FINANCIAL:

How much money do you earn in a week? _____

How much money do you spend on alcohol and/or drugs in a week? _____

Where do you obtain your money from to purchase alcohol and/or drugs? _____

	YES	NO
Have you ever sold alcohol and/or drugs?		
Have you ever traded things for alcohol and/or drugs?		
Have you ever pawned items for alcohol and/or drugs?		
Have you ever borrowed money to purchase alcohol and/or drugs?		
Have you ever went without other things to buy alcohol and/or drugs?		

Have you ever had to file for bankruptcy?   Yes _____   No _____   If yes, explain: _____
_____
_____

LEGAL HISTORY:

Have you ever been arrested?   Yes _____   No _____   If yes, how many convictions? _____
_____

List all of the charges that you can remember with dates and years:

Convictions	Year(s)	Convictions	Year(s)	Convictions	Year(s)
Assault		Breaking & entering		Burglary	
CHINS		Curfew violation		Destruction of property	
Disorderly conduct		Failed urinalysis (UA)		Grand theft	
Grand theft auto		Hit & run		Vandalism	
Minor in consumption		Petty theft		Possession	
Convictions	Year(s)	Convictions	Year(s)	Convictions	Year(s)
Public intoxication		Robbery		Runaway	
Shoplifting		Truancy		Other	
DUI		Ingestion of a controlled substance			

How old were you when you experienced your first contact with the law? _____
_____

Do you have any current legal problems? Yes _____ No _____ If yes, explain (date of arrest, court date & charge, etc.)? _____

_____

Do you have a probation officer/parole officer (PO)/court services officer (CSO)/juvenile court authority (JCA)?

Yes_____ No_____ If yes, answer the following:

Name of person listed: _____

Address of person listed: _____

Telephone number of person listed: _____

	YES	NO
Have you ever stolen alcohol and/or drugs?		
Have you ever used alcohol and/or drugs while in placement?		
Have you ever violated your probation due to alcohol and/or drug use?		
Have you ever shoplifted for money to buy alcohol and/or drugs?		
Have you ever committed a burglary for alcohol and/or drugs?		
Are you more involved in criminal activities due to your alcohol and/or drug use?		

****

SOCIAL/LEISURE:

	YES	NO
Do any of your friends use alcohol and/or drugs?		
Do your friends try to talk you into drinking alcohol and/or using drugs?		
Do your friends try to talk you out of drinking alcohol and/or using drugs?		
Is it hard for you to trust others?		
Do you have any friends who you can trust?		
Do you have close friends?		
Have you withdrawn from your friends?		
Have you lost friends due to your alcohol and/or drug use?		
Do your friends express concern about your alcohol and/or drug use?		
Have you stopped or reduced the time you spend on hobbies due to your alcohol and/or drug use?		

****

FAMILY:

Name of Relationship	Alive	Deceased	Cause of Death	Chemical Dependency (CD) Problems (Yes or No)
Father (Biological)				
If applicable: Stepfather				
Mother (Biological)				
If applicable: Stepmother				
Biological siblings:				
If applicable: Step Siblings				

What is your birth order? _____

Name of the town and state where you were raised: _____
_____

Name the people who raised you: _____
_____

Name the person and their relationship to you that you felt closest to while growing up: _____
_____

Describe your childhood (happy, sad, normal, etc.): _____

How were you disciplined, and who disciplined you? _____

Did you feel that you were loved while growing up? Yes _____   No _____

What is or was your parents' relationship like? _____

Are you married? Yes _____   No _____   If yes, what is your wife/husband's name: _____
_____

Does your wife or husband use or abuse alcohol and/or drugs? Yes _____   No _____

Have you been previously married? Yes _____   No _____   If yes, explain: _____
_____

Do you have children?   Yes _____   No _____   If yes, please list the children:

Children's Names	Ages of Children	Do your children live with you?		Do your children have a CD problem?	
		YES	NO	YES	NO

Who will be caring for your children while you are in treatment? _____

With whom do you currently live? _____

Number of people in the household? _____

Does anyone in your family have any emotional or physical problems?   Yes _____   No _____   If yes, explain:
_____
_____

Are there any family conflicts?   Yes _____   No _____

How do you get along with your family? _____

Have family members expressed concern over your alcohol and/or drug use?   Yes _____   No _____   If yes, who expressed the concern and why? _____
_____

Has anyone in your family gone to alcohol and/or drug and/or gambling treatment?   Yes _____
No _____

Are any of your family members in a 12-step recovery program?   Yes _____   No _____

****

SPIRITUAL:

Do you believe in a Higher Power? (Example: God or Tunkashila)   Yes _____   No _____

Do you have any concerns about your spiritual beliefs/practices?   Yes _____   No _____

	YES	NO
Do you have religious beliefs?		
Have you ever lost your faith in a Higher Power?		
Have you lost your dreams and goals?		
Have you ever done things drunk and/or high that you would not have done if you had been sober or straight?		

What things lift your spirit? _____

What are your strengths? _____

What are your weaknesses? _____

****

MENTAL STATUS EXAMINATION:

Problem Solving:

1. If the flag floats to the south, from which direction is the wind?

   North = 3 points   _____

2. At what time of the day is your shadow the shortest?

   Noon = 3 points   _____

3. Why does the moon look larger than the stars?

   It is lower = 2 points   Nearer objects appear larger = 4 points   _____

4. If your shadow points to the northeast, where is the sun?

   Southwest = 4 points   _____

Knowledge:

5. What are houses made of?

   1 point for each material up to 4 points   _____

6. Tell me the names of some fish.

   1 point for each species up to 4 points   _____

7. Give me the names of some large cities.

   1 point for each city up to 4 points.   Excluded are small towns.   _____

8. What is sand used for?

   Playing = 1 point   Construction = 2 points   Glass = 4 points   _____

9. What metal is attracted by a magnet?

   Steel = 2 points   Iron = 4 points   _____

10. How many stripes are in the U.S. flag?

    13 = 4 points   _____

                                                                              KENT SCORE _____

WILSON SCORE: (Ask the client the following multiple equation questions. Stop at the last correct answer. You do not have to go beyond. Locate the scoring guide on the next page.)

   2 x 12 = _____   2 x 24 = _____   2 x 48 = _____

   2 x 96 = _____   2 x 192 = _____   2 x 384 = _____

   2 x ? = _____

Intelligence Range	KENT SCORE	WILSON SCORE	Approximate IQ
Defective	0–18	2 x 12	Below 70
Borderline	19–20	2 x 24	70–80
Dull normal	21–23	2 x 48	80–90
Average	24–31	2 x 96	90–110
Bright normal	32–33	2 x 192	110–120
Superior	34–35	2 x 384	120–130
Very superior	36	2 x ?	Greater than 130

Instructions: Place a check mark in the box if the item was answered correctly. Write incorrect or unusual answers in the space provided. If necessary, urge client once to complete the task.

	1. What day of the week is this?
	2. What month is this?
	3. What day of the month is this?
	4. What year is this?
	5. What place is this?
	6. Repeat these numbers: 8 7 2.
	7. Say these same numbers backward.
	8. Repeat these numbers: 6 3 7 1.
	9. Listen to these numbers: 6 9 4. Count 1 through 10 out loud, then repeat 6 9 4. (Help if needed. Then use numbers 5 7 3.)
	10. Listen to these numbers: 8 1 4 3. Count 1 through 10 out loud, then repeat 8 1 4 3.
	11. Beginning with Sunday, and say the days of the week backward.
	12. 9 – 3 equals?
	13. Add 6 to the previous answer.
	14. Take away 5 from 18 equals?
	15. Repeat these words after me and then remember them, I will ask for them later: HAT, CAR, TREE, TWENTY-SIX.
	16. The opposite of fast is slow. The opposite of up is what?
	17. The opposite of large is?
	18. The opposite of hard is?
	19. An orange and a banana are both fruits. Red and blue are both what?
	20. A penny and a dime are both what?
	21. What were those words that I asked you to remember? HAT
	22. CAR
	23. TREE
	24. TWENTY-SIX
	25. Take away 7 from 100, then take away 7 from what is left and keep going. 100 – 7 equals?

	26. Minus 7
	27. Minus 7
	28. Minus 7
	29. Minus 7
	30. Minus 7
	31. Minus 7

_____   **TOTAL SCORE:** (If the client's score is less than 20, the medical director and/or the psychologist should be notified.)

Client was cooperative _____ Uncooperative _____ Depressed _____ Lethargic _____ Other _____

Safety Screening Assessment

☐ Admit

☐ Admit with a safety plan. Describe in detail: _____

☐ Do not admit. Explain: _____

Physical appearance on admission: _____

_____

Mental state, behaviors, and attitude on admission: _____

_____

On admission the client was accompanied by _____

Age _____   B/P _____   Temperature _____   Pulse _____

Respirations _____   Height _____   Weight _____

CIWA score on admission _____ Vital sign score on admission _____

Summary _____

_____

_____

_____

_____

_____

DSM–IV **IMPRESSIONS:** _____

_____

_____

_____

_____

_____

_____

Nursing Signature & Title   Date

_____

Physician Signature   Date

Appendix 59

Adolescent Nurses Intake

Julie Braaten, RN, and Carol Regier, RN

Date: _____

What events precipitated your admission to Keystone Treatment Center? _____
_____

Who referred you to Keystone Treatment Center? _____
_____

CHEMICAL USE HISTORY

Have you ever had a previous treatment for chemical dependency? Yes _____ No _____ (If yes, complete the following questions.)

When: Month & Year	Where: Name of Facility & Address	Did you complete treatment? Yes/No	Outpatient Treatment	Inpatient Treatment	Length of Sobriety After the Treatment

Please list any alcohol and/or drug education you may have had such as PPP/IPP classes. _____
_____
_____

Do you have an alcohol and/or drug free environment to live in? Yes _____ No _____ If no, why not?
_____
_____

Have you ever attended Alcoholics Anonymous (AA)/Narcotics Anonymous (NA) or Gamblers Anonymous (GA) meetings in the past?   Yes_____   No_____

ALCOHOL:

Diagnostic and Statistical Manual of Mental Disorders (DSM–IV) DIAGNOSIS: 303.00 Alcohol Intoxication; 291.80 Alcohol Withdrawal; 305.00 Alcohol Abuse; 303.90 Alcohol Dependence with or without Physiological Dependence

What was your age of first use of alcohol? _____

How old were you when you started drinking alcohol on a regular basis? _____
_____

How often are you drinking alcohol? (daily, number of times per week, or number of times per month)
_____

How long have you been drinking alcohol in this pattern? _____
_____

How much alcohol do you usually drink at one time? _____
_____

What is your maximum amount of alcohol that you can drink at one time? _____
_____

When was your last drink of alcohol, and how much alcohol did you consume at that time? _____
_____
_____

Do you feel you have a problem with alcohol?   Yes _____   No _____   If yes, how long has your alcohol use been causing problems? _____
_____
_____

Do you require increased alcohol amounts to achieve intoxication or your desired effect?
Yes _____   No _____

Do you experience a diminished effect with continued use of the same amount of alcohol?
Yes _____   No _____

Have you ever had to go to an emergency room or physician's office for an alcohol related illness or accident?
Yes _____   No _____   If yes, explain: _____
_____
_____

Have you ever experienced alcohol poisoning?   Yes _____   No _____   If yes, explain: _____
_____
_____

Have you ever experienced the following withdrawal symptoms?

	YES	NO
Coarse tremors of hands, tongue, and/or eyelids		
Nausea and/or vomiting		
Malaise/weakness		
Autonomic hyperactivity (tachycardia, sweating, elevated blood pressure)		
Anxiety/nervousness		
Depressed mood		
Irritability		
Transient hallucinations and/or delusions		
Headache		
Insomnia		

Do you drink alcohol or use other drugs to relieve or avoid withdrawal symptoms?   Yes _____   No _____

Have you ever experienced blackouts?   Yes _____   No _____

Have you tried to quit drinking alcohol before?   Yes _____   No _____   If yes, explain: _____

_____

_____

Have you ever tried to control your drinking before?   Yes _____   No _____   If yes, explain: _____

_____

_____

What was the longest period you went without drinking alcohol in the past 12 months? _____

_____

Why did you abstain from drinking alcohol during that time period? _____

_____

_____

Has drinking created any problems with interpersonal relationships in the following areas?

	YES	NO	If yes, explain
With your girlfriend/boyfriend?			
With your children, if applicable?			
With other members of your family?			
With your friends?			

When drinking alcohol have you ever been involved in any of the following:

	YES	NO	If yes, explain
Physical and/or verbal fighting			
Motor vehicle accidents			
Injuries of any kind			

CANNABIS:

DSM–IV DIAGNOSIS: 305.20 Cannabis Abuse; 304.30 Cannabis Dependence with or without Physiological Dependence

Have you ever used cannabis, marijuana, pot, THC, hashish, weed, dope, green goddess, hydro, indo, KGB, locoweed, Mary Jane, sinsemilla, homegrown, etc.? Yes_____ No_____ The following are not applicable if the previous question was answered no.

Name of Drug	Age of First Use	Method(s) of Use: Smoked; Oral	Past/Current Pattern/ Frequency of Use (daily, weekly, monthly— number of times)	How Long Have You Used in This Pattern	Past/Current Usual Consumption	Maximum Consumption	Date of Last Use

Have you ever experienced the following with use or after use of cannabis?

	YES	NO		YES	NO
Chronic cough			Bronchitis		
Headache			Irritability		
Muscle cramps			Sleep disturbances		
Decreased exercise tolerance			Increased heart rate		
Panic attacks					

COCAINE:

DSM–IV DIAGNOSIS: 305.60 Cocaine Abuse; 304.20 Cocaine Dependence with or without Physiological Dependence

Have you ever used crack, coke, powder, white, snow, flake, devil's dandruff, fast white lady, uptown, white boy, white dragon, 24-7, cookies, glo, hard ball, rock, etc.? Yes_____ No_____ The following are not applicable if the previous question was answered no.

Name of Drug	Age of First Use	Method(s) of Use: Smoked; Oral	Past/Current Pattern/ Frequency of Use (daily, weekly, monthly— number of times)	How Long Have You Used in This Pattern	Past/Current Usual Consumption	Maximum Consumption	Date of Last Use

Have you ever seen things that other people could not see, or heard things other people could not hear (hallucinations and/or delusions)?   Yes _____   No _____

Have you experienced the following withdrawal symptoms?

	YES	NO		YES	NO
Fatigue			Agitation		
Nausea/vomiting			Craving for cocaine		
Depression			Insomnia/hypersomnia		
Sweating/chills			Anxiety		
Irritability			Increased appetite		
Preoccupation with obtaining cocaine			Vivid/unpleasant dreams		

HALLUCINOGENS:

DSM–IV DIAGNOSIS: 305.30 Hallucinogen Abuse; 304.50 Hallucinogen Dependence with or without Physiological Dependence

Have you ever used LSD, acid, DMT, peyote, buttons, mushrooms, mescaline, psilocybin, battery acid, dots, zen, window pane, boomers, yellow sunshine, etc.? Yes _____   No _____   The following are not applicable if the previous question was answered no.

Have you ever had a flashback?   Yes _____   No _____

Name of Drug	Age of First Use	Method(s) of Use: Smoked; Oral; Sniffed; Injected; Inhaled	Past/Current Pattern/ Frequency of Use (daily, weekly, monthly— number of times)	How Long Have You Used in This Pattern	Past/Current Usual Consumption	Maximum Consumption	Date of Last Use

OPIOIDS & OTHER ANALGESICS (INCLUDING NARCOTICS):

DSM–IV DIAGNOSIS: 305.50 Opioid Abuse; 304.00 Opioid Dependence with or without Physiological Dependence

Have you ever used heroin, eigth, H, hell dust, horse, junk, poppy, smack, train, thunder, opium, Darvon (propoxyphene hydrochloride), Darvocet (propoxyphene napsylate), Lortab (hydrocodone bitartrate & acetaminophen), Lorcet, Percocet (oxycodone & acetaminophen), Percodan, Roxicet, Roxanol, Tylox, Codeine, Demerol (meperidine hydrochloride), Morphine, Oxycontin, Oxycodone, MS Contin, Oxy IR, Hydrocodone, Flexeril (cyclobenzaprine hydrochloride), Fioricet with Codeine, Fiorinal with Codeine, Fentanyl (Duragesic) patch, Sublimaze (fentanyl citrate), Dilaudid, Methadone, Vicodin, Stadol (butorphanol tartrate), Talwin (pentazocine hydrochloride), Ultram (tramadol hydrochloride)?   Yes_____   No_____   The following are not applicable if the previous question was answered no.

Name of Drug	Age of First Use	Method(s) of Use: Smoked; Oral; Sniffed; Injected	Past/Current Pattern/ Frequency of Use (daily, weekly, monthly— number of times)	How Long Have You Used in This Pattern	Past/Current Usual Consumption	Maximum Consumption	Date of Last Use

Have you experienced the following withdrawal symptoms?

	YES	NO		YES	NO
Craving for an opioid			Nausea/vomiting		
Muscle aches/cramps			Pupillary dilation		
Fever			Goose bumps		
Tremors			Loss of appetite		
Increased heart rate			Lacrimation		
Diarrhea			Rhinorrhea		
Yawning			Sweating		

INHALANTS:

DSM–IV DIAGNOSIS: 305.90 Inhalant Abuse; 304.60 Inhalant Dependence with or without Physiological Dependence

Have you ever sniffed/inhaled aerosols, lighter fluid, gasoline, model cements, solvents, rush, white out, glue, paint, paint thinner, felt tip markers, nail polish, nail polish remover, rubber cement, ether, amyl nitrite, butyl nitrite, nitrous oxide, cooking sprays (like Pam), Freon, markers? Yes_____ No_____   The following are not applicable if the previous question was answered no.

Name of Drug	Age of First Use	Method(s) of Use: Inhaled; Sniffing; Huffing; Bagging; Snappers; Poppers	Past/Current Pattern/ Frequency of Use (daily, weekly, monthly— number of times)	How Long Have You Used in This Pattern	Past/Current Usual Consumption	Maximum Consumption	Date of Last Use

Have you experienced the following?

	YES	NO		YES	NO
Sleep disturbances			Nausea/vomiting		
Shakes/tremors			Sweating		
Abdominal discomfort			Chest discomfort		
Irritability			Being amotivational		
Dizziness			Hallucinations/Delusions		
Belligerence			Apathy		
Impaired judgment			Weight loss		
Muscle weakness			Disorientation/Confusion		
Lack of coordination			Depression		
Rapid pulse			Seizures		
Memory impairment			Slurred speech		

AMPHETAMINES (INCLUDING METHAMPHETAMINES) & STIMULANTS:

DSM–IV DIAGNOSIS: 305.70 Amphetamine Abuse; 304.40 Amphetamine Dependence with or without Physiological Dependence

Have you ever used speed, speeders, ecstasy, methamphetamine, glass, ice, white crosses, ephedrine, crank, crystal, uppers, MDMA, Adderall (dextroamphetamine sulfate), Ritalin (methylphenidate hydrochloride), Dexedrine (dextroamphetamine sulfate), Dexedrine Spansules, Cylert (pemoline)? Yes_____ No_____ The following are not applicable if the previous question was answered no.

Name of Drug	Age of First Use	Method(s) of Use: Oral; Sniffed; Injected; Smoked	Past/Current Pattern/ Frequency of Use (daily, weekly, monthly— number of times)	How Long Have You Used in This Pattern	Past/Current Usual Consumption	Maximum Consumption	Date of Last Use

Have you experienced the following withdrawal symptoms?

	YES	NO		YES	NO
Depression			Anxiety		
Agitation			Irritability		
Insomnia/hypersomnia			Fatigue		
Vivid unpleasant dreams			Decreased or increased appetite		
Increased heart rate			Lacrimation (abnormal secretion of tears)		
Diarrhea			Rhinorrhea (excessive mucous secretion from the nose)		
Yawning			Sweating		

SEDATIVE, HYPNOTIC OR ANXIOLYTIC:

DSM–IV DIAGNOSIS: 305.40 Sedative, Hypnotic or Anxiolytic Abuse; 304.10 Sedative, Hypnotic or Anxiolytic Dependence with or without Physiological Dependence

Have you ever used a barbiturate, downer, sleeping medication, Valium (diazepam), chloral hydrate, Dalmane (flurazepam hydrochloride), Klonopin (clonazepam), Seconal (secobarbital sodium),Restoril (temazepam), Halcion (triazolam), Ambien (zolpidem tartrate), Ativan (Lorazepam), Xanax (alprazolam), Librium (chlordiazepoxide hydrochloride), Tranxene (clorazepate dipotassium), Atarax (hydroxyzine hydrochloride), Serax (oxazepam), etc.? Yes_____ No_____ The following are not applicable if the previous question was answered no.

Name of Drug	Age of First Use	Method(s) of Use: Oral; Injected	Past/Current Pattern/ Frequency of Use (daily, weekly, monthly— number of times)	How Long Have You Used in This Pattern	Past/Current Usual Consumption	Maximum Consumption	Date of Last Use

Have you experienced the following withdrawal symptoms?

	YES	NO		YES	NO
Anxiety			Agitation		
Tremors			Insomnia		
Shakiness			Headaches		
Tinnitus (a sensation of noise, ringing, or roaring & can only be heard by the one affected)			Blurred vision		
Diarrhea			Seizures		
Nausea and/or vomiting			Muscle aching/twitching		
Dizziness			Concentration difficulties		

PHENCYCLIDINE:

DSM–IV DIAGNOSIS: 305.90 Phencyclidine Abuse; 304.90 Phencyclidine Dependence with or without Physiological Dependence

Have you ever used phencyclidine (PCP), angel dust, animal tranquilizer, embalming fluid, ozone, rocket fuel, wack, happy sticks, magic dust, Peter Pan, trank, etc.?   Yes_____   No_____   The following are not applicable if the previous question was answered no.

Name of Drug	Age of First Use	Method(s) of Use: Oral; Injected; Sniffed; Smoked	Past/Current Pattern/ Frequency of Use (daily, weekly, monthly— number of times)	How Long Have You Used in This Pattern	Past/Current Usual Consumption	Maximum Consumption	Date of Last Use

Have you experienced the following?

	YES	NO		YES	NO
Rage/violence			Craving		
Compulsive PCP seeking behaviors			Seizures		
Coma			Accidental injury—related to the drug's effects		
Delusions			Paranoia		
Memory loss			Difficulty with speech		
Difficulty with thought			Depression		
Weight loss					

ANABOLIC ANDROGENIC STEROIDS (AAS):

DSM–IV DIAGNOSIS: (Other or Unknown Substance-Related Disorders) 305.90 Abuse; 304.90 Dependence (You need to specify the individual substance that is being abused in relation to the above abuse & dependence diagnosis. Example: 304.90 AAS Dependence)

Have you ever used steroids, roids, rage, anabolics, juicers, step ups, etc.? Yes _____ No _____ The following are not applicable if the previous question was answered no.

Name of Drug	Age of First Use	Method(s) of Use: Oral; Injected	Past/Current Pattern/ Frequency of Use (daily, weekly, monthly— number of times)	How Long Have You Used in This Pattern	Past/Current Usual Consumption	Maximum Consumption	Date of Last Use

Have you experienced the following?

	YES	NO		YES	NO
Fatigue			Depression		
Muscle pain			Headache		
Craving			Irritability		
Aggressiveness			Changes in levels of energy		

GAMMA HYDROXYBUTYRATE (GHB) & ANALOGS:

DSM–IV DIAGNOSIS: (Other or Unknown Substance-Related Disorders) 305.90 Abuse; 304.90 Dependence (You need to specify the individual substance that is being abused in relation to the above abuse & dependence diagnosis. Example: 304.90 GHB Dependence)

Have you ever used GHB, Georgia home boy, G, goop, liquid ecstasy, cherry meth, fantasy, G-riffic, jib, liquid E, liquid X, salty water, scoop, sleep, sleep – 500, soap, vita – G, etc.?   Yes_____   No_____   The following are not applicable if the previous question was answered no.

Name of Drug	Age of First Use	Method(s) of Use: Oral	Past/Current Pattern/ Frequency of Use (daily, weekly, monthly— number of times)	How Long Have You Used in This Pattern	Past/Current Usual Consumption	Maximum Consumption	Date of Last Use

Have you experienced the following?

	YES	NO		YES	NO
Nausea and/or vomiting			Delusions/hallucinations		
Depression			Seizures		
Respiratory distress			Loss of consciousness		
Slowed heart rate			Lowered blood pressure		
Amnesia			Coma		
Anxiety			Insomnia		
Tremors			Tachycardia		
Delirium			Agitation		

OVER-THE-COUNTER MEDICATION(S):

Do you use and/or abuse antihistamines, Nytol, Nyquil, laxatives, Primatene, diet pills, Mydol, Coricidin Cold & Cough, Robitussin, etc.?   Yes_____   No_____   The following are not applicable if the previous question was answered no.

Name of Drug	Age of First Use	Method(s) of Use: Oral	Current Pattern/ Frequency of Use (daily, weekly, monthly— number of times)	How Long Have You Used in This Pattern	Current Usual Consumption	Maximum Consumption	Date of Last Use

NICOTINE:

Do you smoke cigarettes? Yes _____ No _____

If yes, age of first use of cigarettes? _____

How many packs of cigarettes do you smoke per day? _____

_____

Do you use smokeless tobacco? Yes _____ No _____

How much do you use in one day? _____

Do you experience a chronic cough, possibly related to your tobacco use? Yes _____ No _____

Have you ever coughed up or expectorated blood, possibly related to your tobacco use?

Yes _____ No _____

Do you have any sores on the inside of your mouth? Yes _____ No _____

Have you attempted to quit or control your use of nicotine? Yes _____ No _____ If yes, how long were you able to quit your tobacco use and what were the reason(s) why you attempted to quit? _____

_____

****

Do you use drugs to relieve or avoid withdrawal symptoms? Yes _____ No _____

Do you require increased amounts of your drugs/medications to achieve intoxication or your desired effect?

Yes _____ No _____

Do you experience a markedly diminished effect with continued use of the same amount of drugs/medications?

Yes _____ No _____

Have you ever had to go to an emergency room or physician's office for a drug/medication related illness or accident? Yes _____ No _____ If yes, explain: _____

_____

_____

Have you ever experienced a drug/medication overdose? Yes _____ No _____ If yes, explain: _____

_____

_____

Have you tried to quit your drug use before? Yes _____ No _____ If yes, explain: _____

_____

Have you ever tried to control your drug use before? Yes _____ No _____ If yes, explain: _____

_____

_____

What was the longest period you went without using drugs in the past 12 months? _____

_____

Why did you abstain from using drugs during that time period? _____

_____

Has your drug use created any problems with interpersonal relationships in the following areas:

	YES	NO	If yes, explain
With your girlfriend/boyfriend?			
With your children, if applicable?			
With other members of your family?			
With your friends?			

When using drugs have you ever been involved in any of the following:

	YES	NO	If yes, explain
Physical and/or verbal fighting			
Motor vehicle accidents			
Injuries of any kind			

Additional Critical Life Areas

Yes _____   No _____   Have you ever used injectable drugs/drugs intravenously?

Yes _____   No _____   Have you stayed drunk and/or high for more than one day?

Yes _____   No _____   Have you ever drank alcohol and/or used drugs in dangerous situations (driving, swimming, etc.)?

GAMBLING HISTORY: (312.31 Pathological Gambling)

When was the last time you gambled? _____

_____

Have you ever been assessed and/or had previous treatment for gambling?   Yes _____   No _____   If yes, please answer the following questions in the table.

When: Month & Year	Where: Name of Facility & Address	Did you complete treatment? Yes/No	Outpatient Treatment	Inpatient Treatment	Length of Abstinence After Your Treatment

Have you ever had credit counseling?   Yes _____   No _____   If yes, when and where was the credit counseling completed? _____

_____

What forms of gambling do you participate in?

	YES	NO		YES	NO		YES	NO		YES	NO
Video lottery			Scratch tickets			Slot machines			Pull tabs		
Blackjack			Poker (Cards)			Powerball			Dog racing		
Bingo			Horse racing			Sports			Simulcasting		
Stock market			Table games			Internet			Other(s)		

What was the most dollar amount that you have ever won? _____

What was the most dollar amount that you have ever lost? _____

What was your age of your first gambling episode? _____

If "no" is answered on all of the previous questions, the following questions do not need to be asked.

Do you feel that you have a problem with gambling?   Yes _____   No _____   If yes, how long has gambling been a problem for you? _____
_____

How much money do you spend on an average on gambling per month? _____
_____

How often do you gamble (daily, weekly, monthly, yearly) and how much (number of times weekly and monthly, yearly)? _____
_____

What is your current gambling related debt? _____
_____

Have you ever filed bankruptcy due to your gambling?   Yes _____   No _____   If yes, explain: _____
_____
_____

	YES	NO
Are you preoccupied with gambling (e.g., preoccupied with reliving past gambling experiences, handicapping or planning the next venture, or thinking of ways to obtain money with which to gamble)?		
Have you ever gambled with increasing amounts of money in order to achieve the desired excitement?		
Have you ever tried to control, cut back, or stop gambling?		
Have you ever felt restless or irritable when attempting to cut down or stop gambling?		

	YES	NO
Have you ever gambled as a way of escaping from problems or of relieving a dysphoric mood (e.g., feelings of helplessness, guilt, anxiety, depression)?		
Have you ever gambled the next day to win back your losses (chasing losses)?		
Have you ever lied to family members, therapists, or others to conceal the extent of involvement with your gambling?		
Have you ever committed illegal acts such as forgery, fraud, theft, or embezzlement to finance your gambling?		
Have you ever been arrested because of your gambling, spent time in jail or prison?		
Have you ever jeopardized or lost a significant relationship, job, educational, or career opportunity because of your gambling?		
Have you relied on others to provide money to relieve a desperate financial situation caused by gambling?		
Have you used credit cards to obtain money for gambling?		
Did you ever write bad checks in order to gamble?		
Have you ever gotten behind on bills because of your gambling losses?		
Have you ever gone without necessities because of gambling losses?		
Have you ever sold or pawned anything to obtain money for gambling?		
After winning, have you ever gambled away your winnings or part of it?		
Have you ever felt remorseful after gambling?		

PHYSICAL ASSESSMENT:

Are you currently under the care of a physician(s)?   Yes _____   No _____

When was the last time you saw a physician? _____
_____

What was the reason for the visit? _____
_____

Name and address of family physician: _____
_____
_____

Name and address of other physicians you are seeing: _____
_____
_____

Do you have any medical or physical problems for which you see a physician?   Yes _____   No _____
If yes, what are your problems or concerns? _____
_____
_____

How would you assess your health? Good ( ) Fair ( ) Poor ( )

Do you feel that your alcohol and/or drug use has affected your health? Yes _____ No _____ If yes, explain how your health has been affected. _____
_____

Have you ever been told that the use of alcohol and/or drugs are a serious threat to your health? Yes _____ No _____ If yes, who told you and why? _____
_____

TUBERCULOSIS:

Have you ever had tuberculosis (TB)? Yes _____ No _____ Have you ever had a BCG vaccination? Yes _____ No _____

Have you ever been exposed to someone else who has had tuberculosis? Yes _____ No _____

Have you ever experienced any of the following symptoms within the previous 3 months?

	YES	NO
Productive cough for a 2 to 3 week duration**		
Unexplained night sweats**		
Unexplained fevers**		
Unexplained weight loss**		

**If a client responds yes to any of the previous four questions, he or she shall be referred to the physician for a medical evaluation to determine the absence or presence of active disease. A Mantoux skin test may or may not be given during this evaluation based on the opinion of the evaluating physician.

Have you ever had a TB tine of Mantoux test? Yes _____ No _____

Did you have a reaction to the test? Yes _____ No _____

If you reacted, when was your last chest X-ray and where did you have the chest X-ray taken?_____
_____
_____

****

SEIZURES/CONVULSIONS:

Have you ever had a seizure/convulsion? Yes _____ No _____ If yes, explain: _____
_____
_____

When was your last seizure activity? _____
_____

Was your seizure activity directly related to your alcohol and/or drug use? Yes _____ No _____

Did the seizure occur during your alcohol and/or drug use? Yes _____   No _____

Did the seizure occur during withdrawal from alcohol and/or drug use? Yes _____   No _____

Are you currently taking medication(s) for your seizure activity? Yes _____   No _____

Have you taken medication(s) in the past to control your seizure activity? Yes _____   No _____

* *

Have you had any of the following?

	YES	NO		YES	NO
Whooping cough			Mumps		
Measles			Chicken pox		

* *

Do you currently have any sores, cuts, bruises, or any injuries? Yes _____   No _____   If yes, explain: _____
_____
_____
_____

Do you have any of the following?

	YES	NO		YES	NO
1. Heart problems			12. Medication allergies		
2. High blood pressure			13. Food allergies		
3. Stroke/CVA/TIA			14. Latex allergy		
4. Lung problems/breathing problems COPD/ emphysema/ asthma			15. Edema/swelling		
5. Anemia			16. Headaches		
6. Arthritis/gout			17. Skin problems		
7. Back problems			18. Bowel problems/constipation/ diarrhea/bloody bowel movements/ tarry bowel movements		
8. Diabetes			19. Ulcers/stomach problems/ hematemesis (vomited blood)		
9. Thyroid problems			20. Pancreatitis		
10. Liver problems/ hepatitis			21. Urinary tract problems (frequency of voiding)		
11. Numbness/tingling of extremities			22. Prostate problems (if male)		

(Continued)

(Continued)

	YES	NO		YES	NO
23. Cancer			26. Surgical procedures		
24. Eyes, ears, nose, and throat (EENT) problems			27. Other medical issues not asked		
25. Muscle cramps/weakness					

If yes is answered to any of the previous questions, please write down the number and explain: _____

_____

_____

_____

_____

_____

_____

List medications that the client has previously taken but not taking currently:

Name of Medication	Was Medication Effective?		Reason for Use of Medication
	Yes	No	
	Yes	No	
	Yes	No	

_____ Client unable to recall names of previous medications that he or she has taken.

FEMALES ONLY:

Do you experience any menstrual problems? Yes _____ No _____ If yes, explain: _____

_____

_____

Date of your last menstrual period? _____

_____

Date of your last Pap smear: _____

_____

Are you currently pregnant? Yes _____ No _____ If yes, when is your estimated due date and what physician are you seeing for this pregnancy? _____

_____

Have you ever been pregnant? Yes _____ No _____ If yes, number of pregnancies: _____

_____

Have you ever had a miscarriage? Yes _____   No _____

Have you ever had an abortion? Yes _____   No _____   If yes, give date(s): _____

_____

Describe any complications during your pregnancy(ies): _____

_____

* *

AUDITORY ASSESSMENT:

Do you have a hearing loss? Yes _____   No _____   If yes, which ear is affected? _____

_____

Do you wear any hearing aide devices? Yes _____   No _____

* *

VISUAL ASSESSMENT:

Do you wear contacts and/or glasses? Yes _____   No _____

Is your vision blurred or do you see double? Yes _____   No _____

Eye Chart Results: Both eyes: _____   Right eye: _____   Left eye: _____

* *

NUTRITIONAL ASSESSMENT:

How would you assess your eating habits? Good ( ) Fair ( ) Poor ( )

	YES	NO	EXPLANATION TO A YES RESPONSE
1. Are you on a special diet?			If yes, what type of diet?
2. Have you had any recent weight changes in the past 6 months?			# of pounds lost _____ # of pounds gained _____ Reason for weight loss or gain:
3. Do you skip meals or go without food when you are drinking alcohol and/or using drugs?			
4. Have you ever induced vomiting after eating?			
5. Have you ever been diagnosed as anorexic or bulimic?			

If there is a yes response to questions 1, 2, 4, and/or 5, please inform the dietary staff so that the dietician may visit with the client.

* *

SEXUAL HISTORY:

Age of your first sexual experience: _____

_____

Do you have any concerns about sex and/or your sexuality? Yes _____ No _____ If yes, explain:
_____

_____

Does your alcohol and/or drug use affect your choices about sex? Yes _____ No _____ If yes, explain:
_____

_____

Have you ever been in trouble because of sexual behavior(s)? Yes _____ No _____ If yes, explain:
_____

_____

Do you currently have or ever have been treated for a sexually transmitted disease? Yes _____ No _____
If yes, explain: _____

_____

Do you use protection during sexual intercourse? Yes _____ No _____

Have you had sexual intercourse with more than 1 partner? Yes _____ No _____

* *

PAIN ASSESSMENT:

Pain Level: ☐ 0 ☐ 1 ☐ 2 ☐ 3 ☐ 4 ☐ 5 ☐ 6 ☐ 7 ☐ 8 ☐ 9 ☐ 10
(0 being no pain)

What is your acceptable level of pain: _____

Are you currently experiencing pain? Yes _____ No _____ If yes, answer the following questions:

Location and description of pain: _____

What relief measures do you use to decrease your pain? _____

_____

Pain Management Booklet given to the client: Yes _____ No _____ (In the Client Handbook)

* *

PSYCHOLOGICAL HISTORY/SCREENING/MENTAL HEALTH ISSUES:

Have you ever seen a counselor/psychologist/psychiatrist? Yes _____ No _____ If yes, answer the following questions:

When was your last visit? _____

How long have you been seeing this therapist? _____

Have you ever been hospitalized for mental health issues?   Yes _____   No _____

Name of Person & Facility Name	Reason for Counseling/Hospitalization	Date(s)

Have you ever received treatment for any of the following mental health or psychiatric problems?

	YES	NO		YES	NO		YES	NO
Adjustment disorders			Anxiety disorders (panic disorder, phobias, OCD, post-traumatic stress disorder [PTSD], etc.)			Sexual abuse or sexual assault		
Grief issues			Sleep disorders			Physical and/or emotional abuse		
Fetal alcohol syndrome disorder			Personality disorders (antisocial, avoidant, narcissistic, and/or borderline, schizoid, dependent, paranoid)			Impulse control disorders (intermittent explosive disorder)		
Fetal alcohol effects			Other psychotic disorders			Eating disorders		
Sleep disorders			Attention deficit & disruptive behavior disorders			Bipolar disorders		
Dementia			Depressive disorders			Dissociative disorders (amnesia and depersonalization)		
Schizophrenia & other psychotic disorders			Hyperactivity disorder			Learning disorders		

If yes, please explain: _____

_____

_____

_____

How would you assess your sleeping habits? Good _____ Fair _____ Poor _____

How many hours of sleep do you get per night? _____

Do you have problems with falling asleep? Yes _____ No _____ Do you have problems awakening frequently throughout the night? Yes _____ No _____

Do you feel sad, down, and/or depressed? Constantly _____ Often _____
Occasionally _____ Infrequently _____

    Explain: _____

Do you feel fearful, anxious and/or nervous? Constantly _____ Often _____
Occasionally _____ Infrequently _____

    Explain: _____

Have you ever had a panic attack (suddenly fearful without cause)? Yes _____ No _____ If yes, explain (when was your last panic attack, did you go to the hospital, etc.?): _____
_____

Do you have feelings of uncontrollable anger, rage, or violence? Yes _____ No _____ If yes, explain:
_____
_____

What do you do when you are angry? _____
_____

Are you or have you been in the past physically abusive to others? Yes _____ No _____

    When and explain: _____

    Was this abuse reported? Yes _____ No _____

Have you ever been physically abused? Yes _____ No _____

    When and explain: _____

    Was this abuse reported? Yes _____ No _____

    Did you ever tell anyone? Yes _____ No _____

Have you ever been bullied or bullied others on the Internet? Yes _____ No _____ If yes, explain:
_____

Do you ever physically abuse yourself? Yes _____ No _____ If yes, explain: _____
_____

Are you or have you been in the past sexually abusive to others? Yes _____ No _____

    When and explain: _____

    Was this abuse reported? Yes _____ No _____

Have you ever been sexually abused? Yes _____ No _____

    When and explain: _____

    Was this abuse reported? Yes _____ No _____

    Did you ever tell anyone? Yes _____ No _____

Do you have thoughts of harming other people?   Yes _____   No _____   If yes, when and explain:

_____

_____

Have you ever been verbally aggressive toward others?   Yes _____   No _____   If yes, explain:

_____

_____

Have you ever been physically aggressive?   Yes _____   No _____   If yes, explain (when, where, how violent, was there property destruction, was a weapon involved?): _____

_____

_____

Was law enforcement involved when you were physically aggressive?   Yes _____   No _____   N/A _____   If yes, please explain: _____

_____

Have you ever had thoughts of harming yourself?   Yes _____   No _____   If yes, explain (when was the last time you had these thoughts, etc.?): _____

_____

Are you currently experiencing any thoughts of harming yourself?   Yes _____   No _____   If yes, explain:

_____

_____

Have you made plans for carrying out any of these thoughts?   Yes _____   No _____   If yes, explain:

_____

_____

Have you ever attempted suicide?   Yes _____   No _____   If yes, explain (when was last attempt, etc.?):

_____

_____

Has anyone in your family tried to hurt themselves?   Yes _____   No _____   If yes, please explain:

_____

_____

Have you ever self-mutilated (cutting, burning, etc.)?   Yes _____   No _____   If yes, please explain (describe when, where on body, with what, how long have you engaged in this behavior, and the date of most recent behavior, and if you required medical intervention): _____

_____

_____

Do you use alcohol and/or drugs to relieve or avoid your problems?   Yes _____   No _____

Do you feel unable to change things?   Yes _____   No _____

Do you use alcohol and/or drugs to escape?   Yes _____   No _____

Do you have plans for the future?   Yes _____   No _____

Briefly describe how you react when things do not go your way: _____

_____

****

SCHOOL HISTORY:

Did you drink alcohol and/or use drugs:

	YES	NO
Before school		
During school		
After school		

Are you currently attending school?   Yes _____   No _____

If yes, answer the following questions:

What school are you attending? _____

What grade are you currently in? _____

What are your current grades in the classes you are taking? _____

Has the use of alcohol and/or drugs caused a deterioration of your school grades?   Yes _____   No _____

If yes, explain: _____

If not attending school, are you working on your GED?   Yes _____   No _____

If you quit school, in what grade did you quit? _____

Are you currently active in extracurricular activities?   Yes _____   No _____   If yes, what activities? _____

_____

Have you quit being involved in extracurricular activities?   Yes _____   No _____   If yes, explain: _____

_____

Has the use of alcohol and/or drugs caused absences in your school attendance?   Yes _____   No _____

If yes, explain: _____

Have you ever been suspended or expelled from school?   Yes _____   No _____   If yes, explain: _____

_____

Have you experienced any conflicts with your teachers and/or coaches?   Yes _____   No _____

If yes, explain: _____

Have you ever been intoxicated or high (stoned) at school?   Yes _____   No _____   If yes, explain: _____

_____

Have you ever been caught at school for alcohol and/or drug possession?   Yes _____   No _____

If yes, explain: _____

Have you recently dropped some of your old friends and started going with a new group?

Yes _____   No _____

If yes, explain: _____

Have any of your friends been admitted to an alcohol and/or drug treatment center?   Yes _____   No _____

If yes, explain: _____

****

VOCATIONAL:

Do you currently have a job?   Yes _____   No _____   If yes, answer the following questions:

Do you work full-time?   Yes _____   No _____   Do you work part-time?   Yes _____   No _____

Name of your employer: _____

What is your position/title at work? _____

How long have you been employed with this company/business? _____

Have you ever been placed on probation or suspension at work due to you alcohol and/or drug use and/or gambling?

Yes _____   No _____   If yes, explain: _____

If you are unemployed, how long have you been unemployed? _____

	YES	NO
Have you ever stolen alcohol and/or drugs and/or money from the workplace?		
Have you ever been fired from a job due to your alcohol and/or drug use and/or gambling?		
Have you ever used alcohol and/or drugs or gambled before going to work?		
Have you ever used alcohol and/or drugs or gambled while at work?		
Have you ever just quit going to work?		
Has alcohol and/or drugs caused changes in your performance at work?		
Have you ever called in sick for work due to your alcohol and/or drug use?		

****

FINANCIAL:

How much money do you earn in a week? _____

How much money do you spend on alcohol and/or drugs in a week? _____

Where do you obtain your money from to purchase alcohol and/or drugs? _____

	YES	NO
Have you ever sold alcohol and/or drugs?		
Have you ever traded things for alcohol and/or drugs?		
Have you ever pawned items for alcohol and/or drugs?		
Have you ever borrowed money to purchase alcohol and/or drugs?		
Have you ever gone without other things to buy alcohol and/or drugs?		

* *

LEGAL HISTORY:

Have you ever been arrested? Yes _____ No _____ If yes, how many convictions? _____

_____

List all of the charges that you can remember with dates and years:

Convictions	Year(s)	Convictions	Year(s)	Convictions	Year(s)
Assault		Breaking & entering		Burglary	
CHINS		Curfew violation		Destruction of property	
Disorderly conduct		Failed urinalysis (UA)		Grand theft	
Grand theft auto		Hit & run		Vandalism	
Minor in consumption		Petty theft		Possession	
Convictions	**Year(s)**	**Convictions**	**Year(s)**	**Convictions**	**Year(s)**
Public intoxication		Robbery		Runaway	
Shoplifting		Truancy		Other	
DUI		Ingestion of a controlled substance			

How old were you when you experienced your first contact with the law and what was the charge or incident?

_____

Do you have any current legal problems? Yes _____ No _____ If yes, explain (date of arrest, court date, and charge, etc.)? _____

_____

Do you have a probation officer or parole officer (PO)/court services officer (CSO)/juvenile court authority (JCA)? Yes _____ No _____ If yes, answer the following:

Name of person listed: _____

Address of person listed: _____

Telephone number of person listed: _____

	YES	NO
Have you ever stolen alcohol and/or drugs?		
Have you ever used alcohol and/or drugs while in placement?		
Have you ever violated your probation due to alcohol and/or drug use?		
Have you ever shoplifted for money to buy alcohol and/or drugs?		
Have you ever committed a burglary for alcohol and/or drugs?		
Are you more involved in criminal activities due to your alcohol and/or drug use?		

* *

SOCIAL/LEISURE:

	YES	NO
Do any of your friends use alcohol and/or drugs?		
Do your friends try to talk you into drinking alcohol and/or using drugs?		
Do your friends try to talk you out of drinking alcohol and/or using drugs?		
Is it hard for you to trust others?		
Do you have any friends who you can trust?		
Do you have close friends?		
Have you withdrawn from your friends?		
Have you lost friends due to your alcohol and/or drug use?		
Do your friends express concern about your alcohol and/or drug use?		
Have you stopped or reduced the time you spend on hobbies due to your alcohol and/or drug use?		

* *

FAMILY:

Name of Relationship	Alive	Deceased	Cause of Death	Chemical Dependency (CD) Problems (Yes or No)
Father (Biological)				
If Applicable: Stepfather				

(Continued)

(Continued)

Mother (Biological)				
If Applicable: Stepmother				
Biological Siblings: NAME	**AGE**			
If Applicable: Step Siblings NAME	**AGE**			

What is your birth order? _____

Name of the town and state where you were raised: _____

Name the people who raised you: _____

Name the person and their relationship to you that you felt closest to while growing up: _____

_____

Describe your childhood (happy, sad, normal, etc.): _____

_____

How were you disciplined, and who disciplined you? _____

_____

Did you feel that you were loved while growing up? Yes _____ No _____

What is or was your biological parents' relationship like? _____

_____

If applicable, what is your biological and stepparents' relationship like? _____

_____

Are you married? Yes _____ No _____ If yes, what is your wife/husband's name? _____

_____

Does your wife or husband use or abuse alcohol and/or drugs? Yes _____ No _____

Do you have children? Yes _____ No _____ If yes, please list the children:

Children's Names	Ages of Children	Do your children live with you?		Do your children have a CD problem?	
		YES	**NO**	**YES**	**NO**

Who will be caring for your children while you are in treatment? _____
_____

With whom do you currently live with? _____

Number of people in the household? _____

Does anyone in your family have any emotional or physical problems? Yes _____ No _____ If yes, explain:
_____
_____

Are there any family conflicts? Yes _____ No _____

How do get along with your family? _____

Have family members expressed concern over your alcohol and/or drug use? Yes _____ No _____ If yes,
who expressed the concern and why? _____

Has anyone in your family gone to alcohol and/or drug and/or gambling treatment? Yes _____ No _____

Are any of your family members in a 12-step recovery program? Yes _____ No _____

Have you ever run away from home? Yes _____ No _____ If yes, please explain (was the law involved,
how long were you gone, where did you go, etc): _____
_____
_____

****

SPIRITUAL:

Do you believe in a Higher Power? (Example: God or Tunkashila) Yes _____ No _____

Do you have any concerns about your spiritual beliefs/practices? Yes _____ No _____

	YES	NO
Do you have religious beliefs?		
Have you ever lost your faith in a Higher Power?		
Have you lost your dreams and goals?		
Have you ever done things drunk and/or high that you would not have done if you had been sober or straight?		

What things lift your spirit? _____

What are your strengths? _____

What are your weaknesses? _____

MENTAL STATUS EXAMINATION:

Problem Solving:

1. If the flag floats to the south, from which direction is the wind?

   North = 3 points   _____

2. At what time of the day is your shadow the shortest?

   Noon = 3 points   _____

3. Why does the moon look larger than the stars?

   It is lower = 2 points   Nearer objects appear larger = 4 points   _____

4. If your shadow points to the northeast, where is the sun?

   Southwest = 4 points

Knowledge:

5. What are houses made of?

   1 point for each material up to 4 points   _____

6. Tell me the names of some fish.

   1 point for each species up to 4 points   _____

7. Give me the names of some large cities.

   1 point for each city up to 4 points. Excluded are small towns.   _____

8. What is sand used for?

   Playing = 1 point   Construction = 2 points   Glass = 4 points   _____

9. What metal is attracted by a magnet?

   Steel = 2 points   Iron = 4 points   _____

10. How many stripes are in the U.S. flag?

    13 = 4 points
                                                                             _____

                                                          KENT SCORE _____

(Ask the client the following multiple equation questions. Stop at the last correct answer. You do not have to go beyond. Locate the scoring guide on the next page.)

$2 \times 12 =$ _____ $2 \times 24 =$ _____ $2 \times 48 =$ _____

$2 \times 96 =$ _____ $2 \times 192 =$ _____ $2 \times 384 =$ _____

$2 \times ? =$ _____

Intelligence Range	KENT SCORE	WILSON SCORE	Approximate IQ
Defective	0–18	2×12	Below 70
Borderline	19–20	2×24	70–80
Dull normal	21–23	2×48	80–90

Intelligence Range	KENT SCORE	WILSON SCORE	Approximate IQ
Average	24–31	2×96	90–110
Bright normal	32–33	2×192	110–120
Superior	34–35	2×384	120–130
Very superior	36	$2 \times ?$	Greater than 130

Instructions: Place a check mark in the box if the item was answered correctly. Write incorrect or unusual answers in space provided. If necessary, urge client once to complete the task.

	1. What day of the week is this?
	2. What month is this?
	3. What day of the month is this?
	4. What year is this?
	5. What place is this?
	6. Repeat these numbers: 8 7 2.
	7. Say these same numbers backward.
	8. Repeat these numbers: 6 3 7 1.
	9. Listen to these numbers: 6 9 4. Count 1 through 10 out loud, then repeat 6 9 4. (Help if needed. Then use numbers 5 7 3.)
	10. Listen to these numbers: 8 1 4 3. Count 1 through 10 out loud, then repeat 8 1 4 3.
	11. Beginning with Sunday, say the days of the week backward.
	12. 9 – 3 equals?
	13. Add 6 to the previous answer.
	14. Take away 5 from 18 equals?
	15. Repeat these words after me and then remember them, I will ask for them later: HAT, CAR, TREE, TWENTY-SIX.
	16. The opposite of fast is slow. The opposite of up is what?
	17. The opposite of large is?
	18. The opposite of hard is?
	19. An orange and a banana are both fruits. Red and blue are both what?
	20. A penny and a dime are both what?
	21. What were those words that I asked you to remember? HAT
	22. CAR

(Continued)

(Continued)

	23. TREE
	24. TWENTY-SIX
	25. Take away 7 from 100, then take away 7 from what is left and keep going. 100 – 7 equals?
	26. Minus 7
	27. Minus 7
	28. Minus 7
	29. Minus 7
	30. Minus 7
	31. Minus 7

_____ **TOTAL SCORE** (If the client's score is less than 20, the medical director and/or the psychologist should be notified.)

Client was cooperative _____ Uncooperative _____

Depressed _____ Lethargic _____

Other _____

Physical appearance on admission: _____
_____

Mental state, behaviors, and attitude on admission: _____
_____
_____

On admission the client was accompanied by _____
_____

Age _____ B/P _____ Temperature _____ Pulse _____

Respirations _____ Height _____ Weight _____

CIWA Score on admission _____ Vital sign score on admission _____

Safety Screening Assessment

☐ Admit

☐ Admit with a safety plan. Describe in detail: _____
_____

☐ Do not admit. Explain: _____
_____

Summary _____
_____
_____
_____
_____

***DSM–IV* IMPRESSIONS:** _____

_____

_____

_____

_____

_____

_____

Nursing Signature & Title   Date

_____

Physician Signature   Date

Appendix 60

National Cancer Institute Guide to Quitting Smoking

Introduction

From those of us at the National Cancer Institute: Congratulations! You are taking the first step to quitting cigarette smoking.

We wrote this booklet with the help of ex-smokers and experts. It can help you prepare to quit and support you in the days and weeks after you quit. It also describes problems to expect when you quit. Being prepared can help you through the hard times.

Many tips are offered in this booklet—choose what works best for you. You can quit for good, even if you've tried before. In fact, most smokers try to quit many times before they succeed.

Stay upbeat. Keep trying. Use what you learn each step of the way until you quit for good. Soon, you too will be an ex-smoker.

Source: The National Cancer Institute (NCI) is part of the National Institutes of Health, one of agencies in the U.S. Department of Health and Human Services. NCI is the U.S. Government's principal agency for cancer research and training.

Before you START a Smoke-Free Life

Quitting is hard

Many ex-smokers say quitting was the hardest thing they ever did.

Do you feel hooked? You're probably addicted to nicotine. Nicotine is in all tobacco products. It makes you feel calm and satisfied, yet also alert and focused But the more you smoke, the more nicotine you need to feel good Soon, you don't feel "normal" without nicotine This is nicotine addiction.

It takes time to break free from nicotine addiction. It may take more than one try to quit for good. So don't give up too soon. You *will* feel good again.

Quitting is also hard because smoking is a big part of your life. You may enjoy holding a cigarette and puffing on it. You may smoke when you are stressed, bored, or angry. You may light up when you drink coffee or alcohol, talk on the phone, drive, or are with other smokers. After months and years, smoking has become part of your daily routine. You may light up without even thinking about it.

Quitting isn't easy. Just reading this booklet won't do it. You may try to quit several times before you're finally done with cigarettes. But you will learn something each time you try. It takes willpower and strength to beat your addiction to nicotine. Remember that millions of people have quit smoking for good. You can be one of them.

Just thinking about quitting may make you anxious. But your chances will be better if you get ready first. Quitting works best when you're prepared.

Preparing to quit

Think about why you want to quit

Decide for sure that you want to quit, and then promise yourself you'll do it. It's okay to have mixed feelings. Don't let that stop you. There will be times every day that you don't feel like quitting. You will have to stick with it anyway. Find reasons that are important to you.

Think of health reasons, such as:

- My body will start healing right away.
- I will have more energy and focus.
- I will feel more physically fit.
- I will have whiter teeth and healthier gums.
- I will cough less and breathe easier.
- I will lower my risk of cancer, heart attack, stroke, emphysema, chronic bronchitis, and cataracts.
- I will reduce the risk of fertility problems, premature births, and lower birthweight babies.
- I will no longer expose my family and friends to secondhand smoke.

KEEP IN MIND

Your body gets more than nicotine when you smoke.

Cigarette smoke contains more than 4,000 chemicals. Some of these chemicals are also found in wood varnish, the insecticide DDT, rat poison, and nail polish remover.

The ashes, tar, gases, and other poisons— such as arsenic—in cigarettes harm your body over time. They damage your heart and lungs. They also make it harder for you to taste and smell things and to fight infection.

Source: U.S. Department of Health and Human Services. *Reducing Tobacco Use: A Report of the Surgeon General.* Atlanta, GA: U.S. Department of Health and Human Services, Centers for Disease Control and Prevention, National Center for Chronic Disease Prevention and Health Promotion, Office on Smoking and Health, 2000

KEEP IN MIND

Even a little secondhand smoke is dangerous.

Secondhand smoke—also called environmental tobacco smoke—comes from a burning tobacco product and from the smoke exhaled by smokers. Inhaling secondhand smoke is called involuntary or passive smoking.

Nonsmokers who breathe secondhand smoke may:

- develop cancer or heart disease
- have breathing problems
- get colds and the flu more easily
- die younger than people who don't breathe secondhand smoke

Pregnant women who breathe secondhand smoke may:

- give birth to low-weight babies
- have babies who are more likely to die of sudden infant death syndrome (SIDS)

Children who breathe secondhand smoke may:

- have breathing problems, such as asthma
- get more ear infections
- develop more lung infections, such as pneumonia

Source: U.S. Department of Health and Human Services. *The Health Consequences of Involuntary Exposure to Tobacco Smoke: A Report of the Surgeon General.* Atlanta, GA: U.S. Department of Health and Human Services, Centers for Disease Control and Prevention, Coordinating Center for Health Promotion, National Center for Chronic Disease Prevention and Health Promotion, Office on Smoking and Health, 2006.

Think of some other reasons to quit, such as:

- I will be proud of myself.
- I will make my family, friends, and coworkers proud of me.
- I will be a better role model for others, especially my kids.
- I will feel more in control of my life.
- I will have more money to spend.
- I will save time by not taking cigarette breaks, buying cigarettes, or searching for a light.

Write down why you want to quit

Write down all the reasons you want to quit.
Keep your list where you'll see it often. Good places for your list are:

- where you keep your cigarettes
- in your wallet or purse
- in your kitchen
- in your car

When you reach for a cigarette, find your list of reasons for quitting. It will remind you why you want to stop.

My reasons to quit are

_____

_____

_____

_____

_____

_____

_____

_____

KEEP IN MIND

Pregnancy and smoking are not a good mix.

 If you are pregnant or thinking about having a baby, there's no better time to quit smoking than now. Women who smoke have a harder time getting pregnant. If they do get pregnant, they risk losing the baby or having a stillborn baby. And babies born to mothers who smoke:

- may be smaller than normal at birth
- are more likely to die of sudden infant death syndrome (SIDS)
- may be cranky, restless, and get sick more often
- are more likely to have learning problems as they develop

The good news is that quitting can help you have a healthy baby. It helps to quit any time during your pregnancy, but it's even better to quit before you become pregnant. Information to help you stop smoking is available in English and Spanish at **www.smokefree.gov/resources.html.**

_____

Source: U.S. Department of Health and Human Services. *Women and Smoking: A Report of the Surgeon General.* Atlanta, GA: U.S. Department of Health and Human Services, Centers for Disease Control and Prevention, National Center for Chronic Disease Prevention and Health Promotion, Office on Smoking and Health, 2001.

Learn how much you depend on nicotine

Knowing how addicted you are to nicotine can help you quit. It can help you decide if you need extra support, such as joining a quit-smoking program or taking medication to help you quit.

Answer the six simple questions in this nicotine addiction test. Your score will help you figure out how much you depend on nicotine.

Nicotine Addiction Test

		Points	Your Points
1. How soon after you wake up do you smoke your first cigarette?	Less than 5 minutes	3	
	6-30 minutes	2	
	31-60 minutes	1	
	After 1 hour	0	
2. Do you smoke more frequently in the hours after waking than during the rest of the day?	Yes	1	
	No	0	
3. Do you find it difficult not to smoke?	Yes	1	
	No	0	
4. Which cigarettes would you most hate to give up?	The first one in the morning	1	
	Any other	0	
5. How many cigarettes do you smoke a day?	10 or less	0	
	11-20	1	
	21-30	2	
	31 or more	3	
6. Do you smoke when you're so sick that you're home in bed?	Yes	1	
	No	0	
		Your Score	

Understand what your score means

If you scored even a single point, you may be dependent on nicotine. The higher your score, the more dependent you are. Remember—no matter what your score, you'll have to work hard to quit.

Source: Heatherton, TF, Kozlowski LT, Frecker RC, Fagerstrom KO. The Fagerstrom Test for Nicotine Dependence: a revision of the Fagerstrom Tolerance Questionnaire. *British Journal of Addictions.* 1991; 86:1119 -1127

Understand what makes you want to smoke

Wanting to smoke is not just an unhealthy habit. You want to smoke because your body now relies on nicotine. When the amount of nicotine in your body runs low, it triggers a craving—a strong, almost uncontrollable urge—for another cigarette. You may feel jittery, short-tempered, or anxious when you haven't smoked. Your body wants nicotine.

Triggers—people, places, activities, and feelings you associate with smoking—also make you want to smoke. Your triggers might be hearing the sounds of a party, finishing a task, or smelling coffee. Whatever your triggers, they can make you crave a cigarette.

Know your triggers

If you know your triggers, you have a head start on avoiding situations that tempt you to smoke.
Think about what might tempt you to smoke. Put a check next to the triggers on page 9 that apply to you.
Many smokers find that all these triggers make them want to smoke. You may only check a few. The point is to recognize all the situations that trigger your craving for a cigarette.

- ❑ Waking in the morning
- ❑ Drinking coffee, tea, or alcohol
- ❑ Smelling a cigarette
- ❑ Being with other smokers
- ❑ Seeing someone smoke
- ❑ Taking a break
- ❑ Talking on the phone
- ❑ Checking email
- ❑ Surfing the Internet
- ❑ Watching TV

- ❑ Driving my car
- ❑ Being a passenger
- ❑ After eating
- ❑ After having sex
- ❑ After completing a task
- ❑ Feeling stressed
- ❑ Feeling lonely or depressed
- ❑ Being or feeling less tolerant
- ❑ Feeling bored
- ❑ Feeling angry, irritable, or impatient

Meet your triggers head on

You can get prepared to quit smoking by thinking of ways to avoid some triggers and creating alternatives for others. You'll find that the urge to smoke only lasts a few minutes. Even if it lasts longer, it will go away, whether or not you smoke. Fighting the urge to smoke is easier if you:

- take a deep breath
- keep your hands busy—write, doodle, or hold a coin or pencil
- put something else in your mouth, such as a toothpick, sugar-free lollipop, or celery stick
- go places where smoking isn't allowed, such as a library or nonsmoking restaurant
- hang out with people who don't smoke
- avoid or reduce alcoholic drinks; try to drink water or juice instead

I will deal with my triggers by

_____

_____

_____

_____

_____

_____

_____

Know your options for quitting smoking

Quitting is hard. Success partly depends on how much you depend on nicotine. With many quit methods to choose from, be aware that no single approach works best for everyone. And you may need to try more than one method before you quit for good.

Some quit methods require a doctor's prescription. While others do not, it's always a good idea to discuss your plan to quit smoking with your doctor. Check the box of the options you want to talk about with your doctor.

❑ Cold turkey

For some smokers, "going cold turkey" seems like the easiest way to quit: Just stop smoking and tell yourself you'll never light up again. This works for some smokers—usually those with the lowest level of nicotine dependence—but not many. Fewer than 5 percent of smokers can quit this way. Most people aren't prepared when smoking habits and withdrawal symptoms trigger an intense urge to smoke. Research shows that most smokers have more success with one of the assisted quit methods discussed below. These methods have been tested and all of them are included in the U.S. Public Health Service guidelines for treating tobacco use and dependence.

❑ Over-the-counter medications

You don't need a prescription to buy certain medications that can improve your success with quitting. Nicotine replacement therapy (NRT) products—lozenges, gum, or a patch—provide nicotine to help reduce your craving for nicotine and withdrawal symptoms, if any. This allows you to focus on changing the behavior and habits that trigger your urge to smoke. To read more about NRT, see page 18.

❑ Prescription medications

Your doctor can prescribe medications to help you quit smoking. Some—inhalers and nasal sprays—act much like nonprescription nicotine replacement therapy. Other medications do not contain nicotine and work in different ways to help reduce your urge to smoke. To read more about prescription medications, see page 18.

❑ Counseling and group support

Many smokers quit with support provided by individual counseling or group treatment. You can combine these therapies with over-the-counter or prescription medications. Counseling can help you identify and overcome situations that trigger the urge to smoke. Research shows that success rates for all quit methods are higher when they are combined with a support program that provides encouragement through regularly scheduled one-on-one or group meetings, or quitlines.

❑ Quitlines

Quitlines are free, telephone-based counseling programs that are available nationwide. When you call a quitline, you are teamed with a trained counselor who can help you develop a strategy for quitting or help you stay on the program you have chosen. The counselor often provides material that can improve your chances of quitting. You can call the National Cancer Institute's Smoking Quitline at 1–877–44U–Quit (1–877–448–7848) or the National Quitline at 1–800–QUITNOW (1–800–784–8669) These are national quitlines that can help you anywhere in the United States.

KEEP IN MIND

Not everyone has feelings of withdrawal, but many smokers do. You may experience one or many symptoms of withdrawal and they may last for different periods of time.

Common feelings of smoking withdrawal include:

- feeling down, blue, or depressed
- feeling anxious, nervous, or restless
- having trouble thinking clearly
- being unable to sleep
- feeling tired or run down
- feeling hungry or gaining weight

Now Let's START

START Set a quit date

Finding a time to quit isn't easy. Any time can be a good time to quit when you are ready to try. Some smokers like to pick a day that is meaningful to them, such as:

- a birthday or wedding anniversary
- the first day of vacation
- New Year's Day (January 1)
- Independence Day (July 4)
- World No Tobacco Day (May 31)
- The Great American Smokeout (the third Thursday of each November)

It doesn't have to be a special day to quit. For many people, today is the day. You can choose any day to be your quit day. When you are ready to take the first step toward quitting, take it.

START: Five important steps toward quitting for good
S   Set a quit date
T   Tell family, friends, and coworkers you plan to quit
A   Anticipate and plan for the challenges you will face while quitting
R   Remove cigarettes and other tobacco products from your home, car, and workplace
T   Talk to your doctor about getting help to quit

KEEP IN MIND

Some smokers find it difficult to quit at certain times— after a bad day or personal loss, during a crisis, or at a stressful time, such as a divorce. Examine how you view such times in your life. Can you afford to wait before setting your quit date?

My quit date is

_____

START: Tell your family, friends, and coworkers you plan to quit

Quitting smoking is easier with the support of others. Tell your family, friends, and coworkers you plan to quit and how they can help you.

Some people like to have others ask them how things are going, while some find it annoying. Tell the people you care about exactly how they can help you. Here are some ideas:

- Ask everyone to understand if you have a change in mood; assure them it won't last long.
- Ask smokers who are close to you to quit with you or at least not smoke around you.
- Tell yourself and others: "The longer I go without cigarettes, the sooner I'll feel better ".
- Tell yourself and others: "The worst withdrawal symptoms from smoking—irritability and trouble sleeping—may be over within 2 weeks ".

In addition to the support of family, friends, and coworkers, you can get support if you:

- talk one-on-one or in a group with others who are quitting
- text-message experts on *LiveHelp* at **www.smokefree.gov**
- call the National Cancer Institute Quitline at 1–877–44U–QUIT (1–877–448–7848)
- contact the National Quitline at 1–800–QUITNOW (1–800–784–8669)

The family, friends, and coworkers I want to tell are

_____

_____

_____

_____

_____

_____

_____

_____

_____

_____

START: Anticipate and plan for the challenges you will face while quitting

Expecting challenges is an important part of getting ready to quit. Quitting presents both short- and long-term challenges. You may need different strategies for handling each.

Short-term challenges

Most people who have a hard time quitting and resume smoking do so in the first 3 months after trying to quit. Difficulty quitting is often caused by withdrawal symptoms—the physical discomfort smokers feel when they give up nicotine. It is your body's way of telling you it is learning to be nicotine-free. These feelings will go away in time.

Long-term challenges

Even as your physical withdrawal is decreasing, you may still be tempted to smoke when you feel stressed or down Although it's a challenge to be ready for these times, knowing that certain feelings can trigger a craving to smoke will help you handle the tough times.

Smoking journal

To understand your short- and long-term challenges, start by examining your smoking habits. Keeping a smoking journal can help you track how many cigarettes you smoke a day and what you are doing when you light up.

Check for patterns in your smoking. You may find triggers you aren't even aware of. Perhaps cigarettes you smoke at certain times or circumstances mean different things to you. Some may be more important than others. Understanding what tempts you to smoke in the short and long term will help you control the urge to smoke before it hits.

You can copy the journal in this booklet or make your own. Keep your journal with you so you can easily use it. Be sure to record the time you smoke, where you are, what you are doing, and what you are thinking or feeling. Rate how much you want the cigarette each time you smoke.

Try this activity for at least a few days, making sure to record 1 day during the week and 1 day on the weekend. You may even find that the time you take to complete the journal helps you smoke less.

0 ➡ None

1 ➡ Just a little

2 ➡ Some

3 ➡ A lot

My Smoking Journal

Cigarette Number	Time of Day	Craving Level	Activity	Who I Was With	Mood
Example	10:45	3	At Work	Alone	Stressed
1					
2					
3					
4					
5					
6					
7					
8					
9					
10					
11					
12					
13					
14					
15					
16					
17					
18					
19					
20					

START: Remove cigarettes and other tobacco products from your home, car, and workplace.

Getting rid of things that remind you of smoking also will help you get ready to quit. You should:

- Throw away all your tobacco supplies (cigarettes, lighters, matches, and ashtrays). Don't forget to check your drawers, coats, and bags.
- Make things clean and fresh in your home and car and at work; for instance, clean your drapes, carpets, and clothes.
- Have your teeth cleaned and remove those nicotine stains.

Don't save the "just in case" pack of cigarettes!

Saving one pack just makes it easier to start smoking again.

I can remove reminders of smoking by

_____

_____

_____

_____

_____

_____

_____

_____

_____

_____

KEEP IN MIND

All forms of tobacco are harmful.

Tobacco products and delivery methods come in many forms. However tobacco is packaged or delivered, it causes disease and addiction. Light or low-tar cigarettes are just as harmful as regular cigarettes. Clear your home, car, and workplace of all forms of tobacco.

START: Talk to your doctor about getting help to quit

It is important to tell your doctor when you are ready to quit—especially if you are pregnant, thinking of becoming pregnant, or have a serious medical condition. Your doctor can help you connect with the right resources to make your quit attempt successful. Remember—quitting "cold turkey" isn't your only choice.

Make sure to let your doctor or pharmacist know what medications you are taking. Nicotine changes how some drugs work. Your doctor may need to adjust some of your medications after you quit.

You can learn more about medications before you see your doctor from the summaries below and the up-to-date medication guide at **www.smokefree.gov/quit-smoking/medicationguide.**

Medications to help you quit

The Food and Drug Administration (FDA) has approved nicotine and non-nicotine cessation products to reduce withdrawal symptoms and the urge to smoke. Studies show that these medications, compared with trying to quit without them, can double or triple your chances of quitting for good. You will get the most benefit from these medications when you follow the instructions completely. You should not use any product that has not been tested and approved by the FDA.

Nicotine cessation products

Nicotine cessation products—also called nicotine replacement therapy (NRT)—contain small amounts of nicotine but not the hundreds of other harmful chemicals found in cigarettes. NRT helps you handle the physical symptoms of quitting by providing nicotine at much lower levels than found in cigarettes. This satisfies your nicotine craving and lessens your urge to smoke. Over-the-counter NRT options include a patch, gum, or lozenges that contain nicotine. Nicotine inhalers and nasal sprays are available only by prescription.

Non-nicotine cessation products

Some products that help withdrawal symptoms and nicotine cravings don't contain nicotine. They help by reducing symptoms and smoking urges. A prescription is needed for these medications. See your physician to discuss the details of your medication plan and to get a prescription.

My next doctor's appointment is

Date_____Time_____

KEEP IN MIND

Medications alone can't do all the work. They can help with cravings and withdrawal, but they won't completely prevent withdrawal symptoms. Even if you use medication to help you stop smoking, quitting may still be hard at times.

Many people find it helps to combine medication with behavior strategies. For example, you can keep healthy snacks handy to beat cravings, limit time with smokers, and enroll in a smoking cessation program.

My Quitting Worksheet

Review what you have done so far to prepare yourself to quit smoking successfully.

My reasons to quit are

_____

_____

_____

_____

_____

My nicotine addiction test score is _____

My triggers

❑ Waking in the morning

❑ Drinking coffee, tea, or alcohol

❑ Smelling a cigarette

❑ Being with other smokers

❑ Seeing someone smoke

❑ Taking a break

❑ Talking on the phone

❑ Checking email

❑ Surfing the Internet

❑ Watching TV

❑ Driving my car

❑ Being a passenger

❑ After eating

❑ After having sex

❑ After completing a task

❑ Feeling stressed

❑ Feeling lonely or depressed

❑ Being or feeling less tolerant

❑ Feeling bored

❑ Feeling angry, irritable, or impatient

I will deal with my triggers by

_____

_____

_____

_____

_____

My Quitting Worksheet

The quit method I'm interested in

❑   Cold turkey

❑   Over-the-counter medication (gum, patch, lozenges)

❑   Prescription medication (inhaler, nasal spray)

❑   Counseling and group support

❑   Quitlines

My quit date is _____

The family, friends, and coworkers I want to tell are

_____

_____

_____

_____

_____

_____

I can remove reminders of smoking by

_____

_____

_____

_____

_____

_____

_____

_____

_____

My next doctor's appointment is

Date_____ Time_____

Today's the Big Day–Your Quit Date

So today is the big day—your quit date. Quitting is not easy, so to help you get through your first smoke-free days, we suggest that you:

- keep busy and find new things to do
- stay away from what tempts you
- plan to reward yourself

Keep busy and find new things to do

Keep busy today, spending as much time as you can in nonsmoking places. Create some new habits and mix up your daily routine. Today and the days ahead will be easier if you avoid things that remind you of smoking. Remember—it's harder to smoke if you are keeping yourself busy and finding new things to do.

Here are some examples to get you started.

Go to nonsmoking places

- gyms
- libraries
- malls
- museums
- places of worship
- smoke-free restaurants

Be active

- walk or run
- take a bike ride
- go for a swim
- shoot hoops
- try a yoga class

Distract your hands

- hold something—a tennis ball, pen, or coin
- squeeze Silly Putty®
- knit or crochet

Distract your mind

- do a crossword puzzle
- read a book
- play cards

Drink the right stuff

- avoid alcoholic drinks
- drink a lot of water and low-sugar fruit juice
- replace coffee or tea with a new healthy beverage

Fool your mouth

- write a letter
- try a toothpick or straw
- eat a lollipop
- chew sugar-free gum
- eat carrot or celery sticks
- brush your teeth often and use mouthwash

You may have a hard time concentrating in your early days as a nonsmoker. Mental activities, such as doing crossword puzzles or even reading a book or magazine, may be more challenging. Recognize that it may be difficult to stay mentally focused in the early stages of quitting. Remember—your skill in these activities will return.

Stay away from what tempts you

You now understand that certain things trigger your urge to smoke. Today and as you're trying to quit, review your list of triggers. Then think of how you can avoid them. Other helpful tips to avoid triggers are noted below.

Change your routine

Changes in your routine help you avoid times and places that trigger the urge to smoke. Do things and go places where smoking is not allowed. Keep this up until you feel more relaxed and confident about being smoke-free.

Instead of smoking...	Try...
after meals	getting up from the table, brushing and flossing your teeth, and taking a walk.
while driving	listening to a new radio station, trying a different route, or taking a train, carpool, or bus, if possible.
while drinking coffee	switching to water, juice, or tea. Or, change the time you drink your coffee.
at a party	standing with nonsmokers and keeping your hands busy.

When you really crave a cigarette

Remember—the urge to smoke usually lasts only a few minutes. Try to wait it out. One reason it's important to get rid of all your cigarettes is to give yourself the time you need for these cravings to fade. Drink water or do something else until the urge passes. Look at the plan you made when you were getting ready to quit. You wrote down steps to take at a time like this. Try them! You also can use any of the tips below.

Tips	Examples
Pick up something other than a cigarette.	Try carrot or celery sticks, pickles, popsicles, sunflower seeds, apples, raisins, or pretzels.
Have a list of things you can do at a moment's notice.	Organize your computer files, delete messages from your cell phone, or call a friend to chat.

(Continued)

(Continued)

Tips	Examples
Take a deep breath.	Take 10 slow, deep breaths and hold the last one. Then breathe out slowly. Relax.
Clean something.	Wash your hands or the dishes, vacuum, or clean out your car.
Make a move.	Go outside or to a different room, or change what you are doing or who you are with.

No matter what, don't think, "Just one won't hurt". It will hurt. It will slow your progress toward your goal of being smoke-free. Remember— trying something to beat the urge is always better than trying nothing. The craving will go away, whether you smoke a cigarette or not.

Plan to reward yourself

Don't think of it as stopping smoking. Think of it as starting a new, healthier life style. Staying smoke-free is challenging. It takes some time. Be patient. You will begin to feel better. Set up rewards to remind yourself how hard you're working. For example, you could:

- buy yourself something special to celebrate quitting
- splurge on a massage or dinner at a new restaurant
- see a movie or sporting event
- start a new hobby
- begin exercising

My list of rewards

Make your own list of rewards. If they require a purchase, figure out the cost. Then plan for rewards that equal the amount of time you've succeeded in quitting (1 day, 1 week, 1 month, and so on). Put aside cigarette money to save for or buy some of them. You'll be amazed at how fast the money you used to spend on cigarettes adds up and how soon you'll be able to buy your rewards.

_____

I would like to reward myself by

_____

_____

_____

_____

_____

_____

_____

_____

_____

_____

_____

_____

_____

_____

KEEP IN MIND

You have to be careful with food rewards.

It's a great idea to go out to dinner or have a scoop of ice cream. Just be reasonable. Treat yourself without overeating. Make sure you are really hungry and not just searching for a substitute for a cigarette craving.

Now that you aren't buying cigarettes, you probably have more spending money. For example, if you smoke one pack a day:*

After...	...You've Saved
1 day	$5.00
1 week	$35.00
1 month	$150.00
1 year	$1,825.00
10 years	$18,250.00
20 years	$36,500.00

*Prices are based on an average of $5.00 per pack of cigarettes. The cost of a pack may differ, depending on where they are bought.

Quitting for Good–You Can Do It!

Beating an addiction to nicotine takes a lot more than just willpower and determination. You should feel great about yourself for making it this far. Now's the time to focus on sticking with it. To continue your success, make sure you:

- keep your guard up
- don't get discouraged if you slip
- stay upbeat
- focus on a new, healthier lifestyle

Keep your guard up

Your brain has learned to crave nicotine. Although you have quit, the urge to smoke often hits at the same time as when you smoked. For a long time, you have connected certain people, places, activities, and feelings with smoking a cigarette. Although you have quit, triggers such as drinking coffee or using your cell phone don't just disappear. These triggers may cause you to smoke again.

Be cautious and understand that most of the cravings connected to your triggers should disappear within a few months. But others may last longer. That's why you should never take a puff again, no matter how long it's been since you quit.

Continue to review your smoking journal to see when you might be tempted. Then use the skills you've learned to continue to get through your urges without smoking.

Don't get discouraged if you slip

Don't be discouraged if you slip and smoke one or two cigarettes. It's not a lost cause. One cigarette is better than an empty pack. But that doesn't mean you can safely smoke every now and then, no matter how long ago you quit. One cigarette may seem harmless, but it can quickly lead back to your old smoking habits.

Many ex-smokers tried stopping many times before finally succeeding. When people slip, it's usually within the first few months after quitting, when resisting the urge to smoke can be especially challenging. If you do slip, here are some strategies that can help you get back on track.

Realize you slipped

Acknowledge that you slipped. You've had a small setback. This doesn't make you a smoker again. Feel good about all the time you went without smoking. Focus on strengthening your coping skills.

Don't be too hard on yourself

One slip doesn't make you a failure. It doesn't mean you can't quit for good. But don't be too easy on yourself, either. If you slip, don't say, "Well, I've blown it. I might as well smoke the rest of this pack." It's important to get back on the nonsmoking track right away. Remember, your goal is no cigarettes—not even one puff.

Understand why you slipped

Find the trigger. Exactly what was it that made you smoke? Be aware of that trigger. If you are using medication to help you quit, don't assume that it isn't working if you slip and have a cigarette or two. Stay with it. It will help you get back on track.

Learn from your experience

What has helped you the most to keep from smoking? Make sure to do that on your next try. If you need to visit your doctor or other health professional again, do so. He or she can help motivate you to continue your effort to quit. Talk to your family and friends. It's okay to ask for support.

Know and use the tips in this booklet. People with even one coping skill are more likely to stay ex-smokers than those who don't know any. START to stop again! It's never too late to try.

Stay upbeat

As you go through the first days and weeks without smoking, stay positive. Don't blame yourself if you slip and smoke a cigarette. Don't think of smoking as "all or nothing." Take it one day at a time.

Remember—you didn't learn to smoke overnight. You may have taken months or even longer to adjust your routines to smoking. Quitting is a learning process, too. Staying positive will help you choose new activities and patterns to replace old habits.

Focus on a new, healthier lifestyle

Watch your weight

Many ex-smokers gain some weight because food tastes and smells better after quitting. You may notice that you snack more as a way to cope with the stress of quitting. Because your body uses food more slowly when you first stop smoking, you may gain weight.

If you're worried about gaining weight, remember that the benefits from quitting far outweigh the initial possibility of a few extra pounds. And by being aware of possible weight gain, you can do something about it. Get in shape and eat regular, nutritious meals to prevent unhealthy weight gain. Talk to your doctor or a nutritionist about meals and snacks with healthy amounts of protein, fruits, and vegetables. Also, check the suggestions below.

Get in shape

Exercise is a great distraction from smoking. It lowers the stress and reduces the cravings that make you want a cigarette. Try to make time to be physically active every day. Experts recommend:

- 30 minutes a day of moderate physical activity for at least 5 days a week, or
- at least 20 minutes of vigorous physical activity at least 3 days a week

Keep in mind most physical activities will help you burn calories and control weight gain. When you talk to your doctor about quitting, ask about exercises or activities that can get you back on the road to being fit. Find activities you like to do and that will fit into your schedule. You can also add activity to your day by walking during lunch, taking the stairs, parking farther away from your destination, or stretching during breaks. Possible activities include:

- walking or running
- dancing
- martial arts
- yoga

- tennis
- basketball
- aerobics
- cycling

Eat healthy foods

Don't stress over your eating patterns. Just try to make healthy food choices as you begin to increase your exercise. Any small changes will help. Here are some tips to get you started today:

- replace high-calorie foods with healthy, low-calorie ones, such as fresh fruits, vegetables, juices, yogurt, or air-popped popcorn without butter
- eat sugar-free candy or juice pops, or chew sugar-free gum
- choose foods that take longer to eat and keep your hands busy, such as oranges or sunflower seeds
- try crunchy foods, such as pretzels and rice cakes, so your mouth has to work
- drink water before and between meals

If you need to have something sweet on occasion, choose foods that taste sweet but have reduced fat and sugar, such as low-fat frozen yogurt.

For more information on how to eat healthy foods, talk to your doctor or nutritionist. Remember to be patient. It takes time to get good at eating healthily and staying smoke-free!

Remember The Long-Term Rewards

Tobacco use in the United States causes more than 440,000 deaths each year. Of those deaths, 170,000 are from cancer.

Once you quit smoking, you will add healthy days and years to your life. And you will significantly lower your risk of death from lung cancer and other diseases, including:

- heart disease
- stroke
- emphysema
- cervical cancer
- kidney cancer
- acute myeloid leukemia
- pancreatic cancer

- stomach cancer
- bladder cancer
- esophageal cancer
- laryngeal cancer
- oral cancer
- throat cancer

The health of your loved ones also will benefit from your quitting— they'll no longer be exposed to dangerous secondhand smoke. Finally, by quitting smoking, you're setting a good example. You're showing others, especially young people, that a life without cigarettes is a longer, healthier, happier life.

Within 20 minutes of smoking that last cigarette, your body starts making healthy changes that will continue for years. You can look forward to the following dramatic changes the moment you become an ex-smoker.

CONGRATULATIONS!

20 minutes after quitting

Your heart rate drops.

12 hours after quitting

The carbon monoxide level in your blood drops to normal.

2 weeks to 3 months after quitting

Your heart attack risk begins to drop. Your lung function begins to improve.

1 to 9 months after quitting

Your coughing and shortness of breath decrease.

1 year after quitting

Your added risk of coronary heart disease is half that of a smoker's.

5 years after quitting

Your stroke risk is reduced to that of a nonsmoker's 5–15 years after quitting.

10 years after quitting

Your lung cancer death rate is about half that of a smoker's.

15 years after quitting

Your risk of coronary heart disease is back to that of a nonsmoker's.

Source: U.S. Department of Health and Human Services. *The Health Consequences of Smoking: What It Means to You.* Atlanta, GA: U.S. Department of Health and Human Services, Centers for Disease Control and Prevention, National Center for Chronic Disease Prevention and Health Promotion, Office on Smoking and Health, 2004.

For More Information

National Cancer Institute

- **www.cancer.gov**

The National Cancer Institute (NCI) website provides two key tools to help you quit smoking: *LiveHelp*, an online text messaging service, and the toll-free number to NCI's Smoking Quitline. *LiveHelp* offers you live, online assistance from information specialists who provide cancer information and can help you navigate the NCI website. Click on the *LiveHelp* link, Monday through Friday.

NCI's Smoking Quitline also is staffed by specialists who can help you quit smoking. Call 1–877–44U–Quit (1–877–448–7848), Monday through Friday.

Cancer Information Service

- **http://cis.nci.nih.gov**

NCI's Cancer Information Service provides accurate, up-to-date information on cancer. Information specialists can help you quit smoking and explain the latest cancer information in easy-to-understand English or Spanish. Call 1–800–4–CANCER (1–800–422–6237); TTY, 1–800–332–8615.

American Cancer Society

- **www.cancer.org**

The American Cancer Society (ACS) has volunteers and offices all over the country. ACS can help you learn about the health hazards of smoking and how to become an ex-smoker. Its programs include the Great American Smokeout each November. ACS also has many booklets and other information to help you quit. Check online or call 1–800–ACS–2345 (1–800–227–2345) to find your local office or for more information.

American Heart Association

- **www.americanheart.org**

The American Heart Association (AHA) has thousands of volunteers and 130,000 members—doctors, scientists, and others—in 55 state and regional groups AHA offers books, tapes, and videos on how smoking affects the heart. It also has a guidebook on weight control in quit-smoking programs. Check online or call 1–800–AHA–USA1 (1–800–242–8721) to find your local office or for more information.

American Legacy Foundation

- **www.americanlegacy.org**

The American Legacy Foundation® develops programs that address the health effects of tobacco use. Through grants, training, partnerships, and grassroots marketing, the Foundation aims to help young people reject tobacco and give everyone access to tobacco prevention and cessation services. Vulnerable populations are a key focus. Check online for more information.

American Lung Association

- **www.lungusa.org**

The American Lung Association (ALA) helps smokers who want to quit through its Freedom From Smoking® self-help quit-smoking program. ALA actively supports laws and information campaigns for nonsmokers' rights. It also provides public information programs on the health effects of smoking. Check online or call 1–800–LUNG–USA (1–800–586–4872) to find your local office or for more information.

Centers for Disease Control and Prevention

- **www.cdc.gov/tobacco/osh/**

The Office on Smoking and Health, a program office within the Centers for Disease Control and Prevention (CDC), funds booklets on smoking topics such as relapse, helping a friend or family member quit smoking, the health hazards of smoking, and the effects of parental smoking on teenagers. Check online or call 1–800–CDC–INFO (1–800–232–4636) for more information.

Appendix 61

Post-Traumatic Stress Disorder (PTSD) Checklist Civilian Version

PCL-M for *DSM-IV* (11/1/94)

Name: _____

INSTRUCTIONS TO CLIENT: Below is a list of problems and complaints that people sometimes have in response to stressful experiences. Please read each one carefully, put an X in the box to indicate how much you have been bothered by that problem *in the past month*.

1. Repeated, disturbing *memories, thoughts,* or *images* of a stressful experience?

   1. Not at all   2. A little bit   3. Moderately   4. Quite a bit   5. Extremely

2. Repeated, disturbing *dreams* of a stressful experience?

   1. Not at all   2. A little bit   3. Moderately   4. Quite a bit   5. Extremely

3. Suddenly *acting* or *feeling* as if a stressful experience *were happening again* (as if you were reliving it)?

   1. Not at all   2. A little bit   3. Moderately   4. Quite a bit   5. Extremely

4. Feeling *very upset* when *something reminded you* of a stressful experience?

   1. Not at all   2. A little bit   3. Moderately   4. Quite a bit   5. Extremely

5. Having *physical reactions* (e.g., heart pounding, trouble breathing, sweating) when *something reminded you* of a stressful experience?

   1. Not at all   2. A little bit   3. Moderately   4. Quite a bit   5. Extremely

6. Avoiding *thinking about* or *talking about* a stressful experience or avoiding *having feelings* related to it?

   1. Not at all   2. A little bit   3. Moderately   4. Quite a bit   5. Extremely

7. Avoiding *activities* or *situations* because *they reminded you* of a stressful experience?

    1. Not at all   2. A little bit   3. Moderately   4. Quite a bit   5. Extremely

8. Trouble *remembering important parts* of a stressful experience?

    1. Not at all   2. A little bit   3. Moderately   4. Quite a bit   5. Extremely

9. *Loss of interest* in activities that you used to enjoy?

    1. Not at all   2. A little bit   3. Moderately   4. Quite a bit   5. Extremely

10. Feeling *distant* or *cut off* from other people?

    1. Not at all   2. A little bit   3. Moderately   4. Quite a bit   5. Extremely

11. Feeling *emotionally numb* or being unable to have loving feelings for those close to you?

    1. Not at all   2. A little bit   3. Moderately   4. Quite a bit   5. Extremely

12. Feeling as if your *future* will somehow be *cut short*?

    1. Not at all   2. A little bit   3. Moderately   4. Quite a bit   5. Extremely

13. Trouble falling or staying asleep?

    1. Not at all   2. A little bit   3. Moderately   4. Quite a bit   5. Extremely

14. Feeling irritable or having angry outbursts?

    1. Not at all   2. A little bit   3. Moderately   4. Quite a bit   5. Extremely

15. Having difficulty concentrating?

    1. Not at all   2. A little bit   3. Moderately   4. Quite a bit   5. Extremely

16. Being *"super-alert"* or watchful or on guard?

    1. Not at all   2. A little bit   3. Moderately   4. Quite a bit   5. Extremely

17. Feeling *jumpy* or easily startled?

    1. Not at all   2. A little bit   3. Moderately   4. Quite a bit   5. Extremely

END OF TEST

Scoring: Any answer of 3–5 is considered symptomatic.

Use the following *DSM* criteria for diagnosis:

- Symptomatic response to at least 1 "B" item (Questions 1–5).

- Symptomatic response to at least 3 "C" items (Questions 6–12).

- Symptomatic response to at least 2 "D" items (Questions 13–17).

Source: Weathers, Litz, Huska, & Keane; National Center for PTSD—Behavioral Science Division; This is a government document in the public domain.

Appendix 62

Post-Traumatic Stress Disorder (PTSD) Checklist Military Version

PCL-M for *DSM-IV* (11/1/94)

Name: _____

INSTRUCTIONS TO CLIENT: Below is a list of problems and complaints that veterans sometimes have in response to stressful military experiences. Please read each one carefully, put an X in the box to indicate how much you have been bothered by that problem *in the past month.*

1. Repeated, disturbing *memories, thoughts,* or *images* of a stressful military experience?

   1. Not at all   2. A little bit   3. Moderately   4. Quite a bit   5. Extremely

2. Repeated, disturbing *dreams* of a stressful military experience?

   1. Not at all   2. A little bit   3. Moderately   4. Quite a bit   5. Extremely

3. Suddenly *acting* or *feeling* as if a stressful military experience *were happening again* (as if you were reliving it)?

   1. Not at all   2. A little bit   3. Moderately   4. Quite a bit   5. Extremely

4. Feeling *very upset* when *something reminded you* of a stressful military experience?

   1. Not at all   2. A little bit   3. Moderately   4. Quite a bit   5. Extremely

5. Having *physical reactions* (e.g., heart pounding, trouble breathing, sweating) when *something reminded you* of a stressful military experience?

   1. Not at all   2. A little bit   3. Moderately   4. Quite a bit   5. Extremely

6. Avoiding *thinking about* or *talking about* a stressful military experience or avoiding *having feelings* related to it?

   1. Not at all   2. A little bit   3. Moderately   4. Quite a bit   5. Extremely

7. Avoiding *activities* or *situations* because *they reminded you* of a stressful military experience?

   1. Not at all   2. A little bit   3. Moderately   4. Quite a bit   5. Extremely

8. Trouble *remembering important parts* of a stressful military experience?

   1. Not at all   2. A little bit   3. Moderately   4. Quite a bit   5. Extremely

9. *Loss of interest* in activities that you used to enjoy?

   1. Not at all   2. A little bit   3. Moderately   4. Quite a bit   5. Extremely

10. Feeling *distant* or *cut off* from other people?

   1. Not at all   2. A little bit   3. Moderately   4. Quite a bit   5. Extremely

11. Feeling *emotionally numb* or being unable to have loving feelings for those close to you?

   1. Not at all   2. A little bit   3. Moderately   4. Quite a bit   5. Extremely

12. Feeling as if your *future* will somehow be *cut short*?

   1. Not at all   2. A little bit   3. Moderately   4. Quite a bit   5. Extremely

13. Trouble falling or staying asleep?

   1. Not at all   2. A little bit   3. Moderately   4. Quite a bit   5. Extremely

14. Feeling irritable or having angry outbursts?

   1. Not at all   2. A little bit   3. Moderately   4. Quite a bit   5. Extremely

15. Having difficulty concentrating?

   1. Not at all   2. A little bit   3. Moderately   4. Quite a bit   5. Extremely

16. Being *"super-alert"* or watchful or on guard?

   1. Not at all   2. A little bit   3. Moderately   4. Quite a bit   5. Extremely

17. Feeling *jumpy* or easily startled?

   1. Not at all   2. A little bit   3. Moderately   4. Quite a bit   5. Extremely

END OF TEST

Scoring: Any answer of 3–5 is considered symptomatic.

Use the following *DSM* criteria for diagnosis:

- Symptomatic response to at least 1 "B" item (Questions 1–5).

- Symptomatic response to at least 3 "C" items (Questions 6–12).

- Symptomatic response to at least 2 "D" items (Questions 13–17).

Source: Weathers, Litz, Huska, & Keane; National Center for PTSD—Behavioral Science Division. This is a government document in the public domain.

Appendix 63

Alcohol Abstinence Self-Efficacy Scale

Listed below are a number of situations that lead some people to drink alcohol.

Mark how confident you are that you would abstain from alcohol in each situation.

Circle the number that best describes your feelings of confidence to abstain from alcohol in each situation during the past week according to the following scale:

1 = Not at all confident

2 = Not very confident

3 = Moderately confident

4 = Very confident

5 = Extremely confident

Situation	Confident to abstain from alcohol (not drink any alcohol)				
	Not at all	**Not very**	**Moderately**	**Very**	**Extremely**
1) When I am in agony because of stopping or withdrawing from alcohol use.	1	2	3	4	5
2) When I have a headache.	1	2	3	4	5
3) When I am feeling depressed.	1	2	3	4	5
4) When I am on vacation and want to relax.	1	2	3	4	5

Source: Reprinted with permission from Journal of Studies on Alcohol, vol. 55, pp. 141–148, 1994 (Presently Journal of Studies on Alcohol and Drugs). Copyright by Alcohol Research Documentation, Inc. Rutgers Center of Alcohol Studies, Piscataway, NJ 08854.

(Continued)

(Continued)

Situation	Confident to abstain from alcohol (not drink any alcohol)				
	Not at all	**Not very**	**Moderately**	**Very**	**Extremely**
5) When I am concerned about someone.	1	2	3	4	5
6) When I am worried.	1	2	3	4	5
7) When I have the urge to try just one drink to see what happens.	1	2	3	4	5
8) When I am being offered a drink in a social situation.	1	2	3	4	5
9) When I dream about taking a drink.	1	2	3	4	5
10) When I am feeling a physical need or craving for alcohol.	1	2	3	4	5
11) When I am physically tired.	1	2	3	4	5
12) When I am experiencing some physical pain or injury.	1	2	3	4	5
13) When I feel like blowing up because of frustration.	1	2	3	4	5
14) When I see others drinking at a bar or a party.	1	2	3	4	5
15) When I sense everything is going wrong for me.	1	2	3	4	5
16) When people I used to drink with encourage me to drink.	1	2	3	4	5
17) When I am feeling angry inside.	1	2	3	4	5
18) When I experience an urge or impulse to take a drink that catches me unprepared.	1	2	3	4	5
19) When I am excited or celebrating with others.	1	2	3	4	5

Score: The higher the score, the higher the self-efficacy.

Appendix 64

Hamilton Anxiety Rating Scale

Rating: Clinician-rated

Administration time: 10–15 minutes

Main purpose: To assess the severity of symptoms of anxiety

Population: Adults, adolescents, and children

Commentary

The HAM-A was one of the first rating scales developed to measure the severity of anxiety symptoms, and is still widely used today in both clinical and research settings. The scale consists of 14 items, each defined by a series of symptoms, and measures both psychic anxiety (mental agitation and psychological distress) and somatic anxiety (physical complaints related to anxiety). Although the HAM-A remains widely used as an outcome measure in clinical trials, it has been criticized for its sometimes poor ability to discriminate between anxiolytic and antidepressant effects, and somatic anxiety versus somatic side effects. The HAM-A does not provide any standardized probe questions. Despite this, the reported levels of inter-rater reliability for the scale appear to be acceptable.

Scoring

Each item is scored on a scale of 0 (not present) to 4 (severe), with a total score range of 0–56, where <17 indicates mild severity, 18–24 mild to moderate severity, and 25–30 moderate to severe.

Versions

The scale has been translated into Cantonese for China, French, and Spanish. An IVR version of the scale is available from Healthcare Technology Systems.

Additional References

Maier W, Buller R, Philipp M, Heuser I. The Hamilton Anxiety Scale: reliability, validity and sensitivity to change in anxiety and depressive disorders. J Affect Disord 1988;14(1):61–8.

Borkovec T and Costello E. Efficacy of applied relaxation and cognitive behavioral therapy in the treatment of generalized anxiety disorder. J Clin Consult Psychol 1993; 61(4):611–19

Source: Hamilton, M. (1959). The assessment of anxiety states by rating. *British Journal of Medical Psychology,* *32,* 50–55.

Address for Correspondence

The Hamilton Anxiety Rating Scale (HAM-A) is in the public domain.

Hamilton Anxiety Rating Scale

Below is a list of phrases that describe certain feeling that people have. Rate the clients by finding the answer which best describes the extent to which he/she has these conditions. Select one of the five responses for each of the fourteen questions.

0 = Not present, 1 = Mild, 2 = Moderate, 3 = Severe, 4 = Very severe.

1. **Anxious mood**   0   1   2   3   4

Worries, anticipation of the worst, fearful anticipation, irritability.

2. **Tension**   0   1   2   3   4

Feelings of tension, fatigability, startle response, moved to tears easily, trembling, feelings of restlessness, inability to relax.

3. **Fears**   0   1   2   3   4

Of dark, of strangers, of being left alone, of animals, of traffic, of crowds.

4. **Insomnia**   0   1   2   3   4

Difficulty in falling asleep, broken sleep, unsatisfying sleep and fatigue on waking, dreams, nightmares, night terrors.

5. **Intellectual**   0   1   2   3   4

Difficulty in concentration, poor memory.

6. **Depressed mood**   0   1   2   3   4

Loss of interest, lack of pleasure in hobbies, depression, early waking, diurnal swing.

7. **Somatic** (muscular)   0   1   2   3   4

Pains and aches, twitching, stiffness, myoclonic jerks, grinding of teeth, unsteady voice, increased muscular tone.

8. **Somatic** (sensory)   0   1   2   3   4

Tinnitus, blurring of vision, hot and cold flushes, feelings of weakness, pricking sensation.

9. **Cardiovascular symptoms**   0   1   2   3   4

Tachycardia, palpitations, pain in chest, throbbing of vessels, fainting feelings, missing beat.

10. **Respiratory symptoms**   0   1   2   3   4

Pressure or constriction in chest, choking feelings, sighing, dyspnea.

11. **Gastrointestinal symptoms** 0   1   2   3   4

Difficulty in swallowing, wind abdominal pain, burning sensations, abdominal fullness, nausea, vomiting, borborygmi, looseness of bowels, loss of weight, constipation.

12. **Genitourinary symptoms**   0   1   2   3   4

Frequency of micturition, urgency of micturition, amenorrhea, menorrhagia, development of frigidity, premature ejaculation, loss of libido, impotence.

13. **Autonomic symptoms**   0   1   2   3   4

Dry mouth, flushing, pallor, tendency to sweat, giddiness, tension headache, raising of hair.

14. **Behavior at interview**   0   1   2   3   4

Fidgeting, restlessness or pacing, tremor of hands, furrowed brow, strained face, sighing or rapid respiration, facial pallor, swallowing, etc.

Appendix 65

Strengths, Needs, Abilities, and Preferences

Strengths

List three of your most positive qualities (strengths):

1.

2.

3.

Please check the following comments if you feel they describe yourself.

_____ I believe that I am highly internally motivated to quit all mind-altering substances.
_____ I believe that I am highly externally motivated to finish this course of treatment because of legal issues/problems, relationship issues/problems, and/or job related consequences, etc.
_____ I believe that I have the recovery support of family, significant other(s), and/or friends.
_____ I have a supportive home environment to return to.
_____ I believe that I am highly imaginative and creative.
_____ I am financially stable.
_____ I am in good health.

List three of your greatest achievements:

1.

2.

3.

List three things you hope to achieve or to work on while in treatment:

1.

2.

3.

Please describe what you feel treatment is all about.

Please describe your beliefs and understanding of a Higher Power/God.

My spiritual/religious orientation is open to a "Higher Power" concept as it relates to the 12 steps.

Please check the statement if it applies to you:

Yes   No

Needs

_____ I need help educating my family and/or significant others regarding chemical dependency.
_____ I need help stabilizing my psychological and/or emotional symptoms specifically.
_____ I need help in finding a clean and sober supportive recovery environment to enter when I leave
          the facility. I prefer to live in or near the following town: _____
_____ I need help in identifying my relapse triggers.
          Other needs

Abilities

_____ I believe that I am educated enough to understand this program's printed materials and complete
          written assignments.
_____ I believe that I have natural leadership abilities.
_____ I am usually well organized and able to establish priorities.
_____ I am self-directive and need little external supervision to accomplish tasks or assignments.
          Other abilities/talents/skills

Preferences

Please check and explain any that apply to you. I have specific preferences related to my:

_____ Culture

_____ Ethnicity (Race)_____

_____ Religion_____

_____ Gender

_____ Sexual orientation_____

_____ Age_____

_____ Physical_____

_____ My preferred language is English.

_____ I have English language problems and would prefer that detailed educational materials and program assignments be modified or translated so I can better comprehend.

_____ I prefer to learn by reading materials/articles/books, etc.

_____ I prefer to learn through individual contact with people.

_____ I prefer to learn by watching educational DVDs.

_____ I prefer to learn by _____.

Appendix 66

Daily Craving Record

Rate your cravings every day on a scale of 0 (the least amount of craving possible) to 10 (the most craving possible). Then put down the *situation* or *thoughts* that triggered the craving. Have your counselor or group help you uncover the automatic thoughts or situations that triggered craving. Do this at least for the first 90 days of recovery. Make as many copies of these pages that you need. In treatment, you will replace inaccurate thoughts with accurate thoughts.

0 = no craving   3 = moderate craving   10 = severe craving

Date _____ Craving _____ Triggers _____

Date _____ Craving _____ Triggers _____

Date _____ Craving _____ Triggers _____

Date _____ Craving _____ Triggers _____

Date _____ Craving _____ Triggers _____

Date _____ Craving _____ Triggers _____

Date _____ Craving _____ Triggers _____

Date _____ Craving _____ Triggers _____

Date _____ Craving _____ Triggers _____

Date _____ Craving _____ Triggers _____

Date _____ Craving _____ Triggers _____

Date _____ Craving _____ Triggers _____

Date _____ Craving _____ Triggers _____

Date _____ Craving _____ Triggers _____

Date _____ Craving _____ Triggers _____

Date _____ Craving _____ Triggers _____

Date _____ Craving _____ Triggers _____

Date _____ Craving _____ Triggers _____

Date ____ Craving ____ Triggers _____

Date ____ Craving ____ Triggers _____

Date ____ Craving ____ Triggers _____

Date ____ Craving ____ Triggers _____

Date ____ Craving ____ Triggers _____

Date ____ Craving ____ Triggers _____

Date ____ Craving ____ Triggers _____

Date ____ Craving ____ Triggers _____

Date ____ Craving ____ Triggers _____

Date ____ Craving ____ Triggers _____

Date ____ Craving ____ Triggers _____

Date ____ Craving ____ Triggers _____

Date ____ Craving ____ Triggers _____

Date ____ Craving ____ Triggers _____

Date ____ Craving ____ Triggers _____

Date ____ Craving ____ Triggers _____

Date ____ Craving ____ Triggers _____

Date ____ Craving ____ Triggers _____

Date ____ Craving ____ Triggers _____

Date ____ Craving ____ Triggers _____

Date ____ Craving ____ Triggers _____

Date ____ Craving ____ Triggers _____

Date ____ Craving ____ Triggers _____

Date ____ Craving ____ Triggers _____

Date ____ Craving ____ Triggers _____

Date ____ Craving ____ Triggers _____

Date ____ Craving ____ Triggers _____

Date ____ Craving ____ Triggers _____

Date ____ Craving ____ Triggers _____

Date ____ Craving ____ Triggers _____

Date ____ Craving ____ Triggers _____

Date ____ Craving ____ Triggers _____

Date ____ Craving ____ Triggers _____

Date ____ Craving ____ Triggers _____

Date ____ Craving ____ Triggers _____

Date ____ Craving ____ Triggers _____

Date ____ Craving ____ Triggers _____

Date ____ Craving ____ Triggers _____

Date ____ Craving ____ Triggers _____

Date ____ Craving ____ Triggers _____

Date ____ Craving ____ Triggers _____

Date ____ Craving ____ Triggers _____

Date ____ Craving ____ Triggers _____

Date ____ Craving ____ Triggers _____

Date ____ Craving ____ Triggers _____

Date ____ Craving ____ Triggers _____

Date ____ Craving ____ Triggers _____

Date ____ Craving ____ Triggers _____

Date ____ Craving ____ Triggers _____

Date ____ Craving ____ Triggers _____

Date ____ Craving ____ Triggers _____

Date ____ Craving ____ Triggers _____

Date ____ Craving ____ Triggers _____

Date ____ Craving ____ Triggers _____

Date ____ Craving ____ Triggers _____

Date ____ Craving ____ Triggers _____

Date ____ Craving ____ Triggers _____

Date ____ Craving ____ Triggers _____

Date ____ Craving ____ Triggers _____

Date ____ Craving ____ Triggers _____

Date ____ Craving ____ Triggers _____

Date ____ Craving ____ Triggers _____

Date ____ Craving ____ Triggers _____

Date ____ Craving ____ Triggers _____

Date ____ Craving ____ Triggers _____

Date ____ Craving ____ Triggers _____

Date ____ Craving ____ Triggers _____

Date ____ Craving ____ Triggers _____

Date ____ Craving ____ Triggers _____

Date ____ Craving ____ Triggers _____

Date ____ Craving ____ Triggers _____

Date _____ Craving _____ Triggers _____

Date _____ Craving _____ Triggers _____

Date _____ Craving _____ Triggers _____

Date _____ Craving _____ Triggers _____

Date _____ Craving _____ Triggers _____

Date _____ Craving _____ Triggers _____

Date _____ Craving _____ Triggers _____

Date _____ Craving _____ Triggers _____

Date _____ Craving _____ Triggers _____

Date _____ Craving _____ Triggers _____

Date _____ Craving _____ Triggers _____

Date _____ Craving _____ Triggers _____

Date _____ Craving _____ Triggers _____

Date _____ Craving _____ Triggers _____

Date _____ Craving _____ Triggers _____

Date _____ Craving _____ Triggers _____

Appendix 67

National Association of Alcohol and Drug Abuse Counselors (NAADAC) Code of Ethics

Principle 1: Nondiscrimination

- *I shall affirm diversity among colleagues or clients regardless of age gender, sexual orientation, ethnic/racial background, religious/spiritual beliefs, marital status, political beliefs, or mental/physical disability.*
- *I shall strive to treat all individuals with impartiality and objectivity relating to all based solely on their personal merits and mindful of the dignity of all human persons. As such, I shall not impose my personal values on my clients.*
- *I shall avoid bringing personal or professional issues into the counseling relationship. Through an awareness of the impact of stereotyping and discrimination, I shall guard the individual rights and personal dignity of my clients.*
- *I shall relate to all clients with empathy and understanding no matter what their diagnosis or personal history.*

Principle 2: Client Welfare

- *I understand that the ability to do good is based on an underlying concern for the well being of others. I shall act for the good of others and exercise respect, sensitivity, and insight. I understand that my primary professional responsibility and loyalty is to the welfare of my clients, and I shall work for the client irrespective of who actually pays his/her fees.*
- *I shall do everything possible to safeguard the privacy and confidentiality of client information except where the client has given specific, written, informed, and limited consent or when the client poses a risk to himself or others.*
- *I shall provide the client his/her rights regarding confidentiality, in writing, as part of informing the client of any areas likely to affect the client's confidentiality.*
- *I understand and support all that will assist clients to a better quality of life, greater freedom, and true independence.*

Source: Retrieved from www.ndbace.org/forms/NAADACCodeofEthics-2004.pdf.

- *I shall not do for others what they can readily do for themselves but rather facilitate and support the doing. Likewise, I shall not insist on doing what I perceive as good without reference to what the client perceives as good and necessary.*
- *I understand that suffering is unique to a specific individual and not of some generalized or abstract suffering, such as might be found in the understanding of the disorder. I also understand that the action taken to relieve suffering must be uniquely suited to the suffering individual and not simply some universal prescription.*
- *I shall provide services without regard to the compensation provided by the client or by a third party and shall render equally appropriate services to individuals whether they are paying a reduced fee or a full fee.*

Principle 3: Client Relationship

- *I understand and respect the fundamental human right of all individuals to self-determination and to make decisions that they consider in their own best interest. I shall be open and clear about the nature, extent, probable effectiveness, and cost of those services to allow each individual to make an informed decision of their care.*
- *I shall provide the client and/or guardian with accurate and complete information regarding the extent of the potential professional relationship, such as the Code of Ethics and professional loyalties and responsibilities.*
- *I shall inform the client and obtain the client's participation including the recording of the interview, the use of interview material for training purposes, and/or observation of an interview by another person.*

Principle 4: Trustworthiness

- *I understand that effectiveness in my profession is largely based on the ability to be worthy of trust, and I shall work to the best of my ability to act consistently within the bounds of a known moral universe, to faithfully fulfill the terms of both personal and professional commitments, to safeguard fiduciary relationships consistently, and to speak the truth as it is known to me.*
- *I shall never misrepresent my credentials or experience.*
- *I shall make no unsubstantiated claims for the efficacy of the services I provide and make no statements about the nature and course of addictive disorders that have not been verified by scientific inquiry.*
- *I shall constantly strive for a better understanding of addictive disorders and refuse to accept supposition and prejudice as if it were the truth.*
- *I understand that ignorance in those matters that should be known does not excuse me from the ethical fault of misinforming others.*
- *I understand the effect of impairment on professional performance and shall be willing to seek appropriate treatment for myself or for a colleague. I shall support peer assistance programs in this respect.*
- *I understand that most property in the healing professions is intellectual property and shall not present the ideas or formulations of others as if they were my own. Rather, I shall give appropriate credit to their originators both in written and spoken communication.*
- *I regard the use of any copyrighted material without permission or the payment of royalty to be theft.*

Principle 5: Compliance With Law

- *I understand that laws and regulations exist for the good ordering of society and for the restraint of harm and evil, and I am aware of those laws and regulations that are relevant both personally and professionally and follow them, while reserving the right to commit civil disobedience.*
- *I understand that the determination that a law or regulation is unjust is not a matter of preference or opinion but a matter of rational investigation, deliberation, and dispute.*
- *I willingly accept that there may be a penalty for justified civil disobedience, and I must weigh the personal harm of that penalty against the good done by civil protest.*

Principle 6: Rights and Duties

- *I understand that personal and professional commitments and relationships create a network of rights and corresponding duties. I shall work to the best of my ability to safeguard the natural and consensual rights of each individual and fulfill those duties required of me.*
- *I understand that justice extends beyond individual relationships to the community and society; therefore, I shall participate in activities that promote the health of my community and profession.*
- *I shall, to the best of my ability, actively engage in the legislative processes, educational institutions, and the general public to change public policy and legislation to make possible opportunities and choice of service for all human beings of any ethnic or social background whose lives are impaired by alcoholism and drug abuse.*
- *I understand that the right of confidentiality cannot always be maintained if it serves to protect abuse, neglect, or exploitation of any person or leaves another at risk of bodily harm.*

Principle 7: Dual Relationships

- *I understand that I must seek to nurture and support the development of a relationship of equals rather than to take unfair advantage of individuals who are vulnerable and exploitable.*
- *I shall not engage in professional relationships or commitments that conflict with family members, friends, close associates, or others whose welfare might be jeopardized by such a dual relationship.*
- *Because a relationship begins with a power differential, I shall not exploit relationships with current or former clients for personal gain, including social or business relationships.*
- *I shall not under any circumstances engage in sexual behavior with current or former clients.*
- *I shall not accept substantial gifts from clients, other treatment organizations, or the providers of materials or services used in my practice.*

Principle 8: Preventing Harm

- *I understand that every decision and action has ethical implication leading either to benefit or harm, and I shall carefully consider whether any of my decisions or actions has the potential to produce harm of a physical, psychological, financial, legal, or spiritual nature before implementing them.*
- *I shall refrain from using any methods that could be considered coercive such as threats, negative labeling, and attempts to provoke shame or humiliation.*

- *I shall make no requests of clients that are not necessary as part of the agreed treatment plan.*
- *I shall terminate a counseling or consulting relationship when it is reasonably clear that the client is not benefiting from the relationship.*
- *I understand an obligation to protect individuals, institutions, and the profession from harm that might be done by others. Consequently, I am aware that the conduct of another individual is an actual or likely source of harm to clients, colleagues, institutions, or the profession and that I have an ethical obligation to report such conduct to competent authorities.*

Principle 9: Duty of Care

- *I shall operate under the principle of Duty of Care and shall maintain a working/therapeutic environment in which clients, colleagues, and employees can be safe from the threat of physical, emotional, or intellectual harm.*
- *I respect the right of others to hold opinions, beliefs, and values different from my own.*
- *I shall strive for understanding and the establishment of common ground rather than for the ascendancy of one opinion over another.*
- *I shall maintain competence in the area of my practice through continuing education, constantly improving my knowledge and skills in those approaches most effective with my specific clients.*
- *I shall scrupulously avoid practicing in any area outside of my competence.*

Appendix 68

Gambling History

Robert R. Perkinson, PhD

This exercise will help you to become more aware of how gambling has affected your life and the lives of those around you. Answer the questions as completely as you can. It is time to get completely honest with yourself. Write down exactly what happened.

1. How old were you when you first gambled? Describe what happened and how you felt.

2. List all of the types of gambling you have ever participated in and the age at which you first gambled.

   Video lottery

   Blackjack

   Bingo

   Scratch tickets

   Poker (Cards)

   Horse racing

   Slot machines

   Powerball

   Sports betting

   Pull tabs

   Dog racing

   Other

3. What are your gambling habits? Where do you gamble? With whom? Under what circumstances?

4. Was there ever a period in your life when you gambled too much? Explain.

5. Has gambling ever caused a problem for you? Describe the problem or problems.

6. When you were gambling, did you find that you gambled more, or for a longer period of time, than you had originally intended? Give some examples.

7. Do you have to gamble more now to get the same effect you want? How much more than when you first started?

8. Did you ever try to cut down on your gambling? Why did you try to cut down, and what happened to your attempt?

9. What did you do to cut down? Did you change the time, place, or game? Limit the amount ("I'll only spend twenty dollars tonight")? Restrict your gambling to a certain time of day ("I'll only gamble after five o'clock")?

10. Did you ever stop completely? What happened? Why did you start again?

11. Did you spend a lot of time getting over your losses?

12. Were you ever so obsessed with gambling that you had problems doing something dangerous such as driving a car? Give some examples.

13. Did you ever gamble so much that you missed work or school? Give some examples.

14. Did you ever miss family events or recreation because you were gambling? Give a few examples.

15. Did your gambling ever cause family problems? Give some examples.

16. Did you ever feel annoyed when someone talked to you about your gambling? Who was this person, and what did he or she say? Give some examples.

17. Did you ever feel bad or guilty about your gambling? Give some examples.

18. Did gambling ever cause you any psychological problems such as being depressed? Explain what happened.

19. Did gambling ever cause you any physical problems or make a physical problem worse? Give a few examples.

20. Did you ever have lose track of time when gambling? Give some examples.

21. Did you ever get sick because you were gambling? Give some examples.

22. Did you ever have intense guilt because of gambling? Give some examples about how you felt.

23. Did you ever get nervous or suffer withdrawal symptoms when you quit gambling? Describe what happened to you when you stopped gambling.

24. Did you ever gamble to avoid symptoms of withdrawal? Give some examples of when you used gambling to control withdrawal symptoms.

25. Have you ever sought help for your gambling problem? When? Who did you see? Did the treatment help you? How?

26. Why do you continue to gamble? Give five reasons.

27. Why do you want to stop gambling? Give 10 reasons.

28. Has gambling ever affected your reputation? Describe what happened and how you felt.

29. Describe the feelings of guilt you have about your gambling. How do you feel about yourself?

30. How has gambling affected you financially? Give a few examples of how you wasted money in your addiction.

31. Has your ambition decreased due to your gambling? Give an example.

32. Has your addiction changed how you feel about yourself?

33. Are you as self-confident as you were before?

34. Describe the reasons why you want treatment now.

35. List all of the types of gambling you have been involved in, in the past 6 months.

36. List how often and in what amounts you have gambled in the past 6 months.

37. List the life events that have been affected by your gambling (e.g., school, marriage, job, children).

38. Have you ever had legal problems because of your gambling? List each problem.

39. Have you ever lost a job because of your gambling? Describe what happened.

40. Do you want treatment for your gambling problem? List a few reasons.

References

Abelson, H. I., Fishburne, P., & Cisin, I. H. (1977). *National Survey on Drug Abuse, 1977: A nationwide study—Youth, young adults, and older adults, Vol. 1: Main findings* (Publ. No. [ADM] 78–618). Washington, DC: U.S. Government Printing Office.

Adams, R. D., & Victor, M. (1981). *Principles of neurology.* New York: McGraw-Hill.

AIDS and Chemical Dependency Committee. (1988). *Guidelines for facilities treating chemical dependency clients at risk for AIDS and HIV infection* (2nd ed.). New York: American Medical Society on Alcoholism and Other Drug Dependencies.

Aigner, T. G., & Balster, R. L. (1978). Choice of behavior in rhesus monkeys: Cocaine versus food. *Science, 201,* 534–535.

Alberti, R. E., & Emmons, M. L. (1995). *Your perfect right: A guide to assertive living.* Atascadero, CA: Impact Publishers.

Alcoholics Anonymous. (1976). *Alcoholics Anonymous.* New York: Alcoholics Anonymous World Services.

Alcoholics Anonymous. (1981). *Twelve steps and twelve traditions.* New York: Alcoholics Anonymous World Services.

Alcoholics Anonymous. (2001). *Alcoholics Anonymous.* New York: Alcoholics Anonymous World Services.

Alcoholics Anonymous. (2002a). *Alcoholics Anonymous* (4th ed.). New York: Alcoholics Anonymous World Services.

Alcoholics Anonymous. (2002b). *Twelve steps and twelve traditions.* New York: Alcoholics Anonymous World Services.

Alexander, E. J. (1951). Withdrawal effects of sodium amytal. *Diseases of the Nervous System, 12,* 77–82.

Alexander, J. F. (1974). Behavior modification and delinquent youth. In J. C. Cull & R. E. Hardy (Eds.), *Behavior modification in rehabilitation settings.* Springfield, IL: Charles C Thomas.

Alexander, J. F., & Parsons, B. V. (1973). Short term behavioral intervention with delinquent families. *Journal of Abnormal Psychology, 81,* 219–255.

American Cancer Society. (2011). *Guide to quitting smoking.* Atlanta, GA: Author.

American Psychiatric Association. (1994). *Diagnostic and statistical manual of mental disorders* (4th ed.). Washington, DC: American Psychiatric Press.

American Psychiatric Association. (2000). *Diagnostic and statistical manual of mental disorders* (Rev. ed.). Washington, DC: American Psychiatric Press.

Anderson, J. (1941, March). Alcoholics Anonymous. *The Saturday Evening Post.*

Anglin, M. D., & Hser, Y. (1990). Treatment of drug abuse. In M. Tonry & J. Q. Wilson (Eds.), *Drugs and crime* (pp. 339–460). Chicago: University of Chicago Press.

Annual causes of death in the United States. (2011). *Common sense for drug policy.* Retrieved from http://drugwarfacts.org/cms/?q=node/30

Anthenelli, R. M., & Schuckit, M. A. (1994). Genetic influences in addiction. In N. S. Miller & M. C. Doot (Eds.), *Principles of addiction medicine* (sec. 1, chap. 6, pp. 1–14). Chevy Chase, MD: American Society of Addiction Medicine.

Appenzeller, O., Standefer, J., Appenzeller, J., & Atkinson, R. (1980). Neurology of endurance training: V. Endorphins. *Neurology, 30,* 418–419.

Arria, A. M., Kuhn, V., Calderia, K. M., O'Grady, K. E., Vincent, K. B., & Wish, E. D. (2008). High school drinking mediates the relationship between parental monitoring and college drinking: A longitudinal analysis. *Substance Abuse Treatment, Prevention and Policy, 7*, 6.

Atkinson, R. M., & Kofed, L. L. (1984). Substance use and abuse in old age. *Substance Abuse, 5*, 30–42.

Balster, R. L., & Chait, L. D. (1978). The behavioral effects of phencyclidine in animals. In R. C. Petersen & R. C. Stillman (Eds.), *PCP phencyclidine abuse: An appraisal* (Publ. No. [ADM] 78–728, pp. 53–65). Washington, DC: U.S. Government Printing Office.

Barlow, D. H., & Craske, M. G. (2006). *Mastery of your anxiety and panic: Workbook*. New York: Oxford University Press.

Baum, R., & Iber, F. L. (1980). Initial treatment of the alcoholic client. In S. E. Gitlow & H. S. Peyser (Eds.), *Alcoholism: A practical treatment guide*. New York: Grune & Stratton.

Bearman, S. K., Presnall, K., Martinez, E., & Stice, E. (2006). The skinny on body dissatisfaction: A longitudinal study of adolescent girls and boys. *Journal of Youth and Adolescence, 35*, 217–229.

Beattie, M. (1987). *Codependent no more: How to stop controlling others and start caring for yourself*. Center City, MN: Hazelden.

Beck, A. T. (1967). *Depression: Clinical, experimental, and theoretical aspects*. New York: Harper & Row.

Beck, A. T. (1972). *Depression: Causes and treatment*. Philadelphia: University of Pennsylvania Press.

Beck, A. T. (1976). *Cognitive therapy and the emotional disorders*. New York: International Universities Press.

Beck, A. T., & Emery, G. (1979). *Coping with anxiety and panic: SCT method*. Philadelphia: Center for Cognitive Therapy.

Beck, A. T., & Greenberg, R. (1974). *Coping with depression*. Philadelphia: Center for Cognitive Therapy.

Beck, A. T., Rush, J. A., Shaw, B. F., & Emery, G. (1979). *Cognitive therapy of depression*. New York: Guilford Press.

Beitman, B. D., Carlin, A. S., & Chiles, J. C. (1984). Pharmacotherapy-psychotherapy triangle: A physician, a non-medical psychotherapist, and a client. *Journal of Clinical Psychiatry, 45*, 458–459.

Benson, H. (1975). *The relaxation response*. New York: William Morrow.

Benson, H. (2000). *The relaxation response*. New York: Harper Paperbacks.

Berne, E. (1964). *Games people play: The psychology of human relationships*. New York: Grove.

Bettet, P. S., & Maloney, M. J. (1991). The importance of empathy as an interviewing skill in medicine. *Journal of the American Medical Association, 266*, 1831–1832.

Blakemore, J. E. O., Berenbaum, S. A., & Liben, L. S. (2009). *Gender development*. Clifton, NJ: Psychology Press.

Block, J. (1971). *Lives through time*. Berkeley, CA: Bancroft Books.

Blumenthal, S. J. (1990). An overview and synopsis of risk factors, assessment, and treatment of suicidal clients over the life cycle. In S. J. Blumenthal & D. I. Kupfer (Eds.), *Suicide over the life cycle: Risk factors, assessment, and treatment of suicidal clients*. Washington, DC: American Psychiatric Press.

Bradshaw, J. (1988). *Healing the shame that binds you*. Deerfield Beach, FL: Health Communications.

Bradshaw, J. (1990). *Homecoming: Reclaiming and championing your inner child*. New York: Bantam Books.

Braunwald, E., Isselbacher, K. T., Petersdorf, R. G., Wilson, J. D., Martin, J. B., & Fauci, A. S. (1987). *Harrison's principles of internal medicine*. New York: McGraw-Hill.

Brostoff, W. S. (1994). Clinical diagnosis. In N. S. Miller & M. C. Doot (Eds.), *Principles of addiction medicine* (sec. 4, chap. 1, pp. 1–4). Chevy Chase, MD: American Society of Addiction Medicine.

Brown, B. W., Monck, E. M., Carstairs, G. M., & Wing, J. K. (1962). Influence of family life on the course of schizophrenic illness. *British Journal of Preventative Social Medicine, 16*, 55–68.

Burant, D. (1990). Management of withdrawal. In A. Geller (Ed.), *Syllabus for the review course in addiction medicine*. New York: Signet.

Burling, T. A., Reilly, P. M., Molten, J. O., & Ziff, D. C. (1989). Self-efficacy and relapse among inpatient drug and alcohol abusers: A predictor of outcome. *Journal of Studies on Alcohol, 50*(4), 354–360.

Burns, D. D. (1999). *The feeling good handbook*. New York: Penguin.

Busto, U. E., Sykora, K., & Sellers, E. M. A. (1989). A clinical scale to assess benzodiazepine withdrawal. *Journal of Clinical Psychopharmacology, 9*, 412.

Cameron, J. L. (2004). Interrelationships between hormones, behavior, and affect during adolescence: Understanding hormonal, physical, and brain changes occurring in association with pubertal activation of the reproductive axis. Introduction to Part III. *Annals of the New York Academy of Sciences, 7027*, 110–123.

Caracci, L., Megone, P., & Dornbush, R. (1983). Phencyclidine in an East Harlem psychiatric population. *Journal of the National Medical Association, 75*, 869–874.

Carroll, M., & Comer, S. (1994). The pharmacology of phencyclidine and the hallucinogens. In N. S. Miller & M. C. Doot (Eds.), *Principles of addiction medicine* (sec. 2, chap. 7, p. 153). Chevy Chase, MD: American Society of Addiction Medicine.

Carroll, M., & Comer, S. (1998). Phencyclidine and the hallucinogens. In A. W. Graham, T. K. Schultz, & B. B. Wilford (Eds.), *Principles of addiction medicine* (sec. 2, chap. 7, pp. 1–9). Chevy Chase, MD: American Society of Addiction Medicine.

Centers for Disease Control. (1990). *HIV/AIDS surveillance report*. Atlanta, GA: Author.

Centers for Disease Control and Prevention. (2009). *Causes of death*. Atlanta, GA: Author.

Centers for Disease Control and Prevention. (2010). *Tobacco use: Targeting the nation's leading killer at-a-glance 2010*. Atlanta, GA: Author.

Chatlos, J. C., & Jaffe, S. L. (1994). A developmental biopsychosocial model of adolescent addiction. In N. S. Miller & M. C. Doot (Eds.), *Principles of addiction medicine* (sec. 17, chap. 1, pp. 1–5). Chevy Chase, MD: American Society of Addiction Medicine.

Chopra, G. S., & Smith, J. W. (1974). Psychotic reactions following cannabis use in East Indians. *Archives of General Psychiatry, 30*, 24–27.

Cloptin, P. L., Janowsky, D. S., Cloptin, J. M., Judd, L. L., & Huey, L. (1979). Marihuana and the perception of affect. *Psychopharmacology, 61*, 203–206.

Cohen, H. L., & Filipczak, J. A. (1971). *A new learning environment*. San Francisco: Jossey-Bass.

Cohen, S. (1979). Inhalants. In R. I. DuPont, A. Goldstein, & J. O'Donnell (Eds.), *Handbook on drug abuse* (pp. 213–220). Washington, DC: U.S. Government Printing Office.

Conigliaro, J., Reyes, C.D., Parran, T. V., & Schultz, J. E. (2003). Principles of screening and early intervention. In A. W. Graham, T. K. Schultz, M. F. Mayo-Smith, & R. K. Ries (Eds.), *Principles of addiction medicine* (3rd ed.). Chevy Chase, MD: American Society of Addiction Medicine, Inc.

Conte, H. R., Plutchik, R., Wild, K. V., & Karasu, T. B. (1986). Combined psychotherapy and pharmacotherapy for depression: A systematic analysis of the evidence. *Archives of General Psychiatry, 43*, 471–479.

Cook, R. F., Hostetter, R. S., & Ramsay, D. A. (1975). Patterns of illicit drug use in the army. *American Journal of Psychiatry, 132*, 1013–1017.

Courtwright, D. T. (2001). *Forces of habit: Drugs and the making of the modern world*. Cambridge, MA: Harvard University Press.

Craske, M. G., Antony, M. M., & Barlow, D. H. (2009). *Mastering your fears and phobias: Workbook*. New York: Oxford University Press.

Creager, C. (1989, July–August). SASSI test breaks through denial. *The Professional Counselor*, 65.

Csikszentmihalyi, M., & Larson, R. (1984). *Being adolescent*. New York: Basic Books.

Custer, R. L. (1984a). *Forward in sharing recovery through Gamblers Anonymous*. Los Angeles: Gamblers Anonymous Publishing.

Custer, R. L. (1984b). Profile of a pathological gambler. *Journal of Clinical Psychiatry, 45*(12, Pt. 2), 35–38, 998–1011.

Dahl, R. E. (2004). Adolescent brain development: A period of vulnerabilities and opportunities. *Annals of the New York Academy of Sciences, 1021*, 1–22.

Davidson, W. S., & Seidman, E. (1974). Studies of behavior modification and juvenile delinquency: A review, methodological critique, and social perspective. *Psychological Bulletin, 81*, 998–1011.

Davis, B. C. (1982). The PCP epidemic: A critical review. *International Journal of Addiction, 17*, 1137–1155.

Dickinson, W. E., & Eickelberg, S. J. (2009). Management of sedative-hypnotic intoxication and withdrawal. In R. K. Miller & S. C. Miller (Eds.), *Principles of addiction medicine* (sec. 6, chap. 43). Chevy Chase, MD: American Society of Addiction Medicine.

DiClemente, C. C. (2006a). *Addiction and change: How addictions develop and addicted people recover.* New York: Guilford Press.

DiClemente, C. C. (2006b). Natural change and the troublesome use of substances: A life-course perspective. In W. R. Miller & K. M. Carroll (Eds.), *Rethinking substance abuse: What the science shows, and what we should do about it.* New York: Guilford Press.

DiClemente, C. C., Carbonari, J. P., Montgomery, R. P. G., & Hughes, S. O. (1994). The Alcohol Abstinence Self-Efficacy Scale. *Journal of Studies on Alcohol, 55*, 141–148.

Dietch, J. (1983). The nature and extent of benzodiazepine abuse: An overview of recent literature. *Hospital and Community Psychiatry, 34*, 1139–1145.

Domino, E. F. (1978). Neurobiology of phencyclidine: An update. In R. C. Peterson & R. C. Stillman (Eds.), *PCP phencyclidine abuse: An appraisal* (Publ. No. [ADM] 17–728, pp. 18–43). Washington, DC: U.S. Government Printing Office.

Dorland's illustrated medical dictionary. (1965). Philadelphia: W. B. Saunders.

Dorus, W., Kennedy, J., Gibbons R. D., & Raci, S. D. (1987). Symptoms and diagnosis of depression in alcoholics. *Alcoholism, 11*, 150–154.

Douvan, E., & Adelson, J. (1966). *The adolescent experience.* New York: John Wiley.

DuPont, R. L. (1994). Laboratory diagnosis. In N. S. Miller & M. C. Doot (Eds.), *Principles of addiction medicine* (sec. 4, chap. 2, pp. 1–8). Chevy Chase, MD: American Society of Addiction Medicine.

Earley, P. H. (2009). Physician health programs and addiction among physicians. In R. K. Ries (Ed.), *Principles of addiction medicine, fourth edition.* Chevy Chase, MD: American Society of Addiction Medicine.

Ellis, A. (1962). *Reason and emotion in psychotherapy.* New York: Lyle-Stuart.

Emrick, C. D. (1987). Alcoholics Anonymous: Affiliation process and effectiveness as treatment. *Alcoholism, 11*, 416–423.

Evans, M. A., Marty, R., Brown, D. J., Rodda, B. E., Kippinger, G. F., Lemberger, L., & Forney, R. B. (1973). Impairment of performance with low doses of marijuana. *Clinical Pharmacological Therapy, 14*, 936–940.

Ewing, J. A. (1984). Detecting alcoholism: The CAGE questionnaire. *Journal of the American Medical Association, 252*, 1905–1907.

Eysenck, H. J., & Eysenck, S. B. J. (1976). *Personality structure and measurement.* London: Routledge & Kegan Paul.

Featherly, J. W., & Hill, E. B. (1989). *Crack cocaine overview, 1989.* Washington, DC: U.S. Department of Justice.

Fischman, M. W., Schuster, C. R., Rosnekov, L., Shick, J. F. E., Krasnegor, N. A., Fennell, W., & Freedman, D. X. (1976). Cardiovascular and subjective effects of intravenous cocaine administration in humans. *Archives of General Psychiatry, 33*, 983–989.

Florentine, R., & Hillhouse, M. P. (2000). Drug treatment and 12-step program participation. The effects of integrated recovery activities. *Journal of Substance Abuse Treatment, 18*, 64–74.

Folkins, C. H., & Sime, W. E. (1981). Physical fitness training and mental health. *American Psychologist, 36*, 373–389.

Folstein, M. F., Folstein, S. W., & McHugh, P. R. (1975). Mini-mental state: A practical method of grading the cognitive state of clients for the clinician. *Journal of Psychiatric Research, 12*, 189–198.

Frances, R. J., Bucky, S., & Alexopolos, G. S. (1984). Outcome study of familial and nonfamilial alcoholism. *American Journal of Psychiatry, 141*, 11.

Frances, R. J., & Franklin, J. E., Jr. (1988). Alcohol and other psychoactive substance use disorders. In J. A. Talbott, R. E. Hales, & S. C. Yudofsky (Eds.), *The American Psychiatric Press textbook of psychiatry*. Washington, DC: American Psychiatric Press.

Freedman, D. X. (1968). The use and abuse of LSD. *Archives of General Psychiatry, 18*, 300–347.

Freud, S. (2000). *The standard edition of the complete psychological works of Sigmund Freud*. New York: Norton.

Fultz, J. M., & Senay, E. C. (1975). Guidelines for the management of hospitalized narcotics addicts. *Annals of Internal Medicine, 82*, 815–818.

Gabel, R. H., Barnard, N., Norko, M., & O'Connell, R. A. (1986). AIDS presenting as mania. *Comparative Psychiatry, 27*, 251–254.

Gambert, S. R. (1992). Substance abuse in the elderly. In J. H. Lowinson, P. Ruiz, R. B. Millman, & J. G. Langrod (Eds.), *Substance abuse: A comprehensive textbook* (2nd ed.). Baltimore: Williams & Wilkins.

Gamblers Anonymous. (1989a). *The combo book*. Los Angeles: G.A. Publishing.

Gamblers Anonymous. (1989b). *G.A.: A new beginning*. Los Angeles: G.A. Publishing.

Gary, V., & Guthrie, D. (1972). The effect of jogging on physical fitness and self-concept in hospitalized alcoholics. *Quarterly Journal of Studies on Alcohol, 33*, 1073–1078.

Gawin, F. H., & Ellinwood, E. H. (1988). Cocaine and other stimulants: Actions, abuse, and treatments. *New England Journal of Medicine, 318*, 1173–1182.

Gawin, F. H., & Kleber, H. S. (1986a). Abstinence symptomatology and psychiatric diagnosis in cocaine abusers. *Archives of General Psychiatry, 43*, 107–113.

Gawin, F. H., & Kleber, H. S. (1986b). Pharmacologic treatments of cocaine abuse and substance abuse. *Psychiatry in Clinics of North America, 9*, 573–583.

Geller, A. (1990). Protracted abstinence. In A. Geller (Ed.), *Syllabus of the review course in addiction medicine*. Washington, DC: American Society of Addiction Medicine.

Geller, A. (1994). Management of protracted withdrawal. In N. S. Miller & M. C. Doot (Eds.), *Principles of addiction medicine* (sec. 11, chap. 2, pp. 1–6). Chevy Chase, MD: American Society of Addiction Medicine.

Gerstein, D. R., & Harwood, H. J. (Eds.). (1990). *Treating drug problems*. Washington, DC: National Academy Press.

Gessner, P. K. (1979). Drug withdrawal therapy of the alcohol withdrawal syndrome. In E. Majchowicz & E. Moble (Eds.), *Biochemistry and pharmacology of ethanol* (Vol. 2). New York: Plenum.

Gilman, A. G., Goodman, L. S., & Gilman, A. (1980). *Goodman and Gilman's the pharmacological basis of therapeutics*. New York: Macmillan.

Glynn, T. J. (1990). Methods of smoking cessation: Finally some answers. *Journal of the American Medical Association, 263*, 2795–2796.

Gold, M. S. (1994a). Marijuana. In N. S. Miller & M. C. Doot (Eds.), *Principles of addiction medicine* (sec. 2, chap. 8, pp. 1–6). Chevy Chase, MD: American Society of Addiction Medicine.

Gold, M. S. (1994b). Opioids. In N. S. Miller & M. C. Doot (Eds.), *Principles of addiction medicine* (sec. 2, chap. 4, pp. 1–6). Chevy Chase, MD: American Society of Addiction Medicine.

Goldman, A. R. (1989). *Accreditation and certification: For providers of psychiatric, alcoholism, and drug abuse services*. Bala Cynwyd, PA: Practical Communications.

Goodwin, D. W. (1971). Blackouts and alcohol induced memory dysfunction. In N. K. Mello & J. H. Mendelson (Eds.), *Recent advances in studies in alcohol*. Rockville, MD: National Institute on Mental Health.

Goodwin, D. W. (1985). Alcoholism and genetics. *Archives of General Psychiatry*, *42*, 171–174.

Goodwin, D. W., Crane, J. B., & Guze, S. B. (1969). Alcoholic blackouts: A review and clinical study of 100 alcoholics. *American Journal of Psychiatry*, *126*, 174–177.

Gorski, T. T. (1989). *Passages through recovery*. Center City, MN: Hazelden.

Gorski, T., & Miller, M. (1982). *Counseling for relapse prevention*. Independence, MO: Independence Press.

Gottschalk, L. A., McGuire, F. L., Heiser, J. F., Dinovo, E. C., & Birch, H. (1979). *Drug abuse deaths in nine cities: A survey report* (Research Monograph No. 29). Rockville, MD: National Institute on Drug Abuse.

Gould, L. C., & Keeber, H. D. (1974). Changing patterns of multiple drug use among applicants to a multimodality drug treatment program. *Archives of General Psychiatry*, *31*, 408–413.

Graziano, A. M., & Mooney, K. C. (1984). *Children and behavior therapy*. New York: Aldine.

Greenberg, R. L., & Beck, A. T. (1987). *Panic attacks: How to cope, how to recover*. Philadelphia: Center for Cognitive Therapy.

Greenfield, S., Hufford, M., Vagge, L., Muenz, L., Costello, M., & Weiss, R. (2000). The relationship of self-efficacy expectations to relapse among alcohol dependent men and women: A prospective study. *Journal of Studies on Alcohol*, *61*, 345–351.

Greist, J. H., Klein, M. H., Eischins, R. R., Faris, J., Gurman, A. S., & Morgan, W. P. (1979). Running as treatment for depression. *Comprehensive Psychiatry*, *20*, 41–54.

Griffith, J. D., Cavanaugh, J., Held, J., & Oates, J. A. (1972). Dextroamphetamine. *Archives of General Psychiatry*, *26*, 97–100.

Group for the Advancement of Psychiatry Committee on Alcoholism and the Addictions. (1991). Substance abuse disorders: A psychiatric priority. *American Journal of Psychiatry*, *148*, 1291–1300.

Gunderson, J. G., & Zanarine, M. C. (1987). Current overview of the borderline diagnosis. *Journal of Clinical Psychiatry*, *48*(Suppl. 8), 5–11.

Hamilton, M. (1959). The assessment of anxiety states by rating. *British Journal of Medical Psychology*, *32*, 50–55.

Hamilton, M. (1960). A rating scale for depression. *J Neurol Neurosurg Psychiatry*, *23*, 56–62. Retrieved from http://ajp .psychiatryonline.org/cgi/external_ref?access_num=14399272&link_type=MED

Hardman, J., Limbird, L. E., Molinoff, P. B., Ruddon, R. W., & Gilman, A. G. (1996). *Goodman and Gilman's the pharmacological basis of therapeutics* (9th ed.). New York: McGraw-Hill.

Harris, M. J., Jeste, D. V., Gleghorn, A., & Sewell, D. D. (1991). New-onset psychosis in HIV-infected clients. *Journal of Clinical Psychiatry*, *52*, 369–376.

Havens, L. (1978). Explorations in the use of language in psychotherapy: Simple empathetic statements. *Psychiatry*, *41*, 336–345.

Henningfield, J. E. (1984). Pharmacologic basis and treatment of cigarette smoking. *Journal of Clinical Psychiatry*, *45*, 24–34.

Herbert, M. (1982). Conduct disorder. In A. E. Kazdin & B. B. Lahey (Eds.), *Advances in clinical and child psychology* (Vol. 5). New York: Plenum.

Heron, M., Hoyert, D. L., Murphy, S. L., Xu, J., Kochanek, K., & Tejada-Vera, B. (2009, April 17). Deaths: Final data for 2006. *National Vital Statistics Reports*, *57*(14), 11. Retrieved from www.cdc.gov/nchs/data/nvsr/nvsr57/nvsr57_14.pdf

Hesselbrock, M. N., Meyer, R. E., & Kenner, J. J. (1985). Psychopathology in hospitalized alcoholics. *Archives of General Psychiatry*, *46*, 3–5.

Hingson, R. W., Heeren, T., & Winter, M. R. (2006). Age at drinking onset and alcohol dependence: Age at onset, duration, and severity. *Archives of Pediatric and Adolescent Medicine*, *160*, 739–746.

Hirschfeld, R. M. A., & Goodwin, F. K. (1988). Mood disorders. In J. A. Talbott, R. E. Hales, & S. C. Yudofsky (Eds.), *The American Psychiatric Press textbook of psychiatry*. Washington, DC: American Psychiatric Press.

Hoffmann, N. G. (1991, June). *Treatment outcomes from abstinence based programs*. Paper presented at the meeting of the International Institute on the Prevention and Treatment of Alcoholism, Stockholm, Sweden.

Hoffmann, N. G. (1994). Assessing treatment effectiveness. In N. S. Miller & M. C. Doot (Eds.), *Principles of addiction medicine* (sec. 9, chap. 5, pp. 1–9). Chevy Chase, MD: American Society of Addiction Medicine.

Hoffmann, N., & Harrison, P. (1987). *A 2-year follow-up of inpatient treatment*. St. Paul, MN: Chemical Abuse Treatment Outcome Registry.

Hollister, L. E. (1974). Interactions in man of delta-9-tetrahydrocannabinol. I: Alphamethylparatyrosine. *Clinical Pharmacological Therapy, 15*, 18–21.

Hollister, L. E. (1986). Health aspects of cannabis. *Pharmacology Review, 38*, 1–20.

Hubbard, R. L. (1992). Evaluation and treatment outcome. In J. H. Lorvinson, P. Ruiz, R. B. Millman, & J. G. Langrod (Eds.), *Substance abuse: A comprehensive textbook*. Baltimore: Williams & Wilkins.

Hubbard, R. L., & Anderson, J. A. (1988). *Follow-up study of individuals receiving alcoholism treatment*. Research Triangle Park, NC: Research Triangle Institute.

Hubbard, R. L., & DesJarlais, D. C. (1991). Alcohol and drug abuse. In E. E. Holland, R. Petels, & G. Knox (Eds.), *Oxford textbook of public health* (Vol. 3, 2nd ed.). London: Oxford University Press.

Hubbard, R. L., Marsden, M. E., Rachel, J. V., Harwood, H. J., Cavanaugh, E. R., & Ginzburg, H. M. (1989). *Drug abuse treatment: A national study of effectiveness*. Chapel Hill: University of North Carolina Press.

Hughes, J. R., & Hatsukami, D. (1986). Signs and symptoms of tobacco withdrawal. *Archives of General Psychiatry, 43*, 289–294.

Hunt, W. A., Barnett, L. W., & Branch, L. G. (1971). Relapse rates in addiction programs. *Journal of Clinical Psychology, 27*, 455–456.

Inaba, D., & Cohen, W. E. (2007). *Uppers, downers, all arounders*. Monterey, CA: CNS Publications.

Institute of Medicine. (1989). *Research effectiveness in the prevention and treatment of alcohol related problems*. Washington, DC: National Academy Press.

Institute of Medicine. (1995). *Federal regulation of methadone treatment*. Washington, DC: National Academy Press.

Institute of Medicine, Committee for the Study and Treatment and Rehabilitation Services for Alcoholism and Alcohol Abuse. (1990). *Broadening the base of treatment for alcohol problems*. Washington, DC: National Academy of Science.

Jacobs, J. W., Bernhard, M. R., Delgado, A., & Strain, J. J. (1977). Screening for organic mental syndromes in the medically ill. *Annals of Internal Medicine, 86*, 40–46.

Jaffe, J. H. (1980). Drug addiction and drug abuse. In A. G. Gilman, L. S. Goodman, & A. Gilman (Eds.), *Goodman and Gilman's the pharmacological basis of therapeutics*. New York: Macmillan.

Jay, D. (2006). *No more letting go: The spirituality of taking action against alcoholism and drug addiction*. New York: Bantam.

Johnston, L. D., O'Malley, P. M., Bachman, J. G., & Schulenberg, J. E. (2008). Monitoring the future: National results on adolescent drug use, National Institute on Drug Abuse. Bethesda, MD: U.S. Department of Health and Human Services.

Joint Commission on Accreditation of Healthcare Organizations. (1988). *Consolidated standards manual*. Chicago: Author.

Joint Commission on Accreditation of Healthcare Organizations. (1992). *Client records in addiction treatment: Documenting the quality of care*. Oakbrook Terrace, IL: Author.

Jones, R. T. (1971). Marijuana-induced "high": Influence of expectation, setting, and previous drug experience. *Pharmacological Review, 23*, 359–369.

Jones, R. T., Bennowitz, N., & Bachman, J. (1976). Clinical studies of cannabis tolerance and dependence. *Annals of the New York Academy of Science, 282*, 221–239.

Juergens, S. M. (1994). Sedative-hypnotics. In N. S. Miller & M. C. Doot (Eds.), *Principles of addiction medicine* (sec. 2, chap. 3, pp. 1–10). Chevy Chase, MD: American Society of Addiction Medicine.

Kagan, J. (1989). Temperament contribution to social behavior. *American Journal of Psychology, 44*, 668–674.

Kagan, J., Reznick, J. S., & Gibbons, J. (1989). Inhibited and uninhibited types of children. *Child Development, 60*, 838–845.

Kagan, J., Reznick, J. S., & Snidman, N. (1987). The physiology and psychology of behavioral inhibition in children. *Child Development, 58*, 1459–1473.

Kalant, H., Engel, J. A., Goldberg, L., Griffiths, R. R., Jaffe, J. H., Krasnegor, N. A., Mello, N. K., Mendelson, J. H., Thompson, T., & Van Ree, J. M. (1978). Behavioral aspects of addiction: Group report. In J. Fishman (Ed.), *The basis of addiction: Report of the Dahlem workshop on the basis of addiction* (pp. 463–495). Berlin: Abakon Verlagsgesellschaft.

Kaminer, Y., Bukstein, O. G., & Tarter, R. E. (1991). The teen addiction severity index: Rationale and reliability. *International Journal of Addiction, 26*, 219–226.

Kandel, D. (1978). Antecedents of adolescent initiation into stages of drug use. In D. Kandel (Ed.), *Longitudinal research on drug use*. Washington, DC: Hemisphere.

Karasu, T. B. (Chair). (1989). *Treatments of psychiatric disorders*. Washington, DC: American Psychiatric Press.

Kasser, C. L., Geller, A., Howell, E., & Wartenberg, A. (1998). Principles of detoxification. In A. W. Graham, T. K. Schultz, & B. B. Wilford (Eds.), *Principles of addiction medicine* (2nd ed., sec. 6, chap. 7, p. 423). Chevy Chase, MD: American Society of Addiction Medicine.

Kazdin, A. E., & Weisz, J. R. (2003). *Evidence-based psychotherapies for children and adolescents*. New York: Guilford Press.

Khantzian, E. J., & Treece, C. (1985). *DSM-III* psychiatric diagnosis of narcotics addicts: Recent findings. *Archives of General Psychiatry, 42*, 1067–1071.

King, G. S., Smialick, J. E., & Troutman, W. G. (1985). Sudden death in adolescents resulting from the inhalation of typewriter correction fluid. *Journal of the American Medical Association, 253*, 1604–1609.

Klein, D. F., Gittelman, R., Quitkin, F., & Rifkin, A. (1980). *Diagnosis and drug treatment of psychiatric disorders: Adults and children*. Baltimore: Williams & Wilkins.

Klerman, G. L., Weissman, M. M., Rounsaville, B. J., & Chevron, E. S. (1984). *Interpersonal psychotherapy of depression*. New York: Basic Books.

Kosten, T. R., Rounsaville, B. J., & Kleber, H. D. (1985). Comparison of clinical ratings to self-reports of withdrawal during clonidine detoxification of opiate addicts. *American Journal of Drug and Alcohol Abuse, 11*, 1–10.

Kranzler, H. R., Ciraulo, D. A., & Jaffe, J. H. (2009). Medications for use in alcohol rehabilitation. In R. K. Miller & S. C. Miller (Eds.), *Principles of addiction medicine* (sec. 7, chap. 46). Chevy Chase, MD: American Society of Addiction Medicine.

Larson, R. W., Brown, B. B., & Mortimer, J. T. (Eds.). (2003). *Adolescents' preparation for the future: Perils and promise: A report of the study group on adolescence in the 21st century*. New York: Wiley.

Leaper, C., & Friedman, C. K. (2007). The socialization of gender. In J. E. Grusec & P. D. Hastings (Eds.), *Handbook of socialization*. New York: Guilford Press.

Ledwidge, B. (1980). Run for your mind: Aerobic exercise as a means of alleviating anxiety and depression. *Canadian Journal of Behavioral Science, 12*, 127–140.

Lerner, R. M., & Steinberg, L. (2009). *Handbook of adolescent psychology* (2-vol set). New York: Wiley.

Leshner, A. L. (1997). Addiction is a brain disease, and it matters. *Science, 278*, 45–47.

Leshner, A. L. (1998, May–June). Research advances in treating heroin addiction. *The Counselor*, p. 8.

Lesieur, H. R., & Blume, S. D. (1987). The South Oaks Gambling Screen (SOGS): A new instrument for the identification of pathological gamblers. *American Journal of Psychiatry, 144*, 1184–1188.

Linehan, M. M. (1993). *Skills training manual for treating borderline personality disorder*. New York: Guilford Press.

Littleton, J. (1995). Acamprosate in alcohol dependence: How does it work? *Addiction, 90*, 1179–1188.

Littleton, J. (1996). The neurobiology of craving: Potential mechanisms for acamprosate. In M. Soyka (Ed.), *Acamprosate in relapse prevention of alcoholism* (pp. 27–46). Berlin: Springer-Verlag.

Lowinson, J. H., Marion, I. J., Herman, J., & Dole, V. P. (1992). Methadone maintenance. In J. Lowinson, P. Ruiz, R. B. Millman, & J. G. Langrod (Eds.), *Substance abuse: A comprehensive textbook*. Baltimore: Williams & Wilkins.

Manthey, M. (1991). Commitment to my co-workers. In S. Cox & D. Miller (Eds.), *Leaders empower staff*. Minneapolis, MN: Creative Management.

Marlatt, A. G., & Donovan, D. M. (2008). *Relapse prevention: Maintenance strategies in the treatment of addictive behaviors*. New York: Guilford Press.

Marlatt, A. G., & Gordon, J. R. (1985). *Relapse prevention*. New York: Guilford Press.

Masterson, J. F., Jr., & Costello, J. (1980). *From borderline adolescent to functioning adult: The test of time*. New York: Brunner/Mazel.

Mayer, J., & Filstead, W. J. (1979). The Adolescent Alcohol Involvement Scale: An instrument for measuring adolescents' use and misuse of alcohol. *Journal of Studies on Alcohol, 40*, 291–300.

Mayo-Smith, M. (2009). Management of alcohol intoxication and withdrawal. In R. K. Ries & S. C. Miller (Eds.), *Principles of addiction medicine* (4th ed., sec. 5, chap. 42, pp. 431–440). Chevy Chase, MD: American Society of Addiction Medicine.

McCauley, K. (2009). *Pleasure unwoven* [DVD]. Salt Lake City, UT: The Institute for Addiction Study.

McKay, J. R. (2005). Is there a case for extended interventions for alcohol and drug disorders. *Addiction, 100*, 1594–1610.

McKay, M., Rogers, P. D., & McKay, J. (1989). *When anger hurts: Quieting the storm within*. Oakland, CA: New Harbinger.

McLellan, A. T. (2006). What we need is a system: Creating a responsive and effective substance abuse treatment system. In W. R. Miller & K. M. Carroll (Eds.), *Rethinking substance abuse: What the science shows and what we should do about it*. New York: Guilford Press.

McLellan, A. T. (2010). On science and service: An interview with Tom McLellan, Ph.D., Deputy Director White House Office of National Drug Control Policy by Bill White. *Counselor: The Magazine for Addiction Professionals, 10*(4), 24–35.

McLellan, A. T., Luborsky, L., & Woody, G. E. (1980). An improved diagnostic evaluation instrument for substance abuse clients: The Addiction Severity Index. *Journal of Nervous and Mental Disease, 168*, 26–33.

Mee-Lee, D. (1985). The Recovery Attitude and Treatment Evaluator (RAATE): An instrument for client progress and treatment assignment. *Proceedings of the 34th International Congress on Alcoholism and Drug Dependence* (pp. 424–426).

Mee-Lee, D. (1988). An instrument for treatment progress and matching: The Recovery Attitude and Treatment Evaluator (RAATE). *Journal of Substance Abuse Treatment, 5*, 183–186.

Mee-Lee, D. (Ed.). (2001). *ASAM PPC-2R ASAM client placement criteria for the treatment of substance-related disorders, second edition revised*. Chevy Chase, MD: American Society of Addiction Medicine.

Mee-Lee, D., Hoffmann, N. G., & Smith, M. B. (1992). *The recovery attitude and treatment evaluator manual*. St. Paul, MN: New Standards, Inc.

Melges, F. T., Tinklenberg, J. R., Hollister, L. E., & Gillespie, H. K. (1970). Temporal disintegration and depersonalization during marijuana intoxication. *Archives of General Psychiatry, 23*, 204–210.

Mid-America Addiction Technology Transfer Center. (2008). *Psychotherapeutic medications 2008: What every counselor should know* (7th ed.). Kansas City, MO: Author. Retrieved from www.narha.org/images/pdf/resources/PsychotherapeuticMedications2008.pdf

Miller, G. A. (1985). *The Substance Abuse Subtle Screening Inventory manual*. Bloomington, IN: SASSI Institute.

Millon, T. (1981). *Disorders of personality: DSM-III Axis II*. New York: John Wiley.

MMWR. (2006, June 9). *Youth risk behavior surveillance—United States, 2005* (Vol. 255). Atlanta: Centers for Disease Control and Prevention.

Monti, P. M., Kadden, R. M., Rohsenow, D. J., Cooney, N. L., & Abrams, D. B. (2002). *Treating alcohol dependence: A coping skills training guide* (2nd ed.). New York: Guilford Press.

Morrison, M. A., & Smith, Q. T. (1990). Psychiatric issues of adolescent chemical dependence. In A. Geller (Ed.), *Syllabus for the review course in addiction medicine*. Washington, DC: American Society of Addiction Medicine.

Morse, R. M. (1994). Elderly clients. In N. S. Miller & M. C. Doot (Eds.), *Principles of addiction medicine* (sec. 18, chap. 2, pp. 1–6). Chevy Chase, MD: American Society of Addiction Medicine.

Mueser, K. T., Drake, R. E., Turner, W., & McGovern, M. (2006). Comorbid substance use disorders and psychiatric disorders. In W. R Miller & K. M. Carroll (Eds.), *Rethinking substance abuse: What the science shows, and what we should do about it*. New York: Guilford Press.

Naditch, M. P., & Fenwick, S. (1977). LSD flashbacks and ego functioning. *Journal of Abnormal Psychiatry, 86*, 352–359.

Nahas, G. G. (1973). *Marihuana: Deceptive weed*. New York: Raven.

Narcotics Anonymous. (1988). *Narcotics Anonymous*. Van Nuys, CA: Narcotics Anonymous World Service Office.

Nathan, P. E., & Gorman, J. M. (2007). A guide to treatments that work (3rd ed.). New York: Oxford University Press.

National Institute on Drug Abuse. (2005, May). *Heroin abuse and addiction* (Rev. ed.). Bethesda, MD: Author.

National Sleep Foundation. (2006). *2006 Sleep in America Poll*. Washington, DC: Arthor.

National Vital Statistics Reports. (2008, June 11). Table 7. Deaths and death rates for the 10 leading causes of death in specified age groups. United States, preliminary 2006. *National Vital Statistics Reports, 56* (No. 16), 30.

Nestler, E. J. (1998). Neuroadaptation in addiction. In A. W. Graham, T. K. Schultz, & B. B. Wilford (Eds.), *Principles of addiction medicine* (2nd ed., sec. 1, chap. 5, pp. 57–71). Chevy Chase, MD: American Society of Addiction Medicine.

Nunes, E. V., & Weiss, R. D. (2009). Co-occuring addiction and affective disorders. In R. K. Miller & S. C. Miller (Eds.), *Principles of addiction medicine* (sec. 11, chap. 84). Chevy Chase, MD: American Society of Addiction Medicine.

Offer, D. (1986). Adolescent development: A normative perspective. In *American Psychiatric Association annual review* (Vol. 5). Washington, DC: American Psychiatric Press.

Offer, D., & Offer, J. B. (1975). *From teenage to young manhood: A psychological study*. New York: Basic Books.

Offer, D., Ostrov, E., & Howard, K. I. (1981). *The adolescent: A psychological self-portrait*. New York: Basic Books.

Ollendick, T. H., & Cerny, J. A. (1981). *Clinical behavior therapy with children*. New York: Plenum.

O'Malley, S. S., Jaffe, A. J., Chang, G., Schottenfeld, R. S., Meyer, R. E., & Rounsaville, B. (1992). Naltrexone and coping skills therapy for alcohol dependence: A controlled study. *Archives of General Psychiatry, 49*, 881–887.

Patterson, G. R. (1977). *Families: Applications of social learning to family life* (Rev. ed.). Champaign, IL: Research Press.

Patterson, G. R., & Gullion, M. E. (1976). *Living with children: New methods for parents and teachers* (Rev. ed.). Champaign, IL: Research Press.

Perkinson, R. R. (2000). *God talks to you*. Bloomington, IN: 1st Books Library.

Perkinson, R. R. (2003a). *Chemical dependency counseling: A practical guide* (2nd ed.). Thousand Oaks, CA: Sage.

Perkinson, R. R. (2003b). *The gambling addiction patient workbook*. Thousand Oaks, CA: Sage.

Perkinson, R. R. (2003c). *The alcoholism and drug abuse patient workbook*. Thousand Oaks, CA: Sage.

Perkinson, R. R. (2004). *Treating alcoholism: How to help your clients enter recovery*. New York: John Wiley.

Perkinson, R. R. (2008). *A communication from God* [CD]. cdbaby

Perkinson, R. R. (2011). *The alcoholism and drug abuse client workbook*. Thousand Oaks, CA: Sage.

Perkinson, R. R., & Jongsma, A. E. (2006). *The chemical dependence treatment planner with disk*. New York: John Wiley.

Perkinson, R. R., & Jongsma, A. (2009). *The addiction treatment planner* (4th ed.). New York: John Wiley.

Perkinson, R. R., & LaCour, J. (2004). *Faith-based addiction curriculum*. Orlando, FL: The Net Institute.

Perry, S. W., & Jacobsen, P. (1986). Neuropsychiatric manifestations of AIDS-spectrum disorders. *Hospital and Community Psychiatry, 37*, 135–142.

Phillips, E. L. (1968). Achievement place: Token reinforcement procedures in a home-style rehabilitation setting for "predelinquent" boys. *Journal of Applied Behavior Analysis, 1*, 213–223.

Pierce, J. P., Fiore, M. C., Novotny, T. E., Hatziandreu, E. J., & Davis, T. (1989). Trends in cigarette smoking in the United States: Projections to the year 2000. *Journal of the American Medical Association, 261*, 61–65.

Plutchik, R. (1980). *Emotion: A psychoevolutionary synthesis*. New York: Harper & Row.

Post, R. M., Kotin, J., & Goodwin, F. K. (1974). The effects of cocaine in depressed clients. *American Journal of Psychiatry, 131*, 511–517.

Prochaska, J. O. (2003). Enhancing motivation to change. In A.W. Graham, T. K. Schultz, M. F. Mayo-Smith, & R. K. Ries (Eds.), *Principles of addiction medicine* (3rd ed.). Chevy Chase, MD: American Society of Addiction Medicine, Inc.

Prochaska, J. O., & DiClemente, C. C. (1983). Stages and processes of self-change of smoking: Toward an integrative model of change. *Journal of Consulting and Clinical Psychology, 51*, 390–395.

Prochaska, J. O., & DiClemente, C. C. (1984). *The transtheoretical approach: Crossing the traditional boundaries of therapy*. Malabar, FL: Krieger.

Prochaska, J. O., DiClemente, C. C., & Norcross, J. C. (1992). In search of how people change: Applications to the addictive behaviors. *American Psychologist, 47*, 1102–1114.

Prochaska, J. O., Norcross, J. C., & DiClemente, C. C. (1994). *Changing for good*. New York: William Morrow.

Reifler, B., Raskind, M., & Kethley, A. (1982). Psychiatric diagnosis among geriatric clients seen in an outreach program. *Journal of the American Geriatrics Society, 30*, 530–533.

Richels, K., Case, W. G., Downing, R. W., & Winokur, A. (1983). Long-term diazepam therapy and clinical outcome. *Journal of the American Medical Association, 12*, 767–771.

Ries, R. K., & Miller, S. C. (Eds.). (2009). *Principles of addiction medicine* (sec. 1, chap. 1). Chevy Chase, MD: American Society of Addiction Medicine.

Rosenbaum, J. F., Biederman, J., Hirshfeld, D. R., Bolduc, E. A., & Chaloff, J. (1991). Behavioral inhibition in children: A possible precursor to panic disorder or social phobia. *Journal of Clinical Psychiatry, 52*(11, Suppl.), 5–9.

Sanders, M. R., & Glynn, T. (1981). Training parents in behavioral self-management: An analysis of generalization and maintenance. *Journal of Applied Behavior Analysis, 14*, 223–237.

Santrock, J. W. (2010). *Adolescence: Thirteenth edition*. New York: McGraw-Hill.

Schore, A. N. (2003). *Affect dysregulation and disorders of the self*. New York: Norton.

Schuckit, M. A. (1984). *Drug and alcohol abuse: A clinical guide to diagnosis and treatment*. New York: Plenum.

Schuckit, M. A. (1994). Dual diagnosis: Psychiatric pictures among substance abusers. In N. S. Miller & M. C. Doot (Eds.), *Principles of addiction medicine* (sec. 6, chap. 1, pp. 1–4). Chevy Chase, MD: American Society of Addiction Medicine.

Secretary of Health, Education, and Welfare. (1977). *Marihuana and health: Seventh annual report to the U.S. Congress*. Washington, DC: U.S. Government Printing Office.

Sells, S. (2001). *Parenting your out-of-control teenager: 7 steps to reestablish authority and reclaim love*. New York: St. Martin's Griffin.

Selye, H. (1956). *The stress of life*. New York: McGraw-Hill.

Selzer, M., Winokur, A., & van Rooijen, C. (1975). A self-administered Short Michigan Alcoholism Screening Test. *Journal of Studies on Alcohol, 36*, 117–126.

Shaffer, H. J., & LaPlante, D. A. (2008). Treatment of gambling disorders. In A. G. Marlatt & D. M. Donovan (Eds.), *Relapse prevention: Maintenance strategies in the treatment of addictive behaviors*. New York: Guilford Press.

Sharp, C. W., & Brehm, M. L. (Eds.). (1977). *Review of inhalants: Euphoria to dysfunction* (Publ. No. [ADM] 77–553). Washington, DC: U.S. Government Printing Office.

Sharp, C. W., & Carroll, L. T. (Eds.). (1978). *Voluntary inhalation of industrial solvents* (Publ. No. [ADM] 79–779). Washington, DC: U.S. Government Printing Office.

Short Michigan Alcoholism Screening Test. (1975). *Journal Studies of Alcohol, 36,* 117–126.

Siever, L. J., & Davis, K. L. (1991). A psychobiological perspective on the personality disorders. *American Journal of Psychiatry, 148,* 1647–1658.

Siever, L. J., Llar, H., & Coccaro, E. (1985). Psychobiology substrates of personality. In *Biological response styles: Clinical implications.* Washington, DC: American Psychiatric Press.

Simmons, R. G., & Blyth, D. A. (1987). *Moving into adolescence.* Hawthorne, NY: Aldine.

Skipper, G. E. (1997). Treating the chemically dependent health professional. *Journal of Addictive Disorders, 16*(3), 67–73.

Skipper, G. E., & Dupont, R. L. (2010). Physician health programs: A model of successful treatment of addictions. *Counselor: The Magazine for Addiction Professionals, 11*(6).

Smith, C. M. (1977). The pharmacology of sedative/hypnotics, alcohol, and anesthetics: Sites and mechanisms of action. In W. R. Martin (Ed.), *Drug addiction: I. Morphine, sedative/hypnotics, and alcohol dependence.* Berlin: Springer-Verlag.

Soujanen, W. W. (1983). Addiction and the minds of adolescents. In R. C. Bersinger & W. W. Suojanen (Eds.), *Management and the brain: An integrative approach to organization behavior* (pp. 77–92). Atlanta: Georgia State University Press.

Spalt, L. (1979). Evidence of an X-linked recessive genetic characteristic in alcoholism. *Journal of the American Medical Association, 241,* 2543–2544.

Spelberger, C. D. (1983). *Manual for the State-Trait Anxiety Inventory.* Palo Alto, CA: Consulting Psychologists Press.

Spitzer, R. L. (1987). *Diagnostic and statistical manual of mental disorders* (3rd ed., Rev. ed.). Washington, DC: American Psychiatric Press.

Spon, A.R. (1999). *Blueprint for change: Corrective thinking facilitator's guide.* Roscoe, IL: Truthought, LLC.

Stern, M. J., & Cleary, P. (1981). National Exercise and Heart Disease Project: Psychosocial changes observed during a low-level exercise program. *Archives of Internal Medicine, 141,* 1463–1467.

Stimmel, B., Goldberg, J., Rotkopf, E., & Cohen, M. (1977). Ability to remain abstinent after methadone detoxification: A six year study. *Journal of the American Medical Association, 237,* 1216–1220.

Stuart, R. B. (1971). Behavioral contracting within the families of delinquents. *Journal of Behavior Therapy and Experimental Psychology, 2,* 1–11.

Stulis, C. A. (2009). HIV, TB and other infectious diseases related to alcohol and other drug use. In R. K. Ries & S. C. Miller (Eds.), *Principles of addiction medicine* (sec. 10, chap. 77). Chevy Chase, MD: American Society of Addiction Medicine.

Substance Abuse and Mental Health Services Administration. (2006). *Addiction counseling competencies: The knowledge, skills, and attitudes of professional practice.* Retrieved from www.samhas.gov

Substance Abuse and Mental Health Services Administration. (2007). *Results from the 2007 National Survey on Drug Use and Health: National findings.* Retrieved from www.oas.samhsa.gov

Substance Abuse and Mental Health Services Administration. (2009a). *Results from the 2008 National Survey on Drug Use and Health: National findings* (Office of Applied Studies, NSDUH Series H-36, HHS Publication No. SMA 09-4434). Rockville, MD.

Substance Abuse and Mental Health Services Administration. (2009b). The role of biomarkers in the treatment of alcohol use disorders. *Substance Abuse Treatment Advisory, 5*(4) 1–8.

Sue, D. W., & Sue, D. (1999). *Counseling the culturally different: Theory and practice* (3rd ed.). New York: John Wiley.

Talbott, J. A., Hales, R. E., & Yudofsky, S. C. (Eds.). (1988). *American Psychiatric Press textbook of psychiatry*. Washington, DC: American Psychiatric Press.

Tarasoff v. Regents of the University of California, 551 P.2d, 334 at 340 (1976).

Tarokh, L., & Carskadon, M. A. (2008). Sleep in adolescents. In L. R. Squire (Ed.), *New encyclopedia of neuroscience*. Oxford, UK: Elsevier.

Tasker, F.L., & Golombok, S. (1997). *Growing up in a lesbian family: Effects on child development*. New York: Guilford Press.

Tennant, F. S., Jr., & Grossbeck, C. J. (1972). Psychiatric effects of hashish. *Archives of General Psychiatry, 27*, 133–136.

Tetrault, J. M., & O'Connor, P. G. (2009). In R. K. Miller & S. C. Miller (Eds.), *Principles of addiction medicine* (sec. 6, chap. 44). Chevy Chase, MD: American Society of Addiction Medicine.

Thacore, V. R., & Shukla, R. S. P. (1976). Cannabis psychosis and paranoid schizophrenia. *Archives of General Psychiatry, 33*, 383–386.

Thompson, T., & Pickens, R. (1970). Stimulant self-administration by animals: Some comparisons with opiate self-administration. *Federal Processes, 29*, 6–12.

Turner, C. E. (1980). Chemistry and metabolism. In R. L. Peterson (Ed.), *Marijuana research findings* (Research Monograph No. 13, Publ. No. [ADM] AD-1001). Rockville, MD: National Institute on Drug Abuse.

Uhl, G. R., & Grow, R.W. (2004). The burden of complex genetics in brain disorders. *Archives of General Psychiatry, 61*, 223–229.

U.S. Department of Health and Human Services. (1999). *National Household Survey on Drug Abuse 1999*. Washington, DC: Department of Health and Human Services, Substance Abuse and Mental Health Services Administration.

U.S. Department of Health and Human Services. (2009). *National Household Survey on Drug Abuse 2009*. Washington, DC: Department of Health and Human Services, Substance Abuse and Mental Health Services Administration.

U.S. Department of Justice. (1983). *Let us all work to fight drug abuse*. Washington, DC: Author.

U.S. Department of Labor. (1994). *America in jeopardy: The young employee and drugs in the workplace*. Washington, DC: U.S. Department of Labor, Office of the Assistant Secretary for Policy.

U.S. Surgeon General. (1979). *Smoking and health* (Publ. No. [PHS] 79–50066). Washington, DC: U.S. Government Printing Office.

U.S. surgeon general releases advisory on alcohol use in pregnancy. (2005, February 21). *U.S. Department of Health & Human Services, Office of the Surgeon General*. Retrieved from www.surgeongeneral.gov/pressreleases/sg02222005.html

Vaillant, G. E. (1977). *Adaptation to life*. Boston: Little, Brown.

Vaillant, G. E. (2003). Natural history of addiction and pathways to recovery. In A. W. Graham, T. K. Schultz, M. F. Mayo-Smith, & R. K. Ries (Eds.), *Principles of addiction medicine* (3rd ed.). Chevy Chase, MD: American Society of Addiction Medicine, Inc.

van den Berg, S. M., & Boomsma, D. I. (2007). The familial clustering of age at menarche in extended twin studies. *Behavior Genetics, 37*, 661–667.

Vardy, M. M., & Kay, F. R. (1983). LSD psychosis or LSD induced schizophrenia? *Archives of General Psychiatry, 40*, 877–883.

Volkow, N. D., & Li, T.-K. (2009). Drug addiction: The neurobiology of behavior gone awry. In R. K. Ries & S. C. Miller (Eds.), *Principles of addiction medicine* (sec. 1, chap. 1). Chevy Chase, MD: American Society of Addiction Medicine.

Volpicelli, J. R., Alterman, A. L., Hayashida, M., & O'Brian, C. P. (1992). Naltrexone in the treatment of alcohol dependence. *Archives of General Psychiatry, 49*, 876–880.

Walker, R. (1992). *Twenty-four hours a day*. Center City, MN: Hazelden.

Wallach, J. (1992). *Interpretation of diagnostic tests: A synopsis of laboratory medicine* (5th ed.). Boston: Little, Brown.

Weedman, R. (1992). *Dancing the tightrope*. Naples, FL: Healthcare Network.

Weinhold, B. K., & Weinhold, J. B. (1989). *Breaking free of the co-dependency trap*. Walpole, NH: Stillpoint.

Weiss, R. D., Mirin, S. N., Griffin, M. L., & Michaels, J. K. (1988). Psychopathology in cocaine abusers: Changing trends. *Journal of Nervous and Mental Disorders, 176,* 719–725.

Wells, K. C., & Forehand, R. (1981). Childhood behavior problems in the home. In S. M. Turner, K. S. Calhoun, & H. E. Adams (Eds.), *Handbook of clinical behavior therapy*. New York: John Wiley.

Wells, K. C., & Forehand, R. (1984). Conduct and oppositional disorders. In P. H. Bornstein & A. E. Kaydin (Eds.), *Handbook of clinical behavior therapy with children*. New York: Dorsey.

Wesson, D. R., & Smith, D. E. (1977). Cocaine: Its use for central nervous system stimulation including recreational and medical uses. In R. C. Peterson & R. C. Stillman (Eds.), *Cocaine: 1977* (Research Monograph No. 13, pp. 137–150). Washington, DC: U.S. Government Printing Office.

Westley, W. A., & Epstein, N. B. (1969). *The silent majority*. San Francisco: Jossey-Bass.

White, W. L. (2009). Recovery-oriented systems of care: scientific rationale and promising practices. *Counselor: The Magazine for Addiction Professionals, 10*(1), 1–152.

White, W. L. (2010). Interviews with pioneers: Robert L. Dupont, MD on addiction, treatment, recovery and a life of service. *Counselor: The Magazine for Addiction Professionals, 11*(1), 38–48.

Widiger, T., & Frances, A. (1989). Epidemiology, diagnosis, and comorbidity of borderline personality disorders. In *American Psychiatric Association annual review* (Vol. 8). Washington, DC: American Psychiatric Press.

Wikler, A. (1976). Aspects of tolerance to and dependence on cannabis. *Annals of the New York Academy of Science, 282,* 126–147.

Wilcox, R. E., Gonzales, R. A., & Erickson, C. K. (1994). In N. S. Miller & M. C. Doot (Eds.), *Principles of addiction medicine* (sec. 1, chap. 3, p. 4). Chevy Chase, MD: American Society of Addiction Medicine.

Wilkins, J. N., Danovitch, I., & Gorelick, D. A. (2009). In R. K. Miller & S. C. Miller (Eds.), *Principles of addiction medicine* (sec. 6, chap. 45). Chevy Chase, MD: American Society of Addiction Medicine.

Wilson, B.J. (2008). Media and children's aggression, fear and altruism. *The Future of Children, 18*(1), 87–118.

Wise, R. A., & Kelsey, J. E. (1998). Behavioral models of addiction. In A. W. Graham, T. K. Schultz, & B. B. Wilford (Eds.), *Principles of addiction medicine* (2nd ed., sec. 1, chap. 3, pp. 37–49). Chevy Chase, MD: American Society of Addiction Medicine.

Woods, J. H., & Carney, J. (1977). Narcotic tolerance and operant behavior. In N. A. Krasnegor (Ed.), *Behavioral tolerance: Research and treatment implications* (Publ. No. [ADM] 78–551, pp. 54–66). Washington, DC: U.S. Government Printing Office.

Woodward, J. J. (1994). Alcohol. In N. S. Miller & M. C. Doot (Eds.), *Principles of addiction medicine* (sec. 2, chap. 2, pp. 1–12). Chevy Chase, MD: American Society of Addiction Medicine.

Woody, G. G., Lubrorsky, L., McLellan, T., O'Brien, C. P., Beck, A. T., Blaine, J., Herman, I., & Hole, A. (1984). Psychotherapy for opiate addicts: Does it help? *Archives of General Psychiatry, 40,* 639–643.

Zegans, L. S. (1982). Stress and the development of somatic disorders. In L. Goldberger & S. Brenznitz (Eds.), *Handbook of stress: Theoretical and clinical aspects*. New York: Free Press.

Zung, W. W. K. (1971). A rating instrument for anxiety disorders. *Psychosomatics, 12,* 371–379.

Index

About the Author

Robert R. Perkinson is the clinical director of Keystone Treatment Center in Canton, South Dakota. He is a licensed psychologist; licensed marriage and family therapist; internationally certified alcohol and drug counselor; South Dakota certified chemical dependency counselor, Level III; and a nationally certified gambling counselor and supervisor. His specialty areas focus on treating alcoholics, addicts, and pathological gamblers. He is the author of *Chemical Dependency Counseling: A Practical Guide* (2nd ed.) (2003a), which is the leading treatment manual in the world for chemical dependency counselors. With Dr. Arthur E. Jongsma Jr. (2001) he is the coauthor of *The Addiction Treatment Planner*, which is the best-selling treatment planner and computer software program for mental health and addiction professionals. He has also written *The Alcoholism and Drug Abuse Patient Workbook* (2003c) and the *Gambling Addiction Patient Workbook* (2003b). These workbooks have all of the exercises patients need to enter a stable recovery. His book entitled *Treating Alcoholism: How to Help Your Clients Enter Recovery* (2004) trains professionals how to treat patients with alcohol problems. He is the author of the book *God Talks to You* (2000) and the meditation tape *A Communication From God* (2008) by cdbaby, which help addicts make their first conscious contact with a Higher Power of their own understanding. He is a composer and has completed his second CD, *Peace Will Come*, music that helps addicts learn the essentials of a spiritual journey. With Dr. Jean LaCour (2004), he wrote the *Faith-Based Addiction Curriculum* to teach professionals of faith how to treat addiction. Dr. Perkinson is an international motivational speaker and regular contributor to numerous professional journals. He is the webmaster of several Web pages, including www.robertperkinson.com, www.alcoholismtreatment.org, and www.godtalkstoyou.com, where he gets over 2.6 million hits a year and answers questions on addiction for free. His biographies can be found in *Who's Who in America, Who's Who in Medicine and Healthcare, Who's Who in Science and Engineering,* and *Who's Who in the World.*

SAGE Research Methods Online

The essential tool for researchers

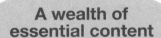